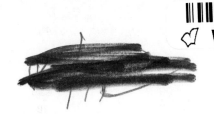

Major Problems in the History
of the Vietnam War

MAJOR PROBLEMS IN AMERICAN HISTORY SERIES

GENERAL EDITOR
THOMAS G. PATERSON

Major Problems in the History of the Vietnam War

DOCUMENTS AND ESSAYS

EDITED BY

ROBERT J. McMAHON

UNIVERSITY OF FLORIDA

D. C. HEATH AND COMPANY
Lexington, Massachusetts   Toronto

For Alison

Preface

American intervention in Vietnam grew slowly in the first years after the Second World War—almost imperceptibly so to most Americans. But a pattern of ever-deepening commitment soon became evident. By the early 1950s, the United States was underwriting approximately 80 percent of France's colonial war against Vietnamese nationalists; following the collapse of French rule in 1954, Washington became the principal source of support for a new, struggling South Vietnamese government. By the early 1960s, the United States was providing that regime with thousands of military advisers in an effort to check a renewed guerrilla insurgency. Just a few years later, American ground troops joined the fray, and the United States found itself bogged down in a major land war.

In the ten-year period bracketed by the introduction of American combat forces in 1965 and the collapse of the United States-backed Saigon regime in 1975, the Vietnam War dominated the political, social, cultural, and intellectual life of the United States. Probably no issue since the Civil War divided Americans more deeply than the Indochina conflict. Certainly few, if any, episodes in contemporary history have had a more profound impact on American society or compelled a more searching examination of America's role in the world. A precise accounting of the war's deeper costs, however, remains elusive. The passions it unleashed have not yet ebbed, nor has the nation fully absorbed its consequences.

Recent years have witnessed a tremendous outpouring of Vietnam-era reflections in the United States, testifying both to the continued public preoccupation with the war and to the absence of a broad consensus on its meaning. Movies, television series, documentaries, novels, and memoirs have proliferated, competing for the public's attention with books and articles by scholars, policy analysts, military officers, civilian policymakers, and journalists. The viewpoints expressed in these diverse efforts have varied as widely as the lessons drawn. Significantly, this continuing fascination with the Vietnam years has not been confined to those with vivid memories of that turbulent time. Indeed, college students, many born well after the major U.S. escalations of the mid-1960s and most not old enough to have begun kindergarten when the last American troops withdrew, have flocked to enroll in courses on the Vietnam War. By the late 1980s, the number of such courses has been estimated at over 400, prompting some educators to label student interest in the war a cultural phenomenon of major proportions.

This volume seeks to stimulate critical thinking about the Vietnam War and its meaning for Americans. The essays and documents in this book, like those that appear in the other anthologies in D. C. Heath's Major Problems in American History Series, are intended to introduce students to the major controversies and debates surrounding the subject. Because the Vietnam War represents a major episode in the American national experience, the principal focus of these documents and essays is on three America-centered questions: Why was the United States drawn into the Vietnam War? How did the United States seek to accomplish its goals in Vietnam from the 1940s to the 1970s? And what have been the lessons and consequences of the war for the United States?

The war, of course, forms not just a chapter in American history, but a chapter in the history of modern Asia—and the world. Nor was the United States the only significant actor in the drama. In an effort to present students with a balanced perspective on the war and with the context necessary for understanding American decisions, I have included three chapters that deal exclusively with Vietnamese topics. Throughout the chapters, essays and documents place American policy in the broadest possible framework. The book's primary focus remains, nonetheless, on the *American* experience in Vietnam.

Each chapter opens with a brief introduction to the topic at hand. The introduction is followed by a series of primary-source documents and two or three interpretive essays by historians, political scientists, participants, or other authorities. The documents reveal the flavor of the time and the range of contemporary issues and retrospective assessments. The essays present the more significant debates and controversies generated by the war. Readers are encouraged to weigh conflicting arguments, assess evidence carefully, and form their own opinions. Suggestions for additional reading follow each chapter, providing guideposts to those interested in probing issues more deeply.

Many individuals helped in the preparation of this book. I am especially grateful to Thomas G. Paterson for first suggesting this project to me, and for his valuable suggestions at every stage. For general advice, specific recommendations, and constructive criticism, I thank Edward P. Crapol, William J. Duiker, George C. Herring, Gary R. Hess, Richard H. Immerman, John Israel, Melvyn P. Leffler, Gary May, Kell Mitchell, Samuel L. Popkin, Donald W. Rogers, Sandra C. Taylor, and William S. Turley. I acknowledge Ted Snow's help in locating certain materials and the expert assistance of the secretarial staff at the University of Florida's History Department. I thank Heath's editors, Sylvia L. Mallory and James Miller, for providing a marvelous combination of professionalism, enthusiasm, and support. I join them and the series editor in welcoming suggestions for improving this volume.

Most of all, I am indebted to my family. My sons, Tommy and Michael, tolerated with characteristic cheerfulness their father's occasional absences and more-than-occasional preoccupations. And my wife, Alison, as always, provided indispensable support, understanding, and encouragement.

R. J. M.

Contents

C H A P T E R   4
Dwight D. Eisenhower and Vietnam: Deepening the Commitment
Page 117

C H A P T E R   5
John F. Kennedy and Vietnam: Incremental Escalation
Page 177

C H A P T E R 6
Lyndon B. Johnson's Decisions for War
Page 224

C H A P T E R 7
U.S. Military Strategy
Page 262

C H A P T E R 11
Richard M. Nixon's Strategy for Withdrawal
Page 441

C H A P T E R 12
The Antiwar Movement and Public Opinion
Page 475

CHAPTER 15
Consequences and Lessons of the War
Page 599

Commonly Used Acronyms

ARVN	Army of the Republic of Vietnam
CIA	Central Intelligence Agency
CINCPAC	U.S. Commander in Chief, Pacific
COSVN	Central Office for South Vietnam of the Communist Party
DMZ	Demilitarized Zone
DRV	Democratic Republic of Vietnam (North Vietnam)
GVN	Government of Vietnam (South Vietnam)
ICP	Indochinese Communist Party
JCS	Joint Chiefs of Staff
MAAG	U.S. Military Assistance Advisory Group
MACV	U.S. Military Assistance Command, Vietnam
MR	Military Region
NLF	National Liberation Front
NSC	National Security Council
NVA	North Vietnamese Army
NVN	North Vietnam
PAVN	Peoples' Army of Vietnam (regular army of North Vietnam)
PLAF	Peoples' Liberation Armed Forces (regular army of the NLF, then PRG)
PRG	Provisional Revolutionary Government
RVN	Republic of Vietnam (South Vietnam)
RVNAF	Republic of Vietnam Armed Forces
SEA	Southeast Asia
SEATO	Southeast Asia Treaty Organization
SVN	South Vietnam
VC	Vietcong

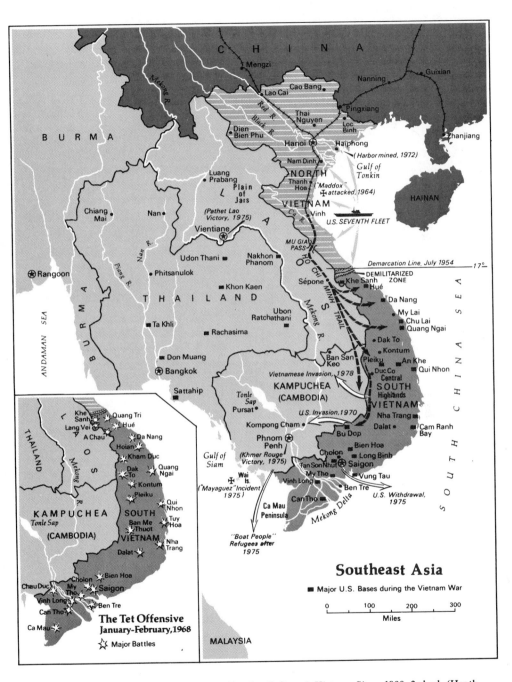

Southeast Asia

■ Major U.S. Bases during the Vietnam War

0   100   200   300
Miles

The Tet Offensive
January–February, 1968
☆ Major Battles

From Thomas G. Paterson, *American Foreign Policy: A History, Since 1900*, 3rd ed. (Heath, 1988), p. 559.

Major Problems in the History
of the Vietnam War

CHAPTER

1

Vietnam and America:

An Introduction

✗

America's longest war, the Vietnam conflict also was one of its most divisive. As American troop levels swelled to over half a million by the late 1960s, American society split sharply over the morality and efficacy of the war effort. The war's inconclusiveness and unpopularity spawned not only a broad-based antiwar movement but also a reexamination of America's purpose as wrenching and far reaching as any other since the Civil War. Neither President Richard M. Nixon's decision in 1969 to begin withdrawing U.S. troops nor the fall of Saigon to the communists in April 1975 did much to resolve the debate or ease the traumas that it unleashed.

The selections in this opening chapter explore the larger boundaries of that debate by focusing on the following questions: Why did the United States intervene in Vietnam: to defend freedom and liberty or to protect imperial interests dictated by America's world position? What did the United States seek to accomplish in Vietnam? Were its goals attainable? Who were its enemies? its allies? Can U.S. actions there be characterized as moral—or immoral? In the larger scope of U.S., Asian, and world history, how should the Vietnam War be interpreted and judged?

✗ *E S S A Y S*

In the first essay, Leslie H. Gelb, a prominent journalist and former assistant secretary of state, and Richard K. Betts of the Brookings Institution summarize and critique the various interpretations analysts have offered to explain U.S. involvement in Vietnam. They conclude that the decision-making system actually worked far better than most of its critics realize. It worked, they believe, because it achieved its stated purpose of preventing a communist victory in Vietnam until the U.S. domestic consensus shifted in 1974–1975.

In the next essay, Norman Podhoretz, editor of *Commentary* and author of numerous books about contemporary American society, insists that the United

1

States went into Vietnam for idealistic, not selfish, reasons: to save the southern half of Vietnam from the evils of communism. He finds vindication for the moral soundness of America's commitment in the "hideous consequences" for the Vietnamese people of the U.S. defeat.

The final essay offers a radical perspective on the origins and consequences of the war. Gabriel Kolko of York University (Toronto) sees U.S. intervention as an essential part of Washington's overall strategy for guiding and integrating the world's political and economic system. He contends that America's defeat exposed the limitations of modern arms and armies against the force of revolutionary nationalism, making the Vietnam War one of this century's seminal events.

The System Worked

LESLIE H. GELB AND RICHARD K. BETTS

Writing history, especially history as recent and controversial as the Vietnam War, is a treacherous exercise. One picks away at the debris of evidence only to discover that it is still alive, being shaped by bitterness and bewilderment, reassurances and new testimony. Consequently answers to certain questions will forever remain elusive. Were U.S. leaders right or wrong in involving the nation in Vietnam? Did they adopt the best strategy for fighting the war? Were they genuinely seeking a compromise peace? Each succeeding generation of historians will produce its own perspective on the rights and wrongs of the war, and each perspective will be different from the others. This has happened with every other war, and it will happen with Vietnam.

What the historian can legitimately seek to do at this point is to begin to piece together the whats and whys. What were the patterns that characterized the war in Vietnam? What policy dilemmas did U.S. leaders face? Why were their choices indeed dilemmas? Why did they choose the way they did?

Four basic and recurring patterns marked what was happening in Vietnam from 1947 to 1969.

The first pattern was that of the French, the Saigon government, and their military forces. The military forces always got better, but they never got good enough. Each Vietminh or North Vietnamese offensive, whatever the immediate results, showed again and again that first the French and then the Saigon forces could not defend themselves without ever larger doses of massive American assistance. (The invasion of South Vietnam by the North Vietnamese across the demilitarized zone in 1972 was a partial exception.) These anti-Communist forces could never translate their advantages in total air superiority, dominance in mobility and firepower, and a sizable edge in manpower into victory. In fact they spent most of the time on the defensive until mid-1968. Something was wrong somewhere. Something always was wrong.

Leslie H. Gelb and Richard K. Betts, *The Irony of Vietnam: The System Worked* (Washington: Brookings Institution, 1979), pp. 9–26. Reprinted by permission.

Military power without political cohesiveness and support is an empty shell. The non-Communist Vietnamese, to be sure, invariably had a solid strike against them: it could not be an easy task to coalesce the forces of nationalism while depending militarily on the French or the Americans. Yet the non-Communist groups never were able to submerge their own differences in a single, unified purpose and to gather support from the peasant masses. Before the end, the regime of President Nguyen Van Thieu gained in stability but seemingly not in legitimacy. Without this legitimacy—and the quest for it seemed never-ending—the anti-Communist Vietnamese perpetually required American support.

A second pattern characterized the Vietminh and later the Hanoi government. While the annual hopeful prediction was that the Communists were about to expire, their will to fight seemed undiminished and they kept coming back. When the going got rough in Vietnam, they would divert temporarily to Laos and Cambodia. One need not glorify the Communists to face this fact. The brutality of their methods of warfare matched, if not exceeded, Saigon's. And certainly Hanoi received massive doses of aid from the Soviet Union and China, although only a fraction of the aid the United States gave to France and Saigon. But something always went right for them somewhere.

The Communist leaders always had their differences, but they could put them aside in the pursuit of their goal of an independent and unified Vietnam. Although as dictatorial as their foes, if not more so, they were nevertheless able to organize and marshal their efforts effectively year after year. They were, in short, more *effectively* dictatorial than the Saigon mandarins, especially because after World War II they captured much of the banner of nationalism. The non-Communist nationalists never achieved the same degree of ideological cohesion, organizational discipline, and grass roots activism. For these reasons the Communists crept near to victory on several occasions.

Victory would have been theirs on these occasions had it not been for a third pattern—that of increasing American involvement. As U.S. involvement increased, appearing at times to raise the possibility of a Communist defeat, the Soviet Union and China would step up aid to their ally. Whenever one Vietnamese side or the other in this conflict was in danger of losing, one of the superpowers would step in to redress the balance. The war could not end as long as these outside powers wanted to keep their clients from losing.

The upshot was a fourth pattern—stalemate. From time to time negotiating initiatives were launched, serving only to emphasize that the war was basically a civil war in which neither side would risk genuine compromise. Each side tried more force. The other side would match it. The anti-Communist Vietnamese, though inefficient and corrupt, always had enough support and resiliency to hang on. The Communist Vietnamese, though battered, always possessed the determination to drive on. Death fast became a way of life in Vietnam as stalemate continued but the war got bigger.

Back in Washington, these patterns created, and were in part created by, the conflicting goals that posed a rack of interlocking policy dilemmas.

Stakes versus leverage. U.S. stakes in avoiding a Communist takeover in Vietnam were as great as the stakes of Paris and Saigon. Thus, occasional threats from Washington to "shape up or else" were never taken seriously, for leaders in Paris and Saigon realized that the United States stood to lose as much as they from withdrawal. As the stakes grew, leverage shrank. American goals and strength were therefore paradoxically a fundamental source of bargaining weakness.

Pressure versus collapse. At various times U.S. leaders believed that neither the French nor the South Vietnamese would undertake necessary reforms without hard pressure from Washington, and that pressing too hard might lead to complete collapse of the anti-Communist position. If the Americans pushed the French into granting genuine independence to Vietnam, France would have no incentive to continue the fight against communism and would withdraw. If the Americans pushed the Saigon government too hard on land reform, corruption, and the like, Saigon's administrative structure would become overburdened, its power base would be placed in jeopardy, and its ever-fragile unity might come apart. Thus the weakness of the French and the South Vietnamese was the source of their bargaining strength.

Vietnamese reform versus American performance. Truman, Eisenhower, Kennedy, and Johnson each made clear that reforms would be a precondition for further U.S. assistance. Each violated his own preconditions. The dilemma was this: if the United States performed before the French and the Saigon government reformed, they would never reform, but if the United States did not perform first and the situation further deteriorated, reforms would become academic. Thus at the end of 1964 American leaders concluded that the Saigon government was too precarious to warrant additional U.S. help but was unlikely to survive without it.

Involvement or not—a loss either way. U.S. strategists recognized over the years that greater involvement by outside powers was sure to run against the grain of Vietnamese nationalism, thereby making the war unwinnable. Eisenhower realized that getting further involved in France's colonial war was a losing proposition. Kennedy saw in 1961 that sending in American combat troops and making the American presence more visible could only transform the situation into "a white man's war," again a losing proposition. But Eisenhower, Kennedy, and the other presidents also believed that France and Saigon were certain to fail without greater U.S. involvement.

Restraint versus signals. U.S. leaders correctly calculated that increasing American involvement in Vietnam would trigger heightened domestic criticism of the war. Thus each President sought to postpone and then to downplay escalatory actions or even to conceal the significance of those actions as long as possible. But at the same time, they calculated with equal correctness that restraint for domestic political purposes would convey the wrong signal to the Vietminh, Hanoi, and their supporters. It could only be read by the Communists as a sign of U.S. weakness and ultimate irresolution.

The damned if do, damned if don't dilemma. At bottom, the presidents acted as if they were trapped no matter what they did. If they escalated to avoid defeat, they would be criticized. If they failed to escalate, they would be criticized for permitting defeat. Theirs was the most classic of all dilemmas: they were damned if they did and damned if they didn't. There seemed to be no course of action that would not risk domestic support, although until 1968 criticism for softness seemed less bearable than criticism for excessive involvement. The dilemma lay not only in balancing left-wing domestic constituencies against right-wing ones, but also in the contradictory demands of the Right. Republican rightists at various times criticized Democrats both for being the "war party" *and* for "selling out" countries to communism.

In sum, given the constant goal of a non-Communist South after the Korean War, these six U.S. dilemmas in Vietnam melded into three historically phased ones. At first, U.S. leaders realized that there was no chance of defeating the Vietminh unless France granted true independence to Vietnam, but that if France did so, it would not remain and fight the war. So the United States could not win with France and could not win without it. Then American leaders recognized that although President Ngo Dinh Diem was losing the support of the people, he nevertheless represented the only hope of future political stability. So the United States could not win with Diem and could not win without him. Later the American view was that the Saigon regime would not reform with U.S. aid and could not survive without massive U.S. involvement, and that the North Vietnamese effort seemed able to survive despite U.S. efforts. Once again, the war could neither be won with U.S. help nor without it. Why, then, did the United States continue throughout these phases to put its resources into an ever-expanding *and* never-ending war?

Nations at war and after a war, win or lose, try to scratch away at the traditions or values that hold their societies together to see what they are made of. Are they wise and just nations? Or are they foolish and aggressive? Merciless or humane? Well led or misled? Vital or decadent? Hopeful or hopeless? It is arguable whether a society should indulge in such self-scrutiny. Societies are, as Edmund Burke wrote, "delicate, intricate wholes" that are more easily damaged than improved when subjected to the glare of grand inquisitors.

But in the case of the United States and the war in Vietnam, many people have sought answers to which they are entitled, and many others are only too eager to fill in the blanks. The families and friends of those who were killed and wounded want to know whether it was worth it. This answer is clear to most by now: No. Intellectuals still want to know "Why Vietnam?" Policy analysts want to know whether the failure was conceptual and strategic (the realm of ends) or organizational and operational (the realm of means). The answers to these questions will themselves become political facts and forces, shaping the U.S. role in the world and the lives of Americans at home for years to come.

Central to this inquiry are the wide-ranging explanations of U.S. involvement given in the Vietnam War literature. Nine seem to stand out. Different authors combine them in different ways, although none presents a complete answer. The nine basic explanations are as follows:

1. The arrogance of power—idealistic imperialism. Richard Hofstadter has argued that Americans have had a misleading historical experience with warfare and that unlike the Europeans, they have not learned to live with minor setbacks and limited successes, since they have known only victory. This led to the "illusion of American omnipotence" in U.S. foreign policy.

This view holds that a driving force in American involvement in Vietnam was that the United States is a nation of enormous power and, like comparable nations in history, sought to use this power at every opportunity. To have power is to want to employ it and, eventually, is to be corrupted by it. The arrogance derived from the belief that to have power is to be able to do anything. It was also an idealistic arrogance, an imperialism more ingenuous than malevolent, a curious blend of Wilsonianism and realpolitik that sought to make the world safe for democracy even if this meant forcing Vietnam to be free. Power invokes right and justifies itself. Vietnam was there, a challenge to this power and an opportunity for its exercise, and no task was beyond accomplishment.

2. The rapacity of power: economic imperialism. This explanation, a variant of the domestic politics interpretation given below, is that special-interest groups, such as the industrial and financial elite, maneuvered the United States into war. This elite's goal was to capture export markets and natural resources at public expense for private economic gain. Gabriel Kolko's neo-Marxist analyses are the best examples of this approach.

Michael Klare, mixing the power elite model of C. Wright Mills with the economic determinism of Noam Chomsky, put the argument this way:

U.S. policy in general and U.S. intervention in Vietnam in particular were "the predictable outcome of an American drive to secure control over the economic resources of the non-Communist world." American businessmen held key posts in the executive branch. Senators, congressmen, academics, scientists, think-tankers, and the military were their hirelings. They all longed for the almighty dollar. They could not make enough "honest dollars" in the United States, so they enlisted the power of Washington to guarantee foreign markets for the export of goods and capital and access to raw materials. They hoodwinked the rest of the nation into believing that the protection of their profits was in the U.S. national interest. They needed military capability. The military-industrial complex responded with sensors, defoliants, automatic battlefields, helicopters, and the like, and tested them in the laboratory of Vietnam. Put it all together with an adversary who would do everything he could to resist, and you have a war without end.

3. Bureaucratic politics. There are several, not mutually exclusive, approaches within this view. One, a quasi-Freudian version, has it that national security bureaucrats—the professionals who make up the military services, civilians in the Defense Department, the Agency for International Development, the State Department, and the Central Intelligence Agency (CIA)—are afflicted with the curse of machismo, the need to assert and prove manhood and toughness. This instinct compounded misunderstanding and organizational failure. The bureaucrats' career advancement and acceptability within the government depended on showing that they were not afraid to propose the use of force. Another more conspiratorial approach has it that bureaucrats purposefully misled their superiors about the situation in Vietnam and carefully constructed policy alternatives so as to circumscribe their choices, thus forcing further involvement in Vietnam.

The first approach has been set forth by Richard Barnet and James C. Thomson, Jr. According to Barnet, the national security manager quickly learns that "toughness is the most highly prized virtue." Thomson drove the point home: "Those who doubted our role in Vietnam were said to shrink from the burdens of power, the obligations of power, the uses of power, the responsibility of power. By implication such men were soft-headed and effete." Citing the lack of informed judgment on Indochina because of the "banishment of real expertise" on Asia, the "domestication of dissenters," the "effectiveness trap" whereby bureaucrats refrain from protesting for fear of losing their influence, the "curator mentality," and "bureaucratic detachment" from moral isues, Thomson observed that the conflict was bound to lead to "a steady give-in to pressures for a military solution."

Of the second approach, Stavins, Barnet, and Raskin noted:

> The deliberate inflation and distortion of issues in the advocacy process leads to what I call the bureaucratic model of reality . . . the final purpose of which is to induce the President to do something or to make him feel comfortable about something the bureaucracy has already done. . . . The shrewd adviser tailors his advice to the President's prejudices as best he knows them.

David Halberstam emphasized this bureaucratic duplicity, particularly in regard to the role of military reporting from the field in the early 1960s. A similar variant of bureaucratic politics is posed by the Committee of Concerned Asian Scholars: "The Indochina war is in large part a product of sheer institutional momentum." According to this interpretation, bureaucrats develop a stake in their solution to a problem; a change in the solution is difficult because it means a repudiation of a previous chain of decisions and is therefore an admission of personal failing in the past. As another analyst argued, the crisis managers advising the President became so involved they "would not, perhaps could not, let go." This fairly unified vision of bureaucracy contrasts with a fourth and final view of organizational determinism: bureaucratic bargaining. In this explanation the cautious approach of the State Department and the CIA gradually lost out in the councils of decision to the arguments of the professional military.

4. Domestic politics. This explanation is quite complicated, and authors argue their cases on several different levels. The magnanimous view sees American presidents fending off the Communists in Vietnam in order to save the country from another round of right-wing McCarthyism and to retain domestic support for a continuing U.S. role in the world. Chroniclers who have been close to presidents have stressed this interpretation.

Another more complex portrait was sketched by Daniel Ellsberg, who saw domestic politics as putting U.S. leaders in a bind between two conflicting imperatives: "Rule 1 . . . *Do not lose the rest of Vietnam to communist control before the next election,*" and "Rule 2 . . . *Do not commit U.S. ground troops to a land war in Asia, either.*" The former drove the presidents on and the latter constrained them. The presidential rule that "*this is a bad year for me to lose Vietnam to Communism,*" said Ellsberg, along with rules 1 and 2,

> amounts to a *recurrent* formula for calculating Presidential decisions on Vietnam realistically, given inputs on alternatives, any time from 1950 on. The mix of motives behind this judgment can vary with circumstances and Presidents, but since 1950 a variety of domestic political considerations have virtually always been present. These have been *sufficient* underpinning even in those years when . . . "strategic" concerns were not also urgent.

These constraints can also be seen as reinforced by the underlying urge, especially in Johnson's case, not to be "the first President to lose a war."

5. Pragmatic security managers. This interpretation is closely linked to the bureaucratic and arrogance-of-power explanations. It is the view that U.S. leaders over the years were not inspired by any particular ideology but were essentially pragmatists weighing the evidence and looking at each problem on its merits. According to this perspective, these leaders knew they were facing tough choices, and their decisions always were close ones. But having decided 51 to 49 to go ahead, they tried to sell and implement their policies 100 percent.

Pragmatists are problem-solvers, and in the words of Joseph Kraft: "The war is peculiarly the war of the Whiz Kids and their friends and supporters in the liberal, business, and academic community. It is the war of those of us who thought we could manage force, and tune violence finely."

6. Ethnocentricity and misperception. Some analysts emphasize the naïveté and insensitivity of policymakers who did not understand the significance of cultural differences, and who therefore did not see that America's Vietnamese allies would not and could not live up to U.S. expectations. Communist revolution in the context of Vietnamese society was simplistically and falsely equated with the earlier challenges in Western Europe. Policymakers assumed that the stakes and solutions were similar, ignoring the complexity, uniqueness, and much greater foreignness of the Vietnamese setting. The United States failed in Vietnam because Americans thought they could treat it like any other Western country and were oblivious to the constraints of the traditional Vietnamese culture and character and to the reasons for the vitality of Vietnamese communism. A related view is that which stresses misunderstanding of Hanoi's and the Vietcong's motives and the miscalculation of policy based on this misperception. Better anthropology and psychology would have helped. In short, had the United States really known who it was dealing with and had it really comprehended how *they* viewed the war, it would not have gotten in so deeply.

7. *The slippery slope.* Tied to the pragmatic approach, the balance of power, and the arrogance of power, but attributing more to the process than to the underlying assumptions, is the explanation that holds that U.S. involvement in Vietnam is the story of the slippery slope. According to this view Vietnam was not always critical to U.S. national security; it became so over the years as each succeeding administration piled commitment on commitment. Each administration not quite knowingly slid further into the Vietnam quagmire, not really understanding the depth of the problems in Vietnam and convinced that it could win. The catchwords of this view are optimism, miscalculation, and inadvertence.

The most vocal advocate of this thesis has been Arthur M. Schlesinger, Jr., who in 1967 expressed it as follows:

And so the policy of "one more step" lured the United States deeper and deeper into the morass. In retrospect, Vietnam is a triumph of the politics of inadvertence. We have achieved our present entanglement, not after due and deliberate consideration, but through a series of small decisions. It is not only idle but unfair to seek out guilty men. President Eisenhower, after rejecting American military intervention in 1954, set in motion the policy of support for Saigon which resulted, two Presidents later, in American military intervention in 1965. Each step in the deepening of the American commitment was reasonably regarded at the time as the last that would be necessary. Yet, in retrospect, each step led only to the next, until we find ourselves entrapped today in that nightmare of American strategists, a land war in Asia—a war which no President, including President Johnson, desired or intended. The Vietnam story is a tragedy without villains.

Schlesinger went on to say: "By continually increasing what the Pentagon calls the 'quotient of pain,' we can, according to the administration theory, force Hanoi at each new stage of widening the war to reconsider whether the war is worth the price." But "the theory that widening the war will shorten it . . . appears to be based on three convictions: first, that the war will be decided in North Vietnam; second, that the risk of Chinese or Soviet entry is negligible; and third, that military victory in some sense is possible" (at least in suppressing the resistance in the South). All these convictions, he concluded, were dangerous forms of illusion and self-deception. Marvin Kalb and Elie Abel agreed when they stated that America stumbled "step by downward step, into the longest, most costly, and most disruptive war Americans have ever fought, in the misguided belief that when things go wrong anywhere in the world the commitment of sufficient American dollars and—if need be—of American soldiers, must surely put them right."

Other writers have been less charitable. Bernard Fall, referring to Schlesinger's theory that "error creates its own reality," said that "it would not be unfair to state that the official reports on the situation from 1954 to the present depict a well-nigh unbroken series of seemingly 'unavoidable' decisions, all made with the best of intentions and for the noblest of purposes—but each gone awry at the last moment because of outside factors beyond one's control." He added, however, that "official reactions to warnings about the surely catastrophic end results of the course upon which the Saigon authorities—both Vietnamese and American—were embarked fell upon both deaf and resentful ears, as differences of view between the trained outside observers and officialdom became irreconcilable."

According to Theodore Draper:

> As a result of one miscalculation after another, we have gradually been drawn into making an enormous, disproportionate military and political investment in Vietnam. This investment—not the vital interests of the United States in Vietnam—has cast a spell on us. The same thing would happen if we should decide to put 500,000 troops in Mauritania or even Ruritania. Once American resources and prestige are committed on such a profligate scale, the "commitment" develops a life of its own and, as the saying goes, good money must be thrown after bad.

8. International power politics and containment—policing the world. The desire to maintain some perceived balance of power among nations is an explanation that is intimately related to that of pragmatism but places more emphasis on the traditional imperatives of international relations. According to Donald Zagoria: "For the Americans—as for the Russians and Chinese—Vietnam has been a pawn in a global ideological and power struggle." The United States, he said, was "intent—particularly after the Korean War—on drawing a Cold War line in Asia."

The principal considerations in pursuing the balance-of-power goal were seeing that "the illegal use of force" was not allowed to succeed, honoring commitments, and keeping credibility with allies and potential adversaries. The underlying judgment was that failure to stop aggression in one place would tempt others to aggress in ever more dangerous places. As the most powerful non-Communist nation, the United States had no choice but to serve as the world's policeman. Intervention in Vietnam, in this view, was not aggressive, adventurous, idealistic, or naive, but simply the ineluctable result of the American power position in the world, the same response that great powers have historically made to challenges from other powers.

Kalb and Abel, for example, noted that after Lyndon Johnson won his election, he *could* have considered changing U.S. policy. But he was determined not to lose Vietnam and thus rejected the possibility of a quiet withdrawal. "To him, that would have meant going back on the nation's pledged commitment." Townsend Hoopes described numerous times during the period October 1967 through March 1968 when pressures were brought to bear on the President that might have changed U.S. policy. But the President's reaction was that the struggle was a test of wills between

Washington and Hanoi and that the United States must not relent. Relenting was regarded as tantamount to a resounding defeat to worldwide U.S. policy and prestige and as a green light to the Soviet Union and China to foster more Communist wars of national liberation around the world.

9. *Ideological anticommunism.* The analysts who offer this explanation hold that anticommunism was the central fact of U.S. foreign policy from at least 1947 until the end of the 1960s. After World War II global competition between East and West began. An ideology whose very existence seemed to threaten basic American values had combined with the national force of first Russia and then China. This combination caused American leaders to see the world in "we-they" terms and to insist that peace was indivisible. Going well beyond balance-of-power considerations, every piece of territory became critical and every besieged nation a potential domino. Communism came to be seen as an infection to be quarantined rather than a force to be judiciously and appropriately balanced. Vietnam in particular became the cockpit of confrontation between the Free World and totalitarianism; it was where the action was for twenty years.

Hoopes, for example, observed that although the United States was confronted by a genuine and serious Soviet threat following World War II (and one aggravated in particular by the Korean War), unfortunately "the American response to the cold war generated its own momentum and, in doing so, led us . . . beyond the rational requirements of our national security." Anticommunism degenerated into a religious obsession despite numerous indications that the Communist bloc was no longer monolithic. U.S. aid to Vietnam continued to be based on the conviction that any Communist expansion threatened the security of the United States. The graduated escalation of the war, beginning around 1965, reflected the continuing influence of the cold war beliefs and resulted in wanton destruction grossly disproportionate to the goal sought.

Chester Cooper, in tracing the history of U.S. involvement in Vietnam since World War II, showed how the anti-Communist strain evolved through the different administrations. The residue of democratic antitotalitarian militancy of World War II, directed against fascism, carried over into cold war anticommunism.

> The issue of the "Free World vs. International Communism" made decisions about international relations seem simple and, what is more, cast a mantle of morality and righteousness over all our actions abroad. The Soviet Union and its friends, by their deeds and their words, provided the spark that launched an American crusade to save the world from Communism.

Each of these explanations provides some insight into particular issues, particular people, and the workings of bureaucratic organizations at certain times. But however these explanations are combined, they are better as answers to the question of why the United States originally became involved and committed in Vietnam than as analyses of the process of involvement, the strategy for fighting the war, and the strategy for ending it.

The most prevalent and popular combination of explanations—pragmatic security managers, domestic politics, anticommunism, and slippery slope—is misleading in three crucial respects: it sees commitment as essentially stemming from involvement, the stakes building with each successive escalation—the simple investment trap model; it does not sufficiently emphasize the constraints in fighting the war, nor does it tie these constraints in a coherent way to the strategy of gradualism; and in stressing the factor of Washington's optimism about victory, it seriously distorts official American appraisals of, and expectations about, the war. Explanations 8 and 9, which see involvement as the rational product of given premises about the international balance of power and American ideals, are closer to the mark if any are. But Vietnam, according to most observers, is a story about how the U.S. system failed because the people who ran it blundered. According to this conventional wisdom the American leaders were a collection of moderate pragmatists and cold war ideologues who were trapped by their own philosophies and their ignorance of Vietnam. Pragmatists and ideologues alike foundered, so the stories go, because neither understood that Vietnam was an endless war, a quagmire.

Both stereotypes are compelling in some ways. The pragmatic one gives comfort to those who see where the United States wound up in Vietnam and conclude that no one could have wished this result. It must have been a mistake. The ideological one offers proof to those who look at Vietnam as one more act in the American drama about communism. It was necessary to fill the bill. These general pictures of blundering and blustering are also compelling in a sense as glimpses of the organizational minds of the State Department and the armed services.

Yet the stereotypes fail. They fail because the decisionmaking system they purport to describe *did achieve its stated purpose* of preventing a Communist victory in Vietnam until the domestic balance of opinion shifted and Congress decided to reduce support to Saigon in 1974–75—that is, until the consensus, and hence the purpose, changed and the United States decided to let Vietnam go.

The system worked. The story of U.S. policy toward Vietnam is either far better or far worse than supposed. Presidents and most of those who influenced their decisions did not stumble into Vietnam unaware of the quagmire. U.S. involvement did not stem from a failure to foresee that the war would be a long and bitter struggle. Vietnam was indeed a quagmire, but most American leaders knew it. Of course, there were periods when many were genuinely optimistic. But these infrequent and short-lived periods (late 1953, 1957–59, 1962 and early 1963, and late 1967) were invariably followed by deep pessimism. Very few persons, to be sure, envisioned what the Vietnam situation would be like by 1968. Most realized, however, that the light at the end of the tunnel was very far away, if not unreachable. Nevertheless, the presidents persevered. Given the international compulsions to "keep our word" and "save face," domestic prohibitions against losing, and high personal stakes, U.S. leaders did "what was necessary," did it about the way they wanted to, were prepared to pay the costs each administration could foresee for itself, and plowed on with a mixture of hope and doom. They saw no acceptable alternative until 1968, when the President decided to deescalate, and again in 1974–75, when Congress decided to trim the aid cord.

[In summary, we advance three propositions.] The first proposition tells why and how the United States became involved in Vietnam. The second explains both why "winning" strategies could not be adopted and why the process of involvement was gradual. The third offers answers about expectations.

Proposition 1. U.S. involvement in Vietnam is not mainly a story of inadvertent descent into unforeseen quicksand but of why U.S. leaders considered it vital not to lose Vietnam by force to communism. They believed Vietnam to be vital, not for itself, but for what they thought its "loss" would mean internationally and domestically. Previous involvement made further involvement harder to avoid, and to this extent initial commitments were compounded. But the basic pressures, stakes, and objectives, and the judgments of Vietnam's vitalness—after the fall of China and beginning with the Korean War—were sufficient in themselves to set the course for escalation.

Proposition 2. The presidents, Congress, public opinion, and the press all both reinforced the stakes against losing and introduced constraints against winning. Until the summer of 1965 the presidents did less than those who were urging military victory recommended and rejected policies that could lead to disengagement—in effect they did what they deemed to be minimally necessary at each stage to keep Vietnam and later South Vietnam out of Communist hands. After the summer of 1965, as the war dragged on and the consensus began to dissipate, President Johnson remained a true believer and pushed for the maximum feasible, given diplomatic and domestic constraints as he saw them. Throughout, however, the presidents met the pressures of the system as brakemen, doing less than what they were being told was necessary for victory. While each President was one of the key architects of this consensus, he also was a part and a prisoner of the larger political system that fed on itself, trapping all its participants in a war they could not afford to lose and were unable to win quickly.

Proposition 3. The presidents and most of their lieutenants were not deluded by reports of progress and did not proceed on the basis of optimism about winning a near-term or even longer-term military victory. A feeling of pessimism characterized most of these men most of the time. Occasional optimism or flushes of hope that took temporary precedence over actual analysis only punctuated the general atmosphere of resignation. Policymakers recognized that the steps they were taking were inadequate to win the war and that unless Hanoi relented they would have to do more and more. In effect they chose a course of action that promised stalemate, not victory or peace. The presidents, at times, sought to escape the stalemated war through a negotiated settlement but without fully realizing (though realizing more than most of their critics) that a civil war cannot be ended by political compromise. Their strategy was to persevere in the hope that their will to continue—if not the practical effects of their actions—would cause the Communists to relent.

A Moral and Necessary Intervention

NORMAN PODHORETZ

On April 30, 1975, when the last American helicopter scurried desperately off the roof of the American Embassy in Saigon as the city fell to the invading North Vietnamese army, the Washington *Post* said that it was a day of "deliverance" for the United States. In some sense, of course, it was. For nearly fifteen years, Americans had been working, fighting, and dying in Vietnam; and from this, surely, they were delivered on April 30, 1975.

They were also delivered from something else on that fateful day— something less bloody than the war itself but in some ways no less anguished and anguishing. This was the debate over the war that had been raging with an intensity that escalated along with American involvement, bursting from time to time out of the confines of words and ideas and arguments into the demonstrations, the skirmishes, and the more violent confrontations of what had come to be called "the war at home." Overnight, it seemed, Vietnam, the great obsession of the past decade and more, disappeared from the national consciousness. The newspapers and magazines and television stations carried what were in effect obituary notices, and the debate, along with the war that had provoked it, was then hastily interred in the forensic equivalent of an unmarked grave.

But of course nothing in history ever really happens overnight. In the case of the debate over Vietnam, by the time it was buried, it had long since lost its right to be called a debate. For at least the last five years of American involvement in Vietnam, hardly any voices had been raised in defense of our continued participation in the war. The arguments all came from the other side, and for the most part they remained unanswered. Entering office in 1969, Richard Nixon, like Lyndon Johnson in the last phase of his Presidency, spoke mainly of how to get the United States out of Vietnam. Rarely did he, or anyone else in those days, attempt to justify the intervention itself. Nixon had supported the decision of John F. Kennedy's Administration to go into Vietnam; he had supported the deepening of American involvement under Johnson; and then, by resisting the temptation to withdraw immediately upon becoming President, he had taken the onus of Vietnam upon himself, turning it (in an act that many thought foolish from the point of view of his own political fortunes) into "his" war. Yet he never really made it "his" war in the sense of defending it politically and morally. There was no point, he and his people kept saying, in arguing over how and why we had got into Vietnam; the only question was how

Norman Podhoretz, *Why We Were in Vietnam.* Copyright © 1982 by Norman Podhoretz, pp. 9–15, 195–199, 210. Reprinted by permission of Simon & Schuster, Inc.

best to get out. Thus what Nixon mainly did was defend his strategy of gradual withdrawal against the demand for an immediate end to the American presence. The effect was to concede the moral and political arguments to the antiwar forces—by now a coalition that included people who had led the country into Vietnam in the first place and were eager to atone by leading it out.

Even before April 30, 1975, then, Vietnam had become perhaps the most negatively charged political symbol in American history, awaiting only the literal end of American involvement to achieve its full and final diabolization. From a narrowly political point of view, it had become to the generation that had experienced it what Munich had been to an earlier generation: the self-evident symbol of a policy that must never be followed again.

Indeed, for many people whose original support of American intervention in Vietnam had been based on memories of Munich, Vietnam not only replaced it but canceled it out. To such people the lesson of Munich had been that an expansionist totalitarian power could not be stopped by giving in to its demands and that limited resistance at an early stage was the only way to avoid full-scale war later on. Prime Minister Neville Chamberlain, returning to England from the conference in Munich at which Nazi Germany's claims over Czechoslovakia had been satisfied, triumphantly declared that he was bringing with him "peace in our time." But as almost everyone would later agree, what he had actually brought with him was the certainty of a world war to come—a war that Winston Churchill, the leading critic of the policy of appeasement consummated at Munich, would later call "unnecessary." According to Churchill, if a line had been drawn against Hitler from the beginning, he would have been forced to back away, and the sequence of events that led inexorably to the outbreak of war would have been interrupted.

Obviously, Vietnam differed in many significant ways from Central Europe in the late 1930s. But there was one great similarity that overrode these differences in the minds of many whose understanding of such matters had been shaped by the memory of Munich. "I'm not the village idiot," Dean Rusk, who was Secretary of State first under Kennedy and then under Johnson, once exploded. "I know Hitler was an Austrian and Mao is a Chinese. . . . But what is common between the two situations is the phenomenon of aggression." In other words, in Vietnam now as in Central Europe then, a totalitarian political force—Nazism then, Communism now—was attempting to expand the area under its control. A relatively limited degree of resistance then would have precluded the need for massive resistance afterward. This was the lesson of Munich, and it had already been applied successfully in Western Europe in the forties and Korea in the fifties. Surely it was applicable to Vietnam as well.

When, however, it began to become evident that, in contrast to the cases of Western Europe and Korea, the differences between Vietnam now and Central Europe then were more decisive than the similarities, the relevance of Munich began to fade, and a new set of lessons—the lessons of Vietnam—began to take hold. The legacy of Munich had been a disposition, even a great readiness, to resist, by force if necessary, the expansion of totalitarianism; the legacy of Vietnam would obversely be a reluctance, even a refusal, to resist, especially if resistance required the use of force.

For some of the older generation who rejected the tutelage of Munich in favor of the tutelage of Vietnam, the new pedagogic dispensation was generally limited to lessons of a strictly political character. When they said, or (less given to being so explicit) nodded in agreement as others said, "No More Vietnams," they had in mind a new foreign policy that would base itself on more modest expectations of American power than had prevailed in the years of Kennedy and Johnson. For them the main lesson of Vietnam was that the United States no longer should or could play the role of "policeman of the world." We had certain core interests—Western Europe, Japan, Israel—that we were, and must remain, committed to defend. But however desirable it might ideally be to undertake more than that, we lacked the power, the will, and the wisdom to carry out a more ambitious strategy with any hope of success. In this view, Vietnam represented the great cautionary argument against the "arrogance of American power."

In addition to humility about the extent of American power, Vietnam persuaded many, or perhaps most, converts from the school of Munich that humility was also required in defining the purposes for which this limited American power could and should be used. Even assuming that it might be desirable to contain the spread of Communism—and many by now had lost their former conviction that it was desirable—Vietnam showed that the United States was unable (or indeed unqualified) to go on making the effort with any hope of success. On this issue Vietnam was taken to be an irrefutable piece of evidence showing the folly of an ideologically based foreign policy in general and of an anti-Communist "crusade" in particular.

But these were only the blandest of the lessons of Vietnam. For, unlike Munich, Vietnam became the symbol of something much broader than a mistaken foreign policy. Especially for younger people who had no personal memory of the Second World War, Vietnam did not so much reverse the legacy of Munich as it succeeded to the legacy of Auschwitz. Only the most extreme elements within the antiwar movement took to spelling the name of the country as "Amerika," but many who shied away from so open an identification of the United States under Johnson with Germany under Hitler tacitly acquiesced in (if only by failing to object to) the idea that American involvement in Vietnam was an evil fully comparable to the evils done by Nazi Germany.

Sometimes the evil was taken to be the American intervention itself: an act of aggression against a people fighting to liberate themselves from a corrupt and repressive regime. Far from resisting the spread of totalitarianism, we were propping it up. We were the counterrevolutionaries, we were the imperialists, we were the enemies of freedom and self-determination.

As time went on, however, the emphasis shifted from the original "Amerikan" sin, the evil of the intervention, to the atrocities and crimes we were said to be committing in the fighting of the war itself. Within South Vietnam, the country we were allegedly trying to defend, we were uprooting villages, indiscriminately bombing and bombarding areas populated by civilians, defoliating forests and destroying crops, setting women and children on fire with napalm and other incendiary weapons, and committing random atrocities like the massacre of My Lai; and when, after 1965, we extended the war to North Vietnam, we became guilty of terror-bombing aimed at harmless civilian targets. All this added up to the great crime of genocide. Some Americans agreed with Europeans like Jean-Paul Sartre and Bertrand Russell that the United States was deliberately "wiping out a whole people and imposing the Pax Americana on an uninhabited Vietnam"; others thought that the policy was not deliberate but that (in the words of the American writer Frances FitzGerald) it "had no other military logic" and that the results were in any case "indistinguishable" from genocide.

So well and widely established did this view become, and so halfhearted and ineffective were the replies, that the word Vietnam became serviceable as a self-evident symbol of evil even outside the context of politics. (Here, for example, was how it would later seem natural for a member of the Vietnam generation to speak of himself: "Sometimes my life seems like my own personal Vietnam policy. A rap sheet so heinous that I wonder why those hooded judges of my conscience did not condemn me long ago. . . .")

But within the context of politics, the idea that the American intervention into Vietnam had been a crime led, as we would expect, to sterner lessons than those that followed from the idea that the intervention had merely been a mistake. Instead of learning humility about the extent of their power, Americans were to learn renunciation. Until we could teach ourselves to intervene on the side of good—the side of revolutionary change—the best thing we could do both for ourselves and for the rest of the world was not to intervene at all. Oppressed peoples everywhere were rising and demanding their rights, and everywhere they encountered American opposition. The lesson of Vietnam was that the United States, not the Soviet Union and certainly not Communism, represented the greatest threat to the security and well-being of the peoples of the world.

Thus it was that by April 30, 1975, the debate over Vietnam had already been settled in favor of the moral and political position of the antiwar movement. At best Vietnam had been a blunder; at worst it had been a crime. At best it exposed the folly of trying to contain the spread of Communism anywhere outside Western Europe; at worst it demonstrated that we were and always had been on the wrong side of a worldwide struggle.

That the United States was defeated in Vietnam is certain. But did that defeat truly mean what the antiwar movement seems to have persuaded everyone it meant? Do the policies that led the United States into Vietnam deserve the discredit that has been attached to them? Does the United

States deserve the moral contumely that Vietnam has brought upon it in the eyes of so many people both at home and abroad? Is it true, as the German novelist Guenter Grass has said, that America "lost in Vietnam its right to appeal to morals"? The only way to answer these questions is to reopen the debate over Vietnam from which the United States was prematurely delivered in the closing years of the war. But before the political and moral issues can be properly engaged, it will be necessary to retell the story of how and why the United States went into Vietnam and how and why it was driven out. . . .

Here then we arrive at the center of the moral issue posed by the American intervention into Vietnam.

The United States sent half a million men to fight in Vietnam. More than 50,000 of them lost their lives, and many thousands more were wounded. Billions of dollars were poured into the effort, damaging the once unparalleled American economy to such an extent that the country's competitive position was grievously impaired. The domestic disruptions to which the war gave rise did perhaps even greater damage to a society previously so self-confident that it was often accused of entertaining illusions of its own omnipotence. Millions of young people growing to maturity during the war developed attitudes of such hostility toward their own country and the civilization embodied by its institutions that their willingness to defend it against external enemies in the future was left hanging in doubt.

Why did the United States undertake these burdens and make these sacrifices in blood and treasure and domestic tranquillity? What was in it for the United States? It was a question that plagued the antiwar movement from beginning to end because the answer was so hard to find. If the United States was simply acting the part of an imperialist aggressor in Vietnam, as many in the antiwar movement professed to believe, it was imperialism of a most peculiar kind. There were no raw materials to exploit in Vietnam, and there was no overriding strategic interest involved. To Franklin Roosevelt in 1941 Indochina had been important because it was close to the source of rubber and tin, but this was no longer an important consideration. Toward the end of the war, it was discovered that there was oil off the coast of Vietnam and antiwar radicals happily seized on this news as at last providing an explanation for the American presence there. But neither Kennedy nor Johnson knew about the oil, and even if they had, they would hardly have gone to war for its sake in those pre-OPEC days when oil from the Persian Gulf could be had at two dollars a barrel.

In the absence of an economic interpretation, a psychological version of the theory of imperialism was developed to answer the maddening question: *Why are we in Vietnam?* This theory held that the United States was in Vietnam because it had an urge to dominate—"to impose its national obsessions on the rest of the world," in the words of a piece in the *New York Review of Books*, one of the leading centers of antiwar agitation within the intellectual community. But if so, the psychic profits were as illusory as the economic ones, for the war was doing even deeper damage to the national self-confidence than to the national economy.

Yet another variant of the psychological interpretation, proposed by the economist Robert L. Heilbroner, was that "the fear of losing our place in the sun, of finding ourselves at bay, . . . motivates a great deal of the anti-Communism on which so much of American foreign policy seems to be founded." This was especially so in such underdeveloped countries as Vietnam, where "the rise of Communism would signal the end of capitalism as the dominant world order, and would force the acknowledgment that America no longer constituted the model on which the future of world civilization would be mainly based."

All these theories were developed out of a desperate need to find or invent selfish or self-interested motives for the American presence in Vietnam, the better to discredit it morally. In a different context, proponents of one or another of these theories—Senator Fulbright, for example—were not above trying to discredit the American presence politically by insisting that *no* national interest was being served by the war. This latter contention at least had the virtue of being closer to the truth than the former. For the truth was that the United States went into Vietnam for the sake not of its own direct interests in the ordinary sense but for the sake of an ideal. The intervention was a product of the Wilsonian side of the American character—the side that went to war in 1917 to "make the world safe for democracy" and that found its contemporary incarnations in the liberal internationalism of the 1940s and the liberal anti-Communism of the 1950s. One can characterize this impulse as naive; one can describe it, as Heilbroner does (and as can be done with any virtuous act), in terms that give it a subtly self-interested flavor. But there is no rationally defensible way in which it can be called immoral.

Why, then, were we in Vietnam? To say it once again: because we were trying to save the Southern half of that country from the evils of Communism. But was the war we fought to accomplish this purpose morally worse than Communism itself? Peter L. Berger, who at the time was involved with Clergy and Laymen Concerned About Vietnam (CALCAV), wrote in 1967: "All sorts of dire results might well follow a reduction or a withdrawal of the American engagement in Vietnam. Morally speaking, however, it is safe to assume that none of these could be worse than what is taking place right now." Unlike most of his fellow members of CALCAV, Berger would later repent of this statement. Writing in 1980, he would say of it: "Well, it was *not* safe to assume. . . . I was wrong and so were all those who thought as I did." For "contrary to what most members (including myself) of the antiwar movement expected, the peoples of Indochina have, since 1975, been subjected to suffering far worse than anything that was inflicted upon them by the United States and its allies."

To be sure, the "bloodbath" that had been feared by supporters of the war did not occur—not in the precise form that had been anticipated. In contrast to what they did upon taking power in Hanoi in 1954 (when they murdered some 50,000 landlords), or what they did during their brief occupation of Hué during the Tet offensive of 1968 (when they massacred 3,000 civilians), the Communists did not stage mass executions in the newly conquered South. According to Nguyen Cong Hoan, who had been an NLF [National Liberation Front] agent and then became a member of the National Assembly of the newly united Communist Vietnam before disillusionment drove him to escape in March 1977, there were more executions in the provinces than in the cities and the total number might well have reached into the tens of thousands. But as another fervent opponent of the war, the New York *Times* columnist Tom Wicker was forced to acknowledge, "what Vietnam has given us instead of a bloodbath [is] a vast tide of human misery in Southeast Asia—hundreds of thousands of homeless persons in United Nations camps, perhaps as many more dead in flight, tens of thousands of the most pitiable forcibly repatriated to Cambodia, no one knows how many adrift on the high seas or wandering the roads."

Among the refugees Wicker was talking about here were those who came to be known as "the boat people" because they "literally threw themselves upon the South China Sea in small coastal craft. . . ." Many thousands of these people were ethnic Chinese who were being driven out and forced to pay everything they had for leaky boats; tens of thousands more were Vietnamese fleeing voluntarily from what Nguyen Cong Hoan describes as "the most inhuman and oppressive regime they have ever known." The same judgment is made by Truong Nhu Tang, the former Minister of Justice in the PRG [Provisional Revolutionary Government] who fled in November 1979 in a boat loaded with forty refugees: "Never has any previous regime brought such masses of people to such desperation. Not the military dictators, not the colonialists, not even the ancient Chinese overlords."

So desperate were they to leave that they were willing to take the poor chance of survival in flight rather than remain. Says Nguyen Cong Hoan: ". . . Our people have a traditional attachment to their country. No Vietnamese would willingly leave home, homeland, and ancestors' graves. During the most oppressive French colonial rule and Japanese domination, no one escaped by boat at great risk to their lives. Yet you see that my countrymen by the thousands and from all walks of life, including a number of disillusioned Vietcongs, continue to escape from Vietnam; six out of ten never make it, and for those who are fortunate to make it, they are not allowed to land." Adds one of the disillusioned who did make it, Doan Van Toai: "Among the boat people who survived, including those who were raped by pirates and those who suffered in the refugee camps, nobody regrets his escape from the present regime."

Though they invented a new form of the Communist bloodbath, the North Vietnamese (for, to repeat, before long there were no Southerners in authority in the South, not even former members of the NLF and the PRG) were less creative in dealing with political opposition, whether real or imagined. The "re-education camps" they had always used for this purpose in the North were now extended to the South, but the result was not so much an indigenous system of Vietnamese concentration camps as an imitation of the Soviet Gulag. (*The Vietnamese Gulag*, indeed, was the name Doan Van Toai gave to the book he published about the camps in

1979.) The French journalist Jean Lacouture, who had supported the Communists during the war to the point (as he now admitted) of turning himself into a "vehicle and intermediary for a lying and criminal propaganda, [an] ingenuous spokesman for tyranny in the name of liberty," now tried to salvage his integrity by telling the truth about a re-education camp he was permitted to visit by a regime that had good reason to think him friendly. "It was," he wrote, "a prefabricated hell."

In May 1977, two full years after the Communist takeover, President Jimmy Carter—a repentant hawk, like many members of his cabinet, including his Secretary of State and his Secretary of Defense—spoke of "the intellectual and moral poverty" of the policy that had led us into Vietnam and had kept us there for so long. When Ronald Reagan, an unrepentant hawk, called the war "a noble cause" in the course of his ultimately successful campaign to replace Carter in the White House, he was accused of having made a "gaffe." Fully, painfully aware as I am that the American effort to save Vietnam from Communism was indeed beyond our intellectual and moral capabilities, I believe the story shows that Reagan's "gaffe" was closer to the truth of why we were in Vietnam and what we did there, at least until the very end, than Carter's denigration of an act of imprudent idealism whose moral soundness has been so overwhelmingly vindicated by the hideous consequences of our defeat.

The Limits of American Power

GABRIEL KOLKO

The Vietnam War was the United States' longest and most divisive war of the post-1945 epoch, and in many regards its most important conflict in the twentieth century. Obviously, the Vietnamese Communist Party's resiliency made Vietnam distinctive after 1946, but that the United States should have become embroiled with such formidable adversaries was a natural outcome of the logic and objectives of its role in the modern era. In retrospect, it is apparent that there existed two immovable forces, one of which had no conceivable option but to pursue the policy it had embarked on, and that it was far more likely for America to follow in the footsteps of the French than to learn something from their defeat. How and why it made that momentous decision and what it perceived itself to be doing reveals much about our times and the social and political framework in which contemporary history is made. For Vietnam was ultimately the major episode in a larger process of intervention which preceded and transcended it. All of the frustrations and dilemmas which emerged in Vietnam existed for Washington before 1960, and they persist to this day. The only thing that made the Vietnam War unique for the United States was that it lost completely.

The hallmark of American foreign policy after 1945 was the universality

From *Anatomy of A War* by Gabriel Kolko, pp. 72–79, 547–551. Copyright © 1985 by Gabriel Kolko. Reprinted by permission of Pantheon Books, a Division of Random House, Inc.

of its intense commitment to create an integrated, essentially capitalist world framework out of the chaos of World War Two and the remnants of the colonial systems. The United States was the major inheritor of the mantle of imperialism in modern history, acting not out of a desire to defend the nation against some tangible threat to its physical welfare but because it sought to create a controllable, responsive order elsewhere, one that would permit the political destinies of distant places to evolve in a manner beneficial to American goals and interests far surpassing the immediate needs of its domestic society. The regulation of the world was at once the luxury and the necessity it believed its power afforded, and even if its might both produced and promised far greater prosperity if successful, its inevitable costs were justified, as all earlier imperialist powers had also done, as a fulfillment of an international responsibility and mission.

This task in fact far transcended that of dealing with the USSR, which had not produced the world upheaval but was itself an outcome of the first stage of the protracted crisis of the European and colonial system that had begun in 1914, even though the United States always held Moscow culpable to a critical extent for the many obstacles it was to confront. The history of the postwar era is essentially one of the monumental American attempts—and failures—to weave together such a global order and of the essentially vast autonomous social forces and destabilizing dynamics emerging throughout the world to confound its ambitions.

Such ambitions immediately brought the United States face to face with what to this day remains its primary problem: the conflict between its inordinate desires and its finite resources, and the definition of realistic priorities. Although it took years for the limits on American power to become clear to its leaders, most of whom only partly perceived it, it has been this problem of coherent priorities, and of the means to implement them, rather than the ultimate abstract goals themselves that have divided America's leaders and set the context for debates over policy. What was most important for much of the post-1945 era was the overweening belief on the part of American leaders that regulating all the world's political and economic problems was not only desirable but also possible, given skill and power. They would not and could not concede that the economic, political, and social dynamics of a great part of the world exceeded the capacities of any one or even a group of nations to control. At stake were the large and growing strategic and economic interests in those unstable nations experiencing the greatest changes.

The interaction between a complex world, the constraints on U.S. power, and Washington's perceptions, including its illusions and ignorance, is the subject matter for most of the history of contemporary American foreign policy. The "accidental" nature of that policy after 1946 was a consequence of the intrinsic dilemmas of this ambition rather than its cause. To articulate its priorities was quite simple. Europe was, and still is, at the top of the list of America's formally defined economic, strategic, and political interests. The dilemma of priorities was that none precluded others wholly, so that America's leaders never excluded intervention in any major part of the world. In the last analysis, it was the sheer extent of its objectives, and the inevitable crises and issues which emerged when the process of intervention began, that imposed on the United States the loss of mastery over its own priorities and actions.

By the late 1940s the United States had begun to confront the basic dilemmas it was to encounter for the remainder of the century. The formulation of priorities was an integral part of its reasoning, and so was resistance to communism in whatever form it might appear anywhere in the world. Its own interests had been fully articulated, and these found expression in statements of objectives as well as in the creation of international political, military, and economic organizations and alliances the United States effectively dominated, with American-led "internationalism" becoming one of the hallmarks of its postwar efforts.

Describing the various U.S. decision makers' motives and goals is a necessary but inherently frustrating effort because American capitalism's relative ideological underdevelopment produces nuances and contradictions among men of power which often become translated into the tensions and even ambivalences of American diplomacy. But the complex problem of explaining the causes of U.S. foreign policy can never obviate a description of the real forces and considerations which lead to certain actions and to an optimizing of specific, tangible interests rather than of others. Complexity in serious causal explanations has existed since time immemorial and is intrinsic to the analytic process, yet the importance many care to assign to caprice and accident itself looks frivolous on closer examination of the historical facts and political options. There are, ultimately, main trends and forces, and these must be respected regardless of coincidental related factors.

Prevention of the expansion of communism, the "containment" doctrine, became formally enshrined no later than 1947, and in 1950 the "rollback" of communism was secretly adhered to in the famous National Security Council 68 policy. In 1947 the so-called domino theory first emerged in the form of the Truman Doctrine on Greece. Were Greece to fall, Secretary of State George C. Marshall argued in February of that year, Turkey might follow and "Soviet domination might thus extend over the entire Middle East and Asia." Later that year the same logic required the reconstruction of West Germany, lest its weakness create a vacuum of power into which communism could enter and thereby spread throughout Europe. An area was, by this calculation, no stronger than its weakest link, and the domino mode of analysis, involving interconnections and linkages in estimating the effects of major political upheavals, well before Indochina was becoming the first and probably the most durable of conventional U.S. doctrines on the process of change and power in the modern world.

Such perceptions led irresistibly to the official decision in mid-1949, when the Communists triumphed in China, to draw a line against any new communist states in Asia, even though Washington was then preoccupied with European problems. But in Indochina the interaction of European with Asian affairs was always important to American leaders, for France's

growing absorption with Indochina was causing it to veto West German rearmament, and the more quickly France won and brought its troops back
home to balance projected German power, the sooner it could be brought
into existence. No less crucial was the future position of Japan in Asia and
in the world economy should it lose access to Southeast Asian raw materials
and markets.

In a word, intervening in Vietnam never generated original international
political dilemmas and issues for the United States. America's leaders clar-
ified their ideas about dominoes, the credibility of their power, or the raw-
materials system in the world long before their action on Indochina had
more than a routine significance. It was precisely because of the repeated
definitions of containment, dominoes, intervention, and linkages of seemingly discrete foreign policy questions elsewhere in the world that the United
States made the irreversible decision to see the war in Vietnam through to
the end. Even many of the purely military dilemmas that were to emerge
in Vietnam had been raised earlier in Korea. Until well into the 1960s
Vietnam was but one of many nations the United States was both involved
in and committed to retaining in friendly hands, and from 1953 through
1962 it provided more military and economic aid to Turkey, South Korea,
and Taiwan, about as much to Pakistan, and only somewhat less to Greece
and Spain. Given its resources and goals, America was deeply involved
throughout the world as a mattter of routine. This fact encouraged a new
intervention to the extent that it succeeded in maintaining client regimes
but could also be a restraint once the demands of one nation became so
great as to threaten the United States' position elsewhere.

The domino theory was to be evoked initially more than any other
justification in the Southeast Asian context, and the concept embodied both
strategic and economic components which American leaders never separated. "The fall of Indochina would undoubtedly lead to the fall of the
other mainland states of Southeast Asia," the Joint Chiefs of Staff argued
in April 1950, and with it Russia would control "Asia's war potential . . .
affecting the balance of power." Not only "major sources of certain strategic materials" would be lost, but also communications routes. The State
Department maintained a similar line at this time, writing off Thailand and
Burma should Indochina fall. Well before the Korean conflict this became
the United States' official doctrine, and the war there strengthened this
commitment.

The loss of Indochina, Washington formally articulated in June 1952,
"would have critical psychological, political and economic consequences.
. . . the loss of any single country would probably lead to relatively swift
submission to or an alignment with communism by the remaining countries
of this group. Furthermore, an alignment with communism of the rest of
Southeast Asia and India, and in the longer term, of the Middle East (with
the probable exceptions of at least Pakistan and Turkey) would in all probability progressively follow. Such widespread alignment would endanger
the stability and security of Europe." It would "render the U.S. position
in the Pacific offshore island chain precarious and would seriously jeop-

ardize fundamental U.S. security interests in the Far East.'' The ''principal world source of natural rubber and tin, and a producer of petroleum and other strategically important commodities'' would be lost in Malaya and Indonesia. The rice exports of Burma and Thailand would be taken from Malaya, Ceylon, Japan, and India. Eventually, there would be ''such economic and political pressures in Japan as to make it extremely difficult to prevent Japan's eventual accommodation to communism.'' This was the perfect integration of all the elements of the domino theory, involving raw materials, military bases, and the commitment of the United States to protect its many spheres of influence. In principle, even while helping the French to fight for the larger cause which America saw as its own, Washington's leaders prepared for greater intervention when it became necessary to prop up the leading domino—Indochina.

There were neither private nor public illusions regarding the stakes and goals for American power. Early in 1953 the National Security Council reiterated, ''The Western countries and Japan need increased supplies of raw materials and foodstuffs and growing markets for their industrial production. Their balance of payments difficulties are in considerable part the result of the failure of production of raw materials and foodstuffs in non-dollar areas to increase as rapidly as industrial production.'' ''Why is the United States spending hundreds of millions of dollars supporting the forces of the French Union in the fight against communism?'' Vice-President Richard Nixon explained publicly in December 1953. ''If Indo-china falls, Thailand is put in an almost impossible position. The same is true of Malaya with its rubber and tin. The same is true of Indonesia. If this whole part of Southeast Asia goes under Communist domination or Communist influence, Japan, who trades and must trade with this area in order to exist, must inevitably be oriented towards the Communist regime.'' Both naturally and logically, references to tin, rubber, rice, copra, iron ore, tungsten, and oil were integral to American policy considerations from the inception. As long as he was President, Eisenhower never forgot his country's dependence on the importation of raw materials and the need to control their sources. When he first made public the ''falling domino'' analogy, in April 1954, he also discussed the dangers of losing the region's tin, tungsten, and rubber and the risk of Japan's being forced into dependence on communist nations for its industrial life—with all that implied. Always implicit in the doctrine was the assumption that the economic riches of the neighbors of the first domino, whether Greece or Indochina, were essential, and when the United States first intervened in those hapless and relatively poor nations, it kept the surrounding region foremost in its calculations. This willingness to accept the immense overhead charges of regional domination was constantly in the minds of the men who made the decisions to intervene.

The problem with the domino theory was, of course, its intrinsic conflict with the desire to impose priorities on U.S. commitments, resources, and actions. If a chain is no stronger than its weakest link, then that link has to be protected even though its very fragility might make the undertaking that much more difficult. But so long as the United States had no realistic sense of the constraints on its power, it was ready to take greater risks. The complex interaction of the America's vast goals, its perception of the nature of its power, the domino vision of challenges, and the more modest notions implicit in the concept of priorities began in 1953 to merge in what became the start of the permanent debate and crisis in American strategic and diplomatic doctrine.

Washington had by 1947 become wholly convinced that the Soviet Union was in some crucial manner guiding many of the political and social upheavals in the world that were in fact the outcome of poverty, colonialism, and oligarchies, and that it was, thereby, seriously subverting the United States' attainment of its political and economic objectives of a reformed, American-led capitalist world order. Toward the end of the Korean War, the incipient conflicts built into such a definition of the world were paralleled and aggravated by a crisis in U.S. military technology and doctrine. These two threads inevitably intertwined late in 1953 in the "New Look" debate and in the beginnings of a perpetual search for a global strategy that could everywhere synthesize America's objectives and resources.

The Korean War tested the U.S. military's overwhelming superiority of firepower and technology, along with its capacity to sustain the economic and political costs of protracted war. Given the inconclusive end of the war along the thirty-eighth parallel after three years of combat, and given the total failure of Washington's September 1950 goal of reuniting the country by force of arms, the war had fully revealed the limits of American power. The domestic political controversy it created was less decisive, but it, too, disclosed the formidable political liabilities that such dismal struggles brought to the party in power. And in fiscal 1953, with military spending at 13.8 percent of the gross national product—three times the 1950 proportion—inflation and budget deficits exposed the constraints on American economic resources. In a word, the United States had undertaken a massive effort and achieved only inconclusive results; this reality raised the issue of the credibility of its power. No less important was the fact that it had become bogged down in Asia at the very moment its main priorities and attention were focused on Europe and the Middle East. To resolve these dilemmas became an obsession in Washington, one that affected every area of the world and influenced the U.S. strategy debate for the remainder of the century.

The effort to define a "New Look" for American foreign policy, culminating in Dulles's famous January 12, 1954, speech, was stillborn, for the Soviet test of a hydrogen bomb in August 1953 decisively broke the U.S. monopoly of strategic nuclear weapons. Land war, Dulles declared, could be fought with the forces of America's allies but the United States itself would rely on its "massive retaliatory power . . . by means and at places of our choosing." It was the only "modern way of getting maximum protection at bearable cost," for limited conventional war in Korea had involved potentially unlimited costs. The dark intimation that America might destroy Peking or Moscow because of events in some distant place was the beginning of a search for a new strategy, but the internal contradictions of that view were immediately criticized in Washington. That quest did not preclude relatively minimal responses to what seemed to be small challenges, and even as the weight of military spending on the national economy was reduced substantially over the remainder of the decade and as strategic weapons became more prominent, the White House increased its reliance on covert warfare waged by the CIA—the success of which in Iran and Guatemala greatly encouraged this relatively low-cost, often inconspicuous form of intervention. For whatever the theory, in practice the United States continued to be deeply involved in very different political contexts in every corner of the globe. Throughout the 1950s Washington never husbanded finite resources rationally to attain its primary goals, because, while it could reduce the role of military spending in the economy, it was unwilling and unable to scale down its far more decisive political definitions of the scope and location of American interests in the world.

To a remarkable extent, America's leaders perceived the nature of the contradiction but never ceased to believe that they could find a solution. The intense defense debates of the middle and late 1950s, which made the reputations of numerous articulate and immensely self-confident military intellectuals like Henry Kissinger, Maxwell Taylor, and W. W. Rostow, inconclusively contradicted and neutralized each other. But what was constant in all such theories was the need to be active rather than passive in responding to new problems and challenges, for American power both to appear and to be credible, and to seek to control and direct, rather than be subject to the dictates of, highly fluid outside forces and events. To develop a sense of mastery was the objective, but the fact that the technologies and strategies for attaining it were constantly being debated produced a perpetual dilemma.

It was in this larger context of a search for a decisive global strategy and doctrine throughout the 1950s that the emerging Vietnam issue was linked to so many other international questions. Washington always saw the challenge of Indochina as just one part of a much greater problem it confronted throughout the world: the efficacy of limited war, the danger of dominoes, the credibility of American power, the role of France in Europe, and much else. Vietnam became the conjunction of the postwar crisis of U.S. imperialism at a crucial stage of America's much greater effort to resolve its own doubts about its capacity to protect the larger international socioeconomic environment in which its interests could survive and prosper. By 1960 every preceding event required that the credibility of U.S. power be tested soon, lest all of the failures and dilemmas since 1946 undermine the very foundations of the system it was seeking to construct throughout the world. It was mainly chance that designated Vietnam as the primary arena of trial, but it was virtually preordained that America would try somewhere to attain successes—not simply one but many—to reverse the deepening pattern of postwar history. . . .

The Vietnam War was for the United States the culmination of its frustrating postwar effort to merge its arms and politics to halt and reverse the emergence of states and social systems opposed to the international order Washington sought to establish. It was not the first serious trial of either its military power or its political strategy, only the most disastrous. Despite America's many real successes in imposing its hegemony elsewhere, Vietnam exposed the ultimate constraints on its power in the modern era: its internal tensions, the contradictions between overinvolvement in one nation and its interests and ambitions elsewhere, and its material limits. Precisely because of the unmistakable nature of the defeat after so long and divisive an effort and because of the war's impact on the United States' political structure and aspirations, this conflict takes on a significance greater than that of either of the two world wars. Both of them had only encouraged Washington's ambition to guide and integrate the world's political and economic system—a goal which was surely the most important cause of its intervention in the Vietnam conflict after 1950.

While the strategic implications of the war for the future of American military power in local conflicts was the most obvious dimension of its defeat, it had confronted these issues often since 1946. What was truly distinctive was the collapse of a national consensus on the broad contours of America's role in the world. The trauma was intense; the war ended without glory and with profound remorse for tens of millions of Americans. Successive administrations fought the war so energetically because of these earlier frustrations, of which they were especially conscious in the early 1960s, scarcely suspecting that rather than resolving them, they would only leave the nation with a far larger set of military, political, and economic dilemmas to face for the remainder of this century. But by 1975 the United States was weaker than it had been at the inception of the war in the early 1960s, a lesson hardly any advocate of new interventions could afford to ignore.

The limits of arms and armies in Vietnam were clear by Tet 1968. Although the United States possessed nominally good weapons and tactics, it lacked a military strategy capable of overcoming its enemy's abilities and appropriate to its economic resources, its global priorities, and its political constraints in Vietnam, at home, and in the rest of the world. Although its aims in South Vietnam were never to alter, it was always incapable of coping with the countless political complexities that irrevocably emerge from protracted armed conflict. America's political, military, and ideological leaders remained either oblivious or contemptuous of these until the war was essentially lost. Even today they scarcely dare confront the war's meaning as Washington continues to assert aggressively its classic postwar objectives and interests in Latin America and elsewhere. America's failure was material, of course, but it was also analytic, the result of a myopia whose importance greatly transcended bureaucratic politics or the idiosyncrasies of Presidents and their satraps. The dominating conventional wisdom of American power after 1946 had no effective means of inhibiting a system whose ambitions and needs increasingly transcended its resources for achieving them. They remained unable and unwilling to acknowledge that these objectives were intrinsically unobtainable and irrelevant to the socioeconomic forms much of the Third World is adopting to resolve its economic and human problems, and that the United States' effort to alter this pervasive reality was certain to produce conflict.

✗ *F U R T H E R   R E A D I N G*

Loren Baritz, *Backfire* (1985)
Peter Braestrup, ed., *Vietnam as History* (1984)
Bernard Brodie, *War and Politics* (1973)
Michael Charlton and Anthony Moncrief, *Many Reasons Why* (1978)
Chester A. Cooper, *The Lost Crusade* (1970)
Bernard Edelman, ed., *Dear America: Letters Home from Vietnam* (1985)
Daniel Ellsberg, *Papers on the War* (1972)
Gloria Emerson, *Winners and Losers* (1976)
Frances FitzGerald, *Fire in the Lake* (1972)
William C. Gibbons, *The U.S. Government and the Vietnam War* (1986–1987)
James William Gibson, *The Perfect War* (1986)
David Halberstam, *The Best and the Brightest* (1972)
James Pinckney Harrison, *The Endless War* (1982)
George C. Herring, *America's Longest War* (1986)
Hugh Higgins, *Vietnam* (1982)
Paul Joseph, *Cracks in the Empire: State Politics in the Vietnam War* (1981)
George McT. Kahin, *Intervention* (1986)
George McT. Kahin and John W. Lewis, *The United States in Vietnam* (1969)
Paul M. Kattenburg, *The Vietnam Trauma in American Foreign Policy, 1945–1975*
    (1980)
Guenther Lewy, *America in Vietnam* (1978)
Timothy J. Lomperis, *The War Everyone Lost—and Won* (1984)
Michael Maclear, *The Ten Thousand Day War* (1981)
George K. Osborn et al., eds., *Democracy, Strategy, and Vietnam* (1987)
John Clark Pratt, *Vietnam Voices* (1984)
Arthur M. Schlesinger, Jr., *The Bitter Heritage* (1966)
James Thomson, "How Could Vietnam Happen? An Autopsy," *Atlantic Monthly*,
    221 (1968), 47–53
William S. Turley, *The Second Indochina War* (1986)

The Development of Vietnamese Nationalism

History and geography exert a powerful influence on all peoples and nations. Vietnam is no exception. American officials were often accused of approaching Vietnam with little understanding of its culture and language and even less appreciation of its rich history—forces that, specialists now agree, contributed mightily to the ultimate outcome of the war.

One of the ironic effects of the war is that it generated an explosion of new scholarship on Vietnamese history, especially in the United States. Recent historical literature has paid particular attention to the genesis of modern Vietnamese nationalism, which is the focus of the selections in this chapter. In their endeavors, scholars have sought to account for elements of continuity and discontinuity in Vietnam's long history; tried to assess the impact of French colonial rule on the social structure, economic life, and intellectual outlook within the country; and struggled to explain the emergence of a strong Communist party within the larger nationalist movement.

✗ D O C U M E N T S

The initial document is a selection from the prison notes of Phan Boi Chau, still revered as one of Vietnam's great nationalists. These reflections were written in 1914 while Chau was imprisoned in China, at the request of the French, for nationalist activities. From his release in 1917 until his death in 1941, he continued to agitate for Vietnamese independence. The second document contains comments made by Nguyen Ai Quoc (more commonly known by his adopted name, Ho Chi Minh) at a National Congress of the French Socialist party held at Tours in December 1920. After denouncing French imperialism in his native land, he approved the resolution to found the French Communist party and join the Third International. On February 3, 1930, Ho helped establish the Communist party of Indochina. In the next document, he exhorts his countrymen to join the party and forge a revolution against French rule. On September 2, 1945, Ho declared an independent Democratic Republic of Vietnam; the declaration, which borrowed deliberately from the American Declaration of Independence, appears in the final document.

Phan Boi Chau's Prison Reflections, 1914

The great victory of Japan in the Russo-Japanese war [1904–05] had a tremendous impact upon us. For it was like a new and strange world opening up.

Before the time of the French Protectorate, Vietnam only knew a world with China. And when the French arrived we only knew a world with France. But the world had changed. A strange new wave as yet undreamed of had arrived.

We had been caught up in our internal affairs for so long that even if our heads were cut off and our bodies lost we still had no fear. We were that way only because we cared for our country and our conscience forced us to be so. As for a way to build independence, at that time we were still dreaming in a very thick fog.

Alas! In the middle of the nineteenth century, even though the universe was shaken by American winds and European rains, our country was still in a period of dreaming in a deep sleep. Our people were still blind and resigned to their lot. We cannot blame them, for even well-known people from the higher classes like myself were like frogs in the bottom of a well or ants at the bottom of their hole. We knew nothing about life. I think that there must be no more tragic-comic people in the world than our people.

It is only because in former times we shut our doors and stayed at home, going round and round in circles of literary knowledge, examinations and Chinese studies. To say frankly that our people were deaf and blind is no exaggeration.

Even after the French invasion our people were still deaf and blind. If we had not been awakened by the violent sound of the guns at Port Arthur, perhaps we should not yet know that there were other foreign countries besides France.

After the beginning of the Russo-Japanese hostilities, during the years of the Dragon [1904] and the Serpent [1905], the competition and struggle between the Europeans and the Asians, between the white-skinned people and the yellow-skinned people, forced us to wake up with a start. We became increasingly enthusiastic and intense in our commitment to our ideals. The only problem we still sought to overcome was that of obtaining weapons. . . .

When in jail, it is of course no use to lament one's pain. But there is the sorrowful fact that I have had to be separated from my brothers, without any news, with only myself to speak Vietnamese for myself to hear, thinking

Phan Boi Chau and Ho Chi Minh, *Reflections from Captivity*, David G. Marr, ed., pp. 22–23, 55–56. Reprinted with the permission of The Ohio University Press, Athens.

only of my sad destiny. I think of my failures and weep, my tears falling like torrents of rain. Truly, from the day I was born until now I have never known the taste of suffering as I know it now.

But I have arrived at this suffering because of the ambition that I have held for these last thirty years. And what has this ambition been?

It has been but a yearning to purchase my freedom even at the cost of spilling my blood, to exchange my fate of slavery for the right of self-determination.

Ah! With such an ambition I took in my own hands the supreme responsibility of speaking on behalf of my people. Is there anyone who dares say I should not have done this? Yet if such an ambition is to achieve anything great, we must rely on the toughness of our muscles, the excellence of our learning, the skill of our planning, and the careful manipulation of conditions. Instead, I wondered if at best I wasn't just a blind man leading the blind. Now I have failed simply because I am unskilled. I need complain no more.

However, I think that in this world there is no reason why a stream of water once it has flowed downward can never come up again, or why a life once set on its course cannot change. Who knows but that my failure today will not be good fortune for my people tomorrow? . . .

Let the thousands, ten thousands, even hundreds of thousands of my people who bear an ambition such as mine take heed from my failure. Let them become people who can take care of themselves. We must not wait until our finger has been cut the ninth time before we find the bandage.

I realize that I am a man who has not obtained steel weaponry worth holding on to, that on this earth I have laid down no strategy worth standing on. At most I am an empty-handed rogue with nothing to my name, weak in force and feeble in ability. Yet I am ready still to fight long-toothed tigers and sharp-clawed panthers. Those who understand my inner soul might console me by saying:

"What a brave man!"

Those who wish to look at my mistakes might well look down and say:

"What a stupid man!"

To sum up, in this world there is truly no one as stupid as I. If this be the last day of my life and if, upon my death, I still be called by such a forbidden name as "the most stupid," then this is very correct. It is impossible to call me anything else. But if I have the good fortune to survive and if, afterwards, I see tigers and panthers, then surely I will fight. May my people learn their lesson from my example.

Ho Chi Minh Deplores "Imperialist Crimes," 1920

Chairman: Comrade Indochinese Delegate, you have the floor.

Indochinese Delegate [Nguyen Ai Quoc]: Today, instead of contributing, together with you, to world revolution, I come here with deep sadness to speak as a member of the Socialist Party, against the imperialists who have committed abhorrent crimes on my native land. You all have known that French imperialism entered Indochina half a century ago. In its selfish interests, it conquered our country with bayonets. Since then we have not only been oppressed and exploited shamelessly, but also tortured and poisoned pitilessly. Plainly speaking, we have been poisoned with opium, alcohol, etc. I cannot, in some minutes, reveal all the atrocities that the predatory capitalists have inflicted on Indochina. Prisons outnumber schools and are always overcrowded with detainees. Any natives having socialist ideas are arrested and sometimes murdered without trial. Such is the so-called justice in Indochina. In that country, the Vietnamese are discriminated against, they do not enjoy safety like Europeans or those having European citizenship. We have neither freedom of press nor freedom of speech. Even freedom of assembly and freedom of association do not exist. We have no right to live in other countries or to go abroad as tourists. We are forced to live in utter ignorance and obscurity because we have no right to study. In Indochina the colonialists find all ways and means to force us to smoke opium and drink alcohol to poison and beset us. Thousands of Vietnamese have been led to a slow death or massacred to protect other people's interests.

Comrades, such is the treatment inflicted upon more than 20 million Vietnamese, that is more than half the population of France. And they are said to be under French protection! The Socialist Party must act practically to support the oppressed natives. . . .

Indochinese Delegate: On behalf of the whole of mankind, on behalf of all the Socialist Party's members, both left and right wings, we call upon you! Comrades, save us!

Chairman: Through the applause of approval, the Indochinese Delegate can realize that the whole of the Socialist Party sides with you to oppose the crimes committed by the bourgeois class.

Ho's Appeal at the Founding of the Communist Party of Indochina, 1930

Workers, peasants, soldiers, youth, and pupils!
Oppressed and exploited compatriots!
Sisters and brothers! Comrades!
Imperialist contradictions were the cause of the 1914–18 World War. After this horrible slaughter, the world was divided into two camps: One is the revolutionary camp including the oppressed colonies and the exploited working class throughout the world. The vanguard force of this camp is the Soviet Union. The other is the counterrevolutionary camp of international capitalism and imperialism whose general staff is the League of Nations.

During this World War, various nations suffered untold losses in property and human lives. The French imperialists were the hardest hit. Therefore, in order to restore the capitalist forces in France, the French imperialists have resorted to every underhand scheme to intensify their capitalist exploitation in Indochina. They set up new factories to exploit the workers with low wages. They plundered the peasants' land to establish plantations and drive them to utter poverty. They levied many heavy taxes. They imposed public loans upon our people. In short, they reduced us to wretchedness. They increased their military forces, firstly to strangle the Vietnamese revolution, secondly to prepare for a new imperialist war in the Pacific aimed at capturing new colonies, thirdly to suppress the Chinese revolution, fourthly to attack the Soviet Union because the latter helps the revolution of the oppressed nations and the exploited working class. World War II will break out. When it breaks, the French imperialists will certainly drive our people to a more horrible slaughter. If we give them a free hand to prepare for this war, suppress the Chinese revolution, and attack the Soviet Union, if we give them a free hand to stifle the Vietnamese revolution, it is tantamount to giving them a free hand to wipe our race off the earth and drown our nation in the Pacific.

However the French imperialists' barbarous oppression and ruthless exploitation have awakened our compatriots, who have all realized that revolution is the only road to life, without it they will die out piecemeal. This is the reason why the Vietnamese revolutionary movement has grown even stronger with each passing day. The workers refuse to work, the peasants demand land, the pupils strike, the traders boycott. Everywhere the masses have risen to oppose the French imperialists.

The Vietnamese revolution has made the French imperialists tremble with fear. On the one hand, they utilize the feudalists and comprador bourgeois in our country to oppress and exploit our people. On the other, they terrorize, arrest, jail, deport, and kill a great number of Vietnamese revolutionaries. If the French imperialists think that they can suppress the Vietnamese revolution by means of terrorist acts, they are utterly mistaken. Firstly, it is because the Vietnamese revolution is not isolated but enjoys the assistance of the world proletarian class in general and of the French working class in particular. Secondly, while the French imperialists are frenziedly carrying out terrorist acts, the Vietnamese Communists, formerly working separately, have now united into a single party, the Communist Party of Indochina, to lead our entire people in their revolution.

Workers, peasants, soldiers, youth, pupils!

Oppressed and exploited compatriots!

The Communist Party of Indochina is founded. It is the party of the working class. It will help the proletarian class to lead the revolution in order to struggle for all the oppressed and exploited people. From now on we must join the Party, help it and follow it in order to implement the following slogans:

1. To overthrow French imperialism, feudalism, and the reactionary Vietnamese capitalist class.
2. To make Indochina completely independent.
3. To establish a worker-peasant and soldier government.
4. To confiscate the banks and other enterprises belonging to the impe-

rialists and put them under the control of the worker-peasant and soldier government.

5. To confiscate the whole of the plantations and property belonging to the imperialists and the Vietnamese reactionary capitalist class and distribute them to poor peasants.
6. To implement the eight-hour working day.
7. To abolish public loans and poll tax. To waive unjust taxes hitting the poor people.
8. To bring back all freedoms to the masses.
9. To carry out universal education.
10. To implement equality between man and woman.

The Vietnamese Declaration of Independence, 1945

All men are created equal; they are endowed by their Creator with certain unalienable Rights; among these are Life, Liberty, and the pursuit of Happiness.

This immortal statement was made in the Declaration of Independence of the United States of America in 1776. In a broader sense, this means: All the peoples on the earth are equal from birth, all the peoples have a right to live, to be happy and free.

The Declaration of the French Revolution made in 1791 on the Rights of Man and the Citizen also states: "All men are born free and with equal rights, and must always remain free and have equal rights."

Those are undeniable truths.

Nevertheless, for more than eighty years, the French imperialists, abusing the standard of Liberty, Equality, and Fraternity, have violated our Fatherland and oppressed our fellow citizens. They have acted contrary to the ideals of humanity and justice.

In the field of politics, they have deprived our people of every democratic liberty.

They have enforced inhuman laws; they have set up three distinct political regimes in the North, the Center, and the South of Viet-Nam in order to wreck our national unity and prevent our people from being united.

They have built more prisons than schools. They have mercilessly slain our patriots; they have drowned our uprisings in rivers of blood.

They have fettered public opinion; they have practiced obscurantism against our people.

To weaken our race they have forced us to use opium and alcohol.

In the field of economics, they have fleeced us to the backbone, impoverished our people and devastated our land.

They have robbed us of our rice fields, our mines, our forests, and our raw materials. They have monopolized the issuing of bank notes and the export trade.

They have invented numerous unjustifiable taxes and reduced our people, especially our peasantry, to a state of extreme poverty.

They have hampered the prospering of our national bourgeoisie; they have mercilessly exploited our workers.

In the autumn of 1940, when the Japanese fascists violated Indochina's territory to establish new bases in their fight against the Allies, the French imperialists went down on their bended knees and handed over our country to them.

Thus, from that date, our people were subjected to the double yoke of the French and the Japanese. Their sufferings and miseries increased. The result was that, from the end of last year to the beginning of this year, from Quang Tri Province to the North of Viet-Nam, more than two million of our fellow citizens died from starvation. On March 9 [1945], the French troops were disarmed by the Japanese. The French colonialists either fled or surrendered, showing that not only were they incapable of "protecting" us, but that, in the span of five years, they had twice sold our country to the Japanese.

On several occasions before March 9, the Viet Minh League urged the French to ally themselves with it against the Japanese. Instead of agreeing to this proposal, the French colonialists so intensified their terrorist activities against the Viet Minh members that before fleeing they massacred a great number of our political prisoners detained at Yen Bay and Cao Bang.

Notwithstanding all this, our fellow citizens have always manifested toward the French a tolerant and humane attitude. Even after the Japanese *Putsch* of March, 1945, the Viet Minh League helped many Frenchmen to cross the frontier, rescued some of them from Japanese jails, and protected French lives and property.

From the autumn of 1940, our country had in fact ceased to be a French colony and had become a Japanese possession.

After the Japanese had surrendered to the Allies, our whole people rose to regain our national sovereignty and to found the Democratic Republic of Viet-Nam.

The truth is that we have wrested our independence from the Japanese and not from the French.

The French have fled, the Japanese have capitulated, Emperor Bao Dai has abdicated. Our people have broken the chains which for nearly a century have fettered them and have won independence for the Fatherland. Our people at the same time have overthrown the monarchic regime that has reigned supreme for dozens of centuries. In its place has been established the present Democratic Republic.

For these reasons, we, members of the Provisional Government, representing the whole Vietnamese people, declare that from now on we break off all relations of a colonial character with France; we repeal all the international obligation that France has so far subscribed to on behalf of Viet-Nam, and we abolish all the special rights the French have unlawfully acquired in our Fatherland.

The whole Vietnamese people, animated by a common purpose, are determined to fight to the bitter end against any attempt by the French colonialists to reconquer their country.

We are convinced that the Allied nations, which at Teheran and San Francisco have acknowledged the principles of self-determination and equality of nations, will not refuse to acknowledge the independence of Viet-Nam.

A people who have courageously opposed French domination for more than eighty years, a people who have fought side by side with the Allies against the fascists during these last years, such a people must be free and independent.

For these reasons, we, members of the Provisional Government of the Democratic Republic of Viet-Nam, solemnly declare to the world that Viet-Nam has the right to be a free and independent country—and in fact it is so already. The entire Vietnamese people are determined to mobilize all their physical and mental strength, to sacrifice their lives and property in order to safeguard their independence and liberty.

✗ E S S A Y S

In the opening essay, John T. McAlister, Jr., formerly of Princeton University, provides a brief overview of Vietnam's historical development up to the imposition of French colonial rule in the late nineteenth century. He emphasizes several persistent themes in the nation's history, including regionalism and village autonomy. Next, David G. Marr of Australian National University states that the Vietnamese revolution of 1945 cannot be understood without reference to prior changes in Vietnam's social structure and intellectual outlook. Particularly significant to later developments were ideological transformations within the intelligentsia—shifts that preceded and ultimately contributed to the success of the Vietminh. William J. Duiker, a historian at Pennsylvania State University, contends in the last selection that the key to communist success was the utilization of Vietnamese nationalism in the struggle to evict the French. His essay helps explain how communism became the most vital element within the Vietnamese nationalist movement by the 1930s.

Vietnam: A Historical Overview

JOHN T. McALISTER, JR.

For a people with a two-thousand-year heritage of occupation, rebellion, and a troubled search for order, the revolution launched in August 1945 represented a major landmark. It not only inaugurated a new approach to politics in Viet Nam, but also marked a millennium of freedom from Chinese occupation. Before the year 939, when the Vietnamese threw off China's direct control over their affairs, they had been ruled as a Chinese province for a thousand years. Yet the tortuous history of the country even predates

From *Vietnam: The Origins of Revolution* by John T. McAlister, Jr., pp. 17–31, 42–43, 46–47. Copyright © 1969 by the Center of International Studies, Princeton, N.J. Reprinted by permission of Alfred A. Knopf, Inc.

Chinese control. The record goes back to 208 B.C., when the Vietnamese first appeared in official annals as a minority people in the kingdom of Nam Viet, known in Chinese history as Nan-yüeh.

Covering wide areas of present-day northern Viet Nam and southern China, the kingdom of Nam Viet was created by a renegade Chinese warlord. He had taken advantage of the decay of China's first imperial dynasty to assert his marginal power based on regional military occupation. His political creation, Nam Viet, remained autonomous for nearly a century because the power of the emerging Han dynasty was restricted to north and central China, where it was struggling to consolidate dynastic control. In the pattern that was to become familiar on China's southern periphery when its imperial regimes were weak or preoccupied internally, Nam Viet was recognized as an autonomous kingdom over which the Han retained a nominal though unenforceable sovereignty. Within the loose structure of the kingdom, the forebears of the Vietnamese were permitted their own administration. This structure consisted of fiefs governed by hereditary chiefs in the sort of feudal system that still exists among the mountain peoples of northern Viet Nam. However, after 111 B.C., when the Han dynasty was strong enough to extend its power southward and absorb Nam Viet into the Chinese empire, the Vietnamese fiefs became provinces of China.

Despite the deep imprint made on them by Chinese culture of the Han and T'ang dynasties, these early Vietnamese possessed a zeal for political autonomy. Among the numerous peoples on the southern periphery of China, only the Vietnamese adopted Chinese culture without becoming a part of the Chinese political system. Only in Viet Nam "did the [Chinese] culture outpace the [Chinese] political unit. The Vietnamese speak a Sinitic language related to Chinese; they derived their higher culture from China; and they were for a long period under Chinese rule." Yet eventually they managed to establish their identity as a separate country within East Asian civilization. Indeed it may be that the adoption of Chinese culture made it possible for the Vietnamese to free themselves from political control by China. In the view of the noted scholar Henri Maspéro, Viet Nam was able to assert its autonomy because Chinese occupation, "by breaking the power of particularist institutions and local groups, and by introducing Chinese ideas and social organization, gave it a cohesion and formal structure which its neighbors lacked." Whether or not the imposition of Chinese culture was instrumental in winning the Vietnamese their autonomy, it seems certain that the way the culture was imposed provided the motivation for them to seek an end to rule by China.

Efforts to absorb the Vietnamese into the Chinese empire were carried on sporadically and haphazardly throughout a millenium of occupation. In fact it seems that the Chinese overlords were more concerned with pacifying these peripheral minority peoples than in assimilating them. As the pressure of the Chinese occupation progressively curtailed the influence of Vietnamese feudal leaders, they were afforded virtually no compensating opportunities to join the broader political and cultural world of the Chinese empire. Because the local aristocracy saw that a continuation of Chinese policy threatened to wipe them out, their hostility toward the occupation rose sharply until it culminated in a rebellion in A.D. 40. Crushed by an expedition of Chinese reinforcements, this desperate revolt by a decaying feudal regime was followed by one of the most thorough attempts to implant Chinese culture among the Vietnamese ever undertaken. Perhaps the most important result of this program was to speed the intermarriage of Vietnamese with Chinese settlers and functionaries. A new elite emerged with a commitment to Chinese language and culture that would have been difficult to obtain by coercion alone. Although this new racially mixed local elite enjoyed none of the privileges or influence of their feudal predecessors, they too were a hereditary aristocracy, but with family ties now based on Chinese customs.

The emphasis on cultural assimilation which had produced a Chinese-oriented aristocracy among the Vietnamese was not matched by efforts to absorb them into Chinese politics. Only gradually and hesitantly was this local elite allowed to participate in the Chinese provincial administration over the Vietnamese. They had to qualify for appointment by mastering the same examinations in Chinese literature and philosophy that were required of Chinese administrative officials. But, as the Han dynasty was in the decline, these administratively qualified Vietnamese demanded and were granted a status—equal to that of any qualified Chinese—which entitled them to be assigned anywhere in the empire. Mixed-blood Vietnamese were actually appointed as subprefects in two Chinese provinces. But these promising beginnings in cultural and political integration came abruptly to an end with the fall of the Han dynasty in A.D. 220.

Thereafter, China suffered several centuries of internal political disintegration. Not only did Chinese preoccupation with domestic politics reduce pressures on the Vietnamese, but it also encouraged them to seek their own political identity separate from China. Significantly, the abortive attempts to establish an autonomous Vietnamese kingdom between 542 and 602 were led by the local racially mixed aristocracy. Their short-lived kingdom was an expression of the political consciousness and skills they had acquired through Chinese culture but had been able to use only slightly within the Chinese empire. Although their flimsy kingdom was easily destroyed by the Chinese, little was done to resolve the underlying causes of the uprising. When China was once again brought under centralized control, in 618 by the T'ang dynasty, little effort was made to integrate the Vietnamese into Chinese political life. The T'ang simply used their burgeoning power to impose the most severe occupation the Vietnamese had ever known. But the power of the T'ang, like that of previous dynasties, had its limits and when it had run its course the resultant weakness in China coincided with an increasing political strength among the Vietnamese. By 939 an autonomous Vietnamese kingdom was able to defend itself against direct Chinese control.

This assertion of local strength did not mean complete independence for Viet Nam. Reimposition of Chinese rule—as was threatened during the

Mongol invasion of 1285, and as occurred briefly, 1413–37, during the Ming dynasty—was always a factor in Vietnamese politics. Instead of asserting their independence of China, which would have run the risk of frequent struggles over the reintroduction of Chinese military occupation, the Vietnamese had earlier become one of China's tributary states. Until France gained control in 1885, the Vietnamese ritually acknowledged the supremacy of China and periodically sent missions bearing tribute. Moreover, these ritual ties contained a fiber of strength in the recognized prerogative of the Chinese court to invest the Vietnamese emperors with their legitimacy to rule. Rather than stimulating Chinese interference in Vietnamese affairs, this symbolic investiture contributed to stability because of the careful scrutiny given to new claimants of political legitimacy.

Once the Vietnamese had freed themselves of a millennium of Chinese domination, they struggled for another millennium with the consequences of their own autonomy. The ending of Chinese control did not mean that the Vietnamese had achieved political unity and stability. For nearly ten centuries they fought among themselves in attempting to institutionalize political power into a unified government having authority over all the Vietnamese. Significantly, the incipient dynasty that was instrumental in asserting Vietnamese autonomy from China was unable to consolidate its power in Viet Nam. Persisting feudal groups thwarted the ephemeral Ngo dynasty (A.D. 939–69) in its ambition to unify the Vietnamese. Even less durable regimes followed the Ngo as competing families sought to subdue their rivals by military force and impose their hereditary rule on the country. Not until 1009, nearly a century after Chinese rule ended, did one group prevail over its rivals and consolidate political power into a durable regime.

The leaders of the resilient Ly dynasty (1009–1225) succeeded in institutionalizing their power by stages. First they established a military administration to translate their predominant strength into territorial control over the country. But the durability of the dynasty for over two centuries undoubtedly resulted from their capacity to transform coercive force into a governmental authority widely accepted as having the legitimate use of power. This institutionalized strength was achieved by sharing power more widely and making the access to power more orderly than under military control. Specifically, a civil administration was established with recruitment based on the Chinese examination system. From this procedure a bureaucracy was created that represented those most thoroughly knowledgeable in Chinese language and culture.

Selection to the bureaucracy, or mandarinate, as the Europeans baptized this scholar-administration, was theoretically open without regard to social standing to all who could satisfy the qualifications. Since education in Chinese culture became the primary criterion for political mobility, some members of the mandarinate, called mandarins by the Europeans, did come from modest social origins. However, since only those with extensive resources could afford the leisure of long years of preparation for these examinations, the bureaucracy in fact institutionalized the power of the families with the greatest wealth and cohesion. Instead of turning their resources into military power with which to fight for dynastic succession, the Vietnamese families gradually accepted competition for political power on a more orderly basis. But despite the rigor of the examinations, power in Viet Nam was still largely hereditary.

For nearly four hundred years, between the eleventh and the fourteenth centuries, the mandarin system of bureaucracy provided relative internal order under conditions of almost constant threat of invasion by aggressive neighbors and dynastic usurpation at home. Domestic challenges to dynastic rule, often militant in character, were never sufficient to bring down the mandarin system, at least not until other factors weakened internal order. Even when the long rule of the Ly dynasty came to an end in 1225 for lack of a male heir, there was no outbreak of internal war. The Tran dynasty (1225–1400) succeeded to dynastic rule by arranging a marriage with the female heir of the Ly family, but it was by preserving the mandarinal system that they maintained the continuity of power. The Tran thus perpetuated a period of political coherence, nearly four centuries long, that was in sharp contrast to the turmoil of both earlier and later epochs.

The institutionalization of power that the mandarinal system had helped to achieve was eventually undermined by critical requirements for external defense. While the threat of invasion was a perennial dilemma, it was not until the late fourteenth century that a sustained external challenge appeared. Until then China and the other bordering states periodically attacked the Vietnamese. But in the fourteenth century, as well as in earlier periods, the main threat came from Champa, a hostile kingdom founded about A.D. 192 on Hindu cultural traditions. Champa was located just south of the Red River Delta in present-day central Viet Nam. The great Vietnamese vulnerability to spoiling attacks by Champa was reduced only after autonomy from China had been won in A.D. 939 and the forces necessary for external defense had been mobilized. By the middle of the eleventh century the Vietnamese were able to sack Champa's capital and kill its king in retaliation for a Cham invasion. As a result of such military strength the Vietnamese acquired in 1069 their first portion of Champa's territory in what was to become a steady southward expansion. Under relentless pressure the Chams were diminished by the twentieth century to a minority status in a greatly enlarged Viet Nam.

Ultimately the Vietnamese had reacted to Cham invasions by a program of territorial expansion aimed at destroying the kingdom of Champa and absorbing its domain. Yet this action was not without its political costs. They emerged when a series of Cham campaigns over a thirty-year period (1360–90) brought an unexpected military challenge to institutionalized political power in Viet Nam. The threat came not from the invaders, who were effectively repulsed, but from a trusted military leader, Le Quy Ly. He had saved the Vietnamese kingdom from destruction and occupation, yet in the process his power had gone beyond the level that could be controlled by dynastic political authority; so had his ambitions. In 1400 he overthrew the Tran dynasty, proclaimed himself Emperor Ho Quy Ly and in effect returned the country to a competition for political power through control of military force. His actions set in motion a sequence of events that increased Viet Nam's reliance on military might and made a return to institutionalized political power increasingly difficult.

After Ho Quy Ly's usurpation the resulting turmoil among the Vietnamese weakened them internally and invited the intervention of China. The former overlords came ostensibly to restore the Tran, but in fact they wished to annex the country. For two decades, 1408–28, a fierce resistance against Chinese occupation was carried on through guerrilla warfare until Le Loi—a great hero of Vietnamese history and the founder of the Le dynasty (1428–1527)—recaptured control over the country and obtained recognition of autonomy from China. Although his successors made great strides in restoring order to the war-ravaged country, their most enduring achievements were also in the field of military operations. An invasion of Champa succeeded in destroying the political viability of the rival kingdom in 1471. Severely diminished in territory, Champa lingered on for another two hundred years before the Vietnamese finally occupied and settled the whole of its territory. However, in the course of this occupation the expansiveness of Vietnamese military power merely posed more sharply the challenge to Vietnamese political ingenuity. Could the Vietnamese consolidate their gains through resilient institutions?

Southward migration (known as *Nam Tiên* in Vietnamese), following in the wake of the conquest of Champa, altered Vietnamese life fundamentally. Vietnamese territory almost doubled its original size, and the country's population, formerly concentrated in the Red River Delta, became scattered throughout areas more than six hundred miles away. The problems of increased scale produced parochial pressures too great for traditional politics to manage, and Viet Nam's central institutions gave way. Though these institutions were modeled on those of the Chinese empire—within which the total area of Viet Nam would have been no more than a province or two—the Vietnamese, as their territory expanded, could not make these institutions work effectively. Even through military administration the Le, unlike previous dynasties, could no longer maintain territorial control over the whole country. Regionalism had become the stronger force.

By 1516 three families had emerged with a disproportionate amount of armed strength in the society while the ruling dynasty had virtually no power at all. The country fell into a state of anarchy, with rich agricultural areas being pillaged by mercenary troops hired by rival families; farming was interrupted and famine spread over the land. It seemed impossible to repeat the previously successful strategy in which the Ly dynasty (1009–1225) had achieved control over the whole country by force and then transformed military power into political institutions. With the expansion of Vietnamese territory it had become easier for more numerous and formidable military groups to develop from fertile agricultural bases; regionalism was ascendant.

In the midst of this breakdown of central authority, one of the three dominant families, the Mac, attempted in 1527 to unify the country under its dynastic control. Instead, their bid for power precipitated a fratricidal internal war that continued spasmodically until just before the French intervened in Viet Nam, almost three hundred years later. As the war became more protracted, the conflict was gradually stabilized by a partition of the country into defined territories controlled by the rival families. The beginning of this trend toward partition occurred in 1592 when the Mac were driven out of the Red River Delta by the force protecting the vestigial Le dynasty. Rather than restoring unity, the victory over the Mac merely aggravated an already strong spirit of enmity between the Trinh and the Nguyen, the two other dominant families. While they were united in opposing the Mac, these two families were divided by their desire to exercise unchallenged influence over the impotent Le rulers. They both regarded the Le as the only legitimate authority in the country, yet each accused the other of fomenting rebellion. On the outcome of this dynastic impasse rested the unity and stability of Viet Nam for more than two centuries.

Lines between the two rival families hardened as the Nguyen steadily consolidated their strength south of the Red River Delta along the strategic coastal plain. Unable to reconcile their struggle for dynastic influence and regional power, in 1620 the two adversaries confronted each other with fierce combat. This conflict persisted tenaciously for fifty years until it subsided into an armed stalemate which divided the country, north and south, into distinct areas of political-military control. The disintegration of the country into two warring states was symbolized by a wall built across the narrow waist of Viet Nam at the 18th parallel, near the town of Dong Hoi, just north of Hue. Erected by the Nguyen, the wall of Dong Hoi rose to a height of eighteen feet, extended a distance of eleven miles, and in 1672 proved strong enough to withstand a major military test from the Trinh in the north. Thereafter the country remained divided for another century on almost the same territorial basis as it is today.

Besides stimulating divisive political tendencies, territorial expansion also brought to Viet Nam an unusual geographic shape—one especially conducive to regionalism and rebellion. The striking dimensions of the territory that has resulted from relentless southward movement are its length of approximately one thousand miles and its width of only three hundred miles at its widest and about forty-five miles at its narrowest. Striking as they are, these dimensions do not reflect the fact that Viet Nam lacks geographic unity. Overall, it is an S-shaped country fragmented with mountain chains and held together by a thin coastal plain loosely connecting two deltas at extreme ends of the territory. Except for the generous extent of seacoast with frequent harbors, few natural avenues of communication span the length of the country. Isolated areas—especially those in the narrow central coastal plain, but also in the mountainous regions surrounding the deltas—have historically posed difficulties for central administration and given a haven to rebels.

In creating problems of regionalism and rebellion, the character of the terrain has been emphasized by the pattern of population settlement. If military conquest alone had been the instrument of Viet Nam's expansion, it is doubtful the Vietnamese would occupy the territory they do today.

Close behind the military forces were the settlers ready to bring the land under cultivation. Yet the terrain, in addition to limiting communications, also restricted the locations in which the Vietnamese population could settle. Only land permitting the cultivation of rice under irrigation, the very foundation of the country's agricultural society, was suitable for Vietnamese migration. Such areas were extensive in the deltas located at either end of the territory; but in the approximately six hundred miles in between there were only small and frequently isolated fragments of land, snatched from the encroachment of the mountains on one side and the sea on the other. Not only was it difficult to adapt the Vietnamese style of wet rice agriculture to the surrounding mountains, but these highlands were infested with the malaria-carrying anopheles mosquito.

The overall limits these barriers imposed upon Vietnamese settlement are best seen in the curious pattern of population distribution that has emerged from southward migration. Today, roughly 30,000,000 Vietnamese are crowded into less than 20,000 of the country's approximately 128,000 square miles of territory. More than 90 per cent of the population is concentrated in less than 20 per cent of the land area, a fact which results in some of the densest population clusters anywhere in the world. Because of their rice agriculture and vulnerability to upland malaria, the Vietnamese live in the fertile lowlands. The remaining 100,000-plus square miles of plateau and mountains are sparsely populated by non-Vietnamese ethnic minorities, who are less advanced culturally than the lowlanders. Thus a major dichotomy between the upland and the lowland areas is reinforced by ethnic as well as other cultural differences.

A focus on this settlement pattern of the Vietnamese people—their reliance on irrigated rice agriculture and their history of territorial expansion—illuminates much that is complex and obscure in their past. Such a perspective sheds light on strengths and weaknesses of Vietnamese politics and society. A hypothesis of the geographer Pierre Gourou is that in a tropical country the cultivation of rice in flooded fields is what alone gives rise to the development of an advanced civilization, while at the same time limiting it both culturally and geographically. In Viet Nam these strengths and limits are best seen through the prime module of social development— the village. It was due primarily to the cohesion and flexibility of the Vietnamese village that popular migration followed upon military conquest. The village was the institution that translated the potential of the newly occupied land into the reality of productive habitation.

A system of sponsored settlement developed in which established villages sent out pioneers. They were usually young people or others without land who were eager to get new fields and create new villages. Support from the parent villages continued until the offspring were self-sufficient. Then official recognition was requested from the emperor, who bestowed a name, a communal seal, and a guardian spirit upon the new village. These imperial articles were traditionally kept in a communal house (known as the *dình*) which was in effect the symbol of village unity: a place for religious ceremonies and public occasions and in a sense a ritual link with the rest of the country.

Through this process the Vietnamese village facilitated the southward territorial advance that simply went beyond the country's capacity to consolidate its gains through political centralization. The experience after 1500, of nearly three centuries of regionalism and disunity—trends never fully resolved before France assumed control over the country—raises several fundamental questions about traditional politics in Viet Nam. Perhaps the key question is why the village was such an effective instrument of cultural expansion while central institutions were not. The answer seems to lie in the deeply rooted autonomy of the village, which, though guaranteed by statute, had evolved through custom and practice. According to an old Vietnamese proverb, "the laws of the emperor yield to the customs of the village."

The substance behind this proverb came from the restraint village institutions imposed on the power of the central authorities. The development of these local institutions, it seems, predated those of the central administration; their origins are often traced to the period before China's occupation was overthrown. . . .

By the end of the eighteenth century a stalemate had endured for a century between the northern (Trinh) and southern (Nguyen) regimes without there having been a major military engagement. But this lack of conflict did not indicate that the sources of rebellion had been resolved. During the seventeenth and eighteenth centuries the Nguyen had continued Vietnamese expansion southward until they had occupied the Mekong Delta over the opposition of its Cambodian inhabitants. Just as this expansion was reaching its apogee, a rebellion broke out in the Nguyen territory south of Hue, in central Viet Nam. Breaking a century of stalemate, this uprising gave the northerners, the Trinh, an unexpected opportunity to extend their control over the whole of Viet Nam. Through ineptness, however, the Trinh alienated the southern rebels, known as the Tay Son, who turned on the Trinh while also fighting the Nguyen. Except for the male heir to their familial leadership, the Nguyen had been virtually eliminated by 1777, and less than a decade later, Trinh rule in the north had been defeated decisively by the Tay Son.

Although rebellion had brought disunity in the sixteenth century, it was out of this Tay Son rebellion that Viet Nam found unity in the nineteenth. At the conclusion of the Tay Son rebellion in 1802, Vietnamese territory was united from the China border to the Gulf of Siam for the first time in history. But this historic achievement was not accomplished by the Tay Son. In an epic conflict the surviving heir to the Nguyen regime capitalized on the Tay Son's preoccupation in the north to return from exile, recapture the Mekong Delta, and in 1788, seize control over the strategic region around Saigon. The heir, who later proclaimed himself Emperor Gia Long, might have been unable to consolidate these territorial gains and unify the country had it not been for the arrival of substantial military and naval reinforcements from France. Arranged by the French missionary prelate, Bishop Pigneau de Behaine, this vital aid marked the revival of a dormant interest in Viet Nam by the French church.

Opportunities for outside involvement in Viet Nam's internal conflict had existed since warfare divided the country in 1620. French interests in Viet Nam had stemmed from this earlier period in which the Nguyen regime had also been dependent on external aid. French priests had been in the country since the early seventeenth century, when the Nguyen's initial weakness against the Trinh had led them to seek sophisticated weaponry from the Portuguese. These French priests, part of a Portuguese Jesuit mission, were so successful in winning converts that they were expelled when the armed stalemate reduced the Nguyen's dependency on foreign aid. Not until the 1780's with the outbreak of the Tay Son rebellion, did France's freedom from world-wide commitments coincide with an opportunity for influence in Viet Nam. But the French revolution cut short the participation of forces raised by the influence of the French clergy at Versailles. Once again France's interest in Viet Nam subsided.

When Emperor Gia Long unified Viet Nam in 1802, the country's capacities for political centralization reached a high-water mark. Realizing that this unity had been essentially a military achievement, the new emperor tried to overcome the regionalism that had divided the country for centuries. Institutions were created to promote the political integration of the Vietnamese people, but regional and parochial identities continued to exert stronger pressures. Beneath the surface of apparent political unity the governors of the various regions held the real power while formally acknowledging the sovereignty of the emperor. Unfortunately for the future of Vietnamese politics, even this promising trend toward unification was ended with Gia Long's death, and in 1820 an authoritarian and xenophobic policy was inaugurated by his heirs.

Once again internal tensions created opportunities for outside intervention. Through the xenophobic policies of Gia Long's successors, the French were denied the influence in Vietnamese affairs they had enjoyed during the fight for unification and had come to expect during the period of consolidation. Not surprisingly, it was the Catholic missionaries who were the hardest hit. Gia Long's successors saw Christianity as a threat to the Confucian traditions upon which Vietnamese politics were founded. They proscribed Christian missions and eventually put some of the French clergymen to death. Since protection by the Far Eastern fleet for French missionaries became a significant issue in France, the Vietnamese attacks on the church provided a convenient opportunity for Napoleon III to solidify the tenuous domestic position of the Second Empire.

After initial setbacks, the intervention in Viet Nam launched by Napoleon III in response to domestic religious sentiment became the special interest of the French navy. More interested in acquiring territory than religious converts, the navy's enthusiasm resulted in the occupation of Viet Nam and the ethnic and culturally distinct areas of Cambodia and Laos. These disparate countries were formed, in 1897, into a territory known thereafter as Indochina—a name chosen as a semantic compensation for French colonial failures in India and China at the hands of the British.

In administering their territorial acquisition, the French created a state in which colonial administration virtually supplanted indigenous politics. Obviously, the primary French concern was to prevent Vietnamese opposition from threatening their colonial rule. Although they could not stop rebellion entirely, the French did neutralize it through military and administrative control. Yet the effect of these preventives was to eliminate all but the most circumscribed and stylized political activity. In becoming the country's incumbent government, the French suppressed the energies that had gone into centuries of political conflict among the Vietnamese. Almost no legitimate channels for political expression existed; the politics of the Vietnamese became synonymous with sedition in French Indochina. Unintentionally, however, Vietnamese political energies were enlarged by the unexpected social consequences of colonial programs. Ultimately, when French strength wavered in the 1940s, pent-up political energies erupted in a revolution that no amount of French force could subdue.

The suppression of Vietnamese political life was begun by the administrative partitioning of the country, which occurred initially through the uneven pattern of French military occupation. Viet Nam would have been occupied all at once except for the limits on French resources imposed by other foreign commitments; a combination of far-flung imperial ambitions and domestic counter-pressures made the French occupation a piecemeal affair. By the treaty of June 1862, the southernmost portion of Viet Nam, called Cochinchina by its French occupiers, came under French control. The central and northern parts of the country, known to the French as Annam and Tonkin, did not become parts of the French empire until more than twelve years after Cochinchina was occupied. Annam—the former Chinese name for all Viet Nam and a term considered derogatory by the Vietnamese—and Tonkin were acquired through treaties of 1884–5 with the Vietnamese government at Hue and the Chinese at Peking. The resulting fragmentation of the country was perpetuated by a colonial mythology which regarded Viet Nam not as one country but three: Annam, Tonkin, and Cochinchina. Even the name *Viêt Nam*, with which the country had been baptized by Gia Long in 1802, was outlawed and uttered only as a rallying cry of revolutionaries.

Partitioning Viet Nam into three parts aided the security of France's colonial state against countrywide uprisings. Administrative barriers were imposed to discourage the Vietnamese from unifying their potential resources against the French. Such obstacles helped to perpetuate the traditional pressures of regionalism and parochialism that had previously limited Vietnamese political unity. . . .

Besides reinforcing old—mainly regional—tensions, French colonial policies created new ones. Although colonially sponsored social change became clustered regionally, it was not planned that way. A reinforced regionalism was a by-product of changes that resulted from programs directed toward other, primarily economic, purposes. In broad outline these

changes occurred from the creation of an export economy in primary products—mainly rice and rubber, but some minerals—with a protected market
for French manufactured imports; from the introduction of taxation in
money to finance expenditures of the colonial budget; and from the expansion of primary education. While these changes held out the promise
of modernization, they were insufficient to achieve that goal; they left Viet
Nam halfway between the traditional and modern worlds. Viet Nam's colonial economy was vulnerable to fluctuations in international commodity and
monetary markets and did not possess the institutional structure for sustained economic growth. Moreover, it lacked a self-generating industrial
sector to absorb the people drawn into the towns in hopes of gaining access
to the monetary economy. . . .

Under the impact of French colonialism, Viet Nam became "a nation
off balance." Social changes had been induced by colonial programs, but
there was hardly a harmonious relationship between the new society and
the old Viet Nam. These changes had "dislocated the traditional mode of
life and produced a poorly integrated society in which a small, urban-
oriented Westernized elite was largely alienated from the bulk of the village
based population." Although harmony had been intermittent in traditional
Viet Nam, it seems to have been a widely shared ideal, especially in the
life of the villages. The basis for this harmony had been a structure of
authority based on Confucian precepts and buttressed by strong patrilineal
kinship ties. The social changes wrought during colonial rule were undoubtedly necessary if Viet Nam were to participate in the interdependent
life of the modern world. However, too little attention was given to the
effects of this process on the structure of authority or popular compliance.
Since the village has been and continues to be the foundation of Vietnamese
society, the deterioration of its resiliency was certain to have a strong
impact on the stability of the society as a whole. Because the villages lay
outside the modern sector that France was creating in the urban centers,
this social instability was not apparent. French administration, commerce,
and military force once provided a veneer of stability on a society halfway
between the traditional and the modern world.

The Colonial Impact

DAVID G. MARR

In 1938 at least eighteen million Vietnamese were being kept in check by
a mere 27,000 colonial troops. Yet a scant sixteen years later, colonial
forces totalling 450,000 were unable to avoid tactical disaster at Dien Bien
Phu and compulsory strategic evacuation south of the seventeenth parallel.
Finally, in the years 1965–1975, various combinations of American, Republic of Vietnam, South Korean, and other allied armed forces totalling

David G. Marr, *Vietnamese Tradition on Trial, 1920–1945*, pp. 1–13, 413–416. Copyright ©
1981, The Regents of the University of California. Reprinted by permission.

up to 1.2 million men were outfoxed, stalemated, and eventually vanquished by the National Liberation Front and the People's Army of Vietnam.

A host of explanations have been offered for this dramatic transformation in the capabilities of both sides. French and American generals have argued that massive attacks in the early stages of Vietnamese revolutionary activity could have nipped resistance in the bud. Possibly. Nevertheless, those same generals discovered that political and economic realities at home, first in Paris, then in Washington, ruled out such a Draconian solution. Other participants or observers have variously stressed the strength of primordial Vietnamese patriotism, the fury of any oppressed people lashing out at its oppressors, sophisticated communist organizing techniques, an increased Vietnamese capability to assimilate and employ modern technology, substantial international support, French and American ignorance of Vietnamese conditions, and the mass media explosion, which may have heightened revulsion in the "home" country.

None of these answers should be ignored by serious students of the struggle in Vietnam. Yet none really succeeds in explaining how, in a matter of a few years, hundreds of thousands of Vietnamese changed from seemingly docile French colonial subjects to experienced political cadres, pith-helmeted soldiers (*bo-doi*), literacy instructors, hygienists or soil technicians—all dedicated to driving out the foreigner and establishing an independent, strong, egalitarian nation. Patriotism and angry reactions to oppression may well have provided the emotional foundations, yet neither could tell Vietnamese how, when, or where to act. Organization and modern technology were certainly important, but to employ both effectively demanded some degree of conceptual transformation. Although international support was valuable, psychologically as well as materially, ultimately it was what the Vietnamese did with this backing that made the difference. As for weaknesses in enemy ranks, Vietnamese revolutionaries tried to comprehend and to exploit these wherever possible. However, they also learned from painful experience that simply to wait for enemy contradictions to manifest themselves was often to leave the initiative in the hands of others.

. . . All such developments in the twentieth-century history of Vietnam must be understood within the context of fundamental changes in political and social consciousness among a significant segment of the Vietnamese populace in the period 1920–45. These changes, while not necessarily decisive, were at least one precondition for mass mobilization and successful people's war strategies from 1945 onward. To cite only one example, there was the growing conviction that one's life was not preordained, that one need not eat dirt forever, that one could join with others to force change. Victory would not occur in a blinding flash, as assumed by many earlier Vietnamese political and social movements. Yet victory was inevitable, the fruit of millions of Vietnamese perceiving their self-interests and uniting against the common enemy, foreign and domestic.

Such ideas were only the beginning of a new consciousness. What was to be the nature of that victory? Certainly it was not seen by most to be the transferring of a heavenly mandate from one ruler to another. Nor was it to be simply destruction of the colonial system. Often the objective was said to be transforming Vietnam into a "civilized" (*van minh*) nation. Although this concept meant different things to different people, it generally encompassed mastery over nature, a spirit of civic responsibility, full development of the individual's mental, physical, and moral faculties, and the ability of Vietnamese to stand proud among other peoples of the world.

These were not tasks to be accomplished overnight. Indeed, much time was spent in the early stages questioning Vietnamese capacities to do much of anything except obey fate, squabble incessantly, and scramble for petty personal gains. Beneath this severe self-criticism, even psychological flagellation, however, lurked the belief that people could change dramatically. Otherwise, why bother to publish hundreds of pamphlets and articles challenging readers to renovate themselves? At any rate, by the late 1920s both the mood of self-disparagement and the emphasis on moral rearmament were being replaced by the belief that history was moving in Vietnam's direction, and that social forces would accomplish what individual regeneration could not.

This new faith was badly shaken by the French colonial repression of 1929–32. It recovered in the Popular Front period of 1936–39. It suffered again in the Japanese-Vichy crackdowns of 1940–44. And then it burst forth as never before in the August 1945 Revolution. Through all these ups and downs a growing number of Vietnamese were learning to combine optimism and patience, moral suasion and social mobilization, theory and practice. The intelligentsia also rediscovered pride in Vietnamese culture—on a selective basis.

Without a variety of economic and social changes from precolonial to colonial times in Vietnam there would probably not have been major changes in consciousness, or, if such changes had occurred, they would have been limited to a much smaller group of people, perhaps "enlightened" members of the royal family, trusted mandarins, and a handful of foreign-language interpreters, merchants, and literate Catholics. To carry this speculation a bit further, such men might have employed their newly acquired knowledge to engineer and to justify a range of institutional reforms. They might even have ended up sharing power with small new military and business elites, as happened in Thailand. But, just as in Thailand, the depth and breadth of intellectual transformation would have been far less substantial.

Vietnam never had that choice. From the 1850s Vietnam was under severe military threat. It was dismembered in the 1860s and 1870s, then swallowed completely by the French in the 1880s. By 1897 all armed resistance had been quelled. During the next five years Governor General Paul Doumer laid down the foundations and framework which were to characterize Indochina (Cambodia and Laos included) for the next four decades. These included a centralized and rather top-heavy administration, an expanded and greatly reinforced tax and corvée system, continued growth of the primary export sector by means of large land grants (often disregarding prior ownership or occupancy), near-monopoly status for French finance capital and product imports, and the construction of an impressive if not always economically viable network of railroads, roads, and canals.

Already before World War I three major changes were apparent in the lives of ordinary Vietnamese. First, the French had capacities to control and to coerce never dreamed of by previous rulers. For this reason less attention was devoted to the conciliatory political arts, to understanding local grievances, compromising, or sharing power with subordinates. It also meant that traditional village obligations to the ruler, in particular, taxes, corvée service, and military service, were no longer the subject of discreet negotiations, but could now be enforced with unprecedented efficiency. Nor was there still an open frontier beyond reach of the system, where aggrieved families could flee. It followed, too, that those Vietnamese who attached themselves to the new rulers and quickly grasped alien procedures could advance to positions of considerable wealth and self-esteem (but little real authority), without having to trouble themselves much about popular anger or any ethic of responsible government. In short, the French can be said to have strengthened some aspects of the traditional hierarchical structure to the detriment of the majority of Vietnamese, while allowing a new indigenous minority to share in the returns as long as they remained obedient and necessarily insensitive to popular grievances.

Secondly, through a policy of granting large land concessions to French companies and Vietnamese collaborators, together with the introduction of French concepts of private property and individual legal responsibility, the colonial government stimulated fundamental changes in village economic and social relations. Phrased most simply, there were now unprecedented pressures toward concentrated wealth, land alienation, and the growth of a class of landless and land-poor Vietnamese. For example, peasant families who had devoted one or more generations to clearing, tilling, and improving land now found themselves being evicted or converted into tenants, perhaps simply because they had not learned the new administrative rules as quickly as others. Small proprietors, who thought they had protected themselves legally, could still be outmaneuvered by means of usurious loans, cadastral manipulations, seizure for back taxes, or simply the duplicity of corrupt local officials. To cry out for redress in such situations was usually hopeless, and sometimes dangerous, since colonial retaliatory power was normally at the disposal of any landlord or official who kept in the good graces of his superiors.

As a corollary of this economic process, the corporate character of Vietnamese villages was gradually eroded. Communal lands—traditionally the basis of village social welfare palliatives, as well as providing modest support for local temples, schools, and routine administrative tasks—now increasingly became the private property of several well-placed families, or even came under the control of non-village members. As disparities in wealth increased, the selection of village notables, the observance of village festivals, the organizing of weddings, funerals, ceremonies to honor returning scholars and the like, became ever more the sources of contention and conspicuous consumption (both of which had always been present to some degree), and ever less the vital ritual reinforcements of community self-consciousness and solidarity. Simultaneously, richer and poorer members of clans and extended families drew further apart, the former mostly interested in special status to reflect their new wealth, the latter trying to borrow money cheaply and loosely according to outmoded lineage rationales. The ultimate breakdown of corporate ties often occurred, as one might expect, in those areas where individuals amassed enough land to leave the villages entirely. Such absentee landlords, particularly prevalent in south Vietnam, controlled the fates of hundreds or thousands of local people without ever having to meet them face to face, or, perhaps even more upsetting, showing up only at rent- or loan-collection times.

Finally, it may well be that the most important transformation of all had to do with the penetration of a cash economy into even the most isolated hamlets of Vietnam. While the implications of this change took several decades to become apparent, there is no doubt that from the turn of the century (earlier in Cochinchina) traditional multiple and personal forms of socio-economic interaction were being replaced by the single, essentially impersonal commercial exchange system. Central taxes were the cutting edge in most cases, levied on individuals rather than corporate villages as before. While several Vietnamese dynasties had experimented with taxes in cash, particularly portions of the land tax, payment in kind had always remained dominant. Now the French ordered that both the entire land tax and the even more onerous head tax be paid in silver—not the copper, zinc, or paper money recognized for other transactions, but solid silver piasters, which peasants often had to acquire solely for this purpose at marked-up rates of exchange from the money lenders or landlords. Corvée obligations could also be rendered in cash, for those who had it. On top of these payments there were diverse indirect taxes (marketing, stamp, consumer goods, transit, entrepot, navigation, etc.) as well as the government-controlled salt and liquor monopolies—all being more rigorously enforced than any comparable taxes of precolonial days. Even if a peasant continued to think of himself as essentially a subsistence farmer, he was being drawn further into the money economy by the tax system.

The preeminent economic objective of the French was to develop a modern export sector. They focused particularly on rice and mining, then later rubber as well. Taxation, monopoly, and market mechanisms soon worked relentlessly against the interests of peasants whose output had previously met the more diverse needs of an autonomous economy, but who were now non-competitive in an imperial operation controlled from Paris. Vietnamese might still need to eat something other than rice, but there were now financial disincentives in many regions to specializing in non-rice production. The same process hit traditional artisans hard, indeed wiping them out entirely if their specialty happened to compete with French imports. Peasants who derived some off-season income from making handicrafts, tools, or other simple essentials also found such opportunities drying up. Rice was now king—not just any rice, but rice in quantities and qualities suitable for export, and sent through channels dominated by non-local interests. A modicum of capital and contacts with officialdom were the two essential ingredients to success. Those who failed became part of the cheap labor pool, another essential ingredient if any company or family wished to set up a new plantation or start a new mining project.

With the outbreak of war in Europe in 1914 investments terminated abruptly. Vietnamese were pressed to help defeat the "Huns." As many as 100,000 peasants and artisans were rounded up and shipped to France to serve in labor battalions, and provided a source of some worry to the colonial authorities when they returned. Meanwhile, in Vietnam during the war, people were strongly "encouraged" to buy war bonds, in effect yet another tax. Rice exports increased. Locally produced goods were allowed temporarily to substitute for normal French imports. Larger numbers of Vietnamese were permitted to enter the bottom rungs of the colonial bureaucracy, and a modest expansion of the public school system was ordered. With that special French penchant for idealistic overstatement, Governor-General Albert Sarraut spun all of these changes into a vision of Franco-Vietnamese collaboration, complete with references to Liberty, Equality, and Fraternity. France, he said, was ready to act as "elder brother" in transmitting the full benefits of modern civilization, and to consider the possibility of native self-rule at some unspecified point in the future. After Germany was defeated, the French Government conveniently ignored these grandiloquent promises. But for many educated Vietnamese the cat had been let out of the bag. If the French needed reminding, they would be the ones to do it. If that did not work, they would try pursuing the ideal of "civilization" on their own.

In 1922, as France itself was slowly managing to pull out of a postwar depression, the Ministry of Colonies organized a grand exposition in Marseilles to try to revitalize in people's minds the French "mission" overseas and to attract new investment capital. Looked at in terms of overall twentieth-century historical trends, France had been permanently weakened by the Great War. The French people were probably more divided than ever on the colonial question. Nevertheless, viewed from the perspective of the 1920s, the response to the Marseilles exposition and other forms of colonial propaganda was nothing short of spectacular. While thousands of ordinary French citizens amused themselves by tasting strange foreign dishes, ogling native dancers, and laughing at the clothing and manners of diverse oriental potentates, potential capital investors concentrated their attention on government promises of monopoly privileges, tax shelters, cheap labor, and solid social order.

Close to three billion francs was invested in Indochina between 1924 and 1930, almost sixty per cent of the total since French arrival. Rubber cultivation, begun very modestly before the war, now was seen by investors as the new bonanza, some 700 million francs being advanced between 1925 and 1929. To provide the physical labor, somewhere between 100,000 and 200,000 Vietnamese were deceived or dragooned into the "red earth" rubber-growing region of Cochinchina during the boom years of the 1920s. Conditions were abysmal, including endemic malaria, contaminated or insufficient food and water, long hours, the docking of wages, and vicious punishments. Consequently the turnover rate due to death, escape, and non-renewal of contracts was extraordinarily high, as indicated by the fact that the rubber plantation work force never exceeded 41,000 in any one year.

Conditions were only slightly better for the miners, of whom there were at least 50,000 during peak years, mostly in the Hon Gay pits of north Vietnam. Here the formula for profit-making included dirt-cheap labor, company stores, 12- to 14-hour shifts, physical brutality, and the absence of safety precautions. Yet French economists still complained that it was "carelessness," "lack of conscientiousness," and "delicate constitution(s)" that caused Vietnamese miners to produce at only one-quarter the rate of their French or Japanese counterparts. New coffee and tea plantations were established in the same way, and more land was cleared and drained so that more Vietnamese tenants and wage laborers could produce more rice for export. Significant expansion occurred in rice milling, distilling, sugar refining, and the production of cement, textiles, and timber. On top of this economic pyramid sat a handful of directors of prestigious French financial institutions. As of 1924, Paris and Saigon were linked by direct transoceanic cable for the first time. Direct airmail service soon followed. Indochina was now a classic colony, her economic fibers attuned to the demands of the "mother country" and the international marketplace.

With the advent of the Great Depression the bottom fell out of the rubber and rice markets. By early 1931 the Indochina economy was in serious trouble—landowners defaulting on bank loans, companies going into bankruptcy, *colons* banging on government doors demanding assistance, and uncounted thousands of Vietnamese tenants, agricultural laborers, plantation hands, miners, and factory workers thrown out of employment, roaming to and fro in search of survival. Not until 1936 did the economy begin to pick up again. Then, a mere four years later, Nazi Germany occupied France, the Vichy-sympathizing authorities in Indochina subordinated themselves to the Japanese, and the economy underwent dislocation once again. By the winter of 1944/45, a tragic but quite predictable situation had developed, whereby hundreds of thousands of tons of rice remained in warehouses in the south (or was converted to alcohol to propel motor vehicles), while somewhere between one and two million Vietnamese people died of starvation in the north.

Looked at from the perspective of eighty years of French colonial activity, the only period when truly favorable conditions existed for full-scale capitalist economic exploitation of Indochina was from 1922 to 1929—a mere eight years. Economic fragility combined with administrative uncertainty underlay the entire colonial operation. No governor-general ever spent a term of more than five and one-half years in Indochina, and the average tenure was a scant two years and eight months. Conservative politicians spoke grandly about colonial restoration while socialists talked vaguely of provisional tutelage. Projects were begun and left uncompleted, or altered in such a way that profits survived but not the ameliorative social trimmings. This fundamental weakness of French colonialism, hardly sensed previously by even the most astute Vietnamese observers, was to become a subject of serious analysis among the new generation of intellectuals.

Vietnam has had three generations of intellectuals since 1900. Scholar-gentry or literati (*si phu*) intellectuals realized during the first decade of the twentieth century that Vietnam was being transformed whether it liked it or not. They tried desperately with whatever weapons, physical or mental, that came to hand to face up to altered conditions. By the end of World War I, however, it was obvious that they were unable to formulate either a penetrating new view of the world or a realistic program of action. Even the most sophisticated and experienced scholar-gentry members remained suspended between the Neo-Confucian classics, which they knew intimately but had come to doubt, and the ideas of Montesquieu, Rousseau, Smith, and Spencer, which they understood only vaguely but assumed to be essential to Vietnam's future. What they did manage to convey to the next generation, nevertheless, was a sense of historical crisis, a profound respect for knowledge, a commitment to action, and faith in the perfectability of humankind.

The intelligentsia (*gioi tri thuc*) that emerged during the 1920s faced many of the same problems as the scholar-gentry, but in yet another social and economic context and with very different intellectual equipment. While not divorced from the villages and the lives of the literati, small farmers, and handicraft workers, the intelligentsia was indubitably a product of the colonial system, just as were the big landlords, tenants, miners, and plantation laborers. Young intelligentsia graduating from French and Franco-Vietnamese schools in increasing numbers generally sought employment as clerks, interpreters, primary teachers, or journalists. As career aspirations exceeded colonial possibilities, there was considerable disenchantment and unrest. To assume a correlation between job frustration and anticolonial attitudes among the intelligentsia would be risky, however. There were well-employed Vietnamese who ended up opposing the French, just as there were thwarted journalists who joined the colonial police or signed on as overseers for landlords, mine supervisors, and plantation administrators.

Unlike the scholar-gentry, the intelligentsia understood the neo-Confucian classics only vaguely but were impatient to digest two millennia of European learning in a matter of a few years. The great advantage, and simultaneously the primary weakness, of these young men and women was that they stood unsteadily between two worlds and tried hard to envisage a third. Most of them had either grown up in villages or had meaningful rural kinship ties. Their parents still believed in ghosts, arranged marriages, and strict social harmony. However, in school, and increasingly through extracurricular means, they learned of cameras, germs, atoms, galaxies, free love, class struggle, and biological evolution. Many found the advice of their elders to ignore the obvious contradictions between old and new and to concentrate on passing examinations and securing a clerkship morally and intellectually repulsive. They wanted to look further, to explain the contradictions, and to fashion a new consciousness for themselves and for the Vietnamese people at large. Often they used the image of discovering a conceptual "lodestone" (*kim chi nam*) that would guide everyone to a brighter future. Although the enthusiasm, aggressive curiosity, and iconoclasm of the intelligentsia were themselves repulsive to many other Vietnamese, social and economic changes were so profound that the latter often felt impotent, incapable of reasserting authority. Youth seized the day.

This was only the beginning, however. One of the most difficult tasks facing the intelligentsia was to distinguish universal insights from the particularities of either European or Vietnamese experience. The traditional Vietnamese preference had been to draw a line between cultured East Asians and the many barbarian peoples, Europeans included, who did not comprehend the way of the universe and hence behaved improperly. Well into the twentieth century some Vietnamese continued to seek comfort in this model of reality, even while being forced to admit that "Eastern spirit" no longer had any claim to universality. At the other extreme, many early products of French colonial schools tended to assume that to be European was civilized and to be Asian barbarian. Yet those who tried simply to imitate Europeans found that they were neither accepted as such by French *colons* nor emulated by the mass of Vietnamese.

The spectacle of China disintegrating into warlordism, of Japan trying to outfox the Western imperialists at their own game, and of the Vietnamese "emperor" on annual salary from the French, made Neo-Confucianism look pathetic. Buddhism and Taoism were seen to be more attractive in such chaotic times, yet only a small minority of the intelligentsia went beyond general knowledge of these philosophies to firm, sustained adherence. On the other side of the world, the spectacle of Europe tearing itself to pieces in World War I undercut those Vietnamese who advocated radical Westernization. If Verdun and the Somme lay at the end of the path of assimilation, then better not try.

During the 1920s Vietnamese writers started to reach beyond the East-versus-West paradigm. They eagerly sought information from anywhere, in the hope that it would help to explain and resolve their own dilemmas. Of particular interest were social upheavals in China, postwar unrest in Europe, the ongoing revolution in Russia, and non-violent resistance in India. Increasingly writers became convinced that there was no qualitative distinction between Europeans and Vietnamese. A vast reservoir of knowledge and techniques was available to anyone in the world. It might often appear to bear a particular national stamp, but that was superficial, capable of being isolated and eliminated. In place of idealized philosophical and cultural systems, Vietnamese writers moved increasingly to historical process as a central explanation of reality. The key question then became one of assessing Vietnam's place in this universal process, and determining how to improve it.

In politics this same historical quest led many Vietnamese writers to conclude that it was not enough to simply exhort people to be patriotic, to unite, and to help save the country. Writers were now poignantly aware of other peoples in the world who presumably loved their homeland and their mother tongue as deeply as did the Vietnamese their own, who even possessed a similar tradition of resisting foreign domination, yet ultimately were completely vanquished and absorbed. Clearly some ethnic groups survived and others did not. Understanding why and how became a major preoccupation. Again, Vietnamese came to the conclusion that much knowledge in the world bore no moral stamp but was available to the evil as well as the good, to colonials and anticolonials, to reactionaries, conservatives, liberals, and radical revolutionaries alike.

The next step was to relate new knowledge and techniques to specific Vietnamese conditions. This proved to be more difficult. First of all, the intelligentsia had to learn a great deal about Vietnam, past and present, that was either unavailable in the colonial schools or had previously been considered irrelevant by young men and women trying first to understand the outside world. Nor was it easy for members of the intelligentsia to move around the country collecting information. The colonial authorities imposed physical restrictions. And a young intellectual in Western dress, speaking with a different accent and having no local relatives, might have to spend months simply gaining the confidence of a few people. When it came time to publish, writers discovered a curious fact about colonial censorship: the authorities were often more charitable toward the printing of esoteric foreign information and theories than they were toward independent data on the Vietnamese experience. Many an article was blanked out precisely at the point where it shifted from foreign generalities to Vietnamese colonial particulars.

Vietnamese intellectuals overseas took the lead in discussing specific political and social developments inside the colony. Ho Chi Minh was the most notable example, but he was followed by scores of other Vietnamese residing for one period of time or another in France, the Soviet Union, and China. While they obviously could not conduct on-the-spot investigations, they did talk intensively with overseas Vietnamese from other provinces and social backgrounds. Publishing was less of a problem than smuggling copies home. Ironically, while most writers in Saigon, Hanoi, or Hue were still grappling with universals, whether in history, philosophy, the social sciences, medicine, or mathematics, writers in Paris, Moscow or Canton were trying to analyze the Bank of Indochina, the conditions of Vietnamese peasants, miners, and plantation workers, or the causes of high infant mortality. Distance from events provided the perspective for sorting the momentous from the trivial, the politically relevant from the intellectually curious.

Eventually, however, this work would have to be carried on inside the country. In the late 1920s a few authors in Saigon and Hue were able to append a bit of specific Vietnamese data to otherwise general discussions of historical evolution, religion, nationalism, and imperialism. In the early 1930s novelists and short-story writers took the lead, describing the lives of Vietnamese functionaries, landlords, intellectuals, shopkeepers, and peasants according to conceptual and stylistic criteria that had not existed in the country several decades earlier. By the late 1930s they had been joined by critical essayists, and the emphasis increasingly was on the lives of poor peasants, tenants, proletarians, beggars, and prostitutes. Collectively these publications amounted to a penetrating indictment of both Vietnamese traditional society and the colonial system.

Preoccupation with the negative could prove self-defeating, however. By the early 1940s many discussions of current conditions were naturalistic caricatures rather than realistic exposés. Sensing an impasse, other writers shifted to selective revitalization of the Vietnamese past and to assertions of a bright future. Vietnam was now seen by even the most radical intelligentsia to possess a history to some degree unique, incapable of being understood simply by reference to universal laws. As might be expected, particular attention was given to military heroes, administrative innovators, and literary giants. Popular culture was mined for evidence of an underlying strength and wisdom among the Vietnamese masses transcending the historical dialectic.

These changes coincided with momentous political developments, including the collapse of the Popular Front (1939), the establishment of the Japanese-Vichy alliance (1940), and the formation of the Communist-led Viet Minh (1941). As a group, the Vietnamese intelligentsia was badly divided on how to respond to these events. Some saw the Japanese as liberators; others hoped for Vietnamese self-rule within a French Union; still others joined the Viet Minh and worked for an allied victory and international recognition of Vietnam's independence. Probably the only thing the intelligentsia shared by 1942–44 was a feeling that the urban milieu of office bureaus, elite societies, coffee shops, and amusement parlors was very constraining, perhaps unreal. The new focus was the Vietnamese village, whether for purposes of preserving its alleged communal character, for suggesting institutional reforms, or for convincing the peasants to seize control of their own destiny.

In 1944–45 members of the intelligentsia joined the Viet Minh by the thousands. Their skills as writers, speakers, teachers, and administrators proved extremely valuable, perhaps essential. They were also competent to ferret out information and to digest and distill it for broad political and military intelligence purposes. The same ability was put to use when learning how to utilize captured materiel, or when devising new equipment and techniques appropriate to primitive conditions. However, intelligentsia linking up with the Viet Minh soon discovered that they were regarded as neither the political nor the intellectual vanguard of society. Those roles were held by the Indochinese Communist Party. Although in 1944 most members of the ICP were probably still of intelligentsia background, the Party took its worker-peasant vision very seriously. The upheavals of 1945 provided a perfect opportunity to identify and enroll thousands of suitable members from these classes.

Members of the ICP, intellectuals or otherwise, had already learned through bitter experience that to will victory, or to analyze the road to victory, was not the same as to achieve victory. They had been forced into agonizing personal choices, endured considerable deprivation, tested a variety of concepts in practice, and tried to reformulate everything in terms meaningful to the majority of their unlettered (but not necessarily ignorant) countrymen. What they wanted from any intelligentsia recruit of 1945 was a willingness to accept group discipline, to concern himself more with means than with ends, and to help the Viet Minh to establish a common frame of reference between the elite and the masses, modernity and tradition, universal and particular. The era of the educated cadre, as distinct from the alienated explorer, had begun.

In the early 1920s Vietnam's young intelligentsia had had a talismanic approach to knowledge. It was to be their invincible weapon to gain independence, freedom, and "civilization." Twenty years later, however, many intelligentsia realized that new ideas might promote or impede change; they might produce unintended as well as intended and dysfunctional as well as functional consequences. Few ideas were inherently good or bad, and even fewer remained as originally conceived. To try to force the "right" ideas in the wrong historical conditions might prove disastrous, yet to wait for the right conditions might be equally dangerous. What was needed was a complex interweaving of ends and means, strategy and circumstance, conscious formulation and spontaneous action. . . .

Between that day in 1925, when several hundred spectators heard a French judge sentence Phan Boi Chau to life imprisonment, and the day in 1945, when a huge crowd listened to Ho Chi Minh proclaim independence, Vietnam underwent a profound transformation. In the mid-1920s, the colonial government had reason to believe that it had found a viable formula for the long-term, peaceful exploitation of Indochina. Only a smattering of Vietnamese dared to disagree openly. The vast majority accepted that change would have to come either by French fiat or by heavenly intervention, not by the actions of ordinary subjects.

Twenty years later, conditions were dramatically different. The French had been forced to drown several Vietnamese uprisings in blood. They had seen the colonial economy completely disrupted. They had been humiliated by the Germans in Europe and incarcerated by the Japanese in Indochina. Even to begin to reassert sovereignty in Indochina, the French were forced to go hat in hand to the Americans, British, and Chinese. Determined to regain pride in themselves, preoccupied by intra-Allied diplomacy, they failed to take accurate measure of Ho Chi Minh, of the new Democratic Republic of Vietnam, or—most importantly—of the political and social revolution sweeping the country. General Leclerc sensed a difficult struggle when he ordered his armored columns to push Vietnamese forces out of Saigon in October 1945. He had no inkling, however, that the end of the road lay at Dien Bien Phu, the ultimate French humiliation. Vietnamese had proven themselves energetic citizens rather than passive subjects.

Neither the August 1945 Revolution nor Dien Bien Phu can be understood without reference to prior changes in social structure and intellectual outlook. The traditional Vietnamese elite had become a pathetic shadow of its former self. Rural life had been altered fundamentally by the decline of the subsistence farmer, the spread of landlordism, the gutting of customary welfare palliatives, and the necessity for ever more family members to seek employment far beyond village boundaries. More than ever before, the tax system took from the poor and gave to the rich.

In place of informal village schools and the classical examination system stood a bewildering variety of French and Franco-Vietnamese educational programs. Fewer than ten percent of the population was able to read in any language, yet this did not prevent a vigorous *quoc ngu* publishing effort from getting under way by the late 1920s. Surprisingly, even workers and peasants gained access to the printed word. [Conservative intellectual] Pham Quynh had reason to be worried when he overheard rickshaw pullers discussing the Phan Boi Chau trial on the basis of press reports. Chanh Thi, the disgruntled teenage peasant in search of a job, became a Communist Party member in part due to his being able to read about the Nghe-Tinh soviets in a heavily censored Hue newspaper. And, like most other literate Vietnamese, he transmitted his discoveries orally to a wider circle of compatriots.

At the heart of the literate constituency was the intelligentsia, perhaps 10,000 in number. Looking at photographs of these self-conscious young men and women in white linen suits and starched frocks it is easy to dismiss the entire group as Westernized misfits. Perusing French-language publications they still appear as rather faddish, over-eager students of Left Bank ideological currents. Only when one reads the profusion of Vietnamese-language materials can they be seen to be grappling with real problems which affected not just themselves but their less-educated countrymen as well. The act of writing in Vietnamese forced members of the intelligentsia to go beyond simple imitation, to experiment culturally, to overcome conceptual problems never dreamt of by their Western mentors. It also linked them to the spoken language, and hence to the intricate world of the Vietnamese village. By the early 1940s, many intellectuals were convinced that the future of Vietnam lay not in the cities but among the 95 percent of the population living in the countryside. The Viet Minh offered intellectuals a timely vehicle for working with peasants, whether as propaganda cadres, military officers, or literacy instructors.

Although the Vietnamese intelligentsia was fascinated by new ideas, eager to expose them to critical debate, to test them in varying contexts, it never defined itself primarily in cerebral terms or allowed a mood of detached scholasticism to prevail. Understanding reality was not enough. One also needed to discover the means to alter reality. In the process of ascertaining what is, one was never to lose sight of what ought to be.

Ideology was seen to provide the essential connection between objective analysis and ethical vision. Confucianism had fulfilled this function until defeat and colonization at the hands of the French rendered its world view unconvincing. At best it survived as a set of moral platitudes. Buddhism offered a subtle alternative to Confucianism, yet it was extremely difficult to reconcile with growing intellectual commitment to science and progress. Social Darwinism appeared to explain a great deal about the contemporary world, to the point where Vietnamese became convinced that they must struggle ruthlessly in order to escape extinction. At the individual and intragroup levels, nonetheless, very few were prepared to concede that might makes right. They continued to believe that evil conduct brings retribution, and that any true ideology had to defend right and attack wrong.

Marxism possessed scientific credentials equal to Social Darwinism plus a firm moral stance. It was also more timely, reaching Vietnamese intellectuals in the wake of the Russian Revolution and the Great Depression. Even conservatives could be found employing Marxist periodization and social categories. Many flocked to Marxism as a new religion, to the point of participating heatedly in international sectarian disputes. Still others focused on Leninist organizational theory and practice. By the early 1940s, whatever their political affiliations, writers were far more concerned with relating foreign models to specific Vietnamese conditions than with proving their global philosophical credentials. For Marxists, the crucial problem was to relate Vietnamese history and culture to group decisions about revolutionary strategy and tactics.

The colonial repression of September 1939 made most intelligentsia activities of the Popular Front period illegal. As had been the case a decade earlier, Vietnamese intellectuals were forced to choose between clamming up, modifying their public positions, or going underground; this time, however, the psychological shock was less profound and the individual readjustments more coherent. Also, the presence of Japanese troops in Indochina and of Allied forces in Kwangsi and Yunnan raised anticolonial stakes to the highest point in fifty years. Members of the Indochinese Communist Party, the Vietnam Nationalist Party, the Dai Viet, Cao Dai, and Hoa Hao each sensed that their moment in history had arrived. The Vichy French, appreciating their vulnerability, offered significant new educational and employment opportunities to those Vietnamese willing to eschew anticolonialism. These wartime developments, combined with the inevitable effects of age, growing family responsibilities, and personality differences, led to the demise of the intelligentsia in the early 1940s.

In 1941 the Indochinese Communist Party was in complete disarray, its members dead, incarcerated, demoralized, or surviving precariously in the forests and swamps. Organizationally it appeared to possess less potential than any of the other groups mentioned above. Yet, only four years later the ICP had devised and implemented a plan to seize power, establish a government, sustain popular enthusiasm, and mobilize millions of people to undertake a wide variety of onerous, often dangerous tasks. Subsequently the ICP was able to stymie all efforts by rival forces, foreign or domestic, to reverse these momentous historical events.

Fortune favored the ICP in several respects. Most notably, the Tokyo-Vichy détente seriously weakened those Vietnamese groups which looked to either the Japanese or the French for political advancement. By the same token, it allowed the ICP to mount violent attacks against French colonial rule without being accused of unfaithfulness to the Allied cause. Communist parties in Malaya, Indonesia, and the Philippines were not so lucky. Important, too, was that Ho Chi Minh returned to Vietnam after thirty years, bringing with him impeccable credentials as an international revolutionary, unrivaled knowledge of world affairs, and a first-hand assessment of national united-front efforts in China.

Neither good fortune nor wise leadership would have counted for much, however, without the ideological transformations that preceded the formation of the Viet Minh and helped the ICP to take the historical initiative. Members of the intelligentsia had long before rejected the mood of bewilderment and pessimism which had characterized their elders. Instead, they possessed an infectious spirit of optimism and cultural pride. From an earlier naive acceptance of all things Western, they moved on to critical investigation and attempts at selective acculturation. Intelligentsia concepts of struggle and progress reached Vietnamese villagers in the 1930s, leading some to look at current conditions in a very different light. The fact that the colonial economy was in turmoil and rural society severely disrupted facilitated this process. When Vietnamese intellectuals and peasants came together in 1945 to uphold national independence and create a new society, there remained significant areas of misunderstanding and disagreement. Yet, there was sufficient consensus to mobilize millions to defeat the French.

Except for Ho Chi Minh, all ranking ICP leaders of the early 1940s had been members of the new intelligentsia. Many took prominent roles in the animated debates of the 1930s and drew heavily on the rhetoric of the Popular Front period in persuading people to join the Viet Minh. They defended the rights of the poor, encouraged women to participate in political struggle, stressed the importance of mass literacy, promised democratic freedoms, and portrayed the contemporary world in terms of a decisive confrontation between good and evil. To these themes were now added selective glorification of the Vietnamese past, praise of particular Vietnamese customs, and the claim that nothing could stand in the way of Vietnamese willpower asserted collectively.

The August 1945 Revolution was the sort of mass voluntarist surge of power that anticolonialists had dreamt of for decades. Even today, participants become excited as they recall the mood and events of 1945. For those who were in their teens or early twenties, it represented the formative experience of their lives, fostering a deep sense of solidarity and readiness to sacrifice; older Vietnamese saw the August Revolution as justification for previous agonies, capping three generations of struggle against unbelievable odds. Nothing that occurred subsequently, not even Dien Bien Phu or the rout of Republic of Vietnam forces in 1975, managed to capture the popular imagination in this way.

Communism and Nationalism

WILLIAM J. DUIKER

With the formation of the Vietminh League at the party's Eighth Plenum in 1941 the communist movement entered its sixteenth year of active ex-

From William J. Duiker, *The Rise of Nationalism in Vietnam, 1900–1941*. Copyright © 1976 by Cornell University Press. Used by permission of the publisher, Cornell University Press.

istence. During that period it had endured a number of major setbacks which would undoubtedly have annihilated an organization of lesser skill and determination. But despite the attempts of the French to eliminate it, it had become a major political force in Vietnam, and certainly the most dynamic and effective organization within the Vietnamese nationalist movement.

Who were these men, and what drew them to communism? We have at this point relatively few sources of information on the backgrounds of the communist party leadership, but such evidence as is available demonstrates that the leadership of the communist movement in the interwar years was composed primarily of intellectuals. While there were undoubtedly workers and peasants in the movement—and particularly in the party's mass associations—few seem to have become professional revolutionaries, and even fewer reached a position of leadership in the party.

From their background it is fairly clear that the founding generation of the communist movement was made up of basically modern men—Vietnamese who had been exposed to Western culture and political ideology. Most of the party's leadership had at one time or another been educated in the Franco-Vietnamese school system and many had received a degree and entered such careers as teaching and journalism. As such, they had become members of the emerging middle class, and were of the same general social stratum as the young Vietnamese who formed the nucleus of the urban nationalist parties that arose in Vietnam after World War I. Why some of these educated young Vietnamese became revolutionaries while others were satisfied to expend their energies in moderate reformism is not an easy question to answer. From the evidence available, however, it appears that moderates tended to come from the relatively affluent section of the bourgeoisie. They were somewhat more likely to have gone to the prestigious schools in the Franco-Vietnamese system and on to France for their higher education, and they were more likely to have joined such lucrative vocations as law, commerce, and medicine, than those who became members of radical parties. It would probably be wrong to view the founding members of the communist movement as totally deprived of opportunities to rise within the system. Many of the leaders of the movement, by their education and background, could have expected to achieve reasonable success in a number of careers open to them—in teaching, government, or journalism. Yet it is probably true that, as John T. McAlister states in his study, *Vietnam: The Origins of Revolution*, many young Vietnamese were drawn to revolution by a sense of being denied access to the status in society they deserved. Many of the careers to which these young men would have aspired were relatively low-paying and did not open the doors to either wealth or political power.

Yet it is not really enough to say that many became revolutionaries simply because reality did not accord with their personal aspirations, for in many cases, they seem to have become radicalized before entering the job market. It is interesting to note that of the top leadership of the communist movement during this period, the vast majority for whom we have biographical information came from scholar-gentry backgrounds. And, where we have information, it often appears that members of their immediate family were active in, or least in sympathy with, the nationalist or protonational organizations opposed to French rule—the Can Vuong, Phan Boi Chau's Exodus to the East, or the Hanoi Free School. If this is the case for the bulk of the early communist leadership, then it is likely that many acquired their resentment of French rule and their activist proclivities from their families even before entering the larger society. From this point of view, the leaders of the communist movement in the 1920s and 1930s can be viewed as direct heirs of the Phan Boi Chau scholar-patriot generation. They were a generation removed, to be sure, and more modern in their outlook and in their solutions, but essentially carried on the tradition of resistance established by their elders.

Eventually the communist movement became more than just the home of the offspring of scholar-gentry families, of course, but it is wise to keep in mind how small and how socially limited the party leadership was in its early years. The Comintern was critical of the petit bourgeois character of the League, and in the 1920s and early 1930s had emphasized the need to build up worker participation in the movement. There is not much indication, however, that this had much effect, at least prior to World War II. Party work in rural areas was similarly plagued with problems. The movement had begun to make inroads among the peasantry in some areas, notably in Annam and in parts of the Mekong delta, but Comintern distrust of the peasantry prevented the communists from following up immediately on the experience in Nghe-Tinh and it could hardly be said that before the anti-Japanese war the ICP had deep roots in the villages.

This early failure to broaden the base of the movement is not the only limitation of the party in the prewar period. Like its predecessors, it suffered from adventurism and factionalism, particularly in the early years. To a degree, such problems were the consequence of inadequate communications, ambiguous Comintern directives, and the zealous activities of the French Sûreté-Général. In retrospect, it is striking to observe how little regional sentiment surfaced in the first decade of the communist movement. In this respect the party had gone beyond its predecessors.

Whatever their early weaknesses, the uniqueness of the communists in the history of Vietnamese nationalism was that, unlike their rivals, they were able to eliminate or minimize obstacles to the ultimate seizure of power. For by the late 1930s, the ICP had begun to formulate a positive strategy which would eventually carry it to victory in the postwar period. And in the process many of the old errors would be eliminated. Some of the major elements of that strategy had already been laid out—by Lenin's theory of a nationalist alliance designed to ally all progressive and anti-imperialist forces in a colonial or semicolonial area in opposition to imperialist control; and by Mao Tse-tung's application of Marxist-Leninist strategy to a specifically Asian setting, involving the deliberate use of the peasantry as a major force in the revolution, and the adoption of guerrilla tactics in an attempt to utilize the strength of the rural population to surround the cities peopled by the bourgeoisie and controlled by the colonial power. The strategy began to become apparent in the years immediately prior to World War II, with the Bac Son uprising and the establishment of the Vietminh front. The new emphasis, the establishment of guerrilla bases along the border, reflected a shift away from the cities and the orthodox, Stalinist-style urban insurrection.

But perhaps the major significance of the formation of the Vietminh League was its solidification of the party's determination to utilize the role of nationalism in the struggle to evict the French. As the brief biographies of . . . countless communist figures . . . seem to show, communism in Vietnam was born out of the nationalist movement. Communist leaders commonly started their revolutionary careers as members of more manifestly nationalist groups—the VNQDD, the Youth Party, the Tam Tam Xa, or the Revolutionary Party—and then turned to Marxist-Leninist doctrine because it seemed like the most effective way to achieve independence.

Communism and nationalism were not always so easily matched, of course. Zealous party members occasionally puristically rejected the emotional appeals of patriotism. Slogans calling for national independence and self-determination, which appealed to the urban bourgeoisie, often had little meaning in rural communities, where a sense of nationalism was only beginning to emerge. On the other hand, as the communists found out in 1930–1931, policies that could win the support of the rural poor risked alienating the middle class in the towns. The challenge for the communists was to tailor their message to the particular target group—national concerns in the cities, economic issues in the rural areas—without destroying the effectiveness of the front as a whole. And, with the formation of the Vietminh, the party had taken a major step towards achieving their goal of building a mass-based movement of national proportions. It had reached the apex of a period of self-education. It was now prepared to commence the struggle to grasp political power in Vietnam. . . .

A relatively mature consciousness of nationalism existed in Vietnam at the beginning of World War II. But the roots of modern nationalism are clearly discernible, well before the beginning of the present century, in Vietnam's historically strong sense of ethnic awareness, an awareness that was tempered by her age-old struggle to resist conquest from the north. Western colonialism, then, did not "create" a sense of separate national or ethnic identity in Vietnam as it did in other societies in Asia; it merely channeled Vietnam's traditional self-awareness along more modern lines.

The protonationalism of the precolonial period met its end in the protracted but undirected struggle against the French in the late nineteenth century. The failure of the Can Vuong illustrated the basic weakness of the traditionalist approach in the face of an invading force endowed with modern weapons, and the next generation of Vietnamese patriots was quick to interpret the French conquest as a sign that the old ways would not work against the new enemy. That Confucian figures such as Phan Boi Chau and Phan Chu Trinh concluded so rapidly that tradition had ceased to have relevance is indicative of the degree to which the Vietnamese gave precedence to national survival over cultural purity. The image of the new society they spun in their dreams was perhaps superficial and naive, but theirs was a sincere attempt to bring Vietnam abreast of the modern world; they took the first step toward modern nationalist movement in Vietnam.

The weakness of the scholar-patriots was inadvertent, but nonetheless fatal. Lacking experience, they did not see all the implications of the changes taking place in the world, and their techniques and actions were heavily laden with traditionalist assumptions and attitudes. Their simple slogans and isolated feats of derring-do were no match for the sophisticated colonial administration. Clearly it took more to build a modern nationalist movement in Vietnam.

The generation that grew to maturity in the wake of World War I was highly conscious of the weakness of its predecessor. With this generation Vietnamese nationalism moved into the cities. Exposed from childhood to French culture, these modern patriots deliberately brought a new Western flavor to Vietnamese nationalism and were often openly contemptuous of traditional institutions. The urbanization of Vietnamese nationalism did not represent a complete break with the past, however. Many of the leading elements in the new nationalist parties which sprang up in Saigon, Hanoi, and Hué were direct offspring of the scholar-patriots and the Can Vuong, and they felt strongly an emotional responsibility to follow the examples of their elders.

The movement into the cities was a necessary phase in the evolution of nationalism in Vietnam, for only urban Vietnamese were truly conscious of the nature of the Western challenge and were capable of devising a strategy to cope with it. But urbanization created a number of new problems. Nationalist activities in urban areas were relatively easily controlled by the authorities, and clandestine operations were more difficult to carry on than in the countryside. Also, the diversity of the urban class structure exposed the resistance movement to the possibility of increased fractionalization and a lack of unity so necessary to the success of their efforts. Intellectuals, of course, are habitually prone to ideological theorizing and the urban nationalist movement seemed to spend more time in inner controversy than in opposing the colonial regime.

Most important, perhaps, the movement into the cities isolated the nationalists intellectually as well as physically from the traditional roots of Vietnamese society in the village. The modern urban Vietnamese, in absorbing Western values and habits, and in seeking a Western vocation, and perhaps even in speaking a Western language in preference to his own, became an alien force in the countryside, where traditional forms still retained considerable vitality. Although members of the scholar-patriot generation were by their education and, frequently, their family background, distinct from the average peasant, they generally had been raised in the village, had absorbed the traditional Sino-Vietnamese heritage, and, in a word, could speak the villager's language. The modern nationalist, by contrast, often grew up in the city, went through the Franco-Vietnamese school system, and frequently spent several years working or studying in Paris. In the process he lost his link with the villagers, who often viewed him with considerable suspicion. The break in communication, of course, frequently worked both ways, for urban nationalists had little comprehension of the problems of peasants, and the urbanite's concern for constitutional democracy and individual liberty, and his desire for more exposure to Western culture, often had little meaning outside the confines of Saigon and Hanoi.

In abandoning Confucianism as a symbol of Vietnamese nationalism, urban nationalists lost the vital emotional link with the village that a religion could provide. Where urban movements elsewhere in South and Southeast Asia maintained the essential link between elites and peasants by relying heavily on an indigenous religious tradition such as Hinduism, Islam, or Buddhism, Vietnamese intellectuals could go to the peasant only with the still alien values of Western science and democracy. The urbanization of Vietnamese nationalism, then, solved some old problems, but created some uncomfortable new ones, and risked putting modern nationalism in a position of permanent weakness. There were few indications that by the beginning of the Pacific War in 1940 the nationalist movement as a whole was on the road to finding a solution.

Out of this social milieu the Vietnamese communist movement arose. . . . Communism in Vietnam began as one answer to the "national" problem, and it was seen as such by much of its early membership, including Ho Chi Minh. As a primarily urban movement it was subject to the problems created by the urbanization of Vietnamese nationalism. Indeed, by the time a formal party was created in 1930, the urban orientation of the movement was deliberately encouraged by Comintern strategy devised in Moscow. During these formative years, the communist movement did relatively well in competing with pure nationalist organizations for support among the workers and urban petty bourgeoisie. If they suffered to a degree for their dependence on a foreign ideology, they made up for this disadvantage by their determination and ability. By the late 1930s they had become the most vital force in Vietnamese nationalism. The striking success of the communists among educated Vietnamese was somewhat unusual in Southeast Asia and deserves further comment. One advantage for the Indochinese Communist Party perhaps, was the colonial tie with France. A large number of Vietnamese intellectuals received their education (and their Marxist beliefs) in Paris, and it is likely that the attraction of the French intellectual to Marxism rubbed off on many French-trained Vietnamese.

Another advantage of Marxism in Vietnam lay in its attractiveness to intellectuals who were in the midst of an identity crisis. As has been observed earlier, nationalists in Vietnam could not build their movement around native religious symbols because Confucianism, closely linked with the reactionary court, never took hold as a symbol of Vietnamese identity within the nationalist movement. The decline of Confucianism in the cities left an emotional and intellectual void in the minds of patriotic intellectuals, and many obviously found Marxist doctrine an attractive modern alternative to the discredited Sino-Vietnamese tradition. As an intricate and sophisticated philosophy, with a universal dogma and a comprehensive explanation of history that was optimistic, scientific, impregnated with moral fervor, and staunchly anti-imperialist, Marxism could be accepted without great difficulty as a modern equivalent of Confucianism.

Still, without a broader base than the urban areas could provide, Vietnamese communism was in the same leaky boat as its nationalist rivals, and it was first and foremost the communists who made the effort to transform nationalism into a mass phenomenon. The experience of the Nghe-Tinh soviets showed, albeit briefly, the potential force of the peasant, but the destruction of the Central Vietnamese apparatus and the emergence into leadership of Stalin School graduates trained in Moscow nipped the early indications of a rural strategy in the bud. By the late 1930s, however, changes were in the wind. The Popular Front showed that the party could work with all classes. The Comintern showed less interest in Indochina and allowed the Indochinese Communist Party greater freedom to design its own strategy. By 1938, two young Communists, Vo Nguyen Giap and Truong Chinh, had written a study of the peasant question which, though unspecific about the peasant's role in the Vietnamese revolution, called him an "invincible force" and intimated that the party should pay more attention to his problems. Then, in 1939–1940, the Indonesian Communist Party was driven from the cities and a new strategy was discovered at Bac Son. In 1941 the leadership caught up with events and at the Eighth Plenum at Pac Bo, put the final touches on the new strategy.

As the Pacific War began, then, the communists had begun the process of building a mass movement for national liberation on the basis of an alliance between the peasantry and the urban intellectuals. The fusing of intellectuals and peasants, if effective, would combine the leadership ability of the former with the tempestuous force of rural discontent. If the Vietminh could successfully attain the pose of an essentially nationalist movement, if it could become the most effective force opposed to French rule in Vietnam, with a finger on the pulse of the discontents of all major strata of Vietnamese society, it would be able to establish itself in the minds of millions of Vietnamese as the legitimate heir to French rule in Vietnam, and the new recipient of the Mandate of Heaven.

Victory would not be rapid or easy, as Ho Chi Minh continually reminded his colleagues. It would take discipline, organization, patience, and willingness to sacrifice. Whether the communists would be able to sustain their momentum after the war was a question only the future could decide, for new times would call for new solutions, new policies. Would the peasant follow the communists? Would the party be able to convince the peasant that it was the heir to the Heavenly Mandate? Would it be able to reconcile the sometimes conflicting demands of city and country, of national self-determination and social reform, in a hard, bitter struggle against its rivals as well as against the French?

In 1941, there were no answers to these questions. Yet the potential for growth was there. The party was small, but it was dedicated and its members were steeled in adversity; their revolutionary zeal was undeniable. And, of course, they were blessed with a leader of singular capacity, for over two decades Ho Chi Minh had shown a striking ability to steer the party from the shoals of factionalism, regionalism, and adventurism. In 1941, the movement, the man, and the moment converged. The communists stood on the brink of grasping victory. They had demonstrated that they alone possessed the understanding, and that indefinable sense of will so necessary to the achievement of victory in human affairs.

✗ *F U R T H E R   R E A D I N G*

Joseph Buttinger, *The Smaller Dragon: A Political History of Vietnam* (1958)
———, *Vietnam: A Dragon Embattled* (1967)
John Cady, *The Roots of French Imperialism in Asia* (1954)
Hoang Van Chi, *From Colonialism to Communism* (1971)
William J. Duiker, *The Communist Road to Power in Vietnam* (1981)
———, *The Comintern and Vietnamese Communism* (1975)
———, *Vietnam: Nation in Revolution* (1983)
Thomas E. Ennis, *French Policy and Developments in Indochina* (1956)
Thomas L. Hodgkin, *Vietnam: The Revolutionary Path* (1981)
Huynh Kim Khanh, "The Vietnamese August Revolution Reinterpreted," *Journal of Asian Studies*, 30 (1971), 761–82
Jean Lacouture, *Ho Chi Minh* (1968)
Ngo Vinh Long, *Before the Revolution: The Vietnamese Peasants Under the French* (1973)
John T. McAlister and Paul Mus, *The Vietnamese and Their Revolution* (1970)
David G. Marr, *Vietnamese Anti-Colonialism* (1971)
Martin Murray, *The Development of Capitalism in Colonial Indochina* (1980)
Charles Robequain, *The Economic Development of French Indochina* (1944)
Virginia Thompson, *French Indochina* (1937)
Robert F. Turner, *Vietnamese Communism* (1975)
Walter F. Vella, ed., *Aspects of Vietnamese History* (1973)
Nguyen Khac Vien, ed., *Tradition and Revolution in Vietnam* (1974)

The Roots of the American Commitment

During World War II, President Franklin D. Roosevelt advanced a series of proposals aimed at liberalizing colonial rule and preparing dependent peoples for ultimate self-government. He often singled out French rule in Indochina as a particularly grievous example of colonial exploitation and advocated a trusteeship system for the postwar period. Yet before his death in April 1945, Roosevelt had begun to retreat from his anticolonial stance. The determination of France and other imperial powers to retain their overseas possessions, and America's need to work with its European allies on a broad range of postwar diplomatic initiatives, forced a modification in the president's plans. FDR consequently did not challenge France's initial efforts to regain sovereignty in Indochina.

The establishment of the independent Republic of Vietnam in the wake of the Japanese surrender and the subsequent outbreak of hostilities between French and Vietminh forces in November 1946 posed daunting policy dilemmas for the administration of Harry S Truman. Initially reluctant to support openly either side in the colonial struggle, the United States clung to a policy of official neutrality throughout the late 1940s. Washington finally abandoned that policy in 1950 and began to supply the French with substantial military and economic assistance.

Most scholars agree that the decision to aid the French in 1950 marks the initial American commitment in Vietnam. But they have offered widely divergent explanations for that decision. Was the American commitment prompted by a growing appreciation of the importance of Southeast Asia to U.S. national security objectives? Or did broader, global concerns shape U.S. thinking? Were economic, strategic, or political factors paramount in American policy making? What impact did the cold war exert on America's policy toward Indochina? This chapter explores these questions.

✗ D O C U M E N T S

The first document presents Secretary of State George C. Marshall's cable of May 1947 to the U.S. Embassy in France, expressing American frustration with French policy in Indochina. In the second document, the State Department reviews and evaluates U.S. policy toward Indochina, emphasizing that a balance must be struck between Vietnamese aspirations and French interests. On March 8, 1949, the Elysée Agreement established the State of Vietnam and the kingdoms of Laos and Cambodia as associated states within the French union. A public statement of American suport for that agreement is the next document.

The next two documents contain the State Department's recommendation of February 1, 1950, to provide military aid to the French in Indochina and the recommendation of the National Security Council in its Paper No. 64. Secretary of State Dean Acheson's announcement that American assistance would be forthcoming is contained in the sixth document. Ho Chi Minh's angry denunciation of that decision during a press interview, in which he called U.S. assistance imperialist intervention, is the last document.

George C. Marshall on the Indochina Dispute, 1947

We becoming increasingly concerned by slow progress toward settlement Indochina dispute. We fully appreciate French are making effort reach satisfactory settlement and hope visit Commissioner Bollaert to Indochina will produce concrete results. The following considerations, however, are submitted for your use any conversations you may have with French authorities at appropriate time this subject. We recognize it might not be desirable make such approach to newly constituted government in first days its reorganization, but nevertheless feel early appropriate opportunity might be found inform French Gov of our concern in this matter.

Key our position is our awareness that in respect developments affecting position Western democratic powers in southern Asia, we essentially in same boat as French, also as British and Dutch. We cannot conceive setbacks to long-range interests France which would not also be setbacks our own. Conversely we should regard close association France and members French Union as not only to advantage peoples concerned, but indirectly our own.

In our view, southern Asia in critical phase its history with seven new nations in process achieving or struggling independence or autonomy. These nations include quarter inhabitants world and their future course, owing sheer weight populations, resources they command, and strategic location, will be momentous factor world stability. Following relaxation European controls, internal racial, religious and national differences could plunge new nations into violent discord, or already apparent anti-Western Pan-Asiatic tendencies could become dominant political force, or Communists could capture control. We consider as best safeguard against these eventualities a continued close association between newly-autonomous peoples and powers which have long been responsible their welfare. In particular we recognize Vietnamese will for indefinite period require French material and technical assistance and enlightened political guidance which can be provided only by nation steeped like France in democratic tradition and confirmed in respect human liberties and worth individual.

We equally-convinced, however, such association must be voluntary to be lasting and achieve results, and that protraction present situation Indochina can only destroy basis voluntary cooperation, leave legacy permanent bitterness, and irrevocably alienate Vietnamese from France and those values represented by France and other Western democracies.

While fully appreciating difficulties French position this conflict, we feel there is danger in any arrangement which might provide Vietnamese opportunity compare unfavorably their own position and that of other peoples southern Asia who have made tremendous strides toward autonomy since war.

While we are still ready and willing to do anything we can which might be considered helpful, French will understand we not attempting come forward with any solution our own or intervene in situation. However, they will also understand we inescapably concerned with situation Far East generally, upon which developments Indochina likely have profound effect.

Plain fact is that Western democratic system is on defensive in almost all emergent nations southern Asia and, because identified by peoples these nations with what they have considered former denial their rights, is particularly vulnerable to attacks by demagogic leaders political movements of either ultra-nationalist or Communist nature which promise redress and revenge past so-called wrongs and inequalities. Signs development anti-Western Asiatic consciousness already multiplying, of which Inter-Asian Conf an example. Unanimity support for Vietnamese among other Asiatic countries very striking, even leading to moves Burma, India, and Malaya send volunteer forces their assistance. Vietnam cause proving rallying-cry for all anti-Western forces and playing in hands Communists all areas. We fear continuation conflict may jeopardize position all Western democratic powers in southern Asia and lead to very eventualities of which we most apprehensive.

We confident French fully aware dangers inherent in situation and therefore venture express renewed hope they will be most generous attempt find early solution which, by recognizing legitimate desires Vietnamese, will restore peace and deprive anti-democratic forces of powerful weapon.

For your info, evidence that French Communists are being directed accelerate their agitation French colonies even extent lose much popular support France may be indication Kremlin prepared sacrifice temporary gains with 40 million French to long range colonial strategy with 600 million dependent people, which lends great urgency foregoing views. . . . Dept much concerned lest French efforts find "true representatives Vietnam" with whom negotiate result creation impotent puppet Govt along lines Cochinchina regime, or that restoration Baodai may be attempted, implying democracies reduced resort monarchy as weapon against Communism. You may refer these further views if nature your conversations French appears warrant.

Statement of U.S. Policy Toward Indochina, 1948

Objectives

The immediate objective of US policy in Indochina is to assist in a solution of the present impasse which will be mutually satisfactory to the French and the Vietnamese peoples, which will result in the termination of the present hostilities, and which will be within the framework of US security.

Our long-term objectives are: (1) to eliminate so far as possible Communist influence in Indochina and to see installed a self-governing nationalist state which will be friendly to the US and which, commensurate with the capacity of the peoples involved, will be patterned upon our conception of a democratic state as opposed to the totalitarian state which would evolve inevitably from Communist domination; (2) to foster the association of the peoples of Indochina with the western powers, particularly with France with whose customs, language and laws they are familiar, to the end that those peoples will prefer freely to cooperate with the western powers culturally, economically and politically; (3) to raise the standard of living so that the peoples of Indochina will be less receptive to totalitarian influences and will have an incentive to work productively and thus contribute to a better balanced world economy; and (4) to prevent undue Chinese penetration and subsequent influence in Indochina so that the peoples of Indochina will not be hampered in their natural developments by the pressure of an alien people and alien interests.

Policy Issues

To attain our immediate objective, we should continue to press the French to accommodate the basic aspirations of the Vietnamese: (1) unity of Cochinchina, Annam, and Tonkin, (2) complete internal autonomy, and (3) the right to choose freely regarding participation in the French Union. We have recognized French sovereignty over Indochina but have maintained that such recognition does not imply any commitment on our part to assist France to exert its authority over the Indochinese peoples. Since V-J day, the majority people of the area, the Vietnamese, have stubbornly resisted the reestablishment of French authority, a struggle in which we have tried to maintain insofar as possible a position of non-support of either party.

While the nationalist movement in Vietnam (Cochinchina, Annam, and Tonkin) is strong, and though the great majority of the Vietnamese are not fundamentally Communist, the most active element in the resistance of the local peoples to the French has been a Communist group headed by Ho

Chi Minh. This group has successfully extended its influence to include practically all armed forces now fighting the French, thus in effect capturing control of the nationalist movement.

The French on two occasions during 1946 attempted to resolve the problem by negotiation with the government established and dominated by Ho Chi Minh. The general agreements reached were not, however, successfully implemented and widescale fighting subsequently broke out. Since early in 1947, the French have employed about 115,000 troops in Indochina, with little result, since the countryside except in Laos and Cambodia remains under the firm control of the Ho Chi Minh government. A series of French-established puppet governments have tended to enhance the prestige of Ho's government and to call into question, on the part of the Vietnamese, the sincerity of French intentions to accord an independent status to Vietnam.

Political.   We have regarded these hostilities in a colonial area as detrimental not only to our own long-term interests which require as a minimum a stable Southeast Asia but also detrimental to the interests of France, since the hatred engendered by continuing hostilities may render impossible peaceful collaboration and cooperation of the French and the Vietnamese peoples. This hatred of the Vietnamese people toward the French is keeping alive anti-western feeling among oriental peoples, to the advantage of the USSR and the detriment of the US.

We have not urged the French to negotiate with Ho Chi Minh, even though he probably is now supported by a considerable majority of the Vietnamese people, because of his record as a Communist and the Communist background of many of the influential figures in and about his government.

Postwar French governments have never understood, or have chosen to underestimate, the strength of the nationalist movement with which they must deal in Indochina. It remains possible that the nationalist movement can be subverted from Communist control but this will require granting to a non-Communist group of nationalists at least the same concessions demanded by Ho Chi Minh. The failure of French governments to deal successfully with the Indochinese question has been due, in large measure, to the overwhelming internal issues facing France and the French Union, and to foreign policy considerations in Europe. These factors have combined with the slim parliamentary majorities of postwar governments in France to militate against the bold moves necessary to divert allegiance of the Vietnamese nationalists to non-Communist leadership.

In accord with our policy of regarding with favor the efforts of dependent peoples to attain their legitimate political aspirations, we have been anxious to see the French accord to the Vietnamese the largest possible degree of political and economic independence consistent with legitimate French interests. We have therefore declined to permit the export to the French in Indochina of arms and munitions for the prosecution of the war against the Vietnamese. This policy has been limited in its effect as we have allowed the free export of arms to France, such exports thereby being available for re-shipment to Indochina or for releasing stocks from reserves to be forwarded to Indochina. . . .

Policy Evaluation

The objectives of US policy towards Indochina have not been realized. Three years after the termination of war a friendly ally, France, is fighting a desperate and apparently losing struggle in Indochina. The economic drain of this warfare on French recovery, while difficult to estimate, is unquestionably large. The Communist control in the nationalist movement has been increased during this period. US influence in Indochina and Southeast Asia has suffered as a result.

The objectives of US policy can only be attained by such French action as will satisfy the nationalist aspirations of the peoples of Indochina. We have repeatedly pointed out to the French the desirability of their giving such satisfaction and thus terminating the present open conflict. Our greatest difficulty in talking with the French and in stressing what should and what should not be done has been our inability to suggest any practicable solution of the Indochina problem, as we are all too well aware of the unpleasant fact that Communist Ho Chi Minh is the strongest and perhaps the ablest figure in Indochina and that any suggested solution which excludes him is an expedient of uncertain outcome. We are naturally hesitant to press the French too strongly or to become deeply involved so long as we are not in a position to suggest a solution or until we are prepared to accept the onus of intervention. The above considerations are further complicated by the fact that we have an immediate interest in maintaining in power a friendly French government, to assist in the furtherance of our aims in Europe. This immediate and vital interest has in consequence taken precedence over active steps looking toward the realization of our objectives in Indochina.

We are prepared, however, to support the French in every way possible in the establishment of a truly nationalist government in Indochina which, by giving satisfaction to the aspirations of the peoples of Indochina, will serve as a rallying point for the nationalists and will weaken the Communist elements. By such support and by active participation in a peaceful and constructive solution in Indochina we stand to regain influence and prestige.

Some solution must be found which will strike a balance between the aspirations of the peoples of Indochina and the interests to the French. Solution by French military reconquest of Indochina is not desirable. Neither would the complete withdrawal of the French from Indochina effect a solution. The first alternative would delay indefinitely the attainment of our objectives, as we would share inevitably in the hatred engendered by an attempted military reconquest and the denial of aspirations for self-government. The second solution would be equally unfortunate as in all likelihood Indochina would then be taken over by the militant Communist group. At best, there might follow a transition period, marked by chaos and terroristic activities, creating a political vacuum into which the Chinese inevitably would be drawn or would push. The absence of stabilization in China will continue to have an important influence upon the objective of a permanent and peaceable solution in Indochina.

We have not been particularly successful in our information and education program in orienting the Vietnamese toward the western democracies and the US. The program has been hampered by the failure of the French to understand that such informational activities as we conduct in Indochina are not inimical to their own long-term interests and by administrative and financial considerations which have prevented the development to the maximum extent of contacts with the Vietnamese. An increased effort should be made to explain democratic institutions, especially American institutions and American policy, to the Indochinese by direct personal contact, by the distribution of information about the US, and the encouraging of educational exchange.

The United States Praises the Elysée Agreement, 1949

The formation of the new unified state of Vietnam and the recent announcement by Bao Dai that the future constitution will be decided by the Vietnamese people are welcome developments which should serve to hasten the reestablishment of peace in that country and the attainment of Vietnam's rightful place in the family of nations.

The United States Government hopes that the agreements of March 8 between President Auriol and Bao Dai, who is making sincere efforts to unite all truly nationalist elements within Vietnam, will form the basis for the progressive realization of the legitimate aspirations of the Vietnamese people.

The State Department Recommends Military Aid to the French, 1950

The Problem

Should the United States provide military aid in Indochina and, if so, how much and in what way.

Assumption

A. There will not be an effective split between the USSR and Communist China within the next three years.

B. The USSR will not declare war on any Southeast Asian country within the next three years.

C. Communist China will not declare war on any Southeast Asian country within the next three years.

D. The USSR will endeavor to bring about the fall of Southeast Asian governments which are opposed to Communism by using all devices short of war, making use of Communist China and indigenous communists in this endeavor.

Facts Bearing on the Problem

1. When the Mutual Defense Assistance Act of 1949 was being written, the question of providing military aid to Southeast Asia was examined and it was decided not to include specific countries in that area, other than the Republic of the Philippines.

2. The attitude of the Congress toward the provision of military and economic aid to foreign countries recently has stiffened due to both economy and to policy considerations.

3. At the same time, the Congress has shown considerable dissatisfaction with policies which are alleged to have contributed to the Communist success in China and which are involved in the current United States' approach toward the question of Formosa.

4. Section 303 of the Mutual Defense Assistance Act of 1949 makes available to the President the sum of $75 million for use, at the President's discretion, in the general area of China to advance the purposes and policies of the United Nations.

5. Section 303 funds are unrestricted in their use.

6. The British Commonwealth Conference recently held at Colombo recognized that no SEA [Southeast Asia] regional military pact now exists due to divergent interest and that such an arrangement was now unlikely.

7. Communism has made important advances in the Far East during the past year.

8. Opposition to Communism in Indochina is actively being carried on by the three legally-constituted governments of Vietnam, Cambodia and Laos.

9. Communist-oriented forces in Indochina are being aided by Red China and the USSR.

Discussion

1. Indochina has common border with China and Burma, thus making it subject to invasion by Red China.

2. Its population is some 27 million concentrated in the delta regions of the Mekong and Red Rivers. Of the total population, Chinese account for between 600,000 and a million, concentrated largely in the cities.

3. Indochina has an agricultural economy based principally on rice of which it is an exporter. World War II and its aftermath seriously disrupted the national economy. The country presently has an annual trade deficit of about $85 million.

4. There are three subdivisions of Indochina: Vietnam, Laos, and Cambodia. An agreement was signed March 8, 1949, between France and Vietnam which provides for the latter to become an Associated State within the French Union. Ratification of the Agreement, followed by the recognition of the Vietnam by the West, is expected in the near future. French policy aims at making Laos and Cambodia Associated States within the French Union at the same time.

5. Governmental stability is poor in Indochina. In Vietnam, less than one-third of the country is controlled by the legal government with the French in control of the major cities; in Cambodia and Laos, the French maintain order but unrest is endemic. Before World War II Indochina was made up of four French Protectorates (Tonkin, Annam, Laos and Cambodia) and the colony of Cochinchina. It was occupied after the war by Chinese troops in the north (Tonkin) and by British and later French in the south. In 1946 a (nationalist coalition) government headed by the Moscow-trained Communist agent Ho Chi Minh consented to the return to the north (Tonkin) of the French upon promises of independence within the French Union. French negotiations with Ho were broken off following the massacre of many foreigners in Tonkin and Cochinchina in December 1946 by Ho's forces. Hostilities have continued to date.

6. The French are irrevocably committed in Indochina and have sponsored Bao Dai as a move aimed at achieving non-Communist political stability. It was a case of backing Bao Dai or accepting the Communist government of Ho Chi Minh. This latter alternative was impossible not only because it would obviously make their position in Indochina untenable but would also open the door to complete Communist domination of Southeast Asia. Such a communist advance would have severe repercussions in the non-communist world.

7. Military operations in Indochina represented a franc drain on the French Treasury of the equivalent of approximately $475 million in 1949. This constitutes nearly half of the current French Military Budget.

8. Ho Chi Minh, a Moscow-trained Communist, controls the Viet Minh movement which is in conflict with the government of Bao Dai for control of Vietnam. Ho actually exercises control of varying degree over more than two-thirds of Vietnam territory and his "government" maintains agents in Thailand, Burma and India. This communist "government" has been recognized by Communist China and the USSR.

9. Most Indochinese, both the supporters of Bao Dai and those of Ho Chi Minh, regard independence from the French as their primary objective. Protection from Chinese Communist imperialism has been considered, up to now, a secondary issue.

10. Unavoidably, the United States is, together with France, committed in Indochina. That is, failure of the French Bao Dai "experiment" would mean the communization of Indochina. It is Bao Dai (or a similar anticommunist successor) or Ho Chi Minh (or a similar communist successor); there is no other alternative. The choice confronting the United States is to support the French in Indochina or face the extension of Communism

over the remainder of the continental area of Southeast Asia and, possibly, farther westward. We then would be obliged to make staggering investments in those areas and in that part of Southeast Asia remaining outside Communist domination or withdraw to a much-contracted Pacific line. It would seem a case of "Penny wise, Pound foolish" to deny support to the French in Indochina.

11. The US plans on extending recognition to the newly-created states of Vietnam, Laos and Cambodia, following French legislative action which is expected in early February 1950.

12. Another approach to the problem is to apply the practical test of probability of success. In the present case we know from the complex circumstances involved that the French are going to make literally every possible effort to prevent the victory of Communism in Indochina. Briefly, then, we would be backing a determined protagonist in this venture. Added to this is the fact that French military leaders such as General Cherrière are soberly confident that, in the absence of an invasion in mass from Red China, they (the French) can be successful in their support of the anti-Communist governments in Indochina.

13. Still another approach to the problem is to recall that the United States has undertaken to provide substantial aid to France in Europe. Failure to support French policy in Indochina would have the effect of contributing toward the defeat of our aims in Europe.

Conclusions

A. Significant developments have taken place in Indochina since the Mutual Defense Assistance Act of 1949 was drawn up, these changes warranting a reexamination of the question of military aid.

B. The whole of Southeast Asia is in danger of falling under Communist domination.

C. The countries and areas of Southeast Asia are not at present in a position to form a regional organization for self-defense nor are they capable of defending themselves against military aggressive Communism, without the aid of the great powers. Despite their lack of military strength, however, there is a will on the part of the legal governments of Indochina toward nationalism and a will to resist whatever aims at destroying that nationalism.

D. The French native and colonial troops presently in Indochina are engaged in military operations aimed at denying the expansion southward of Communism from Red China and of destroying its power in Indochina.

E. In the critical areas of Indochina France needs aid in its support of the legally-constituted anti-Communist states.

Recommendations

1. The United States should furnish military aid in support of the anti-Communist nationalist governments of Indochina, this aid to be tailored to

meet deficiencies toward which the United States can make a unique contribution, not including United States troops.

2. This aid should be financed out of funds made available by Section 303 of the Mutual Defense Assistance Act of 1949.

National Security Council Paper No. 64, 1950

The Position of the United States with Respect to Indochina

The Problem

1. To undertake a determination of all practicable United States measures to protect its security in Indochina and to prevent the expansion of communist aggression in that area.

Analysis

2. It is recognized that the threat of communist aggression against Indochina is only one phase of anticipated communist plans to seize all of Southeast Asia. It is understood that Burma is weak internally and could be invaded without strong opposition or even that the Government of Burma could be subverted. However, Indochina is the area most immediately threatened. It is also the only area adjacent to communist China which contains a large European army, which along with native troops is now in armed conflict with the forces of communist aggression. A decision to contain communist expansion at the border of Indochina must be considered as a part of a wider study to prevent communist aggression into other parts of Southeast Asia.

3. A large segment of the Indochinese nationalist movement was seized in 1945 by Ho Chi Minh, a Vietnamese who under various aliases has served as a communist agent for thirty years. He has attracted noncommunist as well as communist elements to his support. In 1946, he attempted, but failed to secure French agreement to his recognition as the head of a government of Vietnam. Since then he has directed a guerrilla army in raids against French installations and lines of communication. French forces which have been attempting to restore law and order found themselves pitted against a determined adversary who manufactures effective arms locally, who received supplies of arms from outside sources, who maintained no capital or permanent headquarters and who was, and is able, to disrupt and harass almost any area within Vietnam (Tonkin, Annam and Cochinchina) at will.

4. The United States has, since the Japanese surrender, pointed out to the French Government that the legitimate nationalist aspirations of the people of Indochina must be satisfied, and that a return to the prewar colonial rule is not possible. The Department of State has pointed out to the French Government that it was and is necessary to establish and support

governments in Indochina particularly in Vietnam, under leaders who are capable of attracting to their causes the non-communist nationalist followers who had drifted to the Ho Chi Minh communist movement in the absence of any non-communist nationalist movement around which to plan their aspirations.

5. In an effort to establish stability by political means, where military measures had been unsuccessful, i.e., by attracting non-communist nationalists, now followers of Ho Chi Minh, to the support of anti-communist nationalist leaders, the French Government entered into agreements with the governments of the Kingdoms of Laos and Cambodia to elevate their status from protectorates to that of independent states within the French Union. The State of Vietnam was formed, with similar status, out of the former French protectorates of Tonkin, Annam and the former French Colony of Cochinchina. Each state received an increased degree of autonomy and sovereignty. Further steps towards independence were indicated by the French. The agreements were ratified by the French Government on 2 February 1950.

6. The Governments of Vietnam, Laos and Cambodia were officially recognized by the United States and the United Kingdom on February 7, 1950. Other Western powers have, or are committed to do likewise. The United States has consistently brought to the attention of non-communist Asian countries the danger of communist aggression which threatens them if communist expansion in Indochina is unchecked. As this danger becomes more evident it is expected to overcome the reluctance that they have had to recognize and support the three new states. We are therefore continuing to press those countries to recognize the new states. On January 18, 1950, the Chinese Communist Government announced its recognition of the Ho Chi Minh movement as the legal Government of Vietnam, while on January 30, 1950, the Soviet Government, while maintaining diplomatic relations with France, similarly announced its recognition.

7. The newly formed States of Vietnam, Laos and Cambodia do not as yet have sufficient political stability nor military power to prevent the infiltration into their areas of Ho Chi Minh's forces. The French Armed Forces, while apparently effectively utilized at the present time, can do little more than to maintain the *status quo*. Their strength of some 140,000 does, however, represent an army in being and the only military bulwark in that area against the further expansion of communist aggression from either internal or external forces.

8. The presence of Chinese Communist troops along the border of Indochina makes it possible for arms, material and troops to move freely from Communist China to the northern Tonkin area now controlled by Ho Chi Minh. There is already evidence of movement of arms.

9. In the present state of affairs, it is doubtful that the combined native Indochinese and French troops can successfully contain Ho's forces should they be strengthened by either Chinese Communist troops crossing the border, or Communist-supplied arms and material in quantity from outside Indochina strengthening Ho's forces.

Conclusions

10. It is important to United States security interests that all practicable measures be taken to prevent further communist expansion in Southeast Asia. Indochina is a key area of Southeast Asia and is under immediate threat.

11. The neighboring countries of Thailand and Burma could be expected to fall under Communist domination if Indochina were controlled by a Communist-dominated government. The balance of Southeast Asia would then be in grave hazard.

12. Accordingly, the Departments of State and Defense should prepare as a matter of priority a program of all practicable measures designed to protect United States security interests in Indochina.

Dean Acheson Urges Aid for Indochina, 1950

The [French] Foreign Minister [Robert Schuman] and I have just had an exchange of views on the situation in Indochina and are in general agreement both as to the urgency of the situation in that area and as to the necessity for remedial action. We have noted the fact that the problem of meeting the threat to the security of Viet Nam, Cambodia, and Laos which now enjoy independence within the French union is primarily the responsibility of France and the Governments and peoples of Indochina. The United States recognizes that the solution of the Indochina problem depends both upon the restoration of security and upon the development of genuine nationalism and that United States assistance can and should contribute to these major objectives.

The United States Government, convinced that neither national independence nor democratic evolution exist[s] in any area dominated by Soviet imperialism, considers the situation to be such as to warrant its according economic aid and military equipment to the associated states of Indochina and to France in order to assist them in restoring stability and permitting these states to pursue their peaceful and democratic development.

Ho Chi Minh Denounces U.S. Intervention, 1950

Question: What is, Mr. President, the present situation of the U.S. imperialists' interventionist policy in Indochina?

Answer: The U.S. imperialists have of late openly interfered in Indochina's affairs. It is with their money and weapons and their instructions that the French colonialists have been waging war in Viet-Nam, Cambodia, and Laos.

However, the U.S. imperialists are intensifying their plot to discard the French colonialists so as to gain complete control over Indochina. That is why they do their utmost to redouble their direct intervention in every field—military, political, and economic. It is also for this reason that the contradictions between them and the French colonialists become sharper and sharper.

Question: What influence does this intervention exert on the Indochinese people?

Answer: The U.S. imperialists supply their henchmen with armaments to massacre the Indochinese people. They dump their goods in Indochina to prevent the development of local handicrafts. Their pornographic culture contaminates the youth in areas placed under their control. They follow the policy of buying up, deluding, and dividing our people. They drag some bad elements into becoming their tools and use them to invade our country.

Question: What measure shall we take against them?

Answer: To gain independence, we, the Indochinese people, must defeat the French colonialists, our number-one enemy. At the same time, we will struggle against the U.S. interventionists. The deeper their interference, the more powerful are our solidarity and our struggle. We will expose their maneuvers before all our people, especially those living in areas under their control. We will expose all those who serve as lackeys for the U.S. imperialists to coerce, deceive, and divide our people.

The close solidarity between the peoples of Viet-Nam, Cambodia, and Laos constitutes a force capable of defeating the French colonialists and the U.S. interventionists. The U.S. imperialists failed in China, they will fail in Indochina.

We are still laboring under great difficulties but victory will certainly be ours.

✗ E S S A Y S

In the first essay, Gary R. Hess of Bowling Green State University concludes that recognition of the Bao Dai government in February 1950 constituted the first significant U.S. political commitment in Indochina. He contends that the Truman administration, although highly critical of French policy, considered a continued French presence in Indochina vital to the preservation of Western interests in Southeast Asia. The administration thus came to accept France's Bao Dai experiment, albeit with some reluctance, as the least objectionable policy option.

Michael Schaller of the University of Arizona emphasizes in the second essay the critical links between Japan and Southeast Asia in American policy making. He argues that it was concern with Japan's economic future, in the face of communist pressures, that set the stage for the initial American commitments in Indochina.

Robert M. Blum, a historian and analyst for the Central Intelligence Agency, calls attention in the last essay to the political dimension of those decisions. Stressing the role of Congress, party politics, and the wider political environment, he suggests that the intense political debates that erupted after the communist triumph in China in 1949 (often referred to as "the loss of China") compelled Truman to act forcefully somewhere in Asia. His answer to a failed China policy became an aggressive Southeast Asian policy.

Acceptance of the "Bao Dai Solution"

GARY R. HESS

The United States recognition in February 1950 of the government headed by Bao Dai constituted the initial American political commitment in Indochina. It brought American resources and prestige to the support of France in its efforts to defeat the communist-led Viet Minh, the predominant force of Vietnamese nationalism. This American decision was based on the calculation that only the success of the so-called "Bao Dai solution" could assure the preservation of a noncommunist, Western-oriented Southeast Asia. The commitment of 1950 came after five years of agonizing reflection over the Indochina situation. Throughout that period, American policymakers deliberated fundamental issues: the relationship of the Viet Minh to the Soviet Union, the influence of the Chinese civil war on Indochina and the remainder of Southeast Asia, the viability of the "Bao Dai solution," and whether France should be pressed to adopt a liberal colonial policy. While disagreements developed within the Department of State over some of these questions, the prevailing consensus by late 1949 held that the United States had to assume the risks inherent in supporting the Bao Dai government. Underlying the commitment, however, was a prevalent sense of its futility—a derivative of France's unwillingness to grant significant concessions to the Vietnamese.

The commitment to the "Bao Dai solution" marked a significant shift in the American approach to Indochina from the position summarized by Secretary of State George C. Marshall in February 1947, shortly after the beginning of the French-Viet Minh war. Commenting on the dilemmas facing the United States, the secretary stated:

> . . . [W]e have fully recognized France's sovereign position in that area and we do not wish to have it appear that we are in any way endeavoring to undermine that position. . . . At [the] same time we cannot shut our eyes to [the] fact that there are two sides to this problem and that our reports indicate both a lack of French understanding of [the] other side . . . and continued existence of a dangerously outmoded colonial outlook and method in [the] area. . . . On [the] other hand we do not lose sight of the fact that Ho Chi Minh has direct Communist connections and it should be obvious that we are not interested in seeing colonial empire administrations supplanted by philosophy and political organization directed from and controlled by [the] Kremlin. . . . Frankly we have no solution of [the] problem to suggest.

Behind Marshall's summary was a previous record of American frustration in Indochina. During World War II, the United States had assumed that it would be instrumental in determining the postwar status of Indochina. President Franklin D. Roosevelt took a strong personal interest in Indo-

Gary R. Hess, "The First American Commitment in Indochina: The Acceptance of the 'Bao Dai Solution'," *Diplomatic History*, 2 (fall 1978), pp. 331–350. Reprinted by permission.

china, opposing the return of the French and favoring the establishment of an international trusteeship. The minimal American influence in Southeast Asia at the end of the war and the priority given to problems in Europe and East Asia, however, resulted in American deference to the reassertion of French sovereignty. In the ensuing tensions between the French and the Viet Minh-organized Democratic Republic of Vietnam, the United States endeavored, through its contacts with both sides, to encourage compromise and a peaceful solution. After the beginning of warfare in late 1946, the State Department extended an offer of mediation, only to be spurned by the French on the grounds that priority had to be given to the reestablishment of order. Thereafter the United States retreated to a position of limited involvement, caught in the dilemmas underscored in Marshall's statement.

From 1947 to 1950, the French sought to convert the struggle into a civil, as opposed to a colonial, war. By the end of 1947, in addition to its initial foothold in Cochin China, the French army had control of a number of towns in Annam including Hanoi, a string of frontier fortresses, and the industrial areas of the Red River delta. But the French had failed to destroy the Viet Minh, who retained the support of the overwhelming majority of the population and remained capable of waging guerrilla warfare throughout the country. To support its precarious position, the French government developed the strategy of working through Vietnamese collaborators, and by late 1947 this search for a noncommunist nationalist alternative had centered on the former emperor Bao Dai. While Bao Dai and other Vietnamese leaders proved reluctant to cooperate unless they were granted genuine self-government, the French took advantage of their strong anti-Viet Minh sentiments to force acceptance of a superficial, diluted independence. In the so-called Elysée Agreement of March 1949, France recognized Vietnam's independence but retained responsibility for foreign affairs and defense as well as various special privileges. Further, Vietnam and the other "associated states" (Laos and Cambodia) were obliged to become members of the French Union. A dissatisfied Bao Dai returned to Vietnam in July 1949 to become "head of state." On 30 December the terms of the Elysée Agreement were formally instituted by the Conventions of Saigon. On 7 February 1950—five days after the French Assembly ratified those agreements—the United States recognized the Bao Dai regime as an "independent state within the French Union." For France, the establishment of this government and its international recognition were important steps toward the preservation of its position in Indochina.

The transition in French policy was paralleled by the change in the American response from that of "no solution to offer" to endorsement of the "Bao Dai solution." Between 1947 and 1950, American calculations of the French-Viet Minh struggle evolved through several distinct, if chronologically overlapping, phases. American policymaking was based on the assumption that the United States could not accept the risks of a Viet Minh-dominated state. Official analyses of the Vietnamese situation repeatedly expressed uncertainty about the nature and orientation of the Viet Minh. Almost without exception, however, it was concluded that the United States had no choice but to calculate its policy on the most unfavorable consequences of a Viet Minh-dominated state—Vietnam becoming a satellite of the Soviet Union. Ho Chi Minh's professed commitment to nationalism, his expressed admiration for the United States, his apparent neutrality in the early cold war as well as the inclusion of noncommunists within the Viet Minh and the apparent lack of contact between the Viet Minh and Moscow led to the possibility that ". . . this government, if confirmed in power, would follow a nationalist rather than a Soviet line." But the communist background of the Viet Minh leadership produced serious anxiety:

> On the other side, there remains the fact that the Vietnamese leaders include seasoned Communists, men who for years collaborated with the Third International—including Ho Chi Minh in particular—and that no change of heart has been publicly confessed by them.

In an effort to gain a more comprehensive overview of the contingencies in Vietnam, the State Department in July 1947 instructed its consuls at Saigon and Hanoi to report fully on the implications of a Viet Minh-controlled government: its orientation toward the Soviet Union, the importance of its sensitivity to American opinion, and the likelihood that it would provide stability with relatively free political expression. The reports from Charles Reed [U.S. Consul] at Saigon and William O'Sullivan [U.S. Consul] at Hanoi both advanced, with much qualification, the viewpoint that the United States could possibly attain influence in and a reasonable relationship with a Viet Minh-dominated state. O'Sullivan argued that the isolation from the Soviet Union and the proximity of American influence in the Philippines would prevent full association with the Communist bloc. While agreeing that the Viet Minh would not immediately become affiliated with the Soviet Union, Reed maintained that an existing remote Soviet control of the Viet Minh would lead eventually to an open association, once the Viet Minh government was firmly established. Both consuls, however, agreed that the Vietnamese admired the United States and that American influence could be established, principally in the form of economic assistance. Neither consul, however, doubted that the Viet Minh would be successful in establishing a one-party state. These reports thus suggested, at best, an uncertain American position in a Viet Minh-dominated state.

Within the State Department, Kenneth Landon, on behalf of the Division of Philippine and Southeast Asian Affairs, pressed the possibility of factionalism undermining the predominance of the Viet Minh. Landon, who following a meeting with Ho Chi Minh in early 1946 had advocated American mediation, suggested in November 1947:

> It is not a foregone conclusion that if the Annamese win their objective they will establish a communist state. If and when they have a victory, the ardent leadership of the small Communist group will become less vital and the various Annamese factions will turn from facing the French to facing one another. Then will come the time for the natural development

of political parties as Annamese regroup themselves for the purpose of self-government.

A marginal comment by Woodruff Wallmer of the Division of Western European Affairs stated the essential department conclusion on risking the consequences of a Viet Minh victory:

> It may not be certain, as Ken Landon says, that Ho and Co. will succeed in setting up a Communist State if they get rid of the French, but let me suggest that from the standpoint of the security of the United States, it is one hell of a big chance to take.

Repeatedly, similar conclusions to analyses of the Vietnamese political situation affirmed that the United States could not risk a Viet Minh-dominated state.

As the Viet Minh emerged as an unreliable source of stability and receptivity to American influence, the Department of State, in the last months of 1947, considered the implications of acquiescing in French military and political strategy. This issue emerged in the context of Reed's 15 September message urging American intervention to avoid a French restoration, by force of arms, of the pre-World War II status quo. In response, Washington requested that its missions in Hanoi and Saigon report on France's ability to defeat the Viet Minh. While both Reed and O'Sullivan were skeptical of France's military prospects, they expressed particular concern that a French victory could be achieved only at the expense of the interests of the United States. In terms similar to those of his Saigon colleague, O'Sullivan argued:

> Such action [a French restoration of its prewar status] would, of course, be catastrophic to United States prestige, would turn Vietnamese who distrust and hate the French into a violent anti-white bloc, and would insure the irretrievable orientation of intellectuals and the people toward communism and Moscow and against the West.

With additional intelligence reports reaching the Division of Philippine and Southeast Asian Affairs projecting the failure of the French military campaign launched that fall, Landon argued that the United States should register with the French its opposition to the use of arms. That initiative, however, received no support at higher levels.

In early 1948 as the French began advancing the "Bao Dai solution" and the futility of the military campaign against the Viet Minh became evident, officials in Washington increasingly realized the necessity of enlarging the American role in Indochina. To some officers in the State Department, American policy in the Dutch-Indonesian war offered a model that could be utilized in the French-Viet Minh impasse. Specifically, a United Nations-sponsored Good Offices Committee, in which the United States held the pivotal position, was making progress toward a resolution of the Indonesian dispute. No such approach, however, was deemed appropriate in Indochina, not only because of French aversion to third-party interference but, more importantly, because any negotiated settlement had to involve the Viet Minh. A French–Viet Minh agreement, American officials had come to believe, would result in the eventual communist domination of Vietnam.

As policymakers concluded that American interests could not countenance a complete victory by either side or a negotiated settlement, this process of elimination of other alternatives led toward acceptance of the "Bao Dai solution." That orientation of American policy, however, resulted in sharp bureaucratic disagreement over the terms of making a commitment with such important implications. As French colonial policy unfolded in 1948 and 1949, the critical question within the Department of State was not whether to back Bao Dai but rather whether the United States should insist on French concessions to Vietnamese nationalism as a condition of American support. Two competing strategies—one "Asian-oriented" and the other "European-oriented"—emerged. The process by which the United States came to recognize the Bao Dai government reflected a struggle between two bureaucratic groups within the Department of State and, in a broader sense, the priorities that each of them represented.

The Asian-oriented strategy was advanced by the consuls at Saigon and Hanoi and received the endorsement of the officers in the Division of Philippine and Southeast Asian Affairs and the Office of Far Eastern Affairs. In a cable of 30 June 1948 George M. Abbott, who had replaced Reed as the consul at Saigon, set forth the basic Asian-oriented approach that called for withholding any support pending significant changes in French policy. In a conclusion that was underlined by his superiors in Washington, Abbott argued:

> If the Bao Dai solution fails, the United States will be on record as advocating a liberal solution crucial to the political problem but in no wise committed to monarchist, as distinct from non-communist, solutions.

In sum, Abbott and other advocates of the Asian-oriented strategy assumed that diplomatic recognition depended upon the Bao Dai government attaining stability and popular support, which could only result from French concessions.

At the base of the Asian-oriented approach was the recognition of the lack of popular support for Bao Dai and the insufficiency of French policy as a means of attracting noncommunist nationalists to his side. Just prior to Abbott's 30 June recommendations, the installation in Hanoi of the French-sponsored government headed by Nguyen Van Xuan—a first phase of the "Bao Dai solution"—provided vivid evidence of the distance between French colonial policy and its puppets and the mass of the Vietnamese people. Reporting on the ceremonies, the American consul in Hanoi wrote to Washington:

> The pervading atmosphere at all these gatherings celebrating the birth of the "first provisional government of Vietnam" was more that of a funeral than a christening. . . . The expressions on the faces of both the participants and the spectators gave one the impression that the whole thing was a rather poorly managed stage show, with the actors merely going through

the motions. The appearance of Xuan, his stocky figure clothed in mandarinal robes which he quite obviously did not know how to handle, almost succeeded in introducing a note of low comedy. Gilbert and Sullivan came to mind. . . . An obvious attempt was made to identify Bao Dai with the proceedings. . . . A gigantic likeness of the ex-emperor imposed on a map of Indochina dominated the entrance way to the presidential palace, and paintings and photographs were in evidence at other points. . . . At the installation ceremony the small number of Vietnamese civilians allowed to watch the affair was in particularly striking contrast to the amazing number of armed men who literally hid behind every bush. . . . No attempt was made at any time to show popular support for the new government. . . . It is difficult to see how even a puppet can serve any useful purpose if the gulf between those who govern and those governed is admittedly so wide that even the briefest visual contacts cannot be permitted.

Although such reports provided abundant support for the imperativeness of the Asian-oriented strategy, two considerations limited America's ability to influence French policy. First, France held a high card in the intimidating effect of the possibility that it would withdraw from Indochina, thus leaving the United States with the choice between intervening itself or accepting a communist victory. Recognizing that Washington would tolerate a continued French presence rather than face the consequences of withdrawal, Paris indeed was in a position to extend less generous terms than the United States advocated. The threat of withdrawal had been expressed in the spring of 1948 when the State Department discussed with the French embassy the implications of congressional criticism of the extent to which the Indochina war was draining French resources and Marshall Plan assistance. In response, an embassy official warned that any congressional reduction in economic assistance might necessitate leaving Indochina and its insoluble problems to the United States. The lingering effect of this threat, which subsequently became a more prominent feature of the Franco-American exchange over Indochina, reduced the feasibility of the Asian-oriented strategy. Second, the United States was also restrained by the imperatives of the cold war, which established the assumption that France was needed to assure the security of Western Europe. The preservation of a close association with a stable French government was a high priority. To many American officials, acquiescence in France's colonial policy was dictated by the cold war. A policy statement, drafted by the Division of Philippine and Southeast Asian Affairs in late July 1948 and subsequently endorsed by Secretary Marshall, stressed the continued impotence of the United States in Indochina:

The objectives of United States policy can only be attained by such French action as will satisfy the aspiration of the peoples of Indochina. . . . Our greatest difficulty in talking with the French and in suggesting what should and should not be done has been our inability to suggest any practicable solution. . . . We are naturally hesitant to press the French too strongly or to become deeply involved as we are not in a position to suggest a solution or until we are prepared to accept the onus of intervention. The above considerations are further complicated by the fact that we have an immediate interest in maintaining in power a friendly French government, to assist in the furtherance of our aims in Europe. This immediate and vital interest has in consequence taken precedence over active steps toward the realization of our objectives in Indochina.

Despite its inherent limitations, the Asian-oriented strategy set the tone of American policy until the discussions leading to the Elysée Agreement. By that time, a European-oriented strategy challenged for predominance in the policymaking process. Advanced by the American embassy in Paris and supported by the Office of Western European Affairs at the State Department, this approach called for virtually unconditional acceptance of French colonial policy, principally on the grounds that the fragile political situation within France prevented significant concessions to Vietnamese nationalism. The only feasible remedy for the acknowledged shortcomings of the "Bao Dai solution" was American recognition and support, not a liberal French colonial policy.

The struggle over Indochina policy crystallized in late February 1949. In a message to the Paris embassy on 25 February, Secretary of State Dean Acheson, expressing the Asian-oriented approach, indicated that the French should be informed that support of the Bao Dai government depended upon concessions vital to its success. Ambassador Jefferson Caffery blunted this approach to the French, arguing that the United States should not prejudge the agreement. After his review of the 8 March letter from President Vincent Auriol to Bao Dai that constituted the Elysée Agreement, Caffery immediately advocated that American support was vital to strengthening Bao Dai's position. While mindful of Bao Dai's weakness, the ambassador argued that his status as the only alternative to Ho Chi Minh necessitated taking risks on his behalf. This European-oriented approach, supported by the Office of Western European Affairs, drew strong criticism from the Division of Philippine and Southeast Asian Affairs, whose chief, the former Saigon consul Charles Reed, maintained:

> Because we have the power to render impotent the Bao Dai solution, we should not delude ourselves into thinking that we therefore have the power to make such an experiment succeed. Merely because he offers at present the only possible non-Communist solution in Indochina is no reason, in view of his very dubious chances of succeeding, in committing the United States at this time to support, as in event he turns out to be a puppet, we then must follow blindly down a dead-end alley, expending our limited resources—in money and most particularly in prestige—in a fight which would be hopeless.

The issues set forth in the February confrontation over Indochina policy were reaffirmed as policymakers anticipated the American response to Bao Dai's return to Vietnam. From Saigon, Abbott suggested the conditions that should be insisted upon prior to recognition or endorsement; these included the French Assembly's linking of Cochin China to Vietnam, thus assuring the nationalist demand of national unity, and the formation by Bao

Dai of a cabinet of men of sufficient caliber to provide a chance of success. In the meantime, he urged pressure on France to implement the Elysée Agreement liberally and rapidly. Underlying Abbott's position was the assumption that "our support will not assure Bao Dai's success but the lack of it will probably make certain his failure." In opposition, the Office of Western European Affairs and the Paris embassy continued to argue that France, given its internal political divisions over colonial policy, could not be expected to grant additional concessions and, more importantly, that the Bao Dai government needed American support, which had to begin with an official statement welcoming the establishment of the Vietnamese state.

In June 1949 the scenario of the preceding February was replayed, as the Paris embassy again prevented a straightforward statement of the Asian-oriented strategy from being presented to the French government. On 6 June the State Department, acting with the knowledge of Acheson (who had left Washington to attend a foreign ministers meeting in Paris), instructed David Bruce, the new ambassador to France, to present a memorandum to the French government maintaining that the Elysée Agreement provided insufficient concessions to attract nationalists away from Ho Chi Minh and to Bao Dai. To save Indochina from communist control and to preserve some French influence there, the French were obliged to give assurances of genuine Vietnamese independence and to provide an early transfer of authority to the Bao Dai government. Taking advantage of Acheson's presence in Paris to gain his support, embassy officials persuaded the secretary that political conditions in France prevented reconsideration of colonial policy and that it was inappropriate to prejudge the Elysée Agreement. In addition to blunting this initiative, the European-centered group also gained important support for its position from Abbott. The Saigon consul, who was impressed with the arguments of the Paris embassy and was also being pressured by Vietnamese associates of Bao Dai, seconded the embassy's call for immediate American support of the Vietnamese state in order to build up Bao Dai as the cohesive figure in uniting noncommunist nationalists. Accordingly, by mid-June the State Department was preparing a public statement expressing its hope that the Elysée Agreement would bring together the "truly progressive elements within Vietnam" and would lead to a full realization of Vietnamese aspirations. Despite the opposition of a number of other important governments (principally Great Britain, India, the Indonesian Republic, and Thailand) to endorsement of French colonial policy, the United States on 21 June issued its statement in support of the Elysée Agreement.

By the end of June, the Asian-centered strategy had been effectively abandoned. In a memorandum of 28 June to his superior to the Division of Philippine and Southeast Asian Affairs, Charlton Ogburn, who had been instrumental in drafting the abortive June 6 memorandum, expressed profound disappointment:

What has happened is that Southeast Asia's policy has been junked, nothing

effective is being done to promote a non-Communist solution in Indochina.
. . . This is the culmination of three years of consistent effort on the part
of Western Europe to set aside all considerations of our position in Asia
and to keep a free hand for the French. This has been done on the grounds
that a stern attitude on the part of the United States would cause the
French government to fall. We have been gagged by this consideration
beyond all reason, in so many contexts that the thing has become a joke.

Comparing the American responses to colonial policies of European allies
in Indochina and Indonesia, Ogburn concluded:

So long as we were hogtied by this fear in our dealings with the Dutch,
developments in Indonesia went from bad to worse. If the situation in
Indonesia is now improving, I believe it is solely because the Dutch were
threatened with the loss of ECA [Economic Cooporation Administration].
. . . We have spoken far more drastically to the Dutch than we have
dreamed of speaking to the French. And there has been no sign of the
Dutch Government's falling. I think we are heading into a very bad mess
in the policy we are now following toward Indochina.

During the next few months, developments in Indochina confirmed
Ogburn's prediction of a "very bad mess" for American policymakers.
Concerned about the lack of international support for the Elysée Agreement,
the United States urged upon officials of the Bao Dai government the need
to establish an effective, popularly backed state. At the same time, officials
in Washington and Manila pressed the Philippine government to recognize
the communist danger in Indochina and the necessity for the success of
the "Bao Dai solution." Nonetheless, by September the Bao Dai regime
remained lacking in popular and international support.

As the United States confronted a worsening situation, its policymakers
were cognizant of, but unequivocally discounted, renewed public affirma-
tions from Ho Chi Minh of his overriding commitment to Vietnamese nationalism. In the summer of 1949, ending two years of isolation from the
West, Ho issued several statements directed toward France and the United
States. Through radio contact, letters, and the Viet Minh propaganda outlet
at Bangkok, Ho reiterated to French and American correspondents many
of the themes that had characterized his earlier appeal to the West between
the end of World War II and the beginning of the French–Viet Minh War.
In particular, he defended the Viet Minh as representative of many political
groups, affirmed his commitment to national independence and neutrality
in the cold war, and promised investment opportunities for foreign capital.
In America, his views received some attention, especially in *The Nation*.
In that journal, Andrew Roth pressed the argument that Ho constituted an
"Asian Tito" worthy of American support and cultivation. In an article of
10 September Roth maintained:

Although there has been much talk in Washington about the possibility of
Chinese Titoism, the situation in Vietnam suggests that the State Department is incapable of recognizing Titoism when it sees it.

In view of the established assumption that the United States could not risk a communist-dominated Vietnam, the State Department declined any consideration of an "Asian Tito."

While the United States dismissed the "Ho Chi Minh alternative," its tendency toward unconditional acceptance of the "Bao Dai solution" continued to present serious problems, principally the possibility of becoming the lone partner of France in a losing colonial enterprise. The meeting of the Big Three foreign ministers and their staffs in Washington during the week of 8 September underscored differences among France, Great Britain, and the United States. The American disposition to proceed with the recognition of Bao Dai—there being "no acceptable alternative"—ran counter to British reservations, which were based on doubt not only of whether the government met established criteria for recognition but also whether international recognition by itself would strengthen the Bao Dai regime internally. Accordingly the British pressured France to interpret the Elysée Agreement liberally as soon as it was ratified. Yet when Acheson met with French Foreign Minister Robert Schuman, the latter took the initiative and pressed for an enlarged American military and economic commitment. Maintaining that the French army was preventing the communist domination of Southeast Asia, Schuman pressed for United States military assistance to the associated states. While he promised a liberal policy, the foreign minister also stressed the lack of preparation for independence and the necessity for early Asian recognition as the key to strengthening the Bao Dai government. In sum, the three foreign secretaries could agree on little more than the necessity for some appropriate French gestures toward Vietnamese nationalism (chiefly the transferring of the administration of Indochina from the Overseas France Ministry to the responsibility of the foreign office), which would be followed by Anglo-American pressures on governments in South and Southeast Asia to recognize Bao Dai. They could also agree that Western recognition by itself would be the "kiss of death" for the "Bao Dai solution." Following the Washington meeting, conversations between American officials and representatives of Asian governments, principally India, underlined the deep-seated antagonism toward the French policy in Indochina and the need for significant changes to gain the vital support of those governments. Moreover, as foreshadowed in the discussion at Washington, the British appeared to be moving toward dissociation from French policy in Indochina. It seemed that the United States might be placed in a very isolated position, committed to a government that lacked popular and international respectability. The situation in Indochina potentially paralleled the American association with the discredited Chiang Kai-shek government in the Chinese civil war.

By late November the Asian-oriented strategists in the Department of State made another effort to increase the pressure on France as a means of salvaging Western influence in Indochina. The Division of Philippine and Southeast Asian Affairs advocated that France be called upon to follow ratification of the Elysée Agreement with a timetable detailing the transfer of authority in Indochina; moreover, an international commission would be established to supervise the transition. Against the background of the

communist victory in China and the Viet Minh's military success against
the French, this plan was viewed favorably by higher officials, with the
result that on 1 December Acheson informed the embassy in Paris of the
department's anticipated representations to the French government. Again,
however, the embassy blunted a plan that called for taking a strong stand
with the French. Bruce argued that no French government could survive
internally if it undertook such commitments. He urged instead more moderate expectations from France: transferring of Indochina from the Overseas
France Ministry, or a statement affirming that the Elysée Agreement constituted an evolutionary step in the changing French-Indochina relationships. In return, Bruce argued, the United States should recognize the Bao
Dai government and provide economic and military assistance. As it had
in similar circumstances in February and June of 1949, the leadership of
the State Department deferred to the basic position of the European-oriented approach, which by this time called for minimal modification of
French policy in return for a substantial American commitment to France's
position in Indochina.

That direction of American policy was reinforced by reports from Indochina and by the diplomatic-military implications of the Chinese civil
war. In December 1949 Washington received some encouraging estimates
of the prospects for Bao Dai's success. Malcolm MacDonald, the British
commissioner general in Southeast Asia, visited Indochina and quickly
became a strong advocate for Bao Dai's position, urging early support as
a means of evidencing Western goodwill. Samuel Welles, a *Time-Life* correspondent who toured Indochina in the fall of 1949, provided State
Department officers with a very optimistic appraisal of Vietnamese developments. From the field, the consuls at Saigon and Hanoi, while remaining
skeptical about the "Bao Dai solution," reported that the situation had
become more stable. Robert S. Folsom, who joined the Saigon consular
staff in November following tours of duty in China and Hungary, stated,
with the strong backing of Consul General Abbott, that recognition need
not depend upon Bao Dai's attaining popular support; instead, the United
States should extend recognition as a means of helping his government gain
credibility and popular backing.

By late 1949 the victory of the communists in the Chinese civil war
provided an irresistible momentum to the movement toward early, unconditional recognition of the Bao Dai government. The outcome of the Chinese
civil war profoundly affected the thinking of American policymakers with
respect to Indochina. Most evidently, it focused attention on Southeast
Asia as the likely next battleground in the struggle with international communism. As a result, American concern with Southeast Asia intensified and
plans were made to utilize economic and military assistance extensively in
the region as a means of assuring the survival of Western-oriented governments in Indonesia, Thailand, Burma, the Philippines, and Indochina.
Moreover, the devastating defeat of America's longtime ally Chiang Kai-
shek threatened to demoralize noncommunist nations throughout the world.
American credibility seemed to be threatened by the communist victory in

China, making a strong stand against communism in Southeast Asia all the more necessary. The National Security Council (NSC), in its policy statement 48/1, set forth clearly the significance of Indochina:

> [T]he extension of communist authority in China represents a grievous political defeat for us. . . . If Southeast Asia is also swept by communism, we shall have suffered a major political rout, the repercussions of which will be felt throughout the rest of the world. . . . The colonial-nationalist conflict provides a fertile field for subversive movements, and it is now clear that Southeast Asia is the target for a coordinated offensive directed by the Kremlin.

With the implications of the Chinese civil war increasingly prominent in the policymaking process, American officials pressed vigorously for the development of a consensus among the noncommunist governments of the region. By the end of 1949, Washington was urging Asian governments to extend diplomatic recognition of Bao Dai as soon as the French Assembly ratified the Elysée Agreement. The principal argument advanced by the United States held that inasmuch as the Bao Dai regime appeared to be gaining strength, recognition could be vital in attracting nationalists away from Ho Chi Minh and in pressuring the French to meet the legitimate demands of the Vietnamese. But the American appeal to the governments of India, the Philippines, Burma, Indonesia, and Thailand failed. Those nations were unwilling to recognize a government whose independence was compromised and which lacked substantial popular support. To Secretary Acheson, this position on the part of Asian leaders reflected an inadequate understanding of the overriding danger of communism; he noted:

> This general indifference or lack of understanding may prove to be disastrous for those nations as Communism relentlessly advances. It is impossible for the United States to help them resist Communism if they are not prepared to help themselves.

In an effort to make the "Bao Dai solution" more acceptable to Asian nations, the United States pressed the French for a commitment to further concessions, but that initiative likewise failed. In response to American suggestion that ratification of the Elysée Agreement be coupled with a statement on the evolutionary progress of Indochina toward independence, French officials repeatedly maintained that internal constraints prevented any elaboration on Indochina policy. Beyond that argument, the French government was cognizant that American and British plans for recognition were already well advanced and that recognition could be expected without additional concessions.

The American momentum toward recognition was enhanced by the Soviet Union's decision, announced in late January, to recognize the government of Ho Chi Minh. That action seemed to provide evidence of a Soviet–Viet Minh link and thus confirmed the assumption of NSC 48 of the necessity of economic and military assistance to Southeast Asia, principally Indochina. By the first week of February 1950, the United States had become fully committed to the "Bao Dai solution" and was prepared to recognize that government unconditionally.

In the weeks after the recognition of the Bao Dai government, the United States became more fully involved in Indochina. "Escalation" quickly followed recognition. From the perspective of Washington, Indochina increasingly became a military question, thus reducing concern with French colonial policy. Contemplating America's options a few days after recognition, Acheson was wary that ". . . our bargaining position disappears the moment we agree to give them aid." But military and economic assistance had already become the essential next step in stabilizing Vietnam. No one questioned the necessity of preventing a Viet Minh victory in Indochina as the key to preventing communist expansion into Southeast Asia. Failure to aid the French would only result in larger expenditures of American resources at a later date. The French were seen as determined to maintain a strong military effort against communism in Indochina, but they needed American assistance. Otherwise, they would become demoralized and would withdraw, leaving the defense of Indochina and the remainder of Southeast Asia to the United States. On 8 May the United States announced the extension of military assistance. One may well agree with Gaddis Smith's observation: "[t]here are many candidates for the precise date the United States went to war in Indochina. May 8, 1950, is the best." With the outbreak of the Korean War the next month, French and American interests merged into virtual agreement, as Korea and Indochina became seen as two fronts of the same war to contain communism in Asia.

Reflecting on the decision to recognize the Bao Dai government, it is evident that the United States accepted a solution that was given little chance of success. To some extent, the prognosis for Indochina improved in late 1949 and early 1950. The encouraging estimates of Bao Dai's prospects provided by Welles, Folsom, and MacDonald were reinforced by the favorable analyses of Ambassador at Large Philip Jessup and the new consul at Saigon, Edmund Gullion. But even Jessup, who met with Bao Dai in Saigon and with high-ranking French officials in Paris, and Gullion acknowledged that the American interests still necessitated French concessions. Indeed, after the recognition of the Bao Dai government, the State Department renewed its efforts to modify French policy, but with little effect.

After as well as before recognition, the United States basically lacked leverage in dealing with France over Indochina—a consequence of the pressures of the cold war and the communist victory in China. The French presence in Indochina, whatever its imperfections, was considered vital to the preservation of Western interests in Southeast Asia. The extent to which the United States had become a captive of the French program was evident in the State Department retreats of February, June, and December 1949 from projected stern representations on behalf of a liberal colonial policy. Whether attaching conditions to American recognition and support of the Bao Dai government would have made any difference in the long run is uncertain, but at the least representations on behalf of significant French concessions would have dissociated the United States from a colonial policy that was anathema to the vast majority of Vietnamese as well as to the independent nations of Asia. At the time, however, Americans perceived only very limited options in Indochina, and the priority, it appeared, had to be given to anticommunism rather than to nationalism.

Analyses of the development of American involvement in Indochina have generally focused on the period after the Geneva Conference and especially on the escalation from 1961 to 1968. Some scholars have seen the Vietnam policy of the United States as representing a quagmire, i.e., a series of steps, each seeming to promise the attainment of American objectives but resulting only in deeper involvement. Following the publication of the Pentagon Papers, the quagmire theory was challenged by those who argued that the documentary record suggested a pattern of intentional stalemate. According to that viewpoint, each step of involvement represented the minimum necessary to avoid defeat, as each administration from Truman to Nixon was determined not to repeat the domestic ramifications of the "loss of China." This stalemate model has been applied directly to the policy calculations of 1949–50. Yet with nearly all of the documents regarding the initial commitment of 1950 now available, it would seem that the decisions to recognize Bao Dai and to extend military assistance three months later resulted from calculations that were neither as simplistic as the quagmire theory nor as cynical as the stalemate model. On the prospects for the success of American policy in 1949–50, policymakers seemed to fall somewhere between the belief in success advanced by the quagmire proponents and the recognition of almost certain failure argued by the stalemate school.

As much of the foregoing appraisal suggests, the policy adopted in Indochina in 1949–50 can be understood as an important component of the emergence of a clearly defined American policy for Southeast Asia, which was derived from the cold war with the Soviet Union and from the Chinese communist victory. As a consequence of the collapse of European authority in Southeast Asia during World War II and the abrupt ending of the Japanese empire in the area, the United States came out of the war with only vague aspirations for the independence of colonial peoples. That objective had to be compromised in the context of the European adjustment to political change in Asia and the imperatives of the cold war. Gradually an American approach to Southeast Asia emerged, one that called for the peaceful transition of authority to Western-oriented elites, which would provide political and economic stability and keep the area free from communism. This pattern was evidenced in the terms by which the United States withdrew from the Philippines and in the American response to the Indonesian revolution. In Indochina as in the Philippines and Indonesia, the American objective centered on an orderly and early transfer of authority to noncommunist, Western-oriented leaders. But unlike those in Indonesia and the Philippines, such leaders in Vietnam could not command public support, as the communists had managed to gain control of the nationalist movement. That was the dilemma American policymakers could not resolve in 1947, 1950, or thereafter.

A Strategic and Economic Perspective

MICHAEL SCHALLER

The links between policy toward Occupied Japan and the origins of containment in Southeast Asia are both intriguing and elusive. While a few historians suggest that these policies sprang from similar roots, most studies contrast the constructive American record in Japan to the military and ideological crusades pursued in China, Korea, and Indochina.

However, planners and policy makers in the late 1940s did not compartmentalize Japan and Southeast Asia, but saw them as linked sectors on a "great crescent" that stretched in an arc from the Kurile Islands to the borders of Iran and Afghanistan. Those most concerned with Japan in the State and Defense Departments, Economic Cooperation Administration, and in Douglas MacArthur's Occupation Headquarters not only accepted the necessity of Japan reassuming a major regional role but eventually supported the joint assumption by Washington and Tokyo of the mantle of empire Americans had wrested from the Japanese at the close of World War II.

Once the Occupation had proclaimed, or pressed the Japanese government to enact, a variety of basic economic and political reforms, American planners faced the problem of how to integrate Japan into the Asian community. By 1948 they envisioned Japan as an industrial hub, sustained by trade with less developed states along an Asian economic defense perimeter. A secure Japan would help support Southeast Asia against Chinese communism, and vice versa. Above all else, the relationship required that Japan have access to secure, affordable raw materials and markets in Southeast Asia, while minimizing trade with China. Although never as formal or explicit as parallel programs in Europe—Truman Doctrine, Marshall Plan, North Atlantic Treaty Organization (NATO)—this idea shaped both policy toward Japan and the growing commitment to Southeast Asia.

A regional approach toward the Far East began incrementally among several groups in Washington. But by the spring of 1947, the rough outline of a policy emerged. Speaking in Cleveland, Mississippi, on May 8, 1947, in a speech foreshadowing the Marshall Plan, Under Secretary of State Dean Acheson called for pushing forward "with the reconstruction of those two great workshops of Europe and Asia—Germany and Japan—upon which the ultimate recovery of the two continents so largely depends." Acheson's public disclosure followed many interagency discussions and

Michael Schaller, "Securing the Great Crescent: Occupied Japan and the Origins of Containment in Southeast Asia," *Journal of American History,* 69 (Sept. 1982), 392–96, 400–07, 413–14. Reprinted by permission.

private warnings regarding the internal economic situation in Japan. While the American public heard General MacArthur boast of his successful "spiritual revolution" and Japan's readiness, in March 1947, for a quick peace treaty, few policy makers shared his optimism.

The former enemy might now enjoy a democratic constitution and a greatly liberalized political structure, but its 1947 production had declined to barely one-third of prewar levels. Japan had lost its merchant fleet, an empire, much productivity capacity and a predominant economic position in East Asia. Synthetic fibers had virtually wiped out its profitable silk exports to the United States while the chaos of postwar Asia, occupation restrictions, and anti-Japanese sentiment prevented the revival of intraregional trade. Only relief aid by the United States Army—"Government and Relief in Occupied Areas" (GARIOA)—at a cost of almost $400 million per year, prevented a total economic collapse.

Aware of this situation and fearful of the "complete collapse of Japan" followed by chaos and communism, leading figures in the State, War, and Navy Departments as well as influential private citizens mobilized against MacArthur's effort to terminate the Occupation. They favored a radically different approach, stressing the fastest possible economic recovery to precede a peace settlement. This required abandonment of most punitive economic controls and guidance by American civilian economic experts.

As early as February 1947, the State Department's Division of Japanese and Korean Affairs, led by Edwin F. Martin, outlined a comprehensive recovery program for Japan. Previous assumptions that a politically reformed Japan would quickly become self-supporting with only minimal American direction were outdated, Martin wrote, by the radical changes that had overtaken the world economy. In its postwar condition, inefficient and outdated, Japanese industry would never be able to sell enough to the United States or Europe to finance food and commodity imports. Since United States relief must eventually terminate, the resulting economic stagnation would quickly undermine democratic reforms and hurt the rest of Asia by depriving it of "markets for their raw materials and sources for cheap manufactured goods." Martin proposed a two-tiered recovery program designed both to stimulate Japanese industry and redirect its long-term sources of trade. His plan entailed temporarily increasing United States financed raw material imports for processing in Japan and export to non-dollar Asian markets. Simultaneously, the previous punitive approach to reparations payments, decartelization, and levels-of-industry limits would be altered to promote rapid recovery. The temporary infusion of dollars and raw materials would prime Japanese production as it promoted intraregional trade. Eventually, as exchanges based on trading Japanese manufactured goods for Asian raw materials expanded, American aid would no longer be required. This "economic crank-up" would solve the chronic dollar-gap problem, reduce occupation costs, and establish a long-term basis for an integrated Asian economy.

By July, Martin's proposal grew into a sixty-page paper submitted by the department to the State-War-Navy Coordinating Committee (SWNCC).

SWNCC 381, "The Revival of the Japanese Economy," proposed a crash $500-million program to revive the "great workshop" of Asia to a state of "self-sufficiency" by about 1950. After pro forma consultation with other Far Eastern Commission members, the United States would eliminate or drastically reduce all economic constraints on Japanese industry. American aid would finance a large volume of raw material imports for production and export. The program would encourage Japanese sales to nondollar Asian markets with payments in raw materials. This process would reverse the current trend of Japanese dependence on dollar imports, while stimulating a major revival of intraregional trade.

The proposal contained a strongly revisionist and favorable description of Japanese economic expansion in Asia before 1941. Overall, it described Japan as a catalyst for Asian development, much like Britain in relation to the industrialization of Western Europe and North America. Specifically, the proposal endorsed Japanese economic expansion into the "natural frontier" of Southeast Asia. The draft looked toward a time when Japan would enjoy a large trade surplus with Southeast Asia. At that point, American dollar aid to both areas could be reduced. The Southeast Asian currency surplus held by Tokyo could be taken by Washington as debt repayment for GARIOA and then recycled in Southeast Asia in some form of aid program.

Although this call for an "economic crank-up" received informal approval on October 20, the army and State Department still debated the language of the document. The army wanted to use the phrase "shift in emphasis" to describe the program and, more seriously, favored enacting the program unilaterally, with virtually no consulting of foreign governments. Army Under Secretary William Draper, an investment banker who played a key role in economic planning for both Germany and Japan, promoted this approach in the army's policy document, SWNCC 384. In any case, both agencies shared a general goal for Japan, and their specific actions over the next year and a half led to basic reversals of policies regarding the purge program, decartelization, reparations of equipment, limits on industry, and promotion of the rights of organized labor.

Strategic concerns mirrored economic considerations, as demonstrated in August 1947, when Under Secretary of State Robert Lovett requested that George Kennan's Policy Planning Staff (PPS) reevaluate a preliminary draft peace treaty for Japan. In a scathing critique, PPS staff member John Davies dismissed the draft as ignorant of the need for a "stable Japan, integrated into the Pacific, friendly to the U.S., and, in case of need, a ready and dependable ally." Instead of concern with liberal reforms and social experiments, MacArthur's headquarters and Washington treaty drafters ought to stress economic recovery and the development of central military forces to resist a Soviet-inspired coup.

Lovett promptly ordered the existing treaty draft to be scrapped while the PPS prepared a new version. During August and September, the PPS worked with army and navy representatives to set an agenda for a post-

Occupation Japan, amenable to American leadership and a powerful economic force in Asia. This new Japan would not "possess an identity of its own" but would "function as" an "American satellite."

The PPS draft asserted what became a major theme of later policy documents: that Japanese recovery could be gravely impaired by communist control of most of Northeast Asia. While communist authorities might encourage trade, this would inevitably be used by the communists "as a lever for Soviet political pressure, unless Japan is able to obtain these raw materials and markets elsewhere—particularly in South Asia and the Western Hemisphere." During the next one or two years, the PPS draft concluded, Washington must compel MacArthur to hasten recovery by accepting expert civilian advice, working with the Japanese government and business community, and ceasing to push a program of economic-social reform.

During the remainder of 1947 and 1948 Kennan and Draper ceaselessly promoted Japanese economic recovery, often over the protest of MacArthur. Through their fact-finding trips to Japan, frequent testimony before Congress, briefings of the press, and recruitment of American businessmen to oversee Supreme Commander for the Allied Powers (SCAP) economic policy, these pivotal State Department and army officials effected a tremendous change in almost all Occupation policies. By the end of 1948, the "shift in emphasis" and "economic crank-up" redefined the direction of economic and social reform in Occupied Japan. Although civilian and military planners continued to disagree violently on questions regarding post-treaty base rights and the development of military forces within Japan, as early as October 1947 they shared an outlook on the pace and direction of economic orientation. . . .

A report on the "Strategic Importance of Japan," prepared by the CIA in May 1948 for circulation in the State Department and armed forces, echoed the theme that whoever controlled Japan held the key to the Far East. Considering Japan's location and industrial potential—especially if integrated with the Soviet Far East and Manchuria—its possession by the Kremlin might actually tip the balance in the Cold War. Communist possession of Northeast Asia, the report warned, would make Japanese recovery slow and difficult. Were access to Southeast Asia also lost, "the ensuing economic distress, with its attendant political instability, might force Japan to align itself with the U.S.S.R." Under the right conditions, Japan could become a powerful, pro-American, "stabilizing force in Asia." But if left a hostage to Soviet control of its trading zones, "the probability that Japan would eventually succumb to Communist domination would become almost a certainty."

Circumscribing both the hopes and fears for Japan's future, of course, lurked the specter of China's civil war. The terms of its outcome, the policy of the Communists, the attitude of the United States—all bore directly on proposed recovery programs. Throughout 1948 and early 1949, intense debates raged between the State Department, which favored a relatively moderate approach to China, and those in the Defense Department and the

Congressional "China bloc" who demanded increased militancy against the communists, including a virtual economic blockade.

In a series of decisions reached by the NSC in March 1949, the State Department's moderate position prevailed. Rather than attempting to reverse the verdict of China's revolution through outside intervention, the United States would neither intervene on the mainland nor use force to defend Taiwan. While trade would not be encouraged, no barriers would be imposed on United States or Japanese nonstrategic trade with China. Finally, in hopes of inducing, or at least not delaying, a Sino-Soviet split, Washington would try to avoid provoking the communist regime.

At the same time, these successful moves by the State Department required that it demonstrate to its many critics a commitment to containment beyond China. The need to show resolve in a threatened area, combined with an awareness that any Asian strategy must promote Japanese recovery, focused attention on Southeast Asia. The region abutted China, was itself in the throes of political upheaval, and held the promise of providing Japan with an economic alternative to Northeast Asia. In a strong parallel to Tokyo's actions of 1940–1941, American policy makers hoped to resolve or escape their dilemmas in China by adopting a "southern strategy" that would contain China even as it opened a new economic zone for Japan.

Until 1949 the United States had not been directly committed to a defense of Indochina. While some military and economic aid to France filtered down to its forces fighting Ho Chi Minh's Viet Minh guerrillas, the State Department remained reluctant to actively support the colonial war. By June 1948, both the State and Defense Departments felt concerned enough by the growing instability throughout the region to convene a "Southeast Asia Regional Conference" in Bangkok. The conference brought together diplomatic officers and military attachés from throughout Asia to discuss the regional impact of nationalism and communism. They quickly concluded that while nationalism had deep local roots, the Kremlin had placed a top priority on capturing control of the movement. Consequently, the United States must forge a counterstrategy to secure the loyalty or Western orientation of Asian nationalism.

Extensive conference reports sent to Washington stressed the often-overlooked economic importance of the region to the world economy. Malaya's tin and rubber exports, for example, formed the mainstay of the British economy's "dollar arsenal." To varying degrees, France and the Netherlands also depended on dollar earnings from colonial investments and the sales of Asian commodities to balance their chronic deficit in trans-Atlantic trade. The dollar gap, the report noted, was one of the main problems which had required the creation of the ERP [European Recovery Program]. To make matters worse, the desperate colonial wars of France and the Netherlands and their refusal to deal with moderate nationalists played into Moscow's hands. Communists who attacked the colonial regimes posed as "Bolivars," while "each additional day of fighting works for Moscow."

Early in 1949, even as the NSC decisions of March 3 confirmed the relatively moderate policy towards China advocated by the State Department, the PPS prepared an outline for a more assertive program in Southeast Asia. Presented for the department's consideration on March 29, PPS 51 called for a comprehensive "U.S. policy toward Southeast Asia." It described a region remarkable for its undeveloped natural wealth, convulsed by nationalism and the "target of a coordinated offensive plainly directed by the Kremlin."

The long report examined the important role Southeast Asia played as a producer of raw materials and arena for investment by European colonial powers. Since 1941, however, military and political disruptions had blocked the region from producing the surplus needed by Europe or for "Indian and Japanese economic self-support." The atavistic colonial policies of the Europeans not only radicalized the region but also enhanced the Kremlin's efforts to gain a foothold.

The report suggested two reasons behind the Soviet offensive. Although Moscow had no direct need for the region's resources, it saw great value in denying the West and Japan access to the area's raw materials and transportation routes. Moreover, a communist victory there, in the wake of the China debacle, would have a tremendous destabilizing impact "throughout the rest of the world, especially in the Middle East and in a then critically exposed Australia." The PPS paper described Southeast Asia as a "vital segment" in a "great crescent" of containment that ran from Japan through island and mainland Southeast Asia, India, and Australia. Each sector of the crescent, in Southeast Asia or Japan, was vital to "the development of an interdependent and integrated counter-force to Stalinism in this quarter of the world."

The United States must compel its European allies to "rationalize" their policies by devolving power onto moderate nationalist regimes, the paper declared. Then genuine nationalists would flock to the western banner. Thereafter, the confrontation throughout the region would pit nationalist against communist, rather than against the West. In Indochina, the strategic key to the region, Kennan's staff predicted a prolonged campaign of "working through a screen of anti-communist Asiatics, to ensure, however long it takes, the triumph of Indochinese nationalism over Red Imperialism."

The long-range goal of this program, the report concluded, lay in fully integrating Southeast Asia (SEA) with the other major units of the great crescent—India, Australia, and Japan. Washington should "develop the economic interdependence between SEA as a supplier of raw materials, and Japan, Western Europe and India as suppliers of finished goods, with due recognition, however, of the legitimate aspirations of SEA countries for some diversification of their economies." When the PPS paper went before the secretary and under secretaries for consideration, the recorded minutes summarized its message in a concise sentence. The political problems of the area must be solved so "the region could begin to fulfill its major function as a source of raw materials and a market for Japan and Western Europe."

During the summer of 1949, despite the absence of an Asian Marshall Plan, two new programs promoted the connection between Japan and Southeast Asia policy. The Mutual Defense Assistance Act of 1949 established a Mutual Assistance Program (MAP) with funds for a wide range of military purposes. At the same time, Secretary of Defense Louis Johnson initiated a major study of Asian policy (NSC 48), which, he hoped, would commit the administration to a more aggressive stance against communism. By early 1950, the NSC 48 guidelines, combined with MAP, forged new links in American policy between Japan and Southeast Asia.

Originating as SWNCC 360 in April 1947, MAP proposed to give the administration a massive $1.5-billion fund for military aid. The program remained in legislative limbo until the autumn of 1949. While most of the proposed aid would go to Western Europe, both the administration and Congress discussed the need for some additional aid to Asia. During congressional testimony, Acheson specifically described MAP as a way to fight communism in Asia outside the bounds of China. The secretary of state and Gen. Omar Bradley urged that Congress give up any illusion that further aid to Chiang Kai-shek would save either China or Asia from conquest. Acheson, especially, pleaded that Americans not "concentrate every thought we have on China." He urged that more attention be paid to how "we can prevent the spread of this Communist menace throughout Southeast Asia." As an example of this new concern, Acheson described the appointment of Ambassador Philip Jessup to head a group of outside experts, the Far Eastern Consultants, who would study regional security.

The secretary followed the lead of PPS 51 in its description of the "vast area that extends from Pakistan to Japan." The United States must encourage moderate nationalism in this zone even as it induced the European allies to abandon colonial power. Rather than appropriating any more money for Chiang or for a guerrilla war in China, Acheson said, Congress ought to "give the administration some money—not very much—that could be used in Asia on a confidential basis. . . . "

While a few diehard Kuomintang supporters in the House and Senate continued to badger the administration, most representatives supported Acheson's suggestion that a special unvouchered fund be created and used for various programs in Southeast Asia and other areas that the Jessup group might recommend. As signed by the president on October 6, 1949, the MAP program contained "Section 303," a unique provision for an unvouchered $75-million fund to promote containment in the "General Area of China," at the president's discretion.

The promise of an initial $75-million MAP for Asia, with the likelihood of subsequent unvouchered funds, generated a scramble for control of the money and for a program to expend it upon. The "303" funds could be applied toward anything—military aid or the formation of a centralized Asia-aid agency so widely discussed. With these considerations in mind, Defense Secretary Johnson requested the NSC to review overall United States policy in Asia. His June 10, 1949, letter to the NSC complained that while America pursued "day to day, country to country" containment, "global" communism gobbled up Asia. The United States he argued, must institute a "comprehensive plan" of containment in Asia based on more effective coordination of current and future political, economic, and military programs. During the next six months, Defense Department aides worked with the small NSC staff to prepare an aggressive, anticommunist program under military control.

The background drafts of the NSC 48, only recently declassified, reveal the Defense Department's concern over the relationship between economic and strategic security. Their analysis of American policy in Asia focused as much on that area's long-term economic relationship to Russia and the West as on its current political and military balance. American security depended in large part on keeping Asian resources available to the West and Japan while preventing Soviet control over those resources. More specifically, the United States must deny the Soviets "the richest economic prize in the Far East," Japan. Defense planners were certain that Moscow intended to integrate Japan with Siberia, Manchuria, and Korea into a "Communist Co-Prosperity Sphere" that would be a "self-sufficient war-making complex" designed to supplement the European Soviet base.

Japan's advanced industrial base, unique in Asia, would add at least 25 percent to Soviet industrial power, the reports estimated. Yet to acquire this prize, the Kremlin need risk no invasion nor even stress subversion. Simply by holding Northeast Asia, Southeast Asia, and Formosa, it could ensure that Japan would soon slip into the Communist orbit. Only by adopting a program of harassing the Chinese communists and, in Formosa and Southeast Asia, organizing a "properly guided anti-communist effort" might a "bulwark" be erected to preserve a vital zone for Japan.

Since any rollback of Chinese communism remained a long-term proposition and since Formosa and Korea could not fill all Japan's raw material requirements, Southeast Asia appeared the most important potential economic partner for Japan. Using a European analogy, a September draft of NSC 48 compared Manchuria to Central Europe and Japan to England.

> The powder keg Southeast Asia (Balkans, Middle East) occupies a similar position, with the more or less secondary, but not to be overlooked India (Iberian Peninsula) in the offing. Therefore, to carry the analogy further, it must be concluded, (tempered only by the broad concept of defense in the East and offense in the West) that a strong Western oriented Japan, with access to the raw materials of as much of the rest of Asia as possible, is essential to the U.S.

A comprehensive economic analysis of Japan's role, prepared by the CIA, compared Japan's dependence on Southeast Asia to the area's prewar importance to the European empires. Promoting the future economic integration of the two regions would embrace "at once a number of economic interests of the U.S." Japan would benefit greatly from access to cheap and secure raw materials, while Japanese exports and technological guidance to Southeast Asia would promote stability in the wake of retreating European influence. Noting the "comparative advantages" of the Japanese economy, the CIA analysis urged that the United States lift Occupation limits on Japanese monopoly and, instead, assist the formation of "a number of rather large financial and trading concerns." Japanese exporters and developers should be encouraged and helped in returning to Southeast Asia where they could "make full use of their special knowledge and experience in these matters." The CIA even favored American funding of Japanese trading companies, which would then load development funds to increase commodity production in Southeast Asia.

The drafts officially circulated by the Defense Department in mid-October portrayed Asia under coordinated Soviet attack. Utilizing its Chinese puppets, the Kremlin planned to acquire Japan through economic strangulation via its control of Northeast and Southeast Asia. In response, the defense planners urged that the United States create a "Pacific Association" to serve as a vehicle for rolling back communism in China, seizing control of Formosa, and coordinating economic affairs in Asia. This formidable program would be supervised by a high-ranking American specifically charged with revitalizing the struggle against communism in Asia.

Not surprisingly, State Department experts expressed shock at this immense undertaking. The commitments to Formosa, the idea of a Pacific Association, and a program for fighting China ran counter to almost everything Acheson and his advisers advocated. In contrast, Acheson, his Far Eastern Consultants, and area specialists like Davies and Butterworth hoped to temper the Chinese Revolution through gradual accommodation. They had no faith in Chiang, saw no Asian support for a Pacific Association, and believed that the Chinese communists would themselves move away from Moscow if only Washington steered clear of any provocations. The danger to Southeast Asia, in turn, came as much from European intransigence toward moderate nationalists as from Moscow's subversion. As for Japan, State Department experts ridiculed the Defense Department for its refusal to acknowledge that the lack of a peace treaty (blocked by Defense Department objections) undercut Japan's faith in America almost as much as did economic insecurity.

During an arduous redrafting process, which continued from October through late-December 1949, State Department Asia specialists pulled the teeth from most of the NSC 48 proposals. Much of the bellicose rhetoric remained, partly as a sop to Secretary Johnson's enthusiasm. The redraft, NSC 48/1, did call for containing and reducing Soviet and Chinese communist power in Asia, but avoided specifics. The paper did not preclude informal trade and discussions with the Chinese Communists, nor did it call for defending Taiwan or for covert warfare in Manchuria. Regarding Japan, the paper now endorsed a prompt peace settlement, permitting limited trade with China, and a general program to encourage trade with Southeast Asia.

The final State-Defense compromise over the Asia paper came in NSC 48/2, approved on December 30. While Acheson succeeded in barring any new aggressive programs toward China, he did agree to the Defense Department's demand that the $75-million MAP fund be "programmed as a matter of urgency." In effect, the scramble of Defense and State Department planners to promote a new Asian policy had been transferred from NSC 48 to the MAP program. Almost at once, a variety of policy-making groups in Washington seized upon the idea of using the MAP funds and authority as a way to create an integrated containment program in Asia.

During the six months that preceded the outbreak of the Korean War, the State Department, the Defense Department, the Joint Chiefs of Staff (JCS), SCAP, and the Department of the Army continued to disagree about most aspects of Asian policy. No consensus could be reached on the timing and nature of a Japanese peace settlement, nor was there agreement on whether the United States ought to "roll back" or merely "contain" Chinese communism. In contrast, almost all the competing policy-making bureaucrats accepted the argument that linked Japan's fate to Southeast Asia.

Testifying in executive session before the Senate Foreign Relations Committee on January 10, 1950, Acheson drew together the diverse strands of policy in Asia. After denouncing Soviet efforts to tie Eastern Europe to its own economy, the secretary boasted of American plans to promote economic and military integration in Western Europe and Asia. As before, Acheson dismissed arguments that the United States ought to move against China or defend Formosa. While it let the dust settle on the Chinese Revolution, Washington would forge a new bulwark based on Japan, Southeast Asia, and India. Japan, the anchor of this bulwark, must be permitted flexible trade with China to meet immediate economic needs while Southeast Asian resources were developed. Economic aid to the region, rather than an exclusive military program, Acheson argued, would serve to isolate China and expand interdependence.

Acheson repeatedly attacked the pleading of Senators Arthur Vandenberg and William Knowland who insisted on linking American security to the defense of Chiang on Formosa. Similarly, when Ambassador-at-Large Jessup testified in March regarding his tour of the region, he admonished the senators that strong economic links between Japan and Southeast Asia would provide the best barrier to Soviet and Chinese expansion. Any program based on defending Chiang, he warned, was doomed.

The JCS, in a report of January 17, described how the MAP program could achieve the goals described by Acheson. The report described Japan as central to the integrated offshore island chain on which United States security in Asia relied. Japan itself depended on access to strategic raw materials—food, fuel, ores, and fibers. Its security required both trade with Pacific islands and a "buffer on the mainland." In "simpler terms," the JCS report declared,

> the security interest of the United States in the Far East, short of military action, hinges upon finding and securing an area to complement Japan as did Manchuria and Korea prior to World War II. Accepting Communist control of China for the foreseeable future and realizing that a Japanese economy depending largely on resources from China and Korea could draw Japan into the communist orbit; or that a Japanese economy depending

for the foreseeable future upon financial assistance and resources from the U.S. is unacceptable; the urgency strategically, of an arrangement with Southeast Asia stands out strongly.

. . . .

Inevitably, the American attitude of linking Japan and Southeast Asia together as an economic unit carried over into the military sphere. The outbreak of fighting in Korea in June swept away most of the factional and tactical disputes concerning the proper balance of economic and military aid, defense of Formosa, and dealing with the Chinese communists. Dulles's October reference to Japan as the real target in Korea voiced the conclusions of most policy makers. General Bradley, Chairman of the JCS, put the issue directly before President Truman in a June 26 memorandum urging that the United States respond to the Korean crisis by defending not only Korea but also Formosa and the rest of Asia. Bradley told Truman of his firm conviction that "Korea, Japan, Okinawa, Formosa, the Philippines and Southeast Asia are all part of the same problem. Since these positions are interdependent, there is an urgent need for a coordinated overall policy in the Far East."

Ultimately, of course, the financial rewards that the Korean War brought to Japan helped spur the economic miracle of the post-Occupation era. As the United States moved to defend all the regions that Bradley named, Japan's industrial exports reentered those American and European markets in which they supposedly could not compete. Two decades later, in the wake of the American disaster in Vietnam, both a bruised United States and an immensely prosperous Japan would turn back toward political and economic links with the long-shunned communist regime in China.

The very scale of these ironies hampers our understanding of how contemporary policy makers viewed the postwar crises of Japan, China, and Southeast Asia. Nevertheless, among those many planners and agencies concerned with charting the future of Japan after 1945, the fate of Southeast Asia stands out as a central issue around which they constructed a regional policy.

A Political Perspective

ROBERT M. BLUM

At the end of the Pacific War in August 1945, the United States' fondest wish for East Asia was that its countries be at peace and independent, that its governments be stable, that its land mass not be dominated by a single power hostile to Western interests, and that the region participate in an economic system beneficial to both itself and the West. Yet, the region was far from enjoying this benign state. In rapid transition from one state of war to another, many parts of East Asia were doomed to suffer internal strife for many years to come. Where the battle lines in World War II had usually been drawn and the enemy singular, the Asian wars of the late 1940s were either civil wars or insurgencies without front lines and with almost bewildering political complexity. To make matters worse, most countries had an active Communist movement presumed to be Soviet controlled.

Despite the gap between its wish and reality, the United States took few direct measures of significance to arrest the chaos or curb communism in East Asia in the first five years after it defeated Japan. Only in conquered territory—Japan and Korea—were American troops stationed. In China, the United States maintained a half-hearted commitment to the survival of a Nationalist regime that was corrupt, unpopular with the Chinese, and losing a civil war to the Communists. In Southeast Asia, a declining bastion of European colonialism, American influence was minimal.

In sharp contrast to the apparent American indifference toward East Asia, the United States pursued a forceful policy in Western Europe designed to thwart Soviet expansion and obtain an enduring peace. Although their numbers were reduced, American troops never left Europe after the close of the war. Within four years Washington had backed its policy in the region with massive economic assistance, a strong political commitment, and the promise of a strong defense treaty and massive military aid.

The reason for the disparity in commitment was not indifference or inattention to Asia. The American press and private reporting channels of the Truman administration adequately described Asia's troubles. The administration's senior officials devoted much of their attention throughout the second half of the 1940s to the region, especially China. Their relative inaction stemmed from several other reasons.

One was the perceived limitations of American power. The military believed that it could not make a significant commitment of American armed forces to both Europe and Asia at the same time for fear that the cold war might become hot in both regions. The budget makers in the Administration, who enjoyed firm backing in the White House and Congress, believed that there were severe limits to the amount of money the United States could apply overseas through economic and military assistance. As a result of the need to set priorities, American policy makers felt compelled to continue the tradition of emphasizing the security of Europe over Asia.

Beyond the constraint of limited resources, American inaction in the Orient in the early postwar years was encouraged by the inability of anybody in or out of government to devise a sensible plan to retrieve the declining situation in Asia. Short of a massive commitment of American ground forces in China, the Nationalists seemed doomed to lose to the Communists. The problems of Southeast Asia were still the responsibility of European colonial powers who resented American interference. Washington was also divided over how hard to push them to divest themselves of their colonies: on the one hand, American officials worried about alienating countries that played a vital role in European recovery and defense; on the other, they did not want the problems of the region dumped in their own laps.

Finally, American politicians and diplomats, who were of European ancestry, who had occasionally traveled to Europe, and who were familiar with its languages and culture, felt much more comfortable dealing with the problems of Western Europe. Their images and understanding of Asia were much more vague. While some had traveled in China and thought they understood it, few had experience elsewhere in Asia. As a result, they turned their attention to Europe first and acted with vigor and imagination. They watched Asia, and especially China, worriedly, but held back from taking an activist role.

In 1949, as Europe appeared to be on its way to recovery and China was rapidly falling to the Communists, Washington's attention began to turn East with an eye toward positive action. By the end of the year, the administration decided to commit American power and prestige to containing the spread of communism throughout the Far East by drawing a line of containment around much of China. By the spring of 1950, months before the outbreak of the Korean War, Washington had begun to implement this policy.

The focus of the new policy was Southeast Asia. The policy arose, however, only in part as the result of the Truman administration's concern for events in the subcontinent. It also owed its creation to the intense debate in American politics in 1949 over the failure to thwart the Communists within China. The debate created both a perceived political need on the part of the administration to act forcefully somewhere in Asia and a $75 million contingency fund that provided money to embark on an activist policy in the region.

The result, which was clear at the time but thrown out of focus for subsequent students of the period by the dramatic American response to the Korean War, was that the United States became committed to playing a significant role in the defense of Southeast Asia against Communist domination months before 27 June 1950. The first crates of American military hardware, received in Saigon in July 1950, had been on their way for many months and owed their presence there to a complicated mixture of bureaucratic infighting within the Truman administration and to the support of a distracted and highly politicized Congress. . . .

The catalyst that stimulated an active American policy in Southeast Asia was the Mutual Defense Assistance Act of 1949. The act authorized funds for the Military Assistance Program (MAP), the first of many omnibus postwar military aid measures. While the 1949 act's main purpose was to "implement" the North Atlantic Treaty's mutual assistance provision, it also contained an authorization for $75 million in unvouchered funds to be used at the president's discretion in the "general area of China." The purpose of the fund, at least as far as the China bloc was concerned, was to finance overt and covert aid to Nationalist forces on the mainland and Taiwan. Little if any money was spent for that purpose. The effect the $75 million had was to stimulate planning for, and ultimately begin financing of, a containment policy in Southeast Asia. . . .

The American containment policy in Southeast Asia arose from the ashes of its failed policy in China. Through 1949, civilian, military, and congressional policy makers had debated over what stands to take toward the emerging communist regime in Peking. By early 1950, hopes for better relations in the foreseeable future collapsed, to the chagrin of some and the delight of others. In the aftermath of this debacle, Washington's several rival power centers threw their energy into doing something all could agree upon—checking the further spread of communism in Southeast Asia. In a few brief months this policy transformed an area that most Americans barely knew into one deemed so vital that its defense justified a major effort to keep it from falling into the Soviet orbit. The rapid discovery of Southeast Asia should be understood as a byproduct of both strategic assessments and bitter internal debate: both within the executive branch and between the executive branch and Congress. The foundation laid in 1949 and 1950 supported the effort of the American containment policy in the region for the next quarter century.

The Rube Goldberg policy-making process that led to the alienating of Communist China and the embrace of Southeast Asia was unique in its detail but not in its general dimensions. It was replete with political infighting, bureaucratic backstabbing, confused lines of authority, and undercutting and lack of follow-through on decisions reached at the highest level. The process reflected the determination of bureaucrats, diplomats, and politicians to pursue their own version of American interests, the special pleading of lobbyists and committed citizens, congressional horse trading, character assassination in pursuit of personal goals and policy objectives, and an underlying bewilderment among the better informed about what to do to protect American interests in East Asia.

During the first eighteen months of the Truman administration, China policy existed on a continuum. At one end dangled a carrot holding out the prospect for normal relations with Peking if it behaved according to the norms of the international community. This approach assumed that, with luck, the Communist leadership might eventually go the way of Marshall Tito. The stick poised at the other end threatened to isolate the Communists, continue to back the Nationalists and other resistance forces, and, generally, make life difficult for the new regime in the hope that it would eventually fall. The State Department, with the significant exception of Dean Rusk, finally settled on a Titoist policy by the end of 1949, and, for a while, Dean Acheson persuaded the president to go along. In contrast, the military establishment championed a punitive approach. Before the Korean War, it succeeded in obtaining a China policy that fell between the two extremes.

The military's ultimate success in June 1950 depended upon the important support of other forces. The congressional China bloc, with its power to embarrass and obstruct the administration, and with its influence on the size and uses of foreign aid funds, shared a significant amount of credit. The China lobby, in its varied dimensions, made an important contribution by feeding its political allies with information and innuendo. More distantly, the Chinese on both sides of the civil war worked in ironic tandem to exacerbate tensions between Washington and Peking and to play into the hands of the activists. Finally, the activists were playing with a politically stacked deck. By 1949, the American public was becoming accustomed to its government taking direct action in coping with national security threats. When North Korea invaded the South, administration officials who had championed the tattered Titoist policy for the previous eighteen months kicked it over in an evening, without much apparent regret and with full public support.

The State Department meanwhile, had begun to focus American attention elsewhere. Ever since the administration had suggested an omnibus European military assistance program in 1947, some officials considered how military aid might promote American interests in Southeast Asia. As prospects for MAP grew in the following months, a few policy planners in the department began studying the situation in the region in greater detail and with increasing alarm. By 1949, the plans of aid budgeters, the calculations of regional planners, and the political necessity for diverting attention from China militated for a more activist approach in the region.

Specifically, the State Department sought to bury the China question and lead Congressional and public attention toward the "great crescent" of nations that formed an arc from Japan to India. In the process of doing so, through publication of the White Paper and the assembly of the "wise men," the department succeeded in stimulating Congress to direct foreign aid money, initially proposed for non-Communist warlords in China's interior, into an unvouchered fund available for use in all of Asia. The consequence of the fund's creation was threefold: it stimulated the executive branch to plan a more activist policy in Southeast Asia; briefly spawned another pitch battle over China policy; and ultimately funded the first American military assistance to non-Communist forces in Vietnam.

Three decades later, the monolithic view of Asian communism lay shattered. Even though Washington had lost a war in Indochina, the Far East was not lost to Soviet influence. Titoism reigned in China as Soviet and Chinese armies faced each other along the Sino-Soviet border; a Soviet-backed Communist Vietnam had invaded and occupied a Chinese-backed Communist Cambodia; China, which had fought a brief war with its former Vietnamese ally, actively courted non-Communist countries in Southwest and Southeast Asia; and more countries in Asia than not remained non-Communist and Western-oriented.

Today it is arguable that the intervening hostility between China and the United States was in part avoidable. With hindsight, one can imagine an American policy that encouraged the emergence of Chinese Titoism while not promoting the spread of communism in other areas of East Asia. The core of this policy might have been what one contemporary observer described as "judicious leaving alone," a policy of allowing China to work out its internal problems without further American interference. The policy would not have meant embracing the Communists or abetting their victory, only accepting what most observers of the day regarded as inevitable. Washington could have recognized the new regime after receiving assurances that American diplomats would not be mistreated. Certainly, economic and cultural ties might have been preserved. Simultaneously, the United States could have made clear its opposition to Chinese efforts to export its revolution to surrounding countries and been prepared to translate that opposition into deeds.

How the Chinese Communists would have responded had the United States consistently followed such a policy can only be guessed at. The answer lies in the internal dynamics of the Chinese Communist Party as composed in the late 1940s. There was, apparently, a debate within the party, along the lines outlined in the Chou demarché, that ended in mid-1949 in triumph for the side arguing for close ties with Moscow. The influence of the "liberal" wing of the party had declined; Soviet advisors were arriving in increasing numbers; Manchuria was under the control of a Chinese Stalinist; the Russians' insistence on special treaty rights in Manchuria threatened to detach it and other areas of the country from Peking's control. Not surprisingly, perhaps, Mao and the party's dominant wing thought it was time to align with Stalin.

It does not follow, however, that a benign American policy would not eventually have had a constructive impact. Decisions reached in the summer of 1949 that favored Moscow were not irreversible, nor even destined to hold for the next decade. While the United States could not have reversed this trend in the short term, a longer-range policy could have been followed that would not have accentuated the lean toward the Soviet Union but kept the way open—and discreetly encouraged—a tilt the other way.

The Truman administration might have also followed a more benign policy toward Communists in Vietnam, but with uncertain results. Had it done so, the short-term outcome would probably have been Vietnamese Communist domination of the former French colonial empire and a wave of shock to non-Communists throughout Southeast Asia. At that point the West could have regrouped around Thailand—as SEA [Office of Southeast Asian Affairs] chief Charles Reed once urged—and hoped that Ho Chi Minh's talk about neutralism was genuine. Also, at that point several unpredictable variables would have come into play to determine subsequent events in the region: the durability of the "militant solidarity" between a Communist Vietnam and China in the absence of pressure from the West; the ability of the non-Communist nations in the region, especially Thailand, to rebound from the psychological blow of Ho's triumph; the willingness of the United States to sustain non-Communist regimes in the region; and the willingness of the Soviet Union and China to furnish the military hardware necessary to sustain Vietnamese dominance in Indochina.

Thirty years later, faced with its uneasy dominance of all Indochina, Hanoi found that many of these variables did not work in its favor. Perhaps the relevant question is whether under Ho Chi Minh, and without the experience of two wars behind them, the Vietnamese might have proved more accommodating to the West. However, since mendacity was a cornerstone in Ho's career and that of his party, one cannot take his words of reassurance given to foreign journalists and diplomats at face value. The answer to what might have been in Vietnam thus remains unclear.

Whatever else might have been, it is clear that the American political environment of 1949 and 1950 did not encourage a flexible policy toward either China or Vietnam. The political environment of those years was created in part by the impact of an unambiguous Soviet challenge in Europe over the preceding three years, in part by the appearance (the reality was somewhat different) of a direct Soviet challenge in Asia, and by the interaction of these events with domestic American politics. The result was a popular American view that held Communist ideology to be a tool of an international Communist conspiracy. It was not a view that allowed for distinctions between Communist leaders who varied only in the degree of their hostility toward the United States; the phenomenon of Titoism, which was still new in 1949 and 1950, had little impact on popular perception of a monolithic Communist bloc. Although the public was made aware of occasional Chinese Communist expressions of interest in the West, it was unaware of the Chou demarché and other behind-the-scenes signs of Chinese Titoism. It would likely have been unimpressed even had it been more fully informed. Ho Chi Minh's comments about seeking better ties with the West were occasionally reported but had no apparent effect on popular perception.

The popular perception of a ubiquitous Soviet threat—the Russians were also believed to be boring from within—lent itself to a low order of domestic political exploitation. Following a time-honored tradition, the Republicans, as the opposition party, attacked a policy that was not yielding prompt, fruitful results. As part of that tradition, they attacked the policy makers, but with a sustained vehemence unusual in modern American politics. The Republicans, and their Democrat associates, not only charged that the policy makers were wrong, but that they were treasonous as well.

The China bloc's attack revealed several strengths and weaknesses in both itself and its administration defenders. Its most notable aspect was its informal, but important, association with the other friends of China: the China lobby, the Nationalist government, and Nationalist sympathizers in various levels of the executive branch. While the whole effort against the administration lacked central coordination, the common goal allowed the various elements to work in tandem, and sometimes in conspiracy, to reverse administration policy and destroy its policy makers.

Also notable was the pitiful effort the congressional Democrats made to defend themselves and the administration. Most senior party members recognized the partisan character of the China bloc's attack and devised numerous schemes to defend the administration's policy, but their efforts failed to quell the drumbeat of criticism. The administration and the majority leadership, with the support of key Republicans, did demonstrate considerable skill in either blocking enactment of China legislation hostile to administration policy or in shaping it to support administration policy in

Southeast Asia. While their public-relations campaign was feeble, their legislative accomplishments were impressive.

The China bloc's attack also revealed the confusion within the Truman administration in both policy and the question of how to deal with Congress. Not until the Korean War did the administration speak with one voice on China policy. Before that, Dean Acheson would, from time to time, attempt to assert his views, both publicly and privately, but he frequently found his instruction undercut by the Pentagon or ignored within his own department; furthermore, his own follow-through was weak.

Until the early fall of 1949, Acheson was unsure of what to do about China, and the uncertainty was reflected throughout the State Department. Only once in this crucial period, in early January 1950, did President Truman make a significant public statement on China policy; he did so in support of the State Department's position and was promptly undercut by his own Defense Department as well as by some officials in the State Department who thought something forceful should be done to save Taiwan. The result of the confusion was a contradictory China policy and a weak defense in the face of a strong congressional attack.

By mid-1949, the administration began to pursue consistently one key strategy in its defense; its answer to charges of a weak China policy became a strong Southeast Asian policy. As conceived in late June, the policy was a combination of dramatic public statements by senior administration officials about the need for dramatic moves in the subcontinent, coupled with substantive action in Southeast Asia. Like its more direct efforts to defend its China policy, the administration's efforts to dramatize its new Southeast Asian policy were not successful in deflecting China bloc criticism.

The administration was, however, successful in obtaining money from Congress to fund the policy and in launching it in the spring of 1950 without opposition, cursory examination, or serious comment by either congressional friends or foes. While Congress largely ignored the question of policy in areas of Asia outside of China, it predictably would have been hostile to any effort to accommodate Ho Chi Minh. Apart from playing this negative role, which discouraged examination of alternatives, Congress showed little interest in questioning the Southeast Asian policy that the administration began to implement in 1950. However, it did not hesitate to fund the program and did so, more or less unwittingly, in the fall of 1949. Only a decade and a half later did Congress begin to question seriously the containment policy it had played a fundamental role in creating.

✗ *F U R T H E R   R E A D I N G*

Lucien Bodard, *The Quicksand War* (1967)
William Borden, *The Pacific Alliance* (1984)
Dorothy Borg and Waldo Heinrichs, *Uncertain Years: Chinese-American Relations, 1947–1950* (1980)
King C. Chen, *Vietnam and China* (1969)

Evelyn Colbert, *International Politics in Southeast Asia, 1941–1956* (1977)
Edward Drachman, *United States Policy Toward Vietnam, 1940–1945* (1970)
Peter M. Dunn, *The First Vietnam War* (1985)
Russell H. Fifield, *Americans in Southeast Asia: The Roots of Commitment* (1973)
John Lewis Gaddis, *Strategies of Containment* (1982)
Lloyd C. Gardner, *Approaching Vietnam* (1988)
George C. Herring, "The Truman Administration and the Restoration of French
    Sovereignty in Indochina," *Diplomatic History*, 1 (1977), 97–117
Gary R. Hess, "Franklin D. Roosevelt and Indochina," *Journal of American History*, 59 (1972), 353–368
——, *The United States' Emergence as a Southeast Asian Power* (1987)
——, "United States Policy and the Origins of the French-Vietminh War, 1945–
    1946," *Peace and Change*, 3 (1975), 21–33
Akira Iriye, *The Cold War in Asia* (1974)
Akira Iriye and Yonosuke Nagai, ed., *The Origins of the Cold War in Asia* (1977)
George McT. Kahin, *Intervention* (1986)
Robert J. McMahon, "The Cold War in Asia: Toward a New Synthesis?" *Diplomatic History*, 12 (1988), 307–27
——, "Toward a Post-Colonial Order: Truman Administration Policies in South
    and Southeast Asia," in Michael J. Lacey, ed., *The Truman Presidency* (1989)
Edgar O'Ballance, *The Indochina War, 1945–1954* (1964)
Ritchie Ovendale, "Britain, the United States, and the Cold War in Southeast Asia,
    1949–1950," *International Affairs*, 63 (1982), 447–64
Archimedes L. Patti, *Why Vietnam?* (1981)
Lisle A. Rose, *Roots of Tragedy* (1976)
Andrew J. Rotter, *The Path to Vietnam* (1987)
Michael Schaller, *The American Occupation of Japan: The Origins of the Cold War
    in Asia* (1985)
Ronald H. Spector, *Advice and Support* (1983)
Marianne P. Sullivan, *France's Vietnam Policy* (1978)
Christopher Thorne, *Allies of a Kind* (1978)

CHAPTER
4

Dwight D. Eisenhower
and Vietnam:
Deepening the Commitment

When Dwight D. Eisenhower assumed the presidency in January 1953, no resolution of the Indochina conflict appeared in sight. Despite a considerable investment in money and materiel to France, the Truman administration had bequeathed to its successor a much more serious and complex problem. The
American stake in the war had grown almost as quickly as the French position
had deteriorated. The United States, which was then bearing nearly 40 percent
of the cost of the conflict, watched with dismay as French territorial control was
reduced to a series of small enclaves around Hanoi, Haiphong, and Saigon and
a narrow strip along the Cambodian border, while the Vietminh, bolstered by
Chinese aid, grew bolder and stronger. Faced with the unsettling prospect of a
French collapse and a communist victory in Vietnam, Eisenhower made a number of momentous decisions that transformed fundamentally the nature of the
American commitment to Vietnam.

First, Eisenhower chose not to attempt a rescue of the trapped French garrison at Dienbienphu with direct U.S. military intervention. When the remnants
of the French defending force at that remote outpost surrendered to their Vietminh attackers on May 7, 1954, the battle served as a potent symbol of France's
imminent defeat. The president next opted to participate in the Geneva Conference on Indochina—and to acquiesce in its results. The Geneva Accords of July
21, 1954, provided for the cessation of hostilities in Indochina, established independent states in Laos and Cambodia, demarcated a temporary division of Vietnam at the seventeenth parallel, and stipulated procedures that would lead to
the eventual unification of the country. Following the Geneva Conference, the
Eisenhower administration constructed the Southeast Asia Treaty Organization
(SEATO) in order to defend the region against possible communist aggression,
and moved to help create in southern Vietnam a viable, noncommunist regime

under the leadership of Prime Minister Ngo Dinh Diem. The all-Vietnam elections called for in the Geneva Accords were never held; soon the temporary geographical division came to appear permanent. During the Eisenhower years, the United States made a vigorous commitment to the Diem regime, providing it with massive amounts of aid. Nevertheless, by 1960, the prime minister faced growing internal opposition from the reborn Vietminh (or "Vietcong") guerrillas, a movement supported by the communist-dominated regime of Ho Chi Minh in the north.

   In recent years, a vigorous scholarly debate about Eisenhower's foreign policy has emerged, and it has had a marked impact on historical assessments of the president's Vietnam policy. The following questions have proved especially controversial. Why did the president choose not to intervene at Dienbienphu? Did the United States violate the Geneva Accords? How should Eisenhower's ambitious nation-building program in South Vietnam be judged: a partial success or an abject failure? Did Washington commit itself to too fragile a leader in Diem? Were there alternatives? What were the principal strengths and weaknesses of Diem's rule? How is the rebirth of a guerrilla movement in the south in the late 1950s best explained? And, in a broader sense, what were the domestic and international forces during the 1950s that catapulted Vietnam to such a position of prominence for the United States?

✗ D O C U M E N T S

In the first document, Eisenhower appeals to British Prime Minister Winston S. Churchill for "united action" to help save the French garrison at Dienbienphu. The second document is a portion of Eisenhower's press conference of April 7, 1954, in which he spelled out what he meant by the "domino theory" and its relationship to Indochina. Vo Nguyen Giap, the victorious Vietnamese commander at Dienbienphu, assesses the significance of that battle in the next document. The final declaration of the Geneva Conference, July 21, 1954, established a temporary division between northern and southern Vietnam and set forth procedures for eventual unification. It is reprinted here as the fourth document.

   The remaining documents in this chapter focus on the regime of Ngo Dinh Diem in South Vietnam. On January 1, 1955, Central Intelligence Agency operative Edward G. Lansdale emphasized the importance of the South Vietnamese experiment in a memorandum to General J. Lawton Collins, the U.S. special representative in Vietnam. In an April 28, 1955, National Security Council discussion of the sect crisis that nearly toppled Diem from power, sharp differences among top U.S. officials on Diem's abilities came to light. The next document is a declaration by the government of Vietnam, issued on August 9, 1955, renouncing any negotiations with the communist regime in the north.

   On January 1, 1957, U.S. Ambassador Elbridge Durbrow alerted Washington to a series of difficulties that plagued Diem's regime. In the final document, a National Security Council discussion of May 9, 1960, Eisenhower and other leading officials ponder South Vietnam's deepening problems.

Dwight D. Eisenhower Appeals for British Help, 1954

Dear Winston:

I am sure that like me you are following with the deepest interest and anxiety the daily reports of the gallant fight being put up by the French at Dien Bien Phu. Today, the situation there does not seem hopeless.

But regardless of the outcome of this particular battle, I fear that the French cannot alone see the thing through, this despite the very substantial assistance in money and matériel that we are giving them. It is no solution simply to urge the French to intensify their efforts, and if they do not see it through, and Indochina passes into the hands of the Communists, the ultimate effect on our and your global strategic position with the consequent shift in the power ratio throughout Asia and the Pacific could be disastrous and, I know, unacceptable to you and me. It is difficult to see how Thailand, Burma and Indonesia could be kept out of Communist hands. This we cannot afford. The threat to Malaya, Australia and New Zealand would be direct. The offshore island chain would be broken. The economic pressures on Japan which would be deprived of non-Communist markets and sources of food and raw materials would be such, over a period of time, that it is difficult to see how Japan could be prevented from reaching an accommodation with the Communist world which would combine the manpower and natural resources of Asia with the industrial potential of Japan. This has led us to the hard conclusion that the situation in Southeast Asia requires us urgently to take serious and far-reaching decisions.

Geneva is less than four weeks away. There the possibility of the Communists driving a wedge between us will, given the state of mind in France, be infinitely greater than at Berlin. I can understand the very natural desire of the French to seek an end to this war which has been bleeding them for eight years. But our painstaking search for a way out of the impasse has reluctantly forced us to the conclusion that there is no negotiated solution of the Indochina problem which in its essence would not be either a face-saving device to cover a French surrender or a face-saving device to cover a Communist retirement. The first alternative is too serious in its broad strategic implications for us and for you to be acceptable. Apart from its effects in Southeast Asia itself, where you and the Commonwealth have direct and vital interests, it would have the most serious repercussions in North Africa, in Europe and elsewhere. Here at home it would cause a widespread loss of confidence in the cooperative system. I think it is not too much to say that the future of France as a great power would be fatally affected. Perhaps France will never again be the great power it was, but a sudden vacuum wherever French power is, would be difficult for us to cope with.

Somehow we must contrive to bring about the second alternative. The preliminary lines of our thinking were sketched out by Foster [Dulles] in his speech last Monday night when he said that under the conditions of today the imposition on Southeast Asia of the political system of Communist

Russia and its Chinese Communist ally, by whatever means, would be a grave threat to the whole free community, and that in our view this possibility should now be met by united action and not passively accepted. He has also talked intimately with [British ambassador] Roger Makins.

I believe that the best way to put teeth in this concept and to bring greater moral and material resources to the support of the French effort is through the establishment of a new, *ad hoc* grouping or coalition composed of nations which have a vital concern in the checking of Communist expansion in the area. I have in mind in addition to our two countries, France, the Associated States, Australia, New Zealand, Thailand and the Philippines. The United States Government would expect to play its full part in such a coalition. The coalition we have in mind would not be directed against Communist China. But if, contrary to our belief, our efforts to save Indochina and the British Commonwealth position to the south should in any way increase the jeopardy to Hong Kong, we would expect to be with you there. I suppose that the United Nations should somewhere be recognized, but I am not confident that, given the Soviet veto, it could act with needed speed and vigor.

I would contemplate no role for Formosa or the Republic of Korea in the political construction of this coalition.

The important thing is that the coalition must be strong and it must be willing to join the fight if necessary. I do not envisage the need of any appreciable ground forces on your or our part. If the members of the alliance are sufficiently resolute it should be able to make clear to the Chinese Communists that the continuation of their material support to the Viet Minh will inevitably lead to the growing power of the forces arrayed against them.

My colleagues and I are deeply aware of the risks which this proposal may involve but in the situation which confronts us there is no course of action or inaction devoid of dangers and I know no man who has firmly grasped more nettles than you. If we grasp this one together I believe that we will enormously increase our chances of bringing the Chinese to believe that their interests lie in the direction of a discreet disengagement. In such a contingency we could approach the Geneva conference with the position of the free world not only unimpaired but strengthened.

Today we face the hard situation of contemplating a disaster brought on by French weakness and the necessity of dealing with it before it develops. This means frank talk with the French. In many ways the situation corresponds to that which you describe so brilliantly in the second chapter of "Their Finest Hour", when history made clear that the French strategy and dispositions before the 1940 breakthrough should have been challenged before the blow fell.

I regret adding to your problems. But in fact it is not I, but our enemies who add to them. I have faith that by another act of fellowship in the face of peril we shall find a spiritual vigor which will prevent our slipping into the quagmire of distrust.

If I may refer again to history, we failed to halt Hirohito, Mussolini and Hitler by not acting in unity and in time. That marked the beginning of many years of stark tragedy and desperate peril. May it not be that our nations have learned something from that lesson?

So profoundly do I believe that the effectiveness of the coalition principle is at stake that I am prepared to send Foster or [Under Secretary of State Walter] Bedell [Smith] to visit you this week, at the earliest date convenient to you. Whoever comes would spend a day in Paris to avoid French pique, the cover would be preparation for Geneva.

Eisenhower Explains the Domino Theory, 1954

Q. Robert Richards, Copley Press: Mr. President, would you mind commenting on the strategic importance of Indochina to the free world? I think there has been, across the country, some lack of understanding on just what it means to us.

The President: You have, of course, both the specific and the general when you talk about such things.

First of all, you have the specific value of a locality in its production of materials that the world needs.

Then you have the possibility that many human beings pass under a dictatorship that is inimical to the free world.

Finally, you have broader considerations that might follow what you would call the "falling domino" principle. You have a row of dominoes set up, you knock over the first one, and what will happen to the last one is the certainty that it will go over very quickly. So you could have a beginning of a disintegration that would have the most profound influences.

Now, with respect to the first one, two of the items from this particular area that the world uses are tin and tungsten. They are very important. There are others, of course, the rubber plantations and so on.

Then with respect to more people passing under this domination, Asia, after all, has already lost some 450 million of its peoples to the Communist dictatorship, and we simply can't afford greater losses.

But when we come to the possible sequence of events, the loss of Indochina, of Burma, of Thailand, of the Peninsula, and Indonesia following, now you begin to talk about areas that not only multiply the disadvantages that you would suffer through loss of materials, sources of materials, but now you are talking about millions and millions and millions of people.

Finally, the geographical position achieved thereby does many things. It turns the so-called island defensive chain of Japan, Formosa, of the Philippines and to the southward; it moves in to threaten Australia and New Zealand.

It takes away, in its economic aspects, that region that Japan must have as a trading area or Japan, in turn, will have only one place in the world to go—that is, toward the Communist areas in order to live.

So, the possible consequences of the loss are just incalculable to the free world.

Vo Nguyen Giap on Dienbienphu (1954), 1964

Paramount Significance of the Great Dien Bien Phu Victory and of the Winter-Spring Victories

The historic Dien Bien Phu campaign and in general the Winter 1953–Spring 1954 campaign were the greatest victories ever won by our army and people up to the present time. These great victories marked a giant progress, *a momentous change in the evolution of the Resistance War for national salvation put up by our people against the aggressive French imperialists propped up by U.S. interventionists. . . .*

The great Dien Bien Phu victory and the Winter-Spring victories as a whole had a far-reaching influence in the world.

While the bellicose imperialists were confused and discouraged, the news of the victories won by our army and people on the battlefronts throughout the country especially the Dien Bien Phu victory, have greatly inspired the progressive people the world over.

The Dien Bien Phu victory was not only a great victory of our people but was regarded by the socialist countries as their own victory. It was regarded as a great victory of the weak and small nations now fighting against imperialism and old and new-colonialism for freedom and independence. Dien Bien Phu has become a pride of the oppressed peoples, a great contribution of our people to the high movement for national liberation which has been surging up powerfully since the end of World War II, and heralded the collapse of the colonial system of imperialism.

Dien Bien Phu was also a great victory of the forces of peace in the world. Without this victory, certainly the Geneva Conference would not be successful and peace could not be re-established in Indo-China. This substantiates all the more clearly that the victory won at Dien Bien Phu and in general the Resistance War put up by our people, and the victorious struggle for liberation waged by the oppressed people against imperialism and colonialism under all forms, played a role of paramount importance in weakening imperialism, thwarting the scheme of aggression and war of the enemy and contributing greatly to the defence of world peace. . . .

The aggressive war unleashed by the French imperialists in Indo-China dragged on for eight or nine years. Though they did their best to increase their force to nearly half a million men, sacrificed hundreds of thousands of soldiers, spent in this dirty war 2,688 billion French francs, squandered a great amount of resources, shed a great deal of blood of the French people, changed 20 cabinets in France, 7 high commissars and 8 commanders-in-chief in Indo-China, their aggressive war grew from bad to worse, met defeat after defeat, went from one strategic mistake to another, to end in the great Dien Bien Phu disaster. This is because the war made by the French colonialists was an unjust war. In this war the enemy met with the indomitable spirit of an entire people and therefore, no skilful general—be he Leclerc, De Tassigny, Navarre or any other general—could save the French Expeditionary Corps from defeat. Neither there would be a mighty weapon—cannon, tank or heavy bomber and even U.S. atomic bomb—which could retrieve the situation. On the upshot, if in autumn 1953 and winter 1954, the enemy did not occupy Dien Bien Phu by paratroopers or if he occupied it and withdrew later without choosing it as the site of a do-or-die battle, sooner or later a Dien Bien Phu would come up, though the time and place might change; and in the end the French and U.S. imperialists would certainly meet with a bitter failure.

Final Declaration of the Geneva Conference on Indochina, 1954

1. The Conference takes note of the agreements ending hostilities in Cambodia, Laos, and Vietnam and organizing international control and the supervision of the execution of the provisions of these agreements.

2. The Conference expresses satisfaction at the end of hostilities in Cambodia, Laos, and Vietnam; the Conference expresses its conviction that the execution of the provisions set out in the present declaration and in the agreements of the cessation of hostilities will permit Cambodia, Laos, and Vietnam henceforth to play their part, in full independence and sovereignty, in the peaceful community of nations.

3. The Conference takes note of the declarations made by the Governments of Cambodia and Laos of their intention to adopt measures permitting all citizens to take their place in the national community, in particular by participating in the next general elections, which, in conformity with the constitution of each of these countries, shall take place in the course of the year 1955, by secret ballot and in conditions of respect for fundamental freedoms.

4. The Conference takes note of the clauses in the agreement on the cessation of hostilities in Vietnam prohibiting the introduction into Vietnam of foreign troops and military personnel as well as of all kinds of arms and munitions. The Conference also takes note of the declarations made by the Governments of Cambodia and Laos of their resolution not to request foreign aid, whether in war material, in personnel, or in instructors except for the purpose of the effective defense of their territory and, in the case of Laos, to the extent defined by the agreements of the cessation of hostilities in Laos.

5. The Conference takes note of the clauses in the agreement on the cessation of hostilities in Vietnam to the effect that no military base under the control of a foreign State may be established in the regrouping zones of the two parties, the latter having the obligation to see that the zones allotted to them shall not constitute part of any military alliance and shall not be utilized for the resumption of hostilities or in the service of an aggressive policy. The Conference also takes note of the declarations of the Governments of Cambodia and Laos to the effect that they will not join in any agreement with other States if this agreement includes the obligation to participate in a military alliance not in conformity with the principles of the Charter of the United Nations or, in the case of Laos,

with the principles of the agreement on the cessation of hostilities in Laos or, so long as their security is not threatened, the obligation to establish bases on Cambodian or Laotian territory for the military forces of foreign powers.

6. The Conference recognizes that the essential purpose of the agreement relating to Vietnam is to settle military questions with a view to ending hostilities and that the military demarcation line is provisional and should not in any way be interpreted as constituting a political or territorial boundary. The Conference expresses its conviction that the execution of the provisions set out in the present declaration and in the agreement on the cessation of hostilities creates the necessary basis for the achievement in the near future of a political settlement in Vietnam.

7. The Conference declares that, so far as Vietnam is concerned, the settlement of political problems, effected on the basis of respect for the principles of independence, unity, and territorial integrity, shall permit the Vietnamese people to enjoy the fundamental freedoms, guaranteed by democratic institutions established as a result of free general elections by secret ballot. In order to ensure that sufficient progress in the restoration of peace has been made, and that all the necessary conditions obtain for free expression of the national will, general elections shall be held in July 1956 under the supervision of an international commission composed of representatives of the Member States of the International Supervisory Commission, referred to in the agreement on the cessation of hostilities. Consultations will be held on this subject between the competent representative authorities of the two zones from July 20, 1955, onward.

8. The provisions of the agreements on the cessation of hostilities intended to ensure the protection of individuals and of property must be most strictly applied and must, in particular, allow everyone in Vietnam to decide freely in which zone he wishes to live.

9. The competent representative authorities of the North and South zones of Vietnam, as well as the authorities of Laos and Cambodia, must not permit any individual or collective reprisals against persons who had collaborated in any way with one of the parties during the war, or against members of such persons' families.

10. The Conference takes note of the declaration of the Government of the French Republic to the effect that it is ready to withdraw its troops from the territory of Cambodia, Laos, and Vietnam, at the request of the Governments concerned and within periods which shall be fixed by agreement between the parties except in the cases where, by agreement between the two parties, a certain number of French troops shall remain at specified points and for a specified time.

11. The Conference takes note of the declaration of the French Government to the effect that for the settlement of all the problems connected with the re-establishment and consolidation of peace in Cambodia, Laos, and Vietnam, the French Government will proceed from the principle of respect for the independence and sovereignty, unity and territorial integrity of Cambodia, Laos, and Vietnam.

12. In their relations with Cambodia, Laos, and Vietnam, each member of the Geneva Conference undertakes to respect the sovereignty, the independence, the unity, and the territorial integrity of the above-mentioned States, and to refrain from any interference in their internal affairs.

13. The members of the Conference agree to consult one another on any question which may be referred to them by the International Supervisory Commission, in order to study such measures as may prove necessary to ensure that the agreements on the cessation of hostilities in Cambodia, Laos, and Vietnam are respected.

Edward G. Lansdale on the Importance of the South Vietnamese Experiment, 1955

1. Here is some New Year's thinking about the problem you and we face, and a request.

2. As a start, it is worth taking a look at the real value of the chips given to you by President Eisenhower for the game we are playing here. The chips are our direct aid to the Vietnamese. To most Americans, they mean money, material, and technical (advisory) manpower. In the eyes of the world, and especially Asia, they mean something more. In this view, the value of the chips becomes Asia itself and parts of the Middle East.

3. The Asian view is that "direct aid" means that Communism's strongest enemy, the United States, is now in close support of the Free Vietnamese against the Communists. Certainly each of the free nations which has a pact with the United States, in which we will give them close support against the Communists, sees a bit of itself in the situation of the Vietnamese. And, each of those nations, in varying degree, will be measuring what our support actually means. Thus, if we lose here or withdraw however gracefully, politically powerful people in those nations will read their own futures into our action. This means that the do-business-with-China folks of Japan, the anti-American-bases folks of the Philippines, and so on, will find their arguments strengthened locally to the critical strain point for the United States in places we now find difficult enough under neutralist and Communist political pressures. This is far beyond the usual observation of the loss of Vietnam opening Southeast Asia to the impact of Communist dynamism, which is dangerous enough in itself.

4. Thus, I feel that we have too much to lose to consider loosing [*sic*] or withdrawing. We have no other choice but to win here or face an increasingly grim future, a heritage which none of us wants to pass along to our offspring.

5. What will it take to win? It is going to take everything we are now doing and planning to do, plus more—and I believe that the "more" now exists here as a potential awaiting proper employment.

6. I have narrowed down the elements we need for winning the present struggle here to three, which is perhaps over-simplifying. I believe that if we can make these three elements a reality here, the initiative will pass to

us and we will start winning. I feel, further, that we must have clear evidence by June 1955 that we can make the three elements a reality. They are:

a. Successful teamwork
b. Strengthen the free Vietnamese
c. Make the bulk of the population willing to risk all for freedom. . . .

7. *Strengthening Vietnamese.* I am concerned about whether all our aid and efforts here will strengthen the Vietnamese or merely make them more dependent upon us. Certainly none of us who must justify actions eventually at home would desire to place the U.S. in the position of continuing major help here for endless years, on the basis that if our aid were lessened then the enemy would win. Certainly the responsible Americans here would like to see the Vietnamese capably assuming an increasing share of their own burdens in all fields of national life.

8. Thus, I would like to see our efforts here geared as completely as possible to the operating philosophy of helping the Vietnamese to help themselves, not only Vietnamese government or army, but the people themselves. It will mean insisting on more extensive and effective use of our help by the Vietnamese—and our acceptance of workable Vietnamese standards rather than our own perhaps to a greater extent. This will increase proprietary interest in what is constructed (whether it be army division or individual farm), build the muscularity of national abilities, and start giving the Free Vietnamese the confidence in their own competence which the Vietminh have demonstrated so remarkably on their side. These are all factors of strength in a struggle with the Communists. It is also true that a man is more apt to defend what he has constructed for himself—and we will strengthen the Free Vietnamese as we increase the size or amount of what they want to defend from the Communists.

National Security Council Discussion
of the Sect Crisis, 1955

General Collins, accompanied by Mr. Paul J. Sturm of the State Department, entered the Cabinet Room when Item 5 came up for discussion. Mr. Allen Dulles also asked permission for Mr. Kermit Roosevelt of the Central Intelligence Agency to be present while Mr. Dulles briefed the Council on the latest developments in Saigon.

Mr. Dulles explained that last night serious street fighting had broken out in the city of Saigon. A mortar shell had landed on the Presidential Palace, the residence of Prime Minister Diem, at 1:15 P.M. After two further shells had landed in the Palace grounds, Diem had telephoned General Ely and stated that he was ordering counterfire by the Vietnamese national forces. Eleven rounds of such counterfire had been counted by three o'clock in the afternoon. While there had since been rumors that a cease-fire had been arranged, Mr. Dulles doubted the validity of these reports, and said it seemed that Prime Minister Diem had ordered all-out action against the

Binh Xuyen. In other words, Diem was proposing to force a showdown. It was not easy, continued Mr. Dulles, to say which side had actually been responsible for precipitating last night's events, but the real trouble had begun on April 26, when Prime Minister Diem had ordered the removal of the Chief of Police of Saigon, who was a member of the Binh Xuyen gangster group.

In a showdown fight, continued Mr. Dulles, and if the Vietnamese National Army remains loyal to the Prime Minister, there was little doubt that the Army could drive the Binh Xuyen forces out of Saigon. The difficulty was that such an attempt would almost certainly result in disturbances and civil war throughout South Vietnam. In addition, the street fighting might very well result in atrocities against French civilians living in Saigon. Finally, said Mr. Dulles, Diem has advised that he now intends to form a complete new Cabinet, and that he will announce its members tonight.

The President promptly inquired what General Ely was likely to do in the face of the situation which Mr. Dulles had described. General Collins replied that he believed that General Ely would do nothing unless a threat should develop to foreigners resident in Saigon. General Collins then produced a map of the city of Saigon and adjacent areas, and rapidly described the chief features of the city and the deployment of the Binh Xuyen and the National Army forces.

The President then asked General Collins whether the French were likely to interfere with American resupply of Prime Minister Diem's forces. General Collins thought that the French would not so interfere, and pointed out that the French have already offered an ammunition depot in Saigon to the Vietnamese forces.

At this point Mr. Dillon Anderson [special assistant to the president] reminded the Council of the decision with respect to U.S. policy toward South Vietnam which the Council had made in January of this year. While he was doing so, the Executive Secretary handed out a draft record of action prepared in the Department of State, which State suggested should be adopted in lieu of the earlier Council action of January. Secretary Dulles pointed out that the chief difference was that the earlier action had pinpointed Prime Minister Diem as the individual whose government the United States should support.

Secretary Dulles said that he would like to comment in general on the situation in which we found ourselves respecting South Vietnam. In his view, the present difficulties had two fundamental causes. First, the limitations of Prime Minister Diem as the head of a government. While Diem's good qualities were well known and need not be elaborated, it was a fact that he came from the northern part of the country and was not very trustful of other people, perhaps for good reason. Furthermore, he was not very good at delegating authority. Despite these shortcomings, Diem might have proved adequate to the situation if it had not been for the second fundamental limitation—namely, the lack of solid support from the French. While the top leaders of the French Government, such as Mendes-France, Faure and General Ely, have gone along with Diem reluctantly, French colonial officials on the scene in Vietnam have done their best to sabotage him. These two fundamental limitations in conjunction have brought about a situation that has finally induced General Collins to conclude that we must now look for a replacement for Diem.

As a matter of fact, continued Secretary Dulles, we have been telling the French for a considerable period that we would be prepared to consider an alternative to Diem if they could come up with one. They haven't as yet done so. Moreover, the mechanics of effecting a change at this time would be very difficult. A change of Premier would necessarily involve recourse to Bao Dai, and we have always felt that Bao Dai's influence would be invariably exerted in favor of the Binh Xuyen, which supplies his ample funds. We haven't therefore, been inclined to look with very much favor on a new South Vietnam government appointed by Bao Dai. On the contrary, we have felt that it was really essential that a showdown occur between Bao Dai and the rebellious sects. Such a showdown both Bao Dai and the French have consistently tried to avoid.

Late yesterday afternoon, however, we in the State Department dispatched a complicated series of cables to Saigon outlining ways and means of replacing Diem and his government. However, in view of the developments and the outbreak of last night, we have instructed our people in Saigon to hold up action on our plan for replacing Diem. The developments of last night could either lead to Diem's utter overthrow or to his emergence from the disorder as a major hero. Accordingly, we are pausing to await the results before trying to settle on [Pham Huy] Quat or Defense Minister [*sic*] Do as possible replacements. Secretary Dulles confessed that he was not much impressed with the Defense Minister. On the other hand, unless something occurs in the Saigon disorders out of which Diem will emerge as the hero, we will have to have a change. This is the view both of General Collins and General Ely, and Ely has played an honest game with us in this whole affair.

Secretary Dulles then pointed out that Bao Dai had actually threatened to take the matter in his own hands and establish a new government himself. Indeed, we are not absolutely sure that we can restrain him from so doing, since he so to speak represents the only existing source of legitimate governmental authority. Thus we find ourselves obliged to work with him and through him to some extent, until we are in a position to devise some alternative source of authority.

At the conclusion of his statement, Secretary Dulles asked General Collins to present his views. General Collins began by reminding the National Security Council of his earlier appearance before it prior to his departure for Saigon, and of the position he had taken at that time—namely, that there were five major factors on which the future of Free Vietnam would depend. He said that he would briefly run over these same five factors now.

1. The possibility of an overt attack on Free Vietnam by the Vietminh. Of this General Collins stated there was very little danger at the present time.

2. The loyalty of the Vietnamese National Army to Diem. General Collins emphasized that to date the Vietnamese National Army had been loyal to Diem, but that loyalty would almost certainly not extend to supporting the Prime Minister in a civil war. The Army violently disliked the Binh Xuyen, but it also disliked the prospect of engaging in a civil war in South Vietnam which would also include the Hoa Hao and the Cao Dai sects, which were quite strong in the southern portions of Free Vietnam. The great danger of trying to drive the Binh Xuyen from their strongholds in Saigon, said General Collins, was precisely the danger that such an attempt would end in widespread civil war.

3. The problem of the sects. General Collins pointed out that we have feared all along that efforts to cut down the size of the private armies of the sects and to dry up their financial resources would cause trouble. This was probably inevitable, whether Diem or anyone else made the effort. On the other hand, General Collins insisted that Diem's handling of the problem of the sects had been anything but astute.

4. The attitude of the French. General Collins said that since this had been thoroughly covered by Secretary Dulles, he would add no more except to point out that there could be no doubt of the loyal role played with him by General Ely.

5. The personality of Diem. On this point General Collins said that as early as the end of his first week in Saigon he had come to entertain very serious doubts as to Diem's ability to govern. Diem betrayed no political knack whatsoever in his handling of men. His ineptitude in this respect was responsible for the series of resignations from his Cabinet. It was no mere matter of rats quitting a sinking ship. General Collins felt that it was a particular misfortune to lose Minh, the young Secretary of Defense, and Do, the older Secretary of Foreign Affairs, whom General Collins considered to be a man of very good judgment. If, said General Collins, Diem makes good on his statement that he would name a new Cabinet, this Cabinet would almost certainly consist of unknown individuals who had no public standing.

All this induced General Collins to conclude that Prime Minister Diem's number was up. Nor had he ever felt that Diem was the indispensable man. Accordingly, even without Diem the program adopted by the Council for South Vietnam could and should go forward without interruption, even though its estimated costs would be $40 million more this year than previously estimated. General Collins emphasized that he still felt that this U.S. policy and program was a gamble worth taking, although certainly a gamble. A long-term solution of the sect problem was vital to the success of the program. It was likewise vital to take control of the police away from the Binh Xuyen. Finally, it was essential to get genuine French support for the policy and program, no matter who was the Vietnamese Prime Minister.

The President commented that it was an absolute sine qua non of success that the Vietnamese National Army destroy the power of the Binh Xuyen. Otherwise any new government was bound to fail. To this General

Collins replied that the attempt to destroy the Binh Xuyen by military action would almost certainly produce civil war in Vietnam. The Binh Xuyen, if removed from Saigon, would take to the Maquis and raise hell for years to come. Accordingly, General Collins said he personally preferred a political solution. He had wished Diem to form a genuine coalition government. He doubted very much whether Diem could be prevailed upon to try it, but such a political solution seemed most likely to bring success.

Secretary [of the Treasury George] Humphrey inquired how far the Communists were behind the disorders and outbreaks in Saigon. General Collins replied that there could be no doubt that they were stimulating and exploiting the disorders that existed.

At this point Mr. Anderson read the proposed record of action. The President inquired if there were any objections. There being none, the President observed that the proposed action sounded all right to him, and that he could not see what else we could do at this time.

At the close of the discussion, Mr. Allen Dulles commented that if it were any comfort to the Council, there was quite a good deal of evidence that the Vietminh were encountering considerable difficulty in their part of Vietnam.

South Vietnamese Statement on Reunification, 1955

In the last July 1955 broadcast, the Vietnamese national Government has made it clear its position towards the problem of territorial unity.

The Government does not consider itself bound in any respect by the Geneva Agreements which it did not sign.

Once more, the Government reasserts that in any circumstance, it places national interests above all, being resolved to achieve at all cost the obvious aim it is pursuing and eventually to achieve national unity, peace and freedom.

The Viet-Minh leaders have had a note dated July 19 transmitted to the Government, in which they asked for the convening of a consultative conference on general elections. This is just a propaganda move aimed at making the people believe that they are the champions of our territorial unity. Everyone still remembers that last year at Geneva, the Vietnamese Communists boisterously advocated the partition of our territory and asked for an economically self-sufficient area whereas the delegation of the State of Viet-nam proposed an armistice without any partition, not even provisional, with a view to safeguarding the sacred rights of the Vietnamese national and territorial unity, national independence and individual freedom. As the Vietnamese delegation states, the Vietnamese Government then stood for the fulfillment of national aspirations by the means which have been given back to Viet-nam by the French solemn recognition of the independence and sovereignty of Viet-nam, as a legal, independent state.

The policy of the Government remains unchanged. Confronted with the partition of the country, which is contrary to the will of the entire people, the Government will see to it that everybody throughout the country may live free from fear, and completely free from all totalitarian oppression. As a champion of justice, of genuine democracy, the Government always holds that the principle of free general election is a peaceful and democratic means only if, first of all, the freedom to live and freedom of vote is sufficiently guaranteed.

In this connection, nothing constructive can be contemplated in the present situation in the North where, under the rule of the Vietnamese Communists, the citizens do not enjoy democratic freedoms and fundamental human rights.

Elbridge Durbrow Assesses the Diem Regime, 1957

Certain problems now discernible have given us a warning which, if disregarded, might lead to a deteriorating situation in Viet Nam within a few years.

Diem achieved notable successes in the first two years of his regime and remains the only man of stature so far in evidence to guide this country. He has unified free Viet Nam, brought it relative security and stability, and firmly maintains a pro-West, anti-communist position.

In the last year, however, Diem has avoided making decisions required to build the economic and social foundations necessary to secure Viet Nam's future independence and strength. He has made it clear that he would give first priority to the build-up of his armed forces regardless of the country's requirements for economic and social development. Events abroad which increase the danger of communist infiltration and subversion, and which threaten Viet Nam with possible isolation in this area have contributed to his concern and to his determination to strengthen his armed forces.

Certain characteristics of Diem—his suspiciousness and authoritarianism—have also reduced the Government's limited administrative capabilities. He assumes responsibility for the smallest details of Government and grants his Ministers little real authority.

At the same time, discontent is felt in different segments of the population for varied reasons. The base of the regime's popular support remains narrow. The regime might overcome such discontent and finally win over the loyalty of a majority of Vietnamese both in the North and South if it could show its ability to give the country stronger protection and create sound economic and social bases for progress. Progress, which is demanded in Viet Nam as throughout Asia, is perhaps the touchstone of the regime's enduring viability. Yet precisely because Diem is now procrastinating in making decisions affecting fundamental problems of his country's development, the lag between the people's expectations and the Government's ability to show results will grow.

We consider it therefore of importance that we bring strong pressure on the President to reach certain decisions basically in the economic and social fields which have been before him for some months but on which he has not acted. He has resented this and may resent it more, but in ours and his long range interests we must do our utmost to cause him to move forward in these fields.

The purpose of this evaluation of the present situation in Viet Nam is to examine the elements giving rise to some concern regarding certain developments in Viet Nam, to provide the Department [of State] and interested agencies salient background and to set forth conclusions and recommend certain broad courses of action. We feel that a frank discussion of the solution as we see it may be helpful to all concerned.

National Security Council Discussion of Diem's Growing Problems, 1960

Mr. [Robert] Amory [of the CIA] then reported that increasing troubles in South Vietnam were confronting Diem. For months Diem had been facing increased insurgent activity in the countryside similar to that which characterized the last days of the French regime. Moreover, Diem's own ranks had been crumbling. Critics of his one-man rule were becoming more vocal at all levels of government. This criticism asserted that Diem's administration had fostered corruption, condoned maladministration, and permitted dictatorial practices with the result that communism in South Vietnam was being promoted. Criticism of Diem was so far uncoordinated outside government circles but was becoming stronger, as indicated by a recent manifesto made public in Saigon by a group of former officials who called for extensive political reforms.

The President said he had received a stream of reports about South Vietnam. Heretofore we have been proud of Diem and had thought he was doing a good job. Apparently he was now becoming arbitrary and blind to the situation. Mr. Amory said one danger lay in the fact that Diem was not in direct touch with the people since he seldom went out into the countryside to see the people and talk with provincial leaders. He is inclined to leave this kind of activity, as well as the details of administration, to his brothers, who have all the evils and none of the assets needed to do a good job. The President wondered whether we were doing anything to try to persuade Diem to remain in closer touch with the people. Mr. Amory said our Ambassador to South Vietnam and General [Samuel T.] Williams [chief of the Military Assistance Advisory Group in Vietnam] were constantly advising Diem to keep in touch with the people.

Mr. [Livingston] Merchant [under secretary of state for political affairs] said Diem was more and more coming to be surrounded by a small group. He was leaving administration to his two brothers and was losing touch with the grass roots. However, Ambassador Durbrow was keeping in close touch with Diem. Mr. Merchant hoped that what happened to Syngman Rhee in Korea would give Diem pause.

The President said Diem seemed to be calm and quiet and to have an attractive personality unlike Rhee. The President then asked Mr. Merchant to consider whether the situation might be improved by a letter from him (the President) to Diem.

Mr. [Thomas S.] Gates [secretary of defense] remarked that South Vietnam internal security forces were not well equipped to handle insurgent forces in the swampy areas where most of the trouble occurred.

The President said the U.S. ought to do everything possible to prevent the deterioration of the situation in South Vietnam. We had rescued this country from a fate worse than death and it would be bad to lose it at this stage. Mr. Merchant believed that South Vietnam was getting as much economic assistance as it could effectively absorb. The President recalled that when Diem had first been attempting to acquire power in South Vietnam, a recommendation had been made to the Council that the U.S. should oppose him. The President said he hoped the Departments of State and Defense and CIA would consult together to see what could be done about the situation in South Vietnam.

✗ E S S A Y S

In the first essay, George C. Herring of the University of Kentucky and Richard H. Immerman of the University of Hawaii examine the Dienbienphu crisis of 1954. They praise Eisenhower for his decision not to intervene militarily in a desperate effort to save the beleaguered French garrison at Dienbienphu. At the same time, they demonstrate that Eisenhower had been more willing to intervene than he later admitted and most scholars have suspected. Congressional skepticism, British opposition, and Franco-American differences ultimately tied Ike's hands.

George McT. Kahin, a political scientist at Cornell University and a specialist in Southeast Asia, argues in the second selection that in 1954 the United States made the most fundamental decision of its thirty-year involvement in Vietnam: acting unilaterally, it attempted to establish an anticommunist government in South Vietnam under the leadership of Ngo Dinh Diem. Kahin shows that by gambling that Diem could survive with strong U.S. backing, the United States tied itself to an authoritarian ruler with a weak political base.

Ronald H. Spector, a military historian with the U.S. government, analyzes in the final essay the shortcomings of the first American military advisory mission in Vietnam. He depicts the growth of the Vietcong insurgency in the late 1950s as an ominous threat to the South Vietnamese regime, one that American military advisers had not adequately prepared South Vietnam's armed forces to meet.

The Day We Didn't Go to War

GEORGE C. HERRING AND RICHARD H. IMMERMAN

America's role in the Dienbienphu crisis of 1954 has been a source of persisting confusion and controversy. In a *Washington Post* story of June 7, 1954, subsequently expanded into a *Reporter* article provocatively en-

George C. Herring, and Richard H. Immerman, "Eisenhower, Dulles, and Dienbienphu: 'The Day We Didn't Go to War' Revisited," *Journal of American History*, 71 (Sept. 1984), 343–48, 349–54, 355–56, 357–62, 362–63. Reprinted by permission.

titled "The Day We Didn't Go to War," journalist Chalmers M. Roberts divulged that the Dwight D. Eisenhower administration had committed itself to a massive air strike to relieve the Vietminh siege of the French fortress at Dienbienphu. The United States would have intervened in the Indochina War, Roberts went on, had not the congressional leadership, after a secret meeting on April 3, made intervention conditional on British participation and had not the British refused. In their memoirs British and American officials confirmed some of Roberts's account. French memoirists went further, charging that Secretary of State John Foster Dulles and Admiral Arthur W. Radford, chairman of the Joint Chiefs of Staff (JCS), had proposed an air strike to save Dienbienphu, had even proposed the loan of atomic weapons, and then had callously reneged, sealing France's defeat in the war. On the other hand, administration officials at the time and Eisenhower later insisted that they had never seriously contemplated military intervention in Indochina. Eisenhower conceded only that he had attempted to put together an allied coalition to resist Communist encroachments in Southeast Asia but had been thwarted by the British.

Despite lingering uncertainty about what actually happened, scholars have advanced numerous interpretations of the administration's handling of the crisis. Early writers typically used it to show how a reckless Dulles nearly pushed the passive Eisenhower into war. In the aftermath of Lyndon B. Johnson's massive intervention in Vietnam, however, scholars increasingly praised Eisenhower for his caution and for his involvement of Congress in policy formation. Some writers speculated that he had cleverly used Congress to restrain his more impulsive advisers. Others argued that the open process established by Eisenhower promoted a high level of "multiple advocacy," thereby producing sound policy. Whatever the perspective, scholars viewed Eisenhower's decision not to intervene as exceptional in the long history of United States escalation in Vietnam.

Recent declassification of an abundance of United States documents permits a new look at one of the most significant episodes of the Eisenhower years. Those documents make clear that the memoirs of the participants are often inaccurate and misleading and that Roberts's standard account, on which most scholars have relied, contains important errors and suffers from the bias of its own sources. The documents compel modification at a number of important points of recent favorable interpretations of Eisenhower's diplomacy.

The Dienbienphu crisis stemmed at least indirectly from Franco-American adoption of the Navarre Plan in September 1953. To prevent the fall of Indochina to the Communist-led Vietminh insurgents, the United States since 1950 had supported France with steadily growing volumes of military and economic assistance. United States officials deplored the cautious, defensive military strategy pursued by France, however, and they feared that as long as France was fighting for essentially colonial goals, it could not win the war. Certain that the Harry S Truman administration had not effectively applied the leverage available to it, Dulles and Eisenhower conditioned further aid on French agreement to fight the war more aggressively and to make firm promises of independence for the states of Indochina.

Uneager to expand the war but unwilling to abandon it, the French bent to American pressure. The government of Joseph Laniel vaguely promised to "perfect" Vietnamese independence. The newly appointed commander of French forces in Indochina, General Henri Navarre, drew up a military strategy tailored to United States specifications, proposing to combine his scattered forces and to launch a major offensive in the Red River delta. Although Navarre himself was skeptical that the plan could produce victory, the French government adopted it to gain additional United States aid. Dubious of French intentions and capabilities, the Eisenhower administration nonetheless felt compelled to go along, fearing that otherwise Laniel's government might be replaced by one committed to negotiations.

Navarre abandoned his ill-fated plan before he had even begun to implement it. To parry a Vietminh invasion of Laos, he had to scatter the forces he had just started to combine. As part of a hastily improvised alternative strategy, he established in late 1953 a position at the remote village of Dienbienphu in northwestern Vietnam, where he hoped to lure the Vietminh into a set-piece battle. In a broad valley surrounded by hills as high as one thousand feet, he constructed a garrison ringed with barbed wire and bunkers and dispatched twelve battalions of regulars supported by aircraft and artillery. Vietminh commander Vo Nguyen Giap soon laid siege to the French fortress. By early 1954 twelve thousand of Navarre's elite forces were isolated in a far corner of Vietnam. Although uncertain that his troops could defend themselves against superior Vietminh numbers, Navarre decided to remain.

Shortly after, the contingency Americans had so feared became reality. Facing growing political opposition at home, an uncertain military situation in Vietnam, and a depleted treasury, the Laniel government decided that it must negotiate a settlement. Over Dulles's vigorous protests, it agreed to place the Indochina question on the agenda of an East-West conference scheduled to meet in Geneva, Switzerland, in late April 1954.

These developments generated great concern in Washington. An American military observer reported from Dienbienphu as late as February that the French fortress could "withstand any kind of attack the Vietminh are capable of launching," but United States officials could not ignore the possibility that the garrison might fall, causing a total French collapse. Reports of increased Chinese aid to the Vietminh raised additional fears that, as in Korea, China might intervene directly in the war. In any event, Americans suspected that French war-weariness might lead to a sellout in Geneva. "If the French were completely honest they would get out of Indochina," Dulles remarked, "and we certainly didn't want that." Accordingly, the administration searched desperately for means to deter Chinese intervention and to bolster French resistance. Eisenhower sent the French forty bombers and two hundred United States Air Force mechanics to service them. Conceding the risk of expanded involvement, he insisted, "My god, we must not lose Asia—we've got to look the thing right in the face."

The administration concurrently began to face the prospect that United States forces might have to be used. Notwithstanding his determination to "keep our men out of these jungles," Eisenhower reminded the National Security Council (NSC) that "we could nevertheless not forget our vital interests in Indochina." He appointed a special committee to examine the circumstances under which direct United States involvement might be required and the means by which it could be made most effective. The study had not been completed by mid-March 1954, but the siege of Dienbienphu and the danger of a French cave-in at Geneva added a sense of urgency. The committee, headed by Under Secretary of State Walter Bedell Smith, had gone so far as to ask the JCS to develop a "concept of operations" for Indochina.

In mid-March the siege tightened. French and American military experts had predicted that the Vietminh would not be able to transport artillery up the hills surrounding the fortress, but by sheer human exertion they did. In a series of attacks beginning on March 13, the Vietminh seized two major hill outposts established by the French to protect the fortress and the airfield below. Heavy Vietminh guns quickly knocked out the airfield, making resupply possible only by parachute drop. The Central Intelligence Agency (CIA) estimated no better than an even chance that the vulnerable French garrison could hold out. It seemed increasingly clear that the United States might have to take drastic steps to save France or, in the event of a French collapse, to continue the struggle for Indochina on its own.

The visit of General Paul Ely to Washington in late March brought these pressing issues to the forefront. The Smith committee had invited the French chief of staff to discuss additional military assistance. It suspected, nevertheless, that he might request intervention. During his initial meetings with Radford and Dulles, Ely estimated a fifty-fifty chance that Dienbienphu might still hold and asked for the loan of twenty-five additional B-26 bombers and American volunteers to fly them. At that point he seems to have been concerned primarily with the threat of Chinese air intervention, and he inquired in writing what the United States would do if China sent aircraft into the war.

Ely's visit took the form of a game of international cat and mouse, graphically revealing the accumulated frustrations of four years of Franco-American collaboration in Indochina. The United States approved Ely's request for the additional bombers (without the pilots), although Radford expressed grave doubts about France's ability to maintain them and use them in combat. When Radford pressed for a larger United States role in training indigenous forces and in determining strategy, Ely complained of the "invading nature" of the Americans and their apparent determination "to control . . . everything of importance."

Dulles and Radford responded noncommittally to Ely's query about

Chinese intervention. They agreed that they would make no commitments until they "got a lot of answers" from the French on issues that divided the two nations. Dulles informed Ely point-blank that the United States would not invest its prestige except under conditions where military success was likely, which would require France to extend to the United States a "greater degree of partnership" than had prevailed in the past. The result was a tightly qualified "agreed minute" that directed "military authorities [to] push their planning work as far as possible so that there would be no time wasted when and if our governments decided to oppose enemy air intervention over Indochina if it took place."

At Radford's request Ely remained in Washington for one more day, at which time the two men discussed the possibility of an air strike to relieve the siege of Dienbienphu. The idea apparently originated from American and French officers in Saigon. Code-named VULTURE, the plan called for massive night bombing attacks on Vietminh positions by as many as 300 United States aircraft launched from carriers in the region and perhaps from air bases in the Philippines. Who first raised the issue and what commitments resulted are impossible to determine. Ely later declared that Radford had enthusiastically endorsed the plan and had intimated that he had Eisenhower's support. Radford admits telling Ely that within two days of a formal French request as many as 350 United States aircraft could be deployed, but he insists that he made clear that intervention would require a decision at the highest level of government and congressional approval. It is possible, of course, that the two men misunderstood each other. They spoke without an interpreter, Ely's English was not good, and he may have missed or minimized the qualifications Radford says he included. Or the French general may have understood the qualifications quite well and only later professed to have been misled. More likely, Radford was less circumspect than he allows. An Asia-firster in the mold of Douglas MacArthur and a firm believer in air power, he often advocated intervention in Indochina and at times even urged the use of atomic weapons against China. Before his last meeting with Ely, he warned Eisenhower that the United States "must be prepared to act promptly and in force possibly to a frantic and belated request by the French for U.S. intervention." Even if he had included the qualifications, as he later maintained, his obvious zeal for intervention might have left the impression that formal authority could be readily obtained, an impression, given certain of Eisenhower's comments, Radford probably believed.

In the week after Ely left Washington, however, Radford was unable to generate support for VULTURE even among the JCS. . . .

Among top civilian leaders there was no enthusiasm for air intervention at Dienbienphu. Vice President Richard M. Nixon has been frequently cited as an advocate of intervention—and he was—but he did not play a consequential role in shaping policy. Dulles, often portrayed as a "hawk" in this crisis as in others, was in fact quite cautious. Deeply concerned that the Chinese might intervene or that France might hand Indochina over to the Communists at Geneva, the secretary was prepared to take risks in Indochina. He seems not to have been persuaded that VULTURE was either feasible or necessary, however. He stated that if the Chinese intervened he would prefer such things as "harassing tactics from Formosa and along the Chinese seacoast," measures, he added, that "would be more readily within our natural facilities than actually fighting in Indochina."

Eisenhower's position is equally interesting, if characteristically elusive. He is typically depicted as at least a closet dove in this crisis, and he later dismissed VULTURE as military folly. Indeed, as early as 1951 he had entered in his diary, "I am convinced that no military victory is possible in that kind of theater [Indochina]." On March 24, nevertheless, he told Dulles that he would not "wholly exclude the possibility of a single strike, if it were almost certain this would produce decisive results." A week later he alluded to the idea again, adding that such an operation would have to be covert and that "we would have to deny it forever." The president was probably thinking out loud. Like Dulles, he seems never to have been persuaded that the plan would work, and he was equally opposed to intervention in any form in the absence of satisfactory military and political agreements with France. In the week after Ely's departure, VULTURE was not discussed seriously at the top levels, and the administration never made a commitment to it.

Still, Eisenhower and Dulles recognized that something must be done, and between March 24 and April 1 they began to formulate an appropriate response. They proceeded with extreme caution, keeping numerous options open and covering their tracks so well that they baffled contemporaries and future scholars. Dulles labeled their plan "United Action." Based on a regional security program he had proposed under Truman when negotiating the peace treaty (Treaty of San Francisco, 1951) with Japan, United Action was designed to meet the many uncertainties and dilemmas of the Indochina crisis. It reflected the perceived lessons of the Korean War as well as the administration's concept of strategic deterrence and its New Look defense policy. The keystone of the plan was the creation of a coalition composed of the United States, Great Britain, France, Australia, New Zealand, Thailand, the Philippines, and the Associated States of Indochina and committed to the defense of Indochina and of the rest of Southeast Asia against the Communist menace. The mere establishment of such a coalition accompanied by stern warnings to the Communists might be sufficient to bolster the French will to resist and to deter Chinese intervention, thus making outside intervention unnecessary. It is even plausible, as one of Dulles's top aides later suggested, that United Action was merely a grand charade of deterrence and that Eisenhower and Dulles never seriously considered United States military involvement.

It is more plausible that United Action was designed to ensure that if the United States intervened it would do so under favorable circumstances. The evidence indicates that although the administration never committed itself to intervention during the Dienbienphu crisis, that option was left open to meet the contingencies of Chinese intervention, a French military collapse, or, preferably, a breakdown of the Geneva negotiations and a continuation of the war. Eisenhower and Dulles agreed that the United States should go in only as part of a genuinely collective effort and that United States ground forces must not become bogged down in Asia. United Action would provide a legal basis for collective action. A multilateral effort would remove the taint of a war for colonialism and would provide additional leverage to force the French to share political and military decision making. If, on the other hand, France pulled out, United Action would ensure that the United States did not have to fight alone. In keeping with the New Look doctrine, local and regional forces would bear the brunt of the ground fighting while the Americans did those things Dulles proclaimed "we can do better," providing air and naval support, furnishing money and supplies, and training indigenous troops.

The major problem was time. The Geneva conference was only a month away. Ely's query about a United States response to Chinese intervention needed to be answered promptly if it was to have the proper political effect in France. And on March 30 the Vietminh initiated the second stage of the battle for Dienbienphu, launching withering artillery barrages and a series of human-wave assaults against the hill outposts that constituted the outer defenses of the fortress. The French held the lines and even managed successful counterattacks at some points, but the decisive battle seemed to be underway. The fate of the fortress and the outcome of the war might be settled in a matter of weeks.

Eisenhower and Dulles hence moved rapidly to lay the groundwork for United Action. In a March 29 speech designed to "puncture the sentiment for appeasement before Geneva," Dulles publicly unveiled the concept in deliberately vague terms. He warned that the Chinese now supported the Vietminh "by all means short of open invasion" and that Communist success in Indochina would lead to further aggression in Southeast Asia, the loss of which could have disastrous consequences for the entire free world. Using words that his aide Robert Bowie described as "deliberately picked" to sound "menacing without committing anybody to anything," the secretary declared that the possibility of a Communist conquest of Southeast Asia "should not be passively accepted but should be met by united action."

Having raised the possibility of intervention, Eisenhower and Dulles next consulted with the congressional leadership. The president has been rightly praised for involving Congress at that stage, but his move was based as much on political exigency as on abstract respect for the Constitution. The administration carefully monitored public opinion, which overwhelmingly opposed United States military involvement. Further, Eisenhower had only the barest majorities in both houses (48-47-1 in the Senate; 221-212-1 in the House). The Republican right wing had been notoriously unreliable, and the Army-McCarthy hearings were soon to begin. Although the Democrats had supported the president faithfully on foreign policy through much of 1953, bipartisanship had begun to erode. Some Democrats were in a vengeful mood. Recalling the vicious attacks on Truman and Dean Acheson, Hubert H. Humphrey warned Dulles, "As ye [sow], so shall ye reap, and, believe me, you have so sown and so you reap." By the time of the Dienbienphu crisis, even moderate Democrats had begun to challenge the administration's Indochina policy. Congressional restlessness had been made abundantly clear in February when Democrats and Republicans attacked the administration for failing to consult before sending United States Air Force mechanics to Vietnam. To calm the legislators, the president had publicly pledged that the United States would not become involved in war "unless it is a result of the constitutional process . . . placed upon Congress to declare it."

Eisenhower and Dulles perceived that whichever way they went they faced problems with Congress. Should they do nothing and Indochina fall, right-wing Republicans might join Democrats in condemning them for losing additional territory to Communism. If United States intervention were required, however, there would be little time for consultation and deliberation, and the experience of Korea left no doubt that intervention without some kind of congressional authorization would leave the administration politically vulnerable. Eisenhower thus had to implicate Congress at an early stage. "It might be necessary to move into the battle of Dien Bien Phu in order to keep it from going against us," he said in late March, "and in that case I will be calling in the Democrats as well as our Republican leaders to inform them." Remaining cautiously in the background, the president had Dulles and Radford arrange an unusual Saturday morning meeting with the legislative leadership on April 3.

Recently declassified documents make clear that notwithstanding Eisenhower's remark he did not seek authority for an immediate air strike to relieve the siege of Dienbienphu, as Roberts and others have long argued. At a top-level White House meeting on April 2, an obviously isolated Radford conceded that the outcome at Dienbienphu would be "determined within a matter of hours, and the situation was not one which called for any U.S. participation." The administration sought, rather, congressional endorsement of a broad, blank-check resolution, not unlike the Formosa Resolution of 1955, that would give the chief executive discretionary authority to use United States air and sea power to prevent the "extension and expansion" of Communist aggression in Southeast Asia. The draft resolution that Dulles brought to the White House and that Eisenhower approved stipulated that the authority would terminate on June 30, 1955, and would in no way "derogate from the authority of Congress to declare war."

Eisenhower and Dulles sought the resolution primarily to meet the immediate needs of United Action. Dulles indicated that he wanted the resolution mainly as a "deterrent" and to strengthen his hand in upcoming discussions with representatives of allied nations. The administration was also notably discreet in handling its presentation. Eisenhower insisted that the "tactical procedure should be to develop first the thinking of Congressional leaders without actually submitting in the first instance a resolution drafted by ourselves."

Dulles followed the script, but the drama took a direction the administration had not intended. Radford briefed the legislators on Dienbienphu, perhaps mistakenly convincing them that the White House wanted to intervene immediately. Dulles then portrayed the threat to Indochina in the gravest terms and urged that the president be given "Congressional backing so that he could use air and sea power in the area if he felt it necessary in the interest of national security." No one challenged the assessment of the crisis, but the legislators, particularly Democratic senators Richard B. Russell and Johnson, insisted that there must be "no more Koreas with the United States furnishing 90 percent of the manpower" and that there must be firm commitments of support from allies, specifically Great Britain. Dulles persisted, affirming that he had no intention of sending ground forces to Indochina and indicating that he could more easily gain commitments from other nations if he could specify what the United States would do. The congressmen were not swayed. "Once the flag is committed," they warned, "the use of land forces would surely follow." Sharing fully the administration's distrust of France, they also insisted that the United States must not go to war for colonialism. They would only agree that if "satisfactory commitments" could be obtained from Britain and other allies to intervene collectively and from France to "internationalize" the war and to grant the Indochinese independence, a resolution authorizing the president to employ United States forces "could be obtained."

Although less dramatic than often assumed, the outcome of the meeting was significant. Neither Eisenhower nor Dulles differed fundamentally with the congressmen on the form intervention ought to take, but the conditions did tie their hands by virtually eliminating any possibility of unilateral intervention, an option that they had not entirely ruled out. The conditions weakened Dulles's position with allied leaders by requiring the allies' commitment prior to action by Congress, an order the administration would have preferred to reverse. Most important, they made collective intervention dependent on British support and French concessions, each of which would be difficult to obtain. Eisenhower and Dulles admitted that the meeting raised some "serious problems."

Ironically, at the very time the congressmen were setting guidelines for United States intervention, the French were concluding that Dienbienphu could be saved only by a United States air strike. Navarre had originally opposed United States involvement, fearing that it might provoke direct Chinese intervention. In the aftermath of the Vietminh offensive of early April, however, he revised his estimate, cabling the French government on April 4 that an air strike might spare the garrison if executed within the following week. After an emergency meeting that night, Foreign Minister Georges Bidault requested VULTURE, emphasizing that the extensive presence of Chinese matériel and advisers met the conditions under which United States involvement had been discussed by Radford and Ely.

It seems unlikely that Eisenhower and Dulles would have approved the request under any circumstances, but the conditions imposed by the congressmen clinched the decision and probably provided a convenient excuse. Manifesting no sense of disappointment, they agreed that approving the request without "some kind of arrangement getting support of Congress, would be completely unconstitutional and indefensible." Expressing some annoyance with Radford for leading the French to believe that the United States would respond positively, Eisenhower instructed Dulles to see "if anything else can be done" to help the French. But, he concluded firmly, "we cannot become engaged in war." . . .

During the following week the administration prepared the way for United Action. Dulles conferred with the British and the French ambassadors, and Eisenhower wrote a personal letter to Prime Minister Winston Churchill urging British support for a coalition that would be "willing to fight" to defend Southeast Asia. At a news conference on April 7, the president outlined what came to be known as the "domino theory," explaining that if Indochina fell the rest of Southeast Asia would "go over very quickly," with "incalculable" losses to the free world. A carrier strike force already on station in the South China Sea was moved to within one hundred miles of Hainan Island and began air reconnaissance of Chinese airfields and staging areas.

On April 10 Dulles traveled to Europe for the first round of three weeks of frantic shuttle diplomacy. Stopping first in London, he encountered immediate opposition. The British did not share the American view that the loss of Indochina would threaten all of Southeast Asia. Convinced that France retained sufficient influence to salvage a reasonable settlement at Geneva, they feared that outside intervention would destroy any hope of a negotiated settlement and perhaps would even provoke war with China. Most important, they had no inclination to entangle Britain in a war that could not be won. The persistent Dulles could get nothing more than Foreign Secretary Anthony Eden's grudging assent to participate in immediate multilateral talks to establish a common bargaining position at Geneva, with a coalition to be included on the agenda.

Dulles met further obstacles in Paris. He held out the prospect of United States intervention but only on condition that France resist a negotiated settlement at Geneva, agree to fight in Indochina indefinitely, concede to the United States a greater role in planning strategy and in training indigenous troops, and accept Vietnamese demands for complete independence. Like Eden, French Foreign Minister Bidault insisted that nothing should be done to jeopardize the success of the Geneva negotiations. He also indicated that French public opinion would not support continuation of the war if the ties between the Associated States of Indochina and France were severed, and he made plain French opposition to internationalizing the war. As from the British, Dulles could obtain from the French an agreement only to join preliminary talks to be held in Washington on April 20.

By the time Dulles returned to the United States, the administration's delicate strategy faced rising opposition at home. The possibility of some kind of intervention in Indochina elicited from members of Congress increasing protest about the danger of joining a war for French colonialism. In an April 6 speech that won praise from both sides of the aisle, Democratic Senator John F. Kennedy warned that victory could not be won so long as the French remained. Echoing Kennedy's sentiments, Senators Estes

Kefauver, Wayne Morse, and Michael J. ("Mike") Mansfield demanded that France clarify its intentions regarding independence for Indochina. On April 7 Senator Henry Jackson hit closer to the point bothering many in Congress when he demanded that the administration reveal its own intentions in Indochina. . . .

The administration's strategy threatened from several directions, Dulles hastened back to Europe for a North Atlantic Treaty Organization (NATO) council session. The issue of United States air intervention at Dienbienphu immediately emerged. The situation of the French fortress had become perilous. Efforts to retake the inner hill positions had failed, costing France all its reserves. The beleaguered garrison had been reduced to about three thousand able-bodied fighting men, and resupply was virtually impossible. On April 22 Bidault, whom Dulles described as "totally exhausted mentally," hinted at French willingness to internationalize the war and warned that nothing short of "massive air intervention by the U.S." could save Dienbienphu. The following day the foreign minister showed Dulles an "urgent" cable from Navarre indicating that in the absence of an air strike Navarre would have no choice but to order a cease-fire.

Bidault's later claim that at that point Dulles offered him the loan of two atomic weapons seems highly implausible. No other evidence of the alleged offer exists in available French or American sources. Dulles did not have the authority to take such a step, and for him to have so exceeded his prerogatives would have been inconsistent with his usual conduct and with the caution he displayed throughout the Dienbienphu crisis. Dulles had shown little interest in JCS contingency plans that called for atomic bombs should the United States intervene. Eisenhower did discuss the possibility of lending France "new weapons" but not until April 30, while Dulles was in Europe. Shocked when he learned of the charges, the secretary could only surmise that as a result of Bidault's highly agitated state of mind or of problems of translation, Bidault had interpreted as an offer a random statement that United States policy now treated nuclear weapons as conventional. Dulles may have been correct. Bidault attempted to blame the Dienbienphu debacle on his American counterpart, and he may have used the alleged offer to damage the reputation of a man he came to despise thoroughly.

Whatever the case, Bidault's second request for United States air intervention sparked a week of the most intense and nimble diplomatic maneuvering in recent history. Hoping to save Dienbienphu and to strengthen their bargaining position at Geneva, the French sought an American air strike without incurring commitments that would restrict their freedom of action. Dulles could not, of course, commit the United States without first extracting agreements from both Britain and France. In any event, he was less concerned with the immediate situation at Dienbienphu than with the long-term defense of Southeast Asia, and he sought to keep France in the war and to use the opening provided by Bidault's overture to revive the flagging prospects of United Action. Unwilling to enter the war under any circumstances, Britain attempted to restrain the United States and to keep

France committed to a negotiated settlement without provoking an irreparable split in the alliance.

From Dulles's standpoint, Britain was the key, and on April 23 and April 24 he relentlessly pressured Eden. He warned that the French would not continue the war without assurance of British and American support and insisted that the mere knowledge that a "common defense system was in prospect" would deter the Communists and would strengthen the allied hand at the Geneva conference. If Britain agreed, he added, the president would seek immediate congressional authorization for United States intervention. When Eden expressed doubt that an air strike would accomplish anything, Radford, who had joined Dulles in Paris, declared that at least it would "stabilize the situation." If the United States intervened, he went on, Navarre might be relieved of his command, and Americans from "behind the scenes" could exercise a "considerable voice" in the conduct of the war. To calm Eden's expressed fears of World War III, Radford minimized the risks of Soviet or Chinese intervention. The Americans also played down the anticipated cost of British participation, indicating that nothing more would be asked than the use of several air squadrons from Malaya and Hong Kong. Making clear his continued personal opposition, Eden agreed to return to London to consult with Churchill.

Even with the fate of Dienbienphu in the balance, the United States and France could not bridge the vast gap that had long separated them. France had finally agreed to Vietnamese independence, but the question of internationalization of the war remained unsettled. Moreover, the two nations differed sharply in their approaches to the short-term issues. Bidault warned Dulles that making intervention conditional on British participation would merely cause delays when speed was of the essence and added that the British contribution would not "amount to much of anything." To secure an immediate air strike, he cleverly played on established American fears. If Dienbienphu fell, he warned, the French people would insist on getting out of the war and would have no use for a coalition, which they would view as a sinister means of keeping them fighting indefinitely.

Not ruling out intervention while scrupulously avoiding anything that could be interpreted as a commitment, Eisenhower and Dulles urged Bidault to stand firm. In a carefully worded letter of April 24, Dulles informed the French foreign minister that an air strike would constitute "active United States belligerency" and would therefore require congressional authorization. That could not be obtained within a matter of hours, he added, and probably not at all except within the framework of United Action. He went on to insist that the fall of Dienbienphu need not cause a total French collapse—indeed, the Vietminh had incurred such heavy losses during the siege that the overall military balance would favor France. Dulles held out the prospect of future support through "collective action." Concurrently Eisenhower wrote Laniel, reminding him that France had "suffered temporary defeats" in the past and had still prevailed.

Anticipating a negative British response, the French pressed for unilateral United States action. Bidault informed Dulles that French military experts had concluded that a massive air strike could deliver a "decisive blow" because the Vietminh had so many men and so much matériel concentrated around Dienbienphu. The French pleaded for "armed intervention" through "executive action" or some other "constitutional way to help," warning of ominous consequences to the war in Indochina and to Franco-American relations if nothing were done.

Eisenhower and Dulles peremptorily rejected the French proposal. Dulles advised the administration that because the security of the United States was not directly threatened, the political risk could in no way be justified. Air intervention might not save Dienbienphu, he continued, and the United States could not be certain that France would continue the fight. Intervention without Britain would "gravely strain" relations with Australia and New Zealand as well as with Britain. There would not be time to "arrange proper political understandings" with the French, and "once our prestige is committed in battle, our negotiating position in these matters would be almost negligible." If necessary, it would be better to let Dienbienphu fall than to intervene "under the present circumstances." Eisenhower agreed. Years later, he contemptuously recalled Bidault's last-minute proposals to "solve . . . our 'constitutional problems' and launch a unilateral air strike—on their terms."

Eden settled the issue on April 25, when he delivered the unwelcome, but not unexpected, news. Not even the "diplomatic" language of a memorandum of conversation can conceal the tension that followed. Eden insisted that an air strike might not be decisive and added that it would be a "great mistake" in terms of world opinion. He assured Dulles that Britain would give France "all possible diplomatic support" toward reaching a satisfactory political settlement at the Geneva conference. If such a settlement could be obtained, he would join the United States in guaranteeing it and would agree to immediate discussions about a collective effort to defend the rest of Southeast Asia. If not, Britain would cooperate with the United States in exploring the possibilities of United Action. Dulles protested vigorously that the British position might lead to total French capitulation. To write off Indochina and to believe the rest of Southeast Asia could be held would be foolish, he argued. Eden retorted that "none of us in London believe that intervention in Indochina can do anything."

Nor did direct appeals sway Churchill. The prime minister told Radford on April 26 that since the British people had let India go they could not be expected to give their lives to hold Indochina for France. At a formal dinner that evening, the old warrior went into a long and emotional discourse, asserting that the Indochina War could be won only by using "that horrible thing"—the atomic bomb—and noting Britain's vulnerability in the event of a nuclear war. "I have known many reverses myself," he concluded. "I have not given in. I have suffered Singapore, Hong-Kong, Tobruk; the French will have Dien Bien Phu." The British would not be drawn into what they feared would be "Radford's war against China."

The British and French responses to the crisis infuriated American leaders. Privately, Eisenhower vented his rage with his allies. The British had shown a "woeful unawareness" of the risks "we run in that region," he confided to his diary. The French had used "weasel words" in promising independence to the Vietnamese, he wrote an old friend, and "through this one reason as much as anything else have suffered reverses that have been really inexcusable." They wanted the Americans "to come in as junior partners and provide materials, etc., while they themselves retain authority in that region," and he would not go along with them "on any such notion."

For several days French and American officials toyed with various expedients. Dulles studied the possibility of proceeding without Britain and working for United Action with France, the ANZUS (Australia, New Zealand, United States) Pact, and the Associated States of Indochina. He also pondered the feasibility of having French forces withdrawn to defensible enclaves, where they could be supported by United States air and sea power, with the United States assuming responsibility for training indigenous forces. The French government warned Dulles that something must be done to compensate for the anticipated blow to French morale, imploring Dulles to create ad hoc machinery for allied consultation on measures to defend Southeast Asia or, as a last resort, to sponsor a public announcement that nations with vital interests in the area were consulting. French and American military officials explored the possibility of using United States C-119s, with American crews, to fly supplies and ammunition into the war zones to support a last-ditch effort to relieve Dienbienphu.

None of those options produced anything of substance, however, and after Eisenhower told the American public that the United States must steer a course between the "unattainable" and the "unacceptable," the decision against immediate intervention was formalized at a long and heated NSC meeting on April 29. The possibility of an air strike was reconsidered, and several of the conferees, led by Harold Stassen, administrator of the Foreign Operations Administration, proposed that the United States intervene unilaterally and with ground troops if necessary to retrieve the situation. Vice-President Nixon suggested the establishment of a "Pacific Coalition" without Britain and the dispatch of a United States Air Force contingent to make plain American determination to resist further encroachments. The Communists must be put on notice that "this is as far as you go, and no further."

As with the April 6 meeting, the result was both inconclusive and anticlimactic. Eisenhower firmly reiterated that unilateral military intervention would be impossible. "Without allies . . . the leader is just an adventurer like Genghis Khan," he asserted. Moreover, "if our allies were going to fall away in any case, it might be better for the United States to leap over the smaller obstacles and hit the biggest one [the Soviet Union] with all the power we had." After extended discussion the NSC decided to "hold up for the time being any military action on Indo-China" pending developments at Geneva. In the meantime, the United States ought to explore the possibilities of establishing a coalition without Britain while urging France to hold on in the hope that "some formula may be found which would permit additional aid of some sort." In brief, there would be "no intervention based on executive action."

The American decision sealed Dienbienphu's doom. The hopelessly outnumbered defenders finally surrendered on May 7 after fifty-five days of heroic, but futile, resistance. The attention of the belligerents and of interested outside parties immediately shifted to Geneva, where the following day the Indochina phase of the conference was to begin. . . .

The evidence presented here permits firm conclusions about the role of the United States in the Dienbienphu crisis. Contrary to Roberts's view, the Eisenhower administration clearly was at no point committed to an air strike at Dienbienphu. Even when faced with a total French collapse in the frantic days of late April, the administration did not deviate from the position it had staked out before Dulles and Radford met with congressional leaders. At the same time, Eisenhower and Dulles seem to have been much more willing to intervene militarily than the president later indicated in his memoirs. United Action was certainly part bluff, but it also involved a willingness to commit United States military power if conditions warranted it and if the proper arrangements could be made.

The praise accorded Eisenhower for consulting with Congress seems overstated. The political situation left him little choice but to consult, and in any event his intent was to manipulate Congress into giving him a broad grant of authority not unlike that which President Johnson secured in 1964. Implicating Congress in the Dienbienphu decisions protected the administration's domestic flank, but it represented at best a hollow victory. Instead of a blank check, the administration got a tightly drawn contract, and Dulles later conceded that Congress had "hamstrung" his policy.

Because of congressional restrictions, British rejection was decisive in the defeat of United Action, but Franco-American differences played a larger role than scholars have recognized. Long divided on Indochina, the two nations never came close to agreeing on the form United States intervention ought to take, on their respective roles in the proposed coalition, or even on the purposes of the war. It seems likely, therefore, that had other conditions been met, Franco-American divisions might still have prevented United States intervention.

Recent praise for the decision-making process may also be misplaced. The NSC structure encouraged a full review of policy and a high level of multiple advocacy and team building, but what is striking about the Dienbienphu crisis is the extent to which the formal machinery was peripheral to the actual decision making. The NSC role was restricted to planning, but even in that realm it consistently lagged behind the unfolding of events in Indochina.

Regarding the quality of the decision, there seems little reason to quarrel with the view that the administration acted wisely in staying out of war in 1954. It may deserve credit only for making a virtue of necessity, however, and after the Geneva conference it made political commitments to South Vietnam fraught with fateful long-range consequences. The "day we didn't go to war'' merely postponed for a decade large-scale United States military involvement in Vietnam, and the decision not to intervene militarily may well loom as less important than the political commitments made after the fall of Dienbienphu.

Gambling on Diem

GEORGE McT. KAHIN

The middle months of 1954 marked a major turning point in the American relationship with Vietnam. It was during this period that the United States made the most fundamental decision of its thirty-year involvement—the critical prerequisite to the subsequent incremental steps that culminated in President Johnson's famous escalation a decade later. Although this first major increase in American intervention was essentially political, it had important and clearly understood military implications. It was sustainable initially only by the threat of U.S. armed intervention and ultimately by its actual execution. So for the second time Washington attempted to establish an anticommunist government in Vietnam; but now it acted alone, no longer in association with France, and its effort was focused primarily on just the southern half of the country.

In this new departure the Eisenhower administration intervened directly in Vietnam, displacing France as the major external power. Rather than working through the French to support the Bao Dai regime, which claimed authority over all Vietnam, the United States took on the mission of establishing a separate noncommunist state in just the southern regroupment zone prescribed by the Geneva Agreements. The administration believed that, without the encumbrance of the old French colonial presence to undermine its nationalist legitimacy, a revamped Bao Dai regime, with Ngo Dinh Diem as its prime minister, could, if given sufficient American support, stand a good chance of competing effectively with the DRV [Democratic Republic of Vietnam—North Vietnam]. In addition, though their hopes on this score were apparently not so strong, senior U.S. officials thought it possible that this American-backed government would ultimately be able to absorb the North into a single anticommunist state. However unrealistic this second proposition, it was still the presidentially endorsed U.S. objective at least as late as 1958. In April of that year the National Security Council reiterated its aim to "work toward the weakening of the Communists in the North and South Viet Nam in order to bring about the eventual peaceful reunification of a free and independent Viet Nam under anti-Communist leadership.''

To understand this major shift in the United States' approach to Vietnam, one must assess the changed pattern of factors influencing American

From *Intervention*, by George McT. Kahin, excerpts from pp. 66–95. Copyright © 1986 by George McT. Kahin. Reprinted by permission of Alfred A. Knopf, Inc.

policy in the immediate post-Geneva period. The original, European-oriented calculations that had propelled the United States into its limited intervention in the early postwar years increasingly yielded place to considerations rooted primarily in the new ascendancy of communist power in China. Europe did still continue to exert an important influence on American Vietnam policy right through the Geneva Conference, however, because of the pivotal importance of the projected European Defense Community to Washington's Soviet containment strategy. But when the French Parliament defeated EDC soon after the close of the conference, European objectives ceased to have a significant effect on American policy toward Vietnam.

Although the French rejection of EDC only temporarily delayed German rearmament, it entailed the loss of most of France's once-formidable leverage with the United States, which had derived from Washington's uncertainty regarding French domestic politics and the extent to which France could be counted on to cooperate with American economic and military objectives in Europe. The potential of communism in France had by now dramatically ebbed, and the balance of her internal politics no longer threatened her continued presence in an American-led military alignment aimed at containing Soviet power in Europe. Indeed, the large noncommunist majority in the Chamber of Deputies saw such an alignment as clearly in their country's self-interest. The shoe was now on the other foot, for, as France began to face mounting militant nationalist pressures in her North African colonies during the fall of 1954, she badly needed American backing to maintain her ascendancy there.

Other factors important to the previous American preoccupation with Vietnam were, however, still operative: the enduring myth that communism was global and monolithic; the conviction that China was expansionist; and American domestic political pressures centering on the "loss of China" syndrome, whereby all administrations feared being accused of losing additional territory to communist control. But it was, of course, against the Democrats—not Eisenhower's Republicans—that the charge of China's "loss" had been leveled. Moreover, in contrast to the American involvement in China's civil war, the congressional and public perception was thus far of primarily French, not American, responsibility for developments in Vietnam, and France stood out clearly as a lightning rod to divert attacks from the administration's record there. At this stage, fear of domestic criticism, although a factor, was not fundamental to the administration's new decision for a major American involvement. It would only become an important consideration after the Eisenhower administration had publicly committed itself to sustaining a separate state free of communist control in the southern half of Vietnam.

What, then, explains the decision to intervene directly in Vietnam? To the three above-mentioned continuing determinants two new major factors had now been added. First was John Foster Dulles's retrospective analysis—subscribed to by Eisenhower—of the American failure in China, and the lessons he derived from this for policy toward Southeast Asia; and second was the inspiration he and Eisenhower drew from a set of analogies between conditions and the potential for American actions in Vietnam, and recent American and British experiences in other parts of the world.

Dulles approached the conflicts between Southeast Asian peoples and the colonial powers with certain strongly held views. Like his predecessor, Dean Acheson, he had little faith in the self-governing capacity of Southeast Asians who gained their independence from colonial powers through revolution. He was convinced that, without the involvement and guidance of the democratic West, nationalist movements in these countries would probably be drawn into communist-controlled political channels—and this, he believed, was likely even after they had attained full independence. With respect to the peoples of Indochina and Indonesia in particular, he felt that until they attained a greater degree of political maturity, the West had an ongoing obligation to help ensure that communists did not take over; and if the Western colonial powers withdrew, the United States had a responsibility to assume this burden.

From Chiang Kai-shek's defeat in China, Dulles drew a lesson that he regarded as applicable to Southeast Asian countries threatened by communist power. One of the main reasons he saw for the failure of American China policy was that "The territorial integrity of China became a shibboleth. We finally got a territorially integrated China—for whose benefit? The Communists." In other words, while certainly aware of the faults of the Kuomintang regime, Dulles saw its defeat by the Chinese communists as largely attributable to American acquiescence in Chiang's shortsighted attempt to win control over the whole of China concurrently. A more effective strategy would have been to accept temporarily a loss of the country's territorial integrity, yielding part of it to communist power, while concentrating Kuomintang and American resources in order to husband as much of the mainland as possible free of Mao's control. Chiang's residual mainland territory would have provided a base for mounting a rollback of communist control.

Some nine months before the beginning of the Geneva Conference on Indochina, this lesson was being applied to the situation in Indonesia. In late 1953 President Eisenhower counseled Hugh S. Cumming, his administration's first ambassador to Indonesia, that "as against a unified Indonesia which would fall to the Communists and a break up of that country into smaller segments he would prefer the latter." Dulles was more explicit, stating to the ambassador, "As between a territorially united Indonesia which is leaning and progressing towards communism and a break up of that country into racial and geographical units, I would prefer the latter as furnishing a fulcrum from which the United States could work later to help them eliminate communism in one place or another, and then in the end, if they so wish arrive back again at a united Indonesia."

If Eisenhower and Dulles considered this lesson from China to have such validity for Indonesia, it must have seemed even more applicable to the situation in Vietnam. In any case, their approach to Vietnam both during and after the Geneva Conference was consistent with, and undoubtedly to a significant extent shaped by, their perception of the causes of the "failure" in China.

But why did Eisenhower and Dulles believe that the United States had the capacity to implement in Vietnam what they considered to be the logical propositions derived from their retrospective analysis of the "failure" in China? That question cannot be answered without reference to the administration's evaluation of earlier American experiences in Greece, Iran, Guatemala, and especially the Philippines, together with what was regarded as an equally relevant British experience in Malaya. Its assessment of recent developments in these countries tended to reinforce an already self-assured and assertive postwar American "can-do" hubris, inclining policymakers to believe that the success of the United States in meeting challenges from communists or other socioeconomic radicals in these other places demonstrated abilities that could be applied in Vietnam. These combined to encourage the Eisenhower administration to intervene directly in Vietnam in the belief that it could work its own political will there to achieve a solution more consistent with American interests than that provided by the Geneva Conference.

A minority of American officials perceived that conditions in Vietnam were in fact fundamentally different from these other situations. But senior policymakers continued to draw inspiration and self-assurance from these precedents until well after the Eisenhower administration had embarked on a much deeper political intervention and commitment of American prestige in Vietnam. The simplistic analogies, sometimes referred to as "models," provided by these experiences continued to inform U.S. policy throughout Kennedy's administration and during the first part of Johnson's.

In Greece, where the United States had taken over from the British in late 1947, Washington believed that the critical factor in turning the tide against a peasant-backed, communist-led insurrection had been the injection of a large amount of American money, weaponry, and a military mission incorporating some five hundred advisers. American officials thought that this intervention, which had relied heavily on forced relocation of peasants, had been decisive in shoring up a faltering anticommunist government and forcing the insurgents to abandon their struggle and fade away into the hills within two years. The belief that this American experience in Greece was pertinent to Vietnam outlasted the Eisenhower administration. It was revived repeatedly under Kennedy and Johnson, especially by Walt Rostow [State Department and National Security Council official], but also, though less insistently, by William P. Bundy, assistant secretary of state for Far Eastern affairs under Johnson, who had been in Greece during the American campaign there and as late as 1967 was still talking about the possibility of "a Greek solution" in Vietnam.

In Iran in 1953—just a year before the Eisenhower administration's major decision on Vietnam—a covert U.S. program mounted primarily by the CIA had brought down a radical, albeit noncommunist, government led by Mohammed Mossadegh that had been bent on ending foreign domination of the country's oil production, and then returned the recently ousted shah to power. The administration also took great satisfaction in the outcome of its largely covert intervention during the spring of 1954 in Guatemala. This had successfully ousted a noncommunist but radical president who had been willing to accept the support of communists as well as other political groups and been regarded as a threat to American economic interests.

Britain's experience in Malaya was at least as important as the Greek precedent. By 1953 the British were finally beginning to gain the upper hand in their effort to subdue an insurgency of some Malayan Chinese that had broken out five years previously. They attributed their success primarily to an extensive program of forced resettlement of rural Chinese, on whom their enemy was or might be reliant for food and intelligence. After 1959, when a communist-led insurgency finally re-emerged in South Vietnam, Washington saw the presumed Malayan analogy as especially relevant, and commenced to emphasize a policy of population resettlement in rural areas. The Kennedy administration was equally insistent on seeing a Malayan analogy and even more attracted to a resettlement strategy, a predilection that continued under Johnson and Nixon.

But the most influential of all these precedents was the recent example of the Philippines. During 1953–54 American officials helped secure the position of secretary of defense in the Philippines for their own candidate, Ramon Magsaysay, and they then worked successfully to ensure his election as president. While he held these positions, they cooperated effectively with him to suppress a potent communist-led, agrarian-based insurgency, the Hukbalahap. The administration believed it could achieve similar results through its own chosen political instrument six hundred miles to the east in Vietnam. And if the CIA's Colonel Edward Lansdale had been so effective in helping to organize this effort in the Philippines, why should he not be equally successful in Vietnam? In January 1964 Assistant Secretary for East Asian Affairs Roger Hilsman was still looking for "a Vietnamese Magsaysay," and well into that year Secretary of Defense McNamara and Secretary of State Rusk, along with several other senior officials, were still seeing pertinent precedents in the Philippine and Malayan experiences.

The truth was that in character and context the Vietnam insurgency was only superficially akin, at best, to those in the Philippines, Malaya, and Greece. Nevertheless, the defeats of these earlier communist-led insurgencies, in combination with the heady American "successes" in Guatemala and Iran, encouraged the Eisenhower administration in its conviction that it had the capacity to work its will in determining Vietnam's political future.

Shaped primarily by Dulles, but with full support from the president, the administration's new Vietnam policy from the outset involved repudiating the two key political features of the Geneva Agreements: the stipulation that the line separating the two military zones "should not in any way be interpreted as constituting a political or territorial boundary," and the reunification elections, which had been an even more central condition for the armistice. The new policy also entailed two major positive steps by the United States. First, a mutual defense pact between it and several allies in effect treated the seventeenth parallel as a political boundary and provided in advance a measure of protection to the southern regroupment zone against attack by forces based in the North or against "internal subversion." Second, the United States displaced France's political and military presence in this area, taking over as paymaster to the Vietnamese civil servants and soldiers who had collaborated with the French and providing American training and advisers to the previously French-officered Vietnamese auxiliary component of the French expeditionary force. Still headed by Bao Dai as "chief of state," the "State of Vietnam" retained its name but was now restricted to the territory south of the seventeenth parallel. Into this area the United States pumped a massive amount of financial support, dwarfing what France had managed to provide.

These twin American efforts at an end run around some of Geneva's central provisions did not emerge fresh and full-blown after the conference. In the months preceding and during it, American policymakers had laid much of the groundwork for the two interdependent policies of building up a separate southern-Vietnamese state and protecting it from external assault and internal political opposition.

The still-unconsummated process of organizing United Action, initiated by the United States during the conference, now merged into an American-sponsored regional defense organization which was finally embodied in the Manila Pact of September 8, 1954 (ratified by the U.S. Congress February 19, 1955). In effect, the threat of an American-led anticommunist military intervention that had provided France with such useful leverage in Geneva was now spelled out with greater precision and institutionalized into a loosely structured alliance. Popularly known as SEATO (Southeast Asia Treaty Organization), it included the United States, Britain, France, Australia, and New Zealand, together with the only three Asian states Washington could induce to join—the Philippines, Thailand, and Pakistan (the last-named expecting that membership would give it leverage against India). Initially, the French were sufficiently scrupulous about Geneva's provisions for the neutralization of Indochina to resist Dulles's attempt to include Cambodia, Laos, and especially South Vietnam (where the stipulation against adherence to any military alliance was explicit) as members of SEATO. But through the device of adding a protocol to the treaty projecting an "umbrella of protection" over these three areas, Dulles was able to circumvent the impediment. The protocol stipulated that the treaty's provisions extended to Cambodia, Laos, and "the free territory under the jurisdiction of the State of Vietnam," even though they were not signatories of the treaty. Prince Sihanouk promptly repudiated Cambodia's inclusion, and with its neutralization in 1962 Laos was officially removed from jurisdiction of the protocol. Predictably, however, this protection was accepted by the French and Bao Dai for the temporary military regroupment zone south of the seventeenth parallel provided for at the Geneva Conference, now referred to as "the free territory of Vietnam." This was made explicit in a joint Eisenhower-Diem communiqué on May 11, 1957, after U.S.

officials were satisfied that Ngo Dinh Diem's authority had been sufficiently established in this half of the country.

SEATO's members saw its main objective as being "to deter massive military aggression," the United States stipulating that its own involvement would be limited to cases where the aggressor was communist. Though all its signatories saw the alliance as a deterrent against a possible attack by China, the United States, France, and at least some other members regarded it as providing a similar deterrent against the possibility of an assault by Hanoi into the regroupment zone of French forces south of the seventeenth parallel.

SEATO's apparently broad international base disguised a decided lack of enthusiasm on the part of some of its participants, and it was never effective as a vehicle for collective action. The formula did, however, provide subsequent American administrations with the basis for inducing Americans to believe that U.S. military involvement in Indochina had international sanction. Much more important, it provided what the executive branch came to assert was congressional authority for direct military intervention there. Indeed, SEATO's significance ultimately lay more in what came to be construed as a congressional licensing of unilateral U.S. anticommunist military intervention in Southeast Asia than in its role as a collective defense organization. This was not what the Senate had had in mind when it approved the treaty, but what happened in practice.

Nevertheless, during the decade prior to the August 1964 Tonkin Gulf Resolution, SEATO provided the major rationale for a U.S. military role in Indochina. And when, within two years, the 1964 resolution had become discredited because of a crystallization of congressional suspicion as to the circumstances surrounding its passage, SEATO once more provided the president with what was asserted to be "the legal basis" for that involvement.

For two decades SEATO was referred to as an American "commitment." Having signed the treaty, the United States was indeed committed to it. But that treaty itself did not—as successive administrations encouraged the public to believe—commit the United States to defend South Vietnam. In fact, no such pledge was made either by the members of SEATO collectively or by the United States unilaterally. The *ex post facto* presidential interpretation of SEATO that alleged it did so departed widely from the mandate actually agreed to by the U.S. Senate and did violence to its intent. Yet this interpretation gradually became the accepted conventional public perception. It was strongly enough established in the Kennedy administration to be used as justification for escalating involvement beyond the largely political and economic dimension pursued by Eisenhower to the level of direct U.S. military intervention. . . .

By granting protection in advance to Vietnam's southern regroupment zone against any attack by communist forces in the North, SEATO endowed the seventeenth parallel with the political character the Geneva Conference had prohibited and laid a foundation for recognizing a separate statehood for this southern area. This was, indeed, the administration's intention, and, five days before the conference concluded, Dulles informed an executive session of the Senate Foreign Relations Committee, "In fact the military regrouping [zones] will be apt to gradually become a live *de facto* political division. . . ."

With SEATO providing the context for establishing an American-protected state in the southern half of Vietnam, the Eisenhower administration concurrently moved ahead with the second prong of its new Vietnam policy. This was the much more straightforward effort to endow that area with the attributes of governmental power, substituting a dependence on the United States for a previous dependence on France, and ensuring a leadership congenial to and shaped by the administration. This new American political venture retained the same name as its French-sponsored predecessor—the "State of Vietnam"—and Bao Dai stayed on as chief of state for some fifteen months after Geneva, thereby providing a transitional bridge. In this politically precarious period, while the French and Vietminh military forces regrouped and Paris incrementally transferred the fundamental attributes of government to the State of Vietnam, an American presence gradually replaced that of France. During this process Bao Dai, still comfortably ensconced on the French Riviera, progressively, albeit reluctantly, yielded more and more power to Ngo Dinh Diem, the Catholic leader and U.S. protégé whom he had appointed as prime minister in June 1954. . . .

The actual transfer of governmental authority by France to Bao Dai was not completed until more than five months after the end of the Geneva Conference. In consolidating the new government in the southern half of Vietnam, Bao Dai proved useful during this transitional period primarily because of his continuing influence with the soldiers and civil servants who had served the French. Bao Dai, however, was certainly not Washington's first choice to lead this government. His undoubtedly sincere efforts to secure independence from France had failed, and many of those South Vietnamese whom the administration hoped to detach from Ho's standard regarded the former emperor as a collaborator with the colonial order. He did not improve this image by remaining in France, from where he conveyed his orders to his subordinates. Nor did he have a large following among the Catholics.

In view of Washington's jaundiced assessment of Bao Dai, and the apparent ineffectiveness of his prime minister, Prince Buu Loc, it is understandable that American officials should have sought an eminent Catholic nationalist, free of any taint of collaboration with the French, to provide more effective anticommunist leadership. And in inducing Bao Dai, apparently without French approval, to appoint Ngo Dinh Diem as his prime minister in mid-May 1954, the Eisenhower administration secured a man with these attributes. Diem was probably in a better position than any other Vietnamese leader to swing the maximum number of Catholics behind the new southern regime. Furthermore, he had given advance assurances that he agreed to the U.S. proposal to take over the training of South Vietnamese armed forces.

Nonetheless, at this stage American officials were by no means euphoric, and still recognized—as they were much less inclined to do a year or two later—his serious limitations. Thus, the U.S. ambassador to Paris cabled Washington on May 24, "On balance we are favorably impressed [by Diem] but only in the realization that we are prepared to accept the seemingly ridiculous prospect that this yogi-like mystic could assume the charge he is apparently about to undertake only because the standard set by his predecessor is so low." Following Diem's arrival in Saigon on June 25, the assessment of the U.S. chargé there was every bit as unenthusiastic: "Diem is a messiah without a message. His only formulated policy is to ask for immediate American assistance in every form, including refugee relief, training of troops and armed intervention. His only present emotion, other than a lively appreciation of himself, is a blind hatred for the French."

Although some American officials hoped that Diem would emerge as Vietnam's Magsaysay, the only attributes he shared with the Filipino were personal honesty, pecuniary incorruptibility, and a strong anticommunism. A mandarin aristocrat, at once arrogant and reserved and shy, Diem had scant understanding of and little rapport with the peasantry. He felt awkward, and acted so, when prevailed upon to visit rural areas, and his espousal of Catholicism appears to have made no dent in his aloofness from the populace. As Joseph Buttinger, who worked closely with him, has written, "Diem's temperament, social philosophy, and political comportment seemed to preclude all prospects of his ever becoming a popular hero. His stiff demeanor would have doomed any attempt to stir the masses by word or gesture, had he ever been persuaded of the necessity to make himself admired and loved. However, what he wanted was not love but the respect and obedience he considered his due as head of state." Moreover, except in his early years, Diem had actually had very little administrative experience. He had served ably and energetically in the French colonial administration, moving from an initial appointment as district chief in 1921, at the age of twenty, to the position of governor of a small province in 1929. Then, beginning in 1933, he was briefly the young emperor Bao Dai's secretary of the interior in the almost powerless rump Imperial Court at Hué, a position from which he resigned on principle because of French interference with his efforts to introduce reforms, and Bao Dai's unwillingness to give him sufficient backing. But for two decades thereafter he held no administrative post, nor did he show great talent as a political organizer.

Diem stood out in that he had not collaborated with the French. Nevertheless, in the eyes of a significant number of Vietnamese, his nationalist credentials had been tarnished by his willingness to work with Japanese occupation authorities. For a brief period he was their leading candidate for the position of premier in the client Vietnamese government with which they planned to replace the French in March 1945. Only when, at the last minute, the Japanese abandoned their plan for replacing Bao Dai with Prince Cuong De as emperor did Diem lose interest in the premiership. His claim to national leadership was further weakened by his absence from the country (he was in Europe and the United States) from August 1950 through the final years of the anti-French struggle.

At least as late as June 1953, Diem appears to have been unknown to Dulles and was unable to get an appointment with him. During that year, however, from a base in the Maryknoll order's headquarters in Lakewood, New Jersey, Diem—encouraged by several American Catholic leaders, the most prominent of whom was Francis Cardinal Spellman—was actively engaged in soliciting American backing. Acknowledging that Ho Chi Minh drew popular support because of his nationalism, he argued that Ho was succeeding primarily because Bao Dai had been so compromised by his association with the French. Only an anticommunist nationalist whose record was free of such collaboration, he argued, could draw this kind of backing away from Ho. (Diem had earlier turned down an offer of a high position in Ho's government, because he regarded the Vietminh as ultimately responsible for the murder of one of his brothers; but Ho's offer itself demonstrated that even he recognized Diem's stature as a nationalist leader.) However dogmatic and narrow in some of his views, Diem appeared completely assured as to his own ability to provide an effective alternative to Ho. He was able to convince a growing number of influential Americans, initially including Congressman Walter Judd and Senators John F. Kennedy and Mike Mansfield—with others such as Hubert Humphrey soon to follow—that he was the man to do this. His campaign to win congressional support was undoubtedly aided by the enthusiastic backing of a remarkably effective lobby of strongly anticommunist, mostly liberal-leaning Americans, which by the fall of 1955 had been organized as the American Friends of Vietnam, and ultimately enlisted these congressmen and a good many others among its members. It is hard to measure how influential Diem's American backers initially were with Dulles and Eisenhower, but as early as February 1954, against the background of Bao Dai's acknowledged incapacity, Under Secretary of State Bedell Smith told an executive session of the Senate Foreign Relations Committee that the administration was thinking of "providing a certain religious leadership."

Although American officials viewed Diem as the most promising candidate available to head the Saigon government, many were at first circumspect in endorsing him publicly or in offering support. This caution stemmed not only from some lingering doubts as to his qualifications but also from the extremely difficult and precarious political situation he was confronting. The administration's circumspection was clearly reflected in the qualified and conditional offer of support embodied in Eisenhower's letter to Diem of October 1, 1954, written in a hesitant tone and not actually delivered until three weeks later.

Eisenhower made his pledge of aid dependent on Diem's "assurances as to the standards of performance . . . in undertaking needed reforms." American assistance was to be "combined with" Diem's own efforts to "contribute effectively toward an independent Vietnam endowed with a strong government," a government that, Eisenhower hoped, would be "so responsive to the nationalist aspirations of its people'' as to attract domestic and international respect. This letter was not the all-out pledge that subsequent American presidents cited to justify their own intervention; it was, however, one of the first in a series of steps by the Eisenhower administration that, starting cautiously, were eventually to constitute a clear, positive, and virtually unqualified commitment to maintain a separate state in the southern half of Vietnam.

But during the first nine months after Geneva, this official circumspection was paralleled by the concurrent pursuit of another option, a second-track, covert policy; and any assessment of the administration's approach must focus heavily on this largely invisible level of policy. As Chester Cooper, then a top CIA official, candidly put it, ''The Central Intelligence Agency was given the mission of helping Diem develop a government that would be sufficiently strong and viable to compete with and, if necessary, stand up to the Communist regime of Ho Chi Minh in the north.'' Appointed to head this effort was Colonel Edward Lansdale, whom Dulles reportedly asked to ''Do what you did in the Philippines.'' During Diem's first months in office, Lansdale and a few other American agents provided him with ''considerable moral support and guidance,'' as well as funds. Lansdale states that on the very day Diem arrived in Saigon he presented him with ''notes on how to be a Prime Minister of Vietnam.'' He and other CIA operatives helped Diem establish dominance over the Vietnamese military forces gradually being turned over by the French, and later gave him critically important assistance in securing the adherence, neutralization, or dispersal of the armed forces of the Cao Dai, Hoa Hao, and Binh Xuyen. . . .

American backing for Diem still remained reserved for a further five months. In early April 1955, Eisenhower's special ambassador, General J. Lawton Collins, sent the president a series of cables highly critical of Diem's performance and abilities. This, combined with criticism from other American quarters, brought Dulles to conclude, reluctantly, that Diem would have to go. A central criticism was Diem's provocative clumsiness in dealing with important elements of the Vietnamese armed forces, even after Hinh's dismissal, and his alienation of leaders of the large Cao Dai and Hoa Hao militias, whose support was regarded as essential if their troops were to be successfully merged into Diem's army. Diem refused to recognize the autonomy of the considerable territories these religious sects had administered (a status that the French had accepted), and he resisted their demands for additional Cabinet posts in his government. But most crucial was his refusal to take over the substantial financial subsidies to them that the French had terminated as of the end of January, and his curtailment of the military supplies that the French had also been providing. At the same time as he was confronting the sects, Diem moved against the Binh Xuyen, the small army of well-armed gangsters who, following payoffs to Bao Dai and certain corrupt French officials, had gained control of Saigon's police force, thereby obtaining lucrative monopolies of the heroin trade, gambling, and prostitution.

Though American officials applauded Diem's plans to oust the Binh Xuyen, many regarded him as politically foolish and militarily reckless to move against them at the same time as he was confronting the two religious sects, possibly risking a military marriage of convenience between the sects and the Binh Xuyen. Influential U.S. officials regarded Diem's strategy— or absence thereof—in this matter as symptomatic of a lack of political realism that was critically undermining the possibility of establishing a viable state. The sects and Binh Xuyen had indeed begun forging a tactical front against Diem when he precipitated an all-out military confrontation with the Binh Xuyen on April 27.

Covert CIA operations paved the way for his actions by favorably altering the balance of military forces between him and his opponents. Large bribes had been judiciously distributed among several key military leaders of the Binh Xuyen, as well as of the Cao Dai and Hoa Hao, presumably with the help of Lansdale and other CIA operatives. Bernard Fall estimated that during March and April 1955 alone, such inducements to leaders totaled as much as $12 million. As a consequence of these bribes, and because they were persuaded that only with Diem as paymaster would the United States take over the subventions previously paid by France, a majority of the leaders of the Cao Dai—the most powerful of the dissidents—were persuaded to join Diem. Ultimately some 80 to 90 percent of the thirty thousand men in their regular army and militia were integrated into Diem's army. A majority of about nine thousand Hoa Hao soldiers were either induced to back Diem or were neutralized, with the remainder ousted from the Saigon area and on the defensive.

With the cards thus reshuffled, Diem's military forces made the culminating move. Colonel Duong Van Minh, with eleven battalions of the best of the French-trained Vietnamese soldiers and three thousand of the Cao Dai's most seasoned fighters, led by Lansdale's well-bribed protégé Trinh Minh Thé, successfully drove out of Saigon that apparently substantial majority of Binh Xuyen who had not been bribed or otherwise persuaded to cooperate. The operation involved heavy fighting and considerable destruction in the capital, but this military victory, together with the extensive ongoing accomplishments of bribery and integration, added up to a victory for Diem that proved decisive in securing him firm American support.

On the eve of Diem's action against the Binh Xuyen, in view of the disastrous situation that seemed to be developing, Dulles had in fact approved a cable withdrawing American support from him. The unexpected news of Diem's success caused him to cancel it. Overnight, in the eyes of most American officials and much of the U.S. press, Diem was metamorphosed from a stubborn, narrow, politically maladroit failure into a wise and clever hero. He was now master of Saigon and had asserted his control over or neutralized practically all of the French-trained Vietnamese military forces, as well as the formerly French-supported Cao Dai and Hoa Hao armies. The Eisenhower administration no longer doubted that Diem was its man, and the only one capable of helping it create a new state.

Domestically, Diem drew his major support, first, from Vietnamese who had served in either the army or the bureaucracy under the French and, second, from the Catholic community in the South. Among the latter, it was the exiles from North Vietnam, now forming a majority of the South's Catholic population, who comprised the most reliable and effective element in the power base he was establishing. In the words of a Pentagon chronicler, they "provided Diem with a claque: a politically malleable, culturally distinct group, wholly distrustful of Ho Chi Minh and the DRV, dependent for subsistence on Diem's government, and attracted to Diem as a co-religionist," who were important primarily as "a source of reliable political and military cadres." In organizing both his armed forces and the civilian administration, Diem showed a clear favoritism toward this group, often installing them in positions above non-Catholics who had had better training and more experience under the French.

A new piece of support came from that socioeconomic class of the South's new order that was developed and nourished by a continuous flow of heavy U.S. funding. Its centerpiece was the expanding bourgeoisie in the South, many times greater than the tiny group that France's colonial economy had sustained. An enormous umbilical cord, tapping into an American economy six thousand miles away, carried the lifeblood of a new "middle class" that South Vietnam's indigenous economic base could never have begun to support on its own. However artificial, the growth of this group effectively changed the class structure of the southern half of Vietnam.

During the entire twenty-year period it was provided, 1955–75, a massive program of U.S. economic assistance was crucial to the operation of the regimes of Diem and his successors. More than that, it conditioned a whole generation of southerners to an environment and a way of life that could not be sustained by the indigenous economic base, and which promptly collapsed once the trans-Pacific cord was cut. The rapidly growing membership of this almost exclusively urban bourgeoisie—both those who were now able to expand the modest wealth they had accumulated under the French and the much more numerous *nouveaux riches* who emerged during the American period—fully realized that their markedly enhanced economic position was fundamentally dependent on continuing U.S. support of the Saigon regime. Consequently, most of them welcomed Saigon's American connection and were disposed to give political backing to whatever government was likely to ensure its continuation. Thus, Diem and subsequent American protégés could count on substantial support from the South's new bourgeoisie.

This element had already begun to grow during the Franco-Vietminh war when mounting American economic aid had permitted increasing local expenditures by the French administration and individual soldiers. Vietnamese entrepreneurs had, however, benefited less from the war's economic fallout than had the country's well-established Chinese business community. But by January 1955, American funding flowed directly to Diem, rather than through the French, and he quickly moved to direct the economy in ways that would divert the entrepreneurial activities stimulated by this aid away from Chinese channels toward the ethnic Vietnamese, especially those whom he regarded as politically supportive. There was sufficient American aid for the million Chinese who lived in the South—about half of them in Saigon's sister city of Cholon—still to prosper, but much of the cream was scooped off by favored Vietnamese.

Crucial to Diem's ability to develop this new base of support was the Commercial Import Program (CIP)—the major component of the American economic aid package. The inception of this new CIP in January 1955 coincided with France's transfer of all residual elements of authority to the Diem-Bao Dai regime, with the exception of control over the Vietnamese auxiliaries of France's expeditionary forces, which began a month later. Eighty-seven percent of the initial U.S. grant to Diem of $322.4 million in 1955 was channeled through CIP, and thereafter, from 1955 through 1961, Washington provided Diem's government with a total of $1,447 million in economic grant aid, preponderantly through the CIP. Until the end of the American presence in 1975, this program remained the heart of the American economic assistance effort. . . .

By the beginning of May 1955, there was no longer any qualification in Washington's commitment to Diem. The remaining obstacle to the consolidation of a separate anticommunist southern state was the Geneva Conference's clear-cut stipulation that national reunification elections be held in mid-1956 and that consultations to prepare for them be conducted in mid-1955. Certainly some American officials acknowledged that the elections constituted a "binding commitment," and they, along with the French and British, were fearful that repudiating them would destroy the most important positive feature of the Geneva Conference—the military armistice. As the NSC reported, the French believed that "failure to hold elections would provoke a resumption of hostilities by the Vietminh in which France would be directly and involuntarily involved due to the probable presence at least of large numbers of the French Expeditionary Corps through 1955 and the first half of 1956." And American officials feared that, if a refusal to hold elections led to an end of the armistice and a renewal of Vietminh military activity, Britain and France might not support forceful U.S. action to counter it. At the SEATO meeting in February 1955, both allies made clear that this would indeed be the case.

A State Department intelligence report of September 15 expected that along with Canada and India of the International Control Commission, Britain and France would "continue to press for action in sufficient conformity with the agreements so that the Communists will have no excuse for breaking the cease-fire." It warned:

> If Diem is emboldened to reject or continue postponement of the elections stipulated in the Geneva Agreements, the DRV can be expected to seek its goal of unification (and control) through other means. Subject to calculation of what is feasible without stimulating U.S. military involvement the DRV would probably be prepared to use any methods necessary and would use pressures as strong as permitted by prevailing conditions in overall bloc relations with the non-communist world. . . . Should the DRV

conclude that elections are unlikely in fact, it is probable that the communists will greatly increase their subversive as well as political pressures against the South. The DRV, however, would probably seek to avoid direct U.S. military intervention and would probably, therefore, choose a maximum guerrilla and subversive effort rather than direct aggression to obtain its objective of control over a unified Vietnam.

As late as the Kennedy administration it was acknowledged internally that, if Diem's government did not consider itself bound by the Geneva Agreements' provision for elections, then the legal basis of a demand for Vietminh compliance with features of the accords advantageous to the U.S. and Diem, "such as respect for [the] demarcation line and ceasefire," could be called into question. In short, one party to an agreement could not ignore a central provision it found unpalatable and expect the other party to adhere to provisions *it* disliked.

It was understood, then, that there were serious risks in supporting Diem's opposition to national elections, but the potential risks if they were held were regarded as even greater, for American intelligence sources were unanimous that Diem would lose any national election. Extensive studies by American intelligence bodies subsequent to the Geneva Conference all reinforced the conclusion that national elections could only lead to the DRV's victory. A report prepared by the State Department's Division of Research on February 1, 1955, considered that "Almost any type of election that could conceivably be held in Vietnam in 1956 would, on the basis of present trends, give the Communists a very significant if not decisive advantage." It went on to point out that the establishment of "conditions of electoral freedom . . . might operate to favor the Communists more than their opponents." Even in the South, it judged, "maximum conditions of freedom and the maximum degree of international supervision might well operate to Communist advantage and allow considerable Communist strength in the South to manifest itself at the polls." This analysis concluded that "It would appear on balance, therefore, seriously questionable whether the South should make a major issue of free political conditions in the period preceding and during whatever type of elections might finally be decided for Vietnam."

The Eisenhower administration could not afford to risk elections, and it encouraged Diem in his own, understandable disposition to avoid them. That the administration was aware of the implications of this decision is clear from a State Department assessment of September 1955: "Only if Diem were to feel sufficiently assured of direct U.S. support against Communist reprisals, and if the U.S. were prepared to accept the consequences of such a development including some degree of alienation of its Western allies and Asian neutrals, would Diem be likely to persist in a position directly opposed to eventual holding of elections."

The administration was prepared to give him those assurances and accept these consequences. The NSC Planning Board had concluded shortly before that, if denial of victory to Hanoi through prevention of all-Vietnam elections resulted in a renewal of hostilities, the United States had to be prepared to oppose the Vietminh "with U.S. armed forces if necessary, and feasible—consulting Congress in advance if the emergency permits—preferably in concert with the Manila Pact allies of the U.S., but if necessary alone." The United States then developed contingency plans for the immediate deployment of air and naval power in Vietnam in the event of "overt aggression by Vietminh forces." This would be followed by the "early movement of mobile U.S. [ground] forces for the purpose of conducting joint operations for tasks beyond the capabilities of South Vietnamese forces."

Sure of U.S. backing, Diem now assumed a bold and confident posture in opposition to the national elections that were so central to the Geneva Agreements (and indeed he now repudiated all of its political provisions that did not suit his interests). He and his American supporters insisted that, since the Bao Dai–Diem government had not itself agreed to the accords, it was not bound by them. Furthermore, they advanced the equally specious argument that the accords had stipulated "fundamental freedoms and democratic institutions" as prerequisites to any election (rather than as their anticipated consequences, as Article 14a actually posited) and that since these conditions did not yet exist it would be impossible for any meaningful voting to take place—even if by secret ballot under the aegis of the International Control Commission, as the agreements provided. . . .

The decisive change in American policy that unfolded during the years immediately following the Geneva Conference was by no means inevitable; certainly it was not something the Eisenhower administration unwittingly backed into. It was a positive, calculated step into a direct and much deeper involvement than the earlier attempts to work through France. Moreover, this step was taken at a time when the United States had a clear option to avoid any direct commitment. Indeed, the Geneva Agreements offered the United States a broad avenue leading away from even the limited and indirect intervention it had pursued during the previous decade. The capitulation recognized at Geneva was, after all, generally viewed as French, not American, entailing responsibilities that were basically French. Instead of seizing on this clear option, the administration had moved assertively into a much more fundamental phase of intervention, and in doing so staked American honor and prestige on a policy that, once undertaken, was difficult to reverse.

Eighteen months after Ngo Dinh Diem had been appointed prime minister, the Eisenhower administration was congratulating itself on its success in consolidating his leadership of a separate anticommunist state. Its increased confidence in this venture was nicely reflected in a National Security Council progress report at the end of December 1955. "U.S. support," this stated, "made it possible for Prime Minister Diem to continue in office, to consolidate his position, and to stimulate international sympathy and support for Free Vietnam . . . induced French and British acceptance of Diem . . . effectively disposed of pressures for undesirable alternative governments." It had "assisted Diem in beginning to consolidate his position internally, in guaranteeing his independence from the French," and helped him "avoid international pressures for face-to-face consultations with the Viet Minh on all Vietnam elections." The report concluded that "U.S. actions during the period were largely responsible for the survival of a government in Free Vietnam with a will and capability to resist accommodation to the Viet Minh." With all this achieved, the National Security Council looked forward to the "implementation of reforms and some long-range planning in U.S. programs."

But the reforms that American officials hoped would broaden and strengthen Diem's popular base went largely unimplemented. He was dogmatically attached to an imperial tradition which required his subjects to give unquestioning obedience to his rule, sanctioned in his mind by right of the office he held. Never was he able to accept the idea, which numerous U.S. officials tried to instill in him, that he needed to consult and interact with his subjects in order to know what was best for them. Despite occasional lip service to democratic ideas to placate these anxious officials, he remained intent on building power in accordance with his own autocratic disposition. In his unceasing effort to do so he self-righteously followed a highly authoritarian route, marked by heavy and often indiscriminate repression, thus narrowing the regime's popular base that American policy sought to expand.

Having secured the backing of the army, civil service, Catholics, and most of the rapidly increasing bourgeoisie—and assured of the American funding necessary to permit the continued subsidies that were a fundamental condition for the backing of all these groups—Diem felt strong enough to manage the society of South Vietnam according to his and his brother's predilections. Sheltered behind the Franco-Vietminh armistice agreement, and confident of American support if Hanoi breached it, Diem moved rapidly and ruthlessly to consolidate his political authority.

Once Washington officials had accepted Diem over rival claimants and settled him in office, they found it difficult to oppose his wishes or to pressure him into following American prescriptions for good governance. The absolute dependence of Diem's state on the American treasury, together with his ongoing need for U.S. military backing, would appear to have given the American government enormous leverage in shaping the character and course of his regime. But the United States saw no prospect of finding a suitable replacement for him who would share its anticommunist goals, oppose national reunification elections, and could at the same time command even the modest indigenous support given to Diem.

Along with his astute brother, Ngo Dinh Nhu, with whom he increasingly shared power, Diem quickly sensed that U.S. officials saw him as indispensable to their objective of building and sustaining a separate anticommunist state. The two men assessed Washington's commitment to this goal as being strong enough to give them considerable leverage in dealing with it. Diem's period of residence in the United States had occurred during the height of McCarthyism, and he had developed some understanding of the importance of anticommunism in American domestic politics and the relevance of the "loss of China" issue to the Eisenhower administration's anticommunist stance in Vietnam; some Americans who worked with him presumably tutored him further in these matters. In any case, his vital economic and military reliance on the United States tended to be offset significantly by the dependence of the administration in Washington on his survival, measured not only in its perceived global strategic requirements and ideological commitment, but also in terms of domestic American political calculations. From this dependency sprang the apt and much-quoted characterization by journalist Homer Bigart of American policy during most of Diem's governance: "Sink or Swim with Ngo Dinh Diem." The tacit conditionality of American assistance expressed in Eisenhower's October 1954 letter to Diem was soon forgotten, and American expectations that aid would be "met by performance on the part of the Government of Vietnam in undertaking needed reforms" became muted, and were largely disregarded by Diem.

American officials continued to hope that Diem would broaden his political base, but this did not occur despite their exhortation and the enormous public-relations effort made in his behalf in Vietnam by the United States Information Service. Though for most of his nine years in power Diem was favorably treated in much of the American press, particularly the Luce publications (*Time* and *Life*), and publicly praised by many officials, internal U.S. government memoranda soon took a more realistic view. As early as July 1956 the NSC's National Coordinating Board referred to the autocratic nature of Diem's regime and saw its "continued trend toward centralized authority" as resulting in the "alienation of potential supporters." Thanks to the weight of American backing, however, it was another four years before the repressiveness of Diem's rule precipitated a strong enough political reaction, running across most of the South Vietnamese political spectrum, to challenge him seriously.

The Failure of Vietnamization

RONALD H. SPECTOR

By 1957 the United States appeared well on the way to achieving its aims in South Vietnam. The government of Ngo Dinh Diem had vanquished the armies of the sects and the Binh Xuyen and had successfully defied North Vietnam on the issue of national elections. In July 1955 Diem had refused even to consult with the Democratic Republic of Vietnam on the subject. The Republic of Vietnam, said Diem, was in no way bound by the Geneva Agreements. His government had declined to adhere to them and, while eager for a "reunification in freedom," would consider no proposals from a regime which subordinated the national interest to the interests of communism.

The United States had never had much enthusiasm for the elections, believing that North Vietnam would never permit a really free expression of political views. Privately, many American officials also acknowledged that even a relatively "fair" election would almost certainly result in a lopsided victory for North Vietnam. Its larger population and superior political organization and control would weigh heavily in favor of the North, as would the personal prestige of Ho Chi Minh and a continuing popular identification of the Viet Minh with nationalism. As a State Department expert on Vietnam observed, the Diem government would "be campaigning against the massive fact of Viet Minh victory, against ubiquitous Viet Minh infiltration, and against the knowledge, shared even by illiterate coolies, that there would be no such independence as now exists had it not been for the Viet Minh." Nevertheless, the United States could hardly oppose or openly obstruct the holding of nationwide elections. To do so would contradict the traditional American stand that nations divided against their will, such as Germany and Korea, should be reunited through free elections supervised by the United Nations. This position had been reiterated by the American representative at Geneva, Walter Bedell Smith. There was also the possibility that the Communists might again resort to arms if elections were denied or postponed.

Eisenhower and his advisers never adopted a firm policy on the question of elections. In general, Washington leaders saw them as something to be delayed rather than eliminated. They counseled Diem to consult about elections, as required by the Geneva Agreements, but then to stall by insisting that elections be held only when, as the agreements specified, "all necessary conditions obtain for a free expression of national will." In the meantime the Diem government would presumably build up the popular support necessary to win the elections, should they take place. When Diem instead opted simply to have nothing to do with elections, the United States, impressed with his recent successes, went along with little protest. Although the Democratic Republic of Vietnam appealed to the cochairmen of the Geneva Conference—Britain and the Soviet Union—and hinted at renewed military action if the elections were not held, the July 1956 deadline for opening consultations passed without incident.

Early in 1957 Diem came to the United States aboard President Eisenhower's personal plane to be hailed everywhere as the savior of Southeast Asia. The South Vietnamese president addressed a joint session of Congress and paid a ceremonial visit to New York, where Mayor Robert F. Wagner pronounced him "a man history may yet adjudge as one of the great figures of the twentieth century." Senator John F. Kennedy referred to South Vietnam as "the cornerstone of the Free World in Southeast Asia, the keystone to the arch, the finger in the dike." The *Saturday Evening Post* called Diem the "mandarin in a sharkskin suit who's upsetting the Red timetable."

Yet even while Diem was receiving those accolades in the United States, members of the country team in Saigon were reaching different conclusions about the achievements of the South Vietnamese government. During the fall of 1957 Ambassador Durbrow, U.S. Operations Mission Chief Leland Barrows, Embassy Counselor Thomas D. Bowie, and Economic Affairs Officer Wesley Haroldson prepared a report sharply critical of the character and policies of the Diem regime. They described Diem as a man unable to delegate responsibility: "He overrides most of his Ministers, reduces their authority, and assumes personal responsibility for the smallest details of government. He is inclined to be suspicious of others; he lacks an understanding of basic economic principles." Economic development and agrarian reform had been neglected while the president concentrated on pet projects related to security. In the countryside, discontent with the government was increasing, and internal security was expected to decline. In the more sophisticated urban areas, there was considerable resentment and fear of Diem's covert Can Lao Party, which, the officials noted, had managed to infiltrate almost all political, social welfare, journalistic, cultural, and other public activities.

Other members of the country team including the CIA station chief and the Army, Navy, and Air Force attaches endorsed the report in general, but [Lieutenant General Samuel T.] Williams [Chief of the U.S. Military Assistance Advisory Group in Vietnam] dissented. He believed that in order to retain Diem's confidence and cooperation it was imperative to avoid associating with his critics and enemies. "Otherwise we would go the way of the French." General Williams also doubted that the situation was as serious as the report indicated. "The receipt [in Washington] of the proposed dispatch," he warned Ambassador Durbrow, "would unquestionably cause alarm and unnecessary concern . . . the reports I have seen do not indicate a state of considerable concern regarding internal security, the economic situation, or the executive ability of the government of Viet Nam." In a lengthy and heated discussion with other members of the country team, Williams insisted that he was unable to "subscribe to the idea that the president was on the way to failure." Even after persuading the foreign service officers to moderate the tone of their report, he refused to concur in its conclusion.

The months to come were to show that the country team had been, if anything, too mild in its criticism of the Diem government. From observing Diem on numerous trips and inspection tours, General Williams had become convinced that the president was extraordinarily popular, but that popularity turned out to be largely a sham. The American consul at Hue, for example, observed that the villagers who were often paraded out to participate in ceremonies honoring Diem and to make appropriate responses to slogans "have virtually no concept of what they are doing." As a British journalist noted, "Diem holds the fort through the Army and the police force provided by U.S. [money]. It is not that the communists have done nothing because Diem is in power, rather Diem has remained in power because the communists have done nothing." . . .

'Although American civilian officials were critical of both the road-building and resettlement projects, they pointed with pride to another South Vietnamese program: land reform. In the summer of 1959, for example,

Ambassador Durbrow told a U.S. Senate subcommittee that the South Vietnamese government was carrying out "the largest land reform program in Asia."

Land reform was clearly a subject of importance in a country where 75 to 80 percent of the population lived in rural areas and large landholdings by absentee landlords were commonplace. The problem was most acute in the Mekong Delta region, where a majority of the rural population owned no land and a small but extremely wealthy class of absentee landlords held much of the fertile land. Most peasants rented land on a sharecropping basis, with the drawbacks attendant to such a system. To a landlord who provided no credit, seed, or fertilizer, the peasant paid one-third to one-half of the expected yield; in the event of crop failure, the landlord still had the right to demand his share of the normal yield.

During the long war against the French, the Viet Minh had driven away or killed many landlords and turned over their land to the poorer peasants. Instead of accepting that situation, the Diem government restored land to the landlords and then tried to regulate the extent of their landholdings and the landlord-tenant relationship. In 1955 the Diem government passed an ordinance setting a maximum of 15 to 25 percent of a crop as the lawful rent, and the following year limited individual landholdings to 247 acres. Acreage exceeding that maximum was to be purchased by the government and sold in small parcels to tenants, laborers, and other landless persons. Whether or not this constituted "the largest land reform program in Asia," it was certainly one of the most conservative. Landlords were allowed to select the lands to be retained, and the 247-acre limit was far greater than that allowed in Japan or Korea. In many provinces peasants were granted the right to purchase land that they had already been given by the Viet Minh. Although the government established loans to enable penniless peasants to buy land, its rigorous enforcement of repayment provisions often resulted in hardship. In Kien Phong Province, for example, farmers were forced to sell their rice at slump prices to meet loan payments. One farmer was reportedly "placed in a cage too small to stand up in and had to remain there until his wife sold their oxen" to pay the loan.

The implementation of the land reform program was so ensnarled in red tape and legalisms that in many areas relatively little land actually changed hands. In one province in the Mekong Delta, the first land redistribution took place only in 1958, almost two years after the land reform law was established. A 1960 census showed that only 23 percent of the farmers in the Mekong Delta owned any land at all, and about 56 percent of those lived on two-acre farms, one acre of which was rented.

Aside from the government's failure in land reform, rural residents were also affected adversely by a strongly promoted "anti-Communist campaign" mounted during 1955 and 1956 against known and suspected members and ex-members of the Viet Minh. The Viet Minh leaders had left Geneva confident that Vietnam would soon be unified under their control either through the scheduled elections or through the precipitate collapse of the South Vietnamese government. Following the Geneva Conference the Communist leadership began actively to prepare for a campaign of political agitation and propagandizing in the South. They summoned many former Viet Minh soldiers and cadres to regroup in North Vietnam while those who remained behind, an estimated 10,000 active agents, began to agitate for elections and reunion with the North. Mass meetings in the villages were organized by Communist cadres who harangued the crowds about "the victory of Geneva." In many villages in the south and southwest, photos of Ho Chi Minh and copies of the Geneva Agreements appeared on the wall of every house. In Saigon and other large cities the insurgents made a determined effort to win over non-Communist leftists, students, and intellectuals through such ostensibly patriotic organizations as the Saigon-Cholon Peace Movement.

The Diem government responded with the Anti-Communist Denunciation Campaign and with armed action against Viet Minh–led organizations and demonstrations. Although the campaign did considerable damage to the Viet Minh's civilian infrastructure, it was conducted in such a brutal, corrupt, and capricious manner that it alienated large segments of the population. Even former members of the Communist Party who were inactive or no longer loyal to the Viet Minh and former Viet Minh who had never been Communists were harassed, arrested, and in some cases executed. In some areas, families with sons who had gone to North Vietnam following the Geneva Agreements or who had relatives involved in insurgent activities were also affected. "Not only were local officials and police agents frequently incompetent at singling out the active Viet Minh agents, but many were also arrogant and venal in the execution of their tasks and by their offensive behavior generated sympathy for the Viet Minh." In one province, villagers could be jailed simply for having been in a rebel district. The people especially resented a curfew, which hampered fishermen and farmers, and a compulsory unpaid labor program to improve roads and perform other public works.

Despite the disruption to Communist Party organizations in many hamlets and districts, party cadres and innocent victims of the purges could often make their way to jungle, swamp, or mountain areas where they easily evaded government forces. By alienating large numbers of non-Communist and neutral peasants, the heavy-handed campaign also made it easy for the Viet Minh to rebuild their organizations and recruit new members.

Nevertheless, the campaign's short-run impact on the Communist apparatus in South Vietnam was severe. By early 1955 most Viet Minh cadres who had escaped arrest had been driven underground, and Communist-organized demonstrations had become infrequent. With many of its military forces regrouped in the North the party was in a poor position to meet the vigorous onslaught of the South Vietnamese government.

Pressure from the Diem government, combined with disappointment at the cancellation of the hoped-for elections, probably led to a decline in membership and morale in the party. At a meeting of top party leaders in the South in March 1956 Le Duan, Secretary of the Central Committee's

Directorate for South Vietnam, expressed strong dissatisfaction with the North Vietnamese government's policy, which emphasized political agitation in the South and diplomatic pressure on the former Geneva conferees. The only way to achieve reunification, said Le Duan, was to wage armed struggle against the Diem regime.

Yet in 1956 many North Vietnamese leaders were reluctant to become involved in a renewed war, wanting first to "build socialism" in North Vietnam. War would retard development and would carry with it a risk of American intervention. Communist leaders in South Vietnam continued to object to that policy, preferring to proceed with overthrowing the Diem regime before Diem became fully established.

Finally Le Duan offered a compromise. In a pamphlet entitled *On the Revolution in South Vietnam* he argued for a long-term approach to the problem of South Vietnam which, while continuing political agitation and subversion, would also lay the groundwork for a future armed uprising against Diem. Le Duan's arguments were favorably received at the Eleventh Plenum of the Central Committee in December 1956.

By 1957, when Le Duan was recalled to fill a senior party position in North Vietnam, a campaign of terrorism and subversion had begun in the South without direct support from the North. During much of this time, Communist units consciously avoided contact with government forces, concentrating instead upon *tru gian* ("the extermination of traitors"), a systematic program of assassination of government officials and anyone considered an obstacle to the movement. In some provinces special assassination squads of about half a dozen men were formed solely for this purpose. Any village official or government functionary was considered a legitimate target for *tru gian*. "In principle," explained a former party leader in Dinh Tuong Province, "the Party tried to kill any [government] official who enjoyed the people's sympathy and left the bad officials unharmed in order to wage propaganda and sow hatred against the government." At times the insurgents terrorized or executed even persons known to be innocent of any pro-government activity to encourage anxiety and distrust among the villages. . . .

Incidents involving insurgents increased throughout 1957 and into 1958. During January 1957, Communist guerrillas clashed with South Vietnamese Army troops seven times in the Mekong Delta provinces. The following month a Viet Cong force of about thirty men attacked a government civic action team in the village of Tri Binh, fifteen miles south of Tay Ninh; the entire team was killed or wounded, and the local government militia force took no action against the raiders. During a single month in the autumn of 1957, 22 village notables and other local government officials were killed or wounded by the Viet Cong, 6 village chiefs were killed, and 11 members of local militia were killed and 14 kidnapped. During the last quarter of 1957 some 140 armed attacks and terrorist acts were reported throughout the country in addition to more than 50 skirmishes initiated by government troops or security forces. Terrorists wounded, assassinated, or killed at least 74 persons, including 20 government officials and 31 police and security personnel.

The Communists concentrated their armed activities in the southern provinces, mainly in the more rugged and inaccessible region along the Cambodian border where the terrain favored concealment and ambush. Toward late 1957 and early 1958 an increasing number of incidents were also reported on the outskirts of medium-sized towns such as Tan An, Can Tho, My Tho, Soc Trang, Rach Gia, and Ca Mau. Although the insurgents were either new recruits to or veterans of the Viet Minh, the Diem government for propaganda purposes renamed them Viet Cong, a derogatory term meaning Vietnamese Communists. By mid-1957 the name had come into general use.

Despite those developments and other signs that the tempo of insurgent activity was quickening, General Williams saw no reason for alarm. "There are no indications of a resumption of large-scale guerrilla warfare at this date," he told Ambassador Durbrow at the end of 1957. "They [the Viet Cong] lack sufficient strength, do not have a popular base and are faced with a central government whose efficiency to deal with the subversion threat has gradually improved since its inception." He estimated the Viet Cong's combat strength in the central provinces at no more than 1,000 including sect forces, plus around 200 political and propaganda cadres. Williams made this assessment of the situation based on the limited information available to him. The Military Assistance Advisory Group had no intelligence unit, so that in the main General Williams had to depend on South Vietnamese sources for information about the insurgents. . . .

While Americans and Vietnamese in Saigon argued over the question of paramilitary forces, the security situation in the countryside continued to deteriorate. Because travel through most parts of South Vietnam was safe and because Viet Cong units continued to avoid South Vietnamese Army units and fortified government positions of any strength, American officials long failed to detect the full extent of the deterioration. Yet signs were there. Early in 1958 South Vietnamese officials notified the advisory group that there were extensive Viet Cong supply trails in the western parts of the northern provinces of Quang Nam and Thua Thien, and along the Laotian border. During a single week in February in An Xuyen Province at the southern tip of South Vietnam, a Viet Cong company of about a hundred men attacked a government post in the town of Thoi Binh; a force of equal size attacked the town of Hung My; and a small South Vietnamese Army patrol was wiped out in an ambush near the town of Ganh Hao. The American embassy observed that "in many remote areas the central government has no effective control."

The Viet Cong were reportedly most active in the region of the Plain of Reeds adjoining the Cambodian border, which included portions of Kien Phong and Kien Tuong Provinces; the old sect strongholds of Tay Ninh, Binh Long, Phuoc Long, Bien Hoa, Binh Duong, Long Khanh, and Phuoc Tuy Provinces; and the Ca Mau peninsula at the southern tip of the country.

The CIA estimated that, together with the remnants of the sect forces, the Viet Cong by early 1958 had an armed strength of some 1,700 men. By the spring there were reports of Viet Cong units operating out of small posts in heavily wooded areas north of Saigon. In June a Viet Cong force of from twenty to fifty men attacked a government detention center at Pleiku in the Central Highlands, releasing some fifty prisoners, many of them "known communists," while incurring no casualties. Diem attributed the failure to the fact that many of the prison guards were Montagnard tribesmen.

Although General Williams could hardly have been unaware of increasing Viet Cong pressure, he remained convinced that countering insurgency was not the primary business of the South Vietnamese Army. "A division on pacification duty goes to pieces fast," he observed. "The guerrillas go underground and soon the troops start sitting around on bridges and in market places and go to pot." When Vice President Nguyen Ngoc Tho warned Diem that the wave of terrorism and assassination was demoralizing the country, Williams insisted that using army units for security operations "is exactly what the communists want us to do." With division maneuvers scheduled to begin in the early spring of 1958, he observed: "If I were Giap, the first thing I would try to do would be to try to prevent these division maneuvers."

Despite Williams' misgivings the South Vietnamese government responded to the increased Viet Cong activity with a major military effort. For the first time Vietnamese Army units penetrated traditional Communist base areas in the Plain of Reeds, in the Ca Mau peninsula, and in War Zone D, the area northeast of Saigon. Many of these operations were slow and ponderous. In the Ca Mau peninsula a battalion of Vietnamese marines was able to capture some Viet Cong suspects and locate hidden caches of food but soon discovered that the Viet Cong had withdrawn to a strongpoint in the vast swamp and salt marsh immediately behind the western tip of the peninsula. The attackers could approach the enemy strongpoint only by a water route that would lead them directly along the line of fire of the defending Viet Cong. At that point the operation ground to a halt while the battalion commander negotiated with the military region commander and the South Vietnamese Air Force for air strikes.

Although slow and indecisive, the government's operations certainly dealt a heavy blow to the Viet Cong. Party membership in the South, which had stood at some 5,000 in mid-1957, fell to about one-third that level by the end of the year. Official party histories refer to the period of late 1958–early 1959 as "the darkest period" of the struggle in the South, a period when "the enemy . . . truly and efficiently destroyed our Party. . . . The political struggle movement of the masses although not defeated was encountering increasing difficulty and increasing weakness, the party bases, although not completely destroyed, were significantly weakened and in some areas quite seriously." In Gia Dinh Province party membership declined from more than 1,000 in mid-1954, to 385 in mid-1957, to about 6 in mid-1959.

By the end of 1958 surviving party cadres in many parts of South Vietnam had apparently decided, on their own initiative, to escalate the struggle beyond armed propaganda and assassinations even though this violated the party line. Armed units were formed into companies or battalions usually numbering less than one hundred men, armed with rifles, grenades, light machine guns, and sometimes merely pikes.

The renewed Viet Cong activity was most intense in War Zone D, a heavily forested region about fifty kilometers northeast of Saigon. Here Viet Cong units no longer always retreated from South Vietnamese Army forces of equal or inferior strength. During March 1959 there were at least ten firefights between army troops and the Viet Cong in which thirteen government soldiers were killed, wounded, or reported missing; five rifles, two automatic weapons, and a jeep were destroyed. In May 1959 a Viet Cong force occupying high ground in War Zone D, northeast of the town of Bien Hoa, successfully stood off attacks by an entire army battalion, then disengaged before the government troops could bring up artillery.

The Party Central Committee had meanwhile convened its fifteenth plenum in January 1959. At the urging of Le Duan, who had just completed an inspection tour of the South, and of other southern Communist leaders the Central Committee adopted a resolution endorsing the use of armed force to overthrow the Diem regime. By May 1959 new directives were on their way from Hanoi to party leaders in the South. Insurgents, specially trained in the North, were infiltrated back into South Vietnam. A new Central Committee Directorate for South Vietnam was established, and communication routes into the South through Laos were improved and expanded. A new stage in the long struggle for South Vietnam had begun. . . .

Many people have come to regard the French Indochina War (1946–1954) as a rehearsal for the Vietnam War (1965–1973). Similarly, the early advisory period (1955–1960) to a degree foreshadows the period of Vietnamization during the Nixon and Ford administrations. True, there were important differences. The Military Assistance Advisory Group under Generals O'Daniel and Williams labored under advantages and disadvantages unknown to its successors in the 1960s and 1970s. The advantages were relative peace and calm in the countryside, especially from 1956 to 1958, and a relatively strong, stable civil government in Saigon. The disadvantages were the restrictions imposed by the Geneva Agreements on the size and activities of the military advisory effort, the strong budgetary constraints of the Eisenhower era, and the lack of attention and interest on the part of Washington leaders to the problems of Vietnam between 1956 and 1960. Another important difference was that in the Vietnamization years the United States was phasing down its military and civilian involvement. During the late 1950s, the degree of American involvement was relatively stable.

Yet despite the differences the two periods share a common overriding theme. In both the early advisory stage and the later period of Vietnamization, American leaders were attempting to help the Vietnamese armed forces attain an ability to hold their own against their enemies without the assistance of large numbers of U.S. or other allied ground forces. In the 1950s this policy was precipitated by the rapid withdrawal of French combat forces from Vietnam and the inability of American forces to replace them because of limitations imposed by the Geneva Agreements and the New Look defense policy of the Eisenhower administration.

In both cases the Vietnamization effort ended in failure. The reasons for the failure of the second Vietnamization are still being assessed; the reasons for the failure of the first are easier to delineate. In the 1950s American military aims in Vietnam were never clearly defined. Although many Washington leaders believed that Communist subversion was a greater threat to South Vietnam than an overt, large-scale invasion, U.S. contingency planning tended to emphasize the latter. The chiefs of the Military Assistance Advisory Group therefore understandably tended to concentrate on building an army geared to resist attack from the North. In doing so they were merely following contemporary thinking, for in the 1950s, in contrast to the 1960s, there was little interest in, or knowledge of, counterinsurgency warfare within the U.S. armed forces.

The need for a capable security force to deal with the threat of internal subversion was not ignored. Yet responsibility for the training and equipping of paramilitary forces such as the Civil Guard and the Self-Defense Corps was vested not in the advisory group but in other agencies of the U.S. country team, agencies which differed radically in their view of the proper mission, composition, and employment of these forces. This disagreement was further complicated by delays, bureaucratic infighting, and personality clashes. The result was that when insurgency once again became a serious threat in 1959, the paramilitary forces were still unprepared, untrained, and unequipped to cope with it.

Consequently, the Vietnamese Army had to be directly committed against the Communist insurgents. Its indifferent performance in combat against the Viet Cong even after four years of U.S. support and training can be attributed to two sets of factors. The first involved weaknesses inherent in the Vietnamese Army as an institution. The rampant politicization in the higher ranks of the officer corps had enabled incompetent but politically reliable officers to attain and retain positions of responsibility and high command. An absence of unifying national spirit, motivation, or patriotism on the part of most Vietnamese soldiers reflected the lack of any widespread popular support for the Diem regime. Another factor was the poor security system of the army and its penetration at all levels by Viet Cong agents. Still another important element was the system of divided authority, routine insubordination, and overlapping responsibility deliberately fostered by Diem within the army's command system to ensure that no military leader became too powerful. Added to this pattern was the inadequate technical competence of the Vietnamese combat soldier, who was often a recent conscript whose training had been interrupted or never started. Contemporary critics also pointed to the lack of specific training for guerrilla warfare, yet the Vietnamese Army's level of proficiency in basic combat skills was often so low as to make the question of specialized training irrelevant.

At the same time, the very organization, composition, and outlook of the Military Assistance Advisory Group ensured that the American advisers would remain either unaware of these inherent deficiencies or powerless to change them. The so-called short tour limited most U.S. advisers to less than eleven months in which to win the confidence of their Vietnamese counterparts and influence them to take needed measures to increase the effectiveness of their units. A wide gap in customs and culture also separated the advisers from their counterparts, a gap made wider by the small number of American officers able to communicate in any language other than English.

The limited ability of U.S. advisers to influence their counterparts holds true even for General Williams. He enjoyed President Diem's trust and confidence to an extent probably equaled by few other Americans, yet Williams' remark that "I can't remember one time that President Diem ever did anything of importance concerning the military that I recommended against" is surely an exaggeration. General Williams was unable to induce Diem to abandon favoritism in the appointment of officers, to rationalize the chain of command, or to abandon the project to create ranger battalions out of existing army formations. Moreover, Williams' closeness to Diem inclined him, in the view of some observers, to identify so closely with the president that he resisted and attempted to blunt all criticism of Diem, whether well founded or otherwise.

The success of an adviser was measured by his ability to influence his Vietnamese counterpart. Few were willing to report forthrightly that they had been unable to bring about needed reforms and improvements in the units to which they were assigned. Since the whole system of rating the performance of the Vietnamese Army was built upon the subjective, non-standardized evaluations made by the advisers and their superiors, Saigon and Washington were guaranteed a superficial assessment. The dogged "Can Do" attitude of most officers and noncommissioned officers who tended to see all faults in the army as correctable, all failures as temporary, only further contributed to overoptimistic reports.

Considering the small size of the Military Assistance Advisory Group and the many limitations imposed upon its activities, its accomplishments with the weak, demoralized, divided, and disorganized army it inherited in 1955 represent a remarkable achievement. The complete reorganization of the Vietnamese Army, the establishment of a well-conceived and comprehensive school and training system, and the introduction, at least on paper, of a rationalized chain of command were only a few of the advisory group's solid contributions. Yet the subsequent failure of the South Vietnamese Army as an effective fighting force can only underline the warning which the Joint Chiefs of Staff gave to Secretary of State Dulles in 1954: that strong and stable governments and societies are necessary to support the creation of strong armies. That the reverse is seldom true would be clearly and tragically demonstrated in the years to follow.

✗ *F U R T H E R   R E A D I N G*

Stephen E. Ambrose, *Eisenhower: The President* (1984)
David L. Anderson, "J. Lawton Collins, John Foster Dulles, and the Eisenhower Administration's 'Point of No Return' in Vietnam," *Diplomatic History*, 12 (1988), 149–163
Victor Bator, *Vietnam: A Diplomatic Tragedy* (1965)
Melanie Billings-Yun, *Decision Against War: Eisenhower and Dien Bien Phu, 1954* (1988)
Philippe Devillers and Jean Lacouture, *End of a War: Indochina, 1954* (1969)
Robert A. Divine, *Eisenhower and the Cold War* (1981)
Bernard B. Fall, *Hell in a Very Small Place* (1966)
Russell H. Fifield, *Southeast Asia in United States Policy* (1963)
Lloyd C. Gardner, *Approaching Vietnam* (1988)
Melvin Gurtov, *The First Vietnam Crisis* (1967)
Ellen J. Hammer, *The Struggle for Indochina* (1966)
Gabriel Kolko, *Anatomy of a War* (1985)
Edward Geary Lansdale, *In the Midst of Wars* (1972)
Peter Lyon, *Eisenhower* (1974)
Robert J. McMahon, "Eisenhower and Third World Nationalism: A Critique of the Revisionists," *Political Science Quarterly*, 101 (1986), 453–73
Richard A. Melanson and David Mayers, eds., *Reevaluating Eisenhower* (1987)
Robert F. Randle, *Geneva 1954* (1969)
Chalmers M. Roberts, "The Day We Didn't Go to War," *Reporter*, 11 (September 14, 1954), 31–35
Jules Roy, *The Battle of Dienbienphu* (1965)
R. B. Smith, *Revolution Versus Containment* (1983)

CHAPTER
5

John F. Kennedy and Vietnam: Incremental Escalation

The administration of John F. Kennedy inherited an increasingly troublesome commitment in Vietnam, a land that the young president had once described as the "cornerstone of the Free World in Southeast Asia." Fearful that the United States had lost the global initiative to the Soviet Union and China, he was intent on pursuing a more activist foreign policy than his Republican predecessors. JFK especially sought to avoid additional cold war defeats. In the spring of 1961, he supported with some reluctance a negotiated settlement in Laos that would eventually lead to communist participation in a coalition government. Eager to avoid a similar compromise in Vietnam, where he believed the stakes were much greater, Kennedy gradually increased the American presence there. In November 1961 he ordered the dispatch of several thousand U.S. military advisers to help avert the collapse of the Diem government. Their number had swelled to more than 16,000 by the end of Kennedy's presidency in 1963. When Diem's regime tottered in late 1963 in the face of challenges by both Vietcong guerrillas and Buddhist protesters, American officials supported a coup led by a group of South Vietnamese military officers. In the wake of the coup, Diem was murdered. Within weeks, Kennedy himself would fall victim to an assassin's bullet.

JFK's role in the growing American involvement in Vietnam has sparked intense scholarly scrutiny. Most historians agree that his decisions brought incremental, but not dramatic, escalation and that he left his successors with deeper, but still limited, ties to South Vietnam. They differ on almost all other critical questions, including the underlying rationale for Kennedy's decisions, the significance of Vietnam to overall American foreign-policy objectives, the nature and strength of both Diem's regime and the Vietcong insurgency, the precise role of the United States in the coup against Diem, and the broader impact of Diem's ouster on the stability of South Vietnam and the U.S.-Vietnamese relationship.

✗ *D O C U M E N T S*

The opening document is a cable of November 1, 1961, sent to President Kennedy by his military adviser, General Maxwell Taylor, recommending the introduction of a U.S. military force into South Vietnam. In a November 11 memorandum to the president, the second document, Secretary of State Dean Rusk and Secretary of Defense Robert S. McNamara also urge the commitment of U.S. troops. They call for the speedy dispatch of support and advisory troops and the development of plans for the possible later commitment of combat forces. In the third document, Jan Barry, a U.S. Army radio technician who served in South Vietnam from December 1962 to October 1963, reflects on his experiences there.

A memorandum from Senator Mike Mansfield to Kennedy is the fourth document. Mansfield, an enthusiastic early supporter of Diem, questions the deepening American commitment in South Vietnam. On September 2, 1963, in a television interview with Walter Cronkite of CBS, Kennedy made a series of critical remarks about Diem's regime. One week later, he expressed similar dissatisfaction in another television interview while reiterating his belief in the domino theory. Kennedy's interviews appear in the fifth and sixth documents.

The next document is a cable of October 25, 1963, from Ambassador Henry Cabot Lodge in Saigon to national security adviser McGeorge Bundy speculating on the prospects for a coup against Diem. The plotters included South Vietnamese General Tran Van Don and CIA agent Lucien Conein. In an October 30 cable to Lodge, the eighth document, Bundy expresses some ambivalence about a U.S. role in any coup. The last document, a transcript of Diem's final telephone conversation with Lodge, records the prime minister's fears for his safety after the outbreak of the rebellion in Saigon.

Maxwell Taylor Recommends the Dispatch of U.S. Forces, 1961

This message is for the purpose of presenting my reasons for recommending the introduction of a U.S. military force into SVN. I have reached the conclusion that this is an essential action if we are to reverse the present downward trend of events in spite of a full recognition of the following disadvantages:

a. The strategic reserve of U.S. forces is presently so weak that we can ill afford any detachment of forces to a peripheral area of the Communist bloc where they will be pinned down for an uncertain duration.

b. Although U.S. prestige is already engaged in SVN, it will become more so by the sending of troops.

c. If the first contingent is not enough to accomplish the necessary results, it will be difficult to resist the pressure to reinforce. If the ultimate result sought is the closing of the frontiers and the clean-up of the insurgents within SVN, there is no limit to our possible commitment (unless we attack the source in Hanoi).

d. The introduction of U.S. forces may increase tensions and risk escalation into a major war in Asia.

On the other side of the argument, there can be no action so convincing of U.S. seriousness of purpose and hence so reassuring to the people and Government of SVN and to our other friends and allies in SEA as the introduction of U.S. forces into SVN. The views of indigenous and U.S. officials consulted on our trip were unanimous on this point. I have just seen Saigon [cable] 575 to State and suggest that it be read in connection with this message.

The size of the U.S. force introduced need not be great to provide the military presence necessary to produce the desired effect on national morale in SVN and on international opinion. A bare token, however, will not suffice; it must have a significant value. The kinds of tasks which it might undertake which would have a significant value are suggested in Baguio [cable] 0005. They are:

a. Provide a U.S. military presence capable of raising national morale and of showing to SEA the seriousness of the U.S. intent to resist a Communist takeover.

b. Conduct logistical operations in support of military and flood relief operations.

c. Conduct such combat operations as are necessary for self-defense and for the security of the area in which they are stationed.

d. Provide an emergency reserve to back up the Armed Forces of the GVN [Government of (South) Vietnam] in the case of a heightened military crisis.

e. Act as an advance party of such additional forces as may be introduced if CINCPAC [U.S. Commander in Chief, Pacific] or SEATO [Southeast Asia Treaty Organization] contingency plans are invoked.

It is noteworthy that this force is not proposed to clear the jungles and forests of VC guerrillas. That should be the primary task of the Armed Forces of Vietnam for which they should be specifically organized, trained and stiffened with ample U.S. advisors down to combat battalion levels. However, the U.S. troops may be called upon to engage in combat to protect themselves, their working parties, and the area in which they live. As a general reserve, they might be thrown into action (with U.S. agreement) against large, formed guerrilla bands which have abandoned the forests for attacks on major targets. But in general, our forces should not engage in small-scale guerrilla operations in the jungle.

As an area for the operations of U.S. troops, SVN is not an excessively difficult or unpleasant place to operate. While the border areas are rugged and heavily forested, the terrain is comparable to parts of Korea where U.S. troops learned to live and work without too much effort. However, these border areas, for reasons stated above, are not the places to engage our forces. In the High Plateau and in the coastal plain where U.S. troops would probably be stationed, these jungle-forest conditions do not exist to any great extent. The most unpleasant feature in the coastal areas would be the heat and, in the Delta, the mud left behind by the flood. The High Plateau offers no particular obstacle to the stationing of U.S. troops.

The extent to which the Task Force would engage in flood relief activities in the Delta will depend upon further study of the problem there. As reported in Saigon 537, I see considerable advantages in playing up this aspect of the TF mission. I am presently inclined to favor a dual mission, initially help to the flood area and subsequently use in any other area of SVN where its resources can be used effectively to give tangible support in the struggle against the VC. However, the possibility of emphasizing the humanitarian mission will wane if we wait long in moving in our forces or in linking our stated purpose with the emergency conditions created by the flood.

The risks of backing into a major Asian war by way of SVN are present but are not impressive. NVN is extremely vulnerable to conventional bombing, a weakness which should be exploited diplomatically in convincing Hanoi to lay off SVN. Both the D.R.V. and the Chicoms [Chinese communists] would face severe logistical difficulties in trying to maintain strong forces in the field in SEA, difficulties which we share but by no means to the same degree. There is no case for fearing a mass onslaught of Communist manpower into SVN and its neighboring states, particularly if our airpower is allowed a free hand against logistical targets. Finally, the starvation conditions in China should discourage Communist leaders there from being militarily venturesome for some time to come.

By the foregoing line of reasoning, I have reached the conclusion that the introduction of [word illegible] military Task Force without delay offers definitely more advantage than it creates risks and difficulties. In fact, I do not believe that our program to save SVN will succeed without it. If the concept is approved, the exact size and composition of the force should be determined by Sec Def in consultation with the JCS, the Chief MAAG [Military Assistance Advisory Group] and CINCPAC. My own feeling is that the initial size should not exceed about 8000, of which a preponderant number would be in logistical-type units. After acquiring experience in operating in SVN, this initial force will require reorganization and adjustment to the local scene.

As CINCPAC will point out, any forces committed to SVN will need to be replaced by additional forces to his area from the strategic reserve in the U.S. Also, any troops to SVN are in addition to those which may be required to execute SEATO Plan 5 in Laos. Both facts should be taken into account in current considerations of the FY [fiscal year] 1963 budget which bear upon the permanent increase which should be made in the U.S. military establishment to maintain our strategic position for the long pull.

Dean Rusk and Robert S. McNamara's Alternative Plan, 1961

1. United States National Interests in South Viet-Nam.

The deteriorating situation in South Viet-Nam requires attention to the nature and scope of United States national interests in that country. The loss of South Viet-Nam to Communism would involve the transfer of a nation of 20 million people from the free world to the Communist bloc.

The loss of South Viet-Nam would make pointless any further discussion about the importance of Southeast Asia to the free world; we would have to face the near certainty that the remainder of Southeast Asia and Indonesia would move to a complete accommodation with Communism, if not formal incorporation with the Communist bloc. The United States, as a member of SEATO, has commitments with respect to South Viet-Nam under the Protocol to the SEATO Treaty. Additionally, in a formal statement at the conclusion session of the 1954 Geneva Conference, the United States representative stated that the United States "would view any renewal of the aggression . . . with grave concern and seriously threatening international peace and security."

The loss of South Viet-Nam to Communism would not only destroy SEATO but would undermine the credibility of American commitments elsewhere. Further, loss of South Viet-Nam would stimulate bitter domestic controversies in the United States and would be seized upon by extreme elements to divide the country and harass the Administration. . . .

3. The United States' Objective in South Viet-Nam.

The United States should commit itself to the clear objective of preventing the fall of South Viet-Nam to Communist [sic]. The basic means for accomplishing this objective must be to put the Government of South Viet-Nam into a position to win its own war against the Guerillas. We must insist that that Government itself take the measures necessary for that purpose in exchange for large-scale United States assistance in the military, economic and political fields. At the same time we must recognize that it will probably not be possible for the GVN to win this war as long as the flow of men and supplies from North Viet-Nam continues unchecked and the guerillas enjoy a safe sanctuary in neighboring territory.

We should be prepared to introduce United States combat forces if that should become necessary for success. Dependent upon the circumstances, it may also be necessary for United States forces to strike at the source of the aggression in North Viet-Nam.

4. The Use of United States Forces in South Viet-Nam.

The commitment of United States forces to South Viet-Nam involves two different categories: (A) Units of modest size required for the direct support of South Viet-Namese military effort, such as communications, helicopter and other forms of airlift, reconnaissance aircraft, naval patrols, intelligence units, etc., and (B) larger organized units with actual or potential direct military mission. *Category (A) should be introduced as speedily as possible.* Category (B) units pose a more serious problem in that they are much more significant from the point of view of domestic and international political factors and greatly increase the probabilities of Communist bloc escalation. Further, the employment of United States combat forces (in the absence of Communist bloc escalation) involves a certain dilemma: if there is a strong South-Vietnamese effort, they may not be needed; if there is not such an effort, United States forces could not accomplish their mission in the midst of an apathetic or hostile population. Under present circumstances, therefore, the question of injecting United States and SEATO combat forces should in large part be considered as a contribution to the morale of the South Vietnamese in their own effort to do the principal job themselves.

4. Probable Extent of the Commitment of United States Forces.

If we commit Category (B) forces to South Viet-Nam, the ultimate possible extent of our military commitment in Southeast Asia must be faced. The struggle may be prolonged, and Hanoi and Peiping may overtly intervene. It is the view of the Secretary of Defense and the Joint Chiefs of Staff that, in the light of the logistic difficulties faced by the other side, we can assume that the maximum United States forces required on the ground in Southeast Asia would not exceed six divisions, or about 205,000 men (CINCPAC Plan 32/59 PHASE IV). This would be in addition to local forces and such SEATO forces as may be engaged. It is also the view of the Secretary of Defense and the Joint Chiefs of Staff that our military posture is, or, with the addition of more National Guard or regular Army divisions, can be made, adequate to furnish these forces and support them in action without serious interference with our present Berlin plans. . . .

In the light of the foregoing, the Secretary of State and the Secretary of Defense recommend that:

1. We now take the decision to commit ourselves to the objective of preventing the fall of South Viet-Nam to Communism and that, in doing so, we recognize that the introduction of United States and other SEATO forces may be necessary to achieve this objective. (However, if it is necessary to commit outside forces to achieve the foregoing objective our decision to introduce United States forces should not be contingent upon unanimous SEATO agreement thereto.)

2. The Department of Defense be prepared with plans for the use of United States forces in South Viet-Nam under one or more of the following purposes:

   a. Use of a significant number of United States forces to signify United States determination to defend Viet-Nam and to boost South Viet-Nam morale.

   b. Use of substantial United States forces to assist in suppressing Viet Cong insurgency short of engaging in detailed counter-guerrilla operations but including relevant operations in North Viet-Nam.

   c. Use of United States forces to deal with the situation if there is organized Communist military intervention.

3. We immediately undertake the following actions in support of the GVN:

   . . . c. Provide the GVN with small craft, including such United States uniformed advisers and operating personnel as may be necessary for quick and effective operations in effecting surveillance and control over coastal waters and inland waterways. . . .

   e. Provide such personnel and equipment as may be necessary to improve the military-political intelligence system beginning at the provincial level and extending upward through the Government and the armed forces to the Central Intelligence Organization.

   f. Provide such new terms of reference, reorganization and additional personnel for United States military forces as are required for increased United States participation in the direction and control of GVN military operations and to carry out the other increased responsibilities which accrue to MAAG under these recommendations. . . .

    i. Provide individual administrators and advisers for insertion into the Governmental machinery of South Viet-Nam in types and numbers to be agreed upon by the two Governments. . . .

5. Very shortly before the arrival in South Viet-Nam of the first increments of United States military personnel and equipment proposed under 3., above, that would exceed the Geneva Accord ceilings, publish the "Jorden report" [a report by State Department official William J. Jorden that was critical of Diem] as a United States "white paper," transmitting it as simultaneously as possible to the Governments of all countries with which we have diplomatic relations, including the Communist states.

6. Simultaneous with the publication of the "Jorden report," release an exchange of letters between Diem and the President.

    a. Diem's letter would include: reference to the DRV violations of Geneva Accords as set forth in the October 24 GVN letter to the ICC [International Control Commission] and other documents; pertinent references to GVN statements with respect to its intent to observe the Geneva Accords; reference to its need for flood relief and rehabilitation; reference to previous United States aid and the compliance hitherto by both countries with the Geneva Accords; reference to the USG statement at the time the Geneva Accords were signed; the necessity of now exceeding some provisions of the Accords in view of the DRV violations thereof; the lack of aggressive intent with respect to the DRV; GVN intent to return to strict compliance with the Geneva Accords as soon as the DRV violations ceased; and request for additional United States assistance in framework foregoing policy. The letter should also set forth in appropriate general terms steps Diem has taken and is taking to reform Governmental structure.

    b. The President's reply would be responsive to Diem's request for additional assistance and acknowledge and agree to Diem's statements on the intent promptly to return to strict compliance with the Geneva Accords as soon as DRV violations have ceased. . . .

An Early U.S. Army Adviser Remembers His Experiences (1962–1963), 1981

I was nineteen and turned twenty when I was there. I joined the Army in May of 1962 and was in Vietnam in December, just as I finished radio school. That was my first assignment. I could've had orders, as everyone else in the class did, to Germany. Two of us had orders to Vietnam. Before

From *Everything We Had* by Al Santoli, pp. 6–11. Copyright © 1981 by Albert Santoli and Vietnam Veterans of America. Reprinted by permission of Random House, Inc.

I even joined the Army I ran into a guy who'd graduated from high school a year or two ahead of me. He had just gotten out of the Army from Alaska. He said, "Wow, the place to go is Vietnam. You get combat pay in addition to overseas pay. You can really clean up." In the Army there was an undercurrent that there was someplace in the world where you could get combat pay. But there was no real discussion in the newspapers, as I can recall.

Some people in the unit had no conception where they were in the world, they didn't care. It wasn't Tennessee. It wasn't the state they came from. So therefore they had no interest in learning anything. Other people were very interested and learned Vietnamese and became very close with a number of Vietnamese people. At some point you began to realize that the people around the military base were clearly cooperating with the guerrillas because they were able to infiltrate the inside of our bases and we hadn't the faintest idea where the guerrillas were.

When the Buddhist demonstrations began against the Diem government [1963], it became very clear to most Americans there who probably hadn't been paying attention that we were supporting a police state which, against its own people who were peaceably having demonstrations, would turn loose tanks and machine guns and barbed wire all over the country. From May of '63 all through the summer we'd get caught up in them, just trying to walk around in civilian clothes to go to bars. . . .

The entire contingent of Americans in Vietnam was so thinly spread out that there probably weren't more than five hundred in any one place. Tan Son Nhut had the highest concentration. And it was becoming apparent that the ARVN [Army of the Republic of Vietnam] might turn on us. That became a real worry in the summer of 1963. It became rather apparent from discussion going on that there was going to be a coup. I recall going to Saigon several times and hearing this undercurrent in bars where Vietnamese officers would be.

I left Vietnam in mid-October 1963 and the coup happened two weeks later. One of the people who was still there said that the night before the coup took place they were told to get packed up, be ready to leave the country, be ready to blow up their equipment. At that point one of the options was to completely leave Vietnam. . . .

Almost no one in the Washington area knew we had anything like what was going on in Vietnam. Those of us who had been there wore our military patches on our right shoulders, which denoted that we had been in the war. Colonels would stop me and say, "What war have you been in, son? Where is that? We have people fighting over there?"

Mike Mansfield Questions American Policy, 1962

Even assuming that aid over a prolonged period would be available, the question still remains as to the capacity of the present Saigon government to carry out the task of social engineering. Ngo Dinh Diem remains a dedicated, sincere, hardworking, incorruptible and patriotic leader. But he is older and the problems which confront him are more complex than those which he faced when he pitted his genuine nationalism against, first, the French and Bao Dai and then against the sects with such effectiveness. The energizing role which he played in the past appears to be passing to other members of his family, particularly Ngo Dinh Nhu. The latter is a person of great energy and intellect who is fascinated by the operations of political power and has consummate eagerness and ability in organizing and manipulating it. But it is Ngo Dinh Diem, not Ngo Dinh Nhu, who has such popular mandate to exercise power as there is in south Vietnam. In a situation of this kind there is a great danger of the corruption of unbridled power. This has implications far beyond the persistent reports and rumors of fiscal and similar irregularities which are, in any event, undocumented. More important is its effect on the organization of the machinery for carrying out the new concepts. The difficulties in Vietnam are not likely to be overcome by a handful of paid retainers and sycophants. The success of the new approach in Vietnam presupposes a great contribution of initiative and self-sacrifice from a substantial body of Vietnamese with capacities for leadership at all levels. Whether that contribution can be obtained remains to be seen. For in the last analysis it depends upon a diffusion of political power, essentially in a democratic pattern. The trends in the political life of Vietnam have not been until now in that direction despite lip service to the theory of developing democratic and popular institutions "from the bottom up" through the strategic hamlet program.

To summarize, our policies and activities are designed to meet an existing set of internal problems in south Vietnam. North Vietnam infiltrates some supplies and cadres into the south; together with the Vietnamese we are trying to shut off this flow. The Vietcong has had the offensive in guerrilla warfare in the countryside; we are attempting to aid the Vietnamese military in putting them on the defensive with the hope of eventually reducing them at least to ineffectiveness. Finally, the Vietnamese peasants have sustained the Vietcong guerrillas out of fear, indifference or blandishment and we are helping the Vietnamese in an effort to win the peasants away by offering them the security and other benefits which may be provided in the strategic hamlets.

That, in brief, is the present situation. As noted, there is optimism that success will be achieved quickly. My own view is that the problems can be made to yield to present remedies, *provided* the problems and their magnitude do not change significantly and *provided* that the remedies are pursued by both Vietnamese and Americans (and particularly the former) with great vigor and self-dedication.

Certainly, if these remedies do not work, it is difficult to conceive of alternatives, with the possible exception of a truly massive commitment of American military personnel and other resources—in short going to war fully ourselves against the guerrillas—and the establishment of some form of neocolonial rule in south Vietnam. That is an alternative which I most emphatically do not recommend. On the contrary, it seems to me most essential that we make crystal clear to the Vietnamese government and to our own people that while we will go to great lengths to help, the primary responsibility rests with the Vietnamese. Our role is and must remain secondary in present circumstances. It is their country, their future which is most at stake, not ours.

To ignore that reality will not only be immensely costly in terms of American lives and resources but it may also draw us inexorably into some variation of the unenviable position in Vietnam which was formerly occupied by the French. We are not, of course, at that point at this time. But the great increase in American military commitment this year has tended to point us in that general direction and we may well begin to slide rapidly toward it if any of the present remedies begin to falter in practice.

As indicated, our planning appears to be predicated on the assumption that existing internal problems in South Vietnam will remain about the same and can be overcome by greater effort and better techniques. But what if the problems do not remain the same? To all outward appearances, little if any thought has been given in Saigon at least, to the possibilities of a change in the nature of the problems themselves. Nevertheless, they are very real possibilities and the initiative for instituting change rests in enemy hands largely because of the weakness of the Saigon government. The range of possible change includes a step-up in the infiltration of cadres and supplies by land or sea. It includes the use of part or all of the regular armed forces of North Vietnam, reported to be about 300,000 strong, under Vo Nguyen Giap. It includes, in the last analysis, the possibility of a major increase in any of many possible forms of Chinese Communist support for the Vietcong.

None of these possibilities may materialize. It would be folly, however, not to recognize their existence and to have as much clarification in advance of what our response to them will be if they do.

This sort of anticipatory thinking cannot be undertaken with respect to the situation in Vietnam alone. The problem there can be grasped, it seems to me, only as we have clearly in mind our interests with respect to all of Southeast Asia. If it is essential in our own interests to maintain a quasi-permanent position of power on the Asian mainland as against the Chinese then we must be prepared to continue to pay the present cost in Vietnam indefinitely and to meet any escalation on the other side with at least a commensurate escalation of commitment of our own. This can go very far, indeed, in terms of lives and resources. Yet if it is essential to our interests then we would have no choice.

But if on the other hand it is, at best, only desirable rather than essential that a position of power be maintained on the mainland, then other courses are indicated. We would, then, properly view such improvement as may be obtained by the new approach in Vietnam primarily in terms of what it might contribute to strengthening our diplomatic hand in the Southeast Asian region. And we would use that hand as vigorously as possible and in every way possible not to deepen our costly involvement on the Asian mainland but to lighten it.

John F. Kennedy Criticizes the South Vietnamese Government, 1963

Mr. Cronkite: Mr. President, the only hot war we've got running at the moment is of course the one in Viet-Nam, and we have our difficulties there, quite obviously.

The President: I don't think that unless a greater effort is made by the Government to win popular support that the war can be won out there. In the final analysis, it is their war. They are the ones who have to win it or lose it. We can help them, we can give them equipment, we can send our men out there as advisers, but they have to win it, the people of Viet-Nam, against the Communists.

We are prepared to continue to assist them, but I don't think that the war can be won unless the people support the effort and, in my opinion, in the last 2 months, the government has gotten out of touch with the people.

The repressions against the Buddhists, we felt, were very unwise. Now all we can do is to make it very clear that we don't think this is the way to win. It is my hope that this will become increasingly obvious to the government, that they will take steps to try to bring back popular support for this very essential struggle.

Mr. Cronkite: Do you think this government still has time to regain the support of the people?

The President: I do. With changes in policy and perhaps with personnel I think it can. If it doesn't make those changes, I would think that the chances of winning it would not be very good.

Mr. Cronkite: Hasn't every indication from Saigon been that President Diem has no intention of changing his pattern?

The President: If he does not change it, of course, that is his decision. He has been there 10 years and, as I say, he has carried this burden when he has been counted out on a number of occasions.

Our best judgment is that he can't be successful on this basis. We hope that he comes to see that, but in the final analysis it is the people and the government itself who have to win or lose this struggle. All we can do is help, and we are making it very clear, but I don't agree with those who say we should withdraw. That would be a great mistake. I know people don't like Americans to be engaged in this kind of an effort. Forty-seven Americans have been killed in combat with the enemy, but this is a very important struggle even though it is far away.

We took all this—made this effort to defend Europe. Now Europe is quite secure. We also have to participate—we may not like it—in the defense of Asia.

Kennedy Reaffirms the Domino Theory, 1963

Mr. Huntley: Mr. President, in respect to our difficulties in South Viet-Nam, could it be that our Government tends occasionally to get locked into a policy or an attitude and then finds it difficult to alter or shift that policy?

The President: Yes, that is true. I think in the case of South Viet-Nam we have been dealing with a Government which is in control, has been in control for 10 years. In addition, we have felt for the last 2 years that the struggle against the Communists was going better. Since June, however— the difficulties with the Buddhists—we have been concerned about a deterioration, particularly in the Saigon area, which hasn't been felt greatly in the outlying areas but may spread. So we are faced with the problem of wanting to protect the area against the Communists. On the other hand, we have to deal with the Government there. That produces a kind of ambivalence in our efforts which exposes us to some criticism. We are using our influence to persuade the Government there to take those steps which will win back support. That takes some time, and we must be patient, we must persist.

Mr. Huntley: Are we likely to reduce our aid to South Viet-Nam now?

The President: I don't think we think that would be helpful at this time. If you reduce your aid, it is possible you could have some effect upon the government structure there. On the other hand, you might have a situation which could bring about a collapse. Strongly in our mind is what happened in the case of China at the end of World War II, where China was lost— a weak government became increasingly unable to control events. We don't want that.

Mr. Brinkley: Mr. President, have you had any reason to doubt this so-called "domino theory," that if South Viet-Nam falls, the rest of Southeast Asia will go behind it?

The President: No, I believe it. I believe it. I think that the struggle is close enough. China is so large, looms so high just beyond the frontiers, that if South Viet-Nam went, it would not only give them an improved geographic position for a guerrilla assault on Malaya but would also give the impression that the wave of the future in Southeast Asia was China and the Communists. So I believe it.

Mr. Brinkley: In the last 48 hours there have been a great many conflicting reports from there about what the CIA [Central Intelligence Agency] was up to. Can you give us any enlightenment on it?

The President: No.

Mr. Huntley: Does the CIA tend to make its own policy? That seems to be the debate here.

The President: No, that is the frequent charge, but that isn't so. Mr. [John A.] McCone, head of the CIA, sits in the National Security Council. We have had a number of meetings in the past few days about events in South Viet-Nam. Mr. McCone participated in every one, and the CIA coordinates its efforts with the State Department and the Defense Department.

Mr. Brinkley: With so much of our prestige, money, so on, committed in South Viet-Nam, why can't we exercise a little more influence there, Mr. President?

The President: We have some influence. We have some influence and we are attempting to carry it out. I think we don't—we can't expect these countries to do everything the way we want to do them. They have their own interest, their own personalities, their own tradition. We can't make everyone in our image, and there are a good many people who don't want to go in our image. In addition, we have ancient struggles between countries. In the case of India and Pakistan, we would like to have them settle Kashmir. That is our view of the best way to defend the subcontinent against communism. But that struggle between India and Pakistan is more important to a good many people in that area than the struggle against the Communists. We would like to have Cambodia, Thailand, and South Viet-Nam all in harmony, but there are ancient differences there. We can't make the world over, but we can influence the world. The fact of the matter is that with the assistance of the United States and SEATO [Southeast Asia Treaty Organization], Southeast Asia and indeed all of Asia has been maintained independent against a powerful force, the Chinese Communists. What I am concerned about is that Americans will get impatient and say, because they don't like events in Southeast Asia or they don't like the Government in Saigon, that we should withdraw. That only makes it easy for the Communists. I think we should stay. We should use our influence in as effective a way as we can, but we should not withdraw.

Henry Cabot Lodge Discusses Coup Prospects, 1963

1. I appreciate the concern expressed by you [national security advisor McGeorge Bundy] in ref. a relative to the Gen. Don/Conein relationship, and also the present lack of firm intelligence on the details of the general's plot. I hope that ref. b will assist in clearing up some of the doubts relative to general's plans, and I am hopeful that the detailed plans promised for two days before the coup attempt will clear up any remaining doubts.

2. CAS [Classified American Source—reference to CIA] has been punctilious in carrying out my instructions. I have personally approved each meeting between Gen. Don and Conein who has carried out my orders in each instance explicitly. While I share your concern about the continued involvement of Conein in this matter, a suitable substitute for Conein as the principal contact is not presently available. Conein, as you know, is a friend of some eighteen years' standing with Gen. Don, and General Don has expressed extreme reluctance to deal with anyone else. I do not believe the involvement of another American in close contact with the generals would be productive. We are, however, considering the feasibility of a plan

for the introduction of an additional officer as a cut-out between Conein and a designee of Gen. Don for communication purposes only. This officer is completely unwitting of any details of past or present coup activities and will remain so.

3. With reference to Gen [Paul D.] Harkins' [chief of MAAG] comment to Gen. Don which Don reports to have referred to a presidential directive and the proposal for a meeting with me, this may have served the useful purpose of allaying the General's fears as to our interest. If this were a provocation, the GVN could have assumed and manufactured any variations of the same theme. As a precautionary measure, however, I of course refused to see Gen. Don. As to the lack of information as to General Don's real backing, and the lack of evidence that any real capabilities for action have been developed, ref. b provides only part of the answer. I feel sure that the reluctance of the generals to provide the U.S. with full details of their plans at this time, is a reflection of their own sense of security and a lack of confidence that in the large American community present in Saigon their plans will not be prematurely revealed.

4. The best evidence available to the Embassy, which I grant you is not as complete as we would like it, is that Gen. Don and the other generals involved with him are seriously attempting to effect a change in the government. I do not believe that this is a provocation by Ngo Dinh Nhu, although we shall continue to assess the planning as well as possible. In the event that the coup aborts, or in the event that Nhu has masterminded a provocation, I believe that our involvement to date through Conein is still within the realm of plausible denial. CAS is perfectly prepared to have me disavow Conein at any time it may serve the national interest.

5. I welcome your reaffirming instructions contained in CAS Washington [cable] 74228. It is vital that we neither thwart a *coup* nor that we are even in a position where we do not know what is going on.

6. We should not thwart a *coup* for two reasons. First, it seems at least an even bet that the next government would not bungle and stumble as much as the present one has. Secondly, it is extremely unwise in the long range for us to pour cold water on attempts at a coup, particularly when they are just in their beginning stages. We should remember that this is the only way in which the people in Vietnam can possibly get a change of government. Whenever we thwart attempts at a coup, as we have done in the past, we are incurring very long lasting resentments, we are assuming an undue responsibility for keeping the incumbents in office, and in general are setting ourselves in judgment over the affairs of Vietnam. Merely to keep in touch with this situation and a policy merely limited to "not thwarting" are courses both of which entail some risks but these are lesser risks than either thwarting all coups while they are stillborn or our not being informed of what is happening. All the above is totally distinct from not wanting U.S. military advisors to be distracted by matters which are not in their domain, with which I heartily agree. But obviously this does not conflict with a policy of not thwarting. In judging proposed coups, we must consider the effect on the war effort. Certainly a succession of fights for

control of the Government of Vietnam would interfere with the war effort. It must also be said that the war effort has been interfered with already by the incompetence of the present government and the uproar which this has caused.

7. Gen. Don's intention to have no religious discrimination in a future government is commendable and I applaud his desire not to be "a vassal" of the U.S. But I do not think his promise of a democratic election is realistic. This country simply is not ready for that procedure. I would add two other requirements. First, that there be no wholesale purges of personnel in the government. Individuals who were particularly reprehensible could be dealt with later by the regular legal process. Then I would be impractical, but I am thinking of a government which might include Tri Quang and which certainly should include men of the stature of Mr. Buu, the labor leader.

8. Copy to Gen. Harkins.

McGeorge Bundy Expresses Reservations, 1963

1. Your [cables] 2023, 2040, 2041 and 2043 examined with care at highest levels here. You should promptly discuss this reply and associated messages with Harkins whose responsibilities toward any coup are very heavy especially after you leave (see para. 7 below). They give much clearer picture group's alleged plans and also indicate chances of action with or without our approval now so significant that we should urgently consider our attitude and contingency plans. We note particularly Don's curiosity your departure and his insistence Conein be available from Wednesday night on, which suggests date might be as early as Thursday.

2. Believe our attitude to coup group can still have decisive effect on its decisions. We believe that what we say to coup group can produce delay of coup and that betrayal of coup plans to Diem is not repeat not our only way of stopping coup. We therefore need urgently your combined assessment with Harkins and CAS (including their separate comments if they desire). We concerned that our line-up of forces in Saigon (being cabled in next message) indicates approximately equal balance of forces, with substantial possibility serious and prolonged fighting or even defeat. Either of these could be serious or even disastrous for U.S. interests, so that we must have assurance balance of forces clearly favorable.

3. With your assessment in hand, we might feel that we should convey message to Don, whether or not he gives 4 or 48 hours notice that would (A) continue explicit hands-off policy, (B) positively encourage coup, or (C) discourage.

4. In any case, believe Conein should find earliest opportunity express to Don that we do not find presently revealed plans give clear prospect of quick results. This conversation should call attention important Saigon units still apparently loyal to Diem and raise serious issue as to what means coup group has to deal with them.

5. From operational standpoint, we also deeply concerned Don only spokesman for group and possibility cannot be discounted he may not be in good faith. We badly need some corroborative evidence whether Minh and others directly and completely involved. In view Don's claim he doesn't handle "military planning" could not Conein tell Don that we need better military picture and that Big Minh could communicate this most naturally and easily to [General Richard] Stilwell [Harkins's Chief of Staff]? We recognize desirability involving MACV [U.S. Military Assistance Command, Vietnam] to minimum, but believe Stilwell far more desirable this purpose than using Conein both ways.

6. Complexity above actions raises question whether you should adhere to present Thursday schedule. Concur you and other U.S. elements should take no action that could indicate U.S. awareness coup possibility. However, DOD [Department of Defense] is sending berth-equipped military aircraft that will arrive Saigon Thursday and could take you out thereafter as late as Saturday afternoon in time to meet your presently proposed arrival Washington Sunday. You could explain this being done as convenience and that your Washington arrival is same. A further advantage such aircraft is that it would permit your prompt return from any point en route if necessary. To reduce time in transit, you should use this plane, but we recognize delaying your departure may involve greater risk that you personally would appear involved if any action took place. However, advantages your having extra two days in Saigon may outweigh this and we leave timing of flight to your judgment.

7. Whether you leave Thursday or later, believe it essential that prior your departure there be fullest consultation Harkins and CAS and that there be clear arrangements for handling (A) normal activity, (B) continued coup contacts, (C) action in event a coup starts. We assume you will wish Truehart as charge to be head of country team in normal situation, but highest authority desires it clearly understood that after your departure Harkins should participate in supervision of all coup contacts and that in event a coup begins, he become head of country team and direct representative of President, with [William] Truehart [Deputy Chief of Mission] in effect acting as POLAD [Political Adviser]. On coup contacts we will maintain continuous guidance and will expect equally continuous reporting with prompt account of any important divergences in assessments of Harkins and Smith.

8. If coup should start, question of protecting U.S. nationals at once arises. We can move Marine Battalion into Saigon by air from Okinawa within 24 hours—if available. We are sending instructions to CINCPAC to arrange orderly movement of seaborne Marine Battalion to waters adjacent to South Vietnam in position to close Saigon within approximately 24 hours.

9. We are now examining post-coup contingencies here and request your immediate recommendations on position to be adopted after coup begins, especially with respect to requests for assistance of different sorts

from one side or the other also request you forward contingency recommendations for action if coup (A) succeeds, (B) fails, (C) is indecisive.

10. We reiterate burden of proof must be on coup group to show a substantial possibility of quick success; otherwise, we should discourage them from proceeding since a miscalculation could result in jeopardizing U.S. position in Southeast Asia.

Diem's Final Appeal for U.S. Help, 1963

Diem: Some units have made a rebellion and I want to know what is the attitude of the U.S.?

Lodge: I do not feel well enough informed to be able to tell you. I have heard the shooting, but am not acquainted with all the facts. Also it is 4:30 A.M. in Washington and the U.S. Government cannot possibly have a view.

Diem: But you must have some general ideas. After all, I am a Chief of State. I have tried to do my duty. I want to do now what duty and good sense require. I believe in duty above all.

Lodge: You have certainly done your duty. As I told you only this morning, I admire your courage and your great contributions to your country. No one can take away from you the credit for all you have done. Now I am worried about your physical safety. I have a report that those in charge of the current activity offer you and your brother safe conduct out of the country if you resign. Had you heard this?

Diem: No. (And then after a pause) You have my telephone number.

Lodge: Yes. If I can do anything for your physical safety, please call me.

Diem: I am trying to re-establish order.

✗ *E S S A Y S*

R. B. Smith of the University of London contends in the first selection that President Kennedy's initial commitments to South Vietnam must be understood within a broad international context. Vietnam became important to the Kennedy administration, he argues, for reasons that had more to do with the global strategies of the Soviet Union and China, and with American vulnerability, than with the exercise of options on the part of the United States. Kennedy had to respond to the Sino-Soviet challenge in Vietnam or risk the surrender and defeat of America to world communism.

In the second essay, Lawrence J. Bassett and Stephen E. Pelz of the University of Massachusetts offer a different assessment. They assert that America's main enemies in South Vietnam were not the Soviet Union, China, or North Vietnam; rather, they were the southern Vietminh, who had suffered or gone into exile under Diem (organized as the National Liberation Front in 1960), and the peasants who supported them. According to Bassett and Pelz, Kennedy profoundly misunderstood Vietnam. His administration's thinking was shaped not by a sophisticated appreciation of the problem of rural revolution in Southeast Asia but by ingrained cold war thinking about American credibility and the need to contain communism.

Responding to the Sino-Soviet Challenge

R. B. SMITH

During the first few months of his presidency Kennedy was determined to reverse the tough anti-Communist line that had emerged in Washington in the second half of 1960. Anxious not to jeopardize the possibility of new negotiations with Khrushchev by overreacting to the Communist "threat" in any specific area of the globe, he was determined above all to avoid committing American combat troops in circumstances where that might lead to a local war. The president probably still believed in the "missile gap" which as a senator he had been among the first to identify, and which was not finally shown to be a fallacy until September 1961. He was also painfully aware that the United States strategic reserve of conventional forces was not large enough to permit the deployment of a substantial number of troops to any one part of the world without endangering the security of other areas. One of the principal tasks he assigned to Secretary of Defense McNamara was that of reorganizing and expanding the American capability for "limited war." Nevertheless his main hope was that bilateral negotiations with the Soviet Union would lead not only to mutual restraint in the field of nuclear weapons but also to an easing of tension throughout the world. In the meantime, having been converted to Maxwell Taylor's ideas about "flexible response," he was inclined to favor wherever possible covert operations rather than overt military intervention as a method of countering any actual threat to American interests. Kennedy was well aware of the risks to American global power—as well as to his own reputation— of failing to make any response at all whenever that power seemed to be challenged.

By early March the new administration faced difficult decisions in two key areas of inherited crisis: Cuba and Laos. Both situations had to be handled in ways that would not impede the three-power talks on banning nuclear tests due to be resumed in Geneva on 21 March. In the case of Cuba, Kennedy had to decide whether to proceed with existing plans to use exile forces to provoke an uprising against Castro; and if so, how far to allow United States combat forces to become directly involved. A series of top-level meetings between 11 and 15 March 1961 worked out a compromise plan which permitted the operation to go ahead, on condition that it was strictly covert and deniable. With that in mind it was decided that the exiles would land in the relatively secluded "Bay of Pigs" rather than

From R. B. Smith, *An International History of the Vietnam War, Vol. 1: Revolution Versus Containment, 1955–61*, excerpts from pp. 244–261. Copyright © 1983. Reprinted by permission of St. Martin's Press.

at the point originally designated on the south-eastern coast of the island. Without more substantial evidence it would be going too far to suggest that Kennedy deliberately allowed the operation to fail; certainly he was determined to prevent it becoming the excuse for direct American military involvement. It is not clear whether he knew for certain that Castro could not be dislodged without such intervention; but he had some idea of the scale of Soviet arms deliveries since October. The president may have decided that if the CIA could bring about a change of regime by means which required *only* the training and supply of indigenous forces, the result would be welcome. He was not prepared to accept the diplomatic repercussions of direct military action, however, and he intended to draw a clear distinction between the two. At a news conference early in April he explicitly ruled out action by American combat forces against Cuba, and he refused to be swayed from that position when the "covert" operation went ahead on 15–19 April and proved a fiasco.

The situation in Laos was more complicated. In Cuba, where a Soviet ally was already in power, there was no question of convening an international conference to guarantee the island's neutrality. Laos on the other hand had already been the subject of international guarantees, whose reaffirmation in some form was the only way to avert deeper external involvement in an ongoing civil war. It could be argued that not only the United States but also the Soviet Union and North Vietnam had by now violated the Geneva settlement beyond redemption. But so far they had done so only in ways which amounted to indirect interference in Laotian politics and the provision of aid to Laotian armies; they had not sent in their own combat forces. The problem for the Americans was that their intervention had not worked: rightist forces were still not strong enough to restore the situation of early 1960. Here too, Kennedy had to decide whether to deploy American troops in order to secure the southern half of Laos once and for all.

The advice he received from the JCS was probably ambivalent. There was no doubt that a Communist Laos, under the full control of the Pathet Lao [communist-led guerrilla movement] and closely allied with North Vietnam, would pose a potential threat to the security of both Thailand and South Vietnam. Militarily therefore if it ever became necessary to deploy combat units at all in the Indochinese Peninsula, Laos was the logical place for them to go. But the generals were far from enthusiastic about risking another major land war in Asia, especially in a country whose existing communications and logistic facilities were as primitive as those of Laos. They insisted that any operation there would require a force of at least 60,000 men; and by April they were talking about 140,000. That order of commitment, they well knew, was impossible without calling up reserves and embarking on an immediate military build-up. Kennedy realized that such action would not only destroy the Geneva framework irreversibly but would also damage the prospect for East-West negotiations or any other issue. Indochina was not worth such extreme consequences.

Therein lay the essence of his dilemma. Military action was impracticable from almost all points of view—unless he wished to plunge the world into crisis at a time when the United States could no longer take for granted the superiority of its own nuclear forces. Negotiations of some kind were therefore imperative; but would negotiations produce a long-term solution? It was by no means certain that *both* Communist powers would be willing to negotiate an agreement acceptable to the United States. Even if they were, would the resulting neutralization of Laos provide adequate protection for South Vietnam and Thailand? For better or for worse Kennedy decided, as in the case of Cuba, to adopt a policy of restraint—but without any guarantee of success. . . .

The American decision not to put combat units into Laos had immediate consequences for Vietnam. Pathet Lao and North Vietnamese control of Eastern Laos, extending to areas bordering directly on South Vietnam, had made it difficult if not impossible to devise any form of "neutralization" which in practice, as opposed to international law, would prevent the expansion of covert infiltration routes from North to South Vietnam. On the other hand, a new international agreement would effectively preclude the Americans themselves from taking retaliatory action beyond the Vietnamese border. Unless they intended to abandon South Vietnam altogether, they must therefore find ways of strengthening both the political confidence and the material capabilities of the Diem regime. Saigon must be provided with the means to cope with both existing guerrilla activity and a possible expansion of the armed struggle. Kennedy may have hoped that his own restraint in Laos would be met by some attempt on the part of the Soviet Union and China to avert an escalation of the conflict in South Vietnam. If so he was proved wrong.

In the aftermath of the "Bay of Pigs," the Americans had to accept that national liberation struggles of the kind which had brought Castro to power could not easily be reversed once they had succeeded. A revolutionary regime already in control could legitimately declare itself an ally of the Soviet Union and China, and obtain sufficient economic and military support to resist any "covert action" against it. Kennedy was alarmed at the prospect of similar struggles in other countries of the third world leading to a gradual expansion of the "socialist camp." In a speech to the American Society of Newspaper Editors on 20 April 1961, he defined what he saw as the changing nature of the "Communist threat" to the existing global balance of power. On the same day he instructed his deputy secretary of defense, Roswell Gilpatric, to convene an interagency task-force which would recommend a new program of action for Vietnam. Throughout the next few months, decision-making on Vietnam was paralleled by a more general discussion of American capabilities in the field of counterinsurgency.

Kennedy was already a convert to Maxwell Taylor's ideas about the need for "flexible response" rather than total reliance on the nuclear deterrent. He had appointed Taylor his special adviser on military affairs and had assigned to McNamara the task of reviving and developing an American capability to wage "limited war." But the president was also convinced that conventional military action by regular combat divisions was inappropriate to situations of the kind that had arisen in Cuba, Laos or Vietnam. He sought to build on ideas about counterinsurgency that had begun to emerge from Pentagon and CIA planning during 1960. . . .

Meanwhile the Gilpatric task-force spent the last ten days of April developing a set of recommendations on Vietnam predicated on the assumption that American troops would not be sent into Laos. Its preliminary memorandum of 26 April argued for a program to be carried out by the task-force itself, which would include an important (if not predominant) role for [Edward] Lansdale. As the Laos ceasefire took shape, however, the State Department began to assert a claim to more influence in Vietnam decision-making; and in early May Under-secretary of State [George] Ball intervened to oblige the task-force to revise its memorandum. There was to be no weakening of the essential commitment to South Vietnam; but the task-force itself, and particularly Lansdale, would no longer have responsibility for action on the ground. This gave Kennedy greater freedom to relate Vietnam decisions to the wider themes of his global strategy. But the principle of interagency control, with stronger participation by the State, meant in the long run that strategy for Vietnam would develop in a less personalized, more bureaucratic fashion. The question whether things might ultimately have gone better for the United States in Vietnam if Lansdale had been allowed to take charge at this point must remain one of those "ifs of history" which no amount of speculation can resolve. Certainly the delay between then and the final approval of a more systematic American policy in October gave the Communist side time to consolidate its position and so keep the initiative.

Kennedy's first substantive decisions on Vietnam (apart from his endorsement of the Eisenhower counterinsurgency plan in January) were formalized in NSAM [National Security Action Memorandum] no. 52 of 11 May 1961. He overruled a proposal from the JCS to deploy United States forces to South Vietnam immediately, to be there in the event of a subsequent crisis. Instead he approved measures to strengthen the Saigon army and civil guard, backed by an expanded program of operations by American special forces, which would now include more careful surveillance of the Laos border and the infiltration of intelligence teams north of the 17th parallel.

In order to reassure South Vietnam and other friendly governments in the region that the decision on Laos did not imply a general weakening of American commitments, Vice-President Johnson was sent on a tour of South-East Asia which took him to Saigon on 12 May. Among the questions he discussed with Diem was that of a bilateral treaty between the Republic of Vietnam and the United States, which would have guaranteed military support in case the SEATO allies again refused to act collectively in a crisis. Any formal treaty, however, would have been a flagrant violation of Article 19 of the Geneva Agreement and the Americans eventually decided against it. They preferred to justify the further expansion of military assistance to Saigon by arguing that the Communist side had violated the ceasefire, rather than by themselves renouncing any specific clause of the Agreement. Future relations between the United States and South Vietnam would be based on a simple exchange of letters between the two presidents defining their respective needs and commitments. Later on, American opponents of the war would emphasize the fact that there had never been a formal treaty obligation—nor even a specific request for Washington to send troops. But in 1961 Kennedy had no intention of becoming so deeply involved; the legality of commitment was less important than the diplomacy of restraint.

On the day originally fixed for the Laos conference to open (12 May), Khrushchev wrote a personal letter to Kennedy proposing a meeting in Vienna the following month. Kennedy's first reaction was one of optimism, but when the encounter actually took place on 3–4 June it proved considerably less productive than he had hoped. Cuba was no longer a problem; and on the question of Laos the Soviet attitude still permitted a measure of conciliation. During the first sessions at Geneva (16 May–26 June) progress was made on a number of issues. But those were areas where the Americans had backed away from active military involvement. Kennedy was no doubt hoping for something in return—if only a tacit understanding that in other areas the Soviet Union would refrain from actions calculated to disturb the global balance of power. Had such reassurances been forthcoming the United States might have been willing to co-operate more fully in spheres where the Russians sought bilateral agreements: trade and credit relations, normalization of consular arrangements, and control of nuclear weapons. However, Khrushchev denied the possibility of a status quo if it meant an end to revolutionary activity throughout the world. He compared Kennedy's proposal with the nineteenth century concept of a "holy alliance" against political change of any kind. Given the current international line agreed between Moscow and Peking the previous autumn, the Soviet leader could hardly have done otherwise. He also reiterated the demand for a German peace treaty, including a revision of the status of West Berlin; there too he may have been under pressure from "hardline" colleagues in Moscow. The effect of the summit in Vienna was to convince Kennedy that direct negotiations with the Soviet Union could not immediately resolve outstanding problems in areas of East-West tension. He must therefore brace himself for a war of nerves, if not for more serious conflict.

The danger of a crisis over Berlin had already been foreseen in an NSAM of 25 April 1961, authorizing contingency planning which was by now under way. In mid-June the Russians began to force the pace, setting in train the confrontation which led to the building of the Berlin Wall in mid-August and which did not finally die away until late October. Yet despite its apparent seriousness, the Berlin crisis was a controlled international game in which each side could make up its mind how far to go— and could equally rapidly retreat if the conflict threatened to get out of hand. At Vienna, Kennedy expressed fears of "miscalculation" in such situations, but on this occasion there was probably no real danger of war. The same controlled conditions had characterized the Taiwan Straits crisis of 1958. But in South-East Asia there was a far greater danger of the conflict developing in ways the superpowers could not control.

By July it was also obvious that the Geneva Conference would not produce rapid results in Laos. Compared with the conference of 1954, that of 1962 lacked any sense of urgency; there was consequently little hope of agreement within a specified time limit. Nor was formal partition a possible solution by this stage. The declared object of the negotiations was to bring the three "parties" in Laos together in order to reunify the country, and then to neutralize it on terms acceptable to both China and the Soviet Union as well as to the Western powers. On 22 June Sihanouk managed to arrange a meeting in Zurich between the "three princes" (Souvanna Phouma, Souphanouvong and Boun Oum), which led to an agreement in principle to work together. But much still remained to be settled when the Geneva Conference itself adjourned four days later. Part of the blame for this may have rested with the Americans, but the Chinese attitude was equally important. Peking's refusal to agree to strong international machinery—on the grounds that it would deprive the Vientiane government of its sovereignty—seems to have arisen from the fear that a virtual Soviet-American condominium in Laos might exclude China's own influence there. Since the Americans insisted on proper international guarantees, the result was stalemate.

The impossibility of achieving rapid agreement on Laos was part of the reason why it also proved impossible to stabilize the situation in Vietnam. On 9 June Ngo Dinh Diem drafted a letter asking Kennedy for increased military support, which his minister of defense delivered in Washington a week later. Kennedy thereupon agreed to set up a joint economic commission composed of American and Vietnamese officials to work out the economic implications of a further expansion of South Vietnam's military capabilities. Presided over by the economist Eugene Staley—but also including several military advisers—it set to work in Saigon during the second half of June and reported at the end of July.

In late July and early August 1961 the various strands of the global conflict came together. On 25 July, just as the American disarmament negotiator John J. McCloy was arriving in Sochi for talks with Khrushchev, Kennedy went on television to announce a call-up of military reserves and an increase in United States military expenditure. Although the president also expressed interest in further negotiations on the German question, Khrushchev was bound to react sharply. In conversation with McCloy, he accused Kennedy of declaring "preliminary war" on the Soviet Union. Two weeks later, on 7 August, the Soviet leader made his own television broadcast which all but reversed the decision of January 1960 to reduce the size of the Soviet armed forces. This amounted to another set-back for his ideas about both "peaceful co-existence" and Soviet economic development. It must also have convinced Washington that Khrushchev alone was not the arbiter of Soviet policy and that the Moscow "hardliners" were still influential.

It is beyond the scope of the present study to determine whether this impasse might have been avoided by some more "moderate" American approach; but the consequences for Soviet and American decision-making on Vietnam are clear. Also in late July 1961, Khrushchev received at Sochi the Vietnamese premier Pham Van Dong, who had arrived in Moscow in late June and had since been touring Eastern Europe. By the time he left for home on 12 August, Dong had secured not only public Soviet endorsement of the revolutionary struggle in South Vietnam but also another major agreement on economic aid. Kennedy meanwhile reached the conclusion that he had no choice but to "make a stand" in Vietnam. Even so, when he came to consider the Staley Report at the beginning of August he was still inclined to accept its "minimum" rather than its "maximum" recommendations. On 11 August another NSAM (no. 65) authorized the support required to increase South Vietnam's regular forces to a level of 200,000, and to accelerate various economic and social programs. If the North Vietnamese had been obliged at that point to submit to renewed Soviet and Chinese constraint, the "Staley program" might just possibly have been adequate to enable Diem to cope with his difficulties. But by now such constraint seemed less likely than ever. The situation on the ground in South Vietnam continued to deteriorate during August and September, and by October Kennedy found himself endorsing a program for even greater United States involvement.

Could Kennedy have done anything to avoid this greater level of commitment? It is easy enough to criticize his actions by invoking generalities: that he overestimated the importance of Indochina in American global strategy; that he was too concerned with theoretical "anti-Communism" and failed to recognize the specific realities of Vietnam; or even, following Khrushchev's line of thinking, that he ought not to have tried to stem the "tide of revolution" in Asia at all. But international decision-making does not allow world leaders the luxury of reassessing basic principles—or redefining the realities of power politics—at every turn of events. If the historian wishes to suggest that Kennedy made some specific error of judgment, it must be identified in terms of the day-to-day sequence of his actual decisions within the limits of choice open to him.

China was probably the key to the situation. The one thing the United States was free to do in mid-1961, and which *might* have made a significant difference to the subsequent course of events throughout Asia, was to permit the Chinese People's Republic to take its seat at the United Nations. In terms of American domestic politics that decision was all but impossible for Kennedy to take: it would have been opposed not only by the extreme right but even by Eisenhower, and his own position as president was still too insecure. When Kennedy and his advisers met on 5 August at Hyannis Port to discuss tactics for the autumn session of the General Assembly, it was taken for granted that they would continue to recognize Chiang Kaishek: a decision which probably determined the shape of China's policy for the next four or five years. Khrushchev himself had appealed to Kennedy at Vienna to recognize Peking; he probably knew better than his adversary the risks that would be run if it did not happen. The Sino-Soviet *rap-*

prochement of 1960 had been possible only because Deng Xiaoping and Liu Shaoqi had been able to persuade their colleagues to compromise with Khrushchev's line. During the spring and early summer of 1961, Zhou Enlai and Chen Yi had likewise persuaded the leadership to accept the ceasefire in Laos and to participate in the conference at Geneva. But the situation was one in which moderation could be justified only by success, and Lin Biao was almost certainly ready to seize any opportunity to reassert the anti-imperialist, anti-revisionist line. Once it became clear that entry into the United Nations was still barred, the "moderates" again lost ground.

On the Soviet side it was beginning to be apparent around the middle of August 1961 that Khrushchev might after all persuade the Soviet Central Committee—and ultimately the CPSU [Communist Party of the Soviet Union] 22nd Congress—to continue its support for détente; the building of the Berlin Wall (17 August) marked the essential turning-point of the crisis there. Two days later the withdrawal of the Soviet ambassador from Tirana represented one more step towards making condemnation of Albania a vehicle for indirectly criticizing the Chinese line on imperialism and war. At the Congress itself, between 17 and 31 October, Khrushchev launched a major ideological attack on Albania. The Chinese were thus forced to decide whether to follow suit or to reaffirm their independent anti-imperialist line. Zhou Enlai, who led the Chinese delegation to the 22nd Congress, failed to secure any modification of the Soviet line—and on 23 October he had a dramatic exit and left for home.

Ho Chi Minh and Le Duan also went to Moscow again in October for the CPSU Congress. They were careful not to criticize Albania, but paid a tactful visit to the Baltic states when Zhou Enlai went home. There was no question of a Soviet-Vietnamese "split," and North Vietnam succeeded in remaining on good terms with both the Soviet Union and China through-out the 1960s. Ironically, whereas in 1960 a Sino-Soviet *rapprochement* had helped North Vietnam to secure international Communist support for a return to armed struggle, the Sino-Soviet breach of 1961 helped them even more. The Chinese were now more inclined than ever to give Hanoi moral support, if not actual military aid; in such circumstances Khrushchev could not afford to sacrifice Vietnam in the cause of détente. Meanwhile a political work conference of the PLA [Peoples' Liberation Army] meeting in Peking from 18 October to 4 November probably endorsed a strongly anti-impe-rialist line, as well as the "Maoist" line on people's war. Zhou himself is said to have addressed the PLA conference on his return. The Sino-Soviet conflict thus came out into the open; but in a form which entirely precluded any détente between China and the United States or Japan.

From Hanoi's point of view international conditions were now favorable for an expanding struggle against Diem. The Americans had therefore to work out an appropriate response or allow South Vietnam to collapse. Between 18 October and 1 November 1961, coinciding precisely with the Soviet Party Congress and the military conference in Peking, Maxwell Taylor undertook a mission to Indochina to find ways of further strength-ening South Vietnam. There was no longer any reason to hope that negotiations with Moscow would lead to any significant Soviet restraint of Hanoi, and the immediate security situation was deteriorating rapidly.

In Laos, Kennedy was satisfied that a combination of diplomacy and covert operations would be sufficient to prevent the fall of Vientiane; and short of an American invasion, there was little to be done about the "Ho Chi Minh trail" along which Communist infiltration was continuing at a growing rate. In Vietnam, however, something more was required. The president was still determined not to commit regular combat troops, and in early November he rejected Taylor's advice to send even a token force of 8000 men whose presence might have been justified by a need for flood relief operations. Instead he approved a new form of counterinsurgency which for the first time would involve a direct role for United States special forces and logistic support units. This was to lead to the deployment of 10,000 Americans during the next twelve months, but all operating within (or in conjunction with) the South Vietnamese command structure. It remained to be seen whether such a program of "limited partnership" with the Vietnamese would prove an effective counter to revolutionary warfare. But by refusing to send combat units to any part of Indochina and by entering into negotiations on Laos, Kennedy had (if nothing else) averted the possibility of a wider war. The struggle would now be confined to South Vietnam. Win or lose, there was still some hope that he and Khrushchev could between them prevent Vietnam from becoming a serious obstacle to negotiation on major bilateral issues when the opportunity returned.

Kennedy was anxious above all to avoid a sequence of moves and counter-moves which might unravel the whole framework of international relations that had evolved since the Second World War. Throughout the years since 1945 the United States had adhered to the principle of upholding the various agreements which had established the geopolitical pattern across the globe after the Second World War, and the ceasefire agreements on Korea and Indochina in 1953–4 had been treated as an extension of the same pattern. The Americans thus found themselves applying the same criteria of importance to Indochina as to other key areas in their global system; the commitment to South Vietnam was in many respects precisely the same as that to the non-Communist halves of Germany and Korea. But militarily, the actual threat to South Vietnam was more comparable with revolutionary struggles elsewhere in the third world. The problem for Kennedy was whether the United States could fulfill its commitment by successfully responding to that threat in its own terms. Hence the vital importance of his strategy of counterinsurgency.

In all this it is not necessary to suppose that Kennedy saw his own decisions as the first rung on a ladder of "escalation." The subsequent influence of [strategist] Hermann Kahn's doctrines, and the application of that term to Johnson's strategy after 1964, should not deceive us into thinking otherwise. Kennedy himself made no assumption that if counterinsurgency failed it would then be logical to proceed to more conventional operations, including the deployment of ground troops. His objective, in Vietnam as elsewhere, was to find a new method of defeating a new type of "threat" to an American ally: a substitute for, not a prelude to, the conventional action which he knew to be inappropriate. Nor is there any reason to suggest that either Kennedy or his generals deliberately *chose* to make Vietnam their "test case" for the doctrine of counterinsurgency, in preference to some other country that would have been more suitable. Those who have suggested that Vietnam was "the wrong war at the wrong time in the wrong place" have ignored the fact that Kennedy was responding to a situation where most of the initiative lay with the Communist side. Vietnam became important in 1960–1 for reasons which had more to do with the global strategies of the Soviet Union and China, and with American vulnerability, than with the exercise of options on the part of the United States. Trouble in Vietnam—or alternatively in Vietnam and Laos together, if there had been no Geneva Conference in 1961—was avoidable only in the same sense that the Korean War might have been avoided: by surrender, in circumstances where negotiation was impossible. There was a war in Vietnam because that was where the challenge arose, at a moment when Kennedy could not ignore the challenge.

The Failed Search for Victory

LAWRENCE J. BASSETT and STEPHEN E. PELZ

Two weeks before the United States's defeat at the Bay of Pigs, John Kenneth Galbraith, John F. Kennedy's new Ambassador to India, warned the President against "the surviving adventurism in the Administration. . . ." The always frank Galbraith recalled that the "futile campaign to the Yalu ruined the Democrats in 1950. . . . We Democrats with our reputation for belligerence and our basically hostile press have far less margin for mistakes than had the Republicans." During the following months, Galbraith also told Kennedy that South Vietnam was "a can of snakes," and speculated that Premier Ngo Dinh Diem's desperate efforts to cling to power might falter and draw the United States deeper into Indochina. Galbraith recommended that Kennedy send an emissary to explain the problem of Diem's pigheadedness to the State Department—"with pictures. . . . We are increasingly replacing the French as the colonial military force and we will increasingly arouse the resentment associated therewith." "Incidentally," he continued, "who is the man in your administration who decides what countries are strategic? I would like to have his name and address and ask him what is so important about this [Vietnamese] real estate in the space age." Galbraith concluded that "it is the political poison that is really at issue. The Korean war killed us in the early 50's; this involvement could kill us now."

John F. Kennedy himself decided that South Vietnam was strategically vital. He did so because he viewed the world and the methods for dealing with it differently from Galbraith, although he certainly agreed with the

Excerpted from *Kennedy's Quest for Victory: American Foreign Policy, 1961–1963*, edited by Thomas G. Paterson, pp. 223–225, 226–234, 237, 245, 252. Copyright © 1989 by Oxford University Press, Inc. Reprinted by permission.

Ambassador about the domestic political dangers of ordering American infantry units to fight in South Vietnam. While Galbraith called for continuing a "conservative, thoughtful, nonbelligerent stance" toward the world, Kennedy wanted to lead his South Vietnamese allies to victory over the Vietnamese Communists without sending large numbers of American troops into battle. To this end the President stated repeatedly and publicly that the United States would help suppress the insurgency in South Vietnam; he warned the Soviets both publicly and privately against assisting the guerrillas; he increased economic aid to South Vietnam; he enlarged the South Vietnamese Army and police forces; he increased the number of American military advisers, logistic units, and pilots from approximately 700 to approximately 16,700; he allowed a number of the advisers to participate in combat; he ordered assistance to the South Vietnamese for covert raids against North Vietnam; he helped launch the South Vietnamese strategic hamlet program; he encouraged the South Vietnamese military to assume political power; and he rejected suggestions that he try to neutralize South Vietnam—a solution which he had been willing to accept in Laos.

Early in his career Kennedy had formed an image of South Vietnam as a nation whose nationalist elite was caught between French colonialists and Communist insurgents. Since Kennedy believed Americans were not seen as colonialists, he expected that American advisers would be able to work with Vietnamese nationalists to establish and defend a pro-Western state in South Vietnam. Drawing the containment line at the South Vietnamese border was all the more important, because he had reluctantly accepted a neutralized Laos. In his determined search for victory in Vietnam, President Kennedy kept trying different tactics and personnel, but his efforts played into the hands of the National Liberation Front (NLF), a coalition of anti-Diem groups for which the Communists provided most of the leaders. By giving Diem money and men, Kennedy backed a system of landlord rule in the countryside, which was deeply unpopular with the peasants, and by aiding the South Vietnamese security forces in their attempts to impose Diem's will on the villages, he identified the Americans with a repressive *ancien regime*.

Peasants joined the NLF in increasing numbers, because the NLF cadres helped them achieve a rural revolution. Kennedy's program of industrialization, rural aid, resettlement, and helicopter assaults carried little appeal in the countryside. Kennedy nonetheless persisted in his quest for victory in Vietnam, even after repeated warnings that his methods were failing. He did so in part because he and his small senior staff did not spend much time searching for the realities behind the flow of daily cables from Saigon. Given the current state of documentation Kennedy's motives for this persistant quest for victory must remain something of a mystery. It appears, however, that he persevered in Vietnam not only to preserve his credibility as a successful practitioner of containment but also to maintain his reputation as an anti-Communist in the face of Republican attacks at home. . . .

In spite of considerable American economic and military aid, Diem was in trouble by 1959. In 1957–1958 he had restored landlord-gentry rule to many of the rural areas and put his northern and central Vietnamese Catholic Can Lao party members in control of much of the government, army, and police. In 1959 the southern Vietminh began reclaiming the countryside for the peasants, while decrying the harsh rule of "American Diem's" minions. In Long An province, not far from Saigon, for example, armed squads drove Diem's officials almost completely out of the villages with a campaign of terror which killed twenty-six people during the New Year's celebration of 1960. Vietminh cadres established peasant committees in the liberated areas and encouraged the newly empowered peasants to reduce land rents and redistribute the land of those Diemist officials who had fled. By 1961 the campaign had swayed about 80 percent of South Vietnam's villages toward their side, and Diem's government had to rely almost totally on American economic and military assistance to replace the taxes and recruits lost in the villages.

The Vietminh offensive in South Vietnam appeared to confirm Kennedy's picture of world politics in 1961. Although the United States was far superior to the Soviet Union in nuclear weaponry, Kennedy believed the United States faced a challenge to the global balance of power from both the Soviets and the Chinese Communists, who he claimed were merely vying with one another over the best way to bury the West. Because the Soviets possessed hydrogen bombs, Kennedy complained, Eisenhower's reliance on nuclear weapons represented a dangerous illusion; neither side could use such weapons for fighting conventional and brushfire wars. Kennedy therefore adopted a flexible response strategy to counter Communist-led insurgencies like the one in South Vietnam. The President and Secretary of State Dean Rusk also became particularly alarmed by the aggressive rhetoric of the People's Republic of China, which seemed to be gaining influence in Hanoi in 1962.

Kennedy had other reasons for taking the NLF challenge seriously. He had learned during the 1950s that he could win political rewards by advocating an anti-Communist counter-offensive. After all, he had grown up in the Massachusetts politics of anti-Communism, and Bay State voters had provided some of Joseph R. McCarthy's most loyal supporters. As a young congressman Kennedy had actually joined Republicans in criticizing the Democrats for losing East Germany, Poland, and China to the Soviets. He had also made headlines by pursuing alleged Communists in labor unions, and during his senatorial campaign of 1952, he charged that Henry Cabot Lodge, Jr., was soft on Communism. During his political campaigns he solicited support from a wide range of anti-Communist ethnic organizations—Italians, Poles, Germans, Hungarians, Czechs, Greeks, Lithuanians, and Russians.

The political arithmetic was simple—ethnic voters had supported Truman by a two-to-one margin in 1948, but they shifted in large numbers to Eisenhower in 1952. Due in part to his public McCarthyism, Kennedy was one of the few Democrats to buck the Republican tide in 1952. Although ethnic voters did not support McCarthyism in larger proportions than the general population, McCarthyism became the bridge over which formerly loyal Democratic voters in critical electoral college states left the decaying

New Deal coalition. In 1956, 35 percent of Catholic *Democrats* voted against Stevenson. Kennedy knew good politics when he saw it. During his campaign, Kennedy portrayed himself as the man who could stand up to the Communists better than the Republicans, whom he accused of losing both Cuba and the Cold War. In the electoral college, Kennedy achieved a net gain of 22 votes due to the fortuitous concentration of ethnic blocs in key Northern and Midwestern states, and these votes were critical in the very close election of 1960.

The Republicans would hold Kennedy to his campaign promises of victories in the Cold War. In 1960, Richard M. Nixon had predicted that Kennedy was "the kind of man Mr. Khrushchev will make mincemeat of," and during his final briefing of the President-elect, Eisenhower told Kennedy he had to intervene militarily in Laos, with or without allies, if the Laotians invoked the Southeast Asia Collective Defense Treaty (SEATO). Kennedy had sought a second meeting with Eisenhower during the transition because he himself was leaning toward escalation in Laos, where leftist guerrillas were defeating American-backed rightists. For Eisenhower, an independent Laos was vital for holding the rest of Southeast Asia. According to one participant in this meeting, however, Eisenhower did leave an opening for a peaceful solution by saying that a coalition government which included the Communists might succeed in keeping Laos neutral indefinitely, but Kennedy concluded from this meeting that Eisenhower would prefer United States military intervention to any substantial Communist success in Laos. During this second meeting neither Eisenhower nor Kennedy thought Vietnam required emergency measures, for they did not mention the country.

At the start of his Administration, Kennedy believed Indochina demanded decisions. In spite of the best efforts of Central Intelligence Agency advisers, America's allies in Laos were in disarray, and the neutralist factions there were tilting toward cooperation with the Communists; the NLF was making steady gains in South Vietnam; Diem's regime was almost complete dependent upon the United States for funds; and the 675 American advisers in South Vietnam could not stir Diem's security forces to fight effectively. With Eisenhower's support, Kennedy might have declared the region a vital security zone and stationed regular American armed forces in South Vietnam, Laos, and Thailand, exposing those units to attrition by the guerrillas. Or he might have decided to increase military, economic, and political aid and advice to the Laotians and Vietnamese and rely on them to hold the line, exposing only American advisers to danger. Or, finally, he might have tried to negotiate a neutralization agreement with the Communist powers, leaving American allies in Laos and Vietnam to fight on with American dollar aid only, while drawing the military containment line at the Thai border. Kennedy chose the middle course— escalation short of sending United States combat troops—though he had to retreat from Laos and apply his strategy to South Vietnam.

Why did Kennedy intervene in Southeast Asia? Domestic politics played its part, but international factors were also important. Kennedy perceived the Laotian civil war as yet another Sino-Soviet challenge, and he became even more alarmed when Premier Nikita Khrushchev placated the Chinese by declaring Soviet support for wars of national liberation. Khrushchev added to Kennedy's uneasiness in 1961 by increasing Soviet airlifts to Congolese and Laotian insurgents and by augmenting aid to Castro's Cuba and to North Vietnam. Even more disturbing was Khrushchev's threat to resume the Berlin blockade. In October, just before the Berlin crisis eased, Kennedy told Arthur Krock of the *New York Times* that "it was a hell of a note . . . that he had to try to handle the Berlin situation with the Communists encouraging foreign aggressors all over the place . . . in Viet-Nam, Laos, etc."

In early 1961 Kennedy believed the United States lacked the strength to intervene with conventional forces in both Southeast Asia and Europe simultaneously, and, with the Berlin crisis looming, he certainly wanted enough troops available for service in Europe. Landlocked Laos presented difficult logistical problems, and the anticommunist Laotians showed little desire for combat. General Maxwell D. Taylor and Walt W. Rostow of the National Security Council (NSC) staff urged the President to commit the United States to direct military intervention if the Communists renewed their Laotian offensive. Kennedy demurred, replying that President Charles de Gaulle of France "had spoken with feeling of the difficulty of fighting in this part of the world." He also "emphasized the reluctance of the American people and of many distinguished military leaders to see any direct involvement of U.S. troops in that part of the world." Consequently, Kennedy chose to negotiate, and in April 1961 the Soviets and Chinese agreed to meet in Geneva to discuss Laos.

By careful maneuvering, Kennedy was able to limit Republican criticism of his plan for a Laotian coalition government. He neutralized Eisenhower by having British Prime Minister Harold Macmillan appeal directly to the ex-President, and on July 20 he arranged for General Douglas MacArthur to lecture congressional leaders on the inadvisability of deploying American troops in Southeast Asia. Kennedy hoped he could persuade the South Vietnamese and Thais to send their own forces into Southern Laos, if the need arose. Rostow concluded that Kennedy wanted "indigenous forces used to the maximum," and "should we have to fight, we should use air and seapower to the maximum and engage minimum U.S. forces on the Southeast Asian mainland." The Geneva Conference on Laos began in May 1961 and lasted until June 1962, when the conferees agreed to set up a neutral government. Although they promised to respect Laotian neutrality and avoid establishing foreign military bases in Laos, by late 1962 both sides were covertly violating the agreement. The shaky arrangement held together, decreasing the need for overt American intervention after June 1962.

Kennedy's concessions in Laos raised the stakes for him in South Vietnam. During the Laos negotiations, Dean Rusk told Andrei Gromyko that "there must be a cessation of the increasingly open attacks against South Viet Nam by the DRV [North Vietnam]. . . . Both the Soviets and the DRV should understand that we are deeply committed to South Vietnam and cannot and will not accept its destruction." In spite of Rusk's claim, the Eisenhower Administration had not formally committed Kennedy to defend South Vietnam. The SEATO treaty required only that member nations consult with one another and meet common dangers according to their own "constitutional processes." Eisenhower had conditioned the large United States aid program on proper performance by Diem—a performance which Elbridge Durbrow, the United States Ambassador in Saigon, 1960–1961, found lacking. Eisenhower's policy toward South Vietnam left Kennedy with options other than to support a Diemist regime, but Kennedy was determined to help the South Vietnamese defeat the Communists.

Even before deciding to negotiate a Laotian settlement, Kennedy had gradually increased American military and economic aid to South Vietnam. At the outset of his Administration Kennedy had expressed doubt that Eisenhower had been doing enough in South Vietnam, and he asked his NSC staff, "How do we change morale; how do we get [South Vietnamese] operations in the north [North Vietnam]; how do we get moving?" In order to shift "from the defense to the offense," Kennedy authorized a 50,000-man increase in ARVN, sent in more American training staff, deployed 400 Green Berets to lead 9,000 border tribesmen against North Vietnam's infiltration routes, ordered the Central Intelligence Agency to organize commando raids against North Vietnam, armed the South Vietnamese provincial Civil Guard forces with heavy weapons, and added $42 million to an aid program which was already spending $220 million per year. In May 1961 Diem assured Vice President Lyndon B. Johnson that this impressive military and economic buildup would enable the ARVN to go on the offensive. Kennedy also prompted SEATO to declare publicly that it would refuse to "acquiesce in [a] takeover of [South Vietnam by] . . . an armed minority . . . supported from outside. . . ." In spite of these emergency actions, 58 percent of South Vietnam was under some degree of Communist control in May 1961, according to the Department of Defense.

When Kennedy personally tried to warn off the Russians, however, he hit a roadblock. At the Vienna summit in June, Kennedy brought up Khrushchev's speech in support of national liberation wars, and he told the Soviet leader that the "problem was how to avoid direct contact between [the] two countries as we support respective groups; [he] referred to Vietnam guerrilla activity and said we do not believe they represent [the] popular will. . . ." Khrushchev said the Soviets found it necessary to support such wars, because they were the only way oppressed peoples could throw off their oppressors. He also warned that American meddling in such wars might bring the "terrible prospect of mutual destruction." While Kennedy found Khrushchev to be threatening in this encounter, the young President may well have misperceived the degree of Soviet aggressiveness. During the Vienna summit, Kennedy gave as good as he got, and Khrushchev's moves in Germany, Laos, and the Congo might well have been defensive. In Berlin, the East Germans were losing growing numbers of refugees to the West; in Laos, the Communists were counterattacking against an American-backed rightist offensive; and in the Congo, Eisenhower had winked at the Belgian-sponsored Katanga secession and had driven Patrice Lumumba, a nationalist leader, to seek Soviet military aid. Even Khrushchev's much quoted speech called for disarmament negotiations and increased East-West trade, not just national liberation wars. The Soviet Union was not a principal opponent in South Vietnam.

Who was the enemy in South Vietnam? The People's Republic of China was hardly a consistent or enthusiastic ally of the Vietnamese Communists, for Beijing had joined Moscow in forcing Ho Chi Minh to accept the division of Vietnam during the 1954 Geneva Conference, and the Chinese Communists continued to compete with the North Vietnamese for influence over the Pathet Lao in Laos. Until 1960 the Chinese had not been enthusiastic about reviving the insurgency in South Vietnam. Given this record, the majority of the North Vietnamese preferred to lean to the side of the more distant Russians rather than to the side of the nearby Chinese. And just before Kennedy decided to escalate American efforts drastically in South Vietnam, Zhou Enlai walked dramatically out of the Twenty-second Congress of the Communist Party of the Soviet Union on October 23, 1961. As the Sino-Soviet dispute widened in 1961–1963, the North Vietnamese were able to play off both Communist powers to secure somewhat increased aid, but even the Chinese stressed that the independent strength of internal revolutionaries, not outside aid, was the prerequisite for victory in national liberation wars. Although the 1950s' line of peaceful coexistence did disappear from Communist rhetoric, neither the Chinese nor the Russians wanted to press national liberation wars to a direct superpower confrontation, and both recognized the centrality of indigenous sources to revolutionary success.

The North Vietnamese were not even the primary enemy in South Vietnam, for they hoped to avoid a full-scale conventional war with the American-advised Army of the Republic of Vietnam. They planned to mobilize the peasantry by a socio-political campaign and convert urban dwellers and disgruntled ARNV officers to their cause by nationalistic appeals, and then set up a coalition government after a general uprising and coup. In order to appeal to nationalists, the North Vietnamese urged the Southern Vietminh to organize the NLF. After the coup, the North Vietnamese probably planned to ease the Americans out of the country and then move the noncommunist elements out of the coalition. This program would let Hanoi finish its new five-year economic plan for the north by 1966. The North Vietnamese, then, did not constitute the *primary* enemy in South Vietnam during the Kennedy Administration, though they certainly provided leadership, some supplies, and encouragement to southern NLF fighters.

The two main enemies of the United States in South Vietnam were the peasants, who supported the NLF for reasons which Kennedy did not understand, and the southern Vietminh (later NLF) leaders who had suffered or gone into exile under Diem. Under Ho Chi Minh's direction from 1945 to 1954 the southern Vietminh had established the legitimacy of their movement by helping to defeat the Japanese, by driving the French colonialists from the country, and by extending the Vietminh revolution to at least 60 percent of the South, only to see Diem re-impose landlord control in the rural areas and arrest those suspected of Communist connections or opposition sympathies. By 1961 the NLF-inspired peasants were steadily liberating themselves from Diemist rule, while supplying their village militias with arms purchased or captured from the ARVN or brought home by numerous ARVN deserters. Although they received trained leaders from among the southerners who had fled North and returned, and although they received some arms from China, the NLF-led peasants could sustain a guerrilla campaign and control the countryside without major infiltration or arms shipments from North Vietnam or China.

The NLF had so many advantages that the insurgency spread rapidly. Its land program carried great appeal in the Delta region, where tenant farmers comprised the great majority, as well as in central Vietnam where landholdings were very small. Tenants customarily paid around 50 to 60 percent of their crop to the landlord, in addition to taxes and bribes, leaving them far poorer than Kennedy and Gullion supposed; the Diemists also represented an old, Westernizing, landlord regime, symbolized by Catholicism, which distinguished it from the majority of its Confucian, Buddhist, and Animist countrymen. By the fall of 1961, the peasant revolutionaries had won control of the villages in many regions of South Vietnam, although some experts have maintained that the Delta region was still hotly contested as late as 1963. Walt Rostow and Roger Hilsman, Kennedy's principal counter-insurgency war theorists, did not understand the attraction of the people's war strategy for the peasantry. They believed the Communists were primarily terrorists and guerrilla fighters, whose challenge was as much military as socio-economic, though Rostow stressed the military side of the struggle more than Hilsman. If Kennedy had felt politically free to do so, and if he had understood the strength of the people's war strategy, he might well have accepted coalition governments in both Laos and South Vietnam and drawn the counter-insurgency line instead in Thailand, a country which had not suffered the social divisions of colonialism and which did not suffer from a major insurgency.

By fall 1961 Diem's regime was in far deeper trouble than Kennedy had realized. In September, NLF armed forces tripled their attacks and consolidated their hold on much more of the countryside. Diem requested a bilateral security treaty with the United States and, with less enthusiasm, the dispatch of regular American combat forces. Kennedy then sent General Taylor, his personal military counselor, and Rostow of the NSC staff, two hawkish advisers, to South Vietnam to explore the seriousness of the setback and the need to meet Diem's requests. After their return the President began to consider his options. Through early November, the debate among Kennedy's principal advisers centered on a variety of escalatory alternatives. There were five main policies suggested, each of which reflected the organizational origins of its sponsor. . . .

Kennedy ruled out neutralization, but he also vetoed the Pentagon's plan to send regular combat troops to South Vietnam. Although the proposal for troops had gained wide support within the Administration, Taylor reported that Kennedy was "instinctively" against it. The CIA supported the President by predicting that the North Vietnamese would match American deployments with increased infiltration. On November 11, Kennedy vetoed sending regular combat troops. Instead, he decided to increase economic aid as well as send more advisers to ARVN and to South Vietnamese intelligence and government agencies. The United States also promised air reconnaissance, air transport, and helicopter units to improve ARVN reactions to NLF movements. Kennedy ordered that American advisers be assigned to ARVN field battalions, rather than division headquarters (thereby allowing them to help plan and direct operations). The President also followed Lansdale's advice by seeking the insertion of American advisers into the South Vietnamese government to provide operational guidance at all levels. The advisory effort, he said, "should be substantial otherwise we will give the wrong impression. . . . Are we prepared to send in hundreds and hundreds of men and dozens and dozens of ships? If we would just show up with 4 or 5 ships this will not do much good. . . . As I said on Saturday concerning Laos—we took actions which made no difference at all." In return for all of this United States assistance Diem would have to mobilize his nation fully, broaden his government, and give his generals the power to move troops without prior clearance from Saigon. Kennedy directed Ambassador Nolting to tell Diem that the "missions being undertaken by our own forces . . . are more suitable for white foreign troops than garrison duty or seeking out of Viet Cong personnel submerged in the Viet-Nam population." Nevertheless, Kennedy had committed Americans to fly helicopters and planes and accompany ARVN troops when they engaged the NLF.

In mid-November, Kennedy tried to dissuade Bundy, Taylor, Rostow, McNamara, and the Joint Chiefs from their campaign to send regular troops by telling them foreign troops were only "a last resort." The President added that he did not want a war with China. He did agree to allow the Pentagon to plan for the introduction of SEATO troops, but that was as far as he would go. Vietnam, he explained, was unlike Korea, because it was not a clear-cut victim of aggression, and, consequently, neither the Democrats in Congress nor the British nor the French would support SEATO intervention there. And the United States did not have enough troops to go around. Nor was it clear why American soldiers should be sent into South Vietnam, but not into Cuba: "The President said that he could even make a rather strong case against intervening in an area 10,000 miles away against 16,000 guerrillas with a native army of 200,000, where millions have been spent for years with no success." The Joint Chiefs remained unconvinced, replying that they favored invading Cuba as well. The Chiefs doubted that the Lansdale counterinsurgency approach would work, for Vietnam was not like the Philippines or Malaya. They told General Taylor in October that the Malay counter-insurgency campaign was not comparable to Vietnam, because the Thais and British were able to control Malaya's borders; because colonial police were able to isolate ethnic

Chinese insurgents from the majority of the population; because food was scarce, enabling strategic hamlet programs to work; and because the British, not the Malays, were in command. In January 1962 the Joint Chiefs reiterated their request for the dispatch of regular American troops, but by then the alternative program was well under way.

Diem expressed disappointment and anger. He had requested a bilateral alliance and massive aid, not an Americanization of his government. He told Nolting, "Viet Nam did not want to be a protectorate." After tense negotiations, he agreed only to *consult* American advisers whom he helped select, and he avoided significant changes in his military command structure, because he remained fearful of a coup. Kennedy was trapped by the contradictions in his own policy toward Diem. He could not force a supposedly independent nationalist leader to accept American tutelage without appearing to undermine him, and Diem was already publicizing Kennedy's demands. Kennedy gave way. On December 15, the two governments announced their joint partnership—but on Diem's terms. A solid political foundation was essential to successful prosecution of the war, but the State Department had lost another round in its fight to make Diem more efficient, democratic, and popular. And on February 18, 1962, Robert F. Kennedy confirmed the State Department defeat by declaring unconditionally during a visit to Saigon, "We are going to win in Viet-Nam. We will remain here until we do win."

Diem regained some favor with Washington by accepting another part of the Kennedy plan for South Vietnam—strategic hamlets. Roger Hilsman, director of the State Department's Bureau of Intelligence and Research, correctly concluded that the villages of South Vietnam willingly provided supplies and the great majority of recruits to the NLF. He argued that the South Vietnamese government had to provide villagers with civic action programs and physical security by creating fortified hamlets linked by radio. The strategic hamlets would receive developmental aid and close police scrutiny. In addition, the hamlets' own militias would defend them and call in roving Civil Guard units if the NLF attacked. Because they lacked food and replacements, the NLF bands would have to attack in strength, rather than starve, and the Civil Guard and newly mobile ARVN could then crush them by ambush or conventional engagement.

While Hilsman had a somewhat more accurate perception of the insurgency than the Pentagon, his proposed solution proved unrealistic. His proposed village militias consisted of the fathers, uncles, and brothers of the NLF village guerrillas, and his expectation that one relative would starve or even shoot another in return for a medical clinic, a school, and a new well was strange at best. Diem, and his brother Ngo Dinh Nhu, who was in charge of the secret police and internal security, pushed the hamlet program rapidly as a means of reclaiming the villages. Land reform was notably absent and other benefits slow in coming, while the peasants often had to purchase the building materials and barbed wire which they used to fence themselves in.

At first, the military side of Kennedy's counter-insurgency campaign appeared to show progress. Aided by helicopters and growing numbers of American advisers, the ARVN bedeviled the NLF in the first half of 1962. With ARVN's fortunes appearing to prosper, the Kennedy Administration flirted briefly with negotiations. In July 1962, Harriman, who was just wrapping up the Laos settlement, offered the North Vietnamese a neutrality agreement similar to the one he had just concluded for Laos. Ho Chi Minh replied that the NLF had already suggested such a plan: the United States would withdraw its advisers; a cease-fire would go into effect; the great powers would guarantee the neutralization and independence of Vietnam; the Vietnamese would establish a coalition government, which would include both Diem and the NLF; and the coalition government would end the strategic hamlet program, hold free elections, and begin talks to reunify the country. In late 1962 the NLF also offered a cease-fire which did not first require the withdrawal of the Americans. Given the strength of the NLF in the countryside, free elections would almost certainly have resulted in a government dominated by the NLF. Although the NLF proposal opened the prospect of a decent interval between the time of American withdrawal and the time of a prospective defeat of Diem, Kennedy rejected the NLF offer. The President preferred to seek victory, rather than accept defeat, however much disguised or delayed.

By the end of 1962 Kennedy had sent 11,000 American military personnel to South Vietnam, along with 300 military aircraft, 120 helicopters, and additional heavy weapons. American pilots helped to fly combat missions, and the Americans supplied napalm bombs to the South Vietnamese air force. At Binh Hoa in January 1962 an air strike killed five civilians, including a two-year-old boy, a five-year-old girl, and a seven-year-old boy. If their parents had not been active supporters of the NLF before the raid, they most probably joined after this tragedy. Kennedy put General Paul D. Harkins, a former tank officer, in charge of the military assistance program in Saigon, and Harkins adopted a strategy based on the United States Army's tradition of achieving victory via attrition and destruction of the enemy's army. Harkins left the problem of village militias largely to the Vietnamese Civil Guards and Self Defense Corps, while he tried to break the enemy's will by using ARVN regulars to smash the enemy's main guerrilla forces. Taylor and Harkins wanted to put continuous pressure on the NLF regulars by exploiting American air mobility—a strategy which they believed had worked against guerrillas in both Greece and Korea. When ARVN succeeded in surrounding the NLF regulars with overwhelming numbers, they were supposed to use artillery and air strikes to flush them into combat with superior blocking forces.

For a variety of reasons ARVN could not implement this strategy. Its divisions were trained and armed to deter a conventional invasion from the north, and they were unsuited to chase lightly armed guerrillas who disappeared into the countryside. Nor did many of the units in the field want to fight. A number of senior officers were mercenaries who had served in the colonial French Army, and Diem compounded the problem by putting his favorite officers in charge of the best units and keeping them in garrison, while sending poorly trained units into combat. American advisers could not energize ARVN because they did not speak Vietnamese, control promotions, make aid allocations (which came through Diem), or command troops (as they had done in Korea). Intelligence operations also faltered. American and South Vietnamese intelligence officers sought order-of-battle information on regular NLF units, rather than try to identify members of the local village militias and political committees, who were the mainstays of the insurgency. In 1962 air mobility allowed ARVN to achieve some early surprise victories, but the NLF soon adapted to the helicopters by making quicker hit-and-run attacks and placing heavy machine guns in village tree lines. Even if ARVN had been able to destroy the main force units which they were vainly chasing, they would still have faced the much more numerous village militias. The only solution to the village militias was to occupy the villages, reduce land rents, and recognize the NLF's land redistributions. But American military advisers believed in the Clausewitzian goal of destroying their enemy's army, not clearing and holding peasant villages, and Diem believed in control by his bureaucrats and the landlords, not reform for peasant hamlets.

Given the advanced state of the NLF revolt, Kennedy's counterinsurgency strategy was proving unworkable. As 1962 gave way to 1963, the strategic hamlet program also developed trouble. Diem, Nhu, and Harkins had pushed the program far out into enemy territory, resettling some hamlets in which as many as one-third of the men were missing—they had probably joined the NLF. The sullen strategic hamlet militias often did not defend their villages against the insurgents, and the Self-Defense Corps and Provincial Civil Guard units were unable or unwilling to take on company-sized NLF attacks. By the spring of 1963 only 1500 of 8500 strategic hamlets remained viable. By contrast, in June 1963 the NLF was levying taxes in 42 of South Vietnam's 44 provinces.

Organizational problems also undermined Kennedy's strategy. General Lyman Lemnitzer, the Chairman of the Joint Chiefs of Staff, and General Earle G. Wheeler, Army Chief of Staff, proved unsympathetic to counterinsurgency ideas. Kennedy failed to appoint anyone of stature to ride herd in South Vietnam on Harkins, Diem, and Nhu, while in Washington the successive Vietnam task force directors also lacked the rank to force independent government departments to coordinate their activities. Consequently the military campaigns and strategic hamlet programs did not mesh well. Kennedy kept most of the decisions in his own hands, and he lacked the time or energy to be an effective Vietnam desk officer. Nor could he play the role of an Under Secretary of State or Defense in seeking intelligence or reviewing policy, except in crises such as occurred during the fall of 1961. His small NSC staff were primarily European-oriented generalists who lacked Asian expertise or the time to develop a sophisticated set of questions which would have revealed the nature of the NLF revolution. The NSC staff members maintained the illusion of being in touch by having mountains of cables routed through the White House, but they lacked the time and background to put them in their proper perspective. Sorensen is correct in saying that Vietnam "never received the attention it should have . . . at the highest levels." Kennedy remained convinced that the methods of counterinsurgency would gradually bring victory in the countryside. In his State of the Union message of 1963, he confidently declared, "The spearpoint of aggression has been blunted in Viet-Nam."

In early 1963 Kennedy's optimism waned briefly after Senator Mansfield reported on his recent trip to Southeast Asia. Mansfield warned that the United States might ultimately be forced to accept a dominant combat role if Kennedy did not withdraw the American advisers. Mansfield's prediction reportedly angered the President, who was even less pleased when he heard of the very poor ARVN showing in combat at Ap Bac in the Delta. With the American press present, a large ARVN force, aided by American-donated helicopters and armored personnel carriers, allowed a much smaller NLF force to escape. In the process, the NLF inflicted heavy casualties on ARVN and shot down five helicopters. Three American advisers died. Kennedy was puzzled by "the Vietnam troops and their lack of courage," and he asked his aides to reassess the rice paddy war. Hilsman and Michael V. Forrestal, the NSC staffer assigned to expedite Vietnam policy, saw no need to "make any sudden and dramatic change," though they questioned Harkins's penchant for large-scale operations. The generals themselves remained optimistic. Wheeler reported that "[we] are winning slowly on the present thrust," and Harkins trumpeted that "improvement is a daily fact . . . and we are confident of the outcome."

Besides ARVN and strategic hamlet failures, Kennedy had to contend with charges that the United States was using "dirty-war" tactics in Vietnam. Kennedy had indeed ordered a limited, experimental program of trail clearing and crop destruction using defoliants and herbicides such as Agent Orange. In doing so, he not only set an unfortunate precedent for much larger applications of chemicals during the Johnson Administration but he also provided the NLF and North Vietnam with an opportunity to launch a propaganda campaign and appeal to the International Control Commission. It was a high political price to pay for a program which proved militarily worthless.

Much worse problems arose when South Vietnamese troops fired into a crowd of Buddhists in Hué on May 8, 1963. The Buddhist marchers were flying religious banners during a celebration of Buddha's birthday, in spite of a ban on such symbols issued by Diem's brother, Ngo Dinh Thuc, the Archbishop of Hué. The ARVN killed nine marchers and wounded many others, triggering Buddhist demonstrations and self-immolations. In the major South Vietnamese cities students took to the streets to support Buddhist charges of religious discrimination and authoritarianism against the Ngos. Diem and Nhu countered with raids on pagodas, mass arrests, and martial law, each of which provoked more marches and self-immolations, creating a cycle which would persist through the fall of the Ngos in November. Madame Ngo Dinh Nhu, the security chief's wife and Diem's sister-in-law, callously dismissed the immolations as "barbecues" and offered to supply matches and gasoline in the future. The Kennedy Administration attempted repeatedly to induce Diem to compromise with the Buddhists. Diem said he would seek reconciliation, but he never kept his promise.

During his first two years in office Kennedy had tried to minimize the seriousness of the Vietnam problem, and he had largely succeeded. In spite of [presidential assistant Theodore C.] Sorensen's advice, Kennedy chose not to make a major speech at the end of 1961 explaining his decision to escalate, and thus he delayed public debate. As American advisors went into combat, congressmen yielded to Kennedy's appeals for support and Congress routinely approved increases in American aid programs to South Vietnam. In the summer of 1963, however, the Buddhist crisis brought increasingly critical newspaper reports from Homer Bigart and David Halberstam of the *New York Times* and Neil Sheehan of United Press International. At first Kennedy believed that having the American mission in Saigon bring reporters "into our confidence" would generate an "accurate story [of] our Viet-Nam program," but the journalists' well-founded distrust of the Diem regime and the American mission doomed the effort. In late October Kennedy even tried to persuade *New York Times* publisher Arthur H. Sulzberger to remove Halberstam from South Vietnam, but to no avail. Vietnam became a big story in August and September 1963, and increasingly the criticism included both Kennedy and Diem. Kennedy finally had to conclude, "The way to confound the press is to win the war."

As the election campaigns for 1964 began, bipartisan support for Kennedy's foreign policy broke down. During the summer and fall of 1963, conservatives attacked the foreign aid bill, the American wheat sale to the Soviet Union, and the nuclear test ban treaty. Nelson Rockefeller, Nixon, and Goldwater were waiting for Kennedy to make serious mistakes in South Vietnam and then exploit such errors in the presidential campaign. Senator Richard Russell of Georgia, a member of the President's own party, presaged the debate by chiding the Administration for "trying to fight this [Vietnam] problem as if it were a tournament of roses." He called for the "dirty-tricks department" to offer rewards for NLF guerrillas—dead or alive. To Kennedy, experienced as he was in the politics of anti-Communism, these criticisms foreshadowed another debate about "who lost China?"

While Kennedy watched the Buddhist crisis in South Vietnam with growing dismay, he faced a similar crisis closer to home: the civil rights conflict in the American South. The civil rights issue worried Kennedy's pollsters and political advisers, who warned that he might lose critical Southern and Midwestern votes in the next election. By August 1963, half of those polled said he was pushing integration too fast. Louis Harris's analysis of the 1960 results indicated the Republicans might make real inroads in the region in 1964, and a Lubell survey of former Kennedy voters in Birmingham, Alabama, turned up only one white who would again vote for Kennedy.

The probable political loss of the South made the retention and expansion of the Democratic vote in the North vital, but Kennedy's advisers warned him he was in trouble there as well. . . .

Thus, in addition to Kennedy's personal and ideological commitment to containment in South Vietnam, there also existed a political imperative to quiet the Buddhist crisis, stabilize the South Vietnamese regime, and convince the South Vietnamese to fight effectively. But Kennedy had little luck with Diem. In fact, Kennedy's efforts to persuade Diem to mollify the Buddhists aggravated the underlying conflict between Saigon and Washington. Diem resented the rapid American advisery buildup and the American advisers' penchant for meddling in Vietnamese decisions. The South Vietnamese dictator also feared—quite correctly—the Americans might encourage his enemies among the South Vietnamese generals to depose him. The CIA reported that Diem might request a reduction in the number of American advisers. When asked about Diem's complaints at a news conference, Kennedy responded that withdrawal of the advisers would be premature, with "still a long, hard struggle to go" and no "brightening in the skies that would permit us to withdraw troops or begin to by the end of this year." Actually, back in 1962 when the war seemed to be going well, the Pentagon had prepared plans for an orderly withdrawal. If Kennedy had wanted to, he might have used these plans to implement a withdrawal of aid and advisers in stages as a means of forcing the generals and Diem to reform.

During June and July intelligence officials warned Kennedy that Diem had alienated the nationalist elites which Kennedy had identified in the 1950s as vital to building a stable Third World. Thomas Hughes of the State Department reported that discontent was widespread in the civil bureaucracy, in the military establishment, among students, and even within the Catholic hierarchy. Hughes, Hilsman, and the CIA warned that a coup against Diem was a distinct possibility, and Hughes and the CIA assured Kennedy that "a reasonably large pool of . . . experienced and trained manpower" existed which "could provide reasonably effective leadership for the government [of South Vietnam] and [for] the war effort."

On June 27 the Administration announced the nomination of Henry Cabot Lodge, former senator from Massachusetts and Republican candidate for Vice President in 1960, as Ambassador to Saigon. According to the CIA, a "considerably disturbed" Diem correctly interpreted the appointment to mean "that the United States [now] planned to wield a 'big stick.' . . ." Lodge's appointment also gave the Administration political sea room to act against Diem; one magazine predicted Lodge's appointment would "make the Republicans think twice before attacking Administration policy in troublesome South Viet Nam." Lodge arrived in Saigon on August 22, the day after Nhu's American-trained Special Forces raided Buddhist pagodas in Saigon, Hué, and elsewhere and made mass arrests. Diem had presented Lodge with a fait accompli: he had curbed the Buddhists before Lodge could press him to accommodate them. Rumors even circulated that Diem and Nhu were considering serious negotiations with North Vietnam.

Kennedy had instructed Lodge to persuade Diem to treat his non-Communist opponents better, and if Diem resisted, work for Diem's removal. In fact, since July a group of ARVN generals led by Duong Van Minh, Tran Van Don, and Tran Thien Khiem had been exploring the possibility of an American-supported coup with American CIA agents.

In Washington, many senior officials were on vacation at the time of the August raids on the pagodas, and the anti-Diem faction in the White House and State Department urged swift action. Forrestal urged the President to "move before the situation in Saigon freezes." With the aid of George Ball, the Under Secretary of State, who was filling in for Rusk, Harriman, Hilsman, and Forrestal persuaded Kennedy over the telephone to instruct Lodge on August 24 to compel Diem to drop Nhu from his administration and accept American advice on how to run his government and army. If Diem did not comply, then the United States was to give "direct support" to the ARVN generals in the event of Diem's ouster. Kennedy assured Lodge, "We will back you to the hilt on actions you take to achieve our objectives." Perhaps with the Bay of Pigs fiasco in mind, Kennedy did want time to review plans for the coup to assure that the American-backed generals would succeed. He warned Lodge on August 29, "I know from experience that failure is more destructive than the appearance of indecision. . . . When we go, we must go to win. . . ." Consequently, Kennedy reserved the right to "change course and reverse previous instructions." But he continued to allow the Ambassador wide discretion in the execution of his Vietnam policy, authorizing Lodge to suspend aid to Diem "at a time and under conditions of your choice." Although Lodge was eager to act immediately, the ARVN generals were unable to line up enough military support in the Saigon area to risk a coup.

Kennedy continued to apply pressure to Diem. On television on September 2 he remarked that the war could not be won without popular support from the South Vietnamese, and, he added, "in my opinion, in the last 2 months, the government has gotten out of touch with the people." Kennedy predicted that Diem could only regain such support "with changes in policy and perhaps with [changes in] personnel." Otherwise, the choices for victory "would not be very good." But Kennedy disagreed "with those who say we should withdraw. That would be a great mistake. . . . Forty-seven Americans have been killed in combat with the enemy, but this is a very important struggle even though it is far away." Between October 2 and October 5, Kennedy signaled his displeasure with Diem by applying a variety of "selective pressures": Kennedy canceled some future economic aid shipments; threatened to cut off American support for Nhu's Special Forces, unless they were placed under the command of the ARVN General Staff and moved from Saigon into the field; recalled the CIA station chief in Saigon, who was too closely identified with Nhu; and announced publicly that 1,000 American advisers would be withdrawn from South Vietnam by the end of 1963 and all American advisers would be out by the end of 1965, provided that the war in the countryside continued to go well.

By cutting aid to Diem, Kennedy helped revive—apparently unwittingly—the ARVN generals' interest in a coup. On October 3, Duong Van Minh, Chief of the General Staff, asked for reassurance that the Americans would not oppose a coup, and he suggested the possibility that the plan might include the assassination of two Ngo brothers, Nhu and Can. Lucien Conein, Minh's CIA contact, assured him that Washington would provide economic and military assistance to a new regime which promised to co-operate with the United States, regain popular support, and try to win the war. CIA Director John McCone neither encouraged nor deplored the recommendation for the assassination of Diem's brothers, although he did warn Saigon that Diem himself should not be killed. On October 25, Lodge alerted Kennedy that a coup would occur sometime before November. In the days just before the coup, Kennedy and McGeorge Bundy worriedly questioned Lodge about prospects for success and the possibility of achieving plausible deniability of the American role in the coup. Once the attempted overthrow began, however, they told Lodge it was "in the interests of the U.S. Government that it should succeed."

On the morning of November 1, Lodge met for the last time with Diem. A few hours later the coup finally began, with CIA agent Conein at coup headquarters to report to the embassy, advise the coup leaders, and distribute cash, if needed. At 4:30 P.M. that same day a frantic Diem telephoned the United States Ambassador. Lodge relayed an offer of safe conduct out of the country from the coup leaders, but he claimed disingenuously that the United States government had no policy toward the coup. While Diem and Nhu escaped to the Cholon section of Saigon, both to die the following day at the hands of General Minh's lieutenants, Lodge went to bed. On November 8, Washington officially recognized the new military regime in Saigon. A week later, in response to a *New York Times* editorial which suggested a negotiated settlement of the war, Rusk instructed Lodge to tell the generals that the United States government "cannot envisage any points that would be negotiable." The Secretary of State reassured the South Vietnamese government that North Vietnam would have to end its "subversive aggression" and allow the new South Vietnamese regime to "extend its authority throughout South Vietnam before the United States would withdraw."

The events of 1963 shattered one expectation—that Diem would listen to American advice, reform his government, and win the war—and created another—that the generals would do the same. Before the coup Kennedy and his Washington advisers simply assumed that the ARVN generals would be an improvement over Diem, but they were wrong. Many of the members of the South Vietnamese Military Revolutionary Council had been collaborators with the French colonialists, and Robert Thompson, the British counter-insurgency expert, thought they "lacked the experience or ability to command much more than a regiment, let alone a country." Within three months, another military faction overthrew Minh and the Revolutionary Council, starting a topsy-turvey pattern of coup and counter-coup which continued for some time. Even the Buddhist protest marches and self-immolations continued to occur.

Before Minh fell, however, Kennedy himself died. His remarks prepared for delivery on November 22 in Dallas, Texas, a destination he never reached, included the words: "We in this country in this generation—by destiny rather than choice—the watchmen on the walls of world freedom. . . . Our assistance to . . . nations can be painful, risky and costly, as is true in Southeast Asia today. But we dare not weary of the task." And in another speech he intended to deliver that night can be seen the outline of his anticipated 1964 campaign. The New Frontier had gotten the country moving again—America's economy was growing, its space effort thriving, its military power expanding, and its containment policy working from Berlin to Latin America to Southeast Asia. On the day he died he still hoped for victory in South Vietnam and vindication of the doctrine of counter-insurgency.

Why did Kennedy persist in Vietnam under such unpromising conditions? After all, many leaders, ranging from Charles de Gaulle and Douglas MacArthur to Mike Mansfield and John Kenneth Galbraith, had warned Kennedy against a deepening Vietnam adventure. He chose to ignore their warnings. His defenders claimed that the Eisenhower Administration left him no choice but to pursue the war in Vietnam. But he might well have drawn the containment line in Thailand, while letting Diem fight his own battles with generous grants of money and arms. Instead, he sent in 16,000 advisers, 100 of whom had died by the end of 1963; he sponsored the strategic hamlet program; he unleashed a war of attrition against the NLF; and he allowed the military to use napalm, defoliation, and helicopter envelopment tactics, rather than a clear and hold strategy. Why did he do it? Both Khrushchev and Mao Zedung may have helped to draw him in, for they had exaggerated their support for national liberation wars, thereby lending substance to Kennedy's fears. In fact, however, the fragmentation of the Communist world was accelerating in these years, as Kennedy could read in his own intelligence reports. If Kennedy had negotiated a deal on South Vietnam, he might have encouraged détente with the Soviet Union and hastened a Sino-Vietnamese split.

Kennedy's self-confident definition of the South Vietnamese problem was an important reason for his persistence. The President believed that Diem and the generals constituted a third force of nationalists who could lead peasants and workers in a fight against Communism. Because Americans were nation-builders, not colonialists, they could persuade the South Vietnamese to apply American technology, tactics, and organizational techniques to the problems of the Vietnamese countryside, with its problems of underdevelopment, terrorism, and guerrilla warfare. The struggle would be long and hard, but success would come eventually—if only the right combination of Vietnamese nationalist leaders could be found. The misapplied analogs of Greece and Malaya reinforced his belief in nation-building and counter-insurgency. Kennedy's image of Vietnam proved false. In the minds of the peasants, Diem and the generals represented the old regime.

The people of the countryside craved land, power, and the promise of economic justice and national liberation, not wells, clinics, films, strategic hamlets, or infantry sweeps through their villages. The NLF program also contained more political and economic change and less coercion and violence than Kennedy comprehended. Kennedy's expectations for the future were unrealistic as well. American advisers could not transform the ARVN into an effective force, nor persuade Diem and Nhu to appeal to the peasantry.

Kennedy's decision-making system failed to correct the President's false image of Vietnam's prospects. His small staff lacked an understanding of the socio-economic appeal of the Chinese and Vietnamese revolutions to the peasantry. The NSC did not produce an accurate picture which would shatter the President's strongly held image of a nationalist elite waiting for outside inspiration to mobilize a neutral peasantry against Communist terrorists. Although Kennedy's collegial style of decision-making has received considerable praise, it also did not work well in the case of Vietnam. Until the Buddhist crisis of 1963 Kennedy usually treated Vietnam as a fairly routine foreign policy problem, which he assumed he could handle with limited resources. His staff, with the exception of the hyperactive Walt Rostow, tended to coast along the lines of established policy, recommending more of the same. Not until November 1961 did a major review of the options emerge. Even then, however, the list of options which were staffed out and fully considered was incomplete, for none of the key debaters, with the brief exception of Harriman, was a serious advocate of neutralization and a retreat to Thailand. Kennedy never gave negotiations a chance. Nor were there many advocates for withholding advisers while giving Diem enough money and arms to sink or swim on his own. Instead of a sophisticated image of the problem of rural revolution in Southeast Asia, ingrained Cold War thinking about the credibility of containment shaped Administration deliberations. Consequently, the debate always centered on escalation, with Kennedy curbing the hawks in the Pentagon and choosing counter-insurgency.

The politics of anti-Communism also played a large role in shaping Kennedy's decisions. He had survived and prospered in the McCarthyite atmosphere of the fifties, and he feared the loss of swing anti-Communist votes to the Republicans and the Dixiecrats in the increasingly turbulent politics of the sixties. The lesson of the so-called loss of China remained with him, and the Republicans repeatedly peppered him with charges of appeasement on a host of issues. During the 1960 campaign he had promised to turn the tide of the Cold War, and he was preparing to claim considerable progress in 1964. With Laos neutralized, Cuba hostile, and East Berlin sealed off, Vietnam became a testing ground by his own definition. Though some of his defenders have claimed he would have withdrawn the United States from Vietnam after being re-elected in 1964, they underestimate the degree to which Kennedy had committed himself and the country to supporting a non-Communist Vietnam. Kennedy would have had to admit the failure of his major counter-insurgency effort, which was designed to discourage national liberation wars everywhere. More likely than with-drawal was a continued search for the right combination of means and men to win the war in South Vietnam. Kennedy would probably have ruled out sending in United States Army infantry divisions, but short of that limit, he would probably have continued to make a major effort to succeed.

In any case, by late 1963 Kennedy had radically expanded the American commitment to Vietnam. By putting American advisers in harm's way and allowing the press to chronicle their tribulations and casualties, he helped to engage American patriotism in a war against Vietnamese people. By arguing that Vietnam was a test of the West's ability to defeat the people's war strategy and a test of American credibility in the Cold War, he raised the costs of withdrawal for his successor. By launching a strategic hamlet program, he further disrupted peasant society. By allowing Harkins and the ARVN to bomb, shell, search, and destroy, he made so many recruits for the NLF that he encouraged North Vietnam and the NLF to move the war into its final military phase. By participating in Diem's removal, he brought warlord politics to Saigon. By downplaying publicly the American role in Vietnam, he discouraged a constitutional debate about the com-mitment of American advisers to battle. By publicly and privately com-mitting the United States to the survival of an anti-Communist state in South Vietnam, he made it much more difficult for his successors to blame the South Vietnamese government for its own failures and to withdraw. And by insisting that military victory was the only acceptable outcome, he ignored the possibility that negotiations might lead to an acceptable process of retreat. Kennedy bequeathed to Lyndon B. Johnson a failing counter-insurgency program and a deepened commitment to the war in South Vietnam.

✗ *F U R T H E R   R E A D I N G*

David Burner, *John F. Kennedy and a New Generation* (1988)
David Halberstam, *The Making of a Quagmire* (1965)
Ellen J. Hammer, *A Death in November: America in Vietnam, 1963* (1987)
Jim F. Heath, *Decade of Disillusionment* (1975)
Roger Hilsman, *To Move a Nation* (1967)
Henry Cabot Lodge, *The Storm Has Many Eyes* (1973)
John Mecklin, *Mission in Torment* (1965)
Herbert S. Parmet, *JFK* (1983)
Thomas G. Paterson, "Bearing the Burden: A Critical Look at JFK's Foreign Policy," *Virgina Quarterly Review*, 54 (1978), 193–212
———, ed., *Kennedy's Quest for Victory* (1989)
Stephen E. Pelz, "John F. Kennedy's 1961 Vietnam War Decisions," *Journal of Strategic Studies*, 4 (1981), 356–385
Walt W. Rostow, *The Diffusion of Power* (1972)
William J. Rust, *Kennedy in Vietnam* (1985)
Arthur M. Schlesinger, Jr., *Robert Kennedy and His Times* (1978)
———, *A Thousand Days* (1965)
Neil Sheehan, *A Bright Shining Lie* (1988) (on John Paul Vann)
Richard J. Snyder, ed., *John F. Kennedy* (1988)

Theodore C. Sorensen, *Kennedy* (1965)

Maxwell D. Taylor, *Swords and Ploughshares* (1972)

Richard Tregaskis, *Vietnam Diary* (1963)

Richard J. Walton, *Cold War and Counter-Revolution: The Foreign Policy of John F. Kennedy* (1972)

Geoffrey Warner, "The United States and the Fall of Diem," Part I: "The Coup that Never Was," *Australian Outlook*, 29 (1974), 245–58

——, "The United States and the Fall of Diem," Part II: "The Death of Diem," *Australian Outlook*, 29 (1975), 3–17

CHAPTER

6

Lyndon B. Johnson's Decisions

for War

✕

In the months following the Diem and Kennedy assassinations, political chaos gripped South Vietnam. Combined with the spreading guerrilla insurgency, this turmoil made American officials worry that the survival of the Saigon government hung in the balance. In December 1963 Defense Secretary Robert S. McNamara warned President Lyndon B. Johnson that without a reversal of current trends within the next two or three months, the most likely result would be a communist-controlled state. Many of Johnson's advisers urged military escalation, recommending bombing reprisals against the North and the dispatch of U.S. combat forces in the South.

In August 1964, in response to alleged attacks against U.S. naval vessels by North Vietnamese warboats in the Gulf of Tonkin, Congress passed a resolution that granted the president sweeping powers. It authorized him to take ''all necessary measures to repel any armed attacks against the forces of the United States and to prevent further aggression.'' Nevertheless, Johnson moved cautiously. In July 1965, fearing the imminence of Saigon's collapse, he acted. After a lengthy deliberative process, LBJ ordered a sustained bombing campaign against North Vietnam and authorized the introduction of combat forces to stem the insurgency in the South. Those decisions committed the United States to a major land war in Asia.

Because Johnson's escalation of U.S. involvement in Vietnam had such profound consequences, his decisions have understandably been the subject of much heated public and scholarly debate. How were the decisions reached? Did Johnson dominate the deliberative process? Or did he simply follow the recommendations of his principal advisers? Why did LBJ and senior policy makers dismiss the doubts raised by Under Secretary of State George Ball? What specific goals did Johnson expect to achieve through the use of combat troops and the air offensive? Did he expect to defeat the communists? Or only to prevent the fall of the South Vietnamese regime? How did he view the stakes involved in Vietnam? Did his concern with the likely domestic political fallout from the loss of South Vietnam to the communists affect his thinking? Did he seek merely to buy time for his Great Society reform program? What did he believe would be the inter-

national ramifications for the United States if its South Vietnamese ally perished?

X *D O C U M E N T S*

The first document contains excerpts from National Security Action Memorandum 288 of March 17, 1964, which set forth U.S. objectives in South Vietnam. The Tonkin Gulf Resolution, which passed the Senate on August 10, 1964, with only two dissenting votes, and reprinted in the second document, authorized the president to use the force he deemed necessary in Vietnam. President Johnson's April 7, 1965, explanation to an audience at Johns Hopkins University why the United States was fighting in Vietnam is the next selection.

The fourth document, a memorandum to the president from Secretary of Defense Robert McNamara, recommended a substantial expansion of U.S. military pressure against the Vietcong in the South and the North Vietnamese in the North. Under Secretary of State Ball offered contrary advice to the president in a memorandum of July 1, the fifth document. An excerpt from Johnson's memoir *The Vantage Point*, in which he reflected on his decision to accept McNamara's advice, is the next document. The final selection offers a soldier's perspective. Reprinted from Philip Caputo's best-selling memoir *A Rumor of War*, it captures the innocence and idealism that some American fighting men brought with them to Vietnam.

Reassessment of U.S. Objectives in South Vietnam, 1964

[The United States' policy is] to prepare immediately to be in a position on 72 hours' notice to initiate the full range of Laotian and Cambodian "Border Control actions" . . . and the "Retaliatory Actions" against North Vietnam, and to be in a position on 30 days' notice to initiate the program of "Graduated Overt Military Pressure" against North Vietnam. . . .

We seek an independent non-Communist South Vietnam. We do not require that it serve as a Western base or as a member of a Western Alliance. South Vietnam must be free, however, to accept outside assistance as required to maintain its security. This assistance should be able to take the form not only of economic and social measures but also police and military help to root out and control insurgent elements.

Unless we can achieve this objective in South Vietnam, almost all of Southeast Asia will probably fall under Communist dominance (all of Vietnam, Laos, and Cambodia), accommodate to Communism so as to remove effective U.S. and anti-Communist influence (Burma), or fall under the domination of forces not now explicitly Communist but likely then to become so (Indonesia taking over Malaysia). Thailand might hold for a period without help, but would be under grave pressure. Even the Philippines would become shaky, and the threat to India on the West, Australia and New Zealand to the South, and Taiwan, Korea, and Japan to the North and East would be greatly increased.

All of these consequences would probably have been true even if the

U.S. had not since 1954, and especially since 1961, become so heavily engaged in South Vietnam. However, that fact accentuates the impact of a Communist South Vietnam not only in Asia but in the rest of the world, where the South Vietnam conflict is regarded as a test case of U.S. capacity to help a nation to meet the Communist "war of liberation."

Thus, purely in terms of foreign policy, the stakes are high. . . .

We are now trying to help South Vietnam defeat the Viet Cong, supported from the North, by means short of the unqualified use of U.S. combat forces. We are not acting against North Vietnam except by a modest "covert" program operated by South Vietnamese (and a few Chinese Nationalists)—a program so limited that it is unlikely to have any significant effect. . . .

There were and are some sound reasons for the limits imposed by the present policy—the South Vietnamese must win their own fight; U.S. intervention on a larger scale, and/or GVN actions against the North, would disturb key allies and other nations; etc. In any case, it is vital that we continue to take every reasonable measure to assure success in South Vietnam. The policy choice is not an "either/or" between this course of action and possible pressure against the North; the former is essential and without regard to our decision with respect to the latter. The latter can, at best, only reinforce the former. . . .

Many of the actions described in the succeeding paragraphs fit right into the framework of the [pacification] plan as announced by Khanh. Wherever possible, we should tie our urgings of such actions to Khanh's own formulation of them, so that he will be carrying out a Vietnamese plan and not one imposed by the United States.

The Tonkin Gulf Resolution, 1964

To promote the maintenance of international peace and security in southeast Asia.

Whereas naval units of the Communist regime in Vietnam, in violation of the principles of the Charter of the United Nations and of international law, have deliberately and repeatedly attacked United States naval vessels lawfully present in international waters, and have thereby created a serious threat to international peace; and

Whereas these attacks are part of a deliberate and systematic campaign of aggression that the Communist regime in North Vietnam has been waging against its neighbors and the nations joined with them in the collective defense of their freedom; and

Whereas the United States is assisting the peoples of southeast Asia to protect their freedom and has no territorial, military or political ambitions in that area, but desires only that these peoples should be left in peace to work out their own destinies in their own way: Now, therefore, be it *Resolved by the Senate and House of Representatives of the United States of America in Congress assembled,* That the Congress approves and supports the determination of the President, as Commander in Chief, to take all necessary measures to repel any armed attack against the forces of the United States and to prevent further aggression.

Sec. 2. The United States regards as vital to its national interest and to world peace the maintenance of international peace and security in southeast Asia. Consonant with the Constitution of the United States and the Charter of the United Nations and in accordance with its obligations under the Southeast Asia Collective Defense Treaty, the United States is, therefore, prepared, as the President determines, to take all necessary steps, including the use of armed force, to assist any member or protocol state of the Southeast Asia Collective Defense Treaty requesting assistance in defense of its freedom.

Sec. 3. This resolution shall expire when the President shall determine that the peace and security of the area is reasonably assured by international conditions created by action of the United Nations or otherwise, except that it may be terminated earlier by concurrent resolution of the Congress.

Lyndon B. Johnson Explains Why Americans Fight in Vietnam, 1965

Why must this nation hazard its ease, its interest, and its power for the sake of a people so far away?

We fight because we must fight if we are to live in a world where every country can shape its own destiny, and only in such a world will our own freedom be finally secure.

This kind of world will never be built by bombs or bullets. Yet the infirmities of man are such that force must often precede reason and the waste of war, the works of peace.

We wish that this were not so. But we must deal with the world as it is, if it is ever to be as we wish.

The world as it is in Asia is not a serene or peaceful place.

The first reality is that North Viet-Nam has attacked the independent nation of South Viet-Nam. Its object is total conquest.

Of course, some of the people of South Viet-Nam are participating in attack on their own government. But trained men and supplies, orders and arms, flow in a constant stream from North to South.

This support is the heartbeat of the war.

And it is a war of unparalleled brutality. Simple farmers are the targets of assassination and kidnaping. Women and children are strangled in the night because their men are loyal to their government. And helpless villages are ravaged by sneak attacks. Large-scale raids are conducted on towns, and terror strikes in the heart of cities.

The confused nature of this conflict cannot mask the fact that it is the new face of an old enemy.

Over this war—and all Asia—is another reality: the deepening shadow of Communist China. The rulers in Hanoi are urged on by Peking. This is a regime which has destroyed freedom in Tibet, which has attacked India and has been condemned by the United Nations for aggression in Korea. It is a nation which is helping the forces of violence in almost every continent. The contest in Viet-Nam is part of a wider pattern of aggressive purposes.

Why are these realities our concern? Why are we in South Viet-Nam?

We are there because we have a promise to keep. Since 1954 every American President has offered support to the people of South Viet-Nam. We have helped to build, and we have helped to defend. Thus, over many years, we have made a national pledge to help South Viet-Nam defend its independence.

And I intend to keep that promise.

To dishonor that pledge, to abandon this small and brave nation to its enemies, and to the terror that must follow, would be an unforgivable wrong.

We are also there to strengthen world order. Around the globe from Berlin to Thailand are people whose well being rests in part on the belief that they can count on us if they are attacked. To leave Viet-Nam to its fate would shake the confidence of all these people in the value of an American commitment and in the value of America's word. The result would be increased unrest and instability, and even wider war.

We are also there because there are great stakes in the balance. Let no one think for a moment that retreat from Viet-Nam would bring an end to conflict. The battle would be renewed in one country and then another. The central lesson of our time is that the appetite of aggression is never satisfied. To withdraw from one battlefield means only to prepare for the next. We must say in Southeast Asia—as we did in Europe—in the words of the Bible: "Hitherto shalt thou come, but no further."

There are those who say that all our effort there will be futile—that China's power is such that it is bound to dominate all Southeast Asia. But there is no end to that argument until all of the nations of Asia are swallowed up.

There are those who wonder why we have a responsibility there. Well, we have it there for the same reason that we have a responsibility for the defense of Europe. World War II was fought in both Europe and Asia and when it ended we found ourselves with continued responsibility for the defense of freedom.

Our objective is the independence of South Viet-Nam and its freedom from attack. We want nothing for ourselves—only that the people of South Viet-Nam be allowed to guide their own country in their own way.

We will do everything necessary to reach that objective and we will do only what is absolutely necessary.

In recent months attacks on South Viet-Nam were stepped up. Thus, it became necessary for us to increase our response and to make attacks by air. This is not a change of purpose. It is a change in what we believe that purpose requires.

We do this in order to slow down aggression.

We do this to increase the confidence of the brave people of South Viet-Nam who have bravely borne this brutal battle for so many years with so many casualties.

And we do this to convince the leaders of North Viet-Nam—and all who seek to share their conquest—of a simple fact:

We will not be defeated.

We will not grow tired.

We will not withdraw, either openly or under the cloak of a meaningless agreement.

We know that air attacks alone will not accomplish all of these purposes. But it is our best and prayerful judgment that they are a necessary part of the surest road to peace.

We hope that peace will come swiftly. But that is in the hands of others besides ourselves. And we must be prepared for a long continued conflict. It will require patience as well as bravery—the will to endure as well as the will to resist.

I wish it were possible to convince others with words of what we now find it necessary to say with guns and planes: armed hostility is futile— our resources are equal to any challenge—because we fight for values and we fight for principle, rather than territory or colonies, our patience and our determination are unending.

Once this is clear, then it should also be clear that the only path for reasonable men is the path of peaceful settlement. . . .

These countries of Southeast Asia are homes for millions of impoverished people. Each day these people rise at dawn and struggle through until the night to wrestle existence from the soil. They are often wracked by diseases, plagued by hunger, and death comes at the early age of forty.

Stability and peace do not come easily in such a land. Neither independence nor human dignity will ever be won though by arms alone. It also requires the works of peace. The American people have helped generously in times past in these works, and now there must be a much more massive effort to improve the life of man in that conflict-torn corner of our world.

The first step is for the countries of Southeast Asia to associate themselves in a greatly expanded co-operative effort for development. We would hope that North Viet-Nam would take its place in the common effort just as soon as peaceful co-operation is possible.

The United Nations is already actively engaged in development in this area, and as far back as 1961 I conferred with our authorities in Viet-Nam in connection with their work there. And I would hope tonight that the Secretary General of the United Nations could use the prestige of his great office and his deep knowledge of Asia to initiate, as soon as possible, with the countries of that area, a plan for co-operation in increased development.

For our part I will ask the Congress to join in a billion dollar American investment in this effort as soon as it is underway.

And I would hope that all other industrialized countries, including the Soviet Union, will join in this effort to replace despair with hope and terror with progress.

The task is nothing less than to enrich the hopes and existence of more than a hundred million people. And there is much to be done.

The vast Mekong River can provide food and water and power on a scale to dwarf even our own T.V.A.

The wonders of modern medicine can be spread through villages where thousands die every year from lack of care.

Schools can be established to train people in the skills needed to manage the process of development.

And these objectives, and more, are within the reach of a cooperative and determined effort.

I also intend to expand and speed up a program to make available our farm surpluses to assist in feeding and clothing the needy in Asia. We should not allow people to go hungry and wear rags while our own warehouses overflow with an abundance of wheat and corn and rice and cotton.

So I will very shortly name a special team of outstanding, patriotic, and distinguished Americans to inaugurate our participation in these programs. This team will be headed by Mr. Eugene Black, the very able former president of the World Bank.

This will be a disorderly planet for a long time. In Asia, and elsewhere, the forces of the modern world are shaking old ways and uprooting ancient civilizations. There will be turbulence and struggle and even violence. Great social change—as we see in our own country—does not always come without conflict.

We must also expect that nations will on occasion be in dispute with us. It may be because we are rich, or powerful, or because we have made some mistakes, or because they honestly fear our intentions. However, no nation need ever fear that we desire their land, or to impose our will, or to dictate their institutions.

But we will always oppose the effort of one nation to conquer another nation.

We will do this because our own security is at stake.

But there is more to it than that. For our generation has a dream. It is a very old dream. But we have the power, and now we have the opportunity to make that dream come true.

For centuries nations have struggled among each other. But we dream of a world where disputes are settled by law and reason. And we will try to make it so.

For most of history men have hated and killed one another in battle. But we dream of an end to war. And we will try to make it so.

For all existence most men have lived in poverty, threatened by hunger. But we dream of a world where all are fed and charged with hope. And we will help to make it so.

Robert S. McNamara Recommends Escalation, 1965

Introduction

Our objective is to create conditions for a favorable settlement by demonstrating to the VC/DRV that the odds are against their winning. Under present conditions, however, the chances of achieving this objective are small—and the VC are winning now—largely because the ratio of guerrilla to anti-guerrilla forces is unfavorable to the government. With this in mind, we must choose among three courses of action with respect to South Vietnam: (1) Cut our losses and withdraw under the best conditions that can be arranged; (2) continue at about the present level, with US forces limited to, say, 75,000, holding on and playing for the breaks while recognizing that our position will probably grow weaker; or (3) expand substantially the US military pressure against the Viet Cong in the South and the North Vietnamese in the North and at the same time launch a vigorous effort on the political side to get negotiations started. An outline of the third of these approaches follows.

I. Expanded Military Moves

The following military moves should be taken together with the political initiatives in Part II below.

A. Inside South Vietnam. Increase US/SVN military strength in SVN enough to prove to the VC that they cannot win and thus to turn the tide of the war. . . .

B. Against North Vietnam. While avoiding striking population and industrial targets not closely related to the DRV's supply of war material to the VC, we should announce to Hanoi and carry out actions to destroy such supplies and to interdict their flow into and out of North Vietnam. . . .

II. Expanded Political Moves

Together with the above military moves, we should take the following political initiatives in order (a) to open a dialogue with Hanoi, Peking, and the VC looking toward a settlement in Vietnam, (b) to keep the Soviet Union from deepening its military involvement and support of North Vietnam until the time when settlement can be achieved, and (c) to cement the support for US policy by the US public, allies and friends, and to keep international opposition at a manageable level. While our approaches may be rebuffed until the tide begins to turn, they nevertheless should be made. . . .

III. Evaluation of the Above Program

A. Domestic US Reaction.   Even though casualties will increase and the war will continue for some time, the United States public will support this course of action because it is a combined military-political program designed and likely to bring about a favorable solution to the Vietnam problem.

B. Communist Reaction to the Expanded Programs.
    1. *Soviet.* The Soviets can be expected to continue to contribute materiel and advisors to the North Vietnamese. Increased US bombing of Vietnam, including targets in Hanoi and Haiphong, SAM [surface-to-air missile] sites and airfields, and mining of North Vietnamese harbors, might oblige the Soviet Union to enter the contest more actively with volunteers and aircraft. This might result in minor encounters between US and Soviet personnel.
    2. *China.* So long as no US or GVN troops invade North Vietnam and so long as no US or GVN aircraft attack Chinese territory, the Chinese probably will not send regular ground forces or aircraft into the war. However, the possibility of a more active Soviet involvement in North Vietnam might precipitate a Chinese introduction of land forces, probably dubbed volunteers, to preclude the Soviets' taking a pre-eminent position in North Vietnam.
    3. *North Vietnam.* North Vietnam will not move towards the negotiating table until the tide begins to turn in the south. When that happens, they may seek to counter it by sending large numbers of men into South Vietnam.
    4. *Viet Cong.* The VC, especially if they continue to take high losses, can be expected to depend increasingly upon the PAVN [People's Army of Vietnam, regular forces of North Vietnam] forces as the war moves into a more conventional phase; but they may find ways of continuing almost indefinitely their present intensive military, guerrilla and terror activities, particularly if reinforced with some regular PAVN units. A key question on the military side is whether POL [petroleum-oil-lubricants], ammunition, and cadres can be cut off and if they are cut off whether this really renders the Viet Cong impotent. A key question on the political side is whether any arrangement acceptable to us would be acceptable to the VC.

C. Estimate of Success.
    1. *Militarily.* The success of the above program from a military point of view turns on whether the increased effort stems the tide in the South; that in turn depends on two things—on whether the South Vietnamese hold their own in terms of numbers and fighting spirit, and on whether the US forces can be effective in a quick-reaction reserve role, a role in which they have not been tested. The number of US troops is too small to make a significant difference in the traditional 10–1 government-guerrilla formula, but it is not too small to make a significant difference in the kind of war which seems to be evolving in Vietnam—a "Third Stage" or conventional

war in which it is easier to identify, locate and attack the enemy. (South Vietnam has 141 battalions as compared with an estimated equivalent number of VC battalions. The 44 US/3d country battalions mentioned above are the equivalent of 100 South Vietnamese battalions.)

2. *Politically*. It is frequently alleged that such a large expansion of US military personnel, their expanded military role (which would put them in close contact and offer some degree of control over South Vietnamese citizens), and the inevitable expansion of US voice in the operation of the GVN economy and facilities, command and government services will be unpopular; it is said that they could lead to the rejection of the government which supported this American presence, to an irresistible pressure for expulsion of the Americans, and to the greatly increased saleability of Communist propaganda. Whether these allegations are true, we do not know.

The political initiatives are likely to be successful in the early stages only to demonstrate US good faith; they will pay off toward an actual settlement only after the tide begins to turn (unless we lower our sights substantially). The tide almost certainly cannot begin to turn in less than a few months, and may not for a year or more; the war is one of attrition and will be a long one. Since troops once committed as a practical matter cannot be removed, since US casualties will rise, since we should take call-up actions to support the additional forces in Vietnam, the test of endurance may be as much in the United States as in Vietnam.

3. *Generally (CIA estimate)*. Over the longer term we doubt if the Communists are likely to change their basic strategy in Vietnam (i.e., aggressive and steadily mounting insurgency) unless and until two conditions prevail: (1) they are forced to accept a situation in the war in the South which offers them no prospect of an early victory and no grounds for hope that they can simply outlast the US and (2) North Vietnam itself is under continuing and increasingly damaging punitive attack. So long as the Communists think they scent the possibility of an early victory (which is probably now the case), we believe that they will persevere and accept extremely severe damage to the North. Conversely, if North Vietnam itself is not hurting, Hanoi's doctrinaire leaders will probably be ready to carry on the Southern struggle almost indefinitely. If, however, both of the conditions outlined above should be brought to pass, we believe Hanoi probably would, at least for a period of time, alter its basic strategy and course of action in South Vietnam.

Hanoi might do so in several ways. Going for a conference as a political way of gaining a respite from attack would be one. Alternatively it might reduce the level of insurgent activity in the hopes that this would force the US to stop its punishment of the North but not prevent the US and GVN from remaining subject to wearying harassment in the South. Or, Hanoi might order the VC to suspend operations in the hopes that in a period of temporary tranquility, domestic and international opinion would force the US to disengage without destroying the VC apparatus or the roots of VC strength. Finally, Hanoi might decide that the US/GVN will to fight could still be broken and the tide of war turned back again in favor of the

VC by launching a massive PAVN assault on the South. This is a less likely option in the circumstances we have posited, but still a contingency for which the US must be prepared.

George Ball Dissents, 1965

1. A Losing War: The South Vietnamese are losing the war to the Viet Cong. No one can assure you that we can beat the Viet Cong or even force them to the conference table on our terms, no matter how many hundred thousand *white, foreign* (U.S.) troops we deploy.

No one has demonstrated that a white ground force of whatever size can win a guerrilla war—which is at the same time a civil war between Asians—in jungle terrain in the midst of a population that refuses cooperation to the white forces (and the South Vietnamese) and thus provides a great intelligence advantage to the other side. Three recent incidents vividly illustrate this point: (a) the sneak attack on the Da Nang Air Base which involved penetration of a defense perimeter guarded by 9,000 Marines. This raid was possible only because of the cooperation of the local inhabitants; (b) the B-52 raid that failed to hit the Viet Cong who had obviously been tipped off; (c) the search and destroy mission of the 173rd Air Borne Brigade which spent three days looking for the Viet Cong, suffered 23 casualties, and never made contact with the enemy who had obviously gotten advance word of their assignment.

2. The Question to Decide: Should we limit our liabilities in South Vietnam and try to find a way out with minimal long-term costs?

The alternative—no matter what we may wish it to be—is almost certainly a protracted war involving an open-ended commitment of U.S. forces, mounting U.S. casualties, no assurance of a satisfactory solution, and a serious danger of escalation at the end of the road.

3. Need for a Decision Now: So long as our forces are restricted to advising and assisting the South Vietnamese, the struggle will remain a civil war between Asian peoples. Once we deploy substantial numbers of troops in combat it will become a war between the U.S. and a large part of the population of South Vietnam, organized and directed from North Vietnam and backed by the resources of both Moscow and Peiping.

The decision you face now, therefore, is crucial. Once large numbers of U.S. troops are committed to direct combat, they will begin to take heavy casualties in a war they are ill-equipped to fight in a non-cooperative if not downright hostile countryside.

Once we suffer large casualties, we will have started a well-nigh irreversible process. Our involvement will be so great that we cannot—without national humiliation—stop short of achieving our complete objectives. *Of the two possibilities I think humiliation would be more likely than the achievement of our objectives—even after we have paid terrible costs.*

4. Compromise Solution: Should we commit U.S. manpower and prestige to a terrain so unfavorable as to give a very large advantage to the enemy—or should we seek a compromise settlement which achieves less than our stated objectives and thus cut our losses while we still have the freedom of maneuver to do so.

5. *Costs of a Compromise Solution:* The answer involves a judgment as to the cost to the U.S. of such a compromise settlement in terms of our relations with the countries in the area of South Vietnam, the credibility of our commitments, and our prestige around the world. In my judgment, if we act before we commit substantial U.S. troops to combat in South Vietnam we can, by accepting some short-term costs, avoid what may well be a long-term catastrophe. I believe we tended grossly to exaggerate the costs involved in a compromise settlement. An appreciation of probable costs is contained in the attached memorandum.

6. With these considerations in mind, I strongly urge the following program:

a. Military Program
 1. Complete all deployment already announced—15 battalions—but decide not to go beyond a total of 72,000 men represented by this figure.
 2. Restrict the combat role of the American forces to the June 19 announcement, making it clear to General Westmoreland that this announcement is to be strictly construed.
 3. Continue bombing in the North but avoid the Hanoi-Haiphong area and any targets nearer to the Chinese border than those already struck.

b. Political Program
 1. In any political approaches so far, we have been the prisoners of whatever South Vietnamese government that was momentarily in power. If we are ever to move toward a settlement, it will probably be because the South Vietnamese government pulls the rug out from under us and makes its own deal *or* because we go forward quietly without advance prearrangement with Saigon.
 2. So far we have not given the other side a reason to believe there is *any* flexibility in our negotiating approach. And the other side has been unwilling to accept what *in their terms* is complete capitulation.
 3. Now is the time to start some serious diplomatic feelers looking towards a solution based on some application of a self-determination principle.
 4. I would recommend approaching Hanoi rather than any of the other probable parties, the NLF, ——— or Peiping. Hanoi is the only one that has given any signs of interest in discussion. Peiping has been rigidly opposed. Moscow has recommended that we negotiate with Hanoi. The NLF has been silent.
 5. There are several channels to the North Vietnamese, but I think the best one is through their representative in Paris, Mai van Bo. Initial feelers of Bo should be directed toward a discussion both of the four points we have put forward and the four points put forward by Hanoi as a basis for negotiation. We can accept all but one of Hanoi's four points, and hopefully we should be able to agree on some ground rules for serious negotiations—including no preconditions.
 6. If the initial feelers lead to further secret, exploratory talks, we can inject the concept of self-determination that would permit the Viet

Cong some hope of achieving some of their political objectives through local elections or some other device.

7. The contact on our side should be handled through a non-governmental cutout (possibly a reliable newspaper man who can be repudiated).

8. If progress can be made at this level a basis can be laid for a multinational conference. At some point, obviously, the government of South Vietnam will have to be brought on board, but I would postpone this step until after a substantial feeling out of Hanoi.

7. Before moving to any formal conference we should be prepared to agree once the conference is started:
   a. The U.S. will stand down its bombing of the North
   b. The South Vietnamese will initiate no offensive operations in the South, and
   c. The DRV will stop terrorism and other aggressive action against the South.

8. The negotiations at the conference should aim at incorporating our understanding with Hanoi in the form of a multinational agreement guaranteed by the U.S., the Soviet Union and possibly other parties, and providing for an international mechanism to supervise its execution.

Johnson Recalls His Decision to Commit Troops (1965), 1971

We discussed Ball's approach for a long time and in great detail. I think all of us felt the same concerns and anxieties that Ball had expressed, but most of these men in the Cabinet Room were more worried about the results, in our country and throughout the world, of our pulling out and coming home. I felt the Under Secretary had not produced a sufficiently convincing case or a viable alternative.

Dean Rusk expressed one worry that was much on my mind. It lay at the heart of our Vietnam policy. "If the Communist world finds out that we will not pursue our commitments to the end," he said, "I don't know where they will stay their hand."

I felt sure they would *not* stay their hand. If we ran out on Southeast Asia, I could see trouble ahead in every part of the globe—not just in Asia but in the Middle East and in Europe, in Africa and in Latin America. I was convinced that our retreat from this challenge would open the path to World War III.

Our consultations had only begun. I met the next day with the Joint Chiefs of Staff and the Secretaries of the military services. In the afternoon I met again for nearly an hour and a half with Rusk, McNamara, Ball, General Wheeler, Bundy, and several civilian advisers, including Clark

From *The Vantage Point: Perspectives of the Presidency, 1963–1969*, by Lyndon Baines Johnson. Copyright © 1971 by HEC Public Affairs Foundation. Reprinted by permission of Henry Holt and Company, Inc.

Clifford, John McCloy, and Arthur Dean. Later that day I went up to Camp David to reflect. I invited several advisers to join me there for further long discussions on Sunday, July 25.

Secretary McNamara, Ambassador to the United Nations Arthur Goldberg, and Clark Clifford, then Chairman of the President's Foreign Intelligence Advisory Board, joined me in the Aspen Lodge at Camp David in the afternoon. One of the things we wanted to discuss was whether we should take any action in the United Nations in connection with Vietnam. The weight of opinion was against a major effort to persuade the United Nations to act at that time. Most of my advisers felt that the leaders in Hanoi would turn down any UN proposal, because they had consistently declared that Vietnam was not a proper matter for UN involvement. Moreover, it was virtually certain that the Soviet Union would veto any proposal Hanoi might have trouble accepting.

At this session my old friend Clark Clifford was in a reflective and pessimistic mood. "I don't believe we can win in South Vietnam," he said. "If we send in 100,000 more men, the North Vietnamese will meet us. If North Vietnam runs out of men, the Chinese will send in volunteers. Russia and China don't intend for us to win the war."

He urged that in the coming months we quietly probe possibilities with other countries for some way to get out honorably. "I can't see anything but catastrophe for my country," he said.

I told Clifford that he was expressing worries that many Americans, including the President, were experiencing. No one was more concerned than I was, but we could not simply walk out. Nor was I prepared to accept just any settlement as a cover-up for surrender. What we needed was a way to start real negotiations and I intended to keep pressing our offer to talk peace.

We continued our review of the military situation and the requirement for additional forces. Our military commanders had refined their estimates and indicated they could meet the immediate demand with 50,000 men. I called a meeting of the National Security Council two days later, on July 27. I asked McNamara at that time to summarize again the current need as he saw it.

McNamara noted that the Viet Cong had increased in size through local recruitment and replacements from the North. Regular North Vietnamese army units had increased in number and strength. Communist control of the countryside was growing. A dozen provincial capitals were virtually isolated from surrounding rural areas. The South Vietnamese army was growing, but not nearly fast enough to keep pace with the expanding enemy forces. Without additional armed strength, South Vietnam would inevitably fall to Hanoi. I told the NSC there were five possible choices available to us.

"We can bring the enemy to his knees by using our Strategic Air Command," I said, describing our first option. "Another group thinks we ought to pack up and go home.

"Third, we could stay there as we are—and suffer the consequences, continue to lose territory and take casualties. You wouldn't want your own boy to be out there crying for help and not get it.

"Then, we could go to Congress and ask for great sums of money; we could call up the reserves and increase the draft; go on a war footing; declare a state of emergency. There is a good deal of feeling that ought to be done. We have considered this. But if we go into that kind of land war, then North Vietnam would go to its friends, China and Russia, and ask them to give help. They would be forced into increasing aid. For that reason I don't want to be overly dramatic and cause tensions. I think we can get our people to support us without having to be too provocative and warlike.

"Finally, we can give our commanders in the field the men and supplies they say they need."

I had concluded that the last course was the right one. I had listened to and weighed all the arguments and counterarguments for each of the possible lines of action. I believed that we should do what was necessary to resist aggression but that we should not be provoked into a major war. We would get the required appropriation in the new budget, and we would not boast about what we were doing. We would not make threatening noises to the Chinese or the Russians by calling up reserves in large numbers. At the same time, we would press hard on the diplomatic front to try to find some path to a peaceful settlement.

I asked if anyone objected to the course of action I had spelled out. I questioned each man in turn. Did he agree? Each nodded his approval or said "yes." . . .

There was more to it than listening to the arguments and dissents, the explanations and justifications of my wisest advisers in and out of government. When a President faces a decision involving war or peace, he draws back and thinks of the past and of the future in the widest possible terms. On his sworn oath, a President pledges he will protect the nation. The security of the whole country is the foremost responsibility of the Chief Executive. The most important question I had to face was: How will the decisions we make in Vietnam or elsewhere affect the security and the future of our nation?

A President searches his mind and his heart for the answers, so that when he decides on a course of action it is in the long-range best interests of the country, its people, and its security.

That is what I did—when I was alone and sleepless at night in the Executive Mansion, away from official cables and advisers; when I sat alone in the Aspen Lodge at Camp David; when I walked along the banks of the Pedernales River or looked out over the Texas hill country. In those lonely vigils I tried to think through what would happen to our nation and to the world if we did not act with courage and stamina—if we let South Vietnam fall to Hanoi.

This is what I could foresee: First, from all the evidence available to me it seemed likely that all of Southeast Asia would pass under Communist control, slowly or quickly, but inevitably, at least down to Singapore but almost certainly to Djakarta. I realize that some Americans believe they have, through talking with one another, repealed the domino theory. In 1965 there was no indication in Asia, or from Asians, that this was so. On both sides of the line between Communist and non-Communist Asia the struggle for Vietnam and Laos was regarded as a struggle for the fate of Southeast Asia. The evidence before me as President confirmed the previous assessments of President Eisenhower and of President Kennedy.

Second, I knew our people well enough to realize that if we walked away from Vietnam and let Southeast Asia fall, there would follow a divisive and destructive debate in our country. This had happened when the Communists took power in China. But that was very different from the Vietnam conflict. We had a solemn treaty commitment to Southeast Asia. We had an international agreement on Laos made as late as 1962 that was being violated flagrantly. We had the word of three Presidents that the United States would not permit this aggression to succeed. A divisive debate about "who lost Vietnam" would be, in my judgment, even more destructive to our national life than the argument over China had been. It would inevitably increase isolationist pressures from the right and the left and cause a pulling back from our commitments in Europe and the Middle East as well as in Asia.

Third, our allies not just in Asia but throughout the world would conclude that our word was worth little or nothing. Those who had counted so long for their security on American commitments would be deeply shaken and vulnerable.

Fourth, knowing what I did of the policies and actions of Moscow and Peking, I was as sure as a man could be that if we did not live up to our commitment in Southeast Asia and elsewhere, they would move to exploit the disarray in the United States and in the alliances of the Free World. They might move independently or they might move together. But move they would—whether through nuclear blackmail, through subversion, with regular armed forces, or in some other manner. As nearly as one can be certain of anything, I knew they could not resist the opportunity to expand their control into the vacuum of power we would leave behind us.

Finally, as we faced the implications of what we had done as a nation, I was sure the United States would not then passively submit to the consequences. With Moscow and Peking and perhaps others moving forward, we would return to a world role to prevent their full takeover of Europe, Asia, and the Middle East—*after* they had committed themselves.

Philip Caputo Remembers His Idealism (1965), 1977

On March 8, 1965, as a young infantry officer, I landed at Danang with a battalion of the 9th Marine Expeditionary Brigade, the first U.S. combat unit sent to Indochina.

For Americans who did not come of age in the early sixties, it may be hard to grasp what those years were like—the pride and overpowering self-assurance that prevailed. Most of the thirty-five hundred men in our brigade,

From *A Rumor of War* by Philip Caputo, excerpts from pp. xii–xx. Copyright © 1977 by Philip Caputo. Reprinted by permission of Henry Holt and Company, Inc.

born during or immediately after World War II, were shaped by that era, the age of Kennedy's Camelot. We went overseas full of illusions, for which the intoxicating atmosphere of those years was as much to blame as our youth.

War is always attractive to young men who know nothing about it, but we had also been seduced into uniform by Kennedy's challenge to "ask what you can do for your country" and by the missionary idealism he had awakened in us. America seemed omnipotent then: the country could still claim it had never lost a war, and we believed we were ordained to play cop to the Communists' robber and spread our own political faith around the world. Like the French soldiers of the late eighteenth century, we saw ourselves as the champions of "a cause that was destined to triumph." So, when we marched into the rice paddies on that damp March afternoon, we carried, along with our packs and rifles, the implicit convictions that the Viet Cong would be quickly beaten and that we were doing something altogether noble and good. We kept the packs and rifles; the convictions, we lost.

The discovery that the men we had scorned as peasant guerrillas were, in fact, a lethal, determined enemy and the casualty lists that lengthened each week with nothing to show for the blood being spilled broke our early confidence. By autumn, what had begun as an adventurous expedition had turned into an exhausting, indecisive war of attrition in which we fought for no cause other than our own survival.

✗ E S S A Y S

The opening selection is from journalist David Halberstam's best-selling book *The Best and the Brightest.* A former *New York Times* reporter whose dispatches from Vietnam earned him the Pulitzer Prize in the early 1960s, Halberstam ascribes President Johnson's decisions for escalation to a combination of personal and political factors. The president, he argues, proved supremely confident of America's ability to prevail against its adversaries. In the second essay, Larry Berman, a professor of political science at the University of California, Davis, maintains that Johnson's principal goal was not to gain a military triumph for the United States but to deny a communist victory. He sees Johnson's determination to buy time for his legislative agenda as the driving force behind his decision to commit American combat troops to Vietnam.

To Achieve a Victory

DAVID HALBERSTAM

Lyndon Johnson had to decide. The pressures were enormous both ways, there was going to be no easy way out. A few friends like [Senator] Dick

From *The Best and the Brightest* by David Halberstam, pp. 641–646, 694–697, 716–718. Copyright © 1972 by David Halberstam. Reprinted by permission of Random House, Inc.

Russell were warning him not to go ahead, that it would never work; Russell had an intuitive sense that it was all going to be more difficult and complicated than the experts were saying, but his doubts were written off as essentially conservative and isolationist, and it was easily rationalized that Russell, like [Senator J. William] Fulbright, did not care about colored people. Besides, Johnson had bettered Russell in the Senate and now here was Johnson surrounded by truly brilliant men (years later when there were free fire zones in the South—areas where virtually uncontrolled air and artillery could be used—which led to vast refugee resettlement, Russell would pass on his doubts about the wisdom of this as policy to the White House, saying, "I don't know those Asian people, but they tell me they worship their ancestors and so I wouldn't play with their land if I were you. You know whenever the Corps of Engineers has some dam to dedicate in Georgia I make a point of being out of state, because those people don't seem to like the economic improvements as much as they dislike being moved off their ancestral land"). But even Russell was telling the President that he had to make a decision, that he had better move, get off the dime, and Russell would support the flag.

Men who knew Johnson well thought of him as a man on a toboggan course in that period. Starting the previous November [1964] and then month by month as the trap tightened, he had become increasingly restless, irritable, frustrated, more and more frenetic, more and more difficult to work with. He was trapped and he knew it, and more than anyone else around him he knew that he was risking his great domestic dreams; it was primarily his risk, not theirs. The foreign policy advisers were not that privy to or that interested in his domestic dreams, and his domestic advisers were not that privy to the dangers ahead in the foreign policy. As a politician Johnson was not a great symbolic figure who initiated deep moral stirrings in the American soul, a man to go forth and lead a country by image, but quite the reverse, and he knew this better than most. His image and his reputation and his posture were against him; at his ablest he was a shrewd infighter. Despite the bombast he was a surprisingly cautious man (in guiding the Senate against [Senator Joseph] McCarthy he had been the epitome of caution, so cautious as to not receive any credit for it, which was probably what he wanted, it was not an issue to be out in front on). He was very good at measuring his resources, shrewdly assessing what was needed for a particular goal: was it there, was it available, was the price of accomplishing it too high? He had advised against going into Dienbienphu in 1954, not because he thought there was anything particularly wrong with intervention, but because he felt that immediately after the Korean War the country simply could not absorb and support another Asian land war; indeed, it was the very psychology of exhaustion with the Korean War which had put Eisenhower into office.

Now he was facing fateful decisions on Vietnam just as he was getting ready to start the Great Society. With his careful assessment of the country, he was sure the resources were there, that the country was finally ready to do something about its long-ignored social problems. The time was right for an assault on them, and he, Lyndon Johnson, would lead that assault, cure them, go down in history as a Roosevelt-like figure. He was keenly aware of these resources, and in late 1964 and early 1965 he began to use the phrase "sixty months of prosperity" as a litany, not just as party propaganda to get credit for the Democrats, but as a way of reminding the country that it had been having it good, very good, that it was secure and affluent, that it now had to turn its attention to the needs of others. Yet he knew he would not have the resources for both the domestic programs and a real war, and as a need for the latter became more and more apparent, he became restless and irritable, even by Johnsonian standards irascible, turning violently on the men around him. Those who knew him well and had worked long for him knew the symptoms only too well; it was, they knew, part of the insecurity of the man, and they talked of it often and gradually among themselves, since they all were subject to the same abuse. Unable to bear the truth about himself if it was unpleasant, he would transfer his feelings and his anger at himself to others, lashing out at Lady Bird [the President's wife], or George Reedy, or Bill Moyers, or particularly poor Jack Valenti [presidential advisers], but really lashing out at himself. And so in early 1965 this great elemental man, seeing his great hopes ahead and sensing also that they might be outside his reach, was almost in a frenzy to push his legislation through, a restless, obsessed man, driving himself and those around him harder and harder, fighting a civil war within himself.

He knew it would not be easy, that the bombing was a tricky business, not as tricky as ground troops, there was, after all, an element of control in bombing ("If they [the Air Force] hit people I'll bust their asses," he said at the start) but tricky nonetheless. And yet, and yet. "If I don't go in now and they show later I should have gone, then they'll be all over me in Congress. They won't be talking about my civil rights bill, or education, or beautification. No sir, they'll push Vietnam up my ass every time. Vietnam. Vietnam. Vietnam. Right up my ass." Cornered, and having what he would consider the Kennedy precedent to stand in Vietnam, a precedent which Kennedy set, but probably never entirely believed, and with all the Kennedy luminaries telling him to go ahead, even Rusk's uneasiness having been resolved ("He would look around him," said Tom Wicker later, "and see in Bob McNamara that it was technologically feasible, in McGeorge Bundy that it was intellectually respectable, and in Dean Rusk that it was historically necessary"), he went forward. Of course he would; after all, it could be done. He was a can-do man surrounded by other can-do men. If we set our minds to something, we did not fail. If Europeans were wary of this war, if the French had failed, and thus were warning the Americans off, it was not because they had lived more history and seen more of the folly of war, it was because they had become cynical, they had lost the capacity to believe in themselves, they were decadent. We were the first team.

So it all came down to Lyndon Johnson, reluctant, uneasy, but not a man to be backed down. Lyndon would not cut and run, if it came to that;

no one was going to push Lyndon Johnson around. Lyndon Johnson knew something about people like this, like the Mexicans back home, they were all right, the Mexicans, but "if you didn't watch they'll come right into your yard and take it over if you let them. And the next day they'll be right there on your porch, barefoot and weighing one hundred and thirty pounds, and they'll take that too. But if you say to 'em right at the start, 'Hold on, just wait a minute,' they'll know they're dealing with someone who'll stand up. And after that you can get along fine." Well, no one would push Lyndon Johnson of Texas around. This was Lyndon Johnson representing the United States of America, pledged to follow in the tradition of Great Britain and Winston Churchill—Lyndon Johnson, who, unlike Jack Kennedy, was a believer, not a cynic about the big things. Honor. Force. Commitments. Who believed in the omnipotence of American power, the concept of the frontier and using force to make sure you were clearly understood, believing that white men, and in particular Americans, were just a bit superior, believing in effect all those John Wayne movies, a cliché in which real life had styled itself on image (paint the portrait of Johnson as a tall tough Texan in the saddle, he had told Pierre Salinger, although he was not a good rider). And in the Dominican crisis he sent word through McGeorge Bundy for Colonel Francisco Caamano Deno, the rebel leader: "Tell that son of a bitch that unlike the young man who came before me I am not afraid to use what's on my hip."

For *machismo* was no small part of it. He had always been haunted by the idea that he would be judged as being insufficiently manly for the job, that he would lack courage at a crucial moment. More than a little insecure himself, he very much wanted to be seen as a man; it was a conscious thing. He was very much aware of *machismo* in himself and those around him, and at a moment like this he wanted the respect of men who were tough, real men, and they would turn out to be the hawks. He had always unconsciously divided the people around him between men and boys. Men were activists, doers, who conquered business empires, who acted instead of talked, who made it in the world of other men and had the respect of other men. Boys were the talkers and the writers and the intellectuals, who sat around thinking and criticizing and doubting instead of doing. There were good boys, like Horace Busby and for a time Dick Goodwin, who used their talent for him, and there were snot noses, and kids who were to be found at the State Department or in the editorial rooms of the Washington *Post* or the *New York Times* using their talents against him. Bill Moyers was a boy who was halfway to becoming a man, a writer who was moving into operational activities. Hubert Humphrey, Vice-President or no, was still a boy, better than most liberals, but too prone to talk instead of act, not a person that other *men* would respect in a room when it got down to the hard cutting; real men just wouldn't turn to Hubert, he didn't have the weight, and so when Humphrey voiced his doubts on Vietnam he was simply excluded from the action until he muffled his dissent.

Now, as Johnson weighed the advice he was getting on Vietnam, it was the boys who were most skeptical, and the men who were most sure and confident and hawkish and who had Johnson's respect. Hearing that one member of his Administration was becoming a dove on Vietnam, Johnson said, "Hell, he has to squat to piss." The *men* had, after all, done things in their lifetimes, and they had the respect of other men. Doubt itself, he thought, was an almost feminine quality, doubts were for women; once, on another issue, when Lady Bird raised her doubts, Johnson had said of course she was doubtful, it was like a woman to be uncertain. Thus as Vietnam came to the edge of decision, the sides were unfair, given Johnson's make-up. The doubters were not the people he respected; the men who were activists were hawks, and he took sustenance and reassurance that the real men were for going ahead. Of the doves, only George Ball really had his respect. Ball might be a dove, but there was nothing soft about him. He had made it in a tough and savage world of the big law firms, and his approach was tough and skeptical. He did not talk about doing good or put Johnson off by discussing the moral thing to do, rather he too was interested in the exercise of power and a real world that Johnson could understand. He was a doer, an activist, and Johnson would tell him again and again, even as Ball dissented, "You're one of these can-do fellows too, George."

Thus the dice were loaded; the advocates of force were by the very nature of Johnson's personality taken more seriously, the doubters were seen by their very doubts as being lesser men. So he would go ahead, despite his own inner instincts, that the rosy predictions were in fact not likely to be so rosy, that it was likely to be tougher and darker, that George Ball's doubts had a real basis. The thrust to go forward was just too great. Everyone else seemed so convinced of America's invincibility. Even Ball, arguing at the time that it was the right moment to cut our losses, sensed this feeling of American invincibility and will, and would write that by negotiating out, the United States could become a "wiser and more mature nation." But those lessons would have to come the hard way; there were too few restraints. All the training of two decades had been quite the reverse. They had come to the end of one path. They were cornered by bad policies on Asia which they had not so much authored as refused to challenge, both in the fifties when out of power, and in the sixties when in power. And so now they bombed. They did this in place of combat troops, and they believed that it would not last long, perhaps a few months. . . .

The forces pushing against Lyndon Johnson as he came closer and closer to a decision seemed terribly imbalanced. On the one side were the Chiefs and the Saigon generals, wanting troops, sure of themselves, speaking for the Cold War, for patriotism, and joined with them were his principal national security advisers, all believers in the use of force. Those committed to peace were not as well organized, not as impressive, and seemingly not as potent politically; if anything, in making their case to him, they seemed to unveil their weaknesses more than their strengths. One incident revealed how frail the peace people seemed to Johnson. On the first weekend in April the Americans for Democratic Action were holding their annual convention, and a group of the leadership asked to see the President, specifically to protest the bombing. The meeting was granted and about a dozen ADA officials went over to see the President. Some of the ADA people were quite impassioned; the bombing of the North, they said, simply had to stop. It was wrong, it was against everything America stood for. Johnson himself tried as best he could to deflect the criticism. He was under great pressure from the military to use more force, he said; he had tried to negotiate, but Hanoi continued to be the aggressor. He read at great length from a speech that he intended to give on the Mekong River development project; he was, he said, trying to do there what he was doing here at home. But he was not able to assuage their feeling. It was a sharp and tough exchange. The ADA people were particularly worried about McNamara's role, and several of them criticized the growing power of the Secretary of Defense, whom they visualized as being a major hawk. Johnson moved to set them at ease. "Why are you people always complaining about McNamara?" he asked. "Why, Mac Bundy here"—pointing to Bundy—"is a much bigger hawk than McNamara." But even the ADA people did not seem to be particularly unified; there were divisions within the group, and John Roche, a Brandeis professor who was the outgoing chairman, seemed quite sympathetic to the Johnson position. As the group was leaving, it passed through the White House press room, and Joe Rauh, one of the ADA officials, told the waiting reporters that the exchanges had been sharp ones, that the ADA had expressed its opposition to the bombing in very strong terms. At that point Roche tried to soften Rauh's statement, and the two clashed over the wording, Roche wanting a more subdued description.

The whole incident immediately convinced Johnson that he could handle the liberals, that they had no real muscle, that they were divided among themselves. Even as he said good-bye to the ADA representatives, he showed in the Joint Chiefs, plus McNamara and Rusk, for one of the pressing meetings on the use of ground troops. Because he liked to begin each meeting by referring to the one which preceded it, the President now reached into the wastebasket and scooped up the notes which the ADA people had brought to the meeting and written to each other during it. Then, mimicking his previous guests to perfection, he began to read the notes to the assembled Chiefs, pausing, showing great relish in ridiculing each, adjusting his voice as necessary, taking particular pleasure in one that Rauh had written: "Why doesn't he take the issue of Vietnam to the United Nations?" That one in particular broke them up. Then the liberals dispensed with, they got down to more serious things, such as the forthcoming decisions on ground troops.

Nor was Johnson's instinct to use force tempered in April by the experience in the Dominican Republic. When the frail political legitimacy of the Dominican government began to fall apart, and when leftist rebels began to make a challenge, Johnson moved quickly to stop another Cuba. Presidents in the past had been soft on Cuba and had paid for it. No one would accuse Lyndon Johnson of that. So despite the fact that the reports from the Dominican were remarkably unclear, with the American ambassador filing wildly exaggerated estimates on the amount of violence taking place, and totally unconfirmed reports on the extent of Communist subversion, Johnson moved swiftly. He would use force. No one at a high level in the Administration dissented, or suggested that the United States had no legal justification for moving in with force, or indeed that it did not even know what was happening. Force it was, overkill, not just the Marines, but the Airborne as well, 22,000 troops, and they went in, and whatever the uprising was—the Administration seemed unclear about that—it was put down. American muscle had determined the outcome. Oh, there had been protests from the left, and from people nervous about things like this, but Johnson had paid no attention and it had worked out—or seemed to work out. So if the same liberals were making the same soft sounds on Vietnam, why pay attention? People forgot about these things if they worked out, and there was no doubt what would happen when real men walked into one of these fourth-rate countries and set things right. So there was, out of the Dominican, an impression confirmed that if you just stood tall, why, things would come your way, though of course the difference between the depth and root of the insurgency in Vietnam and the sheer political frustration and chaos of the Dominican was very, very great. But the Dominican, whatever else, did not discourage Lyndon Johnson from the use of force. Nor, of course, the men around him.

The President was increasingly concerned about the situation in Vietnam, but he was less wary of the French experience than Taylor or Ball; he was more confident of what *Americans* could do. In addition, and this was to be important later as the question of enclave strategy versus search-and-destroy strategy arose, he was not a man to sponsor a defensive strategy, to send American boys overseas, to see American boys killed, and then yet be involved in a long, unrewarding war. He was not a man for that kind of war, a man to be charged with a no-win policy. The political trap of the Korean War was real to him: he knew what it was like to be attacked for failing to win a war, for getting in with a no-win policy. If Americans were going to be there, they had better be aggressive. Clean it all up and get home. Show Ho what Americans could do, and get him to the table. . . .

So Johnson made his decision; it was, he thought, a personal challenge from Ho. If Ho wanted a challenge, a test of will, then he had come to the right man. Lyndon Johnson of Texas would not be pushed around, he would not try to negotiate with Ho and those others, as he said, walking in the streets of Saigon. He was a man to stand tall when the pressure was there. To be counted. He would show Ho his mettle, show the toughness of this country, and then they could talk. Rusk agreed; this was one democracy that was not going to show itself weak, it had the right leader (later during the Glassboro meetings with the Soviet leadership, Karl Mundt, as conservative a senator as could be found, was appalled to find that the Soviet Union's Kosygin did not have the kind of power to go to war that Johnson seemed to have). Johnson would not shirk from this test of wills. Besides, it was above all a political decision and a domestic one at that; it was a question of how he read the country, and when he found doubters on his own staff, some of the younger people, he would tell them, You boys don't understand, you don't know the relationship between the Congress and Asia. It was an emotional thing; they had never seen it because during their political lifetime it had been bottled up, but it was still there. He would lose his presidential possibilities, he said, if Ho was running through the streets of Saigon. Listen, he added, Truman and Acheson had never been effective from the time of the fall of China. Lyndon Johnson had a mandate for the moment. But this way if he failed on Vietnam it would be gone quickly. McNamara and Bundy seemed to be saying it could be done quickly, perhaps in six months, perhaps a little more. And the test cases were also quick. The Cuban missile crisis had gone quickly and that was a dry run for it, and the Dominican Republic, hell, he had sent a few troops in there and he had put out the fire in a few days. Hardly a shot fired. Look what had happened in the Dominican, when American boys had gone ashore. So this one would be quick too. Just give him six months. Of course, six months later he would be unmovable, too deeply involved in something that was going badly to talk rationally. It was one more sad aspect of Lyndon Johnson that there was the quality of the bully, and the reverse quality as well; he was, at his best, most open, most candid, most easy to reach, most accessible when things were going well, but when things went poorly, as they were bound to on Vietnam, he became impossible to reach and talk to. His greatest flexibility and rationality on the subject came before he had dispatched the first bombers and the first troops; from then on it would all be downhill. Doubters would no longer be friendly doubters, they would be critics and soon enemies; and worse, soon after that, traitors. There was no way to reach him, to enter his chamber, to gain his ear, other than to pledge total loyalty. Only one man would be able to change him, to dissent and retain his respect—and even that was a tenuous balancing act which virtually destroyed one of his oldest friendships, and that was Clark Clifford in 1968.

So, cornered, he would go ahead. He was not just reading their country, which was small, Asian, fourth-rate, bereft of bombers and helicopters; he was above all a political animal and he was reading his *own* country and in that he may have misread it; he read the politics of the past rather than the *potential* politics of the country, which his very victory of 1964 illuminated. (He had won as a peace candidate, and it is likely that had a new China policy been openly debated, with Johnson in favor of it and Goldwater opposing, it might have enlarged his margin; at the least it would have had little negative effect, probably would not have cut into his margin in any appreciable sense, and would have liberated him from one of the dominating myths of the past. But as the issue had been dormant by both liberal and conservative consent for a decade—the liberals giving consent, the conservatives owning the policy—there was no desire to change it.) The Democrats, who had been hurt by the issue in the past, were quite content to keep it bottled up. As was Johnson, a good and traditional liberal who was also a man of the fifties and of Texas in the fifties, where McCarthyism had been particularly virulent, an era of potentially monolithic Communism, where the fewer questions about how monolithic it was, the better.

To Avoid a Defeat

LARRY BERMAN

Thirty thousand American troops died in Vietnam between July 28, 1965, and the inauguration of Richard Nixon in January 1969. "How," asked James C. Thomson, Jr., "did men of superior ability, sound training and high ideals—American policymakers of the 1960s—create such a costly and divisive policy?" I believe that the primary source documents provide several answers to Thomson's legitimate query—each of these will be explored below.

The documents show that the principals accepted containment of communism and the domino theory as basic premises for formulating policy and not as hypotheses for analysis. Moreover, the principals approached the problem definition stage with twenty years of intellectual baggage shaped by visions of Soviet-inspired and aggressive communism. There was an almost talmudic adherence to the containment strategy outlined by George Kennan which called for an "unalterable counterforce at every point where they [Communists] show signs of encroachment." But in 1965 the principals expanded significantly on the definition of containment and, for that matter, of world communism. Containment of Soviet aggression was originally conceived as limited in both geographical scope and objective. As Vietnam *became* an increasingly important component in U.S. global interests, not losing Vietnam assumed an equally high stature. According to the BDM [Corporation] study ["The Strategic Lessons Learned in Vietnam"], "Early on, American leadership mistakenly believed Vietnam to be vital not only for itself, but for what they thought its 'loss' would mean internationally and domestically. Once the commitment was made, each subsequent president reaffirmed the commitment rather than reassessing the basic rationale as to whether vital US interests were involved or not."

The cognitive error was not Johnson's alone. Six postwar presidents and their advisors refused to think critically about the changing nature of Asian communism. As the BDM study put it:

> All of the presidents had lived through Manchuria, Munich, Poland, Yalta, the "loss" of China, the Korean War, and the McCarthy era. Each drew the lesson that the United States could not afford to be soft on communism, specifically that he could not be the president who permitted the "loss" of Vietnam to communism. *Their close advisers reinforced their own anticommunist orientation. There is no question that the presidents and their advisers were conditioned by such past experiences when considering how to deal with the conflict in Vietnam.*
>
> Like leaders in any organization, presidents are not immune to confusing dissent with disloyalty. The Vietnam experience should point to some of the dangers in such confusion. *Premises fail to receive the critical examination they require in formulating a sound policy that keeps pace with changes in a dynamic world.* There was a time when monolithic communism may have justified the anticommunist approach of the US in the 1950s. Equally, it seems possible that the US might have tailored its policy toward Vietnam more closely to observable changes in the Sino-Soviet relationship earlier than it did (during the Nixon presidency). Unfortunately, the problem arose that the investment of US political, economic and military prestige, not to mention US casualties, came to override the intrinsic importance of Vietnam to the US.

Decision-makers constantly justified their views on the necessity of Communist containment with references to another "appeasement at Munich" or another "loss of China." These "simplistic adages were often used," according to the BDM study, "in lieu of developing more precise and perhaps more convincing explanations for making a particular policy decision. In addition, they often came to be voiced indiscriminately, leading to generalization, overuse, and misapplication." The BDM study identified a direct cause-and-effect relationship: "The American experience in Vietnam points to the danger of having one fundamental principle—anticommunism—elevated to the status of doctrine for all regions of the world. By elevating a principle to the level of doctrine, further debate of the subject is minimized, thereby reducing the possibility that legitimate dissenting views will receive sufficient attention at the national policy-making level. What tended to happen in Vietnam was that consensus building on the premise of anticommunism was achieved to give coherence to Vietnam policy at the national level, at the sacrifice of a needed closer examination of the accuracy of that premise."

The logical companion to containment was the domino theory. Clark Clifford, for example, referred to the "solid phalanx of advice from [LBJ's] main advisors . . . the unanimous sentiment among his senior advisors that the domino theory was unquestionably so." "The 'domino' theory," according to the BDM study, "saw any conflict with the communists as a test of the US's national resolve and credibility. The communists had threatened to take over 'free world' territory in Berlin, Korea, Iran, Guatemala, Lebanon and the Dominican Republic and actions taken by the US to prevent the loss of these territories were viewed by many as American Cold War successes. Conversely, the communists gaining control over China and Cuba were viewed as Cold War defeats for the US. Each successive US president found himself bound, in large measure, by his predecessor's doctrine and thereafter often analyzed issues from the same perspectives, continuing policies long after they had outlived their usefulness.'' As a result even support for the repressive and authoritarian Diem was justified as a regrettable means to a nobler end—saving the world from Soviet-inspired Communist aggression. Decision-makers eventually abandoned all of the original preconditions for policy—particularly a stable and meritorious GVN—to pursue the ultimate goal of halting communism in Southeast Asia. Acceptance of the containment legacy led decision-makers to become preoccupied with the question of "how" the government of South Vietnam could be saved, and never with "why" the government was worth saving. Moreover, the stakes were simply too great—freedom stood in the balance. Dean Rusk placed the stakes within the parameter of another world war: "My generation of students was led down the trail into the catastrophe of a World War II which could have been prevented. We came out of that war with a strong feeling that collective security was the key to the prevention of World War III. It was written into Article I of the United Nations Charter and reinforced by security treaties in this hemisphere, across the Atlantic, and across the Pacific. Vietnam involved to some of us the integrity of the system of collective security whose main purpose was to prevent World War III.''

One of the best examples of how these views of the world influenced the problem definition stage occurred *just prior to* Secretary McNamara's trip to Saigon, when the president met with his consultants on foreign affairs. Writing under separate cover to his personal friend McGeorge Bundy, consultant and former State Department official Roswell Gilpatric summarized the consensus of these consultants: "The US *has a commitment* in South Vietnam, nonfulfillment of which would have extremely grave consequences not only in Asia but in Europe. (2) Of the courses of action open to the US in order to make good on that commitment, some are either inadequate or undesirable, viz., (a) the role up to now played by US forces, namely, training, supporting, advising, and otherwise assisting the South Vietnamese, is not enough to keep South Vietnam from losing out to the Viet Cong backed up by the North Vietnamese, (b) strikes against the Hanoi-Haiphong area would probably cause the USSR to react positively because it would otherwise be shown incapable of protecting North Vietnam. (3) Hence, in order to hold on in South Vietnam, *the US faces a new role: that is taking a major part in the combat itself.* This means large additional forces and probably much heavier casualties. To carry out this role with some prospect of success calls for the application of whatever amounts of military power may be needed, perhaps as much as brought to bear in Korea fifteen years ago.''

The assumption by McNamara, Westmoreland, and the Joint Chiefs that the Viet Cong were about to abandon their successful guerrilla tactics in favor of more conventional regiment-size confrontations was pivotal to the reasoning of the July 28 decision. According to McNamara, "the enemy clearly was moving into the third phase of revolutionary warfare, committing regiments and subsequently divisions to seize and retain territory and to destroy the government's troops and eliminate all vestiges of government control." In his memoirs Admiral Sharp wrote, "in early June we had become very concerned that the communists might be about ready to increase the intensity of the conflict. Evidence indicated that the North Vietnamese were now capable of mounting regiment-size operations in many locations throughout the country and battalion-size operations almost anyplace."

Secretary McNamara's forty-four–battalion request was predicated on the assumption that U.S. troops, for the most part, would be engaging main force and not guerrilla units. But the president's advisors were in bitter disagreement over the question of a Third Stage. The case provides an excellent example of how a determined president might have shifted the burden of proof to Westmoreland or McNamara and received answers which were totally incompatible with the preferred option. George Ball, the CIA, the State Department, McGeorge Bundy, and William Bundy all recorded their *rejection* of Westmoreland's claim that the so-called Third Stage was underway. Unfortunately, little of the correspondence between advisors ever reached the president's desk, especially since Johnson acknowledged its import ("he seemed to agree") when Ball raised the point during the July 21 meeting.

The debate at the staff level is quite revealing. After reading McNamara's June 26 memorandum, William Bundy instructed the State Department Office of Intelligence and Research to examine whether or not the Communists were moving into the Third Stage phase of warfare as predicted by General Giap. In a July 23, 1965, *Secret—Limited Distribution* report, State Department officials concluded "that their pattern of behavior in Vietnam to date and their probable expectations as to the future argue *against the hypothesis that the communists are preparing to enter the third stage. . . .* We do not believe that the criteria established by Giap for the third stage—size of unit, scale of operation, and nature of attack—have been or are about to be met in South Vietnam. Our examination of Viet Cong capabilities, the campaign against GVN lines of communication, the communist attack pattern, and the content of communist propaganda, persuades us rather that the VC will continue to employ guerrilla tactics with only intermittent recourse to spectacular, multi-battalion attacks against major ARVN reinforcement, and are not now capable of initiating a drastically different phase of warfare. . . ."

George Ball also rejected McNamara's "unproven" assumption of a Third Stage. Writing to the president, Ball noted that "implicit in arguments for greatly augmented United States combat forces in South Vietnam is the assumption that the Viet Cong have entered—or are about to enter—their so-called 'third phase' of warfare, having progressed from relatively small-scale hit and run operations to large unit, fixed position conventional warfare. *Yet we have no basis for assuming that the Viet Cong will fight a war on our terms* (McGeorge Bundy's very point to McNamara) when they can continue to fight the kind of war they fought so well against both the French and the GVN." Ball noted that "we can scarcely expect [General Giap] to accommodate us by adopting our preferred method of combat, regardless of how many troops we send. There is every reason to suppose that the Viet Cong will avoid providing good targets for our massive bombing and superior firepower."

In his July 1 memo to the president, William Bundy agreed with Ball's rejection of McNamara's thesis: "As for major additional ground deployments, the first argument is simply whether they would be militarily effective. As the Ball paper points out, Hanoi is by no means committed to a really conventional type of war and they could easily go on making significant gains while giving us precious few opportunities to hit them."

Even after the July 21 NSC meeting, Chester Cooper tried to convince McGeorge Bundy to convince McNamara that "we and the GVN will be faced with the problem of guerrilla rather than positional warfare." But by now reasonable questions of the Third Stage were listened to but not heard. The momentum was simply too great, the reasons perceived as too just, the lessons of history too clear—for erroneous tactics to have thrown things off schedule.

A great deal of uncertainty pervaded the decision process. On July 2 Secretary McNamara asked General Wheeler to form a small group of experts to address the question "If we do everything we can, can we have assurance of winning in South Vietnam?" General Wheeler asked General Goodpaster, assistant to the chairman, JCS, to chair the group, and John McNaughton, assistant secretary of defense, provided the staff support. McNaughton, McNamara's closest civilian associate, offered a fascinating perspective on the degree of uncertainty facing decision-makers in early July. He believed that the forty-four–battalion program would be sufficient only through 1965 and urged Goodpaster to "produce a clear articulation of what our strategy is for winning the war in South Vietnam, tough as that articulation will be in the nature of the problem." McNaughton raised several important points: "I think we might avoid some spinning of wheels if we simply assumed that the GVN will not be able to increase its forces in the relevant time period. Indeed, from what Westy has reported about the battalions being chewed up and about their showing some signs of reluctance to engage in offensive operations, we might even have to ask the question whether we can expect them to maintain present levels of men—or more accurately, present levels of effectiveness." McNaughton offered a particularly astute assessment of the political situation in Saigon:

> Is it necessary for us to make some assumption with respect to the nature of the Saigon government? History does not encourage us to believe that Ky's government will endure throughout the time period relevant to the study. Ky's behavior is such that it is hard to predict his impact—he could, by his "revolutionary" talk and by his repressive measures generate either a genuine nationalist spirit or a violent reaction of some sort. I would think

that the study must make some observation, one way or the other, as to things which might happen to the government which would have a significant effect on the conclusions of the study. My own thought is that almost anything within the realm of likelihood can happen in the Saigon government, short of the formation of a government which goes neutral or asks us out, without appreciably affecting the conduct of the war. *The key point may be whether the Army rather than the government holds together.*

With regard to the question "If we do everything we can, can we have assurance of winning in South Vietnam?":

One key question, of course, is what we mean by the words "assurance" and "win." My view is that the degree of "assurance" should be fairly high—better than 75% (whatever that means). With respect to the word "win," this I think means that we succeed in demonstrating to the VC that they cannot win; this, of course, is victory for us only if it is, with a high degree of probability, a way station toward a favorable settlement in South Vietnam. I see such a favorable settlement as one in which the VC terrorism is substantially eliminated and, obviously, there are no longer large-scale VC attacks; the central South Vietnamese government (without having taken in the Communists) should be exercising fairly complete sovereignty over most of South Vietnam. I presume that we would rule out the ceding to the VC (either tacitly or explicitly) of large areas of the country. More specifically, the Brigadier Thompson suggestion that we withdraw to enclaves and sit it out for a couple of years is not what we have in mind for purposes of this study.

At the moment, I do not see how the study can avoid addressing the question as to how long our forces will have to remain in order to achieve a "win" and the extent to which the presence of those forces over a long period of time might, by itself, nullify the "win." . . . *I think we should find a way to indicate how badly the conclusions might be thrown off if we are wrong with respect to key assumptions or judgments.*

On July 14 Wheeler informed McNamara that "there appears to be no reason we cannot win *if such is our will*—and if that will is manifest in strategy and tactical operations." This was, of course, the unlimited options/no upper limit strategy—which Johnson refused to accept.

Challenges to the logic of U.S. involvement continued when McNaughton sent McNamara a "numbers game" scenario of possible options—illustrating that the probability for success and failure increased with each increment and each year. U.S. aims were identified as "70%—to preserve our national honor as a guarantor (and the reciprocal: to avoid a show-case success for Communist 'wars of liberation'); 20%—to keep SVN (and then adjacent) territory from hostile expansive hands; 10%—'answer the call of a friend,' to help him enjoy a better life. Also—to emerge from crisis without unacceptable taint from the methods used." . . .

In his concluding prognosis, McNaughton wrote: "even if 'success,' it is not obvious how we will be able to disengage our forces from South Vietnam. It is unlikely that a formal agreement good enough for the purpose could possibly be negotiated—because the arrangement can reflect little more than the power situation. Most likely, in the case of success, is a settling down into a 'compromise'-like situation with a large number— perhaps 2 divisions—of US forces required to stay for a period of years. During that period of time, any number of things can change the picture beyond prediction.''

According to the *Pentagon Papers*, ''the McNaughton memorandum is of interest because it demonstrates several important items. First, the fact that the question about assurance of winning was asked indicates that *at the Secretary of Defense level there was real awareness that the decision to be made in the next few weeks would commit the US to the possibility of an expanded conflict.* The key question then was whether or not we would become involved more deeply in a war which could not be brought to a satisfactory conclusion. Secondly, the definition of 'win,' i.e., 'succeed in demonstrating to the VC that they cannot win,' indicates the assumption upon which the conduct of the war was to rest—that the VC could be convinced in some meaningful sense that they were not going to win and that they would then rationally choose less violent methods of seeking their goals. But the extent to which this definition would set limits of involvement or affect strategy was not clear. Thirdly, the assumptions on the key variables (the infiltration rates, the strength of GVN forces, the probable usefulness of Third Country forces, the political situation in South Vietnam) were rightfully pessimistic and cautious.''

But the expressions of doubt were never to be publicly aired. When Sen. Mike Mansfield wrote with the question ''The main perplexity in the Vietnam situation is that even if you win, totally, you still do not come out well. What have you achieved?'' McNamara's response reflected just how committed he was to a definition which greatly raised the stakes of losing: ''South Vietnam *is vital* to the United States in the significance that a demonstrable defeat would have on the future effectiveness of the United States on the world scene—especially in areas where people are depending upon our guarantee of their independence. It is a *vital US concern* to maintain *our honor* as an ally and our formidability as an opponent. As for how the situation in Vietnam will ultimately come out, we cannot now know. *But there is a range of outcomes—many less than perfect ones— that would satisfy American vital interests.* Our objectives, after all, are quite limited in Vietnam. They are, first, to permit the South Vietnamese to be independent and make a free choice of government and second, to establish for the world that Communist externally inspired and supported wars of liberation will not work.'' No logic to the contrary would be allowed to disrupt that line of reasoning.

In his memoirs Ambassador Taylor asked, ''how were we trapped into such a costly venture? Who or what was responsible for this miscalculation?'' Taylor then excused decision-makers by noting that ''the requirement for a decision always preceded the availability of most of the needed information.'' But Taylor's judgment needs some qualification. The evidence . . . shows that the problem was not necessarily one of information scarcity, but an insensitivity to how expert knowledge should be utilized.

It is not infrequent that one hears the question: If Southeast Asia in general and Vietnam in specific were all that important to U.S. security interests, why didn't the United States (once the Ball scenario had been rejected) just use its power to win and then defend South Vietnam? The primary constraint on U.S. policy was the belief that provocative military measures against the North would bring Chinese troops into the war. President Johnson maintained that it would take only one stray bomb for the cloning of Korea. For that reason he would not risk bombing the dikes or mining Haiphong harbor. According to Doris Kearns, Johnson "lived in constant fear of triggering some imaginary provision of some imaginary treaty" between the Chinese and Hanoi.

There are several different opinions on this important issue. According to Clark Clifford, "the military would have liked to have invaded North Vietnam. President Johnson knew this was wrong because North Vietnam has a mutual assistance pact with Red China and just as soon as we invaded North Vietnam, the North Vietnamese would have triggered that pact and just hordes of Chinese troops would have come over. Every expert that I know in that part of the world agrees to that statement so there he turned the military down." Ambassador Taylor disagreed with this view, arguing that Washington was unduly apprehensive about possible Chinese reinforcements. In Saigon, "we doubted that either Hanoi or the Vietcong would ever request or accept Chinese combat forces in their country. For centuries the Chinese had been regarded as hated, foreign oppressors by all Vietnamese, North and South, and that historical attitude was not likely to change." In his memoirs Admiral Sharp lamented that the military was never allowed to fight the war "to win" because "political and diplomatic circles in Washington were disproportionately concerned with the possibility of communist and Soviet intervention"—characterized by frequent reference to "mythical hordes" of Chinese streaming into Vietnam should the United States pose a threatening glance. The important point is, however, that President Johnson defined the situation in a way which severely constrained his military options and ultimately undid his political base. In doing so he revealed a fundamental misunderstanding of his adversary's goals and purposes. According to Ambassador Taylor, "in 1965 we knew very little about the Hanoi leaders other than Ho Chi Minh and General Giap and virtually nothing about their individual or collective intentions. We were inclined to assume, however, that they would behave about like the North Koreans and the Red Chinese a decade before; that is, they would seek an accommodation with us when the cost of pursuing a losing course became excessive. Instead, the North Vietnamese proved to be incredibly tough in accepting losses which, by Western calculation, greatly exceeded the value of the stake involved." McGeorge Bundy offered a particularly revealing retrospective evaluation of these constraints: "Obviously the President is the chief actor, but I think everyone else has his share of responsibility, including those who differed over this or that part of the problem—or on the basic go-in or get-out question itself. I know I never found out how to connect LBJ's extraordinary abilities and energies to the questions of operational judgment and tactical and political detail that were so crucial. Perhaps there was no way—but then there should have been ways to help McNamara—or to choose more imaginative field leaders—military or political or both—and to deal with some of the constraints that may have been excessive.''

Since the U.S. goal was only to deny the Communists a victory and not to gain a military victory for itself, the principals proceeded from the premise that the greatest military power on the planet would eventually destroy the VC in South Vietnam and hit the DRV hard enough in North Vietnam to force a negotiated settlement on Hanoi. This strategy ignored the basic fact that Hanoi's *national* strategy was based on protracted struggle: "The leaders of the DRV had no rigid timetable for the struggle in the South. Rather the regime was confident that *the longer the war lasted, the more serious the 'inherent contradictions' in the US and US-GVN relationship would become.* Thus, while the North Vietnamese communists spoke of winning the decisive victory, *their definition of victory* did not imply the final seizure of power from the Saigon government. Instead, it meant either decisive victory on the battlefield, causing a turning point in the war, or partial annihilation of US and ARVN forces, forcing an American withdrawal. Decisive victory was, therefore, to take place within the context of protracted armed and political struggle.''

North Vietnam was involved in a total, not limited war. George Ball recalled that "On his first visit to Vietnam, in 1962, Secretary McNamara reported to the President that 'every quantitative measurement we have shows we are winning the war'—a comment that, as I came to understand, illustrated the Secretary's habitual practice of considering problems in quantitative terms. He was a superb Secretary of Defense—brilliantly skilled in planning, budgeting, devising, and administering efficient procurement policies and controlling all aspects of a great, sprawling part-military, part-civilian Department. But the very quantitative discipline that served him so splendidly as Secretary of Defense tended to interfere with his being a thoroughly successful Secretary of War. . . . What the McNamara approach lacked, of course, was any method of quantifying the quintessential advantage of the North Vietnamese and Viet Cong—the incomparable benefit of superior *élan,* of an intense spirit compounded by the elemental revolutionary drives of nationalism and anti-colonialism. Since anything that could not be quantified tended to be left out of the McNamara equation, the answer never came out right.''

We conclude where we started—with questions about the personality of the real principal, Lyndon Johnson. What force did this powerful personality cast over the decision process? Was this the terrifying Caligula whom no one dared challenge? Or was the July 28 decision locked in by events, politics, and human beings unwilling, like most of us, to reject the basis for our political cognitions? Or in a perverse sort of way, was perhaps making a bad military decision in 1965 the best of all available political decisions for a president who still dreamed of increasing his legislative scorecard?

The documents show that the president and his advisors were remarkably consistent in their belief that they had correctly defined the problem and the stakes in Vietnam. Lyndon Johnson was indeed exposed to dissenting views—Ball and Clifford in particular. Ball never held back and neither he nor Clifford was "beaten" into submission—just outnumbered. To wit, McGeorge Bundy's critique of McNamara's June 26 memo contained all the ingredients of a devil's advocacy process—but Bundy was either brought into line by the president or counted heads and realized that he was a loser in this battle. Ball was also outranked by the major principals. It made a great deal of difference that the paper trail on the president's desk included recommendations for escalation from the secretary of defense, the chairman of the Joint Chiefs of Staff, General Westmoreland, and, most important, Ball's boss, the secretary of state.

In the final analysis the president and not his advisors must accept most of the blame. Johnson was the cause of his ultimate undoing. The president was involved in a delicate exercise of political juggling. He "had known when he sent McNamara to Saigon that the purpose was to build a consensus on what needed to be done to turn the tide—not to cover a retreat. Within that purpose he was glad to have all sorts of options . . . [discussed], but his own priority was to get agreement, at the lowest level of intensity he could, on a course that would meet the present need in Vietnam and not derail his legislative calendar." Above all else, Johnson wanted to buy time and McNamara's plan allowed the president to hold on in Vietnam and to continue to build a Great Society at home. Johnson believed that to accept Ball's advice would be political suicide and result in political paralysis for the next three years. The domestic repercussion if the United States abandoned its commitment would be too great for a four-year president ever to recoup. Congress, Johnson believed, would turn on the president and the right-wing backlash would be devastating. Television screens would relay the "Communist carnage" into living rooms across the country. The rights of people to live in freedom would be trampled on. Hanoi's propaganda would focus on the United States as a paper tiger; China and the Soviet Union would laugh in the face of U.S. integrity, and there was always the spectre of China's "picking up the pieces at the fringe." Allies would never again trust the seal on the treaty with the United States. Johnson believed that Ball was wrong. There was no way to lose with honor. On the other hand, the Joint Chiefs' option raised the possibility of nuclear confrontation. Besides, how could the most powerful military apparatus in the world not achieve the relatively simple goal of denying Hanoi a victory? The United States sought no military victory of its own, no territory, nothing except the goal of convincing Hanoi it could not unify Vietnam by force. In 1965 Lyndon Johnson believed that with one or two lucky breaks this relatively simple goal could be achieved.

Thus did Lyndon Johnson commit slow political suicide. Once he decided to fight the war, his greatest tactical error as a *political* leader came when he rejected the advice of civilian and military advisors on the question of mobilizing the nation's resources. In deciding *not* to mobilize the

Reserves, *not* to seek a congressional resolution or declaration of national emergency, *not* to present the program in a prime-time address to Congress or the nation (rather than an afternoon press conference), and *not* to disclose publicly the full extent of the anticipated military call-up, the president's credibility soon came unraveled. This was not the infamous "Caligula," but rather the soft-selling *Homo politicus*—who believed that losing Vietnam in the summer of 1965 would wreck his plans for a truly Great Society. In doing so he apparently gave very little attention to where he would be six months or one year down the road. But for the moment he pulled it off. On July 28 the country gave a sigh of relief. Lyndon Johnson was acting with restraint. The Reserves were not going to war, the nation was not mobilizing—the soft sell brought Johnson time and support.

Time and support for what? Vietnam was *not* the only important item on the president's agenda the week of July 21. As Johnson explained in *The Vantage Point*, Medicare and the Civil Rights Bill were at crucial stages in conference committee. But even more important, the curtain was closing on a historic era: "In all, thirty six major pieces of legislation had been signed into law, twenty six others were moving through the House and Senate, and eleven more awaiting scheduling." A divisive debate would, in the president's opinion, have ruined his vision of a great America. On July 27 Johnson told his Cabinet that the past week had been "the most productive and most historic legislative week in Washington during this century. . . . Thus the books were closing on our campaign to take action against the most pressing problems inherited from the past—the 'old agenda.' " But Johnson now recognized "the urgent and unavoidable need to begin work on a new agenda."

And in the short run Johnson succeeded—only to prove the bankruptcy of his leadership. Six months following the July 28 decision Johnson went to Congress and declared, "I believe we can continue the Great Society while we fight in Vietnam." Johnson wrote in *The Vantage Point*, "in that sentence, to which the Congress responded with heartening applause, the turmoil of months was resolved, and the Great Society moved through midpassage into its final years of creative activity and accomplishment."

In the end Lyndon Johnson was not misled by advisors. He had no reason, no incentive to lead a searching reevaluation of U.S. policy. . . . Could [Johnson] have led America away from war in 1965[?] The documents show that at no stage was this option ever fully staffed out by the president's assistants. No one was planning the politics of getting out by December if the July decision was ineffective. It could and should have been done—it was certainly less a threat than Johnson believed. He sought only to hide in the middle of two extremes. He had weighed all the costs and then used his great talents to forge a marginal consensus—enough to get the United States into war, but insufficient for war termination. Moreover, Johnson did not act indecisively. He chose between short- and long-run risks, and his fatal mistake occurred in that choice. In holding back from total commitment Johnson was juggling the Great Society, the war in Vietnam, and his hopes for the future. He *chose* to avoid a national debate on the war, to keep the Reserves home, and to buy time for a domestic record meriting nothing less than Mount Rushmore (he would later settle for the Johnson Library).

On June 30, 1965, McGeorge Bundy wrote to the president with a comparative analysis of the "French, 1954—United States, 1965 situation." Bundy concluded his memorandum with the following analogy: "The US in 1965 is responding to the call of a people under Communist assault, a people undergoing a non-Communist national revolution; neither our power nor that of our adversaries has been fully engaged as yet. At home we remain *politically strong* and, in general, *politically united.* Options, both military and political, remain to us that were no longer available to the French." How long, however, would a democracy support a limited and hidden war? Yet it need not have been that way. To George Ball, "a determined President might at any point have overruled those advisers, accepted the costs of withdrawal, and broken the momentum, but only a leader supremely sure of himself could make that decision, and Lyndon Johnson, out of his element in the Vietnam War, felt no such certainty." The NSC meeting of July 21 illustrates the point. Ball had just presented his case for cutting our losses. Ambassador Lodge challenged the undersecretary, primarily on the grounds that the central lesson of history was "indolence at Munich," not Korea or the French experience at Dien Bien Phu. Ball argued back—the United States would never win this war. Nobody had yet produced a convincing case that the United States could achieve its military goals and remain politically united at home. Ball was *not blaming Johnson—previous* administrations had underestimated the situation. It would take a long and protracted war, however, to reveal just how bad the strategic errors had been. Ball seemed to grasp the implication for long-term political leadership even better than Johnson, warning the president that should he proceed as recommended by McNamara, public opinion would soon turn against the president. The Great Society would crumble, and bring Johnson down as well.

In *The Vantage Point* President Johnson reflected on the critical choices of July 1965: "The demanding decisions of those trying days relating to Vietnam were decisions involving our nation's integrity and its security. But they also involved what I considered to be the promise of the American future. In a wondrous time of hope and optimism we had begun the building of a better society for our people. The danger that we might have to slow that building in order to take care of our obligations abroad, brought added anguish. *So on that July 27, 1965, two great streams in our national life converged—the dream of a Great Society at home and the inescapable demands of our obligations halfway around the world. They were to run in confluence until the end of my administration.*" They were, in fact, to bring an end to his administration. Lyndon Johnson's greatest fault as a political leader was that *he chose* not to choose between the Great Society and the war in Vietnam. Instead, he sought a pragmatic guns-and-butter solution for avoiding what he believed would have surely been a divisive national debate in order temporarily to protect his Great Society. . . .

The pathos did indeed turn to tragedy. Johnson used the advisory process to legitimize the decision to political elites and the general public. On July 28, 1965, Lyndon Johnson chose a path which turned Vietnam into America's nightmare. But elements of pathos soon manifested themselves. In June 1966 John Kenneth Galbraith wrote to the president, "As you know, I am completely convinced, and now with the Buddhists more than ever, that we have no future in Viet Nam. But I am not writing to argue on this. I am writing to say that, as a matter of political craftsmanship, I fully believe that, should it be your decision, a script could be written— speeches, involvement of Congress and the U.N., discussion and approval of other Asian countries, concern for self-determination and religious freedom, etc., etc.—that would enable your Administration to accept, with dignity and even credit and applause, any bargain we might get down to orderly withdrawal. It would take brains and skill but it could be done.

"Should the time ever come when you want such a hand, I am yours to command. This is the purpose of this letter which involves no false modesty, although you have some idea of my talents in these matters. *I don't for a moment believe that your presidency need be ruined by this misadventure.*"

Johnson responded with a personal letter to Galbraith (written almost one year to the day after the 1965 decision). The letter shows a president heading for personal defeat: "I have never doubted your talent for political craftsmanship, and I am sure you could devise a script that would appear to justify our taking an unjustifiable course in South Vietnam. But I hope that I never have to take you up on it. To get out of Vietnam before the North gives up its support of the war there, in my opinion, would be unfortunate and wrong. I'm not even sure you and I together could convince the other nations of Asia that it would be to their benefit for us to turn around now. I know it wouldn't, so I would be at best a half-hearted persuader.

"I do want to get out—and will, as I said yesterday, when North Vietnam wants to talk about a peaceful settlement or end the fighting. One of these days you are going to see what we are doing and what it means for the rest of Asia, and then, I hope, you will quietly be grateful that I summoned the extraordinary restraint not to accept for the time being your good offer."

By 1968 the president would run *from* office—his dream of a Great Society ruined by the war. In the end Johnson would fail to make the transition described to him by Vice-President Humphrey: "*President Johnson is personally identified with, and greatly admired for, political ingenuity. He will be expected to put all his great political sense to work now for international political solutions. People will be counting on him to use on the world scene his unrivaled talents as a politician. They will be watching to see how he makes this transition from the domestic to the world stage.*"

The personal tragedy was obvious to former President Eisenhower, who on March 31, 1968, following Johnson's announcement that he would not seek reelection, recorded in his diary: "to me it seems obvious that the President is at war with himself and while trying vigorously to defend the actions and decisions he has made in the past, and urging the nation to pursue those purposes regardless of costs, he wants to be excused from the burden of office to which he was elected.'' Therein rested the legacy of July 1965—a personal and national tragedy.

× *F U R T H E R   R E A D I N G*

Anthony Austin, *The President's War* (1971)

George W. Ball, *The Past Has Another Pattern* (1982)

Larry Berman, *Lyndon Johnson's War* (1989)

Vaughan Bornet, *The Presidency of Lyndon B. Johnson* (1983)

Warren I. Cohen, *Dean Rusk* (1980)

Chester L. Cooper, *The Lost Crusade* (1972)

J. William Fulbright, *The Price of Empire* (1989)

John Galloway, *The Gulf of Tonkin Resolution* (1970)

Leslie H. Gelb and Richard K. Betts, *The Irony of Vietnam* (1979)

Philip Geyelin, *Lyndon B. Johnson and the World* (1966)

Joseph C. Goulden, *Truth Is the First Casualty: The Gulf of Tonkin Affair* (1969)

David Halberstam, *The Best and the Brightest* (1972)

Doris Kearns, *Lyndon Johnson and the American Dream* (1976)

Gregory Palmer, *The McNamara Strategy and the Vietnam War* (1978)

Eugene C. Windchy, *Tonkin Gulf* (1971)

CHAPTER
7

U.S. Military Strategy

X

From the introduction of U.S. ground forces in 1965, President Johnson, General William C. Westmoreland, and other top civilian and military officials sought to define a strategy appropriate to U.S. objectives in Vietnam. How could American superiority in firepower and technology be brought to bear on an elusive enemy in an inhospitable climate? Were America's goals primarily military or political? What role, if any, should the United States play in the political stabilization of its South Vietnamese ally? Those essential questions defied easy solutions for LBJ and his successor.

American military strategy in Vietnam provoked an intense debate among scholars, military officers, and politicians. That debate, which began with the escalation of the American commitment in the mid-1960s, has raged unabated since then; it remains nearly as lively today as at the height of the war. Certain issues have proved especially troublesome. Was the attrition strategy wise? Might alternative military tactics have been more effective? Why did the United States adopt the tactics and strategy that it did? To what extend did the United States understand its foe—and its ally? How clear were the objectives for which it was fighting? Did Hanoi and the National Liberation Front evolve tactics and strategy superior to those of Washington? And, perhaps the most controversial question of all, could the United States have won the war? If so, how?

X DOCUMENTS

In the first document, a November 30, 1965, memorandum to President Johnson, Defense Secretary Robert McNamara recommended additional American troop deployments while admitting that even those deployments could not guarantee victory. George F. Kennan, former U.S. ambassador to the Soviet Union and author of the containment strategy that guided much of post–World War II American foreign policy, criticized the U.S. military commitment to Vietnam in a publicized appearance before the Senate Foreign Relations Committee. Excerpts from Kennan's statement are reprinted as the second document. The next document, a Central Intelligence Agency memorandum of May 12, 1967, offers a candid assessment of the American bombing campaign against North Vietnam, acknowledging its shortcomings. A public statement by McNamara on the improved military outlook for the United States in Vietnam follows. Ironically, at the same time he was issuing this optimistic public prognostication, his private doubts about the war effort were growing.

In the next document, General William C. Westmoreland offers a retrospective justification of the attrition strategy. The last selection presents a soldier's perspective on the experience of combat in Vietnam.

Robert S. McNamara Urges Additional Troop Deployments, 1965

The [Nguyen Cao] Ky [Prime Minister of South Vietnam, 1965–67] "government of generals" is surviving, but not acquiring wide support or generating actions; pacification is thoroughly stalled, with no guarantee that security anywhere is permanent and no indications that able and willing leadership will emerge in the absence of that permanent security. (Prime Minister Ky estimates that his government controls only 25% of the population today and reports that his pacification chief hopes to increase that to 50% two years from now).

The dramatic recent changes in the situation are on the military side. They are the increased infiltration from the North and the increased willingness of the Communist forces to stand and fight, even in large-scale engagements. The Ia Drang River Campaign of early November is an example. The Communists appear to have decided to increase their forces in SVN both by heavy recruitment in the South (especially in the Delta) and by infiltration of regular NVN forces from the North. . . . The enemy can be expected to enlarge his present strength of 110 battalion equivalents to more than 150 battalion equivalents by the end of calendar 1966, when hopefully his losses can be made to equal his input.

As for the Communist ability to supply this force, it is estimated that, even taking account of interdiction of routes by air and sea, more than 200 tons of supplies a day can be infiltrated—more than enough, allowing for the extent to which the enemy lives off the land, to support the likely PAVN/VC force at the likely level of operations.

To meet this possible—and in my view likely—Communist buildup, the presently contemplated Phase I forces will not be enough (approx 220,000 Americans, almost all in place by end of 1965). Bearing in mind the nature of the war, the expected weighted combat force ratio of less than 2-to-1 will not be good enough. Nor will the originally contemplated Phase II addition of 28 more U.S. battalions (112,000 men) be enough; the combat force ratio, even with 32 new SVNse battalions, would still be little better than 2-to-1 at the end of 1966. The initiative which we have held since August would pass to the enemy; we would fall far short of what we expected to achieve in terms of population control and disruption of enemy bases and lines of communications. Indeed, it is estimated that with the contemplated Phase II addition of 28 U.S. battalions, we would be able only to hold our present geographical positions. . . .

3. We have but two options, it seems to me. One is to go now for a compromise solution (something substantially less than the "favorable out once" I described in my memo of Nov. 3) and hold further deployments to a minimum. The other is to stick with our stated objectives and with the war, and provide what it takes in men and materiel. If it is decided not to move now toward a compromise, I recommend that the U.S. both send a substantial number of additional troops and very gradually intensify the bombing of NVN. Amb. Lodge, Wheeler, Sharp and Westmoreland concur in this prolonged course of action, although Wheeler and Sharp would intensify the bombing of the North more quickly.

(recommend up to 74 battalions by end-66: total to approx 400,000 by end-66. And it should be understood that further deployments (perhaps exceeding 200,000) may be needed in 1967. Bombing of NVN. . . . over a period of the next six months we gradually enlarge the target system in the northeast (Hanoi-Haiphong) quadrant until, at the end of the period, it includes "controlled" reconnaissance of lines of comm throughout the area, bombing of petroleum storage facilities and power plants, and mining of the harbors. (Left unstruck would be population targets, industrial plants, locks and dams).

4. Pause in bombing NVN. It is my belief that there should be a three- or four-week pause in the program of bombing the North before we either greatly increase our troop deployments to VN or intensify our strikes against the North. (My recommendation for a "pause" is not concurred in by Lodge, Wheeler or Sharp.) The reasons for this belief are, first, that we must lay a foundation in the minds of the American public and in world opinion for such an enlarged phase of the war and second, we should give NVN a face-saving chance to stop the aggression. I am not seriously concerned about the risk of alienating the SVNese, misleading Hanoi, or being "trapped" in a pause; if we take reasonable precautions, we can avoid these pitfalls. I am seriously concerned about embarking on a markedly higher level of war in VN without having tried, through a pause, to end the war or at least having made it clear to our people that we did our best to end it.

5. Evaluation. We should be aware that deployments of the kind I have recommended will not guarantee success. U.S. killed-in-action can be expected to reach 1000 a month, and the odds are even that we will be faced in early 1967 with a "no-decision" at an even higher level. My over-all evaluation, nevertheless, is that the best chance of achieving our stated objectives lies in a pause followed, if it fails, by the deployments mentioned above.

George F. Kennan Criticizes the American Military Commitment, 1966

I have not been anxious to press my views on the public but I gladly 'give them to you for whatever they are worth, claiming no particular merit for them except perhaps that they flow from experience with Communist affairs that runs back now for some thirty-eight years, and also from the deepest and most troubled sort of concern that we should find the proper course, the right course, at this truly crucial moment.

The first point I would like to make is that if we were not already involved as we are today in Vietnam, I would know of no reason why we should wish to become so involved, and I could think of several reasons why we should wish not to. Vietnam is not a region of major military, industrial importance. It is difficult to believe that any decisive developments of the world situation would be determined in normal circumstances by what happens on that territory. If it were not for the considerations of prestige that arise precisely out of our present involvement, even a situation in which South Vietnam was controlled exclusively by the Viet Cong, while regrettable, and no doubt morally unwarranted, would not, in my opinion, present dangers great enough to justify our direct military intervention.

Given the situation that exists today in the relations among the leading Communist powers, and by that I have, of course, in mind primarily the Soviet-Chinese conflict, there is every likelihood that a Communist regime in South Vietnam would follow a fairly independent course. There is no reason to suspect that such a regime would find it either necessary or desirable in present circumstances to function simply as a passive puppet and instrument of Chinese power. And as for the danger that its establishment there would unleash similar tendencies in neighboring countries, this, I think, would depend largely on the manner in which it came into power.

In the light of what has recently happened in Indonesia, and on the Indian subcontinent, the danger of the so-called domino effect, that is the effect that would be produced by a limited Communist success in South Vietnam, seem to me to be considerably less than it was when the main decisions were taken that have led to our present involvement. Let me stress, I do not say that that danger does not exist. I say that it is less than it was a year or two ago when we got into this involvement. From the long-term standpoint, therefore, and on principle, I think our military involvement in Vietnam has to be recognized as unfortunate, as something we would not choose deliberately, if the choice were ours to make all over again today, and by the same token, I think it should be our government's aim to liquidate this involvement just as soon as this can be done without inordinate damage to our own prestige or to the stability of conditions in that area.

It is obvious, on the other hand, that this involvement is today a fact. It creates a new situation. It raises new questions ulterior to the long-term problems which have to be taken into account; a precipitate and disorderly withdrawal could represent in present circumstances a disservice to our own interests and even to world peace greater than any that might have been involved by our failure to engage ourselves there in the first place. This is a reality which, if there is to be any peaceful resolution of this conflict, is going to have to be recognized both by the more critical of our friends and by our adversaries.

But at the same time, I have great misgivings about any deliberate expansion of hostilities on our part directed to the achievement of something called "victory," if by the use of that term we envisage the complete disappearance of the recalcitrance with which we are now faced, the formal submission by the adversary to our will, and the complete realization of our present stated political aims. I doubt that these things can be achieved even by the most formidable military successes.

There seems to be an impression that if we bring sufficient military pressure to bear, there will occur at some point something in the nature of a political capitulation on the other side. I think this is a most dangerous assumption. I don't say that it is absolutely impossible, but it is a dangerous assumption in the light of the experience we have had with Communist elements in the past. The North Vietnamese and the Viet Cong have, between them, a great deal of space and manpower to give up if they have to, and the Chinese can give them more if they need it. Fidelity to the Communist tradition would dictate that if really pressed to extremity on the military level, these people should disappear entirely from the open scene and fall back exclusively on an underground political and military existence rather than to accept terms that would be openly humiliating and would represent in their eyes the betrayal of the future political prospects of the cause to which they are dedicated.

Any total rooting-out of the Viet Cong from the territory of South Vietnam could be achieved, if it could be achieved at all, only at the cost of a degree of damage to civilian life and of civilian suffering, generally, for which I would not like to see this country responsible. And to attempt to crush North Vietnamese strength to a point where Hanoi could no longer give any support for Viet Cong political activity in the South would almost certainly, it seems to me, have the effect of bringing in Chinese forces at some point, whether formally or in the guise of volunteers, thus involving us in a military conflict with Communist China on one of the most unfavorable theaters of hostility that we could possibly choose.

This is not the only reason why I think we should do everything possible to avoid the escalation of this conflict. There is another one which is no less weighty, and this is the effect the conflict is already having on our policies and interests further afield. This involvement seems to me to represent a grievous misplacement of emphasis on our foreign policies as a whole. Not only are great and potentially more important questions of world affairs not receiving, as a consequence of our involvement in Vietnam, the attention they should be receiving, but in some instances assets we already enjoy and hopefully possibilities we should be developing, are being sacrificed to this unpromising involvement in a remote and secondary theater. Our relations with the Soviet Union have suffered grievously, as was to be expected, and this at a time when far more important things were involved in those relations than what is ultimately involved in Vietnam and when we had special reason, I think, to cultivate those relations. And more unfortunate still, in my opinion, is the damage being done to the feelings entertained for us by the Japanese people; the confidence and the good disposition of the Japanese is the greatest asset we have had and the greatest asset we could have in East Asia. As the greatest industrial complex in the entire Far East, and the only place where the sinews of modern war can be produced on a formidable scale there, Japan is of vital importance to us and indeed to the prospects generally of peace and stability in East Asia.

There is no success we could have in Vietnam that would conceivably warrant, in my opinion, the sacrifice by us of the confidence and good will of the Japanese people.

The Central Intelligence Agency's Assessment of the Bombing Campaign, 1967

Through the end of April 1967 the US air campaign against North Vietnam—Rolling Thunder—had significantly eroded the capacities of North Vietnam's limited industrial and military base. These losses, however, have not meaningfully degraded North Vietnam's material ability to continue the war in South Vietnam.

Total damage through April 1967 was over $233 million, of which 70 percent was accounted for by damage to economic targets. The greatest amount of damage was inflicted on the so-called logistics target system—transport equipment and lines of communication.

By the end of April 1967 the US air campaign had attacked 173 fixed targets, over 70 percent of the targets on the JCS list. This campaign included extensive attacks on almost every major target system in the country. The physical results have varied widely.

All of the 13 targeted petroleum storage facilities have been attacked, with an estimated loss of 85 percent of storage capacity. Attacks on 13 of the 20 targeted electric power facilities have neutralized 70 percent of North Vietnam's power-generating capacity. The major losses in the military establishment include the neutralization of 18 ammunition depots, with a loss capacity of 70 percent. Over three fourths of the 65 JCS-targeted barracks have been attacked, with a loss of about one fourth of national capacity. Attacks on 22 of the 29 targeted supply depots reduced capacity by 17 percent. Through the end of April 1967, five of North Vietnam's airfields had been attacked, with a loss of about 20 percent of national capacity.

North Vietnam's ability to recuperate from the air attacks has been of a high order. The major exception has been the electric power industry. One small plant—Co Dinh—is beyond repair. Most of the other plants would require 3–4 months to be restored to partial operations, although two plants—Haiphong East and Uong Bi—would require one year. For complete restoration, all of the plants would require at least a year. Restoration of these plants would require foreign technical assistance and equipment.

The recuperability problem is not significant for the other target systems. The destroyed petroleum storage system has been replaced by an effective system of dispersed storage and distribution. The damaged military target systems—particularly barracks and storage depots—have simply been abandoned, and supplies and troops dispersed throughout the country.

The inventories of transport and military equipment have been replaced by large infusions of military and economic aid from the USSR and Communist China. Damage to bridges and lines of communications is frequently repaired within a matter of days, if not hours, or the effects are countered by an elaborate system of multiple bypasses or pre-positioned spans.

McNamara on the Improved Military Outlook, 1967

On the military field, let me say to start with, the military commanders I met with—and I met with all of the senior military commanders in the field, all of the senior Vietnamese commanders, many of the Allied commanders, Korean, and New Zealanders, for example, and many of the middle-ranking and junior U.S. officers—all of the military commanders stated that the reports that they read in the press of military stalemate were, to use their words, the "most ridiculous statements that they had ever heard."

In their view military progress had occurred and was continuing. How did they measure this? They measured it in particular by the success of what they called the large-unit actions. These are battalion-sized and larger actions.

They felt that these actions that General [William C.] Westmoreland had organized and carried on over the past several months, particularly in II and III Corps, had a spoiling effect on the Viet Cong and North Vietnamese. Before they could concentrate their troops to launch an offensive, Westmoreland, through his intelligence sources, had obtained information about the intended enemy plans and had struck the troop concentrations as they were developing, spoiling the potential of the enemy for carrying out these offensive actions.

Moreover, as you know, it has been General Westmoreland's strategy over the past several months to attack the base areas, particularly those in the II and III Corps, using B-52 strikes in some cases but in particular using a coordinated ground and air attack against these base areas to destroy the facilities, the stocks—the recuperation areas that the Viet Cong and the North Vietnamese had used.

The military commanders felt, as a result of this combination of spoiling attacks and attacks on the base areas, the pressure had been so great on the North Viet Cong that they had tended to shift their area of activity. Whereas up until very recently, the activity had been concentrated primarily in the II and III Corps, the offensive activities more recently—they had moved their area of action to the I Corps.

This is understandable because in the II and III Corps—with the loss of their base areas—they were at the end of a very long line of communication over which their men and supplies moved from the supply centers in North Viet-Nam. This line of communications moved down the panhandle of North Viet-Nam across into Laos, down Laos to the Cambodian border, and across into South Viet-Nam—a very, very long line of communication that was under very intense air attack, as a matter of fact.

And because this was a handicap to them—particularly so in connection with the strategy that Westmoreland was carrying out against them—they shifted their area of activity to I Corps.

This accounts for their military actions there in the past several weeks. Now they have the advantage of short lines of communication extending down to the southern border of Viet-Nam, very close to the point where the troops are now very active.

Perhaps the most dramatic change that I saw that reflects the military situation was the opening of the roads.

Highway No. 1, which is the coastal route that runs from the 17th parallel—the line of demarcation between North Viet-Nam and South Viet-Nam—clear south to Saigon, has been broken for many, many months in literally hundreds of places, and traffic on the route has been minimal.

But within the past several months, as a result of these military actions—planned and carried out by the free-world forces—that route has gradually been reopened in large segments.

As a matter of fact, day before yesterday, the route from the southern border of the II Corps up to Dong Hai, which is very close to the DMZ—just a few miles south of the DMZ—was opened for traffic.

There will continue to be ambushes, I presume, and Viet Cong strikes against it, but as I flew over the road after this long stretch was opened, literally hundreds of bicycles and scores of cars and trucks—civilian cars and trucks—were using it.

The same thing is true of many of the feeder roads in III and IV Corps— roads that are of importance to move vegetables or rice to market or otherwise serving as an underpinning of the day-to-day life of the society.

I don't want to exaggerate this or imply all roads are open—far from it. I don't even want to suggest that many of the roads being used can be used freely night and day. They can't. But there has been a very, very noticeable—when I say "noticeable," I mean one flying over the area can notice a very substantial increase in the miles of roads that are open to traffic and the volume of traffic on the roads.

Perhaps a word about the air operations is in order.

We have suffered materially in air operations because of night vision— the difficulty of acquiring targets at night.

There have been some very significant changes in technology. I don't want to go into the details of them other than to say they have greatly increased the capability of our forces to carry on all-weather attacks on the lines of communication, both in South Viet-Nam and in North Viet-Nam.

These, in conjunction with new weapons, new types of ordnance, that have been designed and developed in recent years and brought into production in recent months in combination have increased the effectiveness of the airstrikes. As a matter of fact, they have reduced the losses of both planes and pilots. The losses of planes, for example, are rather significantly lower than we had previously estimated.

Now a word on the pacification program. You are all aware that within the past few weeks there has been a reorganization of the American effort in pacification, an integration of the civilian and military staffs.

The responsibility for pacification has been assigned to General Westmoreland, whose deputy, Mr. Robert Komer, has been placed in direct charge of it. I was very pleased with what I saw.

The frictions that I had read about in the paper perhaps existed at one time but certainly have been dampened down, if not completely eliminated. Both civilian and military officers that I visited at the sector level, the provinces, and the subsector levels of the villages and hamlets, were working effectively together and appeared to have benefited from this integration and reorganization of the pacification efforts.

However, having said that, I should state to you that to be candid I must report the progress in pacification has been very slow. I think that the momentum will increase as the new organization gains in experience, but what we are really trying to do here is engage in nation-building. It is an extraordinarily complex process. I would anticipate progress in what is really a very significant field would continue to be slow.

I am sure that the first question you would ask me, if I didn't anticipate it, would be about additional military personnel; so I will address myself to that. I think some more U.S. military personnel will be required. I am not sure how many. I am certain of one thing: that we must use more effectively the personnel that are presently there.

When I say that, I am speaking of all free-world personnel. As you know, the Vietnamese, the Koreans, the Australians, the New Zealanders, the Filipinos, as well as we, have all contributed forces to the support of the operations in Viet-Nam.

There has been a very rapid buildup of those forces. We now have in uniform of the free-world forces over 1,300,000 men. As you might expect in any organization that has expanded as fast as this one has, there are bound to be areas of waste and inefficiency that can be corrected and eliminated—that must be corrected when we are considering additional troop requirements.

William C. Westmoreland Reflects on a War of Attrition, 1977

In response to changes in national policy, there were basically six strategies adopted between 1954 and 1969. The first involved bolstering the South Vietnamese by sending advisers and logistical and economic support in the hope that this could stop and reverse the subversive efforts of the Communists within South Vietnam. The second was an overall strategy of gradually escalating pressure against North Vietnam in the hope of convincing the North to halt its support of the insurgency in the South. This

From *The Lessons of Vietnam*, W. Scott Thompson and Donaldson D. Frizzell, eds., 1977, pp. 57–60, 71. Reprinted by permission of Taylor & Francis.

was essentially a strategy based on bombing. The third was a base-security strategy, which was an adjunct of the decision to bomb North Vietnam but which can be called a strategy in that it represented the first commitment of American ground troops to the fighting, albeit in a defensive role. The fourth was an enclave strategy, which assumed protection by American troops of five important areas of South Vietnam but still left most of the fighting to the South Vietnamese. The fifth involved a gradual buildup of forces in the South for purposes of putting maximum pressure on the Communist structure and forces in the South, emphasizing pacification and nation building, expanding control by the South Vietnamese Government over the population, and, at the same time, escalating pressure on the North with air and naval power. The political objective was to bring the enemy to the conference table. The final strategy comprised maximum expansion of the Vietnamese armed forces, increased efforts to pacify all of South Vietnam and to build a viable nation, coupled with gradual withdrawal with or without negotiations.

The decision to launch an air campaign of rising intensity against the North was made against a background of anguished concern over the threat of South Vietnam's imminent collapse. Although the basic objective was to try to convince the North to end its support of the insurgency, another objective was to bolster the morale and strengthen the resolve of the South Vietnamese, who had long been absorbing punishment while the supporters of the insurgency enjoyed impunity.

Two basic considerations lay behind the gradual escalation of the campaign. First, a modest bombing effort might be enough to convince the North of American resolve and, if negotiations developed, might compensate for some of the leverage the Viet Cong victories gave the other side. Secondly, the fear of Chinese Communist intervention was always of immense concern to American officials. Since the Chinese had responded to earlier bombings in muted tones, policy makers in Washington deduced that a gradually increasing campaign might ruffle the Chinese less than would a sudden massive onslaught. The Administration was faced with a dilemma—mobilizing too much support for the war might produce "war fever" and cause the American people to look upon the war as a "great crusade." Nevertheless, I believe a better job could have been done in explaining the nature of our objectives to the American people and the historical background of our involvement.

The strategy of gradually escalating pressure was a new concept; the Joint Chiefs of Staff disagreed with it. It was not, to them, an early "win" policy. Most military men are accustomed to thinking in terms of terminating a war in the shortest practical time and at least cost, following a decision to fight. It is perhaps unnecessary to make the point that there is a relationship between the length of a war and its cost.

By early April 1965, it had become apparent that the new strategy, even with its adjunct of base security, was having no visible effect on the will of the North Vietnamese to continue to support the insurgency. As someone has put it, the United States was signaling Hanoi with a new alphabet that Hanoi could not or would not read. The realization that the air war alone was not doing the job—or at least would take a long time to do it—led to a belief that some new step had to be taken directly against the insurgency in the South. So long as the Viet Cong—reinforced at that point by North Vietnamese troops—continued to win, the leaders in the North, in expectation of ultimate victory, probably would endure the punishment the limited bombing campaign was inflicting.

Taking a new step against the Viet Cong clearly meant actively involving American troops, yet President Johnson and most of his advisers still shied from such a fateful step. Once committed, planes and ships could be readily withdrawn; not so with ground troops. Furthermore, how well would American troops with their sophisticated equipment perform in an Asian insurgency environment? Better to devise some kind of strategy that stopped short of unrestricted commitment, one that would further signal American resolve yet at the same time provide escape valves.

That was the thinking behind the enclave strategy whereby American troops were to take full responsibility for defense of five coastal enclaves and to be prepared to go to the rescue of South Vietnamese forces within fifty miles of the enclaves. Yet, as I pointed out at the time, it put American troops in the unfortunate position of defending static defensive positions with their backs to the sea—in effect, holding five embattled beachheads. It also left the decision of ultimate success or failure in the hands of South Vietnamese troops whose demonstrated inability to defeat the Viet Cong was the reason for committing American troops.

In the face of continuing crisis, my view, and that of the Joint Chiefs of Staff, prevailed. President Johnson's decision of July 1965 carried the United States across the threshold in Vietnam. Before 1965 ended, the United States was to have 184,000 military personnel in Vietnam, including an Army air-mobile division and a Marine division.

Based on my personal experience with the problems on the ground in South Vietnam—political and military—and considering my perception of the aims of the enemy, I anticipated in 1965 that this nation was becoming involved in a protracted war of attrition in which our national will would be sorely tried. As a student of the history of war, and remembering the relatively recent Korean War experience, I was aware of the likelihood that a limited war, fought with limited means for limited objectives, would put special strain on the body politic of a system of government such as ours.

It was in such a context that I recommended continuation of the one-year tour that had been set for advisers. It was my belief that lengthy involuntary tours would more likely bring about a hue and cry to "bring the boys home" than a tour in which the "boys would come home" after one year unless they volunteered to stay longer. Also, in anticipation of a long war, it seemed to me that the burden of service should be shared by a cross section of American youth. I did not anticipate that numbers of our young men would be allowed by national policy to defer service by going to a college campus.

I hoped, perhaps with folly, that an emerging sense of South Vietnamese nationalism and a revitalized national will in South Vietnam—manifested in a viable government and a proficient fighting force—would in the long run compensate for the inevitable waning of public support in the United States for a difficult war. . . .

From a military standpoint, it clearly would have been better to have moved much earlier against the enemy's sanctuaries in Laos and Cambodia and possibly even in the southern reaches of North Vietnam. Yet that is speaking without consideration for the political consequences. Further, if the military could have employed air and naval power in accordance with its best judgment, our strategy could have been accelerated. However, the same caution may not have been exercised and the dangers of provoking China to get more deeply involved could have been enhanced.

The Vietnam conflict was an undeclared and limited war, with a limited objective, fought with limited means against an unorthodox enemy, and with limited public support. The longest war in our history, it was the most reported and the most visible to the public—but the least understood. It was more than a military confrontation; ideological, economic, psychological, political, and nation-building problems were involved. Our national involvement in Southeast Asia became an emotional public controversy and hence a political issue. This new and traumatic experience by our nation should provide lessons for our people, our leadership, the news media, and our soldiers.

A Soldier's Perspective on Combat in Vietnam, 1977

Writing about this kind of warfare is not a simple task. Repeatedly, I have found myself wishing that I had been the veteran of a conventional war, with dramatic campaigns and historic battles for subject matter instead of a monotonous succession of ambushes and fire-fights. But there were no Normandies or Gettysburgs for us, no epic clashes that decided the fates of armies or nations. The war was mostly a matter of enduring weeks of expectant waiting and, at random intervals, of conducting vicious manhunts through jungles and swamps where snipers harassed us constantly and booby traps cut us down one by one.

The tedium was occasionally relieved by a large-scale search-and-destroy operation, but the exhilaration of riding the lead helicopter into a landing zone was usually followed by more of the same hot walking, with the mud sucking at our boots and the sun thudding against our helmets while an invisible enemy shot at us from distant tree lines. The rare instances when the VC chose to fight a set-piece battle provided the only excitement; not ordinary excitement, but the manic ecstasy of contact. Weeks of bottled-up tensions would be released in a few minutes of orgiastic violence, men screaming and shouting obscenities above the explosions of grenades and the rapid, rippling bursts of automatic rifles.

Beyond adding a few more corpses to the weekly body count, none of these encounters achieved anything; none will ever appear in military histories or be studied by cadets at West Point. Still, they changed us and taught us, the men who fought in them; in those obscure skirmishes we learned the old lessons about fear, cowardice, courage, suffering, cruelty, and comradeship. Most of all, we learned about death at an age when it is common to think of oneself as immortal. Everyone loses that illusion eventually, but in civilian life it is lost in installments over the years. We lost it all at once and, in the span of months, passed from boyhood through manhood to a premature middle age. The knowledge of death, of the implacable limits placed on a man's existence, severed us from our youth as irrevocably as a surgeon's scissors had once severed us from the womb. And yet, few of us were past twenty-five. We left Vietnam peculiar creatures, with young shoulders that bore rather old heads. . . .

There is also the aspect of the Vietnam War that distinguished it from other American conflicts—its absolute savagery. I mean the savagery that prompted so many American fighting men—the good, solid kids from Iowa farms—to kill civilians and prisoners. . . . War by its nature, can arouse a psychopathic violence in men of seemingly normal impulses.

There has been a good deal of exaggeration about U.S. atrocities in Vietnam, exaggeration not about their extent but about their causes. The two most popularly held explanations for outrages like My Lai have been the racist theory, which proposes that the American soldier found it easy to slaughter Asians because he did not regard them as human beings, and the frontier-heritage theory, which claims he was inherently violent and needed only the excuse of war to vent his homicidal instincts.

Like all generalizations, each contains an element of truth; yet both ignore the barbarous treatment the Viet Cong and ARVN often inflicted on their own people, and neither confront the crimes committed by the Korean division, probably the most bloody-minded in Vietnam, and by the French during the first Indochina war.

The evil was inherent not in the men—except in the sense that a devil dwells in us all—but in the circumstances under which they had to live and fight. The conflict in Vietnam combined the two most bitter forms of warfare, civil war and revolution, to which was added the ferocity of jungle war. Twenty years of terrorism and fratricide had obliterated most reference points from the country's moral map long before we arrived. Communists and government forces alike considered ruthlessness a necessity if not a virtue. Whether committed in the name of principles or out of vengeance, atrocities were as common to the Vietnamese battlefields as shell craters and barbed wire. The marines in our brigade were not innately cruel, but on landing in Danang they learned rather quickly that Vietnam was not a place where a man could expect much mercy if, say, he was taken prisoner. And men who do not expect to receive mercy eventually lose their inclination to grant it.

At times, the comradeship that was the war's only redeeming quality caused some of its worst crimes—acts of retribution for friends who had been killed. Some men could not withstand the stress of guerrilla-fighting: the hair-trigger alertness constantly demanded of them, the feeling that the enemy was everywhere, the inability to distinguish civilians from combatants created emotional pressures which built to such a point that a trivial provocation could make these men explode with the blind destructiveness of a mortar shell.

Others were made pitiless by an overpowering greed for survival. Self-preservation, that most basic and tyrannical of all instincts, can turn a man into a coward or, as was more often the case in Vietnam, into a creature who destroys without hesitation or remorse whatever poses even a potential threat to his life. A sergeant in my platoon, ordinarily a pleasant young man, told me once, "Lieutenant, I've got a wife and two kids at home and I'm going to see 'em again and don't care who I've got to kill or how many of 'em to do it."

General Westmoreland's strategy of attrition also had an important effect on our behavior. Our mission was not to win terrain or seize positions, but simply to kill: to kill Communists and to kill as many of them as possible. Stack 'em like cordwood. Victory was a high body count, defeat a low kill-ratio, war a matter of arithmetic. The pressure on unit commanders to produce enemy corpses was intense, and they in turn communicated it to their troops. This led to such practices as counting civilians as Viet Cong. "If it's dead and Vietnamese, it's VC," was a rule of thumb in the bush. It is not surprising, therefore, that some men acquired a contempt for human life and a predilection for taking it.

Finally, there were the conditions imposed by the climate and country. For weeks we had to live like primitive men on remote outposts rimmed by alien seas of rice paddies and rain forests. Malaria, blackwater fever, and dysentery, though not the killers they had been in past wars, took their toll. The sun scorched us in the dry season, and in the monsoon season we were pounded numb by ceaseless rain. Our days were spent hacking though mountainous jungles whose immensity reduced us to an antlike pettiness. At night we squatted in muddy holes, picked off the leeches that sucked on our veins, and waited for an attack to come rushing at us from the blackness beyond the perimeter wire.

The air-conditioned headquarters of Saigon and Danang seemed thousands of miles away. As for the United States, we did not call it "the World" for nothing; it might as well have been on another planet. There was nothing familiar out where we were, no churches, no police, no laws, no newspapers, or any of the restraining influences without which the earth's population of virtuous people would be reduced by ninety-five percent. It was the dawn of creation in the Indochina bush, an ethical as well as a geographical wilderness. Out there, lacking restraints, sanctioned to kill, confronted by a hostile country and a relentless enemy, we sank into a brutish state. The descent could be checked only by the net of a man's inner moral values, the attribute that is called character. There were a few—and I suspect Lieutenant [William] Calley [implicated in the My Lai atrocity] was one—who had no net and plunged all the way down, discovering in their bottommost depths a capacity for malice they probably never suspected was there.

Most American soldiers in Vietnam—at least the ones I knew—could not be divided into good men and bad. Each possessed roughly equal measures of both qualities. I saw men who behaved with great compassion toward the Vietnamese one day and then burned down a village the next. They were, as Kipling wrote of his Tommy Atkins, neither saints "nor blackguards too/But single men in barricks most remarkable like you." That may be why Americans reacted with such horror to the disclosures of U.S. atrocities while ignoring those of the other side: the American soldier was a reflection of themselves.

✗ E S S A Y S

Harry G. Summers, Jr., a U.S. army colonel who served as a battalion and corps operations officer in Vietnam, criticizes both military strategy and civilian leadership during the Vietnam War. He believes that a different strategy could have brought victory to the United States. A selection from his influential book *On Strategy* is the first essay. Next, Gary R. Hess of Bowling Green State University summarizes and critiques the alternative strategies suggested by Summers and another military officer, General Bruce Palmer. Finally, Loren Baritz, a historian and administrator at the University of Massachusetts, Amherst, argues that the Vietnam War was a product of American culture. He contends that that culture, with its faith in technological superiority and managerial sophistication, spawned a self-defeating military strategy.

A Critical Appraisal of American Strategy

HARRY G. SUMMERS, JR.

One of the continuing arguments about the Vietnam war is whether or not a formal declaration of war would have made any difference. On the one hand there are those who see a declaration of war as a kind of magic talisman that would have eliminated all our difficulties. On the other hand there are those who see a declaration of war as a worthless anachronism. The truth is somewhere in between. A declaration of war is a clear statement of *initial* public support which focuses the nation's attention on the enemy. (Continuation of this initial public support is, of course, contingent on the successful prosecution of war aims.) As we will see, it was the lack of such focus on the enemy and on the political objectives to be obtained by the use of military force that was the crux of our strategic failure.

Reprinted with permission from the book *On Strategy* by Harry G. Summers, Jr., pp. 21–23, 120–124, 1982, as published by Presidio Press, 31 Pameron Way, Novato, CA 94949.

Further, a declaration of war makes the prosecution of the war a shared responsibility of both the government and the American people. . . . Without a declaration of war the Army was caught on the horns of a dilemma. It was ordered into battle by the Commander-in-Chief, the duly elected President of the United States. It was sustained in battle by appropriations by the Congress, the elected representatives of the American people. The legality of its commitment was not challenged by the Supreme Court of the United States. Yet, because there was no formal declaration of war, many vocal and influential members of the American public questioned (and continue to question) the legality and propriety of its actions.

This dilemma needs to be understood. It transcends the legal niceties over the utility of a declaration of war. It even transcends the strategic military value of such a declaration. It should not be dismissed as a kind of sophisticated "stab in the back" argument. As will be seen, the requirement for a declaration of war was rooted in the principle of civilian control of the military, and the failure to declare war in Vietnam drove a wedge between the Army and large segments of the American public.

It is not as if we did not know better. We knew perfectly well the importance of maintaining the bond between the American people and their soldiers in the field, and that this bond was the source of our moral strength. As early as the Revolutionary War this moral strength was a primary factor in our defeat of the British, then a major world power. As a result of this experience we wrote the rules for invoking the national will into our Constitution. Article I, Section 8 states them clearly:

> The Congress shall have Power . . . To declare War . . . To raise and support Armies . . . To make Rules for the Government and Regulation of the land and naval forces . . .

Implicit in this rule was the rejection of an 18th century-type army answerable only to the Executive. The American Army would be a people's Army to be committed only by the will of the people. As Alexander Hamilton explained:

> The whole power of raising armies [is] lodged in the *Legislature,* not in the *Executive;* This Legislature [is] to be a popular body, consisting of the representatives of the people, periodically elected . . . a great and real security against the keeping of troops without evident necessity.
>
> . . . The power of the President would be inferior to that of the Monarch. . . . That of the British King extends to the *Declaring* of war and to the *Raising* and *Regulating* of fleets and armies; All which by the Constitution . . . would appertain to the Legislature.

Hamilton's remarks highlight a critical distinction. In other nations a declaration of war by the chief executive alone (emperor, king, premier, party chairman) may or may not represent the *substance* of the will of his people. By requiring that a declaration of war be made by the representatives of the people (the Congress), rather than by the President alone, the Founding Fathers sought to guarantee this substance and insure that our armed forces would not be committed to battle without the support of the American people. Ironically, President Johnson seemed to know that. In a peculiar passage in light of what was to follow, he said:

> I believed that President Truman's one mistake in courageously going to the defense of South Korea in 1950 had been his failure to ask Congress for an expression of its backing. He could have had it easily, and it would have strengthened his hand. I made up my mind not to repeat that error. . . .

Like President Truman in 1950, President Johnson could probably have had a declaration of war in August 1964 after the Gulf of Tonkin incidents when two American destroyers were attacked by North Vietnamese patrol boats. Instead of asking for a declaration of war, however, President Johnson asked Congress for a resolution empowering him to "take all necessary measures to repel an armed attack against the forces of the United States and to prevent further aggression." . . .

Because they made the cardinal military error of underestimating the enemy, our military leaders failed in their role as "the principal military advisors to the President." There are some who have yielded to the temptation to blame everything on the Commander in Chief, President Johnson. But even his severest critics would have to admit that he certainly did not set out to put the nation in turmoil, ruin his political career, and lose the Vietnam war. It was the duty and responsibility of his military advisors to warn him of the likely consequences of his actions, to recommend alternatives, and, as Napoleon put it, to tender their resignations rather than be the instrument of their army's downfall. In failing to press their military advice they allowed the United States to pursue a strategic policy that was faulty from the start. Instead of deliberately adopting the *strategic defensive,* and tailoring our strategies and tactics to that posture, we slipped into it almost unaware and confused it with the *strategic offensive*. In so doing we lost sight of our strategic purpose and found the truth in the Clausewitzian observation: "Defense without an active purpose is self-contradictory both in strategy and in tactics." By their own failure to understand what we were about, our military leaders were not able to warn our civilian decision-makers that the strategy we were pursuing could never lead to conclusive results.

Although from 1965 until 1975 (with the exception of Tet-68 and the ill-fated Eastertide Offensive of 1972) the North Vietnamese were also in a defensive posture, there was a critical difference. The North Vietnamese were on the tactical defensive as part of a strategic offensive to conquer South Vietnam. Our adoption of the strategic defensive was an end in itself and we had substituted the negative aim of counterinsurgency for the positive aim of isolation of the battlefield. This was a fatal flaw. As Clausewitz said, "A major victory can only be obtained by positive measures aimed at a *decision,* never by simply waiting on events. In short, even in the defense, a major stake alone can bring a major gain." The North Vietnamese had a major stake—the conquest of Indochina. It was the United States that was "simply waiting on events."

. . . Clausewitz defined critical analysis as "not just an evaluation of the means actually employed, but of *all possible means*. . . . One can, after all, not condemn a method without being able to suggest a better alternative." From a "purely military" standpoint it might appear that the better alternative would have been a strategic offensive against North Vietnamese armed forces and their will to fight. But, as Clausewitz warned, there is no such thing as a "purely military" strategy. Military strategy exists to serve political ends, and, . . . for a variety of very practical political reasons an invasion of North Vietnam was politically unacceptable.

We were faced with essentially the same dilemma we had faced in the Korean war. Our political policy was to contain the expansion of communist power, but we did not wish to risk a world war by using military means to destroy the source of that power. We solved that dilemma in Korea by limiting our political objectives to containing North Korean expansion and successfully applied our military means to achieve that end. In Vietnam we began with just such limited objectives. Our mistake was in failing to concentrate our military means on that task. It would appear that we sensed this deficiency, since the Korean war model was essentially the alternative that General Vien, General Westmoreland and the JCS recommended. It was not identified as such because it did not fit the frame of reference we had established for ourselves. For one thing, establishment of a Korean war–type objective in the mid-1960s would have branded Army leadership as hopelessly anachronistic. . . . From the perspective of our total victory in World War II, Korea still looked like a defeat and it is only from the perspective of our actual defeat in Vietnam that we can see that Korea was actually a victory. Further, there was the tyranny of fashion. Counterinsurgency, not conventional tactics, appeared to be the wave of the future. Finally, their plans hinged on the mobilization of the Reserves, a political price President Johnson was not prepared to pay.

Time and bitter experience has removed these distortions from our frame of reference. In 1977, General Bruce Palmer, Jr. (USA, Retired), former commander of U.S. Army Vietnam and former Vice Chief of Staff, U.S. Army, saw clearly what should have been done. In a seminar at the U.S. Army War College, he said that, together with an expanded Naval blockade, the Army should have taken the tactical offensive along the DMZ across Laos to the Thai border in order to isolate the battlefield and then *deliberately* assume the strategic and tactical defensive. While this strategy might have entailed some of the same long-term costs of our Korean strategy, it would (like that strategy) have furthered our political objective of containing communist expansion. He said that in his opinion this could have been accomplished *without reserve mobilization*, without invading North Vietnam and running the risk of Chinese intervention, and with substantially fewer combat forces than were actually deployed to Vietnam.

In brief, General Palmer's strategic concept called for a five-division force (two U.S., two ROK [Republic of Korea] and one ARVN along the

DMZ with three more U.S. divisions deployed to extend the defensive line to the Lao-Thai border. An additional U.S. division would have been used to stabilize the situation in the central highlands and in the Saigon area. The Marine divisions would have been held in strategic reserve, to be available to reinforce the DMZ and to pose an amphibious threat, thereby tying down North Vietnamese forces in coastal defense.

General Palmer believed that the advantages of such a strategy would have been enormous. It would have required four fewer divisions than the ten and two-thirds divisions we actually deployed. "Moreover," he said, "the bulk of these forces would have fought on ground of their choosing which the enemy would be forced to attack if he wanted to invade South Vietnam. [This would have provided U.S. forces with a clear and understandable objective—a peace-keeping operation to separate the belligerents.] In defending well-prepared positions, U.S. casualties would have been much fewer. . . . The magnitude and likelihood and intensity of the so-called 'Big War,' involving heavy fire power, would have been lessened [one of the main causes of U.S. public disenchantment with the war]." He went on to say that a much smaller U.S. logistics effort would have been required and we would have avoided much of the base development that was of no real value to the South Vietnamese. "Cut off from substantial out-of-country support, the Viet Cong was bound to wither on the vine and gradually become easier for the South Vietnamese to defeat," he concluded. This conclusion was recently reinforced by statements of former South Vietnamese leaders who believed that by providing a military shield behind which South Vietnam could work out its own political, economic, and social problems, the United States could have provided a reasonable chance for South Vietnamese freedom and independence.

Writing after the U.S. withdrawal from Vietnam, Brigadier Shelford Bidwell, editor of *RUSI*, the distinguished British military journal of the Royal United Services Institute, commented on the view that the war in Vietnam was unwinnable. "This is rubbish," he said, blaming our failure on our election of a strategy which "not only conferred on the North Vietnamese the privilege of operating on safe exterior lines from secure bases but threw away the advantages of a tactical and strategic initiative." He went on to note that by "using firepower of crushing intensity" we succeeded in defeating both the insurgency and the 1972 North Vietnamese offensive but at the strategic price of "American society in turmoil. . . . All this . . . would have been avoided," he said, "by adopting the classical principles of war by cutting off the trouble at the root. . . . If this was not politically realistic, then the war should not have been fought at all."

Just as the North Koreans and their Chinese allies were the "root of the trouble" in the Korean war, so the root in the Vietnam war was North Vietnam (*not* the Viet Cong). In Vietnam as in Korea our political objectives dictated a strategic defensive posture. While this prevented us from destroying the "root" at the source through the strategic offensive, Korea proved that it was possible to achieve a favorable decision with the strategic defensive. It restored the status quo ante, prevented the enemy from achieving his goals with military means, and provided the foundation for a negotiated settlement. All of this was within our means in Vietnam.

Were There Viable Alternative Strategies?

GARY R. HESS

The tenth anniversary of the fall of Saigon occasioned an outpouring of reflections on the American experience in Vietnam. When contrasted with the national sentiments of a decade earlier, the recent press and television analyses of the Vietnam War underline the extent to which scholarly and popular attitudes have changed. With the collapse of South Vietnamese military resistance in the spring of 1975, American soul-searching followed what had become conventional thinking about U.S. involvement in Southeast Asia. The commitment to South Vietnam, it was generally assumed, had been a mistake, a tragic gamble to save a weak and unpopular regime. An immoral and seemingly endless war, forced upon the country by deceitful leaders, was over at last, and with ominous implications for America's global position. The titles of the essays in a special issue of the *New Republic* reflected the national mood. The lead editorial was entitled "On the Disaster," followed by essays with these suggestive titles: "Our SOBs . . . The End is the Beginning . . . Grand Illusion . . . Pushing Sand . . . The Secret War . . . Myths and Interests . . . Hubris: National and Personal . . . The Elite Protects Itself . . . Lies and Whispers."

In those essays and others by prominent foreign policy analysts, the meaning of Vietnam typically found expression in references to the illusions of anti-communism, ignorance of Vietnamese culture and history, and the arrogance of power. Within a decade, however, the terms of thinking about Vietnam have shifted dramatically. Writing from various perspectives, revisionists have defended U.S. intervention, exculpated American warfare of any wrongdoing, and judged the military effort a success. Illusions, and ignorance, and arrogance have given way to hints of a "stab in the back" by the media, Congress, or critics of the war. In its 29 April 1985 issue, marking the tenth anniversary of the fall of Saigon, the *New Republic* embodied, as it had in 1975, the predominant intellectual trend. The editors found the "right lesson" in what they titled "The Myths of Revolution." Other essays, contributed mostly by writers little known in 1975, included a former war critic reflecting on "My Change of Heart" and a Vietnamese dissident coauthoring "Vietnam's Opposition Today." Reflecting the reassessment of the military effort, the issue included "How We Lost." Finally, "Reconsideration of *Fire in the Lake*" criticized the romantic idealization of Vietnamese communism in Frances FitzGerald's prize-winning 1972

Gary R. Hess, "The Military Perspective on Strategy in Vietnam: Harry G. Summers's *On Strategy* and Bruce Palmer's *The 25-Year War*," *Diplomatic History*, 10 (Winter 1986), pp. 91–106. Reprinted by permission.

book. (FitzGerald had been a contributor to the journal's 1975 Vietnam issue.)

Revisionism and political developments in Indochina and the United States have been mutually reinforcing. Hanoi's imposition of rigid control over the south and its invasion of Cambodia have made the Vietnamese government increasingly repugnant to Americans, even those who had criticized U.S. intervention. The "silent majority" of Americans demanded— and eventually achieved in the leadership of President Ronald Reagan—a reaffirmation of pride, patriotism, and militant anti-communism. As part of this conservative resurgence, the Vietnam War has been elevated, in the president's words, to a "noble cause."

An important force in the reinterpretation of the American experience in Vietnam has been the extensive writings from the military perspective. This literature is comprised of two types: the accounts of fighting men and the reflections of higher commanders. In the popular consciousness, the former have been especially influential. Never before have the horrors of a particular war become so widely known in such a short time. Ignored a decade ago, the soldiers have since told their stories to a receptive audience. Vietnam veterans typically portray themselves as the victims of betrayal by the American government and society. In a spate of individual and collective memoirs and novels, several of which have been dramatized on television, Americans have been reminded of how hundreds of thousands of patriotic youth went to Vietnam only to become quickly disillusioned in a mindless war that measured success by the "body count" and taught contempt for "gooks." Survival became an obsession, but those who did survive returned to an America that was, at best, indifferent and, at worst, hostile to those who had fought in an unpopular war. The image of the betrayed Vietnam soldier has been widely cultivated by television and motion pictures, especially in the popular and controversial films *Apocalypse Now*, *Coming Home*, and *The Deer Hunter*.

The views of military commanders have reinforced the bitter recollections of the troops. Frustrated by the confusing directives from the Pentagon and by the restraints imposed upon American power, high-ranking officers generally have placed responsibility for failure on ineffective civilian leadership. General William C. Westmoreland's memoir, *A Soldier Reports*, criticizes especially the Johnson administration's refusal to provide the support necessary to achieve objectives in Vietnam and the ineffectiveness of U.S. negotiations with North Vietnam. In a more comprehensive history of the war, *Summons of the Trumpet*, Major General Dave Richard Palmer, who was an adviser to the South Vietnamese Army (ARVN), likewise traced American frustrations principally to ineffective political leadership in Washington. In *The War Managers*, Brigadier General Douglas Kinnard, who served in Vietnam from 1966 to 1967 and again from 1969 to 1970, documented the extent of the military leadership's disillusionment. In their responses to an extended questionnaire, over one hundred generals, who had commanded in Vietnam, saw their mission hampered by confusing objectives (only 29 percent considered them to be "clear and understandable"), slowness in building up ARVN (73 percent believed that Vietnamization should have been emphasized much earlier), and by hostile reporting of the war (52 percent characterized television coverage as "not a good thing . . . sensational . . . counterproductive"). These findings related closely to the generals' responses as to what should be changed "if we had to do it again": fully 91 percent identified, as overriding priorities, "defining the objectives" and "improving the ARVN."

Besides revealing sympathy with many of Westmoreland's reflections on the war, the generals in *The War Managers* also implicitly criticized his leadership. They divided sharply over the concept and execution of the search-and-destroy strategy, criticized the kill ratio as a measure of success (55 percent judged it a "misleading device"), and decried an inadequate understanding of the enemy (56 percent observed that its "will and determination . . . [were] not sufficiently considered").

Reservations about U.S. strategy are central to the extended critiques provided by Colonel Harry G. Summers, Jr., and General Bruce Palmer, Jr. Like many analysts of the Vietnam War, Summers and Palmer essentially ask what went wrong. Unlike others who agree that the war was winnable, they do not focus blame on Congress, the media, or the antiwar movement. Neither do they see the war as "won" in 1967–68 or 1972–73 and "lost" because of irresolute leadership. There is no hint of a congressional "stab in the back" after "victory" in the Paris peace negotiations, as Richard Nixon self-servingly argues in *No More Vietnams*. Instead, Summers and Palmer place the responsibility for failure on both the nation's civilian and military leadership. What clearly emerges are the efforts of two thoughtful officers to come to grips with the most wrenching experience in the history of the institution to which they dedicated their lives.

The Summers and Palmer arguments are similar, each having influenced the other. In his book, Palmer refers approvingly to *On Strategy*, while Summers praises Palmer's basic views on Vietnam as set forth in a 1977 lecture. Recently, Summers described *The 25-Year War* as "especially valuable" for its stress on "the need for intellectual honesty and moral quality" on the part of army officers.

In analyzing the army's failure to measure up to national expectations, Summers and Palmer follow different approaches. *On Strategy* resulted from Summers's research at the Strategic Studies Institute at the U.S. Army War College, Carlisle Barracks, Pennsylvania, where he later held the General Douglas MacArthur Chair of Military Research. Beginning in 1981 as a War College project to examine the "application of military science to the national defense," *On Strategy* has become an influential book, and Summers has become something of a celebrity. Originally published by the Army War College, then by Presidio Press in 1981, *On Strategy* has since been issued in a Dell paperback edition. Summers's views have received much attention in major journals and on television; he was omnipresent during the tenth anniversary media reflections, and he was the author of the aforementioned *New Republic* article on "How We Lost." Recently he became a columnist for *U.S. News and World Report*. Summers's combat experience lends authority to his arguments. An infantry squad leader during the Korean War, he served as a battalion and company operations officer in Vietnam. What makes his argument most compelling, however, is his application of the principles of warfare set forth by Carl von Clausewitz to U.S. tactics and strategy in Vietnam. As Summers relentlessly demonstrates in case after case, the Americans failed especially to follow the principles of the objective, offensive, mass, economy of force, and maneuver. While observing that the enemy almost consistently adhered to those principles, Summers views the "lesson" of Vietnam as self-evident.

Palmer builds principally upon his considerable experience in Washington and Vietnam between 1963 and 1974. Few officers enjoyed a comparable opportunity to observe both the conflict itself and the decision-making process. As a staff officer of Lieutenant General Harold K. Johnson, deputy chief of Staff for Army Operations from September 1963 to April 1965, Palmer was in a position to follow the concerns and the influence of the Joint Chiefs of Staff (JCS) during the critical first steps of direct U.S. involvement. In early 1965, President Lyndon B. Johnson sent him on a tour of Vietnam, Laos, Cambodia, and Thailand. Like other observers at that time, Palmer was distressed by South Vietnam's vulnerability. After one year as commander of U.S. forces in the Dominican Republic, which brought him into contact with Ambassador Ellsworth Bunker, and then one year at Fort Bragg, Palmer was given command of II Field Force in Vietnam in March of 1967. (He is included among the generals in the Kinnard survey.) Subsequently he was made Westmoreland's deputy at the headquarters of the U.S. Army in Vietnam. After experiencing the tumultuous events of 1967–68, Palmer returned to Washington with Westmoreland in July 1968, becoming the army's vice-chief of Staff. From that position he followed the American withdrawal and the Vietnamization policy before retiring in 1974. Although throughout his memoir Palmer leaves little doubt of his judgment of the men whom he observed—high regard for Dean Rusk, Westmoreland, and Bunker; disdain for the arrogance of Lyndon Johnson, Henry Kissinger, and (mixed with some respect) Alexander Haig—he generally sticks to the larger question of understanding the Vietnam failure. His views already have attracted considerable attention, and *The 25-Year War*, first published by the University Press of Kentucky, is now also available in a Simon and Schuster paperback edition.

Since the arguments of Summers and Palmer move along similar lines and tend to be mutually reinforcing, piecing them together should provide an overview of what has become a widely held perspective on the Vietnam War. Summers and Palmer stress several related themes: the deficiency of preintervention military planning and advice, the failure to issue a declaration of war, the ineffectiveness of Westmoreland's strategy, and the potential success of strategic alternatives. Their analyses seek to explain what Summers labels the American record of "tactical victory, strategic defeat" and to show how the army, operating under the constraints imposed by Washington, could have attained the nation's basic objectives.

Much of the U.S. frustration in Vietnam can be traced to the failure of the nation's military leadership to fulfill basic responsibilities. Strategic planning was not prepared for the Vietnam contingency. Accordingly, when the Joint Chiefs should have expressed doubts about intervention, they muted their serious reservations and endorsed air and ground operations of dubious effectiveness.

Ill-conceived strategic planning, Summers argues, was at the base of U.S. frustration. The army learned the wrong lesson from the Korean War. In that conflict the Chinese intervention forced a fundamental change in strategic operations; no longer could war be carried to the homeland of the enemy. The army had adjusted and brought political and military objectives into balance by waging a war against the Chinese that resulted in the restoration of the prewar status quo. Still bound by World War II concepts of "victory," however, the army drew the incorrect conclusion that Korea "taught" the necessity to avoid a land war with China. A second factor guiding strategy was the overriding fear of nuclear destruction, which placed limits on American options and meant the loss of "escalation dominance." Summers sees pre-Vietnam strategy directed by the "counsel of our fears":

> Instead of seeing that it was possible to fight and win a limited war in Asia regardless of Chinese intervention, we again (as we had done with nuclear war) took counsel of our fears and accepted as an article of faith the proposition that we should never again become involved in a land war in Asia.

Then, as the Johnson administration was moving in 1964–65 to take the United States to war, Palmer contends that the military leaders failed in their obligations to civilian authority. During the deliberations of the JCS, General Earle G. Wheeler, as chairman, insisted upon an "agreed-position" system of recommendations, pressuring those who disagreed with the majority, or with the direction of administration policy, to forego their objections. Therefore, a consensual "no harm in trying . . . it's worth the effort" mentality contributed to the JCS recommendation for air warfare, thus ignoring the reservations of army and navy leaders. Subsequent questions about the functions of ground troops also were not considered adequately. At no point did the service chiefs warn the president and secretary of defense of the likelihood of failure. No one wanted to appear "disloyal," and a "can-do" attitude overwhelmed objections. The civilian leadership needed to know the points of disagreement, but the JCS ignored its responsibilities.

Palmer's criticism of the JCS raises the intriguing question of whether or not reservations about intervention would have restrained President Johnson. He would have had good reason to reflect because the JCS had been assigning increased strategic importance to Indochina. At the time of the 1954 crisis the JCS had urged restraint, holding that "Indochina is devoid of decisive military objectives and the allocation of more than token U.S. armed forces in Indochina would be a serious diversion of limited U.S. capabilities." By 1961, in the words of Leslie Gelb and Richard Betts, the JCS had "[done] an apparent somersault." Embracing the "domino theory," they recommended in 1962 that the United States "take expeditiously all actions necessary to defeat communist aggression in South Vietnam." In justifying their stand, they argued:

> The immediate strategic importance of Southeast Asia lies in the political value that can accrue to the Free World through a successful stand in that area. Of equal importance is the psychological impact that a firm position by the United States will have on the countries of the world—both free and communist. On the negative side, a United States political and/or military withdrawal . . . would have an adverse psychological effect of even greater proportion, and one from which recovery would be both difficult and costly.

While the JCS record of support for increased U.S. commitments to Indochina should have given added credence to any reservations, had they been expressed in 1965, it is questionable whether any words of caution would have altered the momentum toward intervention. Indeed, Palmer's insights add to an understanding of a policymaking process that President Johnson dominated and which discouraged debate over Vietnam initiatives. Concerns about the costs of attaining American objectives and doubts about the chances for success were common within the Department of State, Department of Defense, National Security Council, and elsewhere, but the system did not allow for debate. Recent studies have emphasized the extent to which Johnson took the initiative in Vietnam decision making in 1964–65, forcing consideration of issues in ways that led seemingly inescapably to U.S. intervention. Characteristically manipulating the civilian and military advisers, Johnson evidently had become convinced that the Vietnam problem could be solved quickly through sufficient American power to force North Vietnam to end its war in the south. In the charged atmosphere prevailing in Washington at the time of the Gulf of Tonkin and Pleiku incidents, Johnson would have likely dismissed any JCS reservations against intervention just as he did those of Vice-President Hubert Humphrey and Undersecretary of State George Ball. The president's humiliation of Humphrey was not lost on those who sought influence in the Johnson White House.

When the United States made its crucial decisions of 1965, Summers argues at length, and Palmer concurs, Johnson drastically miscalculated by failing to seek a declaration of war. Only through a declaration could the national attention be focused on the enemy, the war effort become a shared responsibility of government and people, mobilization have resulted appropriately, and sanctions have been imposed against those who aided the enemy. "All of America's previous wars," Summers writes, "were fought in the heat of passion. Vietnam was fought in cold blood, and that was intolerable to the American people." Palmer agrees:

> It seems rather obvious that a nation cannot fight a war in cold blood, sending its men and women to distant fields of battle without arousing the emotions of the people. I know of no way to accomplish this short of a declaration of war by the Congress and national mobilization.

Johnson's decision not to inflame national passions—a result partly of his assumptions about the duration of the war and his determination to focus attention on domestic reform—undermined the war effort from the beginning. Summers and Palmer both cite the president's failure to seek a war declaration as one of their principal indictments of civilian leadership. Their charges raise a number of questions.

First, were all of America's earlier conflicts fought in the "heat of passion," and is that essential? Korea, which Summers refers to as the strategic model for Vietnam, also lacked a declaration of war and was waged without any sustained heat of passion. The dismissed MacArthur's call for victory stirred deep passions during his triumphant American return in 1951. The Korean conflict clearly illustrated the immense difficulties of gaining support for a limited war, and the erosion of Truman's popularity foreshadowed Johnson's fate fifteen years later. Korea also demonstrated, however, that, even in the absence of the level of national commitment implicit in a war declaration, it was possible to attain objectives in a limited war.

Second, would Congress have declared war? According to Summers, Johnson "could probably have had a declaration of war in August 1964 after the Gulf of Tonkin incidents." He cites Arthur M. Schlesinger, Jr., to the effect that Johnson "could certainly have obtained Congressional authorization beyond the Tonkin resolution for a limited war in 1965." But would a declaration of war have been justified in 1964 or 1965 on the basis of national security? Not according to Palmer, who writes: "National security was a legitimate interest . . . but South Vietnam was not vital to the United States." The sketchy "encounters" in the Gulf of Tonkin incident did not touch off a national demand for military retaliation. The passage of the Tonkin resolution should not be interpreted as indicative of congressional willingness to declare war. To members of Congress, as well as the public generally, a declaration of war constitutes a serious commitment; congressional resolutions allowing presidents wide latitude in foreign crises were seen, at least in 1964, as relatively innocuous. In the previous decade, Congress, without serious consequences, had given President Dwight D. Eisenhower such resolutions regarding the Middle East and the Formosa Strait. In the summer of 1964, Johnson's popularity and respect among the American public were overwhelming, and few questioned the sincerity of his campaign promise to avoid war in Vietnam.

Third, would a declaration of war have made a substantial difference in popular support? Would national passions—assuming that they could have been generated in 1964 or 1965—have been sustained? Popular disenchantment with the war developed slowly, reflecting war weariness, disappointment, and distrust. The public still would have witnessed the horrors of war on television, and those images would have been just as compelling had war been declared. The erosion of popular support that became pronounced in late 1967 and early 1968 seems to have been principally the result of mounting frustrations and uncertainties, which a declaration would have reduced only marginally. A declaration of war in 1917 had not precluded substantial opposition to, and criticism of, President Woodrow Wilson's leadership, and a declaration of war in 1941 did not prevent mounting weariness as casualties increased and victory seemed far away, even in the most popular of wars.

Finally, is it not more difficult to keep a declared war safely limited? Arousing the national passions has ominous implications in the nuclear age. The United States, in Vietnam as in Korea and other lesser commitments of its forces in the last forty years, has faced serious dilemmas in using and restricting its power. A declaration of war, even for essentially defensive objectives, increases risks of a wider conflict.

If the strategic planning lacked cohesion and the JCS ignored realities, the American military mission, not surprisingly, had to be improvised. "Insufficient timely discussion" in Washington preceded the dispatch of American forces. General Maxwell Taylor, then ambassador in Saigon, favored a defensive strategy much like the "enclave" approach advocated publicly by Lieutenant General James M. Gavin, which would have restricted American offensive operations to the vicinity of base areas, usually near the coast. Westmoreland, however, advocated taking the war to the enemy, thereby defeating the Vietcong and North Vietnamese units in the south. A war of attrition resulted. To apply General Omar Bradley's famed dictum on MacArthur's Korean strategy to the Summers-Palmer assessment of the Vietnam situation, it amounted to "the wrong war, at the wrong place, at the wrong time, and with the wrong enemy." The attrition strategy, Summers emphasizes, violated basic principles of warfare. By failing to take the offensive, Westmoreland's plan "committed the United States Army . . . to the strategic defensive in pursuit of the negative aim of wearing the enemy down." As it committed itself to counterinsurgency throughout South Vietnam, the army's operations became inefficient and futile; this strategy ignored Clausewitz's principles of mass, economy of force, maneuver, and simplicity.

A central question for both Summers and Palmer concerns the ability of the United States to bring its superior weaponry, especially its massive firepower, to bear against an elusive enemy. They agree that the search-and-destroy strategy was seriously flawed. In Palmer's analysis, search and destroy frequently resulted in heavy American casualties without fully engaging the enemy. While Summers believes that such operations were usually successful tactically, they cost a "fatal strategic price" because much of the domestic opposition to the war focused on the brutality of search-and-destroy tactics. The tragedies at Ben Suc and My Lai resulted from such operations. An alternative approach—gradual extension of control over a large area, such as the methods employed in Operation Junction City—likewise resulted, in Palmer's estimate, in substantial casualties without appreciable long-term gains.

The central flaw of Westmoreland's strategy was its assumption about North Vietnamese determination and capability. The military, Summers argues, made the "cardinal error of underestimating the enemy." Palmer believes that the evidence was there from the beginning to see that attrition would not work. Central Intelligence Agency estimates, which he credits with being consistently more reliable than military intelligence, projected that North Vietnam could indefinitely replace losses inflicted by the Americans.

Committed to this ill-conceived strategy of attrition, the growing U.S. military presence lacked direction and coherence. The "most pernicious policy" was the base camp, an "albatross" draining men and resources. During his tours, Palmer was appalled by the "nine-to-five" routine of officers who were helicoptered twice daily between headquarters at Long Binh and villas at the nearby city of Bien Hoa. The one-year rotation policy resulted in frequent turnover of experienced personnel and in inadequately trained recruits, a situation that could have been avoided had the United States been mobilized and the reserves called for Vietnam duty.

Air operations were as ill-conceived as the war on the ground. The all-out bombing campaign advocated by the JCS was compromised by President Johnson's decision to serve as "target officer." His piecemeal application of the aerial firepower, together with the numerous bombing halts to encourage negotiations, condemned the air arm to discard the Clausewitzian principles of mass, surprise, and consistency. Moreover, civilian leaders, not for the first time, overestimated the effectiveness of bombing campaigns.

A poor command structure, while not the cause of defeat, consistently undermined effective operations. While the North Vietnamese followed Clausewitz's precept of unity of command, Summers contends, the United States lacked a coherent command structure, which was symptomatic of the even greater failure to focus on the military objective. The command problems irritated Palmer during his tours of duty in Vietnam, as well as in Washington, and he details the cumbersome structure. In charge of American operations was the Commander, U.S. Military Assistance Command, Vietnam (COMUSMACV), but that office suffered from poor coordination with ARVN and other allied units in Vietnam. Its chain of command ran from Washington through the Commander in Chief, Pacific (CINPAC) at Hawaii through to Vietnam. COMUSMACV also lacked responsibility for air operations against North Vietnam, these being directed by CINPAC through the Pacific air and naval commanders. Moreover, COMUSMACV was both an army and a joint command; a separate army command was needed. In retrospect, few would question Palmer's assessment that "undivided responsibility and unified direction were conspicuously absent."

These problems in southeast Asia were compounded by other complications in Washington. The JCS lacked sufficient responsibility to direct the war, a situation that Palmer attributes partly to the creation of the Department of Defense which placed the secretary of defense between each of the service chiefs and the president. In this arrangement the JCS function as an indirect advisory group which he describes as a "recipe for destruction in wartime." Based on his observations during the Vietnam War, Palmer argues that, "in time of crises, emergency, or war, the operational chain of command should run from the president/commander-in-chief directly to the JCS and thence to unified commanders."

Management of the army's mission in Vietnam, Palmer readily acknowledges, was consistently undermined by Johnson's disregard of advice. Representing Westmoreland at cabinet meetings in 1968, Palmer observed firsthand the Johnson techniques. At one session the presidential photographer was present throughout, "taking an endless series of snapshots of the president from every conceivable angle." Johnson was "in constant motion, receiving or making phone calls, pressing the buzzer under the top of his desk to give orders . . . and frequently interrupting anyone trying to articulate his views." In an "atmosphere hardly conducive to meaningful discussion," Johnson paid "scant attention" to what was said, for the meeting was evidently a "pro forma gathering designed to support the claim of undivided support." The civilians' disregard for the JCS continued into the Nixon administration, and Kissinger especially dominated decision making.

Still, the American failure flowed ultimately from its flawed strategy. By leaving the initiative to the enemy, the United States invited the Tet Offensive, in which North Vietnamese and Vietcong units achieved their one instance of strategic surprise and won a major strategic victory despite a tactical defeat. The domestic frustrations from the lack of progress in a war of attrition contributed both to the imperative of American withdrawal and to the South Vietnamese believing that their country was being abandoned.

Both Summers and Palmer maintain that the United States should have followed a strategy of carrying the war to strong points in North Vietnam. Counterinsurgency dealt only with the periphery: Hanoi's "screen" in the south. The basic American objective should have been to prevent North Vietnamese infiltration. "If the infiltration could not be brought under control," Summers states, "South Vietnam could never solve its internal problems." In essence, Vietnam was a conventional conflict—a war of North Vietnamese aggression—but the counterinsurgency emphasis of the early 1960s, and the misread "lessons of Korea," blinded the United States to realities. Palmer specifically suggests a strategy of denying North Vietnam access to the Demilitarized Zone (DMZ), which was one of its points of strength throughout the conflict. The United States should have defended the strongest points in the area just to the south of the DMZ and extending across Laos, holding it by developing bases and ports with a substantial international force. If denied authority to send forces into Laos, the United States still could have secured the area through raids into that country. An effective American and South Vietnamese defense of the DMZ would have threatened to trap North Vietnamese units in the south and to cut their lines of supply. Denied support, the Vietcong would have "wither[ed] on the vine." While shielding South Vietnam at the DMZ, the United States could have concentrated on the "primary mission" of building up the ARVN to give it responsibility for countering Vietcong insurgency.

Palmer and Summers also agree that the United States should have kept up continual pressure directly against North Vietnam. Strategic bombing was unnecessary, but air interdiction in sparsely populated areas of North Vietnam and Laos, and along the DMZ, was essential. U.S. air and naval power, moreover, should have blockaded northern ports, and a large amphibious presence should have been maintained in the Gulf of Tonkin to keep the North Vietnamese guessing about American intentions. The "major mistake" of the war, according to Palmer, was signaling North Vietnam that the United States did not intend to invade its territory. That gave the enemy the assurance—one it should not have enjoyed—of realizing that national survival was never at stake. Summers attributes this shortcoming to the publicly expressed fear of nuclear warfare; this cost the United States "a major strategic advantage—*escalation dominance*—the ability to pose a threat to the enemy to raise the level of warfare beyond his ability (or willingness) to respond."

When the Nixon administration finally moved aggressively against the North Vietnamese lines of supply, these analysts found the results generally disappointing because of the earlier strategic shortcomings. The Cambodian incursion of 1970 came too late; its military effect was limited, while its domestic repercussions in the United States were disastrous. Sending ill-prepared ARVN units into Laos in 1971 only revealed the belatedness of Vietnamization; Palmer describes it as "very much [like] sending a boy to do a man's job in an extremely hostile environment." On the other hand, Summers and Palmer both praise Nixon's Christmas 1972 bombing—one of the few times that the United States achieved strategic surprise—because it forced Hanoi into the January 1973 settlement.

The Summers-Palmer alternative seems to offer a means of attaining American objectives at a reasonable cost. It also suggests a mission more compatible with Washington's determination to limit the commitment of U.S. forces. The attrition strategy constantly required additional troops. The cycle of escalation, with each step justified by promises of meeting future needs when, in fact, much intelligence indicated otherwise, led not only to popular disillusionment but also to deep debate within the Johnson administration, culminating in the denial of additional forces in 1968. Furthermore, the alternative approach of restricting the American presence would have been less offensive to the people and leaders of South Vietnam than the virtual Americanization of its government, society, and economy. The prospects for meeting the challenge of nation-building would therefore have been enhanced. Finally, the Summers-Palmer plan seems strategically sound: the enemy is clearly identified; the objective is unequivocal; the logistics are relatively simple; economy of force is practiced; American power is concentrated against enemy strength; and escalation is an option. Moreover, when related to the Summers-Palmer position on a declaration of war, this military mission would have been undertaken with a strong national commitment.

Such reflections on Vietnam hold much relevance as U.S. policymakers confront today's issues. In a 28 November 1984 speech, Secretary of

Defense Caspar Weinberger outlined "six major tests" to be applied when considering the use of American combat forces overseas: the importance of the area to national security; a "clear intention of winning"; well-defined interests; willingness to reassess "size, composition, and disposition" of those forces; recognition that the use of American units was a "last resort"; and, finally, that "[be]fore the U.S. commits combat forces . . . [it has a] reasonable assurance [of] . . . the support of the American people and their elected representatives in Congress." Drawing specifically upon the "lessons" of Vietnam, Weinberger added that "we cannot fight a battle with the Congress at home while asking our troops to win a war overseas, or, as in the case of Vietnam, in effect asking our troops not to win but just to be there." While one may challenge the utility of Weinberger's six major tests, as Secretary of State George Shultz did with respect to the "guaranteed public support in advance" test, such efforts to redefine the terms of military engagement clearly reflect the impact of the Vietnam experience.

The Summers-Palmer alternative, however, also raises a number of military and political questions. From a military viewpoint, was this option feasible, given the situation in Vietnam in 1965? Considering the chronic instability of the Saigon government and the evidence of the Vietcong–North Vietnamese strength in the south, the prospects for a defensive strategy looked bleak at that time. Carrying the war to the enemy seemed imperative.

Could the south have been sealed effectively? Summers draws upon an earlier example: "The United States could (as it had done in Korea) bring the infiltration under control." This is a somewhat facile comparison. The analogy between the North Koreans and North Vietnamese infiltration is open to question. Preventing movement of forces in the terrain of the Korean peninsula was a vastly different mission from deterring small units in jungles in an area with few natural barriers. Stopping North Vietnamese movement into the south likely would have necessitated extending forces over a wider area than the DMZ position. Palmer notes that the DMZ was one of the North Vietnamese points of strength, albeit the most easily defensible. In view of the versatility and determination of the North Vietnamese, the Americans actually might have had to face the situation described by Westmoreland: "Some have considered it practicable to seal the land frontiers against North Vietnamese infiltration. . . . Yet small though [South Vietnam] is, its land frontiers extend for more than 900 miles." To have defended that entire frontier on a scale similar to Korea would have required "many millions of troops." Like others, Westmoreland was skeptical of projects aimed at sealing the DMZ, such as the proposed "McNamara line" of mines, sensors, fortifications, and barbed wire. He argued, however, for the presence of an international force along the DMZ, which could have called immediate attention to North Vietnamese violations of the border. Such a presence might have had an intimidating effect on Hanoi.

Finally, would the alternative strategy have significantly altered political developments? A positive assessment assumes that, given time and support, a lasting national structure could have been established in the south.

Throughout its twenty-five year history, the Republic of Vietnam confronted the immense challenge of trying to build national consciousness in an environment lacking essential characteristics for nation-building. The Saigon government owed its existence to the United States. Opposition to that government and its problems of dependence might have been lessened, but not eliminated, by the concentration of U.S. forces near the DMZ and the buildup of the ARVN. After all, opposition to the Saigon government was not a creation of North Vietnam, and the eventual manipulation and exploitation of the Vietcong by Hanoi should not obscure the southern origins of the insurgency. What were needed were leaders who could have inspired sacrifice, ended the widespread corruption, and brought reforms into rural areas.

Summers and Palmer, like those under whom they served, approach the war with the same assumptions as American policymakers who considered the division of Vietnam to be permanent and expected to dissuade Hanoi from its objective of national unification. Those convictions ran counter to the facts. The government at Hanoi could lay claim to a Nationalist legitimacy that the American client in the south lacked. The determination and resourcefulness of the enemy in Vietnam impressed many Americans who served there, including Palmer and Summers. As they note, the war was "everything" to North Vietnam—the completion of the Communist-Nationalist revolution begun in 1945. Fighting in South Vietnam could never mean as much to the United States, especially since American security was not at stake, as Palmer bluntly acknowledges. This is not intended to romanticize Ho Chi Minh and his followers, for their totalitarian tactics understandably offend U.S. ideals. "What was wrong in backing a weak, corrupt, inefficient regime against a brutally powerful, fanatically puritanical, ruthlessly efficient adversary," David Fromkin and James Chace write, "was that our side was likely to lose." The American effort was consistently undermined by the history of French colonialism and the French–Viet Minh War. "To an incredible degree," David Halberstam once reflected, "we were haunted and indeed imprisoned by the past." Because the South Vietnamese government eventually collapsed does not mean that its political history might not have been changed. The odds against the U.S. effort were substantial, however, and the Vietnam problem most likely defied American solution.

These works are of importance to diplomatic historians. The arguments of Summers and Palmer, by essentially reinforcing the complaints of fighting men about the conduct of the war, will likely help shape popular consciousness concerning the Vietnam conflict. Also, *On Strategy* and *The 25-Year War* are bound to influence military strategists and may come to represent a widely held interpretation on the mistakes of Vietnam.

Summers and Palmer, together with the generals in the Kinnard study, represent the views of one generation of military leaders on America's lost war. Their advice to the next generation of officers is bound to exert influence upon strategic thinking for years to come. Finally, these authors consider the Vietnam War under the conditions that the United States actually faced, and that alone is a singularly useful service. Regardless of whether or not one agrees with their strategic assessments and prescriptions, Summers and Palmer force serious reflection on the objectives and potential of American warfare in Vietnam.

The Limits of Technological Warfare

LOREN BARITZ

War is a product of culture. It is an expression of the way a culture thinks of itself and the world. Different cultures go to war for different reasons and fight in different ways. There is an American way of war. Our Vietnam War was started and fought in ways our culture required.

All the critics of General Westmoreland's ''strategy'' of a conventional big-unit war of attrition argued that he failed to understand that the guerrillas were more important than the conventional forces of North Vietnam. Most of the ''pacification'' devotees made the same point. None of them understood the relationship between American culture and the American way of war.

Lieutenant Colonel Zeb B. Bradford was a better cultural critic than the civilian and academic experts. He explained that Americans could not have fought successfully as guerrillas or antiguerrillas. It was thus necessary for Americans to have concentrated on our own way of war:

> The great strength of US fighting forces historically has been precisely that they have exploited their peculiarly American qualities and attributes. Highly mechanized and technical warfare reinforces our tendencies and talents and serves as a vehicle for evolutionary advance—counterinsurgency goes against the grain. We are a rich, industrial, urban country. Highly technical forces are compatible with our characteristics and resources.

Zeb Bradford wrote what is indisputable: Mostly white, English-speaking soldiers could not fight as guerrillas in Asia. We would make superb guerrillas if we were fighting in the United States.

The counterinsurgency fad was a direct consequence of President Kennedy's uninformed enthusiasm, and it confused the American effort for many years after his death. When the army Chief, General George Decker, told President Kennedy that ''any good soldier can handle guerrillas,'' the President first lectured him and six months later fired him. The military brass got the message. On the surface, counterinsurgency was in. JFK's support of the stylish Green Berets was consistent with his athletic patriotism, and was based on the assumption that military training could somehow overcome culture and race. Peer De Silva, the CIA's chief of station

Excerpts from *Backfire!: A History of How American Culture Led Us into Vietnam* by Loren Baritz, pp. 321–326, 345. Copyright © 1985 by Loren Baritz. Reprinted by permission of William Morrow and Co., Inc.

of Saigon, remembered that Robert and John Kennedy believed that "if a Vietcong *can* lie for hours under water in a rice paddy, breathing air through a straw, so *can* we." It was harder to train them to climb out of the water, mix with the villagers, and remain undetectable. The American way of life and war meant that we could not succeed as counterinsurgents.

American political culture—the self-righteousness of our nationalism— merged with the impulses of our technological culture—tell us what to do and we'll do it, no questions asked. President Kennedy's enthusiasm for counterinsurgency led the nation to assume that we could successfully intervene in Vietnamese politics in ways that were foreign to America's genius. Our managerial sophistication and technological superiority resulted in our trained incompetence in guerrilla warfare.

The conclusion is obvious: If this nation cannot use its managerial and technological strengths in international conflict, it would be wise to avoid engagement. If our expensive weapon systems will not contribute to victory, it would be wise not to pretend that we have other resources.

The only circumstance where this conclusion does not apply is when the imbalance between us and our enemy is ludicrous, as in the adventure on the island of Grenada. This conclusion, however, did apply to our peacekeeping force in Lebanon, where our massed technology could not protect the marines from one terrorist's truck. Our Vietnam experience had revealed that we could not stop what we did not stop in Lebanon. That is because military intelligence, not missiles or an armada of warships, is necessary to stop terrorism. If the intelligence is available, one bullet may be all the technology necessary. If it is unavailable, our soldiers will surely die.

The entire ecology of America's military bureaucracy depends on weapons—increasingly complex, difficult to maintain, and expensive. Thus, General Westmoreland's strategy of conventional war was consistent with the realities of American culture, obviously including its bureaucratic and corporate values. There was nothing else he could do. In a gigantic confusion of means and ends, the Pentagon, both then and now, appears to conceive of its weapons as national strategy and its budget as foreign policy. This is a revealing symptom of the technicians' mentality: Quantity shall overcome. The Israelis and the North Vietnamese might have taught us otherwise. This dependence on quantity has some meaning in conventional warfare, but certainly not in guerrilla war, and, within limits, probably not in the calculus of nuclear deterrence.

The technician's mind is organized around the question *how*. He is motivated by a desire, sometime a need, to solve problems. He is rational, practical, hardheaded, and believes that if an idea can be transformed into a solution that actually works, the idea was true. Most of the war's planners exhibited these traits. Three other attributes of the technological mentality had an even more direct impact on the war. The technician's language is amoral, dispassionate, and optimistic. For example, Secretary McNamara's perception of Vietnam as a limited war reveals all these habits of mind: "The greatest contribution Vietnam is making—right or wrong is beside the point—is that it is developing an ability in the United States to fight a limited war, to go to war without the necessity of arousing the public ire.''

A technician's war would be muddied by the public's passion. Thus, the Vietnam War was cold-blooded. Secretary Rusk said that ''we tried to do in cold blood perhaps what can only be done in hot blood, when sacrifices of this order are involved.'' None of the Presidents attempted to stir passion about this war. General Westmoreland mistakenly said that the reason was that the political leaders ''were more afraid of stirring up the hawks than the doves, a very ironical development. . . . Therefore, a policy decision was made to keep the war low key.'' The war was fought for reasons of state, not out of anger. If the American public was whipped into anger, the political engineers might not have been able to attempt to fine-tune Vietnam to just the right level of death. They might not have been able so precisely to control a more passionate war. The very idea of limited war was at stake.

According to Colonel Harry Summers, an operations officer in Vietnam, the cold-bloodedness was a result of the academic sources of the theories about limited war. ''As we . . . read the writings of the political scientists and systems analysts on limited war, they are noteworthy for their lack of passion. The horror, the bloodshed and the destruction of the battlefield are remarkably absent.'' He quoted Karl von Clausewitz, the classic theorist of war, who wrote about 150 years ago: ''It would be an obvious fallacy to imagine war between civilized peoples as resulting merely from a rational act on the part of the government. . . .'' Crackpot rationalism, to paraphrase C. Wright Mills, was understood a very long time ago. Colonel Summers mistakenly believed that the academics could be forgiven for their bloodless rationalism, ''but we in the military knew better.'' The military was guilty of not talking, of cooperating with the deceptions, and of not forcing the issue when the Presidents decided to avoid exciting the middle class.

The belief that the public should coolly and unemotionally support a war was a result of the desire to make the war conform to the technological mind. We were to fight the war for calculated reasons. This was not war as the American people fondly remembered their good wars, especially The Big One. When the people finally became angry, their anger was more often aimed at the Presidents than at the enemy. Americans, as others, need to perceive the enemy's threat, and the threat needs to be real enough to frighten them, and the fright needs to be metabolized into anger. Then they will support war.

A war over ideology is not enough for the people, however exercised over the abstractions the leaders and other ''responsible'' elites became. These groups believed in abstractions: dominoes, national credibility, and the significance of counterinsurgency. They were merely convinced, not passionate. That is never enough for the people. It is right to insist on becoming fighting mad. Anger could not be factored into the technician's equations.

North Vietnam finally won its war because it was willing to accept more death than we considered rational. That is why the bombing campaigns failed. It is not that our technology failed. Our cultural perceptions failed when so many intelligent men in high positions simply assumed that our enemy's culture was sufficiently like ours that he would quit at a point where we believed we would quit.

We lost the war because we were never clear about the guerrillas, their popular support, the North Vietnamese, or ourselves. Our marvelously clever technology did not help us to understand the war and, in fact, confused us even more because it created our unquestioning faith in our own power. Finally, the North's decision to continue fighting, and our decision to stop, were each consistent with the cultural imperatives of each nation. Because the army of South Vietnam was trained by us to fight in the American style, it was forever dependent on a supply of hardware and fuel. That army was incongruent with the culture it was trying to defend.

This is why the military's continuing claim that we could have won the war if it had been allowed to fight differently is pointless. We could not have fought it differently. The constraints on the tactics of the war, and the absence of a political goal to shape those tactics, were products of American culture at the time. It is meaningless to argue that "next time we'll do it differently and win." The only reasonable prediction about the cultural pressures surrounding a "next time" is that they will at least resemble those that existed in the 1960s and exist now.

Americans continue to believe that managerial expertise and war technology will contribute to the security of the nation and the peace of the world. Such a belief is consistent with who we are, but inconsistent with our experience in Vietnam. We did not know when, where, or how to make use of our tools. It is important to have the right tools. We have them. But it is also important to know when and how to use them. This is why the debate about whether anything useful can be learned from Vietnam is not very enlightening. What we must learn from Vietnam is not tactics or strategy, not technique, but who we are, what our culture requires.

One of the slogans used to tranquilize the people in George Orwell's *Nineteen Eighty-Four* is "Ignorance is Strength." In America since Hiroshima, that slogan turned out to be backward. For postwar America, strength was ignorance. We were so strong, we thought we did not need to know about others. We mistakenly thought we knew ourselves and that was all that mattered. Our power was thought somehow to immunize us against failure, at least against colossal failure.

Because culture creates war, it also creates peace. Some people now argue that the peculiar set of circumstances we encountered in Vietnam will never occur again. There are many ways to remain ignorant about Vietnam. The best way is to remain ignorant about America. Another is to insist that the war was unique, so different from other wars that it holds no important lessons. Every historical event is unique, after all. James Thomson, who resigned from the NSC in 1966, expressed this idea much too cleverly: "The only lesson we should learn from Vietnam is never again to fight a nationalist movement dominated by Communists in a former

French colony." This emphasis on Vietnam's uniqueness has three implications: it ignores American culture; it dismisses Vietnam as an aberration;
and, it does not prevent future intervention on what is now thought to be
the inappropriate model of Vietnam.

For all the criticism that the Vietnam War was unnecessarily militarized,
a parallel fact was that America's managerial fetish "civilianized" the military. General Westmoreland was the chief bureaucratic supervisor who
reported to the bureaucratic Joint Chiefs who reported to Secretary
McNamara who wrote the book on bureaucracy in the Defense Department.
The symptoms of an increasingly managerial military establishment were
evident in the military's conception of itself as just "doing a job," of its
men as managers and workers, and its careerism, bureaucratic sensitivities,
and fixation on accounting controls and statistical indexes. These are the
lasting legacies of Secretary McNamara's indisputably brilliant tenure. The
military's overwhelming investment in engineering was (and is) severely
criticized. But this emphasis was (and is) consistent with our national values. It produced the weapons. The Pentagon could not do otherwise.

Colonel Summers acknowledged that the job of the political leaders of
the war was to provide the political strategy of the war, its reasons and
purpose. The job of the systems analysts was to provide the means to
accomplish the purpose. What was missing was a military strategy for the
use of the available means to accomplish the stated purpose. He thought
we had the *why* and the *what*, but not the *how*. Yet, true to his trade,
Colonel Summers swept politics under the rug. We could no more answer
why we were in Vietnam than we could explain how to use our cascade
of weapons. The single great American accomplishment of the war was in
supplying the weapons, and that was not enough.

Having weapons without a purpose or a strategy led to the policy of
attrition. If we exploded enough bombs and fired enough rounds, we assumed the enemy would quit. At some point, he would have. General
Westmoreland always knew where that point was. The alternative to attrition, he said, was "a war of annihilation." The military struggle could
have succeeded only if all of Vietnam had been utterly devastated, with
the people dead and buried, or at least dead. Someone once said that the
military wanted to carry Vietnam away in the ashtrays of its cars. . . .

. . . The military, despite the agony of Vietnam, felt then and feels now
that they did not lose the war. They think that victory was denied them
by political decision makers who liked to play with soldiers.

The argument that civilian interference prevented the military from
winning has been widely accepted, with almost half of the American public
(and 82 percent of combat vets) agreeing. This easy assignment of blame
obviously permits all of us to growl at the politicians and be done with it.
But the ticket-punching careerist officers were not invented by civilians.
The utter failure to develop military tactics effectively to utilize the technology was not the fault of civilians. The strategy of attrition and the
dizzying rotation of officers were not made in Washington. The cover-ups
and deceptive optimism were the military's own. The interservice rivalries

were not required by politicians. The bureaucratization of William West-moreland's mind was the military's own. The unwillingness to stop the blizzard of heroin was the military's own. The subversion of the Special Forces, the insistence on using B-52s, and spreading the use of Agent Orange were all military decisions.

It is, however, true that the military could not have "won" the war. Neither it nor the politicians knew what *winning* meant. By sheer force of firepower the military won its battles, but it could never have made these victories add up to victory. What was the military's responsibility for the failure of the Presidents and their aides to formulate a strategy? It was not the fault of the politicians that the leading generals and admirals bit their tongues when their candor was indispensable. Unless, of course, they had nothing to say. Colonel Summers, for one, rejected the military's argument that politicians' meddling prevented a victory: "Our problem was not so much political interference as it was the lack of a coherent military strategy—a lack for which our military leaders share a large burden of responsibility." In any case, the military's traditional emphasis on its own experience and judgment was unavailable to the nation's leaders as the Chiefs routinely snapped off a salute with the standard "Can do, sir!" Wind-up bureaucratic dolls should not complain that others did not let them win.

✗ *F U R T H E R   R E A D I N G*

Mark Baker, *Nam* (1981)

Douglas S. Blaufarb, *The Counterinsurgency Era* (1977)

Larry E. Cable, *Conflict of Myths* (1986) (on counterinsurgency)

Cincinnatus, *Self-Destruction: The Disintegration and Decay of the United States Army During the Vietnam Era* (1978)

Mark Clodfelter, *The Limits of Air Power: The American Bombing of North Vietnam* (1989)

Frederick Downs, *The Killing Zone* (1978)

Robert L. Gallucci, *Neither Peace nor Honor* (1975)

Lawrence E. Grinter, "South Vietnam: Pacification Denied," *Southeast Asia Spectrum*, 3 (1975), 49–78

George C. Herring, "American Strategy in Vietnam: The Postwar Debate," *Military Affairs*, 46 (1982), 57–63

Walter L. Hixson, "Containment on the Perimeter: George F. Kennan and Vietnam," *Diplomatic History*, 12 (1988), 149–163

Edwin Hooper et al., *The United States Navy and the Vietnam Conflict* (1976)

Richard A. Hunt and Richard H. Shultz, Jr., *Lessons from an Unconventional War* (1981)

Douglas Kinnard, *The War Managers* (1977)

Andrew F. Krepinevich, Jr., *The Army and Vietnam* (1986)

Guenther Lewy, *America in Vietnam* (1978)

Raphael Littauer and Normal Uphoff, eds., *The Air War in Indochina* (1972)

Robert Mason, *Chickenhawk* (1983)

Drew Middleton, *Air War—Vietnam* (1978)

John Mueller, "The Search for the Breaking Point in Vietnam," *Strategic Studies*, 24 (1980), 497–519

Robert E. Osgood, *Limited War Revisited* (1979)
Bruce Palmer, Jr., *The 25-Year War* (1984)
Dave Richard Palmer, *Summons of the Trumpet* (1978)
Gregory Palmer, *The McNamara Strategy and the Vietnam War* (1978)
Bernard W. Roger, *Cedar Falls–Junction City: A Turning Point* (1974)
U. S. Grant Sharp, *Strategy for Defeat* (1978)
Shelby L. Stanton, *The Rise and Fall of an American Army* (1985)
James C. Thompson, *Rolling Thunder* (1980)
Henry L. Trewhitt, *McNamara* (1971)
Francis J. West, *The Village* (1972)
William C. Westmoreland, *A Soldier Reports* (1976)
Robert H. Whitlow, *U.S. Marines in Vietnam* (1976)

CHAPTER
8

The Enemy: North Vietnam and
the ''Vietcong''

Following the Geneva Conference of 1954, Ho Chi Minh and most of the former Vietminh leadership devoted their energies to the establishment of a socialist state in the territory north of the seventeenth parallel: the Democratic Republic of Vietnam. In the area south of the parallel, Ngo Dinh Diem, with strong American backing, attempted to consolidate his hold on power in the Republic of Vietnam. By 1956, any lingering hope that the all-Vietnam elections promised at Geneva would be held had been dashed, and the two ''regroupment areas'' increasingly resembled independent countries.

The northern leaders had not abandoned the goal of national unification. Opposition to Diem spread throughout the countryside during the late 1950s; a revolutionary guerrilla movement reemerged in the south at that time, composed in part of former Vietminh cadres. At least by 1960, Hanoi was giving active support to that movement, and in November of that year the National Liberation Front (NLF) was founded as a broad populist coalition that sought to appeal to all groups opposed to Diem's regime.

The nature and extent of Hanoi's involvement in the southern revolution stands as one of the most controversial aspects of the Vietnam War. The issue divided scholars, activists, and policymakers at the height of American involvement, and it continues to spark lively debate. The following questions rank among the most significant: Did North Vietnam orchestrate the revolution in the south from its inception? Were the ''Vietcong'' guerrillas and the NLF merely puppets of Hanoi? or did the southern revolution have important internal roots? How and why did the Vietcong gain such a strong foothold in the countryside so quickly? Did the communist program appeal to the peasants, and, if so, how? What role, if any, did the Soviet Union and China play in the deepening conflict in Vietnam? Finally, from the perspective of the United States, who were America's principal enemies in Vietnam?

✗ *D O C U M E N T S*

After the conclusion of the Geneva Agreements, Ho Chi Minh urged his countrymen to follow their provisions. His appeal of July 22, 1954, is printed as the first document. In the second document, Troung Nhu Tang, an opponent of the Diem regime, recalls the events that led to the formation of the National Liberation Front. The NLF's manifesto of December 1960, reprinted here as the third selection, reflected the organization's interest in attracting the broadest possible coalition in opposition to the Diem regime.

In the fourth document, dating from 1961, Vo Nguyen Giap spells out the essential strategy of what he called a "people's war," insisting that an insufficiently equipped people's army, with the right tactics and strategy, could defeat a modern army. Nguyen Chi Thanh, a South Vietnamese communist who would later command all communist forces in the south, offered a similarly optimistic perspective in an article published in July 1963, reproduced here as the fifth document. He stressed that a powerful North Vietnam and an effective revolutionary movement in the south were mutually complementary and required careful coordination. In the final document, a speech delivered over Radio Hanoi on July 17, 1966, Ho displayed characteristic determination in the face of growing American military pressure.

Ho Chi Minh's Appeal After the Geneva Agreements, 1954

The Geneva Conference has come to an end. It is a great victory for our diplomacy.

On behalf of the Government, I cordially make the following appeal:

1. For the sake of peace, unity, independence, and democracy of the Fatherland, our people, armymen, cadres, and Government have, during these eight years or so, joined in a monolithic bloc, endured hardship, and resolutely overcome all difficulties to carry out the Resistance; we have won many brilliant victories. On this occasion, on behalf of the Government, I cordially congratulate you, from North to South. I respectfully bow to the memory of the armymen and people who have sacrificed their lives for the Fatherland, and send my homages of comfort to the wounded and sick armymen.

This great victory is also due to the support given us in our just struggle by the peoples of our brother countries, by the French people, and by the peace-loving people of the world.

Thanks to these victories and the efforts made by the delegation of the Soviet Union at the Berlin Conference, negotiations were opened between our country and France at the Geneva Conference. At this conference, the struggle of our delegation and the assistance given by the delegations of the Soviet Union and China have ended in a great victory for us: The French Government has recognized the independence, sovereignty, unity, and territorial integrity of our country; it has agreed to withdraw French troops from our country, etc.

From now on, we must make every effort to consolidate peace and achieve reunification, independence, and democracy throughout our country.

2. In order to re-establish peace, the first step to take is that the armed forces of both parties should cease fire.

The regroupment in two regions is a temporary measure; it is a transitional step for the implementation of the armistice and restoration of peace, and paves the way for national reunification through general elections. Regroupment in regions is in no way a partition of our country, neither is it an administrative division.

During the armistice, our army is regrouped in the North; the French troops are regrouped in the South, that is to say, there is a change of regions. A number of regions which were formerly occupied by the French now become our free zones. Vice versa, a number of regions formerly liberated by us will now be temporarily occupied by the French troops before they leave for France.

This is a necessity; North, Central, and South Viet-Nam are territories of ours. Our country will certainly be unified, our entire people will surely be liberated.

Our compatriots in the South were the first to wage the war of Resistance. They possess a high political consciousness. I am confident that they will place national interests above local interests, permanent interests above temporary interests, and join their efforts with the entire people in strengthening peace, achieving unity, independence, and democracy all over the country. The Party, Government, and I always follow the efforts of our people and we are sure that our compatriots will be victorious.

3. The struggle to consolidate peace and achieve reunification, independence, and democracy is also a long and hard struggle. In order to carry the day, our people, armymen, and cadres from North to South must unite closely. They must be at one in thought and deed.

We are resolved to abide by the agreements entered into with the French Government. At the same time, we demand that the French Government correctly implement the agreements they have signed with us.

We must do our utmost to strengthen peace and be vigilant to check the maneuvers of peace wreckers.

We must endeavor to struggle for the holding of free general elections throughout the country to reunify our territory.

We must exert all our efforts to restore, build, strengthen, and develop our forces in every field so as to attain complete independence.

We must do our utmost to carry out social reforms in order to improve our people's livelihood and realize genuine democracy.

We further tighten our fraternal relations with Cambodia and Laos.

We strengthen the great friendship between us and the Soviet Union, China, and other brother countries. To maintain peace, we enhance our solidarity with the French people, the Asian people, and people all over the world.

4. I call on all our compatriots, armymen, and cadres to follow strictly the lines and policies laid down by the Party and Government, to struggle

for the consolidation of peace and the achievement of national reunification, independence, and democracy throughout the country.

I eagerly appeal to all genuine patriots, irrespective of their social class, creed, political stand, and former affiliation, to cooperate sincerely with us and fight for the sake of our country and our people so as to bring about peace and achieve reunification, independence, and democracy for our beloved Viet-Nam.

If our people are as one, if thousands of men are like one, victory will certainly be ours.

Long live a peaceful, unified, independent, and democratic Viet-Nam.

Truong Nhu Tang on the Origins of the National Liberation Front (1957–1959), 1985

By the time 1957 merged into 1958, Ngo Dinh Diem had exhausted the patient hopefulness that had initially greeted his presidency. From the first he had moved ruthlessly to consolidate his personal power, crushing the private army of the Binh Xuyen,* then subduing the armed religious sects. From there he attacked those suspected of communist sympathies in what was called the To Cong ("Denounce the Communists") campaign, jailing and executing thousands who had fought against the French. Each of these moves was carried out with surprising energy, and in their own terms they succeeded. As he surveyed the political landscape three years after assuming power, Diem could see no well-organized centers of opposition to his rule. The National Assembly was wholly dominated by his brother's National Revolutionary Movement, the troublesome private armies had been severely handled, and the Communist-dominated resistance veterans were cowed and in disarray.

But Diem's successes had all been of a negative sort. Though he had asserted his authority and gained time, he had done nothing about establishing positive programs to meet the nation's economic and social needs. He had not used the time he had gained. After three years it was apparent that the new president was a powermonger, not a builder. For those who could see, the fatal narrowness of his political understanding was already evident.

In the first place, Diem's armed enemies had for the most part only been mauled, not destroyed. Elements of the defeated sect armies went underground, licking their wounds and looking for allies. Gradually they began to link up with groups of former Vietminh fighters fleeing from the To Cong suppression. The core of a guerrilla army was already in the making.

---

* A tightly run organized crime syndicate that controlled underworld activities in Saigon and Cholon and was not averse to injecting itself into politics.

Excerpted from *A Vietcong Memoir* by Truong Nhu Tang. Copyright © 1985 by Truong Nhu Tang, David Shanoff, and Doan Van Tang, reprinted by permission of Harcourt Brace Jovanovich, Inc.

Even as old enemies regrouped, Diem was busy adding new ones. In the countryside he destroyed at a blow the dignity and livelihood of several hundred thousand peasants by canceling the land-redistribution arrangements instituted by the Vietminh in areas they had controlled prior to 1954. He might have attempted to use American aid to compensate owners and capitalize on peasant goodwill; instead he courted the large landholders. Farmers who had been working land they considered theirs, often for years, now faced demands for back rent and exorbitant new rates. It was an economic disaster for them.

In 1957 Diem promulgated his own version of land reform, ostensibly making acreage available, though only to peasants who could pay for it. But even this reform was carried out primarily on paper. In the provinces it was sabotaged everywhere by landowners acting with official connivance. The result of all this was a frustrated and indignant peasantry, fertile ground for anti-Diem agitation.

Meanwhile, the city poor were tasting their own ration of misery. In Saigon the government pursued "urban development" with a vengeance, dispossessing whole neighborhoods in favor of modern commercial buildings and expensive apartments, which could only be utilized by Americans and the native upper classes. Not a few times, poorer quarters were completely razed by uncontrollable fires (Khanh Hoi and Phu Nuan were particularly calamitous examples). Few thought these fires were accidental; they were too closely followed by massive new construction. The displaced moved onto sampans on the river or to poorer, even more distant districts. In the slums and shanty villages resentment against the Americans mixed with a simmering anger toward the regime.

In the highland regions of the Montagnards too, Diem's policies were cold-blooded and destructive. Attempting to make the tribespeople more accessible to government control, troops and cadres forced village populations down out of the mountains and into the valleys—separating them from their ancestral lands and graves. In Ban Me Thuot and other areas, the ingrained routines of social life were profoundly disrupted by these forced relocations, which seemed to the tribespeople nothing more than inexplicable cruelty.

By the end of 1958, Diem had succeeded brilliantly in routing his enemies and arrogating power. But he had also alienated large segments of the South Vietnamese population, creating a swell of animosity throughout the country. Almost unknown at first, in a few short years he had made himself widely detested, a dictator who could look for support only to the Northern Catholic refugees and to those who made money from his schemes. Most damning of all, he had murdered many patriots who had fought in the struggle against France and had tied his existence to the patronage of the United States, France's successor. To many nationalist-minded Vietnamese, whose emotions were those of people just emerging from a hundred years of subjection to foreigners, Diem had forfeited all claims to loyalty.

In light of Diem's conduct of the presidency, two facts were clear: First, the country had settled into an all too familiar pattern of oligarchic rule and utter disregard for the welfare of the people. Second, subservience to foreigners was still the order of the day. We had a ruler whose overriding interest was power and who would use the Americans to prop himself up—even while the Americans were using him for their own strategic purposes.

As far as I was concerned, this situation was intolerable. Replacing the French despots with a Vietnamese one was not a significant advance. It would never lead to either the broad economic progress or the national dignity which I (along with many others) had been brooding about for years. Among my circle of friends there was anger and profound disappointment over this turn of events. We were living, we felt, in historic times. A shameful, century-long era had just been violently closed out, and a new nation was taking shape before our eyes. Many of us agreed that we could not acquiesce in the shape it was taking. If we were not to be allowed a say about it from within the government, we would have to speak from without.

By the end of 1958, those of us who felt this way decided to form an extralegal political organization, complete with a program and plan of action. We had not moved toward this decision quickly; it was an undertaking of immense magnitude, which would require years of effort before giving us the strength to challenge Diem's monopoly on power. To some, that prospect seemed quixotic at best. But most of us felt we had little choice.

From casual discussions, we began to meet in slightly more formal groups, sometimes only a few of us, sometimes eight or ten together. Two doctors, Duong Quynh Hoa and Phung Van Cung, took active roles, as did Nguyen Huu Khuong, a factory owner, Trinh Dinh Thao, a lawyer, and the architect Huynh Tan Phat. We were joined by Nguyen Van Hieu and Ung Ngoc Ky, who were lycée teachers, and other friends such as Nguyen Long and Tran Buu Kiem. Our first order of business was to identify and make contact with potential allies for what we knew would be a long and bitter struggle.

To do this we formed what we called the mobilization committee, whose members were myself, Hieu, Kiem, Ky, Long, Cung, and architect Phat. Through friends, relatives, business and political contacts we began to establish a network of people who felt as we did about Diem and his policies. Phat and a few of the others were old resisters and had kept their ties with fellow veterans of the French war, many of whom were hiding with friends and family from the To Cong hunters. They too were beginning to organize, and they had colleagues and sympathizers in every social stratum throughout the country. They were natural allies.

Among us we also had people with close ties to the sects, the legal political parties, the Buddhists. In each group we made overtures, and everywhere we discovered sympathy and backing. Sometimes individuals would indicate their desire to participate actively. More often we would receive assurances of quiet solidarity. At the same time, we sent Nguyen Van Hieu to Hanoi to begin working out a channel of support from our Northern compatriots.

At each stage we discussed carefully the ongoing search for allies, wary about how to gather support and still retain our own direction and freedom of action. It was a delicate and crucial problem, of the utmost complexity.

The overwhelming strength of our enemy urged us to acquire whatever assistance we could, from whatever source. In addition, the anticolonial war had not simply ended in 1954; a residual Vietminh infrastructure was still in place and was beginning to come alive again. For better or worse, our endeavor was meshed into an ongoing historical movement for independence that had already developed its own philosophy and means of action. Of this movement, Ho Chi Minh was the spiritual father, in the South as well as the North, and we looked naturally to him and to his government for guidance and aid. . . . And yet, this struggle was also our own. Had Ngo Dinh Diem proved a man of breadth and vision, the core of people who filled the NLF and its sister organizations would have rallied to him. As it was, the South Vietnamese nationalists were driven to action by his contempt for the principles of independence and social progress in which they believed. In this sense, the Southern revolution was generated of itself, out of the emotions, conscience, and aspirations of the Southern people.

The complexity of the struggle was mirrored in the makeup of our group. Most were not Lao Dong ("Workers' Party"—the official name of the Vietnamese Communist Party) members; many scarcely thought of themselves as political, at least in any ideological way. Our allies among the resistance veterans were also largely nationalist rather than political (though they had certainly been led and monitored by the Party). But we also had Party activists among us, some open, some surreptitious. Tran Buu Kiem, the architect Phat, and the teachers Hieu and Ky I knew as politically-minded individuals, who had been leaders of the New Democratic Party during their student years at Hanoi University in the early forties. This militant student union had been absorbed by the Lao Dong in 1951, some of its members enrolling in the Party, some defecting altogether, some simply accepting the change in leadership without themselves becoming Communists. What I didn't know was that Phat had been a secret Party member since 1940 while Hieu, Ky, and Kiem had rallied to the Party in 1951.

But I was not overly concerned at that point about potential conflicts between the Southern nationalists and the ideologues. We were allies in this fight, or so I believed. We needed each other, and the closest ties of background, family, and patriotism united us in respect for each other's purposes. This was my reading of the situation in 1959 as the yet-to-be-named National Liberation Front gathered momentum. I was not alone in drawing this conclusion. And I was not the only one whom time would disabuse.

Manifesto of the National Liberation Front, 1960

Compatriots in the country and abroad!

Over the past hundred years the Vietnamese people repeatedly rose up to fight against foreign aggression for the independence and freedom of their fatherland. In 1945, the people throughout the country surged up in an armed uprising, overthrew the Japanese and French domination and seized power. When the French colonialists invaded our country for the second time, our compatriots, determined not to be enslaved again, shed much blood and laid down many lives to defend their national sovereignty and independence. Their solidarity and heroic struggle during nine years led the resistance war to victory. The 1954 Geneva Agreements restored peace in our country and recognized "the sovereignty, independence, unity and territorial integrity of Viet Nam".

Our compatriots in South Viet Nam would have been able to live in peace, to earn their livelihood in security and to build a decent and happy life.

However, the American imperialists, who had in the past helped the French colonialists to massacre our people, have now replaced the French in enslaving the southern part of our country through a disguised colonial regime. They have been using their stooge—the Ngo Dinh Diem administration—in their downright repression and exploitation of our compatriots, in their maneuvres to permanently divide our country and to turn its southern part into a military base in preparation for war in Southeast Asia.

The aggressors and traitors, working hand in glove with each other, have set up an extremely cruel dictatorial rule. They persecute and massacre democratic and patriotic people, and abolish all human liberties. They ruthlessly exploit the workers, peasants and other labouring people, strangle the local industry and trade, poison the minds of our people with a depraved foreign culture, thus degrading our national culture, traditions and ethics. They feverishly increase their military forces, build military bases, use the army as an instrument for repressing the people and serving the US imperialists' scheme to prepare an aggressive war.

Never, over the past six years, have gun shots massacring our compatriots ceased to resound throughout South Viet Nam. Tens of thousands of patriots here have been murdered and hundreds of thousands thrown into jail. All sections of the people have been living in a stifling atmosphere under the iron heel of the US-Diem clique. Countless families have been torn away and scenes of mourning are seen everywhere as a result of unemployment, poverty, exacting taxes, terror, massacre, drafting of manpower and pressganging, usurpation of land, forcible house removal, and herding of the people into "prosperity zones", "resettlement centres" and other forms of concentration camps.

High anger with the present tyrannical regime is boiling among all strata of the people. Undaunted in the face of barbarous persecution, our compatriots are determined to unite and struggle unflaggingly against the US imperialists' policy of aggression and the dictatorial and nepotic regime of the Ngo Dinh Diem clique. Among workers, peasants and other toiling people, among intellectuals, students and pupils, industrialists and traders, religious sects and national minorities, patriotic activities are gaining in scope and strength, seriously shaking the US-Diem dictatorial regime.

The attempted coup d'etat of November 11, 1960 in Saigon in some respects reflected the seething anger among the people and armymen, and the rottenness and decline of the US-Diem regime. However, there were among the leaders of this coup political speculators who, misusing the patriotism of the armymen, preferred negotiation and compromise rather than to overthrow Ngo Dinh Diem. Like Ngo Dinh Diem, they persisted in following the pro-American and traitorous path, and also used the anti-communist signboard to oppose the people. That is why the coup was not supported by the people and large numbers of armymen and, consequently, ended in failure.

At present, our people are urgently demanding an end to the cruel dictatorial rule; they are demanding independence and democracy, enough food and clothing, and peaceful reunification of the country.

To meet the aspirations of our compatriots, the *South Viet Nam National Front for Liberation* came into being, pledging itself to shoulder the historic task of liberating our people from the present yoke of slavery.

The *South Viet Nam National Front for Liberation* undertakes to unite all sections of the people, all social classes, nationalities, political parties, organizations, religious communities and patriotic personalities, without distinction of their political tendencies, in order to struggle for the overthrow of the rule of the US imperialists and their stooges—the Ngo Dinh Diem clique—and for the realization of independence, democracy, peace and neutrality pending the peaceful reunification of the fatherland.

The *South Viet Nam National Front for Liberation* calls on the entire people to unite and heroically rise up as one man to fight along the line of a program of action summarized as follows:

1. To overthrow the disguised colonial regime of the US imperialists and the dictatorial Ngo Dinh Diem administration—lackey of the United States—, and to form a national democratic coalition administration.

2. To bring into being a broad and progressive democracy, promulgate freedom of expression, of the press, of belief, of assembly, of association, of movement and other democratic freedoms. To grant general amnesty to all political detainees, dissolve all concentration camps dubbed "prosperity zones" and "resettlement centres", abolish the fascist 10-59 law and other anti-democratic laws.

3. To abolish the economic monopoly of the United States and its henchmen, to protect home-made products, encourage home industry and trade, expand agriculture and build an independent and sovereign economy. To provide jobs for the unemployed, increase wages for workers, armymen and office employees. To abolish arbitrary fines and apply an equitable and rational tax system. To help those who have gone South to return to their native places if they so desire, and to provide jobs for those among them who want to remain in the South.

4. To carry out land rent reduction, guarantee the peasants' right to till present plots of land, redistribute communal land and advance toward land reform.

5. To do away with enslaving and depraved US-style culture, build a national and progressive culture and education. To wipe out illiteracy, open more schools, carry out reforms in the educational and examination system.

6. To abolish the system of American military advisers, eliminate

foreign military bases in Viet Nam and build a national army for the defence of the fatherland and the people.

7. To guarantee equality between men and women and among different nationalities, and the right to autonomy of the national minorities; to protect the legitimate interests of foreign residents in Viet Nam; to protect and take care of the interests of Vietnamese living abroad.

8. To carry out a foreign policy of peace and neutrality, to establish diplomatic relations with all countries which respect the independence and sovereignty of Viet Nam.

9. To re-establish normal relations between the two zones, pending the peaceful reunification of the fatherland.

10. To oppose aggressive war; to actively defend world peace.

Compatriots!

Ours are a heroic people with a tradition of unity and indomitable struggle. We cannot let our country be plunged into darkness and mourning. We are determined to shatter the fetters of slavery, and wrest back independence and freedom.

Let us all rise up and unite!

Let us close our ranks and fight under the banner of the *South Viet Nam National Front for Liberation* to overthrow the rule of the US imperialists and Ngo Dinh Diem—their henchmen.

Workers, peasants and other toiling people! The oppression and misery which are now heavily weighing on you must be ended. You have the strength of tens of millions of people. Stand up enthusiastically to save your families and our fatherland.

Intellectuals! The dictatorial rulers have stripped us of the most elementary human rights. You are living in humiliation and misery. For our great cause, stand up resolutely!

Industrialists and traders! A country under the sway of foreign sharks cannot have an independent and sovereign economy. You should join in the people's struggle.

Compatriots of all national minorities! Compatriots of all religious communities! Unity is life, disunity is death. Smash all US-Diem schemes of division. Side with the entire people in the struggle for independence, freedom and equality among all nationalities.

Notables! The interests of the nation are above all else. Support actively the struggle for the overthrow of the cruel aggressors and traitors.

Patriotic officers and soldiers! You have arms in your hands. Listen to the sacred call of the fatherland. Be definitely on the side of the people. Your compatriots have faith in your patriotism.

Young men and women! You are the future of the nation. You should devote your youthful ardour to serving the fatherland.

Compatriots living abroad! Turn your thoughts toward the beloved fatherland, contribute actively to the sacred struggle for national liberation.

At present the movement for peace, democracy and national independence is surging up throughout the world. Colonialism is irretrievably disintegrating. The time when the imperialists could plunder and subjugate the people at will is over. This situation is extremely favourable for the struggle to free South Viet Nam from the yoke of the US imperialists and their stooges. Peace-loving and progressive people in the world are supporting us. Justice is on our side, and we have the prodigious strength of the unity of our entire people. We will certainly win! The US imperialist aggressors and the Ngo Dinh Diem traitorous clique will certainly be defeated. The cause of liberation of South Viet Nam will certainly triumph.

Compatriots around the country!

Let us write and march forward confidently and valiantly to score brilliant victories for our people and our fatherland!

Vo Nguyen Giap on People's War, 1961

The Vietnamese people's war of liberation was a just war, aiming to win back the independence and unity of the country, to bring land to our peasants and guarantee them the right to it, and to defend the achievements of the August Revolution. That is why it was first and foremost a people's war. To educate, mobilise, organise and arm the whole people in order that they might take part in the Resistance was a crucial question.

The enemy of the Vietnamese nation was aggressive imperialism, which had to be overthrown. But the latter having long since joined up with the feudal landlords, the anti-imperialist struggle could definitely not be separated from anti-feudal action. On the other hand, in a backward colonial country such as ours where the peasants make up the majority of the population, a people's war is essentially a peasant's war under the leadership of the working class. Owing to this fact, a general mobilisation of the whole people is neither more nor less than the mobilisation of the rural masses. The problem of land is of decisive importance. From an exhaustive analysis, the Vietnamese people's war of liberation was essentially a people's national democratic revolution carried out under armed form and had twofold fundamental task: the overthrowing of imperialism and the defeat of the feudal landlord class, the anti-imperialist struggle being the primary task.

A backward colonial country which had only just risen up to proclaim its independence and install people's power, Viet Nam only recently possessed armed forces, equipped with still very mediocre arms and having no combat experience. Her enemy, on the other hand, was an imperialist power [France] which has retained a fairly considerable economic and military potentiality despite the recent German occupation [during World War II] and benefited, furthermore, from the active support of the United States. The balance of forces decidedly showed up our weaknesses against the enemy's power. The Vietnamese people's war of liberation had, therefore, to be a hard and long-lasting war in order to succeed in creating conditions for victory. All the conceptions born of impatience and aimed at obtaining speedy victory could only be gross errors. It was necessary to firmly grasp the strategy of a long-term resistance, and to exalt the will to be self-supporting in order to maintain and gradually augment our forces, while nibbling at and progressively destroying those of the enemy; it was necessary to accumulate thousands of small victories to turn them into a great success, thus gradually altering the balance of forces, in transforming our weakness into power and carrying off final victory.

At an early stage, our Party was able to discern the characteristics of this war: a people's war and a long-lasting war, and it was by proceeding from these premises that, during the whole of hostilities and in particularly difficult conditions, the Party solved all the problems of the Resistance. This judicious leadership by the Party led us to victory.

From the point of view of directing operations, our *strategy and tactics had to be those of a people's war and of a long-term resistance.*

Our strategy was, as we have stressed, to wage a long-lasting battle. A war of this nature in general entails several phases; in principle, starting from a stage of contention, it goes through a period of equilibrium before arriving at a general counter-offensive. In effect, the way in which it is carried on can be more subtle and more complex, depending on the particular conditions obtaining on both sides during the course of operations. Only a long-term war could enable us to utilise to the maximum our political trump cards, to overcome our material handicap and to transform our weakness into strength. To maintain and increase our forces, was the principle to which we adhered, contenting ourselves with attacking when success was certain, refusing to give battle likely to incur losses to us or to engage in hazardous actions. We had to apply the slogan: to build up our strength during the actual course of fighting.

The forms of fighting had to be completely adapted that is, to raise the fighting spirit to the maximum and rely on heroism of our troops to overcome the enemy's material superiority. In the main, especially at the outset of the war, we had recourse to guerilla fighting. In the Vietnamese theatre of operations, this method carried off great victories: it could be used in the mountains as well as in the delta, it could be waged with good or mediocre material and even without arms, and was to enable us eventually to equip ourselves at the cost of the enemy. Wherever the Expeditionary Corps came, the entire population took part in the fighting; every commune had its fortified village, every district had its regional troops fighting under the command of the local branches of the Party and the people's administration, in liaison with the regular forces in order to wear down and annihilate the enemy forces.

Thereafter, with the development of our forces, guerilla warfare changed into a mobile warfare—a form of mobile warfare still strongly marked by guerilla warfare—which would afterwards become the essential form of operations on the main front, the northern front. In this process of development of guerilla warfare and of accentuation of the mobile warfare, our people's army constantly grew and passed from the stage of combats involving a section or company, to fairly large-scale campaigns bringing into action several divisions. Gradually, its equipment improved, mainly by the seizure of arms from the enemy—the material of the French and American imperialists.

From the military point of view, *the Vietnamese people's war of lib-*
eration proved that an insufficiently equipped people's army, but an army
fighting for a just cause, can, with appropriate strategy and tactics, combine
the conditions needed to conquer a modern army of aggressive imperialism.

Nguyen Chi Thanh on Communist Strategy, 1963

In 1954, the U.S. imperialists, taking advantage of the French colonialists'
defeat at Dien Bien Phu, drove the French out of south Viet Nam and set
up a puppet regime headed by Ngo Dinh Diem. In essence, this meant that
U.S. neocolonialism replaced French old colonialism and became dominant
in south Viet Nam.

The United States thought that, with its numerous arms, dollars, rich
political and military experience and a faithful lackey Ngo Dinh Diem, it
could solve all the problems in south Viet Nam in a very short time. Events,
however, have proved this to be sheer wishful thinking. . . .

U.S. capital is world-renowned for its cleverness in clicking the abacus
for cold-blooded exploitation. However, it can hardly be found in the annals
of U.S. imperialism where its political and military leaders committed such
serious blunders and long-standing errors as they did in appraising the
situation in south Viet Nam. This is understandable since what is involved
here is not a business calculation but brain-racking "political arithmetic".

Their formula is perhaps something like this:

Step 1. Set up a puppet regime (headed by Ngo Dinh Diem or any other
lackey).

Step 2. Consolidate this puppet regime and take measures to stabilize the
situation in south Viet Nam: direct their main efforts on suppressing
the revolutionary forces and the former Resistance forces, and
gradually eliminate the French influences so as to clear the way
for further U.S. economic, political, military and cultural pene-
trations.

Step 3. Strengthen the puppet regime, turn south Viet Nam into a stable
colony of a new type and a complete military base under absolute
U.S. control.

The above formula appears at first sight to be well thought out. Its
greatest fallacy, however, lies in the fact that it only suits the United States
and disregards all others. The United States does not see the other factors
in this situation.

It is true that U.S. neo-colonialism has scored certain successes in
some parts of the world. In south Viet Nam, however, it is "born at the
wrong time", or to borrow from business language, it will not "pay off".
This is because the United States has overlooked a fundamental factor,
that is, when U.S. neo-colonialism made its way to south Viet Nam, it ran
into certain unexpected circumstances, which may be listed as follows:

• Great, sharp social contradictions exist between U.S. imperialism and
north Viet Nam which is advancing towards socialism.

• With the restoring of peace, social contradictions in south Viet Nam, instead of being eased, have further sharpened and matured. These are contradictions between the south Vietnamese people on the one hand and the U.S. imperialists, the feudal landlord class and comprador capital represented by Ngo Dinh Diem on the other.

• The south Vietnamese people have learned much from their struggle and have been able to utilize correct methods to resolve the social contradictions in south Viet Nam. These methods have been crystallized in the clear-sighted programmes of the South Viet Nam National Liberation Front and of the People's Revolutionary Party of South Viet Nam.

• Generally speaking, the world situation is not favourable to U.S. imperialism. The socialist camp is mightier than the imperialist camp; the movements for democracy and national independence are gaining momentum. These are great and ever-sharpening contradictions, driving the U.S. imperialists into a situation in which they can no longer do as they please.

It appears that south Viet Nam is the focus of many contradictions. The United States should have used algebra in gauging the situation there; instead it used simple arithmetic. Consequently it has run into a blind alley. The United States tries to find a way out by sending a batch of generals and over ten thousand troops to south Viet Nam. This will not help, now or ever. It now appears that the United States may "change the horse in the middle of the stream", but the substitution of one traitor for another will come to nothing. Such a change will not save the U.S.-Diem rule from ruin.

When the U.S. imperialists dispatched ten thousand troops to south Viet Nam, they believed that the rebellious forces could be put down within eighteen months. Later they said it would probably take ten years. Now, some people in the United States are not at all sure if they could succeed in eighteen years.

U.S. imperialism is certainly not ready to reconcile itself to its defeat in south Viet Nam. But it is an indisputable fact that it is being confronted with a crisis in its political line, which has, in turn, given rise to crises in military strategy and tactics.

The causes of these crises lie in the following:

• The fundamental cause is that the U.S. imperialists are doing an unjust thing—invading another country—and therefore they meet with the firm resistance of the south Vietnamese people, are disapproved of by the American people, condemned by other peoples, and even disliked by some of their henchmen in the Ngo Dinh Diem administration.

• Pursuing its aggressive aims, the United States egged Ngo Dinh Diem on to adopt a number of stupid policies, which aggravated the contradictions within the Ngo Dinh Diem regime.

• The U.S.-Diem clique faces an opponent who, although lacking American dollars, arms and other material, is full of anti-imperialist spirit, full of patriotism and revolutionary courage, and experienced in political and military struggles.

Although ultimate conclusions cannot yet be reached insofar as the struggle is still going on in south Viet Nam, we may however put forth the following views:

1. The U.S. imperialists are not invincible. Compared with imperialists of other countries, they are mightier, but compared with the revolutionary forces and the forces of the people of the world, they are not at all strong. If the proletarian revolution and people of the world resolutely struggle against U.S. imperialism, they can surely repel it step by step and narrow down its domain.

We do not have any illusions about the United States. We do not underestimate our opponent—the strong and cunning U.S. imperialism. But we are not afraid of the United States. The strategic concept thoroughly pervades the revolutionary line of south Viet Nam and is the fundamental factor determining the success of the revolution. If, on the contrary, one is afraid of the United States and thinks that to offend it would court failure, and that firm opposition to U.S. imperialism would touch off a nuclear war, then the only course left would be to compromise with and surrender to U.S. imperialism.

2. A powerful north Viet Nam will be a decisive factor in the social development of our entire country. But this does not mean that simply because the north is strong, the revolutionary movement in the south will automatically succeed. The powerful north Viet Nam and the revolutionary movement of the south Vietnamese people are mutually complementary and must be closely coordinated; the building of the north itself cannot replace the resolution of the inherent social contradictions of south Viet Nam. Adhering to this correct view, we have avoided opportunistic mistakes. If, on the contrary, we had feared the United States and had no faith in the success of our struggles against it, we would have called on the people in south Viet Nam to "wait" and "coexist peacefully" with the U.S.-Diem clique, and committed an irreparable error. We have correctly handled the relations between north and south Viet Nam. This is a Marxist-Leninist strategic concept which is in conformity with the latest experience in the world developments and those in our own country.

Ho Vows to "Fight Until Complete Victory," 1966

Compatriots and fighters throughout the country!
The barbarous U.S. imperialists have unleashed a war of aggression in an attempt to conquer our country, but they are sustaining big defeats.

They have rushed an expeditionary corps of about 300,000 men into the southern part of our country. They have used a puppet administration and a mercenary army fostered by them as instruments of their aggressive policy. They have resorted to extremely savage means of warfare—toxic chemicals, napalm bombs, and so forth. With such crimes they hope to subdue our southern compatriots.

But under the firm and wise leadership of the NFLSV [National Front for the Liberation of South Vietnam, or NLF], the South Viet-Nam army and people, closely united and fighting heroically, have scored very glorious victories and are determined to struggle until complete victory with a view to liberating the South, defending the North, and subsequently achieving national reunification.

The U.S. aggressors have brazenly launched air attacks on North Viet-Nam in an attempt to get out of the quagmire in the South and to impose negotiations on us on their terms.

But North Viet-Nam will not falter. Our army and people have shown redoubled eagerness in the emulation to produce and fight heroically. So far we have blasted out of the skies more than 1,200 aircraft. We are determined to defeat the enemy's war of destruction and at the same time to extend all-out support to our dear compatriots in the South.

Of late the U.S. aggressors hysterically took a very serious step further in the escalation of the war: They launched air attacks on the suburbs of Hanoi and Haiphong. That was an act of desperation comparable to the agony convulsions of a grievously wounded wild beast.

Johnson and his clique should realize this: They may bring in 500,000 troops, 1 million, or even more to step up the war of aggression in South Viet-Nam. They may use thousands of aircraft for intensified attacks against North Viet-Nam. But never will they be able to break the iron will of the heroic Vietnamese people to fight against U.S. aggression, for national salvation. The more truculent they are, the further they will aggravate their crime. The war may still last ten, twenty years, or longer. Hanoi, Haiphong, and other cities and enterprises may be destroyed, but the Vietnamese people will not be intimidated! Nothing is more precious than independence and freedom. When victory day comes, our people will rebuild our country and endow it with bigger and more beautiful construction.

It is common knowledge that each time they are about to step up their criminal war, the U.S. aggressors always resort to their peace talks swindle in an attempt to fool world opinion and blame Viet-Nam for unwillingness to enter into peace talks!

President Johnson! Reply publicly to the American people and the peoples of the world: Who has sabotaged the Geneva Agreements which guarantee the sovereignty, independence, unity, and territorial integrity of Viet-Nam? Have Vietnamese troops invaded the United States and massacred Americans: Is it not the U.S. Government which has sent U.S. troops to invade Viet-Nam and massacre the Vietnamese?

Let the United States end its war of aggression in Viet-Nam, withdraw from this country all U.S. and satellite troops, and peace will return here at once. . . .

The Vietnamese people cherish peace, genuine peace, peace in independence and freedom, not sham peace, American peace.

For the defense of the independence of the fatherland and for the fulfillment of our obligation to the peoples struggling against U.S. imperialism, our people and army, united as one man, will resolutely fight until complete victory, whatever the sacrifices and hardships may be. In the past we defeated the Japanese fascists and the French colonialists in much more difficult junctures. Today the conditions at home and abroad are more favorable; our people's struggle against U.S. aggression for national salvation is sure to win a total victory.

✗ *E S S A Y S*

In the first essay, written at the height of the war, Douglas Pike explores the appeal of Vietnamese communism. Currently a member of the Institute of East Asian Affairs at the University of California, Berkeley, he ascribes the National Liberation Front's success to a combination of organizational expertise and revolutionary mystique. Yet Pike also argues that Marxism-Leninism was un-Vietnamese in nature since it stood at variance from the most deeply ingrained Vietnamese views of the universe. In the next essay, independent scholar Frances FitzGerald presents a sharply divergent analysis. Stressing the importance of Ho Chi Minh's leadership role, she argues that Ho's version of Marxism-Leninism successfully blended traditional Vietnamese values with Western optimism. The result was an ideology that offered the surest path to national unity and independence. FitzGerald contends as well that the NLF was a legitimate southern political movement and one with strong appeal to the great mass of rural people, not simply Hanoi's puppet. In the final essay, William J. Duiker of Pennsylvania State University insists on the centrality of North Vietnam's role in the southern revolutionary movement. He concludes that the North Vietnamese directed and controlled the revolution in the south and suggests that northern fears of southern autonomy often generated tensions within the communist camp.

Revolutionary Mystique

DOUGLAS PIKE

To those outside Vietnam there was a general perception, one shared neither by Vietnamese nor by foreigners within the country, that South Vietnam was a place of terror and sudden death, of coups d'état and bombings, of alarms and excursions by night. These things did exist. Yet somehow they remained in perspective and did not dominate the lives of either Americans or Vietnamese, in or out of Saigon. Tolstoy, although writing of another time and place, described exactly how it was:

> The tales and descriptions of that time without exception speak only of the self-sacrifice, patriotic devotion, despair, grief, and the heroism. . . . But it was not really so. It appears so to us because we see only the general historic interest of that time and do not see all the personal human interests that people had. Yet in reality those personal interests of the moment so much transcend the general interests that they always prevent the public interest from being felt or even noticed. Most of the people at that time paid no attention to the general progress of events but were guided only by their private interests. . . .

Thousands of Vietnamese villagers lived through the entire 1960–1965 period without being involved in, and hardly ever being inconvenienced by, either the NLF's armed struggle or the GVN's military operations. Although subjected to great NLF organizational and political attention, the average rural Vietnamese was seldom if ever a direct victim of its violence program. The mental picture held by most Americans of rural Vietnam as a vast, boiling battlefield, of innumerable military engagements by day, of villages again and again torn apart by ARVN-guerrilla clashes, of a people in the midst of constant fighting and bloodshed, with no place to hide, living in a sort of no man's land between two contending armies—that picture simply does not hold up under scrutiny.

A villager of course would be monumentally affected if his village found itself under guerrilla attack, was the scene of a battle between ARVN troops and the guerrillas, or, if in a liberated area, was bombed or napalmed. But the odds of this happening in the 1960–1964 period were not much greater than the odds of being hit by lightning. If, on a statistical basis, a single rural villager was selected at random and studied in terms of how much the war impinged on his life, how often he witnessed combat or even saw combatants, it is most likely that he never would have been directly affected to any degree. The author talked to innumerable villagers in all parts of Vietnam, and most of them spoke of the effects of the war on others but admitted that it had never fallen on them.

The average rural Vietnamese could plant his rice, watch it grow, harvest it, and begin the cycle again, placidly unconcerned, unaffected by the swirl around him. The result was that he did not perceive the situation in Vietnam as a "war" in the same way that Americans regard the Vietnam "war." Thus the frequently stated observation that the Vietnamese peasant "has known nothing but war for twenty years," although technically accurate, is also misleading. An American reading this formed a mental picture of the peasant in "war" under circumstances quite different from reality.

The basic characteristics of the NLF and its activities were the use of a united-front organization to establish a mass base of support; organization of the rural people, employing both rational appeals to self-interest and coercion, and then using the specially created social movements in antigovernmental activity; heavy use of various techniques for the communication of ideas to foment social strife; use of specialized military actions, selective in nature and psychological in intent; use of the Communist party *apparat,* and Communist doctrine among the leaders and full-time cadres, to establish orthodoxy and maintain discipline. The goal was control of the population and, through this control, organization of the people as a weapon against the government. But it was more than this. It was more than simply the inculcation of new beliefs or differing attitudes. The NLF's ultimate objective taken together with other activities was to create a new socialization pattern.

The NLF was concerned with the deepest social values. It sought to create a new system of formal and informal groupings by which the socialization was to be accomplished and behavior regulated. It manipulated economic activities, the base for all human activities, in such a way as to increase the degree of communalism or collectivization and thus to some degree alter the village means of production; it introduced a new political structure to keep internal order and to regulate contact within South Vietnam, particularly with respect to villagers hostile to the NLF; it manipulated educational and other intellectual activities within the village. It apparently attempted to substitute a disguised brand of Marxism for traditional religious beliefs, although in an oblique manner; and it introduced new language terminology, social mythology, and folklore. In short, it attempted to work within the totality of village life and provide a new cultural focus.

Understanding sociopolitical developments in Vietnam involves cataloging the various social and political groups, organizations, cliques, and clans—some of them covert and almost all of them parochial or regional in nature—and then mapping the interrelationships among these various forces. Political infighting consists not so much of open confrontation with one's opponent (or even directly and forcibly destroying him) as it does of drowning, absorbing, splintering, fragmenting, discrediting, turning him aside, or, if necessary, joining him and working at his side to eliminate him. The immediate goal is usually status or prestige more than pure political power. The NLF was superior in this type of political struggle—especially in the rural areas—chiefly because success in this effort depends on good organizational ability and skilled management of social movements. Therefore the secret of NLF success in the early years—and they were many— was organization. Probably the NLF expended more time, money, and manpower on organizational activity than on all other activities combined. Further, this effort was concentrated in what was an organizational vacuum.

In those areas of the country where it had firm and continuous social control the NLF was in effect a society within a society, with its own social structure, values, and coercive instruments. The NLF cadres made a conscious and massive effort to extend political participation, even if it was manipulated, on the local level so as to involve the people in a self-contained, self-supporting revolution. The functional liberation associations at the village level attempted to serve each individual member in terms of his own personal interests while at the same time developing a deep revolutionary consciousness. Ironically, as the result of increased coercion on the part of the NLF, as its popular support dwindled, its actual authority increased. What had been essentially a persuasive mechanism became basically a coercive one, not so much because of the failure of the original NLF social organization pattern as because of the arrival of Northern cadres who were unwilling to trust the original form because they felt in the long run that it would not serve the interests of the Party and indeed might become a threat to it. Once again, the not unfamiliar story of the revolution betrayed. But the organization at all times, whether persuasive or coercive, remained the central NLF activity in the village.

That the leaders of this enterprise were professionals must be evident from the structure they created. It is difficult, however, to estimate the number of NLF leaders and cadres who were professional revolutionaries.

Most of them were vastly experienced, some by choice, some by circumstance. The initial NLF leadership corps was made up of the ex-Viet Minh. Many of these, probably the majority, were professionals such as doctors, lawyers, and teachers. They were competent and enjoyed high status among their followers. Most of them had been in the movement, either Viet Minh or NLF, for most of their lives, although generally the guerrilla leaders had served longer than the civilians. Within the NLF these early leaders came to hold the main-line administrative posts or became the commanders of the Main Force units. They were inclined to be more nationalistic and less doctrinal than those who came after them, and they were far less pro-DRV. Those who rose in prominence after the launching of the NLF, that is, in the early 1960's, were more politically oriented, less apt to have a professional background, and therefore of somewhat lower status in the eyes of the rank and file. They were more doctrinal, more anti-GVN, pro-DRV, and pro-Communist. With the regularization came both cadres and top leaders from the North; their great social trauma had been the Viet Minh war. Most had been young cadres during the Viet Minh war and had climbed the status ladder in the North according to DRV standards, which meant they excelled in Communist virtues, technical competence, zeal, discipline, and unwavering faith in the cause. They had a vested interest in victory through following orders from Hanoi, for it was there that their homes were located, their families lived, and their careers were rooted. Their motivation was quite different; it was North Vietnamese whether or not they had originally come from the South. Above all, these Northern-trained leaders, and they were found chiefly in the NLF military apparatus, were professionals, less marked by the self-righteous puritanism that characterized the earliest NLF leadership group or the individual initiative and revolutionary consciousness that marked those who rose in the ranks during the early stages of the insurgency. They were less moved by the deep sense of frustration that drove the earlier leaders, and their devotion to the cause stemmed more from career building than from ideology or hatred.

One of the most persistent questions asked about the NLF follower was "Why did he join?" The implication in the question is that for one or more rational or emotional reasons the individual Vietnamese decided to enlist in the cause, did so, and thus entered as a believer. . . . Almost the reverse was the case. The Vietnamese youth was first surrounded by a social organization that he had no hand in creating but to which he somehow belonged. Through a process of insinuation the youth came to realize that he was part of the NLF, never quite sure of how this happened and never with any overt choice presented to him. The process of glacially slow recruitment came first, the mystique was developed later. Or, as it has been aptly put, conversion followed subversion. Therefore not motives but circumstances must be considered in understanding the recruitment pattern and its contribution to the NLF mystique.

The most common answer given by a *quy chanh* [defector from the NLF] to questions concerning the circumstances under which he became part of the NLF indicated that he was initially drawn into the organization and later recruited. He might first be asked to act as a messenger, or to take part in a struggle movement, or to deliver leaflets to an agent in the provincial capital. Then he would be urged to join his friends in a study group that might also be a literacy class. Then he would be asked to commit some act of violence; at this point, whether he knew it or not, he was in the net. When handled skillfully, subtly, and gradually, a teen-aged youth did not realize that he was involved until he was already enmeshed. This technique succeeded, for the most part, not in areas where the GVN was exerting itself but in the remote villages where the NLF and the Viet Minh before it were the only visible "government" the youth had ever known. And so the *quy chanh* would say, "Everyone seemed to think it was the correct thing to do," often adding plaintively, "There didn't seem to be any danger. The Saigon government was so far away I didn't think they would ever know about me." Of course a small minority actually sought out and joined the NLF. These included draft dodgers, military deserters, those who hated the government for some personal reason, opportunists, the ambitious who were seeking status, the rejected, the adventurers, and all the others in [philosopher] Eric Hoffer's categories of the True Believer.

For the most part, however, the supporters were recruited under circumstances where there was no alternative. Most recruitment was from among social groups such as the religious sects, with grievances against the government, and less effort was placed on the recruitment of individuals at random. At the same time the NLF sought to create situations that would give rise to grievances among such groups so as to facilitate recruitment. Once the youth was recruited, the training and indoctrination work supplied the rationale for belonging.

Americans and others often assumed that the NLF army members were fanatics. Because they performed well in combat, it was argued, they were highly motivated, which meant dedication to an ideological cause. Thus the search was for the essence of this belief. It proved elusive, largely because it did not exist. The best of the military units—the Main Force units—were highly effective because they were composed of professionals. These were not green young Vietnamese farmers, only recently introduced to the rifle, but experienced guerrillas who had been fighting most of their adult lives. What impelled them was not ideology so much as professional competence, much like the United States Marine or the French Foreign Legionnaire. The men in the best of these units were very good; their discipline was superb; they knew how to use camouflage well, a requirement for survival; they were well skilled in small-unit tactics, especially the ambush in its many variations; they trained hard, rehearsed, and practiced attacks until letter perfect, and then they fought hard. Their mystique should be attributed chiefly to a unit *esprit de corps* that stemmed from the consensus that each man in the unit was a superior and vastly experienced professional.

The strength of the NLF was the result of careful organization building, not the product of some unique spirit or élan. The mystique, to the degree that it existed and bound together the separate building blocks of the movement, resulted from indoctrinational efforts, shared social myths, and leader-led relations. The mystique's functions were, first, identity, stemming from the doctrinal course of the Revolution, the ideology of communism, and the recruitment pattern; and, second, unity, resulting from the nature of the leadership, the indoctrination itself, and individual self-motivating standards of behavior.

The various pseudoscientific laws that the leadership regarded as governing the Revolution were at no time themselves challenged by the NLF followers, nor was the principle that such definitive laws existed, as asserted in these terms in an early NLF document:

> A revolution develops according to objective laws, which exist independently of man's wish. The revolutionary should not rely on his subjective wish but should rely on objective reality, on the objective law of social development, to act and promote the development of history. To lead the Revolution correctly is to act in such a manner that under concrete historical conditions one can mobilize and organize all forces that can be mobilized in order to bring the Revolution to victory. . . .

The leadership considered its chief doctrinal task to be the translation of abstract theory into the setting of a traditional society. It did this by placing prime value on loyalty, as perhaps all such groups must. The Revolution assumed a pragmatic, not greatly intellectual, cast, and it was characterized by an absence of agonizing. It lacked the depth of thought marked by, say, the Russian Revolution and far more resembled the Chinese revolution. To both the NLF and the PRP [People's Revolutionary Party, the Communist Party of South Vietnam], determinants of success were twofold: revolutionary capability, including the proclivity for revolution by the Vietnamese people themselves, and PRP leadership, which is to say Communist leadership. The people's revolutionary capability was more asserted than proven, and the Party's monopolistic leadership imposed rather than prescribed. Both developed into articles of faith, a mystic belief in the power and loyalty of the people and a sense of trust in the omniscience of the Party. What was then required was to put the formula to work: The people would support the Revolution if only the cadres would show them that their interests were identical to the cause, would constantly agitate them so as to prevent loss of ardor, and would develop them into creatures of initiative who would act and not merely react.

No evidence was ever uncovered to indicate that schisms existed in the early years on the proper course of the Revolution. The quarrel that did develop . . . lay in writing the final act of the revolutionary drama— whether it should consist of the General Uprising, the Mao-Giap third stage, or negotiated settlement. The dispute was resolved in favor of the Mao-Giap thesis, not through discussion or by successfully decimating the two other alternatives but because the new supraleadership in Hanoi concluded that it represented the correct course to pursue and used its Northern-trained and Northern-loyal cadres to force acceptance of its decision.

However, even in the days when it was the dominant doctrine, the leadership consistently overestimated its progress and several times erroneously believed that the moment of the General Uprising had arrived. Internal documents from a Lao Dong Youth League conference in June 1961, for example, stated that speakers at that time asserted flatly that the General Uprising would take place in the first three months of 1962 and that all cadres must plan accordingly. After the overthrow of the Diem government and again in the spring of 1965 the leadership apparently believed the moment had come, only to have their hopes again dashed. These failures undoubtedly contributed to the decision to "militarize" the struggle and pursue victory by means of the Mao-Giap third stage. But this triggered a new level of American response, which meant that from a doctrinal standpoint it had failed as much as had the General Uprising thesis.

In sum, from a standpoint of mystique the General Uprising served the NLF well through the golden days of the Revolution. It was not mere window dressing but the justification and rationalization for the insurgency, the cement that held the effort together, and a powerful tool for agit-prop team use in working with villagers. In the end it failed because it was not sufficiently rooted in reality, because it could work only if the Communists' assessment of the social milieu in the South was correct, which it was not.

The NLF and the people it influenced lived in a muzzy, myth-filled world of blacks and whites, good and evil, a simplistic world quite out of character with the one to which the Vietnamese was accustomed. But it created a powerful external image for the Vietnamese immersed in the cause, restructuring his reality, providing him with a new identity and a boundless sense of unity. The elements of this mystique were fourfold.

First, it was characterized by great moralism and was far more moral than ideological. Virtue was the golden word. The cause consisted of moral duties based on moral absolutes, guided by moral imperatives; duty itself, under a virtuous leadership, was the highest value. Preoccupation with law and legality was not simply an effort to establish legitimacy but a justification of the moral correctness of the cause. Because he was virtuous, the NLF supporter was morally superior to the enemy and hence politically and militarily superior. The moralism manifested itself in a spirit of sincerity; the NLF surrounded its words and actions with an aura of sincerity.

Second, it was characterized by extreme romanticism. The NLF leaders, like Mao Tse-tung and Ho Chi Minh before them, were romantic rebels who saw themselves as idealists. Idealistic appeals abounded: the promise of the good life in utopian terms; the opportunity to revolt against all the evil, injustice, and inequity of this world; the chance to be part of a great crusade. But behind these was the romantic lure of the struggle itself; the means not the ends counted. There was more glory along the road than at its end. The clandestine organization made up of multitudes of inner groups, cults, and secret arrangements played on the Vietnamese individual's romantic love of the devious. . . . Yet in general the NLF mystique was less a positive cause than a negation. But this too had lure to the romantic— the lure of anarchy, beyond which, if it failed, lay the lure of martyrdom. The NLF in creating its mystique was acutely sensitive to the age-old Asian attitude of fatalism.

Third, its mystique was imitative and therefore militantly defensive, which probably should be counted as a weakness. The NLF leader was driven by a compulsive search for answers from elsewhere, anywhere. Examples were taken from other places and they were forced, and from other times and they were distorted. If the NLF was not slavishly copying Mao Tse-tung on the Long March, it was employing the Viet Minh's analysis of French Maginot Line thinking as it applied to the Americans, or calling on all cadres to repeat in a literal manner some victory scored a few months earlier in another part of Vietnam. The constant scanning of the horizon was part of a preoccupation with contemplation and self-analysis. Cadres, in a curious form of intellectualism, would explain the Revolution over and over to their most disinterested students—the rural Vietnamese. Copied though it was, it provided the supporter with a worldview that might not be understood but was satisfactory. Through indoctrination and even socialization he received needed psychological support and release from cultural tensions. (The same psychiatrist said the NLF was a father image led by Ho Chi Minh.)

And finally there was a will to believe, perhaps a characteristic of any mystique. It grew from the sense of universality of a movement representing Vietnam, the world, excluding not even a full social class (the enemies in Saigon and Washington). It was based on an assessment of the world environment that the NLF believed made Revolution in Vietnam irresistible and doomed GVN and U.S. prowess to steady deterioration. It was based on faith in the Vietnamese people's revolutionary capability, faith in the doctrinal approach, faith in revolutionary guerrilla warfare consisting of the combined armed and political struggle, and the infallible wisdom of the Party's leaders, who from long experience could divine the laws of history.

Marxism-Leninism as filtered through first Chinese and then Vietnamese thought contributed much to the NLF mystique. After the regularization efforts not only Communist thought but the communist-society goal was proclaimed openly, as previously it had been asserted internally. For example, the PRP asserted in a Radio Liberation broadcast, December 9, 1964, that its ultimate objective was a communist state, and the only question was whether this would come early or late:

> The [enemy] slanders us saying that our Party monopolizes the Front and that our Party's solidarity policy is nothing more than a trick for the present. . . . It says the Party's strategic objectives are against those of the Front, such as national independence, democracy, peace, and neu-

trality, and they say that our Party cannot pursue a sincere and lasting policy of solidarity with the Front. This argument proves that the enemies of our people do not understand anything about our Party of Marxism-Leninism. . . . The general Marxist-Leninist principles of the working class are aimed at rallying the majority of the forces into a united national front, a worker-peasant alliance led by the working class. . . . Our Party does not conceal its ultimate objective, which is to achieve socialism and communism. But our Party has never ceased pointing out that the path leading to that objective is long, and that the objective cannot be achieved in a few years, but several score years. . . .

A Communist condition had prevailed within the NLF from the start and was assumed as a matter of course by Vietnamese of all political shadings. With respect to the mystique the matter of communism's paramountcy became somewhat more complex. Partly it was a matter of definition.

If a Communist is one who believes that man's future is shaped by his tools of production, that history is dominated by a class struggle for control of those means of production, that capitalism must grow increasingly evil, and that a brotherhood of workers and farmers swearing allegiance to an international ideal must unite to seize power and build its own society led by the vanguard, the proletariat, and in turn by the vanguard of the vanguard, the Communist party—if this is a Communist, then there were few Communists among the NLF. If, however, a Communist is one who swears blind allegiance to the world movement whose loci of power are Moscow and Peking, from which in this instance via Hanoi he draws through a political umbilical cord sustenance and strength that he cannot, and does not want to, supply himself, then most of the NLF's leaders, cadres, and true believers were Communists.

It was the difference between philosophic communism and alliance communism. For, in the first instance, to be a Communist meant mastering Marxism-Leninism, which NLF Vietnamese found notoriously difficult to understand since it is distinctly un-Vietnamese in nature and at variance with their most deeply ingrained views of the universe. (For example, it must have been indeed a Herculean task for a cadre to convince a Vietnamese that matter and not God or Spirit is the ultimate reality, or that nothing is inherently unknowable.) The second instance meant simply establishing identity and achieving unity in which an NLF supporter had only to approve of the powerful foreign forces that stood behind him and his cause. Only among the higher-echelon cadres, and even here not with total acceptance, was communism regarded as a new body of wisdom to be learned, understood, and put to use.

Thus the NLF was Communist not because it incorporated Communist doctrine but because it linked itself to foreign states that did. This distinction, or weakness, meant that the strengths that hold Communists and Communist movements together during dark days elsewhere were largely absent in Vietnam.

The Communist Appeal

FRANCES FITZGERALD

The American soldiers in Vietnam discovered their own ignorance in an immediate way. The NLF guerrillas chose the night and the jungles to fight in, similarly, and they chose to work with that part of the population which was the most obscure to the Americans and to the Saigon government officials. For the Americans to discern the enemy within the world of the Vietnamese village was to attempt to make out figures within a landscape indefinite and vague—underwater, as it were. Landing from helicopters in a village controlled by the NLF, the soldiers would at first see nothing, having no criteria with which to judge what they saw. As they searched the village, they would find only old men, women, and children, a collection of wooden tools whose purpose they did not know, altars with scrolls in Chinese characters, paths that led nowhere: an economy, a geography, an architecture totally alien to them. . . .

In an attempt to justify the American bombing of North Vietnam and the dispatch of American troops to the south, the U.S. State Department in February 1965 issued a White Paper entitled *Aggression from the North: The Record of North Vietnam's Campaign to Conquer South Vietnam*. In this paper, State Department officials claimed that the NLF was no more than an instrument of North Vietnam working against the hopes of all the South Vietnamese for peace, independence, prosperity, and freedom. Had these official claims been true, they would have delineated a situation not very different from the civil wars in Nigeria or Pakistan. And a civil war did not, it seemed, always require American intervention—particularly on the weaker side.

But the Vietnam War was not a civil war; it was a revolutionary war that had raged throughout the entire country since 1945. The strength of the revolution had always been in the north, but the Viet Minh had considerable success south of the 17th parallel. In the period of truce following the Geneva Conference the Viet Minh had, in obedience to the military protocols for disengagement, regrouped some ninety thousand soldiers to the north—most of them southerners. Still, below the 17th parallel there remained hundreds of thousands of Viet Minh cadres, local guerrillas, and their sympathizers. The majority of the remaining Viet Minh were not Communists—no more were the majority of the northerners. But many of them had, like the northerners, lived for the years of the war within a political and social system very different from that obtaining in the rest of South Vietnam. In certain areas such as the Ca Mau peninsula, the region west and northwest of Saigon, and northern central Vietnam, villages, often whole districts, belonged to the revolution just as others belonged to the sects. The people of these regions had firmly expected that the end of the war would bring a unified Vietnam under the government of Ho Chi Minh. When six years later the National Liberation Front was formed, the new movement appeared to them only as the logical continuation of the old one. As one village elder told an American in 1964, "The Liberation grew right up from this place. It happened gradually. Another generation started it. Let us say I am now fifty years old, those who are thirty are now going and those who are twenty come to take their place."

And there was a strong element of continuity between the two movements: a continuity of people, of war aims, and of operating methods. The leaders of the NLF worked in close cooperation with the north, even during the years just following the truce, but it was not until the intervention of American combat troops that they became dependent on the north for war materials and for men. In such a situation the notion of "control" becomes ambiguous. (It is difficult, for instance, to imagine that with its own resources and matériel, the NLF had *no* influence in Hanoi.) But even if the NLF had always been "controlled" by Hanoi, the American official conclusion that it was therefore illegitimate as a southern political movement does not by any means follow. The personnel of the NLF was, with few exceptions, southern. Northern troops did not enter the south until the American troops had already arrived. If the north was indeed trying to conquer the south, it was doing so by politics and culture but not by force. But even this case is impossible to make in a clear-cut manner, for there were southerners within the Politburo of Hanoi. The details are incidental.

The National Liberation Front was founded in 1960, but the guerrilla movement in the south began some two or three years earlier. After the Geneva Conference, the active Communist cadres in the south instructed their followers to disband and wait for two years until the national elections were held and a political settlement made. All official Viet Minh activities stopped except for the "legal struggle" for the elections. The NLF leader, Nguyen Huu Tho, later explained this decision of 1954: "There were mixed feelings about the two years' delay over reunification but the general sentiment was that this was a small price to pay for the return to peace and a normal life, free of foreign rule."

Peace did not, however, last very long for most of the southern Viet Minh. In 1955 Ngo Dinh Diem repudiated the Geneva proposals for national elections and began his campaign of terror against the former members of the Resistance. From the accounts of the Viet Minh cadres it appeared that the campaign was largely successful in destroying what remained of the Viet Minh organization and in reducing the villages to subserviency. While some of the Party members fled to Saigon, where they would not be recognized or pursued, others banded together and went into hiding in the jungles and swamps that had served them as base areas during the war. As one cadre remembered, "In those days you could say we were 'based' in the mountains, but these were 'bases' for survival. We had no arms at all and barely the means of existence. . . . Control was so close that it was impossible for us cadres to live among the people. But we came down from the hills at night to try to make contacts."

According to the French historian, Philippe Devillers, the southern cadre at this point pressed for a renewal of the struggle, but the north held back, urging the southerners to give a respite for the consolidation of the DRVN. While Hanoi surely supported the aims of the southern cadre, its judgment on the timing and the policy to be pursued may well have conflicted with that of the southerners. Certainly the northerners then and for several years later limited their aid to the most easily procured commodity of advice. Weapons could be much more easily obtained from the GVN outposts and the Americans than from convoys traveling the long trail down from the north.

In the long run, however, the Diemist repressions only advanced the date of a new armed struggle. They persuaded many of the former Resistance members whose one goal had been to defeat the French that they could not live in physical safety under the Diem regime, that peace was not peace but a continuation of the war. Diemist policy in general threatened the sects and convinced certain intellectuals and rural notables that the new regime would not serve their interests or leave them a hope for future success, as the French and the Bao Daiist administrations once had. A highly trained and dedicated group of soldiers and political instructors, the active Communist cadre in the south went to work on these groups. By 1958 they had established a small network of committees in most of the old Viet Minh strongholds: in the U Minh forest at the southern tip of the Delta, in the jungles west of Saigon and in the west of Quang Nam province. In the next two years they moved out rapidly from their base areas, infiltrating the nearby hamlets, overrunning small GVN outposts to supply themselves with weapons, taking over hamlets, and recruiting again. At the same time they expanded the movement politically, taking in the former Resistance members who did not belong to the hard core and the members of the other political factions alienated by the Diem regime. In December 1960, they formed the National Liberation Front and adopted a ten-point program of "peace, national independence, democratic freedoms, improvement of the people's living conditions, and peaceful national reunification."

Over the next two years the NLF leaders—men who remained for the moment anonymous to the outside world—molded the loose grouping of committees into a close-knit political and military organization. By mid-1961, so American intelligence indicated, its strength had reached fifteen thousand, and half of the guerrillas were fully armed. This military force, known as the People's Self-Defense Forces, developed by a process known to its cadres as "growth and split." A platoon of experienced fighters would split up to train three platoons of new recruits. The company thus formed would split again to train three new companies, and so forth. In the early years these forces remained dispersed in small units, each unit remaining close to the village that formed its own supply base. The plan for expansion included the carefully coordinated activities of propaganda, recruitment,

terrorism against the local GVN officials and soldiers, and the establishment
of governing committees and mass organizations within the newly liberated
villages.

In February 1962, the Front convened a clandestine congress of one
hundred delegates and chose a central committee composed of men of every
political color, from Communists to Saigonese intellectuals to religious
dignitaries from the various sects, including a Catholic priest. Nguyen Huu
Tho, the non-Communist Saigonese lawyer whom Diem imprisoned in 1954
for peace activities, was chosen president. While the makeup of this committee opened the way to a coalition in the event that the United States
should withdraw support from the Saigon government, the "hard-core"
former Resistance fighters formed the only real political party within it—
and thus the controlling element. Until 1962 these men, along with their
colleagues among the southern regroupees, belonged to the Marxist-Leninist
Party of the DRVN, the Lao Dong. At the time of the congress they formed
a new and specifically southern party, the People's Revolutionary Party,
that called itself the "vanguard" and the "steel frame" of the NLF. When
the United States did not withdraw and the Saigon regime did not disin-
tegrate after the fall of the Ngos, the PRP began to expand inside the NLF,
absorbing some of the non-Communists and recruiting new members from
the villages. As the NLF members recognized, the Marxist-Leninist Party
was what gave the Front the strength and discipline to engage in the second
and much more difficult phase of the Liberation war.

By 1962 the NLF had reached an important stage in its development.
At the battle of Ap Bac it showed a group of unbelieving American advisers
that its guerrilla forces could stand up against a multi-battalion ARVN
operation supported by U.S. helicopters and artillery. This military achievement was not an isolated phenomenon. It was the visible expression of an
underlying political reality. By 1962 the NLF had a presence in some 80
percent of the rural communities of South Vietnam. Not only had it retaken
the old Viet Minh territories, but it had expanded outward from them, and
most noticeably into the central regions of the Mekong Delta, where the
Viet Minh had never succeeded in raising more than a collection of guerrilla
bands. It was obviously not just a regional group or a coalition of special
interests, but a national movement with appeal for the great mass of the
rural people. The next war would be something more than a repeat of the
Viet Minh war in the south.

The last point was significant—and somewhat mysterious because of
the very continuity between the Viet Minh and the NLF. The two organizations were more alike than not in organization, program, and technique.
The NLF leaders had the advantage of experience, but they had the disadvantage that the nationalist component of their struggle was not at all as
obvious as that of the Viet Minh. Apart from racial or cultural opposition,
"nationalism" is, after all, a most difficult abstraction. It took a certain
amount of political and economic theory to demonstrate that the American
role in Vietnam was in many ways equivalent to that of the French—
particularly in the early years when there was no American presence in

the countryside. As one Front cadre admitted, the peasants did not grasp the national question as well as the city recruits. And yet it was precisely the peasants who were joining the NLF in large numbers. One explanation, and perhaps the only possible one, was that there were new social and political issues at stake—or issues that the peasants had never felt with such acuity before.

Given the personal view that the Vietnamese take of politics, the stance and personality of Ho Chi Minh had a significance for the political system as a whole that escapes Western political science "concepts." For the Vietnamese, Ho Chi Minh was not only "the George Washington of his country," as an American senator once put it. He was the personification of the revolution—the representative of the new community to itself. For that reason the study of Ho Chi Minh is perhaps more important to an understanding of the Vietnamese revolution than an analysis of all the ideological debates. For Ho was perfectly conscious of his role. He orchestrated his own public gestures just as carefully as the emperors had performed the rites in order to *show* the Vietnamese what had to be done. His reticence was in itself a demonstration.

Quite consciously, Ho Chi Minh forswore the grand patriarchal tradition of the Confucian emperors. Consciously he created an "image" of himself as "Uncle Ho"—the gentle, bachelor relative who has only disinterested affection for the children who are *not* his own sons. As a warrior and a politician he acted ruthlessly upon occasion, but in public and as head of state he took pains to promote that family feeling which Vietnamese have often had for their leaders, and which he felt was the proper relationship between the people and their government. "Our Party," he said, "is great because it covers the whole country and is at the same time close to the heart of every compatriot. . . . It has won so much love in thirty years of struggle and success." Whether in giving sweets to children or in asking the peasants what they received of the hog that was killed for the cadre's birthday, he evoked the world of the old village, where strict patriarchal rule was mitigated by the egalitarian pressure of the small community. The affairs of small nations, he seemed to suggest, are qualitatively different from those of large ones: Vietnam would need none of the great powers' grandiose illusions—or their grandiose brutalities. The Vietnamese style should be that of simplicity combined with inner strength and resiliency. Ho Chi Minh, with his wispy figure, his shorts and sandals, had the sense of irony and understatement so common among Vietnamese. When asked by a European why he had never written a book of his own "Thoughts," he answered with perfect ambiguity that Mao Tse-tung had written all there was to say, hadn't he? In his last will and testament to the Vietnamese people Ho made no claims to singularity. He merely hoped that Vietnam would make a "worthy contribution" to world revolution; he hoped, too, that he would not be given a great funeral lest it "waste the time and money of the people."

Just days before the Tet offensive of 1968, the NLF cadres from the battalions that were to assault Saigon took their men—or so it was reported—to a certain place in the forest to give them their last instructions and words of encouragement. There, where the underbrush had been cleared away for acres, they showed them the hundreds of coffins they had built for the soldiers who would be killed in battle. When they had seen the coffins, the soldiers, it seemed, felt happier and less afraid to die.

As [scholar] Paul Mus once said, the Vietnamese know a great deal better than we do that society is largely made up of its dead. For the Vietnamese, life is but a moment of transition in the unbroken skein of other lives stretching from the past into the future. Death in the absolute sense comes only when there is a break in the society that carries life on through the generations. Such a break had come in the life of the Ngo family; it had by the 1960's occurred to most Vietnamese families of the south. It was not just that so many had lost their sons and their ancestral lands in the war; it was that even before the war so few of the young people had practiced the rites of ancestor worship. They had not practiced the rites because they were, as the young said, "not practical." But the NLF had offered them a new kind of family, a new form of social security. The sight of the coffins reassured the soldiers because it showed them not only that the Front cared about their future, but that it could fulfill its promises. The provision of the coffins was, after all, a logistical triumph and, as such, a sign that the Front had the power to reweave the society and restore its continuity through past, present, and future. The weaver of that unity was Ho Chi Minh.

Upon his return to Vietnam in the 1940's, Ho Chi Minh set up his headquarters in a cave in the northern mountains above a swiftly rushing river. He renamed that mountain Marx and the river Lenin, making a symbolic connection between the ancient Vietnamese image that defined the country and the new history in which that country would live. His method was traditional—the rectification of names. Ho Chi Minh's life made the same connection. As a child he lived in the countryside with his mandarin father, who had engaged in the last resistance of the traditional Confucians to the West. As a young man he had gone West—to Paris, to Moscow, and then back to Vietnam by way of China. As a mature man he had made the synthesis, turning Western theories and methods to use against the Western occupation of his country. Through Marxism-Leninism he provided the Vietnamese with a new way to perceive their society and the means to knit it up into the skein of history. He showed them the way back to many of the traditional values and a way forward to the optimism of the West—to the belief in change as progress and the power of the small people. Through Marxism-Leninism he indicated the road to economic development, to a greater social mobility and a greater interaction between the masses of the people and their government. He reformed the villages, linked them together, and created a nation. Whether or not the system could stand up to the full force of the American war, whether it would last a thousand years, whether it would in the end prove only destructive to Vietnam and the rest of Southeast Asia, it was, nonetheless, a way to national unity and independence, and, by the end of the American war, still the only way the Vietnamese knew.

Hanoi's Southern Strategy

WILLIAM J. DUIKER

For the Party leadership in Hanoi, Diem's performance in the South was probably disconcerting, but not necessarily cause for alarm. Given the realities of the situation, an early resumption of revolutionary struggle in the South was out of the question. Above and beyond the reluctance of the Soviet Union and China to support a renewal of hostilities in Vietnam, there were persuasive domestic reasons to avoid a resumption of the conflict. The D.R.V. would need time to consolidate its authority north of the 17th parallel. With the Party fully in control, the North would soon begin the arduous task of advancing toward socialism. As the Party leadership conceded, this would be a complex and difficult task in an underdeveloped society like North Vietnam. For the foreseeable future, precious natural and human resources would have to be transferred from revolutionary war to nation-building. After a decade of struggle, there was undoubtedly a tangible and natural desire, in the South as in the North, to taste the fruits of peace.

Under the circumstances, it is understandable that for the moment the Party leadership preferred to count on the implementation of the procedures set up at Geneva and to hope that unification elections could be held in order to avoid a costly and bitter struggle. Communist leaders in Hanoi appeared willing, at least for the time being, to pursue a peaceful course. At its Sixth Plenum, held in July 1954, the Central Committee declared its support for a political settlement, but warned that if such means failed it would not hesitate to resort to force once more. Party leaders may have reminded themselves in private (as they did occasionally in public) of the Marxist-Leninist teaching that revolutionary waves come in cycles, that a high tide must be followed by a trough, and that a period of regroupment is necessary before the next revolutionary outbreak. . . .

For the moment, then, the Party attempted to prepare for either contingency [elections being held or not]. According to various estimates, between 50,000 and 90,000 Vietminh sympathizers went to the North after the accords while approximately 10,000 to 15,000 remained in the South. Of the latter, some abandoned political activity, while others were directed to reorganize the Party and the front apparatus on a peacetime basis. Local leaders were instructed to avoid violence and to restrict their activities to peaceful and legal ones, such as the promotion of national elections. On the other hand, the Party leaders in the South should act to protect the

From William J. Duiker, *The Communist Road to Power in Vietnam*. Excerpts from pp. 172–199, 212–214, 233. Reprinted by permission of the author.

remaining revolutionary forces in the area and to maintain the security of the clandestine apparatus. Activities should be conducted on both the legal and semilegal level. Illegal methods were to be used only on a selective basis. . . .

The Party's clandestine organization was not totally dismantled, but it was reduced in size. The Central Office for South Vietnam (COSVN), the southern branch of the VWP [Vietnamese Workers' Party] Central Committee that had been set up in 1951 to provide localized direction for the war in Cochin China, was abolished and replaced by a Regional Committee for the South (Xu uy Nam Bo). Below this committee were three interzone committees, responsible for five to seven provinces each. Le Duan, who had been the principal Party leader in the area during the last years of the war, remained in charge, with another southerner, Pham Hung, as his deputy. As before, headquarters for the secret Party leadership was deep in the Plain of Reeds.

The Party's effort to avoid confrontation with the Saigon government was not particularly successful. Diem refused to play by Hanoi's rules and, far from permitting the old Vietminh apparatus to function on a legal basis, moved vigorously to dig it out root and branch. By the fall of 1954, government security forces had begun to harass the peace movement in Saigon. Several of its leaders were arrested and eventually the headquarters was closed down. In rural areas, Diem launched a "Denounce the Communists" (*To Cong*) campaign, with an emphasis on those areas where the Vietminh organization had traditionally been strong. Communist sources claim that 25,000 suspected Communist sympathizers were arrested, more than 1,000 were killed, and 4,231 were injured. Diem also declared ideological war on communism. Aided by his younger brother and political counselor Ngo Dinh Nhu, he set up several government-sponsored political organizations that were designed to compete with the Communists. Nhu made liberal use of Leninist organizational techniques. To provide an ideological alternative to communism, he attempted to popularize the philosophy of Personalism, a somewhat unwieldy combination of Catholic and Marxist concepts that stressed an amalgamation of Asian communalism and Western libertarianism as the foundation of the new society.

Diem's determined efforts weakened the Communist apparatus in South Vietnam, and his somewhat unorthodox behavior presented the Party leadership with problems. Comments about Diem in a secret Party history of the period are revealing:

> Before Diem unveiled his treacherous face, the people only had a vague idea about him and his administration. Basically, they realized he was just another puppet and they thought he would be in power only for two years. But they did not know that he was dangerously crafty and different from the previous puppets. Some people in the upper strata and many Catholic refugees mistakenly regarded him as a revolutionary scholar. That is why when the U.S.-Diem versus France–Bao Dai clash took place, the people who resented the French and their lackeys were rather pleased to see them defeated by the U.S.-Diem; and a number of people even supported Diem.

Diem paid a high price for his success, however, for his efforts to repress Communist-sponsored activities alienated many non-Communist Vietnamese. Heavy-handed censorship and arbitrary arrests of opposition figures angered Saigon's vociferous corps of intellectuals. In the rural areas corrupt and arrogant officials used their powers indiscriminately and sometimes with brutality. The law was utilized to carry out private vendettas, and the innocent were frequently compelled to pay bribes to avoid arrest.

Such insensitive behavior was undoubtedly a promising sign to Hanoi that the Saigon regime was on the road to self-destruction. In the short run, however, it placed the D.R.V. in an awkward position at a time when Diem's adamant refusal to hold consultations obviously threw Hanoi's political strategy into question. In fact, the Party's immediate options were limited. In August 1955, the Central Committee convened its Eighth Plenum to consider a response and apparently decided that, for the time being, Diem's action should have no effect on the party's strategy toward the South. Primary emphasis would remain on political struggle, and armed activities were to be authorized only in exceptional circumstances. A communiqué issued after the meeting reiterated the Party's preference for unification by "peaceful means" and declared that priority would continue to be assigned to the program of building a socialist society in the North. As if to underline its preference for a peaceful solution, the plenum called for the formation of a broad new Fatherland Front (Mat Tran To Quoc) in the two zones to pressure the United States and the Diem administration to permit reunification elections.

But Diem's declaration of war placed heavy pressure on the revolutionary faithful in the South, who had to bear the full force of the government's repressive activities. Several Communist sources allude to the growing sentiment among the Party rank and file to adopt a more aggressive policy to protect and promote the revolution. Evidently, however, this sentiment was not immediately shared by the new Regional Committee which, in line with official policy in Hanoi, continued to believe that the policy of peaceful political struggle was "the only and correct strategy of struggle." When, in late summer, the committee held its first conference to consider the decisions of the Eighth Plenum in Hanoi, it apparently voiced its approval of existing policy, although it recommended that pressure be placed on the Diem regime to liberalize its policies and hold national elections. The effects of this strategy were apparently beginning to damage the effectiveness of the revolutionary movement in the South. According to the official Party history a number of cadres abandoned their belief in the revolutionary principles of Marxism-Leninism and turned to peaceful reformism. Those who attempted to resist the Diem regime were harassed by government security forces, and their organizations were broken up. . . .

The continuing controversy within the Party leadership over the issue of reunification was reflected in the Tenth Plenum of the Central Committee, held in October of 1956. The Plenum was apparently convened in part to assess policy in the South in light of the international situation and the Diem regime's refusal to hold consultations with the D.R.V. on national elections. But the Central Committee was unable to reach a conclusion on a policy recommendation and asked the Politburo to research the problem for further consideration. According to Vo Nguyen Giap, a report presented by the Politburo at the conference had noted deficiencies in the public understanding of the problem and pointed out that the struggle for reunification was fundamentally a revolutionary task that would require an extended period of time.

It was at this point that Le Duan, head of the Party's Nam Bo Regional Committee, wrote a document that is now described by Hanoi sources as of pivotal importance for the future course of the revolution in South Vietnam. Duan's *The Path of Revolution in the South* [Duong loi cach mang mien Nam] was apparently presented as a proposal to the Eleventh Plenum, held in December. On the surface, Duan's viewpoint appeared to coincide with that of the advocates of a peaceful policy within the Central Committee. He conceded that at its present stage the Vietnamese revolution had two major tasks, building socialism in the North and liberating the South. He further agreed that the existing policy of peaceful political struggle in the South conformed to existing realities (i.e., the current weakness of the Party apparatus in South Vietnam). And the policy of peaceful reunification, he admitted, was in line with the conclusions recently reached at the Twentieth Congress of the CPSU [Communist Party of the Soviet Union] earlier in the year and with the general situation in Vietnam and throughout the world.

Yet Duan's apparent approval of the current line in Hanoi was somewhat deceptive, for in actuality the central thrust of his argument implied the need for a more vigorous approach to the revolution in the South. Although not formally deviating from the existing policy of peaceful struggle, he suggested that there was a difference between reformism, based on "legal and constitutional struggle," and the political struggle of a revolutionary movement which "takes the revolutionary political forces of the masses as its foundation." Clearly, Duan desired a more aggressive and activist approach to political struggle than the one that was currently being followed.

Moreover, Duan contended that the Party, as the vanguard of the revolutionary process, must be ready to lead the masses to seize power. Otherwise, a favorable opportunity to overthrow the reactionary regime in Saigon might be wasted. Such an occasion had arisen in 1945, he pointed out, when the Soviet Union and its allies had defeated the fascist armies of imperial Japan. At that time the Vietnamese revolutionary forces were able to seize power with relative ease, as they had been preparing the ground since 1936. If the party had not readied its strength beforehand, the favorable conditions might have changed and the August Revolution would not have occurred. Today, Duan warned, many cadres responsible for guiding the revolutionary movement regrettably "had not yet firmly understood the strength of the revolutionary masses" and thus failed to lead them in a political struggle against the reactionary regime.

To sum up, Le Duan's pamphlet, although not recommending (as is sometimes asserted) a major shift toward a more military approach in the South, did appeal for an increased effort to promote reunification and, if necessary, to prepare for a possible revolutionary upsurge to come. The vision was more Leninist than Maoist, of an uprising on the model of 1917 or 1945 rather than of a people's war along the lines of the Chinese Civil War or the recent War of Resistance against the French. But it did leave open the possibility that the struggle to complete the unification of the two zones might require the resumption of revolutionary war.

Duan's short treatise was taken up at the Eleventh Plenum of the Central Committee held in December, and it undoubtedly provoked lively discussion. In view of the high regard in which the pamphlet is currently held in Hanoi—it is frequently described as a document of "pivotal importance" in the history of the Vietnamese revolutionary movement—it seems probable that his proposal, which in any event seemed to coincide with the inclination of the Politburo at the October conference, served as the basis for a new consensus within the Party leadership on the need for a more aggressive policy in the South. The plenum apparently did not approve a major shift in the Party line. An article published in *Hoc tap* and reprinted in *Nhan dan* a few days after the conference said that the consolidation of the North was still the primary task. "We must not allow the winning over of the South," it said, "to detract from the requirements of consolidating the North." But the plenum did approve a new policy of punishing selected enemies of the revolution in South Vietnam. According to a Communist defector, the purpose of the new approach was to protect the Party's southern apparatus by throwing fear into the ranks of the enemy and creating confidence among the masses that the revolutionary movement was able to take care of its own. . . .

The results of the new policy in the South began to appear early in 1957, when observers noted a significant increase in terrorist activities directed at government officials or other key personnel in rural areas of South Vietnam. Hanoi sources claimed that those targeted for punishment were normally corrupt officials, "cruel tyrants," "wicked landlords," and "traitors." Critics charged that many of those eliminated were people considered more dangerous to the movement: honest village officials and popular teachers who might lead the masses astray. Corrupt elements, considered by the Party as their best (if unwitting) allies, were frequently left alone. Whether or not that was official policy is not easy to say. Internal Party documents frequently criticized arbitrary terrorism while recognizing the value of a carefully planned policy of "elimination of traitors" as a means of promoting the growth of the movement. . . .

The historian, searching for the roots of what would later be called the "Second Indochina War," could make a persuasive case that the first two steps in the escalation of the conflict occurred in 1955, when Diem launched his "Denounce the Communists" campaign, and in 1956, when Hanoi responded by permitting its followers in the South to take limited measures in self-defense. From this limited "challenge and response" the more dangerous armed confrontation gradually emerged. Before the end of 1957, several hundred GVN officials had been assassinated by revolutionary activists. The Saigon regime was quick to react, and during 1957 it intensified its campaign against the Communists and other groups hostile to the Diem regime. More than 2,000 suspected Communists had been killed and another 65,000 arrested before the end of the year. For the first time, ARVN military units attacked Communist base areas in the Plain of Reeds, on the Ca Mau peninsula, and in Zone D, one of the Party's major base areas, north of Saigon, causing severe losses to the revolutionary infrastructure. In contested villages, carefully constructed self-defense units were broken up and the sect armies were reduced to a mere token force. Party membership in the South, which had stood at about 5,000 in mid-1957, had fallen to one-third that level by the end of the year. Party histories concede the difficulties faced during this period, admitting that GVN efforts reduced the prestige as well as the real strength of the revolutionary movement and "significantly weakened its ability to carry on the struggle." It was, in the words of one historian in Hanoi, "the darkest period" for the revolution in the South.

In desperation, local leaders in many areas began to act on their own initiative. Organized armed units were formed, even though this violated the Party line. Such was the case in Quang Ngai Province, long a stronghold of revolutionary sentiment and a frequent target of ARVN military sweeps. At the other end of the country, several units at company strength began to operate in the U Minh forest in response to Saigon's attacks. By mid-1958 a battalion had been established in Zone D. And by the end of the year, a "command of the People's Armed Forces in Western Nam Bo" was set up to coordinate activities with the General Staff of the remaining sect armed forces who, with two battalions of their own, were still operating in several provinces of the Mekong delta. Tran Van Giau later described this period as the "embryonic stage" of revolutionary war, characterized by unarmed, partially armed, or armed self-defense actions in overt legal struggle of the masses. The primary focus of revolutionary activity was north of Saigon, in the Communist redoubt of Zone D. This area had several advantages for an insurgency movement. It was heavily forested and therefore difficult for the government to penetrate; it was close to the Cambodian border, a classical advantage in Maoist people's war; and it was relatively accessible to the two major potential focal regions of Communist activity, the lower delta provinces and the Central Highlands. Hereafter it would become a key base area for the revolution.

For the most part, the fledgling revolutionary armed forces, soon to become known to the world as the Viet Cong (a derogatory term used by the Saigon government and translated as "Vietnamese Communists"), at first limited their operations to defensive activities. But occasionally they took offensive actions in selected areas, using guerrilla techniques to launch ambushes on ARVN units and on remote GVN-controlled villages or military outposts. Much of this activity took place in the Central Highlands, a region that until now had been relatively uninvolved in the Vietnamese revolution. . . .

Up to now, the Party leadership in Hanoi had resisted a decision to escalate the conflict to a higher level of violence, despite appeals from some quarters in the South. A directive entitled "Situation and Tasks for '59," presumably drawn up by Party strategists in Hanoi for transmission to the southern leadership, conceded the difficulties faced by the revolutionary movement in South Vietnam, but did not approve a change in policy. From the context it seems clear that Hanoi continued to question the revolutionary consciousness of the masses and the ability and readiness of the Party's organization in the South to lead them. According to the directive, the struggle movement against the Diem administration was beginning to develop strongly, but it was still scattered and lacked a strong sense of political awareness. Unrest was widespread, but it was often spontaneous and rarely under Party leadership. Moreover, many members of the Party organization in the South still lacked a clear sense of the current Party line. Although that situation had improved since 1956, when the Eleventh Plenum had approved the new more activist line, many cadres were still too pessimistic in their evaluation of the situation and leaned toward a "reformist" policy rather than one of leading the masses in the political struggle. Others (from the context it appears that this was considered to be a lesser problem) were guilty of a "leftist deviation," that is, of emphasizing the need for armed struggle.

Sometime in late 1958, Le Duan made a secret inspection trip to South Vietnam, presumably to evaluate the situation there in preparation for a major policy review by the Central Committee in Hanoi. Duan's report on his return to the D.R.V. was presented at the Fifteenth Plenum of the Central Committee in January; it had fateful consequences.

There are few published references to this conference in Party histories, and no major documents issued by the meeting have appeared in the Party press. The *Outline History* comments laconically,

> In January 1959, at an important conference, South Vietnam's revolutionary leaders pointed out that South Vietnamese society was a neocolonial and semifeudal one. The Ngo Dinh Diem administration was a reactionary, cruel, war-like one which had betrayed the national interests. It was obviously a U.S. tool for aggression and enslavement. The direction and task of South Vietnamese revolution could not diverge from the general revolutionary law of using revolutionary violence to oppose counter-revolutionary violence, rising up to seize political power for the people. It was time to resort to armed struggle combined with political struggle to push the movement forward.

The failure to identify the "important conference" with the Fifteenth Plenum in Hanoi was probably tied to the decision by VWP leaders to conceal D.R.V. involvement in the rising struggle in the South—a device that would imply that the struggle was indigenous to South Vietnam and, it was hoped, would discourage any increased U.S. involvement. But there is little doubt that the decision was made at the Hanoi plenum. This has been conceded in a history of the Party published in the newspaper *Nhan dan* in early 1980. According to this source the Fifteenth Plenum stressed that the proper course for the Vietnamese revolution at the time was to use "the political force of the masses" in coordination with armed force to topple the Diem regime and lead the revolution to a successful conclusion.

Why was the decision made at this time? Hanoi sources imply that there were two main reasons. On the one hand, popular resentment against the Diem regime had reached significant proportions, creating a potential revolutionary situation. According to the *Outline History*:

> The US imperialists' policy of enslavement and war-provocation, the Ngo Dinh Diem clique's acts or [sic] terrorism and national treachery had caused utter suffering and tensions in the people's life in the South. As 1959 began, the people's life was seriously in danger. The people from various walks of life were seething with anger. Workers and peasants were especially excited and eager to struggle. They felt they could no longer live under the US-Diem regime but should rise up in a life and death struggle with the enemy.

On the other hand, party leaders apparently feared that the GVN's policy of terrorizing the opposition had seriously weakened the revolutionary organization in the South and given a spurious sense of stability to South Vietnamese society. This external impression of stability, Hanoi insisted, only disguised the real weakness within:

> We say that in 1959, the South Vietnamese administration was relatively stable due to the fact that it controlled the administrative machinery at all levels, controlled the army and was able to implement its major policies, etc. However, to attain this temporary stability, it was forced to oppress the masses with extreme cruelty, with police and military terrorism as the essential means. So, stability was acquired at a very high price—*that of complete political failure.*

Under such conditions, the very factors responsible for the regime's stability would lead to its weakening and ultimate disintegration.

The evidence suggests that the Party leadership had come around to the view that the Saigon regime was rapidly deteriorating, creating favorable conditions for a seizure of revolutionary power. On the other hand, it was increasingly clear that Diem could not be overthrown without a commitment to revolutionary violence. The size of Diem's forces and the ferocity of his hostility to the Communists destroyed the possibility that the regime could be transformed or overthrown by peaceful political struggle. But unless the party could protect and expand its forces in the South, it would be very difficult to defeat Ngo Dinh Diem before he succeeded in eliminating all opposition. Hanoi must act, even at the risk of incurring Moscow's displeasure.

The Party was now ready to gamble that a new revolutionary upsurge was in the offing in South Vietnam. But the Fifteenth Plenum was only a first step in formulating a strategy to overthrow the Saigon regime. What forms of violent struggle should be used? How should military and political struggle be combined in the most efficacious way? Was the Maoist three-stage process used during the Franco-Vietminh conflict relevant in the new situation? Unfortunately, Party historians have given us little to go on and we are reduced to speculation. There is some evidence that at the time the basic decision was taken, the Party leadership was uncertain and perhaps divided about the precise forms of struggle to be used. According to one captured document, at the time of the plenum there were "many opinions and hesitancies" about strategy, as "details of the South Vietnamese movement and the revolutionary experience were insufficient to formulate a precise program." Only two years later, it continued, was a specific program drawn up that was based on the revolutionary situation in Laos and Vietnam at that time.

At the least, there seems to have been a minimum consensus in Hanoi that although Diem's growing political weakness was still a major factor—indeed, it was the trump card of the insurgency—a purely political effort would be insufficient to overthrow the Saigon regime. The appointment of Le Duan as secretary general and Hanoi's efforts to persuade the Soviet Union to consider Vietnam as a possible exception to the worldwide application of "peaceful roads to power" suggest that the majority of the Central Committee had by now come to that conclusion. If that was the case, the primarily political armed propaganda units that had characterized the Party's military effort during the August Revolution and that were once again the predominant form of insurgency organization in the South would be unable to counter ARVN forces, which were being armed and trained for conventional combat by the United States. More would be required. How much more would become a matter of debate.

For the moment, then, it is probable that Party strategists in Hanoi were compelled to improvise a response to the needs of their compatriots in the South. In a broad sense, their answer to the problem was the strategy called simply "revolutionary war." This form of conflict was described by one Communist document in general terms as consisting of a protracted war, based on a combination of political and military struggle. In general, the war would gradually progress from small- to large-scale combat and from the rural areas to a final overthrow of the enemy in the cities. But, at least in available documents, there was no specific reference to the classic Maoist three stages of people's war, which may have been somewhat discredited because of its misapplication during the War of Resistance against the French. And there was more than a hint that the Party leadership hoped to use various forms of political struggle more effectively than had been the case at the close of the war against the French. The specific form that this should take was described as "the political force of the masses," which appeared to consist of the use of armed demonstrations by civilians in coordination with armed attacks by military units.

It is also likely that the Party leadership had a different scenario in mind for the final leap to victory than had been applied during the previous conflict. There was apparently considerable optimism that victory could be achieved without resort to a final stage of large-scale military offensive. The underlying weakness of the Diem regime was becoming more apparent day by day. This weakness was the Communists' strength. If the various opportunities for legal and illegal struggle could be effectively utilized, the "political force of the masses" could be mobilized and, in conjunction with the armed strength of revolutionary forces in the South, bring the Saigon regime to its knees through a general uprising launched both in the cities and in the countryside. Alternatively, a progressive disintegration of the Diem regime could lead to negotiations and the formation of a coalition government with active participation by the Communists.

The apparent effort to avoid an open militarization of the struggle in the South was not simply a reflection of Hanoi's desire to limit the costs of the conflict or to accede to Moscow's desire to prevent the Vietnamese revolution from becoming a major issue in East-West relations. More importantly, it probably reflected a desire to dissuade the United States from becoming more openly involved, an occurrence that would change the character of the conflict and possibly lead to a repetition of the high-level military confrontation that had taken place in the struggle against the French. At a minimum, the Fifteenth Plenum had recognized that the existing U.S. presence in the South made a protracted struggle probable. If the civil struggle in the South could be kept from escalating into a major military conflict, the likelihood of increased U.S. involvement could be minimized. . . .

The escalation of struggle in the South made a reinvigoration of the revolutionary apparatus and the formation of a new united front doubly important. In the months following the Third Congress [of September 1960], the Party decided to return to the operational arrangements used in the war against France. COSVN, the old southern branch of the Central Committee that had been abolished in 1954, was reconstituted with General Nguyen Chi Thanh as chairman, and Pham Hung as his deputy. Beneath COSVN were placed five regional Party committees and a sixth for the Saigon metropolitan area. Below the regions, provincial and district committees were created to supervise Party chapters in hamlets and villages. Military units were merged with the aim of forming a revolutionary armed force. At a conference held in Zone D in February under the direction of Tran Nam Trung, military units in the delta and the Western Highlands were merged into the new People's Liberation Armed Forces (PLAF) under unified command, which, in the minds of Party leaders, were probably expected to bear the brunt of the coming struggle against the Saigon regime. Before the end of the month new units, sometimes in coordination with sect forces, had begun to make contact with the enemy.

The revitalization of the mass movement in the South was a more complicated but equally important operation. If indeed the Party hoped to achieve victory by a fairly low level of military activity combined with the active involvement of the revolutionary masses, then the reconstitution of the national front was a crucial element in the process. What was needed above all was a new and dynamic front that could, in the Party's words, "rally all patriotic classes and sections of the people" in the South against the Diem regime. Since 1954, the Party had lacked a front organization in the South with such qualifications. The Saigon-Cholon Peace Movement formed in 1954 had been restricted to urban intellectuals and limited its activities to the promotion of national elections. The Fatherland Front, set up in Hanoi in 1955, was too closely identified with the North and therefore with the Communists. The new alliance should not appear simply as an urban nationalist phenomenon or as a mere appendage of mass organizations in the D.R.V., but as a dynamic organization indigenous to the South that could serve as a magnet for all dissident elements, urban and rural, opposed to the Diem regime.

The character of this projected front was described to the Third Party Congress by Party elder statesman Ton Duc Thang: It would be based on the Leninist concept of the four-class alliance, but in deference to the complexity of South Vietnamese society would also encompass the various religious and ethnic minorities, as well as all patriotic parties and individuals in South Vietnam. The aims of the organization, he pointed out, should be kept correspondingly general in order to appeal to the widest possible range of the population. It would emphasize nationalist and social reformist themes and have as its final objective the creation of a peaceful, unified, democratic, and prosperous Vietnam, beginning with the formation of a national democratic coalition government that would discuss peaceful unification with the North. There would obviously be no mention of communism.

The absence of such a front was remedied on December 20, 1960, with the formation of the National Front for the Liberation of South Vietnam (NLF, or Mat Tran Dan Toc Giai Phong Mien Nam Viet Nam). As described in the *Outline History*, the new organization was founded at a secret conference of representatives of various classes, parties, religious groups, and nationalities "somewhere in the liberated area of South Vietnam." Included in its Central Committee were members of virtually every major segment and class in southern society—the religious sects, Buddhist and Catholic organizations, women's groups, and two puppet political parties created by the Communists, the Radical Socialist Party (Dang Xa Hoi Cap Tien) and the South Vietnam Democratic party (Dang Dan Chu Mien Nam), both counterparts of existing parties in the North. Like its famous predecessor, the Vietminh Front, the NLF was set up administratively at various levels up to its central Presidium but functioned primarily at the village level, where it operated through the familiar mass organizations.

The aims of the new front were set forth in a ten-point program issued at the conference and reflected the objectives previously emphasized by Ton Duc Thang at the Party congress in Hanoi. Repeating the contention of the Third Congress that there were two major enemy forces in South Vietnam, imperialism and feudalism, it asserted that at the moment the sharpest contradiction in the South was between the mass of the population and the U.S. imperialists and their henchmen in Saigon. The operational implication of this belief was that the major emphasis of the new front was to be nationalist rather than revolutionary, aimed at the national democratic rather than the social revolution. To avoid alienating patriotic elements, the front's land policy in liberated areas would be restricted to rent reduction and the confiscation of the land of traitors and cruel landlords. There was, of course, no suggestion that the front was controlled by the Party, or that it had any intimate connections with organizations in the D.R.V. The executive leadership of the front was composed of individuals who were not, for the most part, publicly identified as Communists although some, like Chairman Nguyen Huu Tho, had been closely linked to the Vietminh cause in the South since the 1940s. Most of the top officials were professionals, although there were several representatives of various social or minority groups, such as Nguyen Thi Dinh, heroine of the Ben Tre uprising, and Y Bih Aleo, chairman of the Communist-sponsored Western Highlands Autonomy Movement. To limit identification of the front with the Party, the number of open Party members in leading positions at all levels was strictly limited.

The Party's success in establishing a new united front with no obvious links with the regime in Hanoi had momentous effects on the worldwide image of the insurgency movement. Although most sophisticated foreign observers had little doubt that there were close ties between the leadership of the new front and the Party in the D.R.V., there was a pervasive impression that the NLF possessed at least a modicum of autonomy and thus represented a legitimate alternative to the GVN in expressing the aspirations of the population of South Vietnam. This impression lent substance to the widely held view that the insurgency movement in the South had its roots in the indigenous population and was not simply a creature of the Party leadership in Hanoi. So long as this view prevailed, Washington's insistence that the rising struggle in South Vietnam was an armed attack from the North would appear of dubious validity.

How valid was this impression? As in the case of so many aspects of the Vietnam conflict, the answer all too often depended on the political preference of the individual observer. Today it is possible to obtain a somewhat clearer view. Unquestionably, hostility to the Diem regime among wide strata of the local population was a significant factor in the rising level of insurgency in South Vietnam. The revolutionary movement could hardly have grown and prospered without a solid base of support in both the cities and the countryside. It is also true that the vast majority of cadres sent south in the months following the Fifteenth Plenum were regroupees native to the South. On the other hand, it is also apparent that from the beginning the movement was organized and directed from the North. Although discontent was widespread throughout the South, it is highly unlikely that the unrest would have achieved enough coherence and dynamic force to challenge the power of the Saigon regime without the organizational genius provided by the Party leadership in Hanoi. In that sense, the insurgency was a genuine revolt based in the South, but it was organized and directed from the North.

Did Hanoi, as some claim, deliberately set out to destroy the Saigon regime by force? The evidence here suggests that this was not the case. Party strategy had originally hoped that reunification could take place by peaceful, or at least quasi-peaceful means. Only with reluctance was Hanoi compelled to reassess the situation as a result of the repressive policies put into effect by the Diem government, policies that prevented the revolutionary leaders in South Vietnam from organizing and carrying out a political struggle to achieve the overthrow of the existing government. To say that, of course, is not to deny that Hanoi had every intention of securing control of the South eventually, by whatever means proved necessary. To many outside observers, convinced that the South Vietnamese people deserved the opportunity to control their own destiny, Hanoi's attitude was tantamount to naked aggression. To Party leaders, South Vietnam would not fulfill its national destiny until the reactionary regime in Saigon had been overthrown and a new unified Vietnam established in both zones. Between these two contrasting views, a common understanding of the political and moral realities of the Vietnamese revolution would be virtually impossible to attain.

By the beginning of 1961, the southern insurgents, stimulated from the North, were on the march. Several provinces, including a number in the delta and along the central coast, had come under the partial control of the revolutionary forces. In Hanoi, the initial confusion over policy had been at least temporarily resolved and the foundations of a coherent revolutionary strategy were beginning to emerge. In the world at large, the insurgents now appeared to possess the vocal support of the socialist countries and the sympathy of many others. A new stage of the Vietnamese revolution was about to begin. . . .

While Party leaders groped for a strategy to deal with the growing U.S. presence in South Vietnam, civilian and military cadres at the local level struggled to prepare the forces of the revolution for the challenge. Although Party directives called for intensive efforts to improve capabilities in both military and political fields, it was clear that the immediate objectives must be to increase the size and effectiveness of the revolutionary armed forces in order to cope with GVN repression and, in the words of one Communist historian, to move from the stage of "uniform uprisings to seize power at the local level" to a higher stage of "expanded guerrilla war against enemy sweeps."

By 1961, this process was already well under way. The size of the PLAF exceeded 15,000, well above the total of less than 3,000 two years earlier. Most were in guerrilla units under the direction of the regional Party committees. There were few organized main force units or self-defense units at the village level (the failure to organize at the village level was one of the major criticisms leveled by Party leaders in secret documents). The goal was to set up the PLAF on the familiar three-tiered basis. Fully armed regular units capable of combat operations against ARVN conventional forces and commanded by COSVN or the regional headquarters would form the backbone of the revolutionary army. Below that level would be the full-time guerrillas, usually operating at company size under provincial or district command. The guerrillas would normally restrict their combat activities to operations against the enemy's local units, but when necessary could coordinate their activities with main force units in the area. At the lowest level was the village militia, divided into an armed combat militia (*du kich chien dau*) and the regular village militia (*du kich xa*). The former was composed of vigorous youth in the village and could take part in military operations; the latter usually had older men and was to be used only for defense. The local militia could be used to supplement higher-level units operating in the area and was often a recruiting pool for higher-level units.

During the early years of the insurgency, the vast majority of PLAF recruits were indigenous South Vietnamese. Yet, from the beginning, re-groupees trained in North Vietnam provided a nucleus for the movement. According to U.S. government sources, infiltration rose from approximately 2,000 annually in 1959 and 1960 to a minimum of 3,700 in 1961 and more than 5,000 in 1962. The return of the regroupees did not substantially affect the size of the local forces; by one estimate they made up less than 20 percent of the entire PLAF. But their numbers were no reflection of their importance, for they often served as political cadres or officers, providing an element of experience and ideological steadiness to the young and fre-quently untrained recruits from the rural areas.

It is likely that one of Hanoi's major concerns as it attempted to re-vitalize the movement in the South was to guarantee that leadership re-mained firmly in the hands of Party leaders in the North. Since the 1930s the Party's apparatus in Cochin China had faced unique problems and had tended to operate somewhat independently from the Central Committee, which was usually located in Tonkin. The isolation and autonomy of the southern leadership had created problems, particularly when it was under the control of the ambitious Tran Van Giau, and irritation on the part of top Party figures at Giau's independent policies may have been one of the reasons for his dismissal from the leadership of the movement in the South in the late 1940s. Then, too, traditional cultural and historical differences had long generated a degree of mutual antagonism and distrust between North and South, and from the time of the Franco–Vietminh War com-munism was frequently identified in the minds of southerners as a Northern phenomenon.

In the new conditions of struggle, when the southern leadership would inevitably be operating somewhat independently of Hanoi, the threat of a restoration of southern regionalism undoubtedly concerned Party leaders in Hanoi. The danger would be exacerbated by the fact that the NLF, the overall parent organization of the movement, would consist of thousands, perhaps millions, of Vietnamese who were not members of the Party. For obvious reasons, the NLF leadership itself would be composed primarily of non-Party southerners. To reduce the temptations of autonomy, a number of mechanisms were established to provide guidance from the North. The top COSVN leaders were all Party veterans with a history of loyalty to the organization. At the end of each year a leading COSVN member attended a Politburo meeting in Hanoi to consult with Party leaders and receive directions for future strategy in the South. Party figures also played key roles in the administrative structure of the NLF. Finally, in early 1962 Hanoi decided to set up a southern branch of the VWP, the People's

Revolutionary Party, or PRP (Dang Nhan Dan Cach Mang Viet Nam). The PRP was initially described as an independent party with no formal connections with the VWP in the North; this was a fiction designed to avoid identification of the southern movement with the Party leadership in the North. In reality the PRP was directly subordinate to the parent organization in the D.R.V. through COSVN. There was no attempt to disguise the Marxist-Leninist orientation of the organization. It was described as "a revolutionary party of the working class in South Vietnam," which would be guided by the principles of Marxism-Leninism. . . .

By the end of 1964, for the second time in less than twenty years, the Communists approached the portals of victory. The Johnson administration, in an effort to justify its decision to escalate U.S. involvement, would contend that South Vietnam was the victim of armed aggression from the North. Clearly the revolution in the South was directed from Hanoi, and by the mid-1960s D.R.V. participation had become a major factor in the conflict. But Washington's claim of outside intervention, however justified by the course of future events, could not disguise the fact that the primary source of the revolutionary ferment in the South lay in the political weakness of the Saigon regime and the popularity of the revolutionary cause in the South. The decision of the Kennedy administration to increase its involvement complicated the problem for Hanoi and compelled it to resort to a higher level of revolutionary war, but it did not substantially resolve the underlying political problems in the GVN or arrest the seemingly inexorable slide of the South toward communism.

✗ *F U R T H E R   R E A D I N G*

William Andrews, *The Village War* (1973)
King C. Chen, "Hanoi's Three Decisions and the Escalation of the Vietnam War," *Political Science Quarterly*, 90 (1975), 239–59
Hoang Van Chi, *From Colonialism to Communism* (1964)
Nguyen Thi Dinh, *No Other Road to Take* (1976)
V. C. Funnell, "Vietnam and the Sino-Soviet Conflict," *Studies in Comparative Communism*, 11 (1978), 142–99
Vo Nguyen Giap, *Big Victory, Big Task* (1967)
———, *Unforgettable Days* (1978)
William Darryl Henderson, *Why the Vietcong Fought* (1979)
P. J. Honey, *Communism in North Vietnam* (1963)
Jean Lacouture, *Ho Chi Minh: A Political Biography* (1968)
Edwin E. Moise, *Land Reform in China and North Vietnam* (1983)
Daniel S. Papp, *Vietnam: The View from Moscow, Peking, Washington* (1978)
Douglas Pike, *History of Vietnamese Communism* (1978)
———, *PAVN: People's Army of Vietnam* (1986)
———, *Vietnam and the Soviet Union* (1987)
Samuel L. Popkin, *The Rational Peasant* (1979)
Jeffrey Race, *War Comes to Long An* (1972)
Robert L. Sansom, *The Economics of Insurgency in the Mekong Delta of Vietnam* (1970)

W. R. Smyser, *The Independent Vietnamese: Vietnamese Communism Between Russia and China, 1956–1969* (1980)

Russell Stettler, ed., *The Military Art of People's War* (1970)

James Trullinger, *Village at War* (1980)

Robert F. Turner, *Vietnamese Communism: Its Origins and Development* (1975)

Alexander B. Woodside, *Community and Revolution in Vietnam* (1976)

Donald S. Zagoria, *Vietnam Triangle* (1967)

The Tet Offensive

✗

The Tet lunar holidays of 1968 broke across South Vietnam like a thunderclap as the North Vietnamese and Vietcong launched a series of well-coordinated attacks throughout the country. The offensive heralded a new, much bolder phase in communist military and political strategy. Although American and South Vietnamese forces ultimately repelled the attacks, inflicting heavy casualties on their adversary, the Tet offensive raised fundamental questions about the efficacy of American policy that reverberated throughout the United States. Most important, it forced a wrenching reexamination of Washington policy that culminated in President Johnson's decisions in March 1968 to call for negotiations and to set a ceiling on U.S. troop levels.

Most analysts now agree that the communists suffered heavily for their boldness. They point especially to the devastating losses of Vietcong cadres in the fighting. Following Tet, North Vietnamese troops were compelled to play an increasingly heavy role in the struggle. Specialists agree as well that the offensive dealt the United States a powerful psychological blow, generating strong opposition to the war among elite groups and the general public. They differ, however, in their evaluation of Tet's precise military and political effects. Two questions predominate in recent studies: why was Tet such a turning point for the United States, and should it have been?

✗ D O C U M E N T S

The first three documents reflect the immediate response to Tet. First is an excerpt from Lyndon Johnson's news conference on February 2, 1968, in which the president offers his initial appraisal of the Tet offensive. Two days later, Robert McNamara and Dean Rusk relayed their assessment during a joint television interview. On February 8, Senator Robert F. Kennedy called for a reevaluation of America's Vietnam policy, denouncing the illusions that had been guiding the U.S. war effort. The next document contains extracts from a report by General Earle G. Wheeler, chairman of the Joint Chiefs of Staff, dated February 27. Wheeler evaluated the military situation in the wake of the Tet attacks and repeated General William Westmoreland's request for more than 200,000 additional troops. The fourth document, written in March 1968, presents an early evaluation of the offensive's contributions and shortcomings by the southern branch of the Vietnamese Communist party.

The fifth and sixth documents are personal reminiscences. First, Robert Komer, head of the pacification program in South Vietnam, recalls Tet's impact in Saigon and Washington. Then Clark Clifford, who replaced McNamara as defense secretary on March 1, 1968, remembers the critical questions that he posed to top administration figures at that time.

The last document is Johnson's public address of March 31, in which he called for a bombing halt and the beginning of negotiations with North Vietnam and then stunned his audience with the announcement of his withdrawal from the 1968 presidential race.

Lyndon B. Johnson on the Failed Communist Offensive, 1968

Q. Do you see anything in the developments this week in these attacks in Viet-Nam that causes you to think, to reevaluate, some of the assumptions on which our policies and strategy there has been based? I am thinking in terms of the security ratings, amount of population that is considered under government control? Do you think the basic assumption is still valid?

The President: We do that every week. I would see nothing that would indicate that that should not be done. We must, all the time, try to keep up and to be sure we have not made any mistakes. If you are saying, Have we felt that what happened could not happen? the answer is "No." As a matter of fact, . . . if you have seen any of the intelligence reports, the information has been very clear that two things would happen:

One is that there would be a general uprising, as I stated.

Two, there would be a general invasion and attempt to secure military victory and that the objective would be to get a military victory and a psychological victory. That is one of the great problems the President has to deal with. He is sitting there reading these information reports while his own people, a good many of the best intentioned, are supplying him with military strategy, and the two do not fit in.

So you have to be tolerant and understand their best intentions while you are looking at the other fellow's hole card. That is what General Westmoreland has been doing while all of these Monday morning quarterbacks are pointing out to him that this is the way he should move or this is the way you should not move.

This is part of what happens when you look at history. It may be that General Westmoreland makes some serious mistakes or that I make some. We don't know. We are just acting in light of the information we have. We believe we have information about what they are trying to do there. We have taken every precaution we know of. But we don't want to give you assurance that all will be satisfactory. We see nothing that would require any change of great consequence.

We will have to move men from this place to that one. We will have to replace helicopters. Probably we had 100-odd helicopters and planes seriously damaged, and we will have to replace them. Secretary McNamara told me he could have that done very shortly.

We will have to replace the 38 planes lost, but we have approximately 5,900 planes there. We anticipate that we will lose 25 or 30 every month just from normal crashes and so forth. . . .

I am not a great strategist and tactician. I know that you are not. Let us assume that the best figures we can have are from our responsible military commanders. They say 10,000 died and we lost 249 and the South Vietnamese lost 500. That does not look like a Communist victory. I can count. It looks like somebody has paid a very dear price for the temporary encouragement that some of our enemies had.

We have approximately 5,900 planes and have lost 38 completely destroyed. We lost 100-odd that were damaged and have to be repaired. Maybe Secretary McNamara will fly in 150 shortly. Is that a great enemy victory?

In Peking today they say that we are in panic. You have to judge that for yourself. In other Communist capitals today they say that we have definitely exhibited a lack of power and that we do not have any military strength. You will have to judge that for yourself.

But General Westmoreland evaluating this for us and the Joint Chiefs of Staff reviewing it for him tell me that in their judgment their action has not been a military success.

I am measuring my words. I don't want to overstate anything. We do not believe that we should help them in making it a psychological success either.

Robert McNamara and Dean Rusk Assess the Tet Offensive, 1968

Mr. Able: Secretary McNamara, it is 3 years this week since we started bombing North Viet-Nam. It was also in '65 that we started the big buildup on the ground. What happened this week? How do you relate the ability of the Viet Cong to stage as major an offensive as this one was to the efforts we have been making these past 3 years?

Secretary McNamara: Three years ago, or more exactly, 2½ years ago, in July of 1965, President Johnson made the decision—announced to our people the decision to move significant numbers of combat troops into South Viet-Nam. At that time the North Vietnamese and their associates, the Viet Cong, were on the verge of cutting the country in half and of destroying the South Vietnamese Army. We said so at the time, and I think hindsight has proven that a correct appraisal. What has happened since that time, of course, is that they have suffered severe losses, they have failed in their objective to destroy the Government of South Viet-Nam, they have failed in their objective to take control of the country. They have continued to fight.

Just 4 days ago I remember reading in our press that I had presented a gloomy, pessimistic picture of activities in South Viet-Nam. I don't think it was gloomy or pessimistic; it was realistic. It said that while they had suffered severe penalties, they continued to have strength to carry out the attacks which we have seen in the last 2 or 3 days.

Mr. Abel: Mr. Secretary, are you telling us the fact that the Viet Cong, after all these years, were able to, temporarily at least, grab control of some 20-odd Provincial capitals and the city of Saigon—are you telling us this has no military meaning at all?

Secretary McNamara: No; certainly not. I think South Viet-Nam is such a complex situation—one must always look at the pluses and the minuses, and I don't mean to say there haven't been any minuses for the South Vietnamese in the last several days. I think there have been, but there have been many, many pluses. The North Vietnamese and the Viet Cong have not accomplished either one of their major objectives: either to ignite a general uprising or to force a diversion of the troops which the South Vietnamese and the United States have moved into the northern areas of South Viet-Nam, anticipating a major Viet Cong and North Vietnamese offensive in that area.

And beyond that, the North Vietnamese and the Viet Cong have suffered very heavy penalties in terms of losses of weapons and losses of men in the past several days. They have, of course, dealt a very heavy blow to many of the cities of South Viet-Nam.

Mr. Frankel: Secretary Rusk, the administration has naturally been stressing the things that they think the Viet Cong did not achieve in this week of attacks—didn't cause an uprising, which you say may have been one of their goals, didn't seize cities for any permanent period. But yet we have also been given to understand that the real name of this game out there is "Who can provide safety for whom?" And haven't they in a very serious way humiliated our ability in major cities all up and down this country to provide the South Vietnamese population that is listed as clearly in our control with a degree of assurance and safety that South Vietnamese forces and American forces together could give them?

Secretary Rusk: There is almost no way to prevent the other side from making a try. There is a way to prevent them from having a success.

I said earlier that I thought there would be a number of South Vietnamese who would take a very grumpy view over the inability of the Government to protect them against some of the things that have happened in the last 3 or 4 days. But the net effect of the transaction is to make it clear that the Viet Cong are not able to come into these Provincial capitals and seize Provincial capitals and hold them; that they are not able to announce the formation of a new committee, or a coalition or a federation, and have it pick up any support in the country; that they are not able to undermine the solidarity of those who are supporting the Government.

No; I think there is a psychological factor here that we won't be able to assess until a week or two after the event, and I might say also that we know there is going to be some hard fighting ahead. We are not over this period at all. As a matter of fact, the major fighting up in the northern part of South Viet-Nam has not yet occurred, so there are some hard battles ahead. . . .

Mr. Frankel: Secretary McNamara, let me take advantage of your valedictory mood. Looking back over this long conflict and especially in this rather agonized week in Viet-Nam, if we had to do it all over again, would you make any major changes in our—

Secretary McNamara: This is not an appropriate time for me to be talking of changes, with hindsight. There is no question but what 5 or 10 or 20 years from now the historians will find actions that might have been done differently. I am sure they will. . . . I am learning more and more about Viet-Nam every day. There is no question I see better today than I did 3 years ago or 5 years ago what might have been done there.

On balance, I feel much the way the Asian leaders do. I think the action that this Government has followed, policies it has followed, the objectives it has had in Viet-Nam, are wise. I do not by any means suggest that we have not made mistakes over the many, many years that we have been pursuing those objectives.

Mr. Frankel: You seem to suggest that we really didn't—that none of us appreciated what we were really getting into.

Secretary McNamara: I don't think any of us predicted 7 years ago or 15 years ago the deployment of 500,000 men to Viet-Nam. I know I didn't.

Robert F. Kennedy Calls Vietnam an Unwinnable War, 1968

Our enemy, savagely striking at will across all of South Vietnam, has finally shattered the mask of official illusion with which we have concealed our true circumstances, even from ourselves. But a short time ago we were serene in our reports and predictions of progress.

The Vietcong will probably withdraw from the cities, as they were forced to withdraw from the American Embassy. Thousands of them will be dead.

But they will, nevertheless, have demonstrated that no part or person of South Vietnam is secure from their attacks: neither district capitals nor American bases, neither the peasant in his rice paddy nor the commanding general of our own great forces.

No one can predict the exact shape or outcome of the battles now in progress, in Saigon or at Khesanh. Let us pray that we will succeed at the lowest possible cost to our young men.

But whatever their outcome, the events of the last two weeks have taught us something. For the sake of those young Americans who are fighting today, if for no other reason, the time has come to take a new look at the war in Vietnam; not by cursing the past but by using it to illuminate the future.

And the first and necessary step is to face the facts. It is to seek out the austere and painful reality of Vietnam, freed from wishful thinking, false hopes and sentimental dreams. It is to rid ourselves of the "good company,'' of those illusions which have lured us into the deepening swamp of Vietnam.

We must, first of all, rid ourselves of the illusion that the events of the past two weeks represent some sort of victory. That is not so.

It is said the Vietcong will not be able to hold the cities. This is probably true. But they have demonstrated despite all our reports of progress, of government strength and enemy weakness, that half a million American soldiers with 700,000 Vietnamese allies, with total command of the air, total command of the sea, backed by huge resources and the most modern weapons, are unable to secure even a single city from the attacks of an enemy whose total strength is about 250,000. . . .

For years we have been told that the measure of our success and progress in Vietnam was increasing security and control for the population. Now we have seen that none of the population is secure and no area is under sure control.

Four years ago when we only had about 30,000 troops in Vietnam, the Vietcong were unable to mount the assaults on cities they have now conducted against our enormous forces. At one time a suggestion that we protect enclaves was derided. Now there are no protected enclaves.

This has not happened because our men are not brave or effective, because they are. It is because we have misconceived the nature of the war: It is because we have sought to resolve by military might a conflict whose issue depends upon the will and conviction of the South Vietnamese people. It is like sending a lion to halt an epidemic of jungle rot.

This misconception rests on a second illusion—the illusion that we can win a war which the South Vietnamese cannot win for themselves.

You cannot expect people to risk their lives and endure hardship unless they have a stake in their own society. They must have a clear sense of identification with their own government, a belief they are participating in a cause worth fighting for.

People will not fight to line the pockets of generals or swell the bank accounts of the wealthy. They are far more likely to close their eyes and shut their doors in the face of their government—even as they did last week.

More than any election, more than any proud boast, that single fact reveals the truth. We have an ally in name only. We support a government without supporters. Without the efforts of American arms that government would not last a day.

The third illusion is that the unswerving pursuit of military victory, whatever its cost, is in the interest of either ourselves or the people of Vietnam.

For the people of Vietnam, the last three years have meant little but horror. Their tiny land has been devastated by a weight of bombs and shells greater than Nazi Germany knew in the Second World War.

We have dropped 12 tons of bombs for every square mile in North and South Vietnam. Whole provinces have been substantially destroyed. More than two million South Vietnamese are now homeless refugees.

Imagine the impact in our own country if an equivalent number—over 25 million Americans—were wandering homeless or interned in refugee camps, and millions more refugees were being created as New York and Chicago, Washington and Boston, were being destroyed by a war raging in their streets.

Whatever the outcome of these battles, it is the people we seek to defend who are the greatest losers.

Nor does it serve the interests of America to fight this war as if moral standards could be subordinated to immediate necessities. Last week, a Vietcong suspect was turned over to the chief of the Vietnamese Security Services, who executed him on the spot—a flat violation of the Geneva Convention on the Rules of War.

The photograph of the execution was on front pages all around the world—leading our best and oldest friends to ask, more in sorrow than in anger, what has happened to America?

The fourth illusion is that the American national interest is identical with—or should be subordinated to—the selfish interest of an incompetent military regime.

We are told, of course, that the battle for South Vietnam is in reality a struggle for 250 million Asians—the beginning of a Great Society for all of Asia. But this is pretension.

We can and should offer reasonable assistance to Asia; but we cannot build a Great Society there if we cannot build one in our own country. We cannot speak extravagantly of a struggle for 250 million Asians, when a struggle for 15 million in one Asian country so strains our forces, that another Asian country, a fourth-rate power which we have already once defeated in battle, dares to seize an American ship and hold and humiliate her crew.

The fifth illusion is that this war can be settled in our own way and in our own time on our own terms. Such a settlement is the privilege of the triumphant: of those who crush their enemies in battle or wear away their will to fight.

We have not done this, nor is there any prospect we will achieve such a victory.

Unable to defeat our enemy or break his will—at least without a huge, long and ever more costly effort—we must actively seek a peaceful settlement. We can no longer harden our terms every time Hanoi indicates it may be prepared to negotiate; and we must be willing to foresee a settlement which will give the Vietcong a chance to participate in the political life of the country.

These are some of the illusions which may be discarded if the events of last week are to prove not simply a tragedy, but a lesson: a lesson which carries with it some basic truths.

First, that a total military victory is not within sight or around the corner; that, in fact, it is probably beyond our grasp; and that the effort to win such a victory will only result in the further slaughter of thousands of innocent and helpless people—a slaughter which will forever rest on our national conscience.

Second, that the pursuit of such a victory is not necessary to our national interest, and is even damaging that interest.

Third, that the progress we have claimed toward increasing our control over the country and the security of the population is largely illusory.

Fourth, that the central battle in this war cannot be measured by body counts or bomb damage, but by the extent to which the people of South Vietnam act on a sense of common purpose and hope with those that govern them.

Fifth, that the current regime in Saigon is unwilling or incapable of being an effective ally in the war against the Communists.

Sixth, that a political compromise is not just the best path to peace, but the only path, and we must show as much willingness to risk some of our prestige for peace as to risk the lives of young men in war.

Seventh, that the escalation policy in Vietnam, far from strengthening and consolidating international resistance to aggression, is injuring our country through the world, reducing the faith of other peoples in our wisdom and purpose and weakening the world's resolve to stand together for freedom and peace.

Eighth, that the best way to save our most precious stake in Vietnam— the lives of our soldiers—is to stop the enlargement of the war, and that the best way to end casualties is to end the war.

Ninth, that our nation must be told the truth about this war, in all its terrible reality, both because it is right—and because only in this way can any Administration rally the public confidence and unity for the shadowed days which lie ahead.

No war has ever demanded more bravery from our people and our Government—not just bravery under fire or the bravery to make sacrifices—but the bravery to discard the comfort of illusion—to do away with false hopes and alluring promises.

Reality is grim and painful. But it is only a remote echo of the anguish toward which a policy founded on illusion is surely taking us.

This is a great nation and a strong people. Any who seek to comfort rather than speak plainly, reassure rather than instruct, promise satisfaction rather than reveal frustration—they deny that greatness and drain that strength. For today as it was in the beginning, it is the truth that makes us free.

Earle G. Wheeler's Report on Military Prospects After Tet, 1968

1. The Chairman, JCS and party visited SVN on 23, 24 and 25 February. This report summarizes the impressions and facts developed through conversations and briefings at MACV and with senior commanders throughout the country.

2. *Summary*

• The current situation in Vietnam is still developing and fraught with opportunities as well as dangers.

• There is no question in the mind of MACV that the enemy went all out for a general offensive and general uprising and apparently believed that he would succeed in bringing the war to an early successful conclusion.

• The enemy failed to achieve this initial objective but is continuing his effort. Although many of his units were badly hurt, the judgment is that he has the will and the capability to continue.

• Enemy losses have been heavy; he has failed to achieve his prime objectives of mass uprisings and capture of a large number of the capital cities and towns. Morale in enemy units which were badly mauled or where the men were oversold the idea of a decisive victory at TET probably has suffered severely. However, with replacements, his indoctrination system would seem capable of maintaining morale at a general adequate level. His determination appears to be unshaken.

• The enemy is operating with relative freedom in the countryside, probably recruiting heavily and no doubt infiltrating NVA units and personnel. His recovery is likely to be rapid; his supplies are adequate; and he is trying to maintain the momentum of his winter-spring offensive.

• The structure of the GVN held up but its effectiveness has suffered.

• The RVNAF held up against the initial assault with gratifying, and in a way, surprising strength and fortitude. However, ARVN is now in a defensive posture around towns and cities and there is concern about how well they will bear up under sustained pressure.

• The initial attack nearly succeeded in a dozen places, and defeat in those places was only averted by the timely reaction of US forces. In short, it was a very near thing.

• There is no doubt that the RD [rural development, or pacification] Program has suffered a severe set back.

• RVNAF was not badly hurt physically—they should recover strength and equipment rather quickly (equipment in 2–3 months—strength in 3–6 months). Their problems are more psychological than physical.

• US forces have lost none of their pre-TET capability.

• MACV has three principal problems. First, logistic support north of Danang is marginal owing to weather, enemy interdiction and harassment and the massive deployment of US forces into the DMZ/Hue area. Opening Route 1 will alleviate this problem but takes a substantial troop commitment. Second, the defensive posture of ARVN is permitting the VC to make rapid inroads in the formerly pacified countryside. ARVN, in its own words, is in a dilemma as it cannot afford another enemy thrust into the cities and towns and yet if it remains in a defensive posture against this contingency, the countryside goes by default. MACV is forced to devote much of its troop strength to this problem. Third, MACV has been forced to deploy 50% of all US maneuver battalions into I Corps, to meet the threat there, while stripping the rest of the country of adequate reserves. If the enemy synchronizes an attack against Khe Sanh/Hue-Quang Tri with an offensive in the Highlands and around Saigon while keeping the pressure on throughout the remainder of the country, MACV will be hard pressed to meet adequately all threats. Under these circumstances, we must be prepared to accept some reverses.

• For these reasons, General Westmoreland has asked for a 3 division–15 tactical fighter squadron force. This force would provide him with a theater reserve and an offensive capability which he does not now have.

    3. The situation as it stands today:

        a. Enemy capabilities

            (1) The enemy has been hurt badly in the populated lowlands, but is practically intact elsewhere. He committed over 67,000 combat maneuver forces plus perhaps 25% or 17,000 more impressed men and boys, for a total of about 84,000. He lost 40,000 killed, at least 3,000 captured, and perhaps 5,000 disabled or died of wounds. He had peaked his force total to about 240,000 just before TET, by hard recruiting, infiltration, civilian impressment, and draw-downs on service and guerrilla personnel. So he has lost about one-fifth of his total strength. About two-thirds of his trained, organized unit strength can continue offensive action. He is probably infiltrating and recruiting heavily in the countryside while allied forces are securing the urban areas. . . .

    4. What does the future hold?

        a. Probable enemy strategy. . . . We see the enemy pursuing a reinforced offensive to enlarge his control throughout the country and keep pressures on the government and allies. We expect him to maintain strong threats in the DMZ area, at Khe Sanh, in the highlands, and at Saigon, and to attack in force when conditions seem favorable. He is likely to try to gain control of the country's northern provinces. He will continue efforts to encircle cities and province capitals to isolate and disrupt normal activities, and infiltrate them to create chaos. He will seek maximum attrition of RVNAF elements. Against US forces, he will emphasize attacks by fire on airfields and installations, using assaults and ambushes selectively. His central objective continues to be the destruction of the Government of SVN and its armed forces. As a minimum he hopes to seize sufficient territory and gain control of enough people to support establishment of the groups and committees he proposes for participation in an NLF dominated government.

        b. MACV Strategy:

            (1) MACV believes that the central thrust of our strategy now must be to defeat the enemy offensive and that if this is done well, the situation overall will be greatly improved over the pre-TET condition.

            (2) MACV accepts the fact that its first priority must be the security of Government of Vietnam in Saigon and provincial capitals. MACV describes its objectives as:

• First, to counter the enemy offensive and to destroy or eject the NVA invasion force in the north.

• Second, to restore security in the cities and towns.

• Third, to restore security in the heavily populated areas of the countryside.

• Fourth, to regain the initiative through offensive operations.

c. Tasks:

(1) *Security of Cities and Government.* MACV recognizes that US forces will be required to reinforce and support RVNAF in the security of cities, towns and government structure. At this time, 10 US battalions are operating in the environs of Saigon. It is clear that this task will absorb a substantial portion of US forces.

(2) *Security in the Countryside.* To a large extent the VC now control the countryside. Most of the 54 battalions formerly providing security for pacification are now defending district or province towns. MACV estimates that US forces will be required in a number of places to assist and encourage the Vietnamese Army to leave the cities and towns and reenter the country. This is especially true in the Delta.

(3) *Defense of the borders, the DMZ and the northern provinces.* MACV considers that it must meet the enemy threat in I Corps Tactical Zone and has already deployed there slightly over 50% of all US maneuver battalions. US forces have been thinned out in the highlands, notwithstanding an expected enemy offensive in the early future.

(4) *Offensive Operations.* Coupling the increased requirement for the cities and subsequent reentry into the rural areas, and the heavy requirement for defense of the I Corps Zone, MACV does not have adequate forces at this time to resume the offensive in the remainder of the country, nor does it have adequate reserves against the contingency of simultaneous large-scale enemy offensive action throughout the country.

5. Force Requirements:

a. Forces currently assigned to MACV, plus the residual Program Five forces yet to be delivered, are inadequate in numbers and balance to carry out the strategy and to accomplish the tasks described above in the proper priority. To contend with, and defeat, the new enemy threat, MACV has stated requirements for forces over the 525,000 ceiling imposed by Program Five.

A Communist Party Evaluation, 1968

I. *Great and unprecedented successes recorded in all fields during the first-month phase of the General Offensive and General Uprising.*

Since the beginning of Spring this year, the "Anti-U.S. National Salvation" resistance war of our people in the South has entered a new phase:

In this phase of General Offensive and General Uprising, after a month of continuous offensives and simultaneous uprisings conducted on all battlefields in the South, we have recorded great and unprecedented victories in all fields, inflicting on the enemy heavier losses than those he had suffered in any previous period.

1. We wore down, annihilated and disintegrated almost one-third of the puppet troops' strength, wore down and annihilated about one-fifth of U.S. combat forces, one-third of the total number of aircraft, one-third of

the total number of mechanized vehicles, and an important part of U.S. and puppet material installations; destroyed and forced to surrender or withdraw one-third of the enemy military posts, driving the enemy into an unprecedentedly awkward situation: from the position of the aggressor striving to gain the initiative through a two-prong tactic [military action and rural pacification], the enemy has withdrawn into a purely passive and defensive position, with his forces dispersed on all battlefields in the South for the purpose of defending the towns, cities and the main lines of communications. The struggle potential and morale of U.S. and puppet troops have seriously weakened because our army and people have dealt thundering blows at them everywhere, even at their principal lairs, and because they are facing great difficulties in replenishing troops and replacing war facilities destroyed during the past month.

2. We attacked all U.S.-puppet nerve centers, occupied and exerted our control for a definite period and at varying degrees over almost all towns, cities and municipalities in the South, and destroyed and disintegrated an important part of puppet installations at all levels, seriously damaging the puppet administrative machinery.

3. We liberated additional wide areas in the countryside containing a population of 1.5 million inhabitants; consolidated and widened our rear areas, shifted immense resources of manpower and material, which had been previously robbed by the enemy in these areas, to the support of the front-line and of victory; encircled and isolated the enemy, and reduced the enemy's reserves of human and material resources, driving him into a very difficult economic and financial situation.

4. We have quantitatively and qualitatively improved our armed forces and political forces which have become outstandingly mature during the struggle in the past month. Our armed forces have progressed in many aspects, political organizations are being consolidated and have stepped forward, much progress has been realized in leadership activities and methods and we have gained richer experiences.

The above-mentioned great and unprecedented successes in all fields have strongly encouraged and motivated compatriots in towns and cities and areas under temporary enemy control to arise to seize the state power, have created a lively and enthusiastic atmosphere and inspired a strong confidence in final victory among compatriots in both the North and the South. These successes have moreover won the sympathy and support of the socialist countries and the world's progressive people (including the U.S. progressive people) for our people's revolutionary cause, seriously isolated the U.S. imperialists and their lackeys, deepened their internal contradictions and thereby weakened the U.S. will of aggression.

The above-mentioned great successes in all fields have been recorded thanks to the clear-sighted and correct policy, line and strategic determination of the Party, the wise and resolute leadership of the Party Central Committee, the correct implementation of the Party's policy and line by Nam Truong and Party committee echelons, the sacrifice and devotion of all Party cadres and members who have in an exemplary manner carried out the Party's strategic determination, the eagerness for independence and freedom of the people in the South who are ready to shed their blood in exchange for independence and freedom, the absolute loyalty to the Party's and masses' revolution of the People's armed forces who have fought with infinite courage, the great assistance from the northern rear area and brotherly socialist countries, and the sympathy and support from the world people.

We have won great successes but still have many deficiencies and weak points:

1. In the military field—From the beginning, we have not been able to annihilate much of the enemy's live force and much of the reactionary clique. Our armed forces have not fulfilled their role as "lever" and have not created favorable conditions for motivating the masses to arise in towns and cities.

2. In the political field—Organized popular forces were not broad and strong enough. We have not had specific plans for motivating the masses to the extent that they would indulge in violent armed uprisings in coordination with and supporting the military offensives.

3. The puppet troop proselyting failed to create a military revolt movement in which the troops would arise and return to the people's side. The enemy troop proselyting task to be carried out in coordination with the armed struggle and political struggle has not been performed, and inadequate attention had been paid to this in particular.

4. There has not been enough consciousness about specific plans for the widening and development of liberated rural areas and the appropriate mobilization of manpower, material resources and the great capabilities of the masses to support the front line.

5. The building of real strength and particularly the replenishment of troops and development of political forces of the infrastructure has been slow and has not met the requirements of continuous offensives and uprisings of the new phase.

6. In providing leadership and guidance to various echelons, we failed to give them a profound and thorough understanding of the Party's policy, line and strategic determination so that they have a correct and full realization of this phase of General Offensive and General Uprising. The implementation of our policies has not been sharply and closely conducted. We lacked concreteness, our plans were simple, our coordination poor, control and prodding were absent, reporting and requests for instructions were much delayed.

The above-mentioned deficiencies and weak points have limited our successes and are, at the same time, difficulties which we must resolutely overcome.

II. *The present form of the war between the enemy and us and prospects of future developments.*

1. Our present "Anti-U.S. National Salvation" resistance war has a very new form and is more favorable to us than ever.

a. We are in a completely active and offensive position; we have brought the war into towns and cities, the enemy's rear areas and important and densely populated areas close to towns and cities; our rear areas have increasingly expanded to form a strong, linked-up position which gradually and tightly encircles the enemy's last strong points. Throughout the three areas, the masses have continuously risen up and strengthened their position of mastery with a higher and higher revolutionary spirit. In towns and cities particularly, in the face of the enemy's recent murderous and savage actions against the people, including puppet troops' and civil servants' dependents, the masses, boiling with anger, have been supporting our troops and awaiting favorable occasions to arise, eradicating wicked [enemy] individuals, sweeping the enemy's state power, and building the people's revolutionary state power. All intermediary classes of people are leaning toward the revolution's side.

b. The enemy is in a passive position, being encircled, divided and dispersed on all battlefields. He is facing difficulties in all aspects such as: a stalemate in strategy; passiveness in tactics; difficulties in replenishing troops and replacing war facilities which had been destroyed; difficulties in the economic field because of the restriction of their reserve of manpower and material resources. Because of their serious isolation in the political field and the state of confusion of the puppet army, the puppet regime is gradually losing authority and running toward total failure.

2. Although the enemy is suffering heavy defeat and is in a passive and confused situation, he still has strength and is very stubborn. In his death throes he will resort to more murderous and savage actions. He will massacre the people, thrust out to break the encirclement and create many new difficulties for us. The struggle between the enemy and us will become fiercer, particularly in areas adjoining the towns and cities. Therefore, we must be extremely vigilant, urgently and actively exploit our past successes, overcome all difficulties and hardships with determination to secure final victory and be ready to fight vigorously should the war be prolonged and widened.

However, it must be clearly realized that this will be but the enemy's convulsions before death, his reaction from a weak, not a strong position. The situation will continue to develop in a way favorable to us and detrimental to the enemy with the possibility of sudden developments which we must be ready to take advantage of in order to secure final victory.

Robert Komer Recalls Tet's Impact (1968), 1987

What really surprised us about Tet—and boy it was a surprise, lemme tell you, I was there at Westy's [General Westmoreland] elbow—was that they abandoned the time-tested Mao rural strategy where the guerrillas slowly strangle the city, and only at the end do they attack the seat of imperial power directly. At Tet they infiltrated right through our porous lines and attacked some forty cities. They abandoned the countryside where they were doing very well, and boy did they get creamed in the cities. For once, the enemy, who we could not find out there in the triple canopy jungle, who could control his losses by deciding to cut and run every time we got after him, for once we could find him. He was right there shooting at us in our own headquarters, and the cost to him was enormous militarily.

I always felt that the Tet offensive was a desperate gamble on the part of Hanoi. They saw the American presence going up and up and up, they saw us beginning to get a pacification program going, and they decided they better go for broke. And they did dislocate us. It cost them enormously. They had snuffed out the best of the southern cadre by sending them into the cities. We had a startling success in pacification after the Tet offensive because the enemy had sacrificed the core of his guerrilla movement. After Tet it really became an NVA war.

But he had also fatally weakened us at the center of our political structure. I mean Washington panicked. LBJ panicked. Bus Wheeler, Chairman of the Joint Chiefs, panicked. *We* [American officials in South Vietnam] didn't panic, mainly because we were too goddamn busy. But after the first day we knew we were back on top. The one place where after three days we were still out of control was Hue. Now that was two North Vietnamese divisions. And that was a big problem. They really had to be dug out, and we didn't finish it until February twenty-sixth [nearly a month after the offensive began].

It was the Tet shock to the American psyche that made me first think we might lose. And the shock in Washington was materially increased by the fact that the top command—Bunker and Westmoreland in particular—had come back in late November and reported confidently to the President that "Boss, finally all this stuff you have given us is beginning to pay off, and we look forward to 1968 as a big year of success for us." Westy has great plans for pushing back the NVA. Finally we have an elected government even though it's Thieu and not Ky, and so on.

We were not engaging in deception. We genuinely believed at the end of 1967 that we were getting on top. Hell, I was there in the top three or four Americans in Saigon. Westmoreland believed, Abrams believed, Bunker believed, and I believed that finally, with five hundred thousand goddamn troops and all that air, and pacification finally getting underway, with the Vietnamese having set up a constitution and elections, we really were winning. We couldn't quite see clearly how soon, but this wasn't public relations, this wasn't Lyndon Johnson telling us to put a face on it. We genuinely thought we were making it.

And then boom, forty towns get attacked, and they didn't believe us anymore. Bus Wheeler with his three dwarfs, [Phil] Habib, [George] Carver, and [Gen. William] DePuy, comes out about the twelfth of February. The Chiefs have decided, because they too panicked, that we're losing. Besides which, there's the *Pueblo* incident [the seizure by North Korea of an American naval vessel] in Korea, and maybe there's another Berlin crisis brewing. We have no strategic reserve; it's all either out in Vietnam or on the way. The Chiefs want to go to the President and say "We've got to call up the reserves, because if we get a second front in Korea there's not a goddamn thing we could do about it."

Wheeler comes out and asks Westmoreland "What do you need if we call up the reserves and the wraps are off." Westmoreland says "Look, if you call up the reserves and we've got five hundred thousand more men to play with, I would like two hundred thousand more." He pulls out of the drawer a request he had made in the spring of 1967, which was turned down, and has his guys burn a little midnight oil to update it. He gives it to Wheeler and he says "Look, this is to speed up the pace of victory. We think we have creamed them at Tet. They are on the run now. By God, if you'll give me the resources I'll chase them back into Cambodia, Laos and North Vietnam." He also has some plans that he tells Wheeler about: A hook around the DMZ at Cua Viet and go up there north of Dong Ha. Go into Laos. Go into Cambodia. He wants to hit the enemy in his sanctuaries. He says "We've got them on the run. They're going to retreat to the sanctuaries, and by God let's follow them in there and we'll win this war." Nothing big like taking Haiphong or anything like that. It's a conditional request. Westy is saying "If you're going to call up reserves and the other theater commanders are bidding, I too am going to put in a bid: two hundred thousand more men in two tranches, a hundred thousand in '68 and a hundred thousand in '69. I'll win your war for you in three or four years."

And then they decide not to do anything about the *Pueblo,* and the Berlin crisis proves evanescent. By the time Wheeler gets back, the whole case for calling up the reserves, which the JCS have argued for since the day we entered Vietnam, has disappeared—except the Vietnam case. But the fact that Westmoreland's conditional requisition, which is based on A. calling up the reserves and B. letting him use these troops to go into the sanctuaries, none of that is ever mentioned by Wheeler to either the President or to McNamara. By God they would have thrown him out on his ear. Can you imagine? So the perception in Washington is that we have just suffered a massive defeat and here's the commander saying "Boy, I've just won a massive victory. Give me some more guys and I'll clean this thing up fairly quickly."

So the three gnomes, Habib, Carver, and DePuy, go and talk to the President with Wheeler's patronage, and they say "Those guys in Saigon are smoking opium. We think the situation is much worse than they do. We have just been out there and we disagree with Komer's optimism, with Westmoreland's optimism, with Bunker's optimism and Thieu's optimism. Those guys just got surprised. Who wants to listen to them? We are in deep trouble, and that's why we need more men—not to insure victory but to stave off defeat." And of course this is leaked by some civilian who knows nothing of the conditionality of the request. The Chiefs never tell anybody anything. The goddamn Chiefs of Staff. Wheeler's the evil genius of the Vietnam war in my judgment.

Clark M. Clifford Remembers
His Post-Tet Questions (1968), 1969

I took office on March 1, 1968. The enemy's Tet offensive of late January and early February had been beaten back at great cost. The confidence of the American people had been badly shaken. The ability of the South Vietnamese Government to restore order and morale in the populace, and discipline and esprit in the armed forces, was being questioned. At the President's direction, General Earle G. Wheeler, Chairman of the Joint Chiefs of Staff, had flown to Viet Nam in late February for an on-the-spot conference with General Westmoreland. He had just returned and presented the military's request that over 200,000 troops be prepared for deployment to Viet Nam. These troops would be in addition to the 525,000 previously authorized. I was directed, as my first assignment, to chair a task force named by the President to determine how this new requirement could be met. We were not instructed to assess the need for substantial increases in men and matériel; we were to devise the means by which they could be provided.

My work was cut out. The task force included Secretary Rusk, Secretary Henry Fowler, Under Secretary of State Nicholas Katzenbach, Deputy Secretary of Defense Paul Nitze, General Wheeler, CIA Director Richard Helms, the President's Special Assistant, Walt Rostow, General Maxwell Taylor and other skilled and highly capable officials. All of them had had long and direct experience with Vietnamese problems. I had not. I had attended various meetings in the past several years and I had been to Viet Nam three times, but it was quickly apparent to me how little one knows if he has been on the periphery of a problem and not truly in it. Until the day-long sessions of early March, I had never had the opportunity of intensive analysis and fact-finding. Now I was thrust into a vigorous, ruthlessly frank assessment of our situation by the men who knew the most about it. Try though we would to stay with the assignment of devising means to meet the military's requests, fundamental questions began to recur over and over.

It is, of course, not possible to recall all the questions that were asked nor all of the answers that were given. Had a transcript of our discussions been made—one was not—it would have run to hundreds of closely printed

Clark M. Clifford, "A Vietnam Reappraisal: The Personal History of One Man's View and How It Evolved," *Foreign Affairs* (July 1969), pp. 609–612, 613. Reprinted by permission of *Foreign Affairs*, July 1969. Copyright © 1969 by the Council on Foreign Relations, Inc.

pages. The documents brought to the table by participants would have totalled, if collected in one place—which they were not—many hundreds more. All that is pertinent to this essay are the impressions I formed, and the conclusions I ultimately reached in those days of exhausting scrutiny. In the colloquial style of those meetings, here are some of the principal issues raised and some of the answers as I understood them:

"Will 200,000 more men do the job?" I found no assurance that they would.

"If not, how many more might be needed—and when?" There was no way of knowing.

"What would be involved in committing 200,000 more men to Viet Nam?" A reserve call-up of approximately 280,000, an increased draft call and an extension of tours of duty of most men then in service.

"Can the enemy respond with a build-up of his own?" He could and he probably would.

"What are the estimated costs of the latest requests?" First calculations were on the order of $2 billion for the remaining four months of that fiscal year, and an increase of $10 to $12 billion for the year beginning July 1, 1968.

"What will be the impact on the economy?" So great that we would face the possibility of credit restrictions, a tax increase and even wage and price controls. The balance of payments would be worsened by at least half a billion dollars a year.

"Can bombing stop the war?" Never by itself. It was inflicting heavy personnel and matériel losses, but bombing by itself would not stop the war.

"Will stepping up the bombing decrease American casualties?" Very little, if at all. Our casualties were due to the intensity of the ground fighting in the South. We had already dropped a heavier tonnage of bombs than in all the theaters of World War II. During 1967, an estimated 90,000 North Vietnamese had infiltrated into South Viet Nam. In the opening weeks of 1968, infiltrators were coming in at three to four times the rate of a year earlier, despite the ferocity and intensity of our campaign of aerial interdiction.

"How long must we keep on sending our men and carrying the main burden of combat?" The South Vietnamese were doing better, but they were not ready yet to replace our troops and we did not know when they would be.

When I asked for a presentation of the military plan for attaining victory in Viet Nam, I was told that there was no plan for victory in the historic American sense. Why not? Because our forces were operating under three major political restrictions: The President had forbidden the invasion of North Viet Nam because this could trigger the mutual assistance pact between North Viet Nam and China; the President had forbidden the mining of the harbor at Haiphong, the principal port through which the North received military supplies, because a Soviet vessel might be sunk; the

President had forbidden our forces to pursue the enemy into Laos and Cambodia, for to do so would spread the war, politically and geographically, with no discernible advantage. These and other restrictions which precluded an all-out, no-holds-barred military effort were wisely designed to prevent our being drawn into a larger war. We had no inclination to recommend to the President their cancellation.

"Given these circumstances, how can we win?" We would, I was told, continue to evidence our superiority over the enemy; we would continue to attack in the belief that he would reach the stage where he would find it inadvisable to go on with the war. He could not afford the attrition we were inflicting on him. And we were improving our posture all the time.

I then asked, "What is the best estimate as to how long this course of action will take? Six months? One year? Two years?" There was no agreement on an answer. Not only was there no agreement, I could find no one willing to express any confidence in his guesses. Certainly, none of us was willing to assert that he could see "light at the end of the tunnel" or that American troops would be coming home by the end of the year.

After days of this type of analysis, my concern had greatly deepened. I could not find out when the war was going to end; I could not find out the manner in which it was going to end; I could not find out whether the new requests for men and equipment were going to be enough, or whether it would take more and, if more, when and how much; I could not find out how soon the South Vietnamese forces would be ready to take over. All I had was the statement, given with too little self-assurance to be comforting, that if we persisted for an indeterminate length of time, the enemy would choose not to go on.

And so I asked, "Does anyone see any diminution in the will of the enemy after four years of our having been there, after enormous casualties and after massive destruction from our bombing?"

The answer was that there appeared to be no diminution in the will of the enemy. . . .

And so, after these exhausting days, I was convinced that the military course we were pursuing was not only endless, but hopeless. A further substantial increase in American forces could only increase the devastation and the Americanization of the war, and thus leave us even further from our goal of a peace that would permit the people of South Viet Nam to fashion their own political and economic institutions. Henceforth, I was also convinced, our primary goal should be to level off our involvement, and to work toward gradual disengagement.

Johnson Calls for Negotiations, 1968

Good evening, my fellow Americans. Tonight I want to speak to you of peace in Viet-Nam and Southeast Asia.

No other question so preoccupies our people. No other dream so absorbs the 250 million human beings who live in that part of the world. No other goal motivates American policy in Southeast Asia.

For years, representatives of our Government and others have traveled the world seeking to find a basis for peace talks.

Since last September, they have carried the offer that I made public at San Antonio.

That offer was this: that the United States would stop its bombardment of North Viet-Nam when that would lead promptly to productive discussions—and that we would assume that North Viet-Nam would not take military advantage of our restraint.

Hanoi denounced this offer, both privately and publicly. Even while the search for peace was going on, North Viet-Nam rushed their preparations for a savage assault on the people, the Government, and the allies of South Viet-Nam.

Their attack—during the Tet holidays—failed to achieve its principal objectives.

It did not collapse the elected government of South Viet-Nam or shatter its army, as the Communists had hoped.

It did not produce a "general uprising" among the people of the cities, as they had predicted.

The Communists were unable to maintain control of any of the more than 30 cities that they attacked. And they took very heavy casualties.

But they did compel the South Vietnamese and their allies to move certain forces from the countryside into the cities. They caused widespread disruption and suffering. Their attacks, and the battles that followed, made refugees of half a million human beings.

The Communists may renew their attack any day. They are, it appears, trying to make 1968 the year of decision in South Viet-Nam—the year that brings, if not final victory or defeat, at least a turning point in the struggle.

This much is clear: If they do mount another round of heavy attacks, they will not succeed in destroying the fighting power of South Viet-Nam and its allies.

But tragically, this is also clear: Many men—on both sides of the struggle—will be lost. A nation that has already suffered 20 years of warfare will suffer once again. Armies on both sides will take new casualties. And the war will go on.

There is no need for this to be so.

There is no need to delay the talks that could bring an end to this long and this bloody war.

Tonight I renew the offer I made last August—to stop the bombardment of North Viet-Nam. We ask that talks begin promptly, that they be serious talks on the substance of peace. We assume that during those talks Hanoi will not take advantage of our restraint.

We are prepared to move immediately toward peace through negotiations. So tonight, in the hope that this action will lead to early talks, I am taking the first step to deescalate the conflict. We are reducing—substantially reducing—the present level of hostilities. And we are doing so unilaterally and at once.

Tonight I have ordered our aircraft and our naval vessels to make no attacks on North Viet-Nam, except in the area north of the demilitarized zone where the continuing enemy buildup directly threatens Allied forward positions and where the movements of their troops and supplies are clearly related to that threat.

The area in which we are stopping our attacks includes almost 90 percent of North Viet-Nam's population and most of its territory. Thus there will be no attacks around the principal populated areas or in the food-producing areas of North Viet-Nam.

Even this very limited bombing of the North could come to an early end if our restraint is matched by restraint in Hanoi. But I cannot in good conscience stop all bombing so long as to do so would immediately and directly endanger the lives of our men and our allies. Whether a complete bombing halt becomes possible in the future will be determined by events.

Our purpose in this action is to bring about a reduction in the level of violence that now exists.

It is to save the lives of brave men and to save the lives of innocent women and children. It is to permit the contending forces to move closer to a political settlement.

And tonight I call upon the United Kingdom and I call upon the Soviet Union, as cochairmen of the Geneva conferences and as permanent members of the United Nations Security Council, to do all they can to move from the unilateral act of deescalation that I have just announced toward genuine peace in Southeast Asia.

Now, as in the past, the United States is ready to send its representatives to any forum, at any time, to discuss the means of bringing this ugly war to an end.

I am designating one of our most distinguished Americans, Ambassador Averell Harriman, as my personal representative for such talks. In addition, I have asked Ambassador Llewellyn Thompson, who returned from Moscow for consultation, to be available to join Ambassador Harriman at Geneva or any other suitable place just as soon as Hanoi agrees to a conference.

I call upon President Ho Chi Minh to respond positively and favorably to this new step toward peace.

But if peace does not come now through negotiations, it will come when Hanoi understands that our common resolve is unshakable and our common strength is invincible.

Tonight, we and the other allied nations are contributing 600,000 fighting men to assist 700,000 South Vietnamese troops in defending their little country.

Our presence there has always rested on this basic belief: The main burden of preserving their freedom must be carried out by them—by the South Vietnamese themselves.

We and our allies can only help to provide a shield behind which the people of South Viet-Nam can survive and can grow and develop. On their efforts—on their determinations and resourcefulness—the outcome will ultimately depend. . . .

The actions that we have taken since the beginning of the year to reequip the South Vietnamese forces; to meet our responsibilities in Korea, as well as our responsibilities in Viet-Nam; to meet price increases and the cost of activating and deploying Reserve forces; to replace helicopters and provide the other military supplies we need—all of these actions are going to require additional expenditures.

The tentative estimate of those additional expenditures is $2.5 billion in this fiscal year and $2.6 billion in the next fiscal year.

These projected increases in expenditures for our national security will bring into sharper focus the Nation's need for immediate action, action to protect the prosperity of the American people and to protect the strength and the stability of our American dollar.

On many occasions I have pointed out that without a tax bill or decreased expenditures next year's deficit would again be around $20 billion. I have emphasized the need to set strict priorities in our spending. I have stressed that failure to act—and to act promptly and decisively—would raise very strong doubts throughout the world about America's willingness to keep its financial house in order.

Yet Congress has not acted. And tonight we face the sharpest financial threat in the post-war era—a threat to the dollar's role as the keystone of international trade and finance in the world. . . .

One day, my fellow citizens, there will be peace in Southeast Asia.

It will come because the people of Southeast Asia want it—those whose armies are at war tonight and those who, though threatened, have thus far been spared.

Peace will come because Asians were willing to work for it—and to sacrifice for it—and to die by the thousands for it.

But let it never be forgotten: Peace will come also because America sent her sons to help secure it.

It has not been easy—far from it. During the past 4½ years, it has been my fate and my responsibility to be Commander in Chief. I lived daily and nightly with the cost of this war. I know the pain that it has inflicted. I know perhaps better than anyone the misgivings that it has aroused.

Throughout this entire long period, I have been sustained by a single principle: that what we are doing now in Viet-Nam is vital not only to the security of Southeast Asia, but it is vital to the security of every American.

Surely we have treaties which we must respect. Surely we have commitments that we are going to keep. Resolutions of the Congress testify to the need to resist aggression in the world and in Southeast Asia.

But the heart of our involvement in South Viet-Nam—under three different Presidents, three separate administrations—has always been America's own security.

And the larger purpose of our involvement has always been to help the nations of Southeast Asia become independent and stand alone, self-sustaining as members of a great world community—at peace with themselves and at peace with all others.

With such an Asia, our country—and the world—will be far more secure than it is tonight.

I believe that a peaceful Asia is far nearer to reality because of what America has done in Viet-Nam. I believe that the men who endure the dangers of battle—fighting there for us tonight—are helping the entire world avoid far greater conflicts, far wider wars, far more destruction, than this one.

The peace that will bring them home some day will come. Tonight I have offered the first in what I hope will be a series of mutual moves toward peace.

I pray that it will not be rejected by the leaders of North Viet-Nam. I pray that they will accept it as a means by which the sacrifices of their own people may be ended. And I ask your help and your support, my fellow citizens, for this effort to reach across the battlefield toward an early peace. . . .

Throughout my entire public career I have followed the personal philosophy that I am a free man, an American, a public servant, and a member of my party, in that order always and only.

For 37 years in the service of our nation, first as a Congressman, as a Senator and as Vice President and now as your President, I have put the unity of the people first. I have put it ahead of any divisive partisanship.

And in these times as in times before, it is true that a house divided against itself by the spirit of faction, of party, of region, of religion, of race, is a house that cannot stand.

There is division in the American house now. There is divisiveness among us all tonight. And holding the trust that is mine, as President of all the people, I cannot disregard the peril to the progress of the American people and the hope and the prospect of peace for all peoples.

So I would ask all Americans, whatever their personal interests or concern, to guard against divisiveness and all its ugly consequences.

Fifty-two months and 10 days ago, in a moment of tragedy and trauma, the duties of this Office fell upon me. I asked then for your help and God's, that we might continue America on its course, binding up our wounds, healing our history, moving forward in new unity, to clear the American agenda and to keep the American commitment for all of our people.

United we have kept that commitment. United we have enlarged that commitment.

Through all time to come, I think America will be a stronger nation, a more just society, and a land of greater opportunity and fulfillment because of what we have all done together in these years of unparalleled achievement.

Our reward will come in the life of freedom, peace, and hope that our children will enjoy through ages ahead.

What we won when all of our people united just must not now be lost in suspicion, distrust, selfishness, and politics among any of our people.

Believing this as I do, I have concluded that I should not permit the Presidency to become involved in the partisan divisions that are developing in this political year.

With America's sons in the fields far away, with America's future under challenge right here at home, with our hopes and the world's hopes for peace in the balance every day, I do not believe that I should devote an hour or a day of my time to any personal partisan causes or to any duties other than the awesome duties of this Office—the Presidency of your country.

Accordingly, I shall not seek, and I will not accept, the nomination of my party for another term as your President.

But let men everywhere know, however, that a strong, a confident, and a vigilant America stands ready tonight to seek an honorable peace— and stands ready tonight to defend an honored cause—whatever the price, whatever the burden, whatever the sacrifices that duty may require.

Thank you for listening.

Good night and God bless all of you.

✗ *E S S A Y S*

William S. Turley, a specialist in Vietnamese history who teaches at Southern Illinois University, analyzes the origins and results of the Tet offensive in the first essay. Focusing especially on North Vietnam and the National Liberation Front, he concludes that Hanoi accomplished its minimum objective of sparking a psychological crisis in Washington that hastened American deescalation, but it paid a heavy price of crippling losses. Gabriel Kolko of York University (Toronto) explores Tet's impact on Washington decision-makers in the next essay. He argues that the offensive proved the decisive turning point for U.S. involvement in Vietnam. Kolko contends that the American business and financial communities exerted powerful pressures on the Johnson administration to limit the U.S. commitment because of their concern with the budget deficits and gold and dollar crises spawned by the war. U.S. leaders feared that another escalation in Vietnam would severely damage America's economic position at home and abroad while further eroding its military strength.

Tactical Defeat, Strategic Victory for Hanoi

WILLIAM S. TURLEY

At midnight on January 31, 1968, a million tiny explosions roared across the city. The bright flashes of firecrackers glowed and flickered against the buildings and rising smoke. It was Tet in Saigon, the beginning of the New Year, a sacred time of reunion and renewal. Two and one-half hours later,

William S. Turley, *The Second Indochina War: A Short Political and Military History, 1954–1975*, pp. 99–117. Copyright © 1986, Westview Press. Reprinted by permission.

an old Renault taxi and a small truck crept through the now silent streets and stopped in front of the U.S. Embassy. Nineteen sappers piled out, blew a hole in the compound wall, and rushed in. Meanwhile, some 84,000 communist troops moved toward their targets in five municipalities, thirty-six province capitals, and sixty-four district seats. The Tet Offensive was under way.

For weeks the Communists had meticulously stocked weapons, ammunition, and food in the homes and businesses of urban sympathizers. Vegetable carts bound for market had carried rifles. A ship from Hong Kong had unloaded crates of ammunition marked "firecrackers" onto a dock in Saigon. Combatants and agitators had trickled into the cities one by one or in small groups aboard buses, bicycles, or on foot. Others had gathered at secret locations on the outskirts of the cities. Political cadres had made discreet contact with urban dissidents.

Not every movement went undetected, and by late January, it was apparent that something was about to happen. But the rumors had been heard before, and the evidence hinted at something too audacious to be believed. The attacks achieved almost complete surprise. Despite three years of massive U.S. involvement, the communist offensive was bigger and more complicated than ever before. It struck the very centers of previously inviolable cities. The bulk of the assault forces were indigenous Southern irregulars, and the preparations for the offensive required at least the passive collusion of many of its supposed victims. No matter how the fighting ended, U.S. claims of military victory would not be able to erase the impression that all the blood and expense had been, and always would be, for naught.

The Tet strategy was hardly a new idea for the Vietnamese Communists. Its germ was the August Revolution, in which the Communists had provided a nucleus of armed force for the popular uprisings that had brought the party to power in 1945. Party doctrine subsequently held that surrounding the cities with rural revolution, as Maoists advocated, was insufficient in Vietnam. For if cut off from the countryside, the cities could still hold out with support from the "imperialist" hinterland. Moreover, given Vietnam's cramped geography, enemies that controlled the cities could launch powerful attacks into liberated areas if not distracted by turbulence in their own rear. The strategic solution, called "general offensive and general uprising," was to mount simultaneous armed attacks and popular uprisings at all geographical points. Even if this plan did not sweep the revolution to power, the Communists theorized, it would destroy the enemy's illusion of success.

The idea exercised a powerful hold on revolutionaries who saw themselves as ordained to lead a small, impoverished nation in resistance against more powerful foes. It was especially popular among party members whose revolutionary careers had begun amidst the patriotic fervor that had seized the cities in August 1945. Many believed that the proper stimulus could make the cities explode again. Party leaders had never neglected to consider the cities in their plans and had considered attack in the enemy's most secure areas, in coordination with region-wide popular uprisings, as their ultimate weapon. The Central Committee's resolution 9 in 1963 had foreseen the need for a "general offensive and general uprising," and in 1964, COSVN had drawn up tentative plans, selected targets, and subdivided Saigon into five "lines of attack." Fairly detailed planning was under way by mid-1966.

The Communists realized they could not simply replay the August Revolution, however. The United States and the "puppet" Saigon regime presented a much more formidable obstacle than the shaky Japanese-installed administration a few mobs had overwhelmed in 1945. Much more military power would have to be projected now into the cities to have great effect. But unlike the situation in 1945, power was now available and securely based in the North. The party also had a large organization in the South with which leaders believed they controlled nearly 4 million people. If they bypassed U.S. positions, revolutionary forces stood a chance of destroying the "puppet."

In June 1967, Nguyen Chi Thanh travelled to Hanoi to present a draft plan for attacking the cities to the Political Bureau. Several considerations weighed in the Political Bureau's deliberations. U.S. bombing had taken such toll that communist leaders were impatient for it to end, if only so they could strengthen the North's capacity to support the war in the South. Yet U.S. leaders still appeared to believe in the possibility of military victory, and rural struggle alone seemed unlikely in the near future to make them believe differently. New difficulties would arise if the United States prolonged its involvement or invaded the North. It was imperative to ward off such moves and tilt the United States toward negotiation, which the Communists believed could be done by destroying U.S. confidence. If that effort succeeded, it would be necessary also for the Communists to break up pacification and recover control in the countryside so that "fighting-while-negotiating" could be conducted from a position of strength. After heated discussion, the Political Bureau reached agreement that the time had come for the big blow.

Thanh's plan for an all-out effort apparently encountered resistance, however. General Giap, for one, doubted that Southern irregulars could do the job unaided but was loathe to place precious main forces at risk. Differences over strategy stemmed partly from disagreement over the realism of seeking the immediate termination of U.S. involvement as opposed to preempting further U.S. escalation. Thanh's death on July 6, 1967, may have cleared the way for agreement on a scaled-down version of his plan. In an article serialized in *Nhan dan* (The People) during September, Giap gave his grudging approval but warned against expecting quick victory. Orders went out to Southern command organs the same month. PLAF units and Southern irregulars, those orders made clear, were to bear the main burden of attacking the cities while the PAVN created diversions and stood in reserve.

What, then, did the Communists hope to achieve? Party leaders differed in expectations but agreed it should be possible to jolt the war into a new phase leading toward, if not immediately causing, U.S. withdrawal. The most optimistic hope was that the offensive would paralyze the Thieu regime's military and administrative apparatus, generate popular demand for Thieu to step aside, and end in coalition government. Thus deprived of the "puppet" on whom the United States depended to justify intervention, the United States would have no choice but to fix a date for its withdrawal. Somewhat less sanguine was the hope that the offensive would convince U.S. leaders of the futility of their "limited war" strategy. If, as the Communists surmised, the United States would be unable to escalate further, it would have to give up hope of military victory and seek a way out through negotiations.

The cities up to this time had experienced a few terrorist incidents, but never had the fighting in the countryside pushed into their confines. A person born in Saigon, Hue, Danang, or Can Tho easily could have reached maturity without feeling any direct effect of the war. For many urbanites, U.S. intervention brought jobs and larger pay packets, not pain and suffering. The only sound of combat audible in Saigon was the low rumble of B-52 strikes thirty kilometers away. City youth also were more likely than rural youth to qualify for student draft deferment or to have families with the financial or political means to arrange avoidance of military service altogether. Urbanites were largely oblivious to the terror endured by peasants in "contested" areas and could, if they wished, regard the war as someone else's misfortune.

However, the combined effects of rural insecurity, the destructiveness of U.S. tactics, and economic distortions also had stimulated a cityward migration. The proportion of total population living in the countryside had dropped from 80 to about 70 percent, a trend that would continue and be largely irreversible. This movement threatened to shrink the Communists' base of support in rural areas where they had their main strength. But it also gave them reason to hope that in the bidonvilles spreading in the outskirts and back streets of Saigon and in Danang, Qui Nhon, Cam Ranh, and a dozen lesser provincial capitals, they might find an enlarged pool of urban supporters.

Noteworthy, too, was the changing political scene in Saigon. The era of revolving-door juntas had ended, and Nguyen Van Thieu was safely ensconsed in Independence Palace. On the surface it seemed that a new elite—younger, more career-oriented, and more susceptible to U.S. influence by comparison with the mandarin Francophiles it displaced—had consolidated a firm hold on power. Thieu certainly typified the new group. Born a Buddhist in 1923, Thieu was from a modest, provincial background. Emerging from the first war a major in the French Army, he had transferred to the ARVN and in 1957 had gone for training in the United States. The next year, at the height of the Diem era, he had married into a wealthy Catholic family and converted. With his wife's connections, the right patrons, and a knack for clever maneuver, Thieu was admirably equipped to rise in the armed forces but not to provide inspiring leadership.

The consolidation of the Thieu regime had begun with elections for a Constituent Assembly in 1966 when Thieu as chief of state still shared power with Premier Nguyen Cao Ky. Elections for village councils and hamlet chiefs had followed in spring 1967, a genuine if fragile accomplishment that laid a basis for the rehabilitation of Saigon-sponsored local government. At the top, however, Thieu and Ky had parted over which of them should run for the presidency provided in the new constitution. Leaders of opposing cliques, they threatened to split the military once again. Only when it became clear that the majority of senior officers as well as the United States supported Thieu had Ky agreed in June to run for vice president on Thieu's ticket.

Attention then shifted to culling the civilian candidacies, partly to reduce their exorbitant number but also to remove some genuine electoral threats. Maneuvers in the Constituent Assembly disqualified General Duong Van "Big" Minh, who had announced his intention of returning from exile on the tennis courts of Bangkok. The popular, former minister of economics, Au Truong Thanh, who revealed he once had withheld a gold sales distributorship from the chief of police, also was eliminated. Further manipulations pared down the number of slates to eleven. Of these, the best known of the civilian tickets was headed by Phan Khac Suu and Dr. Phan Quang Dan, both of whom had gained repute by spending time in Diem's jails. Another, headed by Tran Van Huong and Mai Tho Truyen, could count on the aging Huong's prominence as a lay leader of the Southern Buddhist Association to win support among Buddhists in the deep south. A third slate consisting of Truong Dinh Dzu and Tran Van Chieu lacked personal distinction but captured attention by calling for negotiations to end the war. The Dzu-Chieu slate was promptly dubbed the peace ticket.

The campaign was to have begun with a tour of the provinces by all eleven slates of candidates. But Thieu and Ky refused to join, and the air force C-47 that was to carry the other candidates to their first destination delivered them to the wrong airport. Huong claimed that "the government purposely arranged the trip to humiliate us and make clowns out of us." The tour fell apart, and though a second was arranged, the civilians held the military responsible for irregularities that continued down to the end of the campaign. Thieu and his associates, however, were constrained from blatantly rigging the election by the realization that this would create insurmountable problems in Washington and that the election would take place under the scrutiny of a huge foreign press corps and other observers. On September 3, according to the published results, 83.8 percent of the South's registered voters cast ballots. The Thieu-Ky ticket won, but with only 34.8 percent of the votes. The pattern of local results suggested that Thieu and Ky did best where the military felt most free to help; they lost in Hue, Danang, and Saigon. If the results were at all accurate, it was clear that not one of the slates was the first choice of any significant segment of the electorate.

U.S. officials naturally pointed to the turnout as evidence that most

South Vietnamese preferred a noncommunist government. But the election did little to confirm the stature of Thieu as the man to head it. Moreover, it had taken U.S. pressure to assure that elections were held and to unify the military. It was also obvious that civilian elites, once united in opposition to Diem, were now antagonistic to the military government, and the elections had helped to sharpen that antagonism. These elites were also deeply divided among themselves. The threat of collective defeat by the revolution was no more sufficient in 1967 than in 1964 to restrain personal ambition or vanity. Although the city scene was changing, none of this change suggested any worsening of prospects for the Communists.

Communist strategy called for luring U.S. forces away from population centers, and so the Tet Offensive began neither at Tet nor in the cities. It began at Khe Sanh, the remote outpost of a U.S. Marine rifle company near the western end of Route 9. Located on an open plateau, the marine camp and nearby Khe Sanh village faced peaks over 850 meters high, behind which forested hills rolled into Laos and the demilitarized zone. There the marines found the PAVN 325c division digging into the peaks during spring 1967.

The small marine camp was highly vulnerable. Though supported by artillery at the Rock Pile and Camp Carroll, it was just fourteen kilometers from the terminus of an improved road over which the PAVN could move heavy equipment. The marines therefore sent in two battalions of reinforcements. After a few sharp engagements the PAVN division shifted eastward to join other units in feints and jabs along Route 9. Infantry assaults on strongpoints, then artillery barrages, made northern Quang Tri province once again a major focus of U.S. attention.

The 325c was accompanied by the 304th division when it returned to the Khe Sanh area in December 1967. More marine reinforcements plus an ARVN battalion brought the number of base defenders up to 6,000. Finally, on January 21, the two PAVN divisions broke the suspense with attacks on hilltop outposts and a massive artillery barrage that destroyed the base's largest ammunition dump, cratered the runway, and damaged a dozen helicopters. The "siege" of Khe Sanh had begun.

Reports of PAVN divisions maneuvering in the hills around Khe Sanh conjured up the spectre of Dien Bien Phu. The U.S. command pulled 15,000 elite troops from all over the South's five northern provinces to reinforce the Route 9 combat bases, and soon a total of 50,000 U.S. troops were tied down at Khe Sanh or in its support. By the end of January, as communist assault forces assembled on city outskirts, attention in Saigon and Washington was riveted on the mountains. For days after the Tet attacks in the cities, Westmoreland and Thieu believed Khe Sanh was the "real" target and the city attacks the diversion, such a hold did Dien Bien Phu have on their thoughts.

PAVN commanders surely would have been happy to overrun Khe Sanh if given the opportunity. But the victors of Dien Bien Phu could not have been less aware than Westmoreland of the differences between the two battlefields. In the first place, Khe Sanh was not really remote, as Dien Bien Phu had been. It was barely 50 kilometers from the sea and half an hour by air from the huge airbase at Danang. The French, by contrast, had bottled themselves up in rugged mountains over 300 kilometers from their support in Hanoi. Compared to the 325 assorted aircraft available to the French Union force, the United States could draw from 2,000 aircraft including big C-123 and KC-130 transports to supply Khe Sanh with almost constant aerial cover and supplies in excess of need. Second, Khe Sanh was not a valley ringed by mountains but a plateau facing hills on one side only, and the marines held several of the peaks. The possibility of encircling the base from high ground did not exist as it had at Dien Bien Phu. Finally, although the PAVN used more firepower at Khe Sanh (122-mm artillery, 122-mm rockets, 120-mm mortars, Soviet-built PT-76 light amphibious tanks) than in any single engagement up to that time, it faced, aside from the base's own ample artillery, the 175-mm guns of Camp Carroll and massive, all-weather aerial bombardment. By the time the siege eased in mid-April, U.S. aircraft had dropped more than 100,000 tons of bombs (including 60,000 tons of napalm) on a battlefield of a dozen square kilometers.

The 20,000 PAVN troops deployed at Khe Sanh were less than one-half the number used at Dien Bien Phu (a deployment indicative of PAVN strategists' true objectives), though the PAVN had tripled in size since 1954. U.S. estimates of PAVN casualties were less than one-half the 23,000 suffered in the earlier battle. The PAVN attempted to dig siege trenches, but it was a belated effort. The PAVN never tunnelled beneath marine positions as required for an all-out assault. The level of effort was sufficient to sustain a credible diversion, but not to mount a realistic attempt to overrun the base so long as the United States was determined to hold it.

The deputy editor of *Quan doi nhan dan* (People's Army) newspaper, interviewed in Hanoi in 1984, affirmed that Khe Sanh was never intended to be another Dien Bien Phu. The earlier battle took place after seven years of war had worn down the French, whereas the United States in 1968 was at the peak of its military power. Another Dien Bien Phu at Khe Sanh, this officer said, would have been "impossible." Rather, he went on, the Khe Sanh battle, aside from providing a strategic diversion, was a test of the U.S. reaction to the PAVN's use of the demilitarized zone (DMZ). The PAVN command wanted to determine how the United States would respond if the PAVN staged attacks from the zone, specifically whether the United States would send troops into the North.

Hanoi derided the Western preoccupation with the Dien Bien Phu analogy as it applied to Khe Sanh. Communist commentators pointed instead to Lang Vei, a Special Forces/Civil Indigenous Defense Group (CIDG) camp eight kilometers east of the besieged marines. Led by eleven PT-76s, PAVN forces on February 7 completely overran the camp, killing 250 montagnard and 24 U.S. defenders.

As the PAVN hit Khe Sanh and several other highland targets, assault forces slipped around lowland outposts to penetrate the cities. Some struck prematurely at Qui Nhon, Kontum, Pleiku, Darlac, and Nha Trang on January 29, but U.S. and ARVN intelligence missed the attacks' significance. More than one-half the ARVN was on leave for Tet. If a skittish commander had not pulled several U.S. battalions closer to Saigon in early January, the city would have been almost completely devoid of reaction forces. General Westmoreland's intelligence officer later admitted that communist plans seemed so "preposterous" that no one would have believed what was about to happen had anyone known them in detail. The U.S. and ARVN commands so poorly understood the strategy of their enemy that they could not take seriously the evidence of its intentions. So in the wee hours of Tet the cities lay open.

The estimated 67,000 maneuver forces and 17,000 hastily recruited guerrillas that attacked the cities had been led to believe final victory was at hand. Instructions to local party cadres spoke of annihilating Saigon's administrative apparatus and organizing the masses to help consolidate revolutionary power. At higher levels, however, it was understood that these were maximum objectives. During an interview with the author in 1973, a former PLAF colonel who helped plan the attack on Saigon-Cholon remarked that "the party did not say certain places had to be held for so long, but that what could be occupied should be held as long as possible, the longer the better. Any occupation for some length of time was in some measure a success, a victory."

The wave of attacks that broke on January 31 was the first of three violent surges planned for 1968. The assault on the U.S. Embassy was but the tiny if symbolically devastating kickoff. An estimated 4,000 troops joined in the attacks on Saigon, hitting Tan Son Nhut airfield, the ARVN general staff compound, government ministries, and Independence Palace. Battalion-sized forces invested several neighborhoods in Cholon. Tanks and helicopter gunships, sent to evict them, reduced entire city blocks to rubble. Forces that seized large portions of several delta towns were destroyed along with the buildings they occupied. In the large majority of cases, the attacks were beaten back in a few days.

Only in Hue did attacking forces hold out longer. The estimated 7,500-man assault force, one of the few consisting largely of uniformed PAVN regulars, entrenched itself behind the walls of the old city and fought until February 24. Roughly two-thirds of the attackers and nearly 500 ARVN and U.S. troops died in bitter door-to-door fighting, artillery shelling, and aerial bombardment that left 100,000 civilian refugees. In the aftermath, 2,800 bodies were found in mass graves, and another 2,000 people were missing, leaving behind them questions that are hotly disputed to this day (that is, who or what killed them and why).

The first wave of attacks spluttered to an end with mortar and rocket barrages against several cities. Though U.S. and ARVN forces held the streets, half of all U.S. maneuver battalions were tied down in I Corps, and the ARVN had pulled back into defensive positions, leaving the countryside undefended. On April 20, a handful of dissident intellectuals presented themselves as the Vietnam Alliance of National Democratic and Peace Forces and declared adherence to the NLF in a move to broaden the revolution's appeal. A second wave of attacks in early May attempted to build on the momentum of the first, but, lacking surprise, the attacks were quickly beaten back. A third still weaker wave brought the offensive to a close in August.

Despite initial panic, neither the ARVN nor the Saigon government had collapsed. Students and sympathizers had helped to form a "revolutionary administration" in Hué and Tra Vinh, but the population mostly had taken to shelter when banner-waving activists appeared in the streets. Cadres who had freely entered rural communities as ARVN and U.S. forces withdrew to defend the cities found themselves exposed when those forces pushed back out into the countryside to resume pacification. The U.S. estimate of 40,000 communist troops killed in the first wave of attacks was inflated, but the losses were cripplingly high. Communist battalion-sized attacks tapered off, and Washington and Saigon claimed a military victory.

But the military balance hardly mattered. As the fighting subsided in Hué, General Westmoreland claimed the Communists had used up all of their "military chips" in one last "throw of the dice." Now weakened and overextended, he said, they were vulnerable as never before, and their vulnerability presented a "great opportunity" to go for the kill. With the agreement of the Joint Chiefs, Westmoreland proposed an "amphibious hook" around the demilitarized zone to destroy bases and staging areas, attacks on sanctuaries in Laos and Cambodia, and intensified bombing of the North. Westmoreland's proposal required 206,000 more troops, an increase that would require mobilization of the reserves.

Westmoreland's request was submitted in a report by General Earle G. Wheeler, chairman of the Joint Chiefs, which presented a bleak prospect if the request were not granted. Though crafted to win approval, the report, dated February 27, 1968, was more realistic than many that had preceded it. Reproduced in *The Pentagon Papers*, it made the following points:

• The current situation in Vietnam is still developing and fraught with opportunities as well as dangers.

• There is no question in the mind of MACV that the enemy went all out for a general offensive and general uprising and apparently believed that he would succeed in bringing the war to an early successful conclusion.

• The enemy failed to achieve this initial objective but is continuing his effort. Although many of his units were badly hurt, the judgement is that he has the will and the capability to continue.

• Enemy losses have been heavy; he has failed to achieve his prime objectives of mass uprisings and capture of a large number of the capital cities and towns. However, with replacements, his indoctrination system would seem capable of maintaining morale at a generally adequate level. His determination appears to be unshaken.

• The enemy is operating with relative freedom in the countryside, probably recruiting heavily. . . . His recovery is likely to be rapid; his supplies are adequate; and he is trying to maintain the momentum of his winter-spring offensive.

• The structure of the GVN [Government of Vietnam, i.e., Saigon] has held up but its effectiveness has suffered.

• The [ARVN] held up against the initial assault. . . . However, ARVN is now in a defensive posture around towns and cities and there is concern about how well they will bear up under sustained pressure.

• The initial attack nearly succeeded in a dozen places, and defeat in those places was only averted by the timely reaction of U.S. forces. In short, it was a very near thing.

The report then came to its sober conclusion:

• MACV has three principal problems. First, logistic support north of Danang is marginal owing to weather, enemy interdiction and harassment and the massive deployment of U.S. forces into the DMZ/Hué area. Opening Route 1 will alleviate this problem but takes a substantial troop commitment. Second, the defensive posture of ARVN is permitting the VC to make rapid inroads in the formerly pacified countryside. ARVN, in its own words, is in a dilemma as it cannot afford another enemy thrust into the cities and towns and yet if it remains in a defensive posture against this contingency, the countryside goes by default. MACV is forced to devote much of its troop strength to this problem. Third, MACV has been forced to deploy 50 percent of all U.S. maneuver battalions into I Corps, to meet the threat there, while stripping the rest of the country of adequate reserves. If the enemy synchronizes an attack against Khe Sanh/Hue-Quang Tri with an offensive in the Highlands and around Saigon while keeping the pressure on through-out the remainder of the country, MACV will be hard pressed to meet adequately all threats. Under these circumstances, we must be prepared to accept some reverses.

The report was partly a political ploy to alarm the president into expanding the war. But coming less than three months after Westmoreland had said the end of the war was in sight, it only confirmed the pessimism of the new secretary of defense, Clark Clifford, and caused the president to turn to dovish civilians for advice. Disclosure of the troop request on March 10 in the *New York Times* provoked a public uproar. The official optimism of years past suddenly seemed proof of incompetence or deception. Moreover, no one could be certain that even with 206,000 additional troops the United States could impose a military solution or intimidate Hanoi into submission. Something messier seemed just as likely.

The Senate Foreign Relations Committee meanwhile had held hearings on the Tonkin Gulf Incident that cast doubt on Johnson's version of that pivotal event. Hitherto solid congressional support for the war began to ebb away. In mid-March, Senator Eugene McCarthy, the "peace candidate" for the Democratic party's presidential nomination, took 45 percent of the vote in the New Hampshire primary, inspiring Senator Robert Kennedy to join the race on an anti-war platform. Though Johnson won the primary, he sensed impending defeat. If he stood for reelection, the campaign would divide the nation; if he won, his presidency would be ineffectual. So on March 31, Johnson announced he would not seek nomination for another term, declared a bombing halt over the North except for a narrow strip above the demilitarized zone, and called on Hanoi to agree to peace talks. Hanoi accepted on condition that the talks begin by discussing a halt to the bombing altogether, and formal talks opened in Paris in May.

The Tet Offensive demolished the credibility of officials who had claimed progress, improvement, and "light at the end of the tunnel." Dovish opinion gained respectability within the administration itself. But in large measure, it was Lyndon Johnson who had defeated both himself and his policies by refusing to make hard choices. A consensus-seeking, centrist politician, he had sought to hoard the capital of his 1964 landslide victory by antagonizing no one. Fearful of the right, he had refused to "sell out" Saigon and withdraw. Reluctant to antagonize the left, he had given the Joint Chiefs less than what they asked. Needing support for domestic reforms, he had abhorred becoming the first U.S. president to lose a war. At each moment that called for decision, Johnson had chosen only to stave off defeat. But absence of defeat was a recipe for stalemate, and endless war was acceptable to no one.

Public support in the United States for the Vietnam War was about what it had been for the Korean War, though less than for World War II and a good deal more than for World War I. Support fell in response mainly to the rise in casualties and apparent inconclusiveness of the fighting. . . . Vocal opposition was largely confined to the intellectual, nonunion left. As for the anti-war protest movement, it is credited by a student of U.S. wartime opinion with electing Richard Nixon twice: once in 1968 by withholding votes that would have given victory to Hubert Humphrey, and once in 1972 by capturing control of the Democratic party and nominating George McGovern, "the worst presidential candidate any party has put forward in modern times."

How did the Communists view Tet and its aftermath? The first COSVN assessment on January 31 claimed success in "paralyzing" the Saigon administration, confusing the U.S. command, and inflicting heavy damage. But efforts to seize "primary objectives" and to "motivate the people to stage uprisings and break the enemy's oppressive control" were disappointing. The Communists realized from the start that they were unlikely to achieve their maximum aims.

In March, a fuller COSVN assessment directed attention to the successful disruption of the enemy's "two-prong tactic" of military action and rural pacification. U.S. and ARVN forces, the assessment observed, had been forced to disperse in order to defend the towns, cities, and lines of communication. In consequence, "additional wide areas in the countryside containing a population of 1.5 million inhabitants" had been liberated. The revolution had gained access to "immense resources of manpower and material." But the offensive had failed to eliminate much of the enemy armed force, the urban attacks had "not created favorable conditions for motivating the masses to arise,'' and recruitment was insufficient to sustain "continuous offensives and uprisings." Only in a fleeting reference to "internal contradictions" that "weakened the U.S. will of aggression" did the assessment include the Tet Offensive's U.S. domestic scene. Some kind of victory was still sought in altering the actual balance of military and political forces inside South Vietnam.

The Communists barely acknowledged the opening of the Paris talks as they proceeded in May with their second wave of planned attacks. "The Americans," *Quan doi nhan dan* editorialized, "have not given up, so our people will have to suffer more before we can win final victory." In fact, Southern cadres had begun to question whether they should do all of the suffering to obtain relief for the North alone; others wondered why, if negotiations had begun, they had to go on fighting. General Van Tien Dung, the PAVN chief of staff, felt constrained to point out that a bombing halt was essential if the North were to strengthen its role as the "great rear area" for the Southern revolution, and a COSVN directive dated January 10 castigated cadres who had thought the campaign would be a "one-blow affair."

The U.S. agreement to an unconditional bombing halt and to NLF participation in four-party talks allowed the Communist party to claim a satisfactory outcome. The United States, cadres were told, had been forced to deescalate, cease bombing of the North, and join Hanoi at the conference table. Final victory was conceded to lie in an indeterminate future, but the "limited war" strategy had been discredited. U.S. plans to escalate had been preempted, and the war had entered the penultimate phase of "fighting-while-negotiating."

The party's official history describes the Tet Offensive as a great victory, and in the only sense that mattered—the strategic outcome—it was. But many cadres had hoped to turn the tide of battle *inside South Vietnam* and regretted the cost they had had to pay just for psychological impact inside the United States. Former PLAF leader Madame Nguyen Thi Dinh described the post-Tet period to the author as an "especially difficult time" for the Southern revolution. Just why it was difficult has been explained in bitter detail by one of the offensive's chief planners, General Tran Van Tra:

> In Tet 1968, we did not correctly assess the concrete balance of forces between ourselves and the enemy. Nor did we fully realize that the enemy still had considerable capabilities while ours were limited. Consequently, we set requirements that exceeded our actual strength. That is, we based our action not on scientific calculations or careful weighing of all factors but, in part, on an illusion which arose from subjective desire. Although the decision was wise, ingenious and timely . . . and created a significant strategic turning point in Vietnam and Indochina, we suffered heavy losses of manpower and material, especially of cadres at various echelons, which caused a distinct decline in our strength. Subsequently, we not only were unable to preserve all the gains we had made but also had to endure myriad

difficulties in 1969–70 so that the revolution could stand firm in the storm. While it is obvious that the road to revolution is never a primrose path, . . . in Tet, 1968, had we considered things more carefully and set forth correct requirements in conformity with the balance of forces between the two sides, our victory would have been even greater, our cadres, troops and people would have spilled less blood, and the subsequent development of the revolution would have been much different.

Whether Tra blamed himself or others is not clear. But Southern cadres tended to believe that things would have been different if Nguyen Chi Thanh had lived. He, many believed, would have kept the more cautious high command in Hanoi from scaling down his plan, and his genius for mass organization would have guaranteed a better popular response in the cities. The first wave of attacks would have been more powerful, touching off uprisings that would have made the second wave more powerful still. Each successive surge of violence would have been stronger than the last. As it was, complained one former regroupee captain, the campaign had "an elephant's trunk and a snake's tail": It started small and ended smaller. Behind such views lay the firm conviction, held even by defectors, that what had prevented the masses from rising to support the revolution was fear of reprisal. If the enemy's "oppressive apparatus" had been broken, the people would have flocked to the revolution's banner. A short leap of faith sustained Southern cadres' confidence that more force and better organization would inspire greater uprisings next time. As General Tra wrote, "Tet 1968 was an extremely valuable practical experience."

A Decisive Turning Point

GABRIEL KOLKO

The Tet offensive revealed the structural constraints on policy and decision making in contemporary America and compelled the Johnson administration and Congress to acknowledge, to an extent none of their predecessors ever had, the limits that economic, military, and political realities inexorably imposed on them. The sense of crisis that emerged was justified primarily because America's leaders, not only in Washington but in all the major sectors of social power and influence, had to confront candidly the meaning of Vietnam, its symbolism to the region and the world, and its role as a test of national strategy and might. Until 1968 the costs of illusions and errors were not so apparent, and support for a large war existed among the country's leaders.

Only during crises does the real locus of power and interest expose the decisive constraints on political decision makers. To the extent that a society then defines its core needs and goals, the state's alleged autonomy and discretion in the balance of forces and power within a society tend to disappear. The presidency itself is brought to heel before what may roughly be designated as the larger interests of the American system and of those who have the capacity to define it. To the degree that those interests can be clearly and factually articulated, either by those at home or by those foreign nations linked into the U.S.–led world economic, political, and military order, the executive's options are circumscribed. Men whose ideas had earlier led the nation in different directions, as was true of the President's key advisers from 1963 until early 1968, now cease to prove influential. Their myopia, ambitions, or individual styles of work no longer have anything more than incidental interest. Should the institutional order at this point make basic errors of policy, it would be due to broader social illusions and an unrealistic consensus rather than to the caprice of this or that faction or person. In brief, bureaucratic forces are no longer decisive in a framework where choices are visibly not discretionary and the irrationality of conventional wisdom is not yet blind to the dangers of self-destruction. Decisions at this late stage reflect the interests and imperatives of a system. The Tet offensive's most decisive effect was to articulate clearly the fact that the United States was now confronting a potentially grave crisis. The first three months of 1968 were therefore the most important in the history of the entire American aggression in Vietnam.

Just as one must see America's intervention in Vietnam as contextually motivated—with its desire for credibility, regional domination, the propping up of dominoes, and the devising of a successful local-war strategy all evoking greater involvement—so one must comprehend the global events which compelled the infinitely slow process of American disengagement and defeat in the Vietnam War. Even before Tet, increasing institutional and political constraints began casting their shadows on American efforts in Vietnam. The war itself dramatically exacerbated older economic difficulties, but there were yet other dilemmas confronting the administration. These ranged from such intractable problems as the mounting racial tension in American cities and the war's debilitating impact on U.S. military power to the decline of its strategic manpower reserves for other world or even domestic crises. The significance of this erosion was dramatically illustrated in early 1968 when North Korea seized the USS *Pueblo* and its eighty-three crew members on January 23, an act which humiliated the administration and made it appear helpless. Tensions along the thirty-eighth parallel also led the South Koreans at the end of January to consider an immediate withdrawal of their 49,000 men from South Vietnam, and Washington was confronted with the possibility of having to replace them at the very moment of the Tet offensive. The danger of war along Korea's thirty-eighth parallel momentarily appeared real.

Yet it was the gold and dollar crisis that created the most sustained and irresistible pressures on Washington. Although the administration's promises to lower its deficits had managed to keep the gold pool with

Europe alive after December, steady gold purchases showed that Europe's bankers remained extremely nervous. They were especially concerned because Congress refused to act on the President's tax surcharge proposal to reduce the deficits. It was in this context that the President's advisers considered their responses to a possible imminent defeat, and McNamara's parting advice to the President was not to allow another troop escalation in Vietnam to ruin the dollar abroad and the economy at home.

The gold and dollar crisis colored all of Washington's thoughts on responses to the precarious military situation in South Vietnam. At the end of February Senator Jacob Javits of New York called for an end to the gold pool, triggering a panic, and $118 million was withdrawn from the pool in only two days. For two weeks, as the United States reached an impasse in the war in Vietnam, the highly complex and technical dollar-gold problem traumatized Washington and the Western capitals, consuming vast amounts of the time of the President and his advisers. "The specter of 1929 haunted him daily," Doris Kearns reports of her intimate later interviews with him; "he worried that if the economy collapsed, history would subject Lyndon Johnson to endless abuse."

On March 4, Treasury Secretary [Henry] Fowler warned the President that the gold rush and the flight from the dollar were serious and could worsen rapidly, with a gold embargo leading to "exchange rate wars and trading blocs with harmful political as well as economic effects." At the same time other key advisers were carefully and pessimistically assessing the consequences of any additional troop buildup to European bankers' confidence in the dollar. While Europe's gold-pool members had agreed in early March to sustain the dollar, on March 11 banks rushed the pool, which lost nearly a billion dollars in gold before it suspended operations four days later. "We can't go on as is," [National Security Adviser Walt W.] Rostow warned the President on March 14, and on the same day several European nations began to redeem dollars for U.S. Treasury gold to recoup the bullion they had lost in support of the dollar. That afternoon, having lost $372 million that day, and fearing a loss of a billion dollars the following day, the Treasury arranged immediately to close the gold market. With memos and meetings constantly before him and with his chief economic adviser's late January warning of a possible world depression still fresh in his mind, Johnson on March 15 wrote to the European prime ministers that "these financial disorders—if not promptly and firmly overcome—can profoundly damage the political relations between Europe and America and set in motion forces like those which disintegrated the Western world between 1929 and 1933."

At first the White House wanted its allies to accept unlimited amounts of dollars without gold backing, but Fowler and [Federal Reserve Board Chairman William McChesney] Martin opposed this as both unrealistic and a license to continue fiscal irresponsibility. Instead, European central bankers were called to Washington for an emergency meeting on March 16. As antiwar pickets paraded outside their secret sessions, reminding them that the war was the origin of the dollar crisis, the key decisions over the future of the dollar were being made by Europeans. Abolishing the pool altogether, Europe's bankers refused to use their gold to save the dollar. They categorically rejected an American request that they forgo their right to claim gold for dollars from the U.S. Treasury. They offered restraint only if the administration acted more responsibly in managing its economy. In effect, if it refused to place the defense of the dollar above all other considerations, then they reserved the power to demand a reckoning that could profoundly upset America's position in the world economy, with all that this implied for its political leadership.

After Tet the administration finally acknowledged that any increase of troops to Vietnam threatened not just the country's economy but all of its domestic and international priorities. Those in Washington who had for some time opposed the war's overshadowing of other military and regional commitments now became more outspoken. Although they were especially strong among civilians in the Pentagon, there was a near consensus in the government that the war should not cause the nation to sacrifice its other responsibilities, especially to NATO. With America stretched thin globally and with a crisis brewing in Korea, the Joint Chiefs of Staff immediately revived its earlier request for a call-up of reserves—a politically unpopular move for the President—and its chairman, General Wheeler, spent the rest of February conniving to get more men for the military services. In a virtuoso performance he flew to Saigon and after four days was back in Washington on February 27 with an extremely pessimistic report and a demand, allegedly from Westmoreland himself, for 206,000 men. Vietnam had greatly weakened the strategic manpower reserves for crises elsewhere in the world, and Wheeler gambled that he could rebuild them by claiming that the 206,000 were essential to reverse the tide of the war. To deny him the full request, Wheeler argued, was to jeopardize the position of the commander in Vietnam, if not to imperil his forces. One hundred thousand of the new men, however, he planned to send elsewhere than to Vietnam.

The guileless Westmoreland later sharply rebuked Wheeler for pretending that he was the author of the famous 206,000 request, but Wheeler was in fact dissembling largely out of concern for the mounting pressure in Washington over the weakening of the U.S. military elsewhere. Indeed, the President himself was worried that there would be insufficient regular forces to cope with the anticipated summer turmoil in American cities— an anxiety that was justified when huge riots broke out in Washington and in over fifty cities after the Reverend Martin Luther King was assassinated the following April 4. The most immediate result of the request for 206,000 more men, however, was that the President on February 28 asked Clark Clifford, his new Secretary of Defense, to create a committee to study it— and it was this committee's effort to turn its attention to a full-scale review of the war that became the main focus of opposition to further escalation among key Washington decision makers.

When men who have heretofore perceived no limits to their power confront reality, there will always be drama and tension. There were, of course, very dramatic moments during February and March 1968; remorse and doubt led to a debilitating loss of self-confidence unknown among American leaders for decades. But from the inception of Tet to Johnson's epoch-making speech of March 31, there was an inexorability to Washington's command decisions.

The American military's first response was a paralyzing incredulity at their gross underestimation of their enemy's resources and their failure after nearly three years of massive efforts to blunt the Revolution's growing offensive capabilities. Even while Wheeler was actively cajoling Westmoreland to call for reinforcements, the JCS itself on February 12 recommended deferring a decision to send them. By the time Wheeler had mobilized the Joint Chiefs behind him, he confronted other opposition from all sides. While the civilians in the Pentagon were the most aggressive, they had the backing of most of the CIA and the State Department for their immediate contention that sending more troops to South Vietnam would be futile. Not only would more troops encourage the already inefficient ARVN to fight even less well, the opponents of Wheeler's request pointed out, but the critical battles then taking place would be decided long before new soldiers could reach Vietnam. It was also in response to these conflicting views that the President had created the Clifford committee to help him reach his decision.

The Clifford committee began by gathering the basic facts. Initially, it did not intend to question the efficacy of the war. The departing McNamara had warned the President that 400,000 men and $10 billion would be required if he approved the commitment of a large new offensive force. The JCS contended that the 108,000 men definitely intended for South Vietnam out of the 206,000 requested, would tip the scale in the otherwise stalemated war. But even Rostow, who had earlier endorsed the new escalation, now had to admit that the DRV would meet any American buildup. Also crucial in the committee's discussion was the argument that the war was causing the United States to sacrifice its many interests elsewhere in the world, impairing its overall international objectives. Piece by piece, the case for continuing the war by escalating was destroyed. The CIA, especially, argued that the war was stalemated and that the Communists retained the strategic initiative. By the time the Clifford committee's intense discussions and analyses were completed on March 3, Clifford had changed his position and no one favored the 206,000 plan save Wheeler and the JCS. "1968 will be the pivotal year" of the war, Wheeler had correctly argued.

The result was a nominal stalemate among the President's key advisers, which meant a continuation of the status quo, though in fact opinions were changing subtly with the burden of reality. While the possibility of committing 206,000 men was left open on a "week by week" basis, only 22,000 men already authorized were to go immediately as "all we can give at the moment," as the President put it. Johnson later asserted he had rejected the 206,000-man request by early March, but in fact he remained quite ambivalent and unwilling to accept the growing constraints on his freedom of action. Even after the *New York Times* on March 10 revealed the secret debates, he hesitated, although the publicity hurt the advocates of escalation. What the Clifford committee proposed was that the administration do nothing decisive until it could complete a basic reassessment of "political and strategic guidance" of the war. But for two weeks, apart from a desultory consensus that much more had to be done to get the ARVN to assume a far greater role in the war, nothing new was decided on Vietnam, and the President was under the greatest pressure of his life as every conceivable problem weighed on him.

"I felt," he later confided, "that I was being chased on all sides by a giant stampede coming at me from all directions." There was Vietnam, but also the economy. Blacks were rioting, students protesting, and hysterical reporters pressing. "And then the final straw. The thing I feared from the first day of my Presidency was actually coming true. Robert Kennedy had openly announced his intention to reclaim the throne. . . ." The strain on Johnson made his behavior erratic; rumors of his overwrought emotional state and exotic religious experiences abounded—and later enough of them were confirmed to reveal that the President had indeed lost touch. Antiwar Senator Eugene McCarthy's 42 percent vote in the New Hampshire primary on March 12 reinforced the President's desperation.

Politics and economics now merged to affect the future of the war. Clifford, perhaps the shrewdest adviser to Presidents in the post-1945 era, was a critical link in this synthesis. As he was to recount later that month to Rusk and Rostow, "I make it a practice to keep in touch with friends in business and the law across the land. I ask them their views about various matters. Until a few months ago, they were generally supportive of the war. They were a little disturbed about the overheating of the economy and the flight of gold, but they assumed that these things would be brought under control; and in any event, they thought it was important to stop the Communists in Vietnam. Now all that has changed. . . . these men now feel we are in a hopeless bog. The idea of going deeper into the bog strikes them as mad. . . . It would be very difficult—I believe it would be impossible—for the President to maintain public support for the war without the support of these men." In fact, two days after the McCarthy victory, Kennedy approached Clifford and proposed not to run for the presidency if Johnson would create a commission to study and change Vietnam policy. Clifford presented the offer to Johnson, who rejected it brusquely, only to see Kennedy announce his candidacy.

Clifford, meanwhile, was not happy with the President's paralysis and incapacity to reverse the disastrous course toward escalation. The opinions of his corporate friends reinforced his own real but habitually cautious desires to redefine the nation's Vietnam strategy. "I was more conscious each day of domestic unrest in our own country," he wrote the following year. "Just as disturbing to me were the economic implications of a struggle to be indefinitely continued at ever-increasing cost." On March 19 he proposed to Johnson that he call another session of the Senior Advisory Group of the State Department—the so-called Wise Men who the preceding fall had strongly supported the President's war policy. Dean Acheson, its chairman, had since late February, at the President's request, been informally reviewing the war and its conflict with American interests elsewhere in the world, and he had become highly critical of the unlimited commitment. On March 15 he had informed Johnson that the JCS was giving him very poor advice and that it was time to disengage from the unpopular war. Clifford knew he had a powerful friend in the former secretary of state, whose prestige with Johnson was enormous, and he also sensed what his group would advise. Johnson consented to the project probably aware of its likely position, and the Wise Men picked up the debate the Clifford committee had left hanging.

The role of the Wise Men was illustrative of the parameters of power and ideas in the United States in moments of crisis. The basic military, economic, and political facts which so profoundly influenced the Wise Men had already reached most of the President's key advisers and the President himself. Even arch-hawks like Rostow admitted that though putting the country on a war footing in February had been possible, "the changing political environment at home and the international financial crisis of March reduced that possibility." Nothing could change those realities, and in a certain sense the ideas of the Wise Men were anticlimatic, reflecting the tide of events rather than shaping them.

The world of big industry and finance, so amorphous to those outside it but so real to those in it, had been for the war because its members believed in the objectives of American foreign policy which had led to the intervention. Yet key individuals were often called on, both formally and informally, to comment on economic affairs that the war strongly affected, such as budget deficits and inflation. While they had never assumed a critical position on the war before 1968, they consistently favored efforts to eliminate these economic challenges. Such expediency meant that should the nation's financial difficulties become sufficiently serious, they would oppose escalation and might even favor a reduction of the war to economically manageable proportions. Such a stance was strictly pragmatic and graphically revealed the contradictions which led to American involvement in the first place, for its ideal would have been for the United States to have won the war both quickly and cheaply. The Wise Men—who included men with close links to the world of finance, corporate law, and big business like George Ball, Douglas Dillon, Cyrus Vance, John J. McCloy, McGeorge Bundy, Arthur Dean, Robert Murphy, and Henry Cabot Lodge—understood such nuances. It was virtually certain that impersonal calculations of this kind would influence their recommendations. As men used to confronting facts and their implications, they were better able to internalize the larger material balance of forces in the war than most, particularly because it was not their personal reputations that were at stake but their class interests.

Also important during this decisive month was the state of public opinion and that of politicians who instinctively thrive on relating to it, quite unconcerned with their own past inconsistencies on the war. The entry of McCarthy and Kennedy in the race for the Democratic nomination would not have been such a formidable challenge to the President had the polls on March 16 not shown him to be at the lowest point of popularity since he came to office. The public's feelings about the war had become consistently more critical since 1966; by the end of 1967 they were evenly divided. The Tet offensive caused opposition to rise sharply. By the summer of 1968 those Americans who thought the sending of troops to Vietnam was a mistake far outnumbered those in favor of it. This trend profoundly affected many officials, who felt that growing public impatience was imposing a real limit on how long politicians could continue to sustain the war. And the emergence of a larger and more militant antiwar movement on campuses, especially among the children of the elite, struck key defenders of the war personally. By the end of March 1968, it was quite clear that even ignoring the military and economic constraints, the administration was confronting an unprecedented postwar situation in the virtually total collapse of the crucial foreign policy consensus between the executive, the traditional establishment, and the public.

However belligerent or aggressive the President appeared to his advisers or the press at this time, it was clear that he was now implementing the Clifford committee's cautious policy of no further escalation. However, the committee failed to alter the President's basic commitment to an ongoing war. On March 22 the final allotment of new men to South Vietnam was reconfirmed at 24,000 more, nearly half of whom were already there, and the request for 206,000 men was shelved permanently. As with all his fateful March decisions, Johnson later offered the explanation that his freezing the commitment to the war at existing levels after six years of steady escalation was due to a variety of factors, foremost of which was the expectation that there would be no additional NLF offensives and the belief that the ARVN was now fighting harder. But, in fact, both premises proved incorrect, and Johnson still did not escalate when the second Tet wave came, because his other concerns were quite decisive. These included "especially our financial problems," with the gold crisis and budget deficit still hanging over the economy, as well as public opinion. And for a consummate parliamentarian like Johnson, the conviction during March that Congress would no longer support escalation undoubtedly also weighed heavily in his calculations. Whatever his bluster and style, the facts had sunk into the President's consciousness. U.S. policy would get neither worse—nor better.

The famous, often detailed meetings of the Wise Men on March 25–26 only confirmed this reality. Acheson was firmly in command of its proceedings and so preconceived in his judgments that he brooked little opposition from a minority which preferred not to offend the President's martial instincts. The war was stalemated, and the nation could not afford to commit more resources without sacrificing its economy and other global interests in an effort to win it. The public, too, both in South Vietnam and in the United States, was now deeply opposed to the effort. Most of the

Senior Advisory Group favored the ending of escalation and the taking of steps toward disengagement—ranging from less bombing of the DRV to a reduction of American forces and the transfer of greater responsibility for the war to RVN.

For the President, emotionally overwrought during these weeks and merging the greatest personal crisis of his lifetime with the most important failure of American military and foreign policy in this century, the last days of March were excruciating. The shrewdest politician Texas ever produced was for the first time wholly isolated and compelled to assume the burden not simply of his own political errors in Vietnam but also of the failure of an entire class in pursuing the war and the hegemonic goals of American foreign policy, a class that was now abandoning escalation and the President's commitment to it. Carrying the weight of failure, Johnson hesitated and considered persisting with the war without any inhibitions. After terrible days of intense emotional strain, he also decided to withdraw from the race for the 1968 presidential nomination and to retreat to the tranquillity of his Texas ranch.

The President's March 31 speech touched on everything from a bombing halt to negotiations, but the most important and tangible part of it was the announcement of his decision to retire from politics. His erstwhile concessions of a bombing halt in all but vague areas north of the seventeenth parallel in return for reciprocal DRV actions was within only a day to embarrass the administration when planes attacked sites nearly five hundred kilometers north of that line. Rather than extricating himself from the war in a forthright manner, Johnson quickly raised basic doubts about his intentions and further alienated domestic and world opinion. By April and May, bombing attacks against the DRV were far greater than in February or March. From this time until October 31, when Johnson called a total bombing halt over the DRV in a last-ditch effort to win votes for Hubert Humphrey's faltering campaign for the presidency, it was obvious that bombing would both become a tool of public relations and politics for himself and set a precedent for his successor. For while the March 31 speech was an explicit pledge not to escalate the war, the President remained very much committed to sustaining the struggle until he left office, and Rusk and Rostow reinforced his devotion to bombing. Clifford and those who wanted to redefine national policy and scale down the war knew that the President would never agree with them, whatever they said, and all they could do for the remainder of 1968 was try to keep Johnson tied to what they regarded as a schizoid policy and prevent it from becoming something even worse. It was not, in their opinion, to get better.

Johnson's open offer for negotiations was soon mired when the United States retracted its proposal to meet the Communists anywhere, embarrassing the administration even before the long, futile Paris talks were to begin the following May. Conceding that he would not raise troop levels by more than 24,000 or escalate the war, the President asked for Congress's help in solving the budget deficit, the gold and dollar crisis, and the other economic problems that his past escalations had unleashed. The most prominent new proposal in the President's message, which became the basis of Nixon's subsequent Vietnamization policy, was an expanding of the RVN's military forces to take a progressively larger share of combat and, implicitly, lay the basis for a reduced dependency on American troops. It was only here that the advice of the Wise Men may actually have moved the President.

The American presence in Vietnam was directly related to the RVN's chronic military and political weaknesses, and interpreting its performance during the weeks after Tet was central to Washington's definitions of its own role and alternatives. The first, careful reports were highly pessimistic, and the persistent internecine political struggles between Thieu and Ky in the midst of a life-and-death struggle particularly discouraged officials. The CIA believed that the political dimension was critical, but it also confessed that if there was no chance of reform, a U.S. role, regardless of its size, would prove hopeless. The State Department called the RVN's collapse "a strong present possibility over the next few months." By the end of March, however, General Creighton Abrams, who had already been designated quietly to replace Westmoreland, was arguing that the ARVN suddenly had far better morale than earlier. With the bulk of military opinion on the RVN highly skeptical, and the legacy of experience even more negative, the Wise Men focused on the linkage of reconstituting the ARVN and American disengagement, fully aware that it was unlikely to succeed. Yet the notion of a decent interval to conceal the failure of American forces was clearly articulated. Publicly committed to the myth of the RVN's growing successes and strength, the administration saw the claim as the pretense which would justify eventual troop reductions. Even if there was no clear timetable, the unspoken assumption in Washington's plans was that victory was unobtainable and that "Vietnamizing" the war would buy time for whatever diplomatic or political alternatives might arise—or at least postpone the need to confront the very real defeat until after the election.

Given the absence in Johnson's speech of any references to credibility, dominoes, and the like, the implicit shift of emphasis in his statement was crucial. American war aims were neither victory nor some other abstraction but providing the RVN a "shield" behind which it could grow. On the efforts of the RVN's people "the outcome will ultimately depend." This redefinition of basic national objectives conformed both to military, political, and economic necessity and to the overwhelming opinion of leading advisers and decision makers. It was this new American readiness to limit its commitments and later partially to disengage, however amorphously stated and defined at this time, that was the major outcome of the Tet offensive.

Vietnam became America's first foreign war since 1812 to produce a profound domestic social crisis and political polarization. During the First and Second World Wars, political leadership in Washington made key decisions gradually and deliberately as changes occurred in the global balance of forces. Not so with Vietnam. Unlike all earlier wars, it aggravated many of the problems of American capitalism rather than relieving them. Amid a protracted trauma in race relations, the war increasingly became the focus of protest and dissent for millions of people who knew what the President was privately being told: so long as the war absorbed so much money, it was impossible to deal with internal social needs.

The vast bulk of Americans who opposed the war had no basis for analyzing it coherently, and the efforts of the Left within the antiwar movement to explain it failed. While they were incapable of truly perceiving its horror for the average Vietnamese, the gore of television coverage notwithstanding, a sense of this terrible experience nonetheless penetrated their consciousness. The issue of war crimes entered the debates over the war, and the enormity of the damage the United States was inflicting profoundly disquieted the consciences of a small minority. However inchoate opinion and attitudes were, there was a growing appreciation of the vast, ever-larger gap between conventional wisdom and reality, filling some Americans with a deepening sense of outrage and many more with a growing skepticism and sense of alienation. If, in the end, analytic conceptions never caught up with the sheer magnitude of the events, they nonetheless broke the apathy and consensus which had given the successive administrations the freedom from political pressure to test their strategies in Southeast Asia. This growth of skepticism and radicalization accelerated after 1967 to become a serious variable in the politics of the war. Even if protest waned with events and no one group could unify it, the accumulated opposition to the war now became a permanent reality which would emerge periodically to challenge the government in multiple and often exotic and complex ways, ranging from extremely polite middle-class constituents entreating their congressmen to forms of direct action. While no single effort made a difference, collectively all such activity indicated that for the first time in modern American history the national consensus or apathy on foreign policy was irretrievably broken, thereby creating the mass basis for opposition. The politics of opposition evolved not deductively or ideologically but as a part of a cumulative set of choices the state presented to people whose responses were based on an enormous variety of motives. Time and events were shaping consciousness, and thereby action, especially among those who had the most to lose from the war. Vast numbers were being politicized, and Tet was a powerful catalyst in this process. A new reality was being created in the American political universe.

Confronting unprecedented opposition from traditional elites as well as from the public, the White House chose a way out of the impasse that was extremely tortuous but whose direction was clear. It was on the defensive even though no one in government dared to admit total defeat. Only days after Johnson made his March 31 speech, black rioting erupted and for weeks took up much of the administration's attention. In part because the May 1968 riots in France subdued the French ardor for making gold central to the world exchange system, the United States was able to breathe more freely on that question for the remainder of the year, though the precariousness of the dollar remained an inhibition to any costly new adventures.

Yet although its military, economic, and political options had been drastically reduced, the administration made the fateful decision to struggle in a losing context to save its "credibility" by relying on two major, interrelated efforts to gain time during 1968 for alternatives it could only vaguely envision—a policy which was guaranteed to lose the election for virtually any Democrat who chose to run.

The first was merely to continue the war at the same high level of combat and firepower which American forces permitted, with a full awareness of their inability to alter the military equation and shorten the war. This desperate dependence on firepower was symbolic, concealing failure with brutal revenge, as well as a means of obtaining time for the second approach—namely, to begin to transfer the war to the various RVN armies. For Johnson this meant essentially continuing the war within those constraints he abhorred and turning it over to his successor with the strongest military position possible.

American leaders knew that more firepower would not change the position of the Revolution militarily or reduce its ability to mobilize recruits. Still, when the President promised a pause in the bombing of the DRV to encourage negotiated solutions to the war and reciprocity, the Air Force immediately increased its fighter-bomber sorties over the DRV, setting a wartime record during July. The DRV's skepticism toward American initiatives naturally rose with them. The tonnage of bombs dropped on the DRV during 1968 nearly equaled that of 1967, but bombing greatly increased in the south, where a growing part of "the countryside," one American general reported in 1969, "looked like the Verdun battlefields." This emphasis on firepower meant, of course, that the administration would fight what it increasingly knew to be a futile war in ways which could only further wreck South Vietnam's human, social, and economic fabric. As the American generals continued the habitual search-and-destroy tactics throughout 1968, some reported their "coldly realistic, if not pessimistic" conclusions back to Washington that the strategy was still ineffectual.

The successive waves of combat which began on Tet created nearly one million refugees, and over $200 million in capital goods were destroyed during Tet alone. Agricultural output and private-sector output dropped sharply in 1968, as did the revenues of the RVN, which was now more dependent on aid than ever and less able to take over the military responsibilities the Americans proposed to transfer to it. Linked to this mounting economic burden was the accelerating transformation and urbanization of the society. The Americans were impressed that the urban population had shown a distinct apathy toward the RVN's ordeal, even, in some places, engaging in low-level cooperation with the NLF. "The ineffective GVN political response may still further improve the VC cause in the cities, as well as in the countryside," the Clifford committee had presciently warned. In effect, the war created structural forces, such as urbanization, that might define the context of the RVN's politics, so that even if an articulate portion of the urban population did not rally openly to the NLF, the RVN, with its sordid struggles between Thieu and Ky, might nonetheless further alienate them.

The administration's decision to concentrate on strengthening the RVN's various armed forces was crucial both politically and structurally. To the extent that the administration planned to transform the nature of the war from a conflict between Americans and the Revolution to one between the RVN and the Revolution, it was making a fateful choice, since scarcely anyone knowledgeable believed that the RVN had the ability to win such a conflict. The Party had calculated this very question before Tet, and forcing such clarity on the United States was a prime objective of the effort. The new strategy was an excuse for leaving some Americans in South Vietnam at a time when pressure at home was mounting for their removal. While this was a consideration for the White House, many in Washington really saw Vietnamization as a face-saving formula for acknowledging their own failures.

Ironically, the creation of a larger RVN military machine was to become another vehicle for guaranteeing the defeat of its cause. For the RVNAF's growing role goaded the peasantry and urban masses, including many elements indifferent or even hostile to the NLF, to oppose the RVN's war policies. In the spring of 1968 the RVN declared a general mobilization of eighteen- and nineteen-year-olds. All men between eighteen and thirty-eight were now subject to induction and required to stay in a branch of the full-time military until forty-five, while sixteen- and seventeen-year-olds and thirty-nine- to fifty-year-olds were subject to incorporation into the largely unarmed, part-time People's Self-Defense Forces. By 1969, 150,000 new men had been added to the ARVN and 250,000 to the RF/PF [Regional Forces/Provincial Forces]. The mass levee at a time of growing RVN economic difficulties further profoundly distorted the wholly artificial nature of the RVN social system, imposing a vast new tax on it.

The forced recruitment of the nation's sons alienated the people in multiple ways. The most obvious was their personal and economic losses, so that such families more and more perceived the RVN as the main burden on their lives. For the rest of the nation, the ARVN was a growing tax as looting, which had reached new levels during Tet, increased with the mounting economic problems confronting soldiers. "Looting and other misconduct by Republic of Vietnam Armed troops toward the civilian populace have undermined the confidence of the people in RVNAF," the NSC's early 1969 assessment concluded, and they saw no way of reversing it. The ARVN became less cohesive, despite its new arms. The rate of desertions rose substantially, especially among new recruits, and the so-called ghost soldiers became even more common. Their officers were equally unprepared for their tasks, which contributed to growing demoralization. "All agencies agree that the RVNAF could not," the NSC stated early in 1969, "either now or even when fully modernized, handle both the VC and a sizable level of NVA forces without U.S. combat support in the form of air, helicopters, artillery, logistics and some ground forces." Increasing the size of the RVN's army only weakened it as a fighting organization, further undermining the entire social order and leaving its economy more dependent and vulnerable. Unwilling and unable to confront these dilemmas, the Johnson administration preferred to bequeath them all to its successor. . . .

The [Vietnamese Communist] Party has ever since 1968 regarded the Tet offensive as the turning point in the war and as a decisive triumph, the consequences of which would eventually mature in final victory. By 1968 the Vietnam War had become much more difficult to analyze, for the very process of protracted conflict had made it not only a military struggle but one in which the political, economic, and ideological and human domains became increasingly crucial. Of all the factors, none alone was decisive, but their growing interactions were the raw materials that would shape the final outcome of the war.

For the United States, Tet was a long-postponed confrontation with reality; it had been hypnotized until then by its own illusions, desires, and needs. The belated realization that it had military tactics and technology but no viable military strategy consistent with its domestic and international priorities made Tet the turning point in the administration's calculations. Those who had earlier favored the war finally made a much more objective assessment of the balance of forces. To attribute Washington's new perceptions to falsehood on the Communists' part or to naïveté by the American media, as Johnson and various generals were later to do, is to beg the central question of the impact of the military events which imposed a sense of reality on the administration's leading advisers and authorities. For despite the shift in public opinion as a consequence of Tet, it was still not yet so great as to make the difference to those called on to evaluate policy. It was true, of course, that Tet caused the media to become more skeptical of official reports on the war, but they were never to become critical of the imperialist politics that had led to the intervention in the first place. Another reason for their new disbelief, apart from the Revolution's attaining successes the Pentagon had alleged were impossible, was that those U.S. spokesmen who dealt with the media were frequently ignorant of the nature of the war themselves. Having also been treated with condescension and a great deal of intentional distortion, the media's readiness to break with official illusions was quite predictable, not least because many in the administration themselves no longer shared these misconceptions.

Decision making on Vietnam had until 1968 been subject to optional policies because the consequences of those choices had not yet reached insupportable levels, and the magnitude of the costs of errors to the overall stability and interests of the system was still obscure, while the advantages of victory to the assertion of American power geopolitically and militarily were quite clear. The weight of opinion was therefore for war to the extent needed to attain quite rational objectives: the hegemony of American power over social trends in the Third World. By 1968 the costs of the war to the system were measurable, and, whatever their earlier impulses, the small circle of critical advisers reached a basic consensus on the interests of the system. Most of the bureaucrats gave in to the weight of opinion in 1968 for the same reason they had gone along with the dominant conventional wisdom earlier—their own futures depended on operating within a consensus. The dissenters who wanted more war were now just as rare as those who favored less war had been two years earlier.

After Tet it was not the ever-present differences between various groups and personalities which shaped Washington's command decisions but rather the political order's relationship and interaction with all of the powerful economic, political, and social institutions and people which exist in an informal but real fashion to constitute power in the American social system. The chemistry of human and institutional interaction, from ambition to weakness, will always be extremely diverse within predictable parameters. Tet revealed that it was time to focus on the limits of the system. To have pursued the scale of escalation to an even higher level would have wreaked an untold amount of damage on America's economic position at home and abroad, on its military power elsewhere, and on its political life—a price scarcely any serious person proposed to pay.

The offensive brought these processes to a head, and from this viewpoint the Revolution had attained a decisive advantage in its overall struggle. More crucial yet, however, since the wheels of the U.S. political process grind pragmatically and slowly, was its impact on Washington's comprehension of the centrality of the RVN in the war effort. Without exception, all senior officials involved in guiding future policy would have agreed with the CIA when it noted, "The will and capability of the GVN and its armed forces remain the keys to the eventual outcome." The infusion of this understanding more deeply into the American consciousness was perhaps the most important Party goal, and in this regard it succeeded entirely. Even those U.S. generals who later severely criticized the administration's decisions, knew they could not win the war without the RVN's assuming a far greater burden militarily and being far less irresponsible politically. "Vietnamizing" the Vietnam War, ironically, at this late date became the last pillar of American strategy, leaving its position wholly dependent on its own dependents. It was the reluctant acceptance of this unhappy greater reliance on others that guaranteed the Party's eventual victory, for nearly all who were closely connected with the war greatly doubted in private that the RVN could grasp the military victory that had eluded over half a million GIs.

In this sense the Revolution attained the main strategic objectives of the Tet offensive, compelling the United States to leave the realm of desire and confront that of necessity. But the very framework of the epic struggle, for the Revolution as well as for its enemies, was altering. The very process of conflict was disorganizing the entire social order, affecting values and desires. The transformation of the nation, the brutal urbanization, the Americanization of the mores of the youth, and all the scourges of occupation and war were changing the goals of many Vietnamese.

The emergence of new social strata in the burgeoning cities meant that in certain regards both the RVN and the NLF were growing weaker. Yet, while the urban difficulties the Party faced were tactical, and sufficient to undermine its efforts during Tet, for the RVN they were matters of basic survival. As a ruling administrative structure, the RVN needed support and some measure of enthusiasm from those not on its payroll. The passivity and apathy shown to it by the urban population during Tet was extremely ominous. The RVN's potentially fatal dilemma was that it lacked an ideological, economic, and organizational basis for transforming itself into a real political force, able to function and exist independently of the Americans. The very process of egoism and depoliticization which was so troublesome to the Communists was now the RVN's main nemesis, for without a political consensus there could only be cohesion based on repression and avarice. And, given the costliness the economic adhesive of massive corruption which maintained the Thieu regime in power, it was by 1968 quite impossible that the RVN could transcend this fatal contradiction. Indeed, the very nature of the RVN's economic system would eventually produce new issues and grievances around which a new opposition might form. For it had the burden of regulating the social system to minimize the war's dislocations and to meet human needs. In fact it was greatly adding to them.

South Vietnam's rural structure was changing as well, and each mass exodus accelerated this pattern. By the end of 1968 rural Vietnam bore significantly less resemblance to the environment in which the NLF was born. People increasingly desired security from the war's ravages, and this more and more shaped their politics. The collapse or destruction of the NLF infrastructure in many places did not make the RVN any more palatable to the peasants, since what they wanted most—peace—the RVN could not give them. Worse yet, its mounting demands on the peasantry broadened the bases of its grievances even as the land system's traditional economic role altered to make it less onerous. To some extent, and depending on the region, the classic confrontation between the Revolution and its enemies was paralleled by developments in the intricate play of changing peasant values, needs, and politics to which neither the NLF nor the RVN responded wholly. While the NLF's power declined visibly, the RVN could not fill the vacuum. The process of mutual erosion began during Tet, when the Revolution drove the RVN out of a large part of the country yet could not permanently remain there.

Tet was the threshold in the war's development, a major turning point guaranteeing that the Revolution would not be defeated. All the rapidly evolving social, economic, human, and organizational dimensions were increasingly significant for the final outcome, and however nebulous and ambiguous they appeared then, it was clear by the end of 1968 that they would prove decisive.

✗ *F U R T H E R   R E A D I N G*

Larry Berman, *Lyndon Johnson's War* (1989)

Peter Braestrup, *Big Story* (1977)

Bernard Brodie, "The Tet Offensive," in Noble Frankland and Christopher Dowling, eds., *Decisive Battles of the Twentieth Century* (1976), 321–34

William J. Duiker, *The Communist Road to Power in Vietnam* (1981)
Leslie H. Gelb and Richard K. Betts, *The Irony of Vietnam* (1979)
Townsend Hoopes, *The Limits of Intervention* (1970)
Lyndon B. Johnson, *The Vantage Point* (1971)
Guenther Lewy, *America in Vietnam* (1978)
Don Oberdorfer, *Tet* (1971)
Bruce Palmer, Jr., *The 25-Year War* (1984)
Robert Pisor, *The End of the Line: The Siege of Khe Sanh* (1982)
Herbert Y. Schandler, *The Unmaking of a President* (1977)
Harry G. Summers, Jr., *On Strategy: A Critical Analysis of the Vietnam War* (1982)
William C. Westmoreland, *A Soldier Reports* (1976)

CHAPTER
10

The Ally: South Vietnam

X

A consistent aim of American policy from the late 1940s was the creation of an alternative to communist rule in Vietnam. After the defeat of the French, that objective centered on the establishment of an independent regime in the south that would prove capable of resisting both internal and external military threats. It also encompassed the development of effective political, economic, and social institutions, a process often referred to by American officials as nation building. As the American military presence in Vietnam ballooned during the 1960s, America's fate increasingly became tied to the fortunes of its Saigon ally. Washington's military objective in Vietnam—the defeat of the communists—could not easily be dissociated from its political goal—the establishment of a viable state in South Vietnam.

Although the nature of the South Vietnamese regime inspired a flood of polemical tracts in the United States during the 1960s and early 1970s, relatively few scholars have probed deeply into the underlying structure of the government in Saigon. The most basic questions can be posed simply: Did South Vietnam have the potential to emerge as a viable, independent state? or were its inherent weaknesses so great that it can only be characterized as a doomed dependency?

X DOCUMENTS

In the first document, a conversation between Presidents Diem and Eisenhower, the South Vietnamese ruler discusses his country's pressing defense needs and requests additional aid from the United States. The discussion took place at the White House on March 9, 1957. Tran Van Don, one of the leaders in the coup against Diem, reflects in the second document on South Vietnam's need for political and economic reforms following Diem's ouster. The third document, excerpted from the memoirs of former South Vietnamese president Nguyen Cao Ky, reiterates a complaint that South Vietnamese leaders often made of their American allies: that they were insensitive, patronizing, and arrogant. On April 7, 1969, Ky's successor, Nguyen Van Thieu, announced his position on a negotiated settlement to the National Assembly; it appears here as the fourth document. The speech, issued on the eve of the Paris peace talks, left little room for compromise with the communists. In the final document, American serviceman Bobby Muller bitterly recalls his experience with South Vietnamese troops. His blunt disparagement of their fighting ability and commitment to the struggle reflects a viewpoint that many other U.S. soldiers shared.

Ngo Dinh Diem Requests Additional U.S. Aid, 1957

After introductory remarks by the President praising President Diem for the excellent achievements he has brought about in the last three years in stabilizing the situation in Viet-Nam, President Eisenhower asked President Diem to outline the principal problems he is facing today.

President Diem replied that his country has gone through a very grave and serious crisis and has been able to hold on despite strong pressures from all sides. The principal problem of establishing internal security and building up their defense posture has been achieved to a considerable extent. The principal reason Viet-Nam has been able to hold out against these pressures has been because of the sympathy and encouragement given by the United States despite the fact that for a time even some people in the United States did not think that the Diem government could maintain itself.

At the present time Viet-Nam is faced with the possibility of a strong Communist offensive from the Vietminh who have 400 thousand men under arms. Fortunately, however, the Vietminh are faced with serious problems such as high taxes needed to maintain this large force and must have other controls which have caused discontent among the population in the North. Diem feels that Red China is faced with the same problems. They are maintaining a large army which requires heavy taxes and controls over the people, which Diem hopes in the long run will force the Chinese Government to demobilize a considerable portion of their forces and treat the people in a more liberal manner. There is, nevertheless, the possibility that the Vietminh with their large army might try to attack now while they have a superiority in numbers. The Vietminh during the first year after the Geneva Conference did not think it would be necessary to use armed force to take over the South; they thought the government in the South would crumble and they could take over without difficulty. With internal stability in Free Viet-Nam and the build-up of their own armed forces, they have now the possibility of holding out for a few years more during which time Diem reiterated the strain and drain on the economy of the Vietminh may cause them to demobilize some of their forces and adopt a more liberal attitude toward the population. . . .

Diem [stated] that Viet-Nam has attained stability due primarily to the volume of American aid. He pointed out that the magnitude of American aid permitted the US Government to have a large number of advisers and consultants in Viet-Nam who not only can assist Viet-Nam with its problems but also follow closely developments and the use to which aid is placed. In contrast, the small amounts of aid given to other countries, such as 20/30 million dollars, does not permit the US Government to maintain such close control over developments in other countries as is the case in Viet-Nam. Diem pleaded for the maintenance of the present aid level of 250 million dollars a year of which 170 million dollars is allocated for defense purposes. This aid has permitted Viet-Nam to build up its armed strength and thus play an important role in Southeast Asia. If this aid should be cut both the military and economic progress would have to be reduced. This would cause serious repercussions not only in Viet-Nam but among neighboring countries in Southeast Asia who look on Viet-Nam as an example of the good US aid can bring. Any cut would also bring serious political repercussions in Viet-Nam.

Tran Van Don on the Need for Reforms After the Coup Against Diem (1963), 1978

Immediately after the success of the coup d'etat [against Diem], a provisional constitutional charter was proclaimed. It provided for General Big Minh to be the chairman of the MRC [Military Revolutionary Council], which was composed of twelve generals, and for a civilian cabinet of fifteen ministers to be headed by a prime minister who would be responsible to the MRC and to Minh as head of state. This was appropriate because Minh was our leader and known by all as the hero of the coup. Mr. Nguyen Ngoc Tho, former vice president of the republic under the Diem regime was appointed prime minister. He was chosen because of his long administrative experience which would help to smooth this transition phase. In addition, he was a long-time friend of Big Minh and we felt we could trust him.

Having promoted the coup, we were well aware of the difficulties that always follow a sudden change of regime. We understood that this provisional government structure should be replaced as soon as a definitive constitution could be promulgated. Another closely related problem involved our decision to purge the administration and the army of elements we knew to be inept, despotic, or corrupt. We expected a certain breakdown in the functioning of the administration because of this, but thought that the good psychological effect on the people and the purifying influence of new officials would more than overcome any disruptions.

Students, priests, and those politically opposed to the previous government were immediately released from prison and instructions were issued prohibiting arbitrary arrest and confinement. Freedom of the press and of religious belief were solemnly proclaimed and welcomed with enthusiasm. Hard labor in the rural areas was abolished in connection with the strategic hamlet program, and we attempted to obtain support for our new government from the religious sects Hoa Hao and Cao Dai.

The economic and financial situation was disturbing, however, because

American aid had been temporarily suspended during the months preceding the coup. Further, the Tho cabinet was having difficulty since its members could not agree with each other. Part of the problem was that Tho, the former vice president under Diem, was inflexible and narrow in his policies. . . .

Toward the end of January, after a series of contacts with many political, religious, and military leaders, I had been able to plan out the main orientation of our revolutionary program. On January 27, I gave my reform program to Big Minh and [General] Khiem for further submission to the government. It suggested many radical changes, political, economic, social, and cultural, and handed power over to a new revolutionary cabinet under a different prime minister. Especially important were the roles to be entrusted to the youth of the nation for the realization of our revolutionary goals.

I knew that if the war were to be won against the Communists military measures alone would not suffice. Our struggle against the NLF had to be waged with political, economic, cultural, and social considerations as well. The NLF strategy had been to occupy and control the countryside and turn it into a springboard for advancing to the cities. We, therefore, had to make our presence felt in the same rural areas, winning the people's support, seducing them away from Communist influences, and enlisting their participation in a full-scale struggle. My concept was that the war in Vietnam was between two factions of Vietnamese, so it should have been settled between ourselves by all means available. Aid obtained from our Free World friends should have been confined to moral, technical, and material support. Our national policy should have been geared toward solving simultaneously the two overall goals of winning the support of the population and then annihilating the enemy's armed forces.

We also wanted to show the people that we meant what we said, that we truly intended to do away with graft and corruption and special privileges for the governors. I proposed to my colleagues that we lead austere lives, turn in the official limousines so prized by the Diem administration, and sell off the luxurious homes maintained at the expense of the common people. We had to get ourselves used to the idea that we had to get closer to the people, living our lives more like them.

In our military mission we needed to destroy the enemy's secret bases, prevent infiltration of men, weapons, equipment, and supplies, and neutralize his units. Local organizations such as the civil guard and the police were to be responsible for law and order within the local areas. Their purpose was to protect the villages and the people living in them from the political and military cadres of the NLF. In areas that were so rugged that our troops would have unusual difficulty conducting normal military operations, we might have had to request air support such as helicopter transport from our allies.

In winning the support of the populace, we had to remove the insidious influence of the NLF from the villages. This had to be the principal object of the war, with all necessary resources utilized for this purpose. We had to help the people develop their individual capabilities and get them to understand their political rights and enjoy them. To achieve this they needed a great number of well-trained and sympathetic local officials capable of replacing the Communist cadres who had been working with them. Once the people in the countryside, who were 80 percent of our overall population, were won over to the national cause, the NLF could no longer be sustained because it would have lost its main source of support.

I still believe that these objectives were obtainable because the NLF had not yet achieved such power in the countryside as to deny us access to the populace. It is good to remember that no large-scale infiltration of North Vietnamese regular units had yet occurred so that we were faced only by the irregular cadres. The principle we wanted to follow in pacifying the countryside was that of an "oil spot" spreading out from a safe area, making it larger and larger as we gradually made whole provinces secure. Eventually these spots would meet and after a certain time full sections of the country would be thoroughly under government control. Then we would go on to destroy enemy secret bases that had been set up and interrupt the infiltration routes, such as the Ho Chi Minh trail. After all this had been accomplished, we might feel secure enough to contemplate active operations against the North in order to try to unify the national territory.

These plans would, I believe, have permitted our government to secure the countryside and make South Vietnam a safer and better place to live. We had our chance. We had seized power and had the overwhelming mass of the people with us. We were inexperienced, but this probably was in itself something of an advantage. We certainly did not want to continue the sins of the past.

But, our hopes and aspirations were not to be realized.

Nguyen Cao Ky on the Battle for Hearts and Minds, 1976

Alongside the military war, fought with bombs and bullets, we had to fight another war—one to convince our own people that South Vietnam offered a way of life superior to that of the Communists. It was a war for the hearts and minds of the people.

It was not, as some thought, a matter of simple materialism, a philosophy that started with filling bellies. Ambassador Ellsworth Bunker was hopelessly wrong when he told me on one occasion, "People are drifting toward Communism because they are poor. If you give the people everything they want—television sets, automobiles, and so on—none of them will go over to Communism."

Poor Bunker! He was trying to impose American standards of life on people he did not understand, people who basically had no desire for the so-called good things of the American way of life.

Like so many well-meaning Americans, Bunker, when he came to Viet-

From *Twenty Years and Twenty Days* by Nguyen Cao Ky, 1976, pp. 135–138, 154. Stein & Day Publishers.

nam, was unable to grasp the fact that he had made an excursion into a culture as different from America's as an African Negro's is different from that of an Eskimo. No man could hope to span the differences in American and Vietnamese culture and heritage in the short time of his appointment in our land. How could I explain to Bunker's Western mind, for example, that while an American would be lost without a future to conquer, a Vietnamese is lost without the refuge of the past.

"Material goods are not the answer," I replied. "It's much more important to win the hearts and minds of the people than to give them TV sets."

Bunker shook his head disbelievingly, and I felt, watching him, that he was wondering how this young upstart dared to utter such nonsense. But then Bunker no doubt believed in Napoleon's dictum that an army marches on its stomach, and saw no reason why civilians should be any different. But they were.

Among my first priorities when I became prime minister was to introduce some form of social revolution, a term I later amended to "social justice." My aims, my hopes, were very simple: I wanted my people to get a proper reward for their efforts. I wanted a man working eight hours a day to receive twice as much as a man working four hours a day. It takes very little to make the Vietnamese happy. Our needs are simple because we are Asians; we are influenced by the sayings of Confucius. We are not interested in material gain like Westerners; commercial success does not attract us as it does Americans, so we can be happy with little. On the other hand, we do not like to feel exploited, and there lay the root of our problem.

For above all else, the Communist cadres, infiltrating from the North, exploited our corruption and black marketeering as they tried to win over puzzled (yet at heart loyal) peasants to the cause of Ho Chi Minh. They were diabolically clever, for they made no spectacular promises; they held out no bribes. Like Churchill, they offered nothing but blood, sweat, toil, and tears, but they were able to build up the image of a simple, Spartan leader as great in his way as Churchill, and contrast it with our squabbling, corrupt politicians, as squalid in their way as the French politicians in 1940 who bickered among themselves while the Germans streamed across their land.

Yet we had one ace in our hand, if only we could play the hand properly, an ace that did not even exist in the Communist deck of cards. It was freedom, the world's most precious—yet most elusive—treasure. The freedoms that Roosevelt had preached, not only the freedom from fear and want, but the freedom for us to choose our leaders, and the freedom to boot them out if they proved unworthy of the trust reposed in them.

I felt we had to start at the top—and at the bottom. We needed to establish free elections at all levels—in the village tribunal as well as the presidential palace. We needed to introduce fair systems of compensation, provisions for social welfare—all things that are taken for granted in the West.

We achieved more than we were given credit for, though all our efforts were made against a backdrop of a bitter fight for survival. The draft continued in Vietnam until virtually the end, and at the height of the fighting every family in the country had one member, if not two or three, in uniform.

But if we held an ace, we also held a deuce. For while I was preaching the need for freedom, I was not always free myself. True, we were not puppets, yet we never achieved the standing or appearance of an independent, self-governing country. The Americans criticized us for not having a highly developed system of government, but how could we have that when every Vietnamese in Saigon referred to the American ambassador as "the Governor General"?

The Americans did not seek this; they were not colonists, but South Vietnam had been a colony until the defeat of the French, and in many ways it remained virtually a colony, though without the restrictions imposed by the French. We still lacked our own identity.

We never produced a leader to unite the country with its many religious and political factions. The North had one in Ho Chi Minh; rightly or wrongly, the Communists believed in him and fought and died for him. He had a charisma that won many supporters even in the West and not all of them were Communists. Neither Diem, nor Thieu—both backed by the Americans—won the hearts of even the South Vietnamese.

The Americans controlled the fighting of the war. American aid financed the country; without it we could not survive. Americans selected or influenced the selection of our politicians and leaders, even at village level, and had a natural tendency to pick the most compliant rather than the most gifted. American culture—its films, television, and advertising—swamped our own.

Conscious of their dollar-bought superiority, the Americans patronized us at all levels. GIs thoughtlessly but hurtfully referred to Vietnamese as Dinks and Gooks, Slants and Slopes. (Charlie, Chuck, and Claude were reserved for the Viet Cong.)

Their contemptuous attitude was typified by an announcer on the American Forces Radio in 1970: "For those of you staying on in 'Nam, here's a little advice regarding our Vietnamese friends. As you know, they're kind of jumpy now, so please remember the golden rule. Never pat a Vietnamese on the head. Stand on low ground when you talk to them. They kind of resent looking up to you. Okay?"

Certainly the Vietnamese resented being patted on the head. The battle for the hearts and minds of the people was more fundamental to success even than air power or fire power. Yet someone, presumably a GI, painted in white letters on an old warehouse by the river in Saigon the legend: "Just grab the Gooks by the balls and their hearts and minds will follow." . . .

Once more I reiterate that we needed America; we could never have fought the Communists alone. But how much better it would have been if the Americans had never appeared in the picture and we had combined patience with American economic aid and expertise to improve the lot of the average Vietnamese family and the skill of our fighting men. I am convinced that slowly but surely we could have won the war, simply because all the people would have been behind us once the social revolution had been won.

Nguyen Van Thieu's Address
to the National Assembly, 1969

Today, in this forum, I wish to solemnly confirm once more to the world, to our allies, to our fellow countrymen, and to our enemy that in our constant search for a constructive solution to the conflict, we consider that the following six points constitute a reasonable and solid basis for the restoration of peace in Viet-Nam:

1. Communist aggression should stop.

Communist North Viet-Nam should give up its attempts to conquer the RVN by force. It should stop violating the DMZ and the frontiers of the RVN, and stop its wanton attacks against the innocent population of the RVN.

2. Communist North Vietnamese and auxiliary troops and cadres should be completely withdrawn from the Republic of Viet-Nam.

As the military and subversive forces of Communist North Viet-Nam are withdrawn, infiltration ceases, and the level of violence thus subsides, the RVN will ask its allies to remove their forces, in accordance with the Manila joint-communique of seven nations in October, 1966.

3. The territories of the neighboring countries of the RVN should not be violated and used by Communist North Viet-Nam as bases and staging areas for aggression against the RVN.

Communist North Vietnamese troops and cadres illegally introduced and stationed in Laos and Cambodia should be withdrawn from these countries. Communist North Viet-Nam military installations in these countries should be dismantled.

4. The RVN adopts the policy of National Reconciliation.

Those now fighting against us, who renounce violence, respect the laws, and faithfully abide by the democratic processes, will be welcomed as full members of the National Community. As such, they will enjoy full political rights and assume the same obligations as other lawful citizens under the National Constitution.

5. The reunification of the two Viet-Nams is to be decided by the free choice of the entire population of Viet-Nam through democratic processes.

To establish the atmosphere conducive to national reunification, after peace has been reestablished, modalities of economic and cultural exchanges between the two Viet-Nams and other countries of this area, can be actively explored, together with other intermediary measures of peaceful coexistence so that, pending reunification, the two Viet-Nams can participate more fully and more constructively in the various undertakings of the international community.

6. There must be an effective system of international control and re-

liable international guarantees against the resumption of Communist aggression.

The control mechanisms should be freed from the paralyzing effects of the Veto system. It should have sufficient personnel and adequate means to detect any violation of peace agreement. When violations are committed, and aggression is renewed, there should be prompt and effective response from a reliable system of international guarantees, otherwise any peace agreement will be only a sham device used by the Communists to weaken our system of defense, and not a basis for long lasting peace and stability for this part of the world.

An American Serviceman's View of the South Vietnamese Army, 1987

Probably the first two months I was there, I spent out in the bush. Out there the war was easy in a way because there was no ambiguity. Anybody you met out there was hard core NVA regular. No "good guy, bad guy" problem. Later, when we came back to work the coastal area where there were villages and refugees, that's when things started to go "wait a second." Cam Lo, which is one I remember very well, was a refugee village where people had been taken from another place called Gio Linh, ten or fifteen miles away. I didn't understand it then, but for Vietnamese, villagers, their rice paddy and their little ancestral burial ground defines their universe. You take them away as we did and you've totally disrupted what they relate to. And in Cam Lo what I experienced was just hatred in the eyes of people.

The Vietnamese did not like us and I remember I was shocked. I still naively thought of myself as a hero, as a liberator. And to see the Vietnamese look upon us with fear or hatred visible in their eyes was a shock. The only thing we were good for is to sell us something. And frankly every time we operated around Cam Lo we got fucked with. Any patrol, any operation, any convoy passing by would get a smack. So the people that I thought would regard us as heroes were the very people that we were fighting, and all of a sudden my black-and-white image of the world became real gray and confused.

Then I came into contact with the ARVN and that was all the more absurd. First there were some joint operations and then I went with MACV as an advisor and worked with three different ARVN battalions and that's when everything just went screwy in my head. Every night I slept with the battalion commander. We had personal bodyguards and the reason was that a good percentage of the guys in the ranks were VC or even North Vietnamese. The bodyguards were to protect us against getting blown away

From *Everything We Had* by Al Santoli, pp. 111–112. Copyright © 1981 by Albert Santoli and Vietnam Veterans of America. Reprinted by permission of Random House, Inc.

by the guys we were fighting with. We went out into the A Shau valley for what was supposed to be a ten-day operation and it wound up being ten weeks, and we lost a good number of guys not because of firefights but because they took as much rice as they could carry and they split. The A Shau was badlands. It was not a friendly place. And when you leave your unit out in the A Shau you ain't leaving to go bring in the crops back at the farm. You're leaving because you're joining the other side.

It was a joke. The enemy was a tough, hard, dedicated fucking guy, and the ARVN didn't want to hear about fighting. It was LaLa Land. Every, every, every, *every* firefight that we got into, the ARVN broke, the ARVN fucking ran. I was with three different battalions and the story never changed. I almost fell over laughing once. I had an Australian I was working with, and this NVA unit had just ambushed us. We had two companies of ARVN, and finally they got on line to counterattack, and the company commanders give the order to move and nobody moves. And they have to run up and down line with little sticks, beating these guys and kicking them in the fucking rear end to get them up out of their holes. And the Aussie and I look at each other, and we know then and there that this ain't going to work.

✗ E S S A Y S

In the opening essay, based on field research in South Vietnamese villages between 1966 and 1969, Samuel L. Popkin identifies the principal problem facing the Saigon regime: its lack of appeal to the peasantry. He characterizes the Thieu government's post-Tet efforts to offer political reforms at the village level as limited and inadequate. Currently a political scientist at the University of California, San Diego, Popkin predicted in this article that the government would remain unable to legitimize itself in the countryside without a radically altered approach to the peasants.

Gabriel Kolko of York University (Toronto) investigates the inherent structural limitations of the South Vietnamese regime in the second essay. He sees a government hopelessly dependent on American aid and reliant on a pervasive system of corruption for its survival. Such a regime, Kolko argues, had little prospect for widening its narrow political base or blunting the communist appeal to the peasantry.

In the last essay, Bui Diem, former South Vietnamese ambassador to the United States, acknowledges many of the government's shortcomings while insisting that South Vietnam could have evolved into a viable state. Under the most difficult circumstances, real accomplishments were made; others were possible, including the development of a more democratic political system. The United States, he contends, must bear considerable responsibility for failing to use its leverage as a catalyst for reform and for the arrogant manner with which it treated its ally. Bui Diem now serves as a member of George Mason University's Indochina Institute.

Pacification, Politics, and the Village in South Vietnam

SAMUEL L. POPKIN

For years pacification—the "other war"—was touted as the key to a United States-Government of South Vietnam (GVN) "victory" over the National Liberation Front. In the term's most common meaning—physical security—most of South Vietnam is pacified. According to Saigon's statistics, security and control have been extended to over 90% of the rural population. Yet it would be a mistake to assume either that this military progress in the countryside is permanent, or that it is an indication of any fundamental improvement in the relations between the Saigon government and its constituents.

The increase in GVN control results in large measure from a drastic decline in the appeal to peasants of life in areas controlled by the Viet Cong, and from the grave danger of fighting for them. Extensive bombing and shelling, frequent search-and-destroy missions, and defoliation of Viet Cong areas have made life outside the "protection" of the GVN intolerable.

In the early days of the war, peasants—especially the poor—often found themselves better able to survive and prosper under the Viet Cong. Until the strain of war made the Viet Cong unable to charge taxes lower than the landlords' rents and unable to offer anything near the economic advantages of the U.S.-backed GVN, the peasant was often better off with the Viet Cong than with the GVN.

Even as Viet Cong taxes and demands began to increase, the peasant often preferred to live with them and support them. As one peasant explained in an interview in 1967:

> The Viet Cong collect higher taxes but they know how to please the people; they behave politely so people feel that they are more favored. They behave politely and nicely to the people in order to make people like them. They do not thunder at the people like the government soldiers.
>
> People like the government because of freedom, but there is no equality even though the taxes are lower than the Viet Cong's. The thing the people don't like in the government is their behavior. For example, the soldiers often arrest and oppress the people only for revenge—in short it is banditry.

The contrast between living conditions in Viet Cong villages and government villages began to grow as the American presence increased and hurt the Viet Cong badly. It was no longer true that dedicated and virtuous cadres could improve peasant living conditions as much as corrupt cadres backed by United States money. Under the pressures of war the Viet Cong were no longer able to deliver social benefits to the population, while the GVN, living on American resources, was able to begin flooding the countryside with schools, fertilizer, Hondas, infirmaries, and hundreds of thousands of nonagricultural jobs. The peasants, although they often realized the superior quality of Viet Cong government, were nonetheless attracted by the better and safer living conditions in GVN-controlled areas.

The peasant population adjusted to the war by avoiding it. They chose to live in villages with the most economic advantages and, ideally, on the side that would predominate in the end. As Viet Cong forces became more and more strained, they demanded more and more commitment to the struggle, willing or not. "Viet Cong were very good people but forced [the people] to participate in struggle movements. After life under the Viet Cong, government is now preferred."

The Tet offensive of 1968 was the first and most dramatic military demonstration of the unreality of U.S.-GVN claims to approaching victory over the Viet Cong and its North Vietnamese allies. Yet, paradoxically, after Tet, the Viet Cong, though on the international front more formidable, was within Vietnam less stable and less powerful than ever before. Until the Tet offensive, the Viet Cong had been, for many peasants, invincible or at least omnipresent. For over six months they had prepared their supporters for a final victorious confrontation with the GVN and its American supporters. Thus, though the Tet offensive was a shocking demonstration to the West of the precarious U.S.-GVN position, it was, in its failure to achieve a final victory, a blow to Viet Cong supporters within the country.

A Viet Cong defector who had been on the district committee of a long-time Viet Cong stronghold in the delta gave a clear indication of the effect of the Tet offensive on popular expectations and Viet Cong credibility:

> When there was an order to start the fighting at 2 A.M. on the 2nd day of the New Year, the morale of the cadres and population was extremely high; the people were very enthusiastic . . . they thought that after 15 years of participation in and contribution to the Revolution by supporting the cadres, the Offensive General Insur[r]ection in the whole country would bring about a happy end to their efforts. They did not have any fear of death and were very enthusiastic and faithful to their "insurrection duties." . . . [Now] the population had lost confidence in the VC cadres living in their areas. Before the Tet events, the VC said that they only needed seven days to achieve the revolution. They needed the support of the population; they collected very heavy contributions arguing that they needed the contributions to bring about peace and prosperity; but after the anticipated seven days they said that this was only a first stage, the first wave. When the second stage came on the 7th of May (1968) they said there was then an almost complete destruction of the enemy, to step up to the third stage which would be in August, 1968, and which was also to be the final stage; but, as a matter of fact, there has been since no final stage at all. . . . These facts have accounted for the cadres' and the general population's losing confidence in the success of the revolution by the Front.

But the Viet Cong are far from defeated. Though, at present, they are unable to tax, recruit, or propagandize at anything near their pre-Tet rate, their infrastructure is still the most extensive and effective political network in the country.

Contrary to popular opinion, the greatest threat to the Saigon government is not that it will be overrun. A poor army backed with enough planes and artillery can do surprisingly well against even the best opposition army. Saigon's problem has always been the lack of positive support, even though there is often resentment or mistrust of the Viet Cong. And until positive links are made with the peasant population, until they identify with and feel represented by the government in Saigon, the risk of a Viet Cong comeback will remain.

Stunned, indeed shocked, by the possibility of a political settlement and the threat of American troop withdrawals, President Thieu began working to establish a system of rural government capable of meeting the strains of war and of providing political support for his regime. His program to legitimize the GVN in the villages gives control over the village-based Popular Forces (PF) to the Village Chief, grants each village one million piasters to use in any kind of development project approved by the Village Council, and, most important, extends the process of local election for village and hamlet officials begun in 1967.

The success of Thieu's schemes for improving the government's image and developing support in the countryside depends on his ability to attract competent local leadership. The pressures of war have made village and hamlet officials extremely important to the villagers. These officials are responsible for countless papers and permits, and they handle numerous AID [Agency for International Development] programs locally. Whether or not a villager is sympathetic to the GVN and whether or not he cares who wins the war, a friendly local official is a definite asset. Not surprisingly, then, there has been great interest in the elections throughout the countryside.

Under the Diem government, village officials were little more than clerks doing local paperwork for the government. They had no power and were underpaid, yet were expected to uphold their status and that of the regime with various forms of conspicuous consumption. Thus, only the rich could maintain a position in local government, and these did so only temporarily, on the ladder up to a place on the village Cult Committee. This committee, officially responsible for infrequent rituals held at the village *dinh* or communal temple, provided the moral justification for and support of the established government. The Village Council had no power and served almost solely as an apprenticing house for the Cult Committee. The latter, in turn, had no real political power; it depended on the substitution of tradition and convention for political legitimacy.

Even the best Village Chief could not overcome the barriers to social justice and reform which the GVN's bureaucratic structure of government constructed and maintained. One outstanding leader told an interviewer the following:

> As matters stood, tenant farmers had to agree to pay more than the legal rent to enjoy the fruits of their efforts. In my village, one tenant refused

to pay more and he lost his tenancy. This was quite legal since his lease had expired. The village administration could do nothing. This tenant farmer had to make a living elsewhere since each landowner refused to lease his land to him. The village administration knew about that case but could do nothing to protect the interests of the tenant farmer. We were tied up by laws. We could not intervene in the payment of illegal rents unless a tenant farmer brought his case to us. No tenant farmer dared to do so.

As the Viet Cong presented a greater and greater threat in the countryside, village government was abandoned, either to the weak and spineless or to the dishonest. The post of Village Chief became more demanding and more dangerous as officials were asked to enforce more and more unpopular and repressive legislation to try by the GVN's redoubtable methods to control Viet Cong growth. The Cult Committee gradually atrophied and left village officials as the sole extension of the central government in the villages. The position of Village Chief became open to those in search of money or revenge, and, although extortion and the sale of draft deferments may have cost a man his reputation and kept him from a place on the Cult Committee, money bought him an opening in commerce in the city.

As the Cult Committee declined or disintegrated, village government was left in the hands of the dishonest, the indecisive, the powerless, or the puppets of the district official. As village officials found it necessary to cooperate with district and province leaders or lose even a semblance of control, institutional change within the villages became impossible.

There was no organization, save in villages dominated by the Hoa Hao, Cao Dai, or Catholics, to provide a moral counterweight to the established government or to recruit capable men to run for office. The two main sources of recruitment for candidates were the District Chief and members of the previous village administration. To a large extent, therefore, the candidates in local elections were those already deemed acceptable by the old regime.

Slowly, as it now becomes clear that the position of Village Chief has been imbued with new power and prestige, men with leadership ability are stepping forward to run for office. Yet, even if a competent man (or as he is defined by the peasants, "a man who convinces, not a man who orders or threatens") can get the approval of the District Chief to run, he must still overcome several impediments. He must run in an election for the Village Council, and, if he wins, he must be elected Village Chief *by the council*. In four villages, men with overwhelming majorities of the vote in the first election were denied victory in the second one by an old and conventional Village Chief. The process of change is considerably slowed by the discrepancy between ability and power.

At least minimal improvements from the elections can be noted everywhere. Petty bribery, such as the "tea money" peasants give officials for processing papers, involves smaller sums since the elections began. Even where mediocre incumbents have been reinstated due to a lack of meaningful alternatives, the peasant has been afforded some relief—even the worst official has been found to treat the peasants better once his future in office depends on their votes.

The approach of every group that has been successful in the Vietnamese countryside has been to create continuity between village organizations and those of the rest of society. The original difficulties of the GVN were rooted in a division between the village official and the peasants; elections, and other programs have only succeeded in changing the nature of the division, not in mending it. In the days of appointed officials, the Village Chief was nothing more than a lackey of the District Chief with no incentive to try to win support from his peasant constituents. Now that the Village Chief is elected he must cater more closely to the needs of the village voters; yet, by doing so, he widens the gap between himself and the District Chief.

Given the complexities of GVN regulations, it is easy for a District Chief to use the courts against a Village Chief who becomes too staunch a defender of the peasants. One Village Chief allowed the last surviving son of an old blind man to join the village military (even though the unit was full) rather than force him to join ARVN (Army of the Republic of Vietnam) and be separated from his father. The Village Chief explained that:

> While I was at Vung Tau receiving my village chief training, people from my village were forced to do "corvee" labor for the soldiers. When I returned, I went to the District Chief to complain. He said bitterly, 'After your training you seem to know more about the laws than I do . . .' That was all he said, but he kept a grudge.

A few days after the Village Chief's complaint, the youth who had joined the PF was arrested, beaten and forced to confess that he had paid 1,000 piasters to be allowed to stay in the village. The amount alone was enough to suggest that his confession was untrue—the going rate to escape ARVN by joining the village military was closer to 30,000 piasters. Nonetheless, the case was sent to court (where it was finally dismissed), and the youth was shipped off to the ARVN.

Perhaps more serious than any other problem is that of the Phoenix Program, instituted by the CIA in 1967 and officially acknowledged by Thieu after Tet. It was designed to destroy the Viet Cong infrastructure by coordinating the many fragmented intelligence services and making an intensive effort to kill, capture, or cause to defect as many Viet Cong political leaders and agents as possible. It had limited success, at best, in its mission and, in the process, set back the cause of civil justice in the villages and widened the gap between village officials and the central government. To fill the program's quotas of Viet Cong to be 'neutralized,' police agents have arrested many peasants who were guilty of only trivial offenses. The advice of the Village Chief is often ignored; the program gives corrupt police and intelligence officers tremendous leeway for extortion. It has no more precision than a search-and-destroy operation and resembles in its impact Diem's Denunciation of Communism campaign.

The attitude of the GVN has traditionally been that it is better to harm an innocent man than to let a Viet Cong cadre escape. The failure to understand that for the peasant this is not a cut and dried issue, has increased the difficulty of arresting Viet Cong operating within a village. As one village chief explained the problems of a hard-line approach to the political war:

> The VC are now hiding in the mangrove swamp bordering the seacoast. I know they are forcing the village fishermen to supply them with rice and foodstuffs. These people have to go to sea for their living every day. To go to sea they have to cross the mangrove swamp, and they cannot avoid the VC. If they refused to abide by the VC instructions the VC would forbid them to go fishing. Such prohibition might make the man and his relatives starve and the poor man has no choice. Arresting him and putting him in jail would be a bad tactic. This means you simply don't understand the people. You make the people resent you, and meanwhile the VC will force other men to supply them. That's why I didn't arrest these men. But I controlled their activities by asking them to report all they did for the Viet Cong. I then collected free information and know about the VC way of gathering supplies. One man told me that he had to put what the VC wanted in a nylon bag and placed it under a rock. After this occurred many times with many different men I laid an ambush around the place. The result was that I succeeded in capturing two of them when they sneaked out of their hidings and went over to get the supplies.

Had the Village Chief reported the original presence of the Viet Cong, the innocent men who were being forced to supply them would have been arrested, and the Viet Cong themselves would not have been captured.

A good Village Chief, to protect his constituency, looks not only at what a person is doing but also at his motive. It is not a crime, in the eyes of a peasant, to aid the Viet Cong under duress. But only some one well aware of local circumstances can distinguish necessity from choice. Given the difference in the conception of justice between Saigon and the villages, it is not surprising that village soldiers have begun to protect the people of their village from enemies on both sides. It was common in 1969 to find that soldiers stationed in a village had driven out other government agents— usually police and counter terror teams—at gunpoint, and [in] a few provinces, local soldiers had gone so far as to engage in shootouts with rampaging units from ARVN.

It would appear that the present government cannot legitimize itself with the peasants without a radically altered approach to their dilemma. One Village Chief explained that: "This is a very difficult job. If you protect the villager's interests you cannot help hurting the interests of some very influential men. If you try to please these men you must harm the villager's interests." What is missing and what American observers in Saigon keep looking for are channels of political articulation that would carry communications to Saigon from the villages. But there seems to be none about to develop from the current GVN policies. The village programs are designed to substitute local for national politics. As Myron Weiner has noted:

"Fostering participation at the local level has proven to be a useful device of authoritarian regimes for encouraging support for development activities without encouraging the growth of political demands."

That the failure of the GVN to develop a meaningful political structure in the villages is not a result of some debilitating characteristic of peasant life or of Vietnamese culture is made clear by the great strength and flexibility of communities under the direction of the Hoa Hao. The Hoa Hao examples make it clear that where there is organized and dedicated leadership, the strains of war can strengthen village institutions and the commitment of villagers to their leaders. With such a commitment, it is possible to extract a level of sacrifice and labor from villagers that is unheard of in other villages administered by the GVN.

TQ village is a moderately prosperous community of 9,000 people whose principal sources of livelihood are orchards and rice land. After the Tet offensive, nearly 3,000 refugees sought shelter in TQ. Within days the Hoa Hao religious leaders and Village Council members, acting in concert, had recruited the most prominent men in the village to a special "Charity Committee" to take responsibility for the welfare of the refugees. Within weeks the men of the village were building housing for the refugees, providing them with food and clothing, and finding room for their children in the already overcrowded schools. Each "breadwinner" was provided with a job so he could support his family without having to beg or accumulate debilitating debts. The "Charity Committee," with members' families setting the example by their own sacrifices, convinced every farmer to give up a fraction of the land he farmed—whether it was owned or rented—to the refugees.

Instead of raising the religious tax—which has remained at 2 piasters since 1974—the Charity Committee announced to a meeting of the entire village that they were each donating one day's wages to build up a village welfare fund. Over 80% of the families in the village responded to the lead. Since then, participation in other "welfare days" has been even higher. Protected from dishonest GVN officials by a church hierarchy with enough power to enforce civil law, TQ village has been able to hold together as a community and even transform the fanaticism of Tet into constructive work in institutional development.

In contrast, in the capital of the province, chaos was widespread. In response to large-scale looting by an ARVN Ranger Battalion, hundreds of high school students joined the local branch of Vice President Nguyen Cao Ky's Anti-Corruption League. They willingly paid the necessary dues and prepared to slay the proverbial dragon in a provincial version of a Children's Crusade. The movement, however, was disbanded after only a few months when its leader was found to have absconded with the funds.

Comparing the typical Vietnamese village to the Hoa Hao village and measuring their reactions and responses to the disorder of the war is, of course, disingenuous, and cannot help but make GVN efforts look somewhat pathetic. One can see, however, in the Hoa Hao examples that the confusion and ineffectiveness of GVN village government is neither necessary nor indigenous to the Vietnamese people or culture. The Vietnamese peasant, whatever else he may be, is extraordinarily flexible—he can tolerate or support widely differing organizations.

Peasants throughout the country are just as sensitive as the Hoa Hao to corruption, nepotism and inequalities in work assignments and selective service requirements. But after years of rebuff, scorn and intimidation, the average peasant will not risk protest or complaint. The Hoa Hao do not hesitate to denounce bad cadres because, as one peasant said: "We are not afraid because we are Hoa Hao." Hoa Hao villagers have become accustomed to a responsive government; those under GVN control not supported by such an organization will only approach an official once he has shown his willingness to cooperate and his understanding for peasant problems.

The village program in its entirety—elections, shift of control over the PF, and new development programs—is a potent threat to ARVN officers who serve as District and Province Chiefs. ARVN correctly sees its political power threatened by the growth of village government and the development of a viable administration controlled by President Thieu and his cabinet rather than by the South Vietnamese military. The pressures by the peasants, when they are expressed, are directed in large measure against the Saigon government and against the irresponsibility of ARVN in the villages.

President Thieu seems to have realized that the village chiefs are the political base he will need in the national elections in 1971. He has advocated, clearly against the wishes of the ARVN generals, the decentralization of government and the allotment of increased but still minimal powers to Village Chiefs. Thieu's purpose has not been to enact major reforms giving peasants a role in government but rather to develop a power base outside ARVN command.

Thus, Thieu's new emphasis on limited peasant participation has wedged him between two sides, leaving him without the certain support of either. The peasants themselves are still far too dissatisfied with the GVN's intricacies and constraints to support Thieu actively, and the other source of power, the military, is radically opposed to even the mildest of peasant reforms. The impact of peasant demands is likely to be deferred a while longer, but this will not decrease the friction between village officials and district and province chiefs who are appointed from the ranks of ARVN.

The new village programs have begun to stimulate a long dormant village political structure. It is the hope of American pacification officials that this awakening will eventually energize the entire GVN political structure from the village to Saigon. But it is just as likely, or more so, that what will emerge will be similar to the Green Army that fought the Reds and Whites in the Russian Revolution, or to the movement in Bolivia after the mobilization of the peasants by the Chaco War.

It is extremely optimistic and naive to expect a third force to emerge. It is still the far right and the far left who control the guns. It seems probable that ARVN will continue to ignore the welfare of its soldiers and peasants. What support Thieu may get from the people is likely to be insignificant unless ARVN is reformed. For, the essence of the conflict is not between a traditional peasant and a modernizing state, but between a politically sensitive peasantry and a state that is jealous of its own power and prerogatives.

A Doomed Dependency

GABRIEL KOLKO

The war's economic and social impact on South Vietnam between 1965 and 1970 was decisive to its eventual military conclusion. The accumulated effects of war produce their own internal dilemmas and contradictions as well as unintended consequences which may prove far more consequential to a war's outcome than anyone's conscious desires, thereby fixing the boundaries of historical possibilities. The U.S. intervention in Vietnam produced such ironies from the inception, but by the late 1960s their impact was decisive and irreversible.

These economic and social trends appeared less than critical to American leaders, and measured in the form of numbers—the only index available to men whose values preclude empathy—they were quite elusive. Even today, information on South Vietnam's demography, the class structure, or the economy is poor and masks unconscionably the enormous human drama and suffering of fully one-half of a nation. It offends the sense of real human experiences to attempt to reduce such events to aggregate, measurable proportions, but to fathom their meaning and importance is to understand, as fully as frail human capacities allow, controlling factors in war and history, the forces which decide the outcome of the more easily described, much more closely studied world of battles or of decision making.

The nature of South Vietnamese society was not incidental to the U.S. effort, but a critical factor, by itself sufficient to determine whether Washington's fate would be victory or defeat. It explains not only the sources of the Revolution's initial efforts in the south but also the subsequent directions imposed upon it, the nature of its triumph, and the peace that followed. The strength, fragility, and evolution of the U.S. dependent determined the very viability of its undertaking and the extent of the obligation the Americans assumed in their naive optimism.

Firepower shaped the demography of South Vietnam after 1964, reducing the issue for a substantial portion of the peasantry to one of physical survival. At the core of the vast panorama of events emerging from this protracted conflict were men and women whose commitments and lives were ceaselessly affected by innumerable challenges and travails. Their responses ranged across the whole spectrum of possible individual reactions, from heroism and conscious efforts to resolve their problem through collective action against foreign invaders to an elemental decision to survive physically as a person by whatever means necessary. To comprehend that process of constant choice for most of the adults is quite impossible, because the destruction, grief, and physical anguish around them, the extremes of human bravery and human degradation, defy description.

The United States in Vietnam unleashed the greatest flood of firepower against a nation known to history. The human suffering was monumental. The figures on all aspects of this enormous trauma are inadequate, and between 1968 and 1970 the refugee reporting system alone underwent three major revisions. The Pentagon's final estimate of killed and wounded civilians in South Vietnam between 1965 and 1972 ran from 700,000 to 1,225,000, while Senate numbers for the same period were 1,350,000. Deaths in these two assessments ranged from 195,000 to 415,000; "enemy" killed were 850,000 minimum, and a substantial part of these were civilians. The Revolution's figures are much higher. In a nation of about 18 million people in 1970, the war exacted an immensely high toll in killed and wounded.

Munitions was the primary cause of casualties, and the vast bulk of it was employed by the United States and the ARVN which accounted for nearly all the artillery and 100 percent of that delivered by air. In 1969, internal U.S. discussions admitted, "the information available . . . on the overall scale and incidence of damage to civilians by air and artillery . . . is less than adequate." They did know, however, that in the single month of January 1969 over four million people, nearly a quarter of the population, had one or more air strikes within three kilometers of their hamlet. The U.S. and RVN pacification programs sought to empty the NLF-dominated regions of their population, not merely by firepower but also by defoliation, forced removals into strategic hamlets, and other means of separating the peasants from their land. While the reasons for this vast population displacement were both political and military, American officials also considered it "desirable" in making available the huge labor pool they required for their own bases and logistics. And once displaced, the peasants had to be kept, the Americans believed, from returning home. For all these reasons, [Robert] Komer said in April 1967, the United States should "[s]tep up refugee programs deliberately aimed at depriving the VC of a recruiting base."

In essence, a substantial part of the peasantry was consciously forced off the land against its will, permanently transforming the nature of South Vietnamese society. The most conservative estimates are that at least half of the peasants were pushed into refugee camps or urban settings one or more times, many repeatedly. The statistics are, again, far from precise, not least because the United States was hardly inclined to expend the effort to document accurately the brutal consequences of its policies. Senate figures for 1964–72 give only 5.8 million persons as refugees, but additional data show that provinces under the NLF, primarily north of Saigon, and in the Mekong as well, generated the largest proportion of refugees. The correlation between firepower and population displacement is very close.

RVN numbers on refugees or war victims during 1965–72 are substantially higher than U.S. figures, about 7 million people, or about one-third of the population or well over half the peasantry. Once in refugee camps, the peasants saw their standard of living drop by about two-thirds, and their psychic loss was incalculable. The result was the urbanization of a rural society in a manner unique in this century, for it was far more brutal and disorienting to the population than any that a large Third World nation has ever experienced.

Urban Vietnam before 1960 had been remarkably comfortable, its cities scarcely more than colonial enclaves. The French had controlled them until 1954, of course, but the Chinese also were always vital economically and physically. Even in 1966 one-fifth of South Vietnam's urban population, comprising about a million persons, was Chinese. The virtual Chinese monopoly over important economic activities left little space for newcomers, whose commerce was really marginal subsistence. A portion of them made up the most dynamic, entrepreneurial sector, and were in the best position to amass the benefits of the new foreign presence. Into this turbulent world came millions of peasants after 1964.

In 1960, 20 percent of South Vietnam's population lived in urban areas. The proportion had reached 26 percent by 1964, 36 percent by 1968, and 43 percent by 1971—a growth rate of five times that of all less developed nations during the same decade. Saigon's expansion, though great in the surrounding suburbs, was astonishingly small in the metropolitan area, and far less than that of such provincial towns as Can Tho, Danang, Bien Hoa, Hué, and cities closer to actual combat. Danang and Nha Trang grew fourfold between 1960 and 1971, mainly after 1964, while Can Tho's population tripled. . . .

Forced urbanization not only produced a wholly untenable RVN economy but also created a profoundly disturbed human order, fraught with immense political implications. Looked at objectively, the United States in less than a decade did more damage to an entire society than other colonial nations or the urbanization process elsewhere accomplished over generations. No one, the Revolution included, at first fully perceived the magnitude of this cultural assault, which touched the basic question of the nature of politics and individual commitments in a social context of personal and family crisis. By necessity, this experience can affect people in various ways, one of which is egoism, personalism, and *attentisme* or apathy toward politics. The adult peasantry forced into cities became profoundly alienated from a culture and society succumbing to Americans who devoured their sons and daughters, patronized successive juntas, and wreaked havoc on Vietnamese lands and traditions. One split in urban society which emerged was between those who had absorbed the officially sanctioned urban mores and those who remained rural and traditional in either their economic lives or their values. More dangerous, the newly arrived city dwellers were alienated from their children. . . .

A critical problem for the NLF was whether the former peasantry's involuntary rupture with its rural origins and the Revolution was irreversible, but the decisive question for the United States and the RVN was whether it would ever leave its cocoon of private concerns to sustain the RVN in some effective fashion. For while the Revolution had other means of struggling, without a measure of support from the urban population the RVN would remain politically unstable and the cities only a fatal economic burden.

The social order that urbanization created was ultimately the functional outcome of many policies, and though the new society was largely incremental and ad hoc in nature, aspects of it were certainly planned. Urbanization was the unavoidable logic of the high-firepower war, and its cultural form was strongly influenced by the over two million GIs who passed through the country. Many in America and Saigon regarded population reconcentration as both an opportunity and a hidden blessing. That Washington did not understand the critical economic and political implications of the war's demography until it was too late was one of its great miscalculations in the war.

Thousands of Americans were involved in "nation building" projects, including social scientists eager to test their wares in practice. These ranged from the surrounding of air bases with civilians they attempted to make happy with subsidies of every kind so that they would not aid the NLF (a policy that failed dismally) to an effort to write a Vietnamese equivalent of the song "God Bless America" to win over the masses. The radio propaganda that incessantly swept the nation had very little impact, even in the opinion of the RVN's experts, and the most powerful tool that both the United States and the RVN had to consolidate their influence among the masses was the dollar—a weapon which worked best among the youth on the streets but proved also to be finite both in quantity and in effectiveness.

The dollar's assault on the culture, whether traditional or Revolutionary, profoundly alienated a significant element of the older urban dwellers, particularly the students and intelligentsia who had the leisure to observe and think about it. Secondary school and university enrollment increased over ten times between 1954 and 1970, when the RVN claimed there were about 680,000 in the two categories. The children of the petite bourgeoisie, merchants, and even civil servants and RVN functionaries, many transcended their class position and related to their own peer culture in much the same way the children of uprooted peasants did.

The intellectuals, too, were as fragile in South Vietnam as they are anywhere, full of moods, variations, and typical equivocations, but many became increasingly sympathetic to the NLF as they observed what the United States was doing to the nation and its culture, though a significant portion always did what those in power demanded. Many among them, particularly teachers, were poorly paid. The students, especially, reacted to the nightmare of human degradation around them, and some preserved their capacity for action, even as many retreated into their privileged private

worlds. Among people in these social categories, the NLF certainly increased its influence as a by-product of the American cultural offensive,
and a significant portion of this crucial social stratum was always alienated
from the RVN and the United States.

The final test was less the alienated urban intelligentsia's relationship
to the Revolution than its willingness to make those commitments and
sacrifices necessary to maintain the existing order in power, and the effects
of urbanization prevented this from occurring. As a physical solution to
the problem of cooperation between the Revolution and peasantry, the
urbanization of the south appeared sensible to the United States. Despite
its immediate advantages, however, it was by the late 1960s increasingly
alienating the expanding urban population, leaving a growing political, economic, and psychological void. France's struggle against the Communists
had not altered the rural society's structure, character, and values in any
basic way. Even during its entire colonial reign, only a small minority of
the people had been affected ideologically. But the American style of war
was far more damaging to the population's identity and existence. The
reconciliation of the economic and political contradictions in its policies
was almost immediately beyond Washington's abilities. Ultimately, the cumulative effects of urbanization on the RVN's economic, political, and
military system immeasurably aided its total collapse.

The Communist Party's virtual monopoly on the opposition to French
and American imperialism reflected the impact of colonialism on the Vietnamese class structure and its evolution. All of its potential challengers were
too divided, too sectarian, or too ambitious to fill the void in the political
system, and religious differences, especially in the south, gravely weakened
the non-Marxist opposition. Chinese domination of the economy meant that
the stratum with the most to gain from the status quo was unable directly
to relate politically to the rest of the system and was mobile, should need
arise, and no other potential class-based leadership existed. This vacuum
in power and politics was institutionalized for most of the RVN's brief life
in the hands of two men, producing hybrid ruling elites without an autonomous class constituency and dependent ultimately on foreign support.
Diem's nearly decade-long rulership at the inception of the RVN's twenty-
two-year existence, with his systematic attacks on the fragile French bureaucratic legacy and class-based elites, the Chinese particularly, further
narrowed the social basis of rulership, reducing it essentially to his clique
and the military—the only large institutional force he could not abolish or
decrease in functional power. Put simply, the military was the only non-
Communist stratum able to succeed Diem and to aspire to power.

The RVN was very much in the same position as many non-Asian Third
World states dependent on foreign aid or created in a vacuum to perform
a comprador role for a foreign imperialism, and the military in this context
traditionally serves as the political arena and instrument of political succession, even though the sponsoring state—the United States in this case—
hopes also to utilize it primarily as a way of transferring the techniques of
violence and administration necessary to maintain foreign influence. Should

the army's political function become its dominant preoccupation, then its tools of violence will ultimately be crucial only within the military establishment's political process, for arms will become the only real or potential means of political change—making its concern for external threats to the state quite secondary. And where the militarized political structure defines the nature and boundaries of economic development and accumulation to a critical extent, corruption drastically erodes its fighting capacities. In brief, politics neutralizes military capabilities decisively by making all purely military considerations subordinate to the control of political and economic power. The state, the economy, and military and political power all become integrated. The overcoming of this contradiction is the United States' main dilemma every time it creates a dependency on which it in turn becomes dependent to attain its own national objectives.

Such a context makes the social nature and function of the officers a fundamental issue, their class origins and linkages being facts of potentially great significance to their definition of their social and economic role as well as their personal aspirations. This is especially true when the military in underdeveloped nations with a vacuum in institutional power is the dominant mechanism within which rulership is determined. The marginality or stability of a class society at its various levels is critical where a cohesive opposition exists, and it becomes a crucial factor in determining how wars are concluded.

The officers in the RVN's armed forces, some 25,000 by 1967, as well as the tiny elite of senior officers at the rank of major or higher, were homogenous to an astonishing degree. The junior officers, composing 95 percent of the total number of officers, were very young. Since they had to have at least a high school diploma, they were overwhelmingly urbanized and born into families that could afford to educate their children. Soldiers could not rise through the ranks to become officers. A quarter were born in the north, and the percentage of Catholics was double South Vietnam's average, which meant that the military was an important avenue of social mobility for displaced refugees coming from the DRV after 1954. Economically, though, the profession was poorly paid, second lieutenants earning but $55 monthly in 1967 and enjoying few legal perquisites. For the majority who were married and had families, this fact became critical to their real functions. At least one major distinction between officers was their training academy and their year of graduation. Without a definable class or ideological differentiation among the officers, the "school tie" became inordinately important. The National Military Academy at Dalat produced 13 percent of the officers in the military in 1967, but 30 percent of the general-ranking officers graduated from it, while Thu Duc academy graduated two-thirds of the officers and a mere 5 percent of the generals and 30 percent of the field-grade officers. Catholics accounted for a third of the generals.

Of a sample of sixty generals in 1972, one-third were the sons of landowners, another quarter of government officials, and over a quarter of officers and urban professionals and middle- and upper-class elements. They were upwardly mobile; their families were not yet important but at a point where they might aspire to be, and this profoundly affected their use of power. Thieu, for example, was the son of a small landlord, and he graduated from Dalat. A scant majority were graduates of Dalat academy, 14 percent of Thu Duc. Nearly all had begun their careers under the French. The military, given the role of war in the French and the RVN's priorities, was the chief channel of social and economic mobility for an important sector of the marginalized middle classes ready to work for the dominant colonial power.

The motive of the senior officers after Diem's death was simple: power in the form of careers and money. This was just as true of the congeries of civilian miniparties, factions, or religious sects who were always moving in and out of various coalitions or plotting on the sidelines. Where neither coherent class interest nor ideology exists, there is no basis of collective action and responsibility, and personal welfare becomes the motive of politics, resulting in individual corruption as an institutionalized dimension of society.

The Americans always watched this charade with the utmost cynicism. Perhaps the most dangerous aspect of this period was the effort of civilians to link up with military factions and encourage them, which was a guarantee of continuous turmoil and, by mid-1966, of various degrees of warlordism in the four military regions into which the RVN was divided, particularly MR I in the north. Indeed, as the successive military juntas passed through Saigon, mutual suspicions justifiably became axiomatic among those in the perpetual imbroglio the United States was sustaining. As they conspired and as membership in the ruling juntas changed, the system was made ripe for a superior political fixer, and in Nguyen Van Thieu the senior officers met their master.

Thieu was surely the ablest politician to emerge in the RVN's history, and his conversion from Buddhism to Catholicism to advance his career proved he was supremely flexible. He was a member in the June 1965 junta representing the "Young Turks" with no close past ties to the French and Diem. From there he moved unobtrusively to find ways of maneuvering around potential opponents and, above all, to try to find the price or weakness of any who might resist him. Unlike Diem, he had no serious ideological pretensions, and the initial key to his success was his readiness co-optively to share the spoils. Thieu was much more interested in obtaining stable control over power rather than a monopoly of it, and not until 1973 was he to seek total authority in his own hands.

In the wake of Diem's death, one of the most important factors in his rise to power was the aid he obtained from the Chinese business elite. Thieu's sister-in-law married Ly Luong Than, who was already one of the richest Chinese in Saigon, held a U.S. passport in his traditionally abundant collection, and was a key figure in the Fukienese *bang* [Chinese merchant organizations]. Than brought Thieu together with Francis Koo, first secretary of the Taiwanese embassy in Saigon and a senior figure in SEATO intelligence circles. Koo decided Thieu would serve the embattled Chinese community well and provided him funds and contacts to advance his career.

When Nguyen Cao Ky, his main rival, in early 1966 excoriated speculators and had one Chinese publicly executed as a warning to the others, the still nervous Chinese elite gave Thieu massive financial backing and intervened on his behalf with U.S. officials. Thieu was a shrewd operator in his own right, but his access to funds also smoothed his way. He had far more tact and cash to employ than Ky did. The United States' obsessive desire to see military unity was the single most important element in bringing Thieu to power, but his Chinese connection undoubtedly shaped the regime's distribution of economic benefits.

Thieu in 1967 was the sole general with sufficient talent to survive the chaos of Saigon politics and create a powerful political machine. In June 1967 he had the junta nominate him for the new presidency, after he promised to abide by the will of a collective leadership. Even when he was most powerful, Thieu neutralized, co-opted, and pressured many of his military and civilian elite rivals far more gently than Diem did, trying to divide the rewards of office widely to gain time to enjoy the prerogatives of power and, above all, to prevent any threats to his increasingly durable machine from the other senior military commanders. As for the Chinese, one of his first acts in 1967 was to allow them to reestablish their *bangs* and to return their associations' confiscated property.

The moment he came to office, in September 1967, Thieu embarked on building a largely private power machine which integrated the military, the political structure, and the economy in numerous formal and informal ways. Complex in certain aspects and baldly simple in others, his system assured that the RVN's destiny after 1968 would become synonymous with Thieu's ambitions, his power, and, ultimately, his weaknesses.

In an underdeveloped class structure traumatized by the effects of Diem's own power machine, the demography of the war, a subsidized war economy, and an enormous American presence, Thieu temporarily and partially remolded the elastic class system to suit his interests. He unified ambitious, essentially marginal class elements and the rich Chinese around only one common denominator: money and access to privilege. As a Rand Corporation summation of the views of twenty-seven high RVN officers and officials after the war said, "A central feature of the South Vietnamese regime . . . was corruption." His integrative effort encompassed a variety of approaches, ranging from a vast number of people brought into the RVN's employment to a higher elite which was incorporated into the war economy formally and informally, together sharing the main prerogatives of power. The fluid RVN power structure possessed intersecting economic, political, and military components in varying degrees, according to the people and elements involved, but it was never fully formalized before it collapsed both from its own contradictions and from the pressures the Revolution as well as the United States imposed on it.

The analysis of transitional and dependent social orders is potentially misleading if one attributes excess coherence and form to constantly evolving relationships. The task in Vietnam is made all the more difficult because the senior officers, Chinese capitalists, and civilian Vietnamese politicians were each internally divided, and only from 1969 to 1973 (but not later) did Nguyen Van Thieu sufficiently control power to make the structure susceptible to some generalizations. Thieu used his family as much as possible, of course, but his real strength was his ability to find and reward generals ready to cooperate with him loyally in running both the military and the civil administrations. Such a co-optive strategy was successful so long as there was enough to share. It was the sheer enormity of the American economic impact which defined the parameters of the RVN's class development and the political life intimately linked with it.

Both the Revolution and the U.S. government had a handful of analysts who tried to assess the structure of power within the RVN. Their work, as well as that of former RVN officials who have written postmortems, was remarkably parallel in both methods and conclusion. All assigned special significance to the Chinese capitalists in the running of the RVN system. Yet one cannot attribute causal power to them, because it was the French and later the Americans who ultimately controlled the collaborationist system. Without them, Thieu could not have undertaken so much, so well and so quickly. But while it is true that the Chinese by the 1960s were a traditional elite and the generals a distinctly new one, the political leverage the generals possessed made the Chinese highly dependent on their favors. A huge amount of money could be made in the economy and in the state's operations, and the Chinese obtained the major share in the former and a significant proportion of the latter. Opportunities for corruption available from direct control of state positions were vast, and officers and key bureaucrats dominated them.

Thieu was ultimately the functional master of the whole order during four years. His access to money was crucial to political cohesion in the military elite, and it kept most senior civil servants docile until 1973. The hybrid power structure which emerged was really a very personalized synthesis of Thieu and his coalition of loyal generals as well as a Chinese elite, and it is futile to try to determine their relative importance since each without the other was inconceivable. Getting rich was the common consensus which united them, and as Thieu manipulated their avarice, his machine possessed all of the subjective, arbitrary qualities one associates with the accumulation of capital by political means and corruption during a war which was sponsored entirely by a foreign power. Ultimately, the RVN's existence was improvised in an environment of chicanery, desperation, and tragedy which made absurdity and audacity common coin, with marginalized gangsters the mainstay of the social order the United States was attempting to keep in place.

A crucial aspect of America's funding for Thieu's system was mass employment and the perquisites that went with it. When Diem was overthrown, there were 121,000 civilian employees working for the RVN; by 1965 the number had grown to 179,000, increasing very slowly until 1968 (when Thieu took full command of the state administrative apparatus). From 208,000 government employees in 1968, the bureaucracy bounded to 337,000 in 1972 (the police composed 38 percent of this number), its share of the labor force having more than doubled since the early 1960s. The civil service had been fickle and inept in the stormy sea of post-Diemist politics, and Thieu sought to make it a reliable instrument of his power. Although their nominal salaries were low and kept falling, he allocated to them a whole panoply of corrupt practices to deepen his hold on their loyalties. The most common were bribes to obtain essential papers, ranging from normal legal transactions or identification documents to draft deferments, plus numerous petty forms of boodle. Corruption suffused and financially lubricated the state bureaucratic system at all levels.

The junior officer corps also became a major source of support for Thieu, for he satisfied their ambitions far more than any of his predecessors did. The regular military grew rapidly from 1961 to 1965, but the junior officer appointments failed to keep pace with it. When Thieu took power, he increased the number of first lieutenants from 8,764 in 1968 to 17,353 two years later and that of captains from 4,793 to 10,654, at a time when the regular military grew by less than a fifth. They too, of course, were allocated a share of condoned corruption as a supplement to their low salaries, and they often received their appointments because they were beholden to some senior officer for critical recommendations or, more simply, because they bought his favor. Their rackets were generally petty, ranging from the collecting of rice rations and salaries for dead or deserted soldiers to the funneling of military gasoline and supplies into the local markets, some of which the NLF purchased. Along with political officials, some participated in local usury, which during the Thieu period was 50 to 90 percent monthly. Together they could enforce their claims if necessary.

Higher-level officers were far more important, and their appointments were treated more seriously, since they alone could challenge Thieu's growing hegemony. Success in combat or purely military competence was increasingly ignored in senior appointments; political tendencies and personal ambition were far more critical. This made staff rather than combat officers ever-more preponderant at the upper ranks. Friends and relatives were very important. All appointments at the level of major or above had to be carefully approved by one of Thieu's closest allies in Saigon. He alone chose every general officer. There were only 40 generals in 1967, and 82 colonels, and it was to these men that Thieu turned his attention as he consolidated power. Shunting some of them off to powerless positions and avoiding any challenges to powerful generals' corruption, Thieu increased his control over the military apparatus by enlarging the number of generals to 73 and that of colonels to 200 in 1972, but the senior officer corps, in various degrees, remained seriously underbilleted after 1967, as Thieu cautiously filled the higher positions primarily with political appointees and assigned the lower officers duties which far exceeded both their rank and their abilities. Such a bottom-heavy officer corps was designed essentially to prevent a coup d'état. Those at the top were repaid for their devotion with a significant share of the state's diverse economic resources, ranging from normal commerce to sanctioned corruption of every variety, from larceny and graft to import licenses. "We would be left with practically no one to fight the war,'' Thieu's vice-president, Tan Van Huong, admitted, "if all corrupt commanders were to be prosecuted and relieved.'' Thieu's genius was to deflect the ambitions of his select group of senior officers from a desire for real political power and to make them, as two former generals recalled, "motivated by money.'' By the most cautious estimates, fully two-thirds of all generals and colonels were corrupt. . . .

The RVN's military and political machinery increasingly merged in Thieu's hands and could not operate without him, and this fact was far more important to its eventual destiny than the issue whether it was trained to fight conventional or guerilla warfare. The military establishment's primary function was to maintain Thieu's power, and the United States' ability to fight a counterrevolutionary war depended on the durability of a regime which was, in the words of one of Thieu's generals after the war, "intrigue-ridden, dictatorial, and repressive.'' American officials knew by 1971 what was not fully revealed until spring 1975—that Thieu's talent as a military leader was mediocre at best. His role was political, and Washington supported him for this reason.

Thieu understood that by permitting corruption, indeed even encouraging it, he could win loyalty: "The best way of avoiding coups d'etat . . .,'' as one of his aids quoted him. But the fundamental dilemma of such an order for America's anti-Communist crusade remained. The various constituencies Thieu drew into his expanding system were usually linked to him informally rather than institutionally, a fact which somewhat disturbed U.S. officials, although not enough to alter their overwhelming wish to see stability maintained. Elections were, as Nguyen Cao Ky aptly phrased it from his own experience as the victorious vice-president in 1967, "a loss of time and money. They were a joke. They have served to install a regime that has nothing in common with the people—a useless, corrupt regime.'' The National Assembly, which Diem himself created, had no significant powers, and Thieu ignored it. Even the most sympathetic American analysts thought that at least one-third of its members were fortune seekers—and Thieu let them enjoy this search often. . . .

The general dilemma confronting the United States' efforts to expand the military's power and role in numerous underdeveloped nations since 1950 has been the senior officer class' utilization of American support to assume far greater political power. And given the weak economic elite in most nations, the military's political role quickly dominates and exploits the nation's economic development, which ultimately produces instability and crisis politics and thwarts genuine development. In the end, the militarization of the RVN not only monopolized politics but also catalyzed social and human transformations which gravely eroded the coherence and future of the non-Revolutionary ideologies and followers. Those strata of South Vietnamese society without political links could scarcely compete for a large share of the new riches, even though a small number of individuals, mainly Chinese, managed to succeed in the highly fluid context in one way or another. The urban masses lived on the narrowest margins, and even some brothels and bars belonged to the elite that was forming from officers, key bureaucrats, and the Vietnamese and Chinese elements directly allied to them.

American officials always saw clearly the role of the new RVN elite in making vast private gains from political power. They were often informed by various senior generals currying U.S. favor that "corruption exists everywhere, the rich get richer while the mass of the poor Vietnamese see little hope of improvement"—as Marshall Ky told American leaders in July 1965, while jockeying for a greater share of it himself. Far worse than corruption, in American eyes, was tension among the generals and political instability. This consideration caused Washington increasingly to support Thieu, until the officer corps rightly came to believe that he was their surest, perhaps only, link to the Yankee cornucopia. "Patterns of existent political alignments are greatly affected by corruption because of its endemic character in GVN and RVNAF functioning," the National Security Council's early 1969 review of the war concluded. Since reformers could only upset Thieu's cohesive and firmly managed dictatorship, American interest in reform never went beyond occasional subtle changes palatable to Thieu in the aid program.

In this sense, the Americans knew they were ultimately responsible for the Thieu regime, for without their money the RVN would not be able to buy allies who assured stability. The economic basis of its very existence would vanish. "Moreover," the NSC acknowledged in early 1969, "it is natural that many Vietnamese will hold the United States responsible for not controlling its aid so that corruption will not flourish." This relationship was the critical linkage in the social and class structure in the south after 1965, and all else would ultimately prove secondary. Conversely, since the United States now correctly saw that its entire mission was contingent on the RVN's stability, which only Thieu was able to provide, it in turn was wholly dependent on Thieu's remaining in power, a fact he perceived and exploited ruthlessly. Ironically, who was master and who was puppet was increasingly blurred with time.

Analyzed structurally, the apex of the Thieu system was a narrow clique of officers and key civilian officials, not more than several thousand. Immediately below them was a far more numerous set of lower-ranking officials and officers. Directly allied with this elite were various merchants, entrepreneurs in service industries, and businessmen, including a small group of landlords, who collectively channeled money to and from the higher levels via contracts, kickbacks, licenses for imports, and the like. While they never estimated its size, the AID's experts on the upper echelons of this system concluded, "Many of the larger industries in South Vietnam are currently controlled by a small number of coalitions of Chinese businessmen who are allied with strategic Vietnamese government personnel." The Fukienese, according to American officials, were by far the most powerful, Ly Luong Than was their most important leader, and they controlled or had major shares in textiles, scrap metal, construction, banking, insurance, food processing, and imports. Chinese from Swatow were congregated in banking, insurance, diverse manufacturing, and textiles.

All of the analyses of the dominating persons in this system number in the hundreds the officers and senior politicians and officials involved, and their capitalist allies—the large majority being Chinese—could not have been more than one or two thousand. This tiny but critical element accounted for the bulk of the accumulated capital and capital flight. Most of the capitalists had been wealthy before the war, but not on a remotely comparable scale. Directly beneath them was an altogether new group of largely politically based rich whose primary power lay in access to the state's largesse, and these were paralleled by entrepreneurs, mainly Chinese, but with a growing number of Vietnamese, who simply made money in conventional ways inevitable with the boom the American forces brought. . . .

Thieu, of course, never attempted seriously to create a broad class foundation for his regime, but the cumulative effect of Thieu's system was to create a congenial if fickle constituency out of those who were the direct or indirect beneficiaries of the American-funded society. There was never a class base for the Thieu regime in the true sense of class as an institutionally stable and broad element of society. The disintegration of the French legacy and the marginalization of the educated elements who had earlier been ideologically or economically predisposed to anti-Communist politics continued, inevitably conditioning a substantial portion of them for anti-Thieu coalition politics with virtually anyone, including the NLF. The shallow privileged class residues inherited from the French era continued to narrow, especially as inflation after 1965 began to whittle away at the economic resources of all except the Chinese.

The very context in which Thieu's regime developed convinced most of its new elite that it could not endure, and this especially affected its Chinese members, who had traditionally been mobile, prone to keeping wealth highly liquid, and often linked to families and interests elsewhere in Southeast Asia. Between the Chinese and the officers, the basic paradox of the Thieu regime was the opportunism of its most powerful and favored supporters, which took the form of a vast flight of capital, an exodus of children, and a reluctance to invest in long-term economic development. The Chinese capitalists were by definition the weakest class on which the military elite could rely. And precisely because they knew that the generals were vulnerable and transitional, they tried to make certain that their options outside the country were always ready. The Chinese, American officials in Saigon accurately concluded in 1972, for the most part "do not consider themselves a part of the nation in which they live. For the large entrepreneurs, the business decision to invest here or transfer funds abroad is made on business calculations and not on any consideration of national need—exactly, in fact, like any foreign investor does."

The fragile class structure that the French had created and Diem eroded now became even weaker in the flotsam and jetsam of demography, social disintegration, and changes far too rapid to be absorbed coherently. The new lumpen element of war profiteers destroyed the final vestiges of the national and the petite bourgeoisies, plunging them into economic and moral crises which compromised some and radicalized others. And being wholly dependent on American money and support for the very existence of the RVN, the new profiteers had no nationalist or cultural legitimacy for their politics, a fact they could not alter. The underdevelopment of a possible conservative class characterized the pre-Revolutionary order until its end. Both the French and the American colonial legacies made this ephemeral, fluid class development inevitable by their reliance on the Chinese and on dependent, obsequious arriviste generals whose only loyalty in serving comprador roles was ultimately to their own, personal welfare.

Though South Vietnam's economy under Diem was wholly dependent on American aid, after 1964 it was far more fragile. The intensified war and the exponential growth of American GIs posed potentially catastrophic economic challenges to the United States' ambition. For agriculture was being uprooted and the population displaced into cities wholly unable to absorb them with local resources.

The purpose of American economic policy was to stanch the immense economic wounds the war was inflicting long enough to allow its vague military objectives to be attained at a time, as the Agency for International Development later ruefully admitted, when "no one thought the war would last ten years, let alone that we would lose it." The cost to the United States could, if its military assumptions were valid, remain tolerable only for a short period. But to cut its losses was tantamount to military surrender, which was unthinkable. Meanwhile, Washington's temporary economic solutions produced fabulous opportunities for growing corruption, becoming the key to Thieu's political consolidation and, to a lesser degree, the maintenance of more social stability among the masses than would otherwise have been possible. In effect, the RVN's very existence was linked to sufficient economic and military aid, surpassing in importance the outcome of battles or diplomacy, for the very artificiality of the economy and the war's impact left it vulnerable to countless potentially fatal problems.

In retrospect, the AID accurately concluded in 1975, the "period 1965–67 in Viet Nam was unlike anything ever experienced by an underdeveloped country." While the various mechanisms the United States employed may seem complicated to nonspecialists, in essence they were merely manifestations of a simple policy. An escalating war was destroying the existing economy, and Washington made the decision that it was vital to prevent inflation, which could only further radicalize the people and make defeat more certain. The Korean War, which was much smaller in terms both of troops and of areas affected at any one time, had created a runaway inflation, the memory of which was still fresh in Washington in 1964. To combat inflation, the United States decided to maximize imports, neutralizing the vast inflow of dollars accompanying its half a million soldiers, the American expansion of bases and military construction, and the ruination of South Vietnam's traditional productive economic sector. The RVN's seeming prosperity, so illusory for the majority of the nation, was based wholly on this strategy.

Agricultural production by 1968 was a quarter below the already low

1961–65 average. Not until 1970 did it finally surpass it, although per capita output never equaled it. Industrial production, mainly to service U.S. troop demands and provide supplies for construction, rose during 1964–67, dropping sharply in 1968. In 1964–67 imports increased over 100 percent, and imports during 1969–71 exceeded exports by a factor of over fifty-five. By 1967 about 40 percent of the RVN's gross national product was composed of imports entirely dependent on U.S. aid, and by 1970 nearly 50 percent was. Proportionately, the share of gross domestic product devoted to manufacturing dropped dramatically throughout this period—making South Vietnam the only major nation of Asia to experience this form of deindustrialization and leaving it with the lowest proportion in manufacturing of any of them. The South Vietnamese economy was sharply diverted from the production of goods, the only basis of real economic development, into the provision of services, making it structurally very weak and vulnerable to an economic crisis the moment the Americans started to withdraw.

A Viable State

BUI DIEM

Except for the special circumstances that put me close to the center stage of the war in Vietnam, and except for the sheer luck that spared me much of the suffering endured by others, I am not different from other Vietnamese of my generation. In terms of dreams and aspirations, frustrations and disappointments, my life story is essentially theirs.

Vietnamese of my generation came of age in the early forties with the hope that after almost a century as second-class citizens in their own country, they would have a chance to recover their dignity and achieve their independence from France. They dreamed also of peace and a decent life for themselves and their children. It was their misfortune that instead of independence, peace, and a decent life, they saw only revolution, war, and destruction. For three decades they existed in the maelstrom. And even now, when Vietnam no longer has to deal with foreign invaders, their misery continues. Theirs has been a tragedy of historic proportions.

In an interview with Walter Cronkite in 1963, President John Kennedy said, "In the final analysis, it's their war and they are the ones who will either win it or lose it." Much as we might like to, there is no getting away from Kennedy's judgment. The South Vietnamese people, and especially the South Vietnamese leaders, myself among them, bear the ultimate responsibility for the fate of their nation, and to be honest, they have much to regret and much to be ashamed of. But it is also true that the war's cast of characters operated within a matrix of larger forces that stood outside the common human inadequacies and failings. And it was these forces that shaped the landscape on which we all moved.

First among these root causes was the obduracy of France, which in the late forties insisted on retaining control of its former colony rather than conceding independence in good time to a people who hungered for it. Second was the ideological obsession of Vietnam's Communists. Not content with fighting to slough off a dying colonialism, they relentlessly sought to impose on the Vietnamese people their dogma of class warfare and proletarian dictatorship. Finally came the massive intervention by the United States, inserting into our struggle for independence and freedom its own overpowering dynamic. These three forces combined to distort the basic nature of Vietnam's emergence from colonialism, ensuring that the struggle would be more complex and bloodier than that of so many other colonies which achieved nationhood during mid-century.

Caught in the midst of these powerful forces, Vietnam's nationalists found themselves in a succession of precarious situations. In most cases they were forced to choose among unpalatable alternatives; often, indeed, they saw no choice at all. With their survival at stake, they were forced to take refuge in a series of uneasy and uncomfortable compromises that little by little eroded their legitimacy. From one experience to another—first with the French and Bao Dai, then with Ngo Dinh Diem, then with the Americans and the military—they tried to carve out a role for themselves and establish their influence. But always they were pushed to the periphery, and the influence they wielded was never enough to affect the ultimate course of events. To myself and others, for a time it seemed we might be able to develop the nation's economy and build a functioning democracy, even while waging war. But eventually the room to make this kind of contribution diminished, and in the end, against a mechanized North Vietnamese invasion army equipped by the Soviets, all that remained was an alley fight for survival. By then Vietnam's nationalists had been forced to take their place alongside all the other Vietnamese who could only stand by and watch their fate unfold in front of them.

As I look back on the external forces that shaped our lives, it is the American intervention that stands out. French colonialism, after all, is dead and gone, a subject for historians who prefer the inert remains of the past to the passions of the present. As for Vietnamese communism, no one but the fervid or the blind any longer argues the merits of a system that has brought in its wake only war and deprivation and mass flight. (Not that having been right comforts us as we house our refugees and send what sustenance we can back to our families.) But American intervention is a living issue. In the train of failure in Vietnam, and in the face of hard choices elsewhere, the questions of its correctness and its morality still inform American foreign policy debates. Americans still seek to learn the lessons of intervention, and so do America's smaller allies, who cannot help but see in the fate of Vietnam intimations of their own possible futures.

For critics of the Vietnam War, the original decision to intervene was wrong, a result, as one of them put it, of a "steady string of misjudgments." It was wrong because American policymakers in the sixties failed to assess correctly the vital interests of the United States, because they exaggerated the geopolitical importance of Vietnam, and because they had an inflated concept of American capabilities.

Although it is neither my business nor within my competence to pass judgment on how the United States defined its interests at that time, it is my impression that such arguments are made on a distinctly *a posteriori* basis. I remember vividly the political atmosphere in the United States in the summer of 1964, the summer of the Tonkin resolution and Barry Goldwater's nomination, when I first visited this country. At that time the Johnson administration and practically the entire Congress were in favor of the commitment to defend Vietnam (the resolution passed in the Senate, 98 to 2, and in the House, 416 to 0). And so, *mirabile dictu,* were the national news media.

Moreover, the context of international affairs in that period provided good reasons for this nearly unanimous opinion, reasons that went beyond the specific perception of North Vietnamese aggressiveness. It was then the aftermath of the Communist attack in Korea, and China's Communist leaders were broadcasting the most belligerent and expansionistic views, even as they attempted to establish a Peking-Jakarta axis with Indonesia's pro-Communist President Sukarno. For the fragile governments of Southeast Asia the situation seemed serious indeed. Although twenty-five years later it became fashionable among some Americans to belittle Communist threats to the region's stability, among the responsible governments at the time there was deep anxiety.

Even for those South Vietnamese who thought they saw the inherent dangers in American intervention, there was still nothing illogical about it. The American interest in Vietnam, even its land intervention, seemed a natural extension of U.S. policies in Europe (the Marshall Plan, the Berlin airlift, Greece) and Asia (Korea) aimed at preventing the expansion of combined Soviet and Chinese power (at least until the early 1960s, no one could imagine that the two Communist giants would become antagonists). And for the Europeans who were able to rebuild their countries and save their democratic institutions, for the Germans in Berlin, for the Greeks, and for the South Koreans, those policies were not wrong. Nor were they based on misjudgments of geopolitical realities. In Vietnam the policy failed. But that is not to say that it was wrong there either. The disastrous mistakes that were made were mistakes in implementation rather than intention. But the thrust of the policy of containment and protection, that I do not think can be faulted. It is, on the contrary, something for Americans to be proud of.

The more vocal critics of the war in the sixties and seventies characterized the intervention, not just as wrong, but also as immoral. Their charge was based primarily on the theory that the war in Vietnam was a civil war, and that consequently American intervention was an act of aggression against people who were fighting to free themselves from an oppressive regime and unify their country in accord with the aspirations of the great majority of decent-minded Vietnamese.

It is my own belief that this theory held the field for so long primarily because it was a powerful attraction to the many Americans who were angry at their own government and society and were looking for issues to hang their anger on. Certainly, the facts that refuted it were readily available. From early on, both Saigon and Washington knew beyond a doubt that the National Liberation Front—the Vietcong—was a creation of the Communist party, and that without North Vietnamese organization, leadership, supplies, and, starting in 1964, without the North Vietnamese regular army, there would have been no revolution to speak of and no war. It was one of my greatest frustrations that our firm knowledge of this—both from widespread and incontrovertible evidence and also from personal experience among many of us of communist "front" techniques—made no impact on popular understanding in the West. Regardless of what was there to be seen, people saw only what they wished.

After the war, when propaganda no longer mattered, the party dropped its pretense. "Our Party," said Le Duan in his 1975 victory speech, "is the unique and single leader that organized, controlled, and governed the entire struggle of the Vietnamese people from the first day of the revolution." During the war, the North Vietnamese never openly admitted they had troops in South Vietnam. (Le Duc Tho even kept up the pretense with Henry Kissinger, although Kissinger knew the situation as well as he knew his own name, and Tho, of course, knew that he knew it.) But afterward the party treated this subterfuge simply as an excellent piece of public relations and its own role as a matter of intense pride. As the North Vietnamese general Vo Ban told French television interviewers in 1983, "In May 1959 I had the privilege of being designated by the Vietnamese Communist Party to unleash a military attack on the South in order to liberate the South and reunify the fatherland."

During the heyday of the antiwar movement, I marveled at the innocence of its spokesmen in believing something different from this. I wonder even now if they ever feel shame for their gullibility and for their contribution to the tragedy. But they are not heard from. It was, after all, only one chapter in their lives, as it was only a chapter in the book of American history.

The issue of morality, then, comes down to whether it was moral for the United States to have supported an admittedly flawed South Vietnamese regime in its attempt to survive against a totalitarian antagonist. Here, too, the answer seems to me self-evident. However unpalatable leaders like Nguyen Van Thieu might have been, South Vietnam was full of pluralistic ferment and possibilities for change and development. It was a place where good people could hope for something better to evolve, where they could even fight for it, as so many strong-minded opposition politicians, intellectuals, and writers did. None but ideologues can compare such a place with the chilling police state that destroyed it. And none, I think, can fairly question the morality of the effort to prevent its destruction.

To my mind, the lessons of American intervention in Vietnam have to do not so much with the geopolitical or moral underpinning of the war, but rather with the way the intervention was implemented. The real question was not whether to intervene, but how to intervene effectively.

    . . . The salient feature of [the] confused and unclear process (as Bill Bundy characterized it) [by which the Johnson administration decided to bring an American land army to Vietnam] was not that it was ill planned and based on no comprehensive strategy. It was the startling attitude of American decision makers toward their ally. At the top levels of the administration, the State Department, and the Pentagon, there is no evidence to suggest that anyone considered the South Vietnamese as partners in the venture to save South Vietnam. In a mood that seemed mixed of idealism and naïveté, impatience and overconfidence, the Americans simply came in and took over. It was an attitude that would endure throughout the remainder of the conflict. The message seemed to be that this was an American war, and the best thing the South Vietnamese could do was to keep from rocking the boat and let the Americans get on with their business.

The military consequences of this orientation were that the United States took the entire burden on itself instead of searching for ways to make a decisive impact while limiting its exposure. Had the South Vietnamese been consulted in early 1965, it is likely they would have preferred either no intervention or a limited effort sufficient to stabilize the military situation and block the infiltration routes from North Vietnam. An agreement among the United States, South Vietnam, and Laos, allowing U.S. troops to be stationed along the seventeenth parallel as a barrier, would have been quite feasible at the time. With that done, an immediate Vietnamization program could have been undertaken to strengthen and upgrade the South Vietnamese army.

Could such a simple strategy have worked? That is one of the "what if" questions with which the Vietnam War abounds. Colonel Harry Summers, in *On Strategy*, his uncompromising review of American military planning, concludes that it would have, that in fact, isolating the South Vietnamese battlefield from North Vietnamese reinforcement and resupply was the only logical objective for American arms. Whatever the imponderables of war, this approach would at least have had the virtue of establishing the United States as a peace-keeping force protecting South Vietnam from outside aggression. It would have reduced American casualties and precluded the involvement of American firepower in the disconcerting people's war that was such a nightmare for the GIs to fight and that created such powerful antagonism in the arena of international public opinion.

On the political level, too, this American failure to regard the South Vietnamese as people worthy of partnership had destructive results. It meant that the United States never pursued a consistent policy aimed at encouraging the development of a viable democracy in South Vietnam. Certainly, such a thing was possible. Between 1965 and 1967 the South Vietnamese drafted and adopted a constitution, elected a president, vice president, and legislature, and successfully held many local elections—all of this in the middle of a war. It was a substantial achievement, but it would not have happened except that during those years the impulse toward democracy in South Vietnam and the objectives of the Johnson administration coincided.

Unfortunately, thereafter "stability" became the American watchword. As long as the Saigon government demonstrated a modicum of equilibrium, that was all that was asked of it. Several years of progress toward decent government might erode, corruption and autocracy might swell, but these things were not a primary American concern. By 1969 Henry Kissinger and Richard Nixon had embarked on a complex chess game, manipulating big-power diplomacy, military force, and secret negotiations in an attempt to extricate the United States from its quagmire. Amidst this constellation of variables, they needed a government in Saigon that was stable and predictable. If Thieu provided them with that, then whatever else he might do was essentially irrelevant.

It was a fatal error on two counts. First, stigmatized as undemocratic and corrupt, South Vietnam was deemed unworthy of support by an ever-increasing percentage of the American public and Congress. Second, within South Vietnam itself, the unpopular nature of the regime produced apathy, cynicism, and finally, in the anticorruption movement, outrage. Charles Mohr, veteran correspondent of the *New York Times*, summed it up succinctly in a seminar at the American Enterprise Institute. "We lost the war in Vietnam," he said, "not because we did not bring enough pressure to bear on our enemy, but because we did not bring sufficient pressure on our ally." Admittedly, bringing pressure for reform and democracy is a delicate business. But in situations where the United States has significant leverage, the role of catalyst for change, of prodding contending factions toward consensus, beckons to American diplomacy.

To successfully play such a role, there are two prerequisites. One is the will to carry out a strong and consistent advocacy. The other is the determination to accept the consequences if in the end American pressure proves unavailing. The United States must find a way to say to a Ngo Dinh Diem or a Nguyen Van Thieu (or a Ferdinand Marcos or an Augusto Pinochet), "We have no alternative but to stand by our own values. If for your own reasons you find you cannot bring yourselves toward conforming with them, then we are very sorry, but we will have no choice but to leave you to your own devices." With all its power and prestige, the United States simply cannot allow itself to yield to the tyranny of the weak, to authoritarians who believe their importance is so vast that the United States cannot help but support them. If Vietnam has one single lesson to teach, it is that people cannot be saved in spite of themselves. Far better to get out and cut losses before ensnaring treasure, lives, prestige, and all in the service of those whose rule means violent discord and social breakdown.

In Vietnam I always believed that among decent and reasonable people there could be no disagreement about things like corruption, economic and social reforms, and democratic procedures. I believe the same is true elsewhere. Another *New York Times* man, A. M. Rosenthal, in reflecting on his decades of covering American diplomacy, had this to say: "What should our policy be? Simply to act in our belief and interest. Our belief is political freedom and our interest is political freedom. We will not be able to achieve them for others all of the time or even much of the time. But what we can do is stand up for what we believe in, all of the time. . . . That requires two things: vision and constancy. Haitians, Filipinos, Koreans, Afghans seem to have no great confusion about what they really seek from us. Neither do the Czechoslovaks or the Poles." Neither, he might have added, did the South Vietnamese.

The experience of Vietnam suggests that a policy such as Rosenthal recommends would not be simple idealism. After Vietnam it is natural to question the extent to which the United States can sustain any major commitment to a foreign nation unless that nation is capable of eliciting moral support from an idealistic and essentially antimilitaristic American public. The suggestion is that geopolitical considerations by themselves constitute an insufficient grounding for stable, long-term policy. From this perspective, a democratic commitment in foreign policy is not mere idealism; it is also pragmatic self-interest.

From 1965 through 1967, Lyndon Johnson's administration acted according to this concept of idealistic pragmatism. From time to time other administrations did too, but never consistently and never strongly. For all the rhetoric, the American commitment to democracy in South Vietnam was a timid and wavering and sometime thing. That is another way of saying that in South Vietnam American policy neglected the human dimension. It did not accord its allies their requisite dignity as human beings. (I am not speaking here of the thousands of Americans who worked devotedly alongside the Vietnamese.) At the decision-making level, Vietnam was regarded primarily as a geopolitical abstraction, a factor in the play of American global interests. That was true about the way the United States intervened in the war with its land army. It was true about the way the United States conducted the war. And it was especially true about how the United States left the war.

Of all the successive phases of U.S involvement—the intervention of 1965, the Americanization of the war, then its Vietnamization, and finally the disengagement—it is the disengagement that will stick longest in the minds of the South Vietnamese. Major mistakes were made during the war by everyone concerned. But the manner in which the United States took its leave was more than a mistake; it was an act unworthy of a great power, one that I believe will be remembered long after such unfortunate misconceptions as the search and destroy strategy have been consigned to footnotes.

It was not that the leave-taking itself was a disgrace. The United States fought long and hard in Vietnam, and if in the end circumstances required that it withdraw, it may be considered a tragedy but hardly an act of shame. The same cannot be said, however, for the manipulative and callous manner with which the American administration and the American Congress dealt with South Vietnam during the last years of the war. It was not one of

America's finest hours, and there are plenty of lessons in it for both the United States and for other nations, particularly small ones that must rely on the United States for their defense.

As for Henry Kissinger, the architect of the Paris agreement, one can sympathize with his desire for "flexibility," that is, for control. Kissinger was in the middle, attempting to maneuver disparate and obstinate parties (including the North Vietnamese, South Vietnamese, Soviets, Chinese, even, on occasion, his own president) toward the same end. But he had taken on himself an awesome responsibility, negotiating not just for the global interests of the United States but for the existence of South Vietnam. In this context, he and Richard Nixon avoided holding frank discussions on common strategies with the South Vietnamese. They knew that Nguyen Van Thieu could do nothing without American support, yet they chose the unnecessary expedient of keeping developments to themselves until the last moment, then bringing to bear the heavy tactics of promises and threats. They treated a dependent ally of twenty years with finesse and then brutality, instead of with the openness the relationship required.

The fact that Kissinger and Nixon may have believed they had a viable agreement, or at least the best they could get, does not in my view justify their conduct toward South Vietnam. But at the same time, as unique as the Nixon administration's diplomatic style was, it was in effect just another aspect, another face of the American policy that had obtained in Vietnam from the beginning, informed by worthy motives but without an understanding of the human beings who would be affected by its geopolitical goals.

The congresses that in 1973, 1974, and 1975 washed their hands of Vietnam shared fully in this same guilt. Although senators and representatives talked a good deal then about credibility and moral obligation, in fact what they did was to make a geopolitical decision on the basis of what they saw as American self-interest. They did so in callous disregard of the consequences their actions would have on a nation of twenty million people, and they did so although it was no longer a matter of American blood, but only of some hundreds of millions of dollars.

"Is it possible for a great nation to behave this way?" That was the question an old friend of mine asked me in Saigon when news came in August of 1974 that Congress had reduced the volume of aid. He was a store owner whom I had gone to school with in North Vietnam, a totally nonpolitical person. "You are an ambassador," he said. "Perhaps you understand these things better than I do. But can you explain this attitude of the Americans? When they wanted to come, they came. And when they want to leave, they leave. It's as if a neighbor came over and made a shambles of your house, then all of a sudden he decides the whole thing is wrong, so he calls it quits. How can they just do that?" It was a naive question from an unsophisticated man. But I had no answer for it. Neither, I think, would William Fulbright, or George McGovern, or the other antiwar congressmen.

In the end, though, the culpability is hardly theirs alone. So many thought they knew the truth. The newsmen—as arrogant as any—Kissinger, Thieu, Nixon, myself as well. But none of us knew the truth or, knowing it, took it sufficiently to heart. Not we, and certainly not the implacable and ruthless ideologues who were our enemies. The truth is in the millions of Vietnamese families that have suffered the most horrible tragedies, people who understood what was happening only in the vaguest way. The truth of this war lies buried with its victims, with those who died, and with those who are consigned to live in an oppressed silence, for now and for the coming generations—a silence the world calls peace.

✗ F U R T H E R   R E A D I N G

Denis Bloodworth, *An Eye for the Dragon* (1970)
Anthony Bouscaren, *The Last of the Mandarins: Diem of Vietnam* (1965)
Bernard B. Fall, *The Two Vietnams* (1967)
Frances FitzGerald, *Fire in the Lake* (1972)
Allan E. Goodman, *Politics in War: The Bases of Political Community in South Vietnam* (1973)
Lawrence E. Grinter, "Bargaining Between Saigon and Washington: Dilemmas of Linkage Politics During War," *Orbis*, 18 (1974), 837–67
Gerald C. Hickey, *Village in Vietnam* (1964)
George McT. Kahin and John W. Lewis, *The United States in Vietnam* (1969)
Robert W. Komer, *Bureaucracy Does Its Thing* (1972)
Jean Lacouture, *Vietnam Between Two Truces* (1966)
Donald Lancaster, *The Emancipation of French Indochina* (1961)
Jeffrey Race, *War Comes to Long An* (1972)
Robert Scigliano, *South Vietnam: Nation Under Stress* (1964)
Robert Scigliano and Guy Fox, *Technical Assistance in Vietnam* (1965)
Robert Shaplen, *The Road from War* (1970)
James Trullinger, *Village at War* (1980)
Nguyen Thai, *Is South Vietnam Viable?* (1962)
Denis Warner, *The Last Confucian* (1963)

CHAPTER
11

Richard M. Nixon's Strategy
for Withdrawal

✕

Richard M. Nixon assumed the presidency in January 1969 with a clear mandate to end America's commitment to Vietnam. Convinced that a precipitous withdrawal of American troops would jeopardize South Vietnam's prospects for survival as well as America's global prestige and credibility, he opted for a strategy of Vietnamizing the war: withdrawing American forces gradually while turning over the conduct of the war to the South Vietnamese.

Twice Nixon widened the war, at least temporarily, in order, he believed, to hasten its end. In April 1970 he ordered U.S. and South Vietnamese troops into Cambodia in an effort to rout enemy bases there and buy time for Vietnamization. One of the most controversial moves of his presidency, the Cambodian incursion met with passionate opposition, especially on college campuses. Then in February 1971 he approved a major ground operation into Laos.

Nixon simultaneously moved on the diplomatic front. His special assistant for national security affairs, Henry A. Kissinger, began secret negotiations with Le Duc Tho, his North Vietnamese counterpart, in Paris early in 1969. After several years of talks, those efforts appeared ready to bear fruit toward the end of Nixon's first term in 1972. The president, however, considered it necessary to apply additional military pressure on Hanoi—the controversial "Christmas bombings" of 1972—in order to conclude a negotiated settlement. On January 27, 1973, a peace agreement was finally signed in Paris that allowed the total withdrawal of American combat forces.

Although much documentary evidence regarding the Nixon years remains closed to researchers, public and scholarly interest in the president's Vietnam policy has been strong. Interpreters of the Nixon record have differed over such critical matters as the underlying rationale for Vietnamization; the reasons for and consequences of the Cambodian invasion; the relationship between U.S. actions in Vietnam and a global strategy centered on détente with the Soviet Union and normalization of relations with China; and the nature of the Paris peace settlement. Critics on the left have accused Nixon of needlessly prolonging the fighting for a settlement that could have been achieved years earlier; critics on the right have charged him with sacrificing an American ally on the altar of

*expediency and global interests. The documents and essays in this chapter ad-
dress these issues.*

✗ D O C U M E N T S

In early January 1969 Henry Kissinger's National Security Council staff circulated a series of questions about Vietnam policy to concerned agencies within
the executive branch. The answers were summarized in National Security Study
Memorandum No. 1, dated January 21, extracts from which are printed as the
first document. The next document contains a nationwide address by Richard
Nixon, delivered on November 24, 1969, in which the president outlined his
Vietnamization strategy and appealed to the "silent majority" for support. In a
televised national address on May 11, 1970, reprinted as the third document, the
president explained and defended his decision to order U.S. and South Vietnamese troops into Cambodia. The next document contains extracts from Kissinger's news conference of January 26, 1972, in which he discussed previously secret negotiations with North Vietnam, emphasizing the remaining points of
contention between the two sides. On September 11, 1972, the Provisional Revolutionary Government (the title formally adopted by the National Liberation
Front in 1969) released a statement that laid out its negotiating position; it is
reprinted as the final selection.

National Security Study Memorandum No. 1, 1969

The responses to the questions posed regarding Vietnam show agreement
on some matters as well as very substantial differences of opinion within
the U.S. Government on many aspects of the Vietnam situation. While
there are some divergencies on the facts, the sharpest differences arise in
the interpretation of those facts, the relative weight to be given them, and
the implications to be drawn. In addition, there remain certain areas where
our information remains inadequate.

There is general agreement, assuming we follow our current strategy,
on the following—

1. The GVN and allied position in Vietnam has been strengthened
recently in many respects.

2. The GVN has improved its political position, but it is not certain
that GVN and other non-communist groups will be able to survive a peaceful
competition with the NLF for political power in South Vietnam.

3. The RVNAF alone cannot now, or in the foreseeable future, stand
up to the current North Vietnamese-Viet Cong forces.

4. The enemy have suffered some reverses but they have not changed
their essential objectives and they have sufficient strength to pursue these
objectives. We are not attriting his forces faster than he can recruit or
infiltrate.

5. The enemy is not in Paris primarily out of weakness.

The disagreements within these parameters are reflected in two schools
in the government with generally consistent membership. The first school,

which we will call Group A, usually includes MACV, CINCPAC, JCS and Embassy Saigon, and takes a hopeful view of current and future prospects in Vietnam within the parameters mentioned. The second school, Group B, usually includes OSD [Office of the Secretary of Defense], CIA and (to a lesser extent) State, and is decidedly more skeptical about the present and pessimistic about the future. There are, of course, disagreements within agencies across the board or on specific issues.

As illustration, these schools line up as follows on some of the broader questions:

In explaining reduced enemy military presence and activities, Group A gives greater relative weight to allied military pressure than does Group B.

The improvements in RVNAF are considered much more significant by Group A than Group B.

Group A underlines advancements in the pacification program, while Group B is skeptical both of the evaluation system used to measure progress and of the solidity of recent advances.

In looking at the political scene, Group A accents recent improvements while Group B highlights remaining obstacles and the relative strength of the NLF.

Group A assigns much greater effectiveness to bombing in Vietnam and Laos than Group B.

Following is a summary of the major conclusions and disagreements about each of six broad areas with regard to Vietnam: the negotiating environment, enemy capabilities, RVNAF capabilities, pacification, South Vietnamese politics, and U.S. military operations. . . .

Negotiating Environment

There is general U.S. government agreement that Hanoi is in Paris for a variety of motives but not primarily out of weakness; that Hanoi is charting a course independent of Moscow, which favors negotiations, and of Peking, which opposes them; and that our knowledge of possible political factions among North Vietnamese leaders is extremely imprecise. There continues wide disagreement about the impact on Southeast Asia of various outcomes in Vietnam.

Various possible North Vietnamese motives for negotiating are discussed, and there is agreement that the DRV is in Paris for mixed reasons. No U.S. agency responding to the questions believes that the primary reason the DRV is in Paris is weakness. All consider it unlikely that Hanoi came to Paris either to accept a face-saving formula for defeat or to give the U.S. a face-saving way to withdraw. There is agreement that Hanoi has been subject to heavy military pressure and that a desire to end the losses and costs of war was an element in Hanoi's decision. The consensus is that Hanoi believes that it can persist long enough to obtain a relatively favorable negotiated compromise. The respondents agree that the DRV is in Paris to negotiate withdrawl of U.S. forces, to undermine GVN and

USG [U.S. government] relations and to provide a better chance for FV victory in the South. State believes that increased doubt about winning the war through continued military and international political pressure also played a major role. Hanoi's ultimate goal of a unified Vietnam under its control has not changed.

There continues to be a sharp debate between and within agencies about the effect of the outcome in Vietnam on other nations. The most recent NIE [National Intelligence Estimate] on this subject (NIE 50–58) tended to downgrade the so-called "domino theory." It states that a settlement which would permit the Communists to take control of the Government in South Viet-Nam, not immediately but within a year or two, would be likely to bring Cambodia and Laos into Hanoi's orbit at a fairly early state, but that these developments would not necessarily unhinge the rest of Asia.

The NIE dissenters believe that an unfavorable settlement would stimulate the Communists to become more active elsewhere and that it will be difficult to resist making some accommodation to the pressure than generated. They believe, in contrast to the Estimate, these adjustments would be relatively small and insensitive to subsequent U.S. policy.

Factors entering into the judgments are estimates of (1) Hanoi's and Peking's behavior after the settlement; (2) U.S. posture in the regions; (3) Asian leaders' estimates of future U.S. policy; (4) the reactions of the area's non-Communist leaders to the outcome in Viet-Nam; (5) vulnerabilities of the various governments to insurgency or subversion, and (6) the strengths of opposition groups within each state.

The assessments rest more on judgments and assumptions than on tangible and convincing evidence, and there are major disagreements within the same Department. Within the Defense Department, OSD and DIA [Defense Intelligence Agency] support the conclusions of the NIE, while Army, Navy and Air Force Intelligence dissent. Within State, the Bureau of Intelligence supports the NIE while the East Asian Bureau dissents.

Both the majority and the dissenters reject the view that an unfavorable settlement in Viet-Nam will inevitably be followed by Communist takeovers outside Indo China.

Indeed, even the dissenters, by phrasing the adverse results in terms such as "pragmatic adjustments" by the Thais and "some means of accommodation" leave it unclear how injurious the adverse effects would be to U.S. security. . . .

The Enemy

Analyses of various enemy tactics and capabilities reveal both significant agreements and sharp controversies within the Government. Among the major points of consensus:

A combination of military pressures and political tacts explains recent enemy withdrawals and lower levels of activity.

Under current rules of engagement, the enemy's manpower pool and infiltration capabilities can outlast allied attrition efforts indefinitely.

The enemy basically controls both side's casualty rates.

The enemy can still launch major offensives, although not at Tet levels, or, probably, with equally dramatic effect.

Major controversies include:

CIA and State assign much higher figures to the VC Order of Battle than MACV, and they include additional categories of VC/NLF organization.

MACV/JCS and Saigon consider Cambodia (and specifically Sihanoukville) an important enemy supply channel while CIA disagrees strongly. . . .

It is generally agreed that the NVN/VC manpower pool is sufficiently large to meet the enemy's replenishment needs over an extended period of time within the framework of current rules of engagement. According to the JCS, "The North Vietnamese and Viet Cong have access to sufficient manpower to meet their replenishment needs—even at the high 1968 loss rate of some 291,000—for at least the next several years. . . . Present operations are not outrunning the enemy's ability to replenish by recruitment or infiltration."

The South Vietnamese Armed Forces

The emphatic differences between U.S. agencies on the RVNAF outweigh the points of agreement. There is consensus that the RVNAF is getting larger, better equipped and somewhat more effective. And all agree that it could not now, or in the foreseeable future, handle both the VC and sizeable NVA forces without U.S. combat support. On other major points there is vivid controversy. The military community gives much greater weight to RVNAF statistical improvements while OSD and CIA highlight remaining obstacles, with OSD being the most pessimistic. Paradoxically, MACV/CINPAC/JCS see RVNAF as being less capable against the VC alone than does CIA. . . .

Pacification

Two well-defined and divergent views emerged from the agencies on the pacification situation in South Vietnam. One view is held by MACV and Embassy Saigon and endorsed by CINCPAC and JCS. The other view is that of OSD, CIA and State. The two views are profoundly different in terms of factual interpretation and policy implications. Both views agree on the nature of the problem, that is, the obstacles to improvement and complete success. What distinguishes one view from the other is each's assessment of the magnitude of the problem, and the likelihood that obstacles will be overcome.

The first group, consisting of MACV JCS Saigon, maintains that "at the present time, the security situation is better than any time during period in question," i.e., 1961–1968. MACV cites a "dramatic change in the security situation," and finds that the GVN controls three-fourths of the population. JCS suggests that the GVN will control 90% of the population in 1969. The second group, OSD CIA State, on the other hand, is more cautious and pessimistic, their view is not inconsistent with another Tet-offensive-like shock in the countryside, for example, wiping out the much-touted gains of the 1968 Accelerated Pacification Program, or with more gradual erosion. Representing the latter view, OSD arrives at the following conclusions:

(1) "The portions of the SVN rural population aligned with the VC and aligned with the GVN are apparently the same today as in 1962 [a discouraging year]: 5,000,000 GVN aligned and nearly 3,000,000 VC aligned.

(2) "At the present, it appears that at least 50% of the total rural population is subject to significant VC presence and influence."

CIA agrees, and State (INR) [Bureau of Intelligence and Research] goes even further, saying: "Our best estimate is that the VC have a significant effect on at least two-thirds of the rural population."

The Political Scene

This section on the political situation can be boiled down to three fundamental questions: (1) How strong is the GVN today? (2) What is being done to strengthen it for the coming political struggle with the NLF? (3) What are the prospects for continued non-Communist government in South Vietnam?

The essence of the replies from U.S. agencies is as follows: (1) Stronger recently than for many years but still very weak in certain areas and among various elites. (2) Some steps are being taken but these are inadequate. (3) Impossible to predict but chancy at best.

Within these broad thrusts of the responses there are decided differences of emphasis among the agencies. Thus MACV/JCS and Saigon, while acknowledging the problems, accent more the increasing stability of the Thieu regime and the overall political system; the significance of the moves being made by the GVN to bolster its strength; and the possibility of continued non-Communist rule in South Vietnam given sufficient U.S. support. CIA and OSD on the other hand, while acknowledging certain progress, are decidedly more skeptical and pessimistic. They note recent political improvements and GVN measures but they tend to deflate their relative impact and highlight the remaining obstacles. State's position, while not so consistent or clear-cut, generally steers closer to the bearishness of OSD and CIA. . . .

U.S. Military Operations

The only major points of agreement with the U.S. Government on these subjects are:

The description of recent U.S. deployment and tactics;

The difficulties of assessing the results of B-52 strikes, but their known effectiveness against known troop concentrations and in close support operations;

The fact that the Soviets and Chinese supply almost all war material to Hanoi and have enabled the North Vietnamese to carry on despite all our operations.

Otherwise there are fundamental disagreements running throughout this section, including the following:

OSD believes, the MACV/JCS deny, that there is a certain amount of "fat" in our current force levels that could be cut back without significant reduction in combat capability.

MACV/JCS and, somewhat more cautiously CIA ascribe much higher casualty estimates to our B-52 strikes.

MACV/JCS assign very much greater effectiveness to our past and current Laos and North Vietnam bombing campaigns than do OSD and CIA.

MACV/JCS believe that a vigorous bombing campaign could choke off enough supplies to Hanoi to make her stop fighting, while OSD and CIA see North Vietnam continuing the struggle even against unlimited bombing.

Richard M. Nixon on Vietnamization, 1969

Good evening, my fellow Americans: Tonight I want to talk to you on a subject of deep concern to all Americans and to many people in all parts of the world—the war in Viet-Nam.

I believe that one of the reasons for the deep division about Viet-Nam is that many Americans have lost confidence in what their Government has told them about our policy. The American people cannot and should not be asked to support a policy which involves the overriding issues of war and peace unless they know the truth about that policy.

Tonight, therefore, I would like to answer some of the questions that I know are on the minds of many of you listening to me.

How and why did America get involved in Viet-Nam in the first place?

How has this administration changed the policy of the previous administration?

What has really happened in the negotiations in Paris and on the battlefront in Viet-Nam?

What choices do we have if we are to end the war?

What are the prospects for peace?

Let me begin by describing the situation I found when I was inaugurated on January 20.

- The war had been going on for 4 years.
- 31,000 Americans had been killed in action.
- The training program for the South Vietnamese was behind schedule.
- 540,000 Americans were in Viet-Nam, with no plans to reduce the number.

- No progress had been made at the negotiations in Paris and the United States had not put forth a comprehensive peace proposal.
- The war was causing deep division at home and criticism from many of our friends, as well as our enemies, abroad.

In view of these circumstances there were some who urged that I end the war at once by ordering the immediate withdrawal of all American forces.

From a political standpoint this would have been a popular and easy course to follow. After all, we became involved in the war while my predecessor was in office. I could blame the defeat which would be the result of my action on him and come out as the peacemaker. Some put it to me quite bluntly: This was the only way to avoid allowing Johnson's war to become Nixon's war.

But I had a greater obligation than to think only of the years of my administration and the next election. I had to think of the effect of my decision on the next generation and on the future of peace and freedom in America and in the world.

Let us all understand that the question before us is not whether some Americans are for peace and some Americans are against peace. The question at issue is not whether Johnson's war becomes Nixon's war.

The great question is: How can we win America's peace?

Let us turn now to the fundamental issue. Why and how did the United States become involved in Viet-Nam in the first place?

Fifteen years ago North Viet-Nam, with the logistical support of Communist China and the Soviet Union, launched a campaign to impose a Communist government on South Viet-Nam by instigating and supporting a revolution.

In response to the request of the Government of South Viet-Nam, President Eisenhower sent economic aid and military equipment to assist the people of South Viet-Nam in their efforts to prevent a Communist takeover. Seven years ago President Kennedy sent 16,000 military personnel to Viet-Nam as combat advisers. Four years ago President Johnson sent American combat forces to South Viet-Nam.

Now, many believe that President Johnson's decision to send American combat forces to South Viet-Nam was wrong. And many others, I among them, have been strongly critical of the way the war has been conducted.

But the question facing us today is: Now that we are in the war, what is the best way to end it?

In January I could only conclude that the precipitate withdrawal of American forces from Viet-Nam would be a disaster not only for South Viet-Nam but for the United States and for the cause of peace.

For the South Vietnamese, our precipitate withdrawal would inevitably allow the Communists to repeat the massacres which followed their takeover in the North 15 years before.

- They then murdered more than 50,000 people, and hundreds of thousands more died in slave labor camps.
- We saw a prelude of what would happen in South Viet-Nam when the

Communists entered the city of Hue last year. During their brief rule there, there was a bloody reign of terror in which 3,000 civilians were clubbed, shot to death, and buried in mass graves.

- With the sudden collapse of our support, these atrocities of Hue would become the nightmare of the entire nation—and particularly for the million and a half Catholic refugees who fled to South Viet-Nam when the Communists took over in the North.

For the United States, this first defeat in our nation's history would result in a collapse of confidence in American leadership not only in Asia but throughout the world.

Three American Presidents have recognized the great stakes involved in Viet-Nam and understood what had to be done.

In 1963 President Kennedy, with his characteristic eloquence and clarity, said:

> ... we want to see a stable government there, carrying on a struggle to maintain its national independence.
>
> We believe strongly in that. We are not going to withdraw from that effort. In my opinion, for us to withdraw from that effort would mean a collapse not only of South Viet-Nam, but Southeast Asia. So we are going to stay there.

President Eisenhower and President Johnson expressed the same conclusion during their terms of office.

For the future of peace, precipitate withdrawal would thus be a disaster of immense magnitude.

- A nation cannot remain great if it betrays its allies and lets down its friends.
- Our defeat and humiliation in South Viet-Nam without question would promote recklessness in the councils of those great powers who have not yet abandoned their goals of world conquest.
- This would spark violence wherever our commitments help maintain the peace—in the Middle East, in Berlin, eventually even in the Western Hemisphere.

Ultimately, this would cost more lives. It would not bring peace; it would bring more war.

For these reasons I rejected the recommendation that I should end the war by immediately withdrawing all our forces. I chose instead to change American policy on both the negotiating front and the battlefront. . . .

It has become clear that the obstacle in negotiating an end to the war is not the President of the United States. It is not the South Vietnamese Government.

The obstacle is the other side's absolute refusal to show the least willingness to join us in seeking a just peace. It will not do so while it is convinced that all it has to do is to wait for our next concession, and our next concession after that one, until it gets everything it wants.

There can now be no longer any question that progress in negotiation depends only on Hanoi's deciding to negotiate, to negotiate seriously.

I realize that this report on our efforts on the diplomatic front is discouraging to the American people, but the American people are entitled to know the truth—the bad news as well as the good news—where the lives of our young men are involved.

Now let me turn, however, to a more encouraging report on another front.

At the time we launched our search for peace, I recognized we might not succeed in bringing an end to the war through negotiation.

I therefore put into effect another plan to bring peace—a plan which will bring the war to an end regardless of what happens on the negotiating front. It is in line with a major shift in U.S. foreign policy which I described in my press conference at Guam on July 25.

Let me briefly explain what has been described as the Nixon doctrine—a policy which not only will help end the war in Viet-Nam but which is an essential element of our program to prevent future Viet-Nams.

We Americans are a do-it-yourself people. We are an impatient people. Instead of teaching someone else to do a job, we like to do it ourselves. And this trait has been carried over into our foreign policy.

In Korea and again in Viet-Nam, the United States furnished most of the money, most of the arms, and most of the men to help the people of those countries defend their freedom against Communist aggression.

Before any American troops were committed to Viet-Nam, a leader of another Asian country expressed this opinion to me when I was traveling in Asia as a private citizen. He said: "When you are trying to assist another nation defend its freedom, U.S. policy should be to help them fight the war, but not to fight the war for them."

Well, in accordance with this wise counsel, I laid down in Guam three principles as guidelines for future American policy toward Asia:

- First, the United States will keep all of its treaty commitments.
- Second, we shall provide a shield if a nuclear power threatens the freedom of a nation allied with us or of a nation whose survival we consider vital to our security.
- Third, in cases involving other types of aggression, we shall furnish military and economic assistance when requested in accordance with our treaty commitments. But we shall look to the nation directly threatened to assume the primary responsibility of providing the manpower for its defense.

After I announced this policy, I found that the leaders of the Philippines, Thailand, Viet-Nam, South Korea, and other nations which might be threatened by Communist aggression welcomed this new direction in American foreign policy.

The defense of freedom is everybody's business—not just America's business. And it is particularly the responsibility of the people whose freedom is threatened. In the previous administration we Americanized the war in Viet-Nam. In this administration we are Vietnamizing the search for peace.

The policy of the previous administration not only resulted in our assuming the primary responsibility for fighting the war but, even more significantly did not adequately stress the goal of strengthening the South Vietnamese so that they could defend themselves when we left.

The Vietnamization plan was launched following Secretary [of Defense Melvin R.] Laird's visit to Viet-Nam in March. Under the plan, I ordered first a substantial increase in the training and equipment of South Vietnamese forces.

In July, on my visit to Viet-Nam, I changed General Abrams' orders so that they were consistent with the objectives of our new policies. Under the new orders, the primary mission of our troops is to enable the South Vietnamese forces to assume the full responsibility for the security of South Viet-Nam. . . .

We have adopted a plan which we have worked out in cooperation with the South Vietnamese for the complete withdrawal of all U.S. combat ground forces and their replacement by South Vietnamese forces on an orderly scheduled timetable. This withdrawal will be made from strength and not from weakness. As South Vietnamese forces become stronger, the rate of American withdrawal can become greater. . . .

If the level of infiltration or our casualties increase while we are trying to scale down the fighting, it will be the result of a conscious decision by the enemy.

Hanoi could make no greater mistake than to assume that an increase in violence will be to its advantage. If I conclude that increased enemy action jeopardizes our remaining forces in Viet-Nam, I shall not hesitate to take strong and effective measures to deal with that situation.

This is not a threat. This is a statement of policy which as Commander in Chief of our Armed Forces I am making in meeting my responsibility for the protection of American fighting men wherever they may be.

My fellow Americans, I am sure you can recognize from what I have said that we really only have two choices open to us if we want to end this war:

- I can order an immediate, precipitate withdrawal of all Americans from Viet-Nam without regard to the effects of that action.
- Or we can persist in our search for a just peace, through a negotiated settlement if possible or through continued implementation of our plan for Vietnamization if necessary—a plan in which we will withdraw all of our forces from Viet-Nam on a schedule in accordance with our program, as the South Vietnamese become strong enough to defend their own freedom.

I have chosen this second course. It is not the easy way. It is the right way. It is a plan which will end the war and serve the cause of peace, not just in Viet-Nam but in the Pacific and in the world.

In speaking of the consequences of a precipitate withdrawal, I mentioned that our allies would lose confidence in America.

Far more dangerous, we would lose confidence in ourselves. Oh, the immediate reaction would be a sense of relief that our men were coming home. But as we saw the consequences of what we had done, inevitable remorse and divisive recrimination would scar our spirit as a people. . . .

I have chosen a plan for peace. I believe it will succeed.

If it does succeed, what the critics say now won't matter. If it does not succeed, anything I say then won't matter.

I know it may not be fashionable to speak of patriotism or national destiny these days. But I feel it is appropriate to do so on this occasion.

Two hundred years ago this nation was weak and poor. But even then, America was the hope of millions in the world. Today we have become the strongest and richest nation in the world. The wheel of destiny has turned so that any hope the world has for the survival of peace and freedom will be determined by whether the American people have the moral stamina and the courage to meet the challenge of free-world leadership.

Let historians not record that when America was the most powerful nation in the world we passed on the other side of the road and allowed the last hopes for peace and freedom of millions of people to be suffocated by the forces of totalitarianism.

And so tonight—to you, the great silent majority of my fellow Americans—I ask for your support.

I pledged in my campaign for the Presidency to end the war in a way that we could win the peace. I have initiated a plan of action which will enable me to keep that pledge.

The more support I can have from the American people, the sooner that pledge can be redeemed; for the more divided we are at home, the less likely the enemy is to negotiate at Paris.

Let us be united for peace. Let us also be united against defeat. Because let us understand: North Viet-Nam cannot defeat or humiliate the United States. Only Americans can do that.

Nixon Explains the Cambodian Incursion, 1970

Good evening, my fellow Americans. Ten days ago, in my report to the Nation on Viet-Nam, I announced a decision to withdraw an additional 150,000 Americans from Viet-Nam over the next year. I said then that I was making that decision despite our concern over increased enemy activity in Laos, in Cambodia, and in South Viet-Nam.

At that time, I warned that if I concluded that increased enemy activity in any of these areas endangered the lives of Americans remaining in Viet-Nam, I would not hesitate to take strong and effective measures to deal with that situation.

Despite that warning, North Viet-Nam has increased its military aggression in all these areas, and particularly in Cambodia.

After full consultation with the National Security Council, Ambassador Bunker, General Abrams, and my other advisers, I have concluded that the actions of the enemy in the last 10 days clearly endanger the lives of Americans who are in Viet-Nam now and would constitute an unacceptable risk to those who will be there after withdrawal of another 150,000.

To protect our men who are in Viet-Nam and to guarantee the continued success of our withdrawal and Vietnamization programs, I have concluded that the time has come for action.

Tonight I shall describe the actions of the enemy, the actions I have ordered to deal with that situation, and the reasons for my decision.

Cambodia, a small country of 7 million people, has been a neutral nation since the Geneva agreement of 1954—an agreement, incidentally, which was signed by the Government of North Viet-Nam.

American policy since then has been to scrupulously respect the neutrality of the Cambodian people. We have maintained a skeleton diplomatic mission of fewer than 15 in Cambodia's capital, and that only since last August. For the previous 4 years, from 1965 to 1969, we did not have any diplomatic mission whatever in Cambodia. And for the past 5 years, we have provided no military assistance whatever and no economic assistance to Cambodia.

North Viet-Nam, however, has not respected that neutrality.

For the past 5 years . . . North Viet-Nam has occupied military sanctuaries all along the Cambodian frontier with South Viet-Nam. Some of these extend up to 20 miles into Cambodia. The sanctuaries . . . are on both sides of the border. They are used for hit-and-run attacks on American and South Vietnamese forces in South Viet-Nam.

These Communist-occupied territories contain major base camps, training sites, logistics facilities, weapons and ammunition factories, airstrips, and prisoner of war compounds.

For 5 years neither the United States nor South Viet-Nam has moved against these enemy sanctuaries, because we did not wish to violate the territory of a neutral nation. Even after the Vietnamese Communists began to expand these sanctuaries 4 weeks ago, we counseled patience to our South Vietnamese allies and imposed restraints on our own commanders.

In contrast to our policy, the enemy in the past 2 weeks has stepped up his guerrilla actions, and he is concentrating his main forces in these sanctuaries . . . where they are building up to launch massive attacks on our forces and those of South Viet-Nam.

North Viet-Nam in the last 2 weeks has stripped away all pretense of respecting the sovereignty or the neutrality of Cambodia. Thousands of their soldiers are invading the country from the sanctuaries; they are encircling the Capital of Phnom Penh. Coming from these sanctuaries, . . . they have moved into Cambodia and are encircling the Capital.

Cambodia, as a result of this, has sent out a call to the United States, to a number of other nations, for assistance. Because if this enemy effort succeeds, Cambodia would become a vast enemy staging area and a springboard for attacks on South Viet-Nam along 600 miles of frontier, a refuge where enemy troops could return from combat without fear of retaliation.

North Vietnamese men and supplies could then be poured into that country, jeopardizing not only the lives of our own men but the people of South Viet-Nam as well. . . .

In cooperation with the armed forces of South Viet-Nam, attacks are being launched this week to clean out major enemy sanctuaries on the Cambodian-Viet-Nam border.

A major responsibility for the ground operations is being assumed by South Vietnamese forces. For example, the attacks in several areas, . . . are exclusively South Vietnamese ground operations under South Vietnamese command, with the United States providing air and logistical support.

There is one area, however, . . . where I have concluded that a combined American and South Vietnamese operation is necessary.

Tonight American and South Vietnamese units will attack the headquarters for the entire Communist military operation in South Viet-Nam. This key control center has been occupied by the North Vietnamese and Viet Cong for 5 years in blatant violation of Cambodia's neutrality.

This is not an invasion of Cambodia. The areas in which these attacks will be launched are completely occupied and controlled by North Vietnamese forces. Our purpose is not to occupy the areas. Once enemy forces are driven out of these sanctuaries and once their military supplies are destroyed, we will withdraw.

These actions are in no way directed at the security interests of any nation. Any government that chooses to use these actions as a pretext for harming relations with the United States will be doing so on its own responsibility and on its own initiative, and we will draw the appropriate conclusions.

Now, let me give you the reasons for my decision.

A majority of the American people, a majority of you listening to me, are for the withdrawal of our forces from Viet-Nam. The action I have taken tonight is indispensable for the continuing success of that withdrawal program.

A majority of the American people want to end this war rather than to have it drag on interminably. The action I have taken tonight will serve that purpose.

A majority of the American people want to keep the casualties of our brave men in Viet-Nam at an absolute minimum. The action I take tonight is essential if we are to accomplish that goal.

We take this action not for the purpose of expanding the war into Cambodia, but for the purpose of ending the war in Viet-Nam and winning the just peace we all desire. We have made and we will continue to make every possible effort to end this war through negotiation at the conference table rather than through more fighting on the battlefield. . . .

My fellow Americans, we live in an age of anarchy, both abroad and at home. We see mindless attacks on all the great institutions which have been created by free civilizations in the last 500 years. Even here in the United States, great universities are being systematically destroyed. Small nations all over the world find themselves under attack from within and from without.

If, when the chips are down, the world's most powerful nation, the United States of America, acts like a pitiful, helpless giant, the forces of totalitarianism and anarchy will threaten free nations and free institutions throughout the world.

It is not our power but our will and character that is being tested tonight. The question all Americans must ask and answer tonight is this: Does the richest and strongest nation in the history of the world have the character to meet a direct challenge by a group which rejects every effort to win a just peace, ignores our warning, tramples on solemn agreements, violates the neutrality of an unarmed people, and uses our prisoners as hostages?

If we fail to meet this challenge, all other nations will be on notice that despite its overwhelming power the United States, when a real crisis comes, will be found wanting.

During my campaign for the Presidency, I pledged to bring Americans home from Viet-Nam. They are coming home.

I promised to end this war. I shall keep that promise.

I promised to win a just peace. I shall keep that promise.

We shall avoid a wider war. But we are also determined to put an end to this war. . . .

No one is more aware than I am of the political consequences of the action I have taken. It is tempting to take the easy political path: to blame this war on previous administrations and to bring all of our men home immediately, regardless of the consequences, even though that would mean defeat for the United States; to desert 18 million South Vietnamese people who have put their trust in us and to expose them to the same slaughter and savagery which the leaders of North Viet-Nam inflicted on hundreds of thousands of North Vietnamese who chose freedom when the Communists took over North Viet-Nam in 1954; to get peace at any price now, even though I know that a peace of humiliation for the United States would lead to a bigger war or surrender later.

I have rejected all political considerations in making this decision.

Whether my party gains in November is nothing compared to the lives of 400,000 brave Americans fighting for our country and for the cause of peace and freedom in Viet-Nam. Whether I may be a one-term President is insignificant compared to whether by our failure to act in this crisis the United States proves itself to be unworthy to lead the forces of freedom in this critical period in world history. I would rather be a one-term President and do what I believe is right than to be a two-term President at the cost of seeing America become a second-rate power and to see this nation accept the first defeat in its proud 190-year history.

Henry A. Kissinger Reveals the U.S. Negotiating Position, 1972

As you remember from the many briefings that we have had on Viet-Nam, there has been no issue of greater concern to this administration than to end the war in Viet-Nam on a negotiated basis. We have done so because of what we felt the war was doing to us as a people and because we felt that it was essential that whatever differences that may have existed about how we entered the war and how we conducted the war, that we ended it in a way that showed that we had been fair, that we had been reasonable, and that all concerned people could support.

We have not approached these negotiations in order to score debating points. We have not conducted these negotiations in order to gain any domestic benefits. . . .

On the political evolution, our basic principle has been a principle we have been prepared to sign together with them, that we are not committed to any one political structure or government in South Viet-Nam. Our principle has been that we want a political evolution that gives the people of South Viet-Nam a genuine opportunity to express their preferences.

We have pointed out, in innumerable meetings, that we recognize that this is a tough problem. We have indicated with extraordinary repetitiveness, as those of you who have heard me will not challenge, with extraordinary repetitiveness, that we know that Vietnamese traditions are different and that we are prepared to listen to their version of what a free political process might be like.

We have searched our souls to try to come up with a proposal that seems free to us; and after all, the agreement by the existing government—to have a commission comprising the people that wish to overthrow them run, organize, and supervise the election, to put the election under international supervision, and to resign a month before the election—is not just a trivial proposal.

The North Vietnamese position has been that they want us to agree with them, first, on replacing the existing government and, secondly, on a structure in which the probability of their taking over is close to certainty.

They want us, in other words, to do in the political field the same thing that they are asking us to do in the military field, to negotiate the terms of the turnover to them, regardless of what the people may think. . . .

They have said that they want a government composed of people who stand for peace, neutrality, and independence. There is another magic word which eludes me at the moment. And Americans cannot object to this proposal. The only thing is, they are the only ones who know who stands for peace, neutrality, and independence.

Whenever in these negotiations we have said, "All right, you don't like Thieu. How about this fellow, or that fellow, or that fellow?" there is almost no one that we know who they believe stands for peace, neutrality, and independence.

So I would like to express this to you. The issue is to us: We are prepared, in all conscience and in all seriousness, to negotiate with them immediately any scheme that any reasonable person can say leaves open the political future of South Viet-Nam to the people of South Viet-Nam, just as we are not prepared to withdraw without knowing anything at all of what is going to happen next. So we are not prepared to end this war by turning over the Government of South Viet-Nam as part of a political deal.

We are prepared to have a political process in which they can have a chance of winning, which is not loaded in any direction. We have given our views of what this political process might be. We are prepared to listen to their views of what that political process might be. And we said in both notes of last fall, notes that were not intended for publication, at a time when we were hoping to be able to step before you with an agreement, that we are prepared to listen to their points.

Now, there has been some question of, "Did they ask us to replace or overthrow"—or whatever the word is—"the existing government in South Viet-Nam?"

We have every interest in stepping before you with total honesty. They have asked two things of us:

One, an indirect overthrow of the government; that is to say, that we have to withdraw. The way they phrase it, we would have to withdraw all American equipment, even that which the South Vietnamese Army has. They have asked us to withdraw all equipment, all future military aid, all future economic aid; and the practical consequence of that proposal, while they are receiving close to $1 billion worth of foreign aid, would be the indirect overthrow of the Government of South Viet-Nam, something about which there can be no question.

But they have further asked us, and we do not want to be forced to prove it, to change the government directly, generously leaving the method to us, and, therefore, the President's statement was true and is supportable.

We have no interest in engaging in a debate with the North Vietnamese that would force any more of this record into the open. We do have an interest that the American public understand exactly what is at issue today.

Negotiating Position of the Provisional Revolutionary Government, 1972

The provisional Revolutionary Government of the Republic of South Vietnam solemnly declares as follows:

If a correct solution is to be found to the Vietnam problem, and a lasting peace ensured in Vietnam, the U.S. Government must meet the two following requirement:

1. To respect the Vietnamese people's right to true independence and the South Vietnamese people's right to effective self-determination; stop the U.S. war of aggression in Vietnam, the bombing, mining and blockade of the Democratic Republic of Vietnam; completely cease the "Vietnamization" policy; and all U.S. military activities in South Vietnam; rapidly and completely withdraw all U.S. troops, advisors, military personnel, technical personnel, weapons and war materials and those of the other foreign countries in the U.S. camp from South Vietnam; liquidate the U.S. military bases in South Vietnam; end all U.S. military involvement in Vietnam; and stop supporting the Nguyen Van Thieu stooge administration.

2. A solution to the internal problem of South Vietnam must proceed from the actual situation that there exist in South Vietnam two adminis-

trations, two armies, and other political forces. It is necessary to achieve national concord. The sides in South Vietnam must unite on the basis of equality, mutual respect and mutual nonelimination. Democratic freedoms must be guaranteed to the people. To this end, it is necessary to form in South Vietnam a provisional government of national concord with three equal segments to take charge of the affairs in the period of transition and to organize truly free and democratic general elections.

✗ *E S S A Y S*

In the opening essay, Henry Kissinger, Richard Nixon's national security adviser, sets forth the principal concerns and interests that shaped the Nixon administration's approach to Vietnam. He explains that the administration entered office determined to end U.S. involvement in Vietnam, but it needed to do so honorably—with America's prestige and credibility intact. In the next essay, Arnold Isaacs, a journalist who covered the Vietnam War from 1972 to 1975 and traveled extensively throughout Indochina, presents a strong indictment of the Nixon policy. The Nixon administration's preoccupation with America's credibility led to a grievous exaggeration of the regional and global stakes involved in Vietnam. Isaacs suggests that a policy designed to cut U.S. losses by as speedy as possible a withdrawal would better have served American interests. He especially faults Nixon for expanding the war into Cambodia.

Peace with Honor

HENRY KISSINGER

I reached high office unexpectedly at a particularly complex period of our national life. In the life of nations, as of human beings, a point is often reached when the seemingly limitless possibilities of youth suddenly narrow and one must come to grips with the fact that not every option is open any longer. This insight can inspire a new creative impetus, less innocent perhaps than the naive exuberance of earlier years, but more complex and ultimately more permanent. The process of coming to grips with one's limits is never easy. It can end in despair or in rebellion; it can produce a self-hatred that turns inevitable compromises into a sense of inadequacy.

America went through such a period of self-doubt and self-hatred in the late 1960s. The trigger for it was the war in Vietnam. Entered into gradually by two administrations, by 1969 it had resulted in over 31,000 American dead with no prospect of early resolution. It began with overwhelming public and Congressional approval, but this had evolved first into skepticism and then into increasingly hostile rebellion. For too many, a war to resist aggression had turned into a symbol of fundamental American evil. A decade that had begun with the bold declaration that America would pay any price and bear any burden to ensure the survival and success of liberty had ended in an agony of assassinations, urban riots, and ugly demonstrations. The Sixties marked the end of our innocence; this was certain. What remained to be determined was whether we could learn from this knowledge or consume our substance in rebelling against the reality of our maturity.

The turmoil of the 1960s was all the more unsettling to Americans because it came at the end of an extraordinary period of American accomplishment. We had built alliances that preserved the peace and fostered the growth of the industrial democracies of North America, Western Europe, and Japan. We had helped create international economic institutions that had nourished global prosperity for a generation. We had promoted decolonization and pioneered in development assistance for the new nations. In a planet shrunk by communications and technology, in a world either devastated by war or struggling in the first steps of nationhood, the United States had every reason to take pride in its global contribution—its energy, idealism, and enduring accomplishment.

The fact remained that at the end of twenty years of exertion America was not at peace with itself. The consensus that had sustained our postwar foreign policy had evaporated. The men and women who had sustained our international commitments and achievements were demoralized by what they considered their failure in Vietnam. Too many of our young were in rebellion against the successes of their fathers, attacking what they claimed to be the overextension of our commitments and mocking the values that had animated the achievements. A new isolationism was growing. Whereas in the 1920s we had withdrawn from the world because we thought we were too good for it, the insidious theme of the late 1960s was that we should withdraw from the world because we were too evil for it.

Not surprisingly, American self-doubt proved contagious; it is hard for foreign nations to have more faith in a country than it has in itself. European intellectuals began to argue that the Cold War was caused by American as well as by Soviet policies; they urged their governments to break out of the vicious circle by peace initiatives of their own. Many European leaders, catering to this mood, became fervent advocates of détente, playing the role of a "bridge" between East and West—visiting Moscow, exploring ties with Peking, urging disarmament and East-West trade.

These protestations were all very well until the United States, in the late Sixties, began to take them to heart and adopt the policy implicit in them. Suddenly European statesmen reversed course. Now they were fearful of a US-Soviet condominium, a "Super-Yalta" in which American and Soviet leaders would settle global issues over the heads of European governments. In the year that saw the Soviet invasion of Czechoslovakia, the United States was accused by many of its allies of being at one and the same time too bellicose in Southeast Asia and too accommodating in its dealings with the Soviet Union. This ambivalence gnawed at the unity of the Alliance. Unnerved by events in Czechoslovakia, pressed by public opinion toward conciliation, impelled by conviction to strengthen security, the Western Alliance was becalmed like a ship dead in the water.

Similar uncertainty marked our other policies. For two decades our contacts with China had been limited to the reciprocal recriminations of sporadic ambassadorial meetings in Warsaw. The Middle East was explosive, but in the aftermath of the 1967 war no diplomacy was in train. Our domestic divisions prevented decisive initiatives. America seemed reduced to passivity in a world in which, with all our self-doubt, only our power could offer security, only our dedication could sustain hope.

In my view, Vietnam was not the cause of our difficulties but a symptom. We were in a period of painful adjustment to a profound transformation of global politics; we were being forced to come to grips with the tension between our history and our new necessities. For two centuries America's participation in the world seemed to oscillate between overinvolvement and withdrawal, between expecting too much of our power and being ashamed of it, between optimistic exuberance and frustration with the ambiguities of an imperfect world. I was convinced that the deepest cause of our national unease was the realization—as yet dimly perceived—that we were becoming like other nations in the need to recognize that our power, while vast, had limits. Our resources were no longer infinite in relation to our problems; instead we had to set priorities, both intellectual and material. In the Fifties and Sixties we had attempted ultimate solutions to specific problems; now our challenge was to shape a world and an American role to which we were permanently committed, which could no longer be sustained by the illusion that our exertions had a terminal point.

Any Administration elected in 1968 would have faced this problem. It was a colossal task in the best of circumstances; the war in Vietnam turned it into a searing and anguishing enterprise. . . .

I cannot yet write about Vietnam except with pain and sadness.

When we came into office over a half-million Americans were fighting a war ten thousand miles away. Their numbers were still increasing on a schedule established by our predecessors. We found no plans for withdrawals. Thirty-one thousand had already died. Whatever our original war aims, by 1969 our credibility abroad, the reliability of our commitments, and our domestic cohesion were alike jeopardized by a struggle in a country as far away from the North American continent as our globe permits. Our involvement had begun openly, and with nearly unanimous Congressional, public, and media approval. But by 1969 our country had been riven by protest and anguish, sometimes taking on a violent and ugly character. The comity by which a democratic society must live had broken down. No government can function without a minimum of trust. This was being dissipated under the harshness of our alternatives and the increasing rage of our domestic controversy.

Psychologists or sociologists may explain some day what it is about that distant monochromatic land, of green mountains and fields merging with an azure sea, that for millennia has acted as a magnet for foreigners who sought glory there and found frustration, who believed that in its rice fields and jungles some principle was to be established and entered them only to recede in disillusion. What has inspired its people to such flights of heroism and monomania that a succession of outsiders have looked there for a key to some riddle and then been expelled by a ferocious persistence that not only thwarted the foreigner's exertions but hazarded his own internal balance?

Our predecessors had entered in innocence, convinced that the cruel civil war represented the cutting edge of some global design. In four years of struggle they had been unable to develop a strategy to achieve victory— and for all one can know now such a strategy was not attainable. They had done enough to produce a major commitment of American power and credibility but not enough to bring it to a conclusion. In the last year of the Johnson Administration the Communists had launched a massive countrywide offensive. Few students of the subject question today that it was massively defeated. But its scale and sacrifice turned it into a psychological victory. Under the impact of the Tet offensive we first curtailed and then ended our bombing of the North for no return except the opening of negotiations which our implacable adversary immediately stalemated. Public support was ebbing for a war we would not win but also seemed unable to end.

And in our country, opposition grew. It was composed of many strands: sincere pacifists who hated to see their country involved in killing thousands of miles away; pragmatists who could discern no plausible outcome; isolationists who wished to end American overseas involvement; idealists who saw no compatibility between our values and the horrors of a war literally brought home for the first time on television. And these groups were egged on by a small minority expressing the inchoate rage of the 1960s with shock tactics of obscenity and violence, expressing their hatred of America, its "system" and its "evil." All these groups had combined to produce the bitter chaos of the Democratic Convention of 1968, the campus violence, and the confusion and demoralization of the leadership groups that had sustained the great American postwar initiatives in foreign policy.

Richard Nixon inherited this cauldron. Of all choices he was probably the least suited for the act of grace that might have achieved reconciliation with the responsible members of the opposition. Seeing himself in any case the target of a liberal conspiracy to destroy him, he could never bring himself to regard the upheaval caused by the Vietnam war as anything other than a continuation of the long-lived assault on his political existence. Though he sympathized more with the anguish of the genuine protesters than they knew, he never mustered the self-confidence or the largeness of spirit to reach out to them. He accepted their premises that we faced a mortal domestic struggle; in the process he accelerated and compounded its bitterness.

Fairness compels the recognition that he had precious little help. After all, Hubert Humphrey, whose entire life was a reach for reconciliation, had been treated scarcely better during his campaign for the Presidency. And after Nixon took office those who had created our involvement in Vietnam moved first to neutrality and then to opposition, saddling Nixon with responsibility for a war he had inherited and attacking him in the name of solutions they themselves had neither advocated nor executed when they had the opportunity.

The Nixon Administration entered office determined to end our involvement in Vietnam. But it soon came up against the reality that had also bedeviled its predecessor. For nearly a generation the security and progress of free people had depended on confidence in America. We could not simply walk away from an enterprise involving two administrations, five allied countries, and thirty-one thousand dead as if we were switching a television channel. Many urged us to "emulate de Gaulle"; but they overlooked that it took even de Gaulle four years to extricate his country from Algeria because he, too, thought it important for France to emerge from its travails with its domestic cohesion and international stature intact. He extricated France from Algeria as an act of policy, not as a collapse, in a manner reflecting a national decision and not a rout.

Such an ending of the war was even more important for the United States. As the leader of democratic alliances we had to remember that scores of countries and millions of people relied for their security on our willingness to stand by allies, indeed on our confidence in ourselves. No serious policymaker could allow himself to succumb to the fashionable debunking of "prestige" or "honor" or "credibility." For a great power to abandon a small country to tyranny simply to obtain a respite from our own travail seemed to me—and still seems to me—profoundly immoral and destructive of our efforts to build a new and ultimately more peaceful pattern of international relations. We could not revitalize the Atlantic Alliance if its governments were assailed by doubt about American staying power. We would not be able to move the Soviet Union toward the imperative of mutual restraint against the background of capitulation in a major war. We might not achieve our opening to China if our value as a counterweight seemed nullified by a collapse that showed us irrelevant to Asian security. Our success in Middle East diplomacy would depend on convincing our ally of our reliability and its adversaries that we were impervious to threats of military pressure or blackmail. Clearly, the American people wanted to end the war, but every poll, and indeed Nixon's election (and the Wallace vote), made it equally evident that they saw their country's aims as honorable and did not relish America's humiliation. The new Administration had to respect the concerns of the opponents of the war but also the anguish of the families whose sons had suffered and died for their country and who did not want it determined—after the fact—that their sacrifice have been in vain.

The principles of America's honor and America's responsibility were not empty phrases to me. I felt them powerfully. I had been born in Germany in the Bavarian town of Fuerth, six months before Hitler's attempted beer-hall putsch in Bavaria's capital, Munich. Hitler came to power when I was nine years old. Nuremberg, of which Fuerth was a neighbor with the same physical and psychological relationship as Brooklyn has to New York, was known for its Nazi support, massive Nazi Party rallies, and the notorious racial laws. Until I emigrated to America, my family and I endured progressive ostracism and discrimination. My father lost the teaching job for which he had worked all his life; the friends of my parents' youth shunned them. I was forced to attend a segregated school. Every walk in the street turned into an adventure, for my German contemporaries were free to beat up Jewish children without interference by the police.

Through this period America acquired a wondrous quality for me. When I was a boy it was a dream, an incredible place where tolerance was natural and personal freedom unchallenged. Even when I learned later that America, too, had massive problems, I could never forget what an inspiration it had been to the victims of persecution, to my family, and to me during cruel and degrading years. I always remembered the thrill when I first walked the streets of New York City. Seeing a group of boys, I began to cross to the other side to avoid being beaten up. And then I remembered where I was.

I therefore have always had a special feeling for what America means, which native-born citizens perhaps take for granted. I could not accept the self-hatred that took every imperfection as an excuse to denigrate a precious experiment whose significance for the rest of the world had been part of my life. I was enormously gratified to have an opportunity to repay my debt to a society whose blemishes I recognized but also saw in a different perspective; they could not obscure for me its greatness, its idealism, its humanity, and its embodiment of mankind's hopes.

The domestic turmoil of the Vietnam debate therefore pained me deeply. I did not agree with many of the decisions that had brought about the impasse in Indochina; I felt, however, that my appointment to high office entailed a responsibility to help end the war in a way compatible with American self-respect and the stake that all men and women of goodwill had in America's strength and purpose. It seemed to me important for America not to be humiliated, not to be shattered, but to leave Vietnam in a manner that even the protesters might later see as reflecting an American choice made with dignity and self-respect. Ironically, in view of the later charges of "historical pessimism" leveled against me, it was precisely the issue of our self-confidence and faith in our future that I considered at stake in the outcome in Vietnam.

I believed in the moral significance of my adopted country. America, alone of the free countries, was strong enough to assure global security against the forces of tyranny. Only America had both the power and the decency to inspire other peoples who struggled for identity, for progress and dignity. In the Thirties, when the democracies faced the gravest danger, America was waiting in the wings to come to Europe's rescue. There was no one now to come to America's rescue if we abandoned our international responsibilities, or if we succumbed to self-hatred.

Unlike most of my contemporaries, I had experienced the fragility of the fabric of modern society. I had seen that the likely outcome of the dissolution of all social bonds and the undermining of all basic values is extremism, despair, and brutality. A people must not lose faith in itself; those who wallow in the imperfections of their society or turn them into an excuse for a nihilistic orgy usually end up by eroding all social and moral restraints; eventually in their pitiless assault on all beliefs they multiply suffering.

I could never bring myself to think of the war in Vietnam as a monstrous criminal conspiracy, as was fashionable in some circles. In my view our entry into the war had been the product not of a militarist psychosis but of a naive idealism that wanted to set right all the world's ills and believed American goodwill supplied its own efficacy. I had visited Vietnam as a professor. I saw there not ugly Americans—though, as in all wars, these existed too—but dedicated young men facing death daily despite the divisions at home; my recollection was of many idealistic Americans working under impossible conditions to bring government and health and development to a terrified and bewildered people. I thought the country owed something to *their* sacrifice and not only to the vocal protesters. Some of the critics viewed Vietnam as a morality play in which the wicked must be punished before the final curtain and where any attempt to salvage self-respect from the outcome compounded the wrong. I viewed it as a genuine tragedy. No one had a monopoly on anguish.

I saw my role as helping my adopted country heal its wounds, preserve its faith, and thus enable it to rededicate itself to the great tasks of construction that were awaiting it.

The Limits of Credibility

ARNOLD ISAACS

It's time we recognized,'' declared Ronald Reagan, ''that ours was, in truth, a noble cause.'' His campaign advisers had not wanted him to reawaken painful Vietnam memories. But the candidate personally penciled the phrase ''noble cause'' into his speech, it was said, to express his strong view that the nation should not reproach itself for the Vietnam conflict. ''Let us tell those who fought in that war,'' he added, ''that we will never again ask young men to fight and possibly die in a war our government is afraid to win.'' The 5,000 delegates at the Veterans of Foreign Wars 1980 convention—who had earlier broken their organization's long-standing precedent to endorse the Reagan candidacy—responded, one reporter wrote, with ''sustained and boisterous cheers.''

At the start of a new decade, the perception that American actions in Vietnam were a worthy effort, and that they failed not because they were misconceived but only because they were not carried out resolutely enough, seemed to respond to powerful needs in American life and institutions. It was a view that protected the reputations of the political leaders who shaped and executed those actions. It soothed military professionals who could not easily contemplate their own failure to achieve more decisive results

Arnold R. Isaacs, *Without Honor: Defeat in Vietnam and Cambodia.* Copyright © 1983, pp. 488–498. Reprinted by permission of The Johns Hopkins University Press, Baltimore/London.

on the Vietnamese battlefields. And by placing Vietnam in the same framework of conventional patriotic values in which Americans viewed their other wars, it reassured a troubled people that they had not, after all, forfeited the special moral standing America claimed for itself among the world's nations. Shaking off Vietnam guilt seemed essential, too, to officials and commentators who feared, not wholly without reason, that a post-Vietnam reaction was preventing the United States from acting effectively in the world.

Clearly, America could not remain forever immobilized by its memories of Vietnam. But to distort those memories was to risk equal policy errors in the future, arising from the same blindnesses that produced the Vietnam failure. For what the United States really lacked in Vietnam was not persistence but understanding—that, and the flexibility to change policies that had proven bankrupt. From start to finish, American leaders remained catastrophically ignorant of Vietnamese history, culture, values, motives, and abilities. Misperceiving both its enemy and its ally and imprisoned in the myopic conviction that sheer military force could somehow overcome adverse political circumstances, Washington stumbled from one failure to the next in the continuing delusion that success was always just ahead. This ignorance and false hope were mated, in successive administrations, with bureaucratic circumstances that inhibited admission of error and made it always seem safer to keep repeating the same mistakes rather than risk the unknown perils of a different policy.

The wounds of that experience were painful enough. With the war finally over, the revisionist belief that it was lost only because of Washington's timidity, rather than for Vietnamese reasons, was the self-infliction of still another wound—a refusal to learn the lesson that had been so expensively taught.

The delusion of Vietnam policy in the Johnson administration, at least until 1968, was that increasing American military force could not just prevent defeat of an anti-Communist regime in Saigon, but could in time discourage Hanoi from supporting the revolutionary movement in the South, and thus end the conflict. The Nixon administration's delusion was more remarkable. It was that exactly the same objective could be reached while American military force was diminishing.

A good deal of evidence suggests that when Nixon and Henry Kissinger moved into the White House in January 1969, they understood that they were inheriting a failure: that the enormous military effort in Vietnam had ballooned out of all proportion to any conceivable American interest there, and that the spectacle of a huge, expensively-armed U.S. expeditionary force thrashing about in an unavailing contest with a poor, middle-sized Asian Communist state was certainly not serving any American purpose. Vietnam was making the U.S. "look like a paper tiger," Nixon is reported to have acknowledged privately in early 1968, adding his private conclusion that "there's no way to win the war. But we can't say that, of course. In fact, we have to seem to say the opposite, just to keep some degree of bargaining leverage." Henry Kissinger too, by his own later account, believed when he took office that the war was "draining our national strength and had to be liquidated."

It is less clear how squarely Nixon or Kissinger faced the corollary of their logic: if the U.S. couldn't win, then Hanoi, presumably, couldn't lose. Kissinger left many acquaintances with the impression that he saw a Communist victory as tolerable, as long as it was suitably delayed to keep from openly humiliating the United States. Whether or not that was his real view, he certainly thought it useful for Hanoi—and Moscow—to be encouraged to believe so; the Vietnamese Communists, he evidently felt, would surely agree to a negotiated settlement once they understood that the U.S. would not actually seek to achieve its proclaimed goal of preserving a non-Communist regime in Saigon indefinitely. It would only be necessary for Hanoi to conclude, in other words, that Washington did not really mean what it said. To the administration's early offers of "serious talks," however, the North Vietnamese simply repeated their customary demands for total withdrawal of U.S. forces and removal of the Saigon "puppet administration."

Kissinger was shocked and angry at Hanoi's apparent lack of concern for American face. And he appears to have found completely unaccountable the fact that instead of saying one thing in public and something else in private, like the straightforward Americans, Ho Chi Minh and his colleagues kept saying the same unacceptable things no matter in which channel they were conveyed. Others might have considered that perhaps the Vietnamese Communists meant what they were saying. But to Kissinger, their refusal to be duplicitous was inexplicable, even suspect. It reflected a Vietnamese style of communication which he complained in his memoirs, "was indirect and, by American standards, devious or baffling."

Whoever was being devious, Nixon and Kissinger evidently continued to believe for some months that Hanoi would agree to what they saw as a reasonable, even generous, compromise. Journalists accompanying Nixon to his Midway Island summit with Nguyen Van Thieu in June 1969 were given the impression that he had "made up his mind to do whatever he has to do in order to extricate the United States" from the war; the president's and Kissinger's appraisal, newsmen were told, was that Hanoi and the Liberation Front were "just about ready for serious negotiations." Two months after Midway, when he began his secret meetings with North Vietnamese representatives, Kissinger "still half believed that rapid progress would be made" if the Communists could be convinced of American sincerity. As late as the end of September, Nixon expressed his hope publicly. "Once the enemy recognizes that it is not going to win its objectives by waiting us out," he told a press conference, "then the enemy will negotiate and we will end this war before the end of 1970. That is the objective we have."

In part, these expectations seem to have reflected a real belief in the generosity of their own proposals. Apparently, too, Nixon and Kissinger thought the Russians and Chinese could and would deliver a Vietnam settlement in return for American consideration on other matters. Both beliefs were wrong, and rooted in a profound misreading of the adversary U.S. forces had already fought for four frustrating years. Neither the president nor his adviser had yet grasped—possibly they never did—just how intensely the Vietnamese Communists' past had led them to mistrust diplomatic arrangements. ("Never Munich again, in whatever form," North Vietnam's Pham Van Dong vowed in 1966—a comment that not only suggested Hanoi's sense that it was duped in 1946 and 1954, but was also one of those stunning ironies so abundant in the history of the Vietnam conflict, since avoiding a new Munich was also a central theme of the American involvement there.) Nor did the new American president yet understand, apparently, the full measure of the Communists' stubborn belief in their own ultimate triumph. "I think the Americans greatly underestimate the determination of the Vietnamese people." Ho Chi Minh had said, while John F. Kennedy was still in the White House and only a few thousand American soldiers had yet been sent to Vietnam. "The Vietnamese people have always shown great determination when they were faced with a foreign invader."

Neither Kennedy nor Lyndon Johnson gave enough weight to that warning; President Nixon would prove no wiser.

When it finally dawned on Nixon and Kissinger that the North Vietnamese were not interested in a compromise on terms acceptable to the U.S., their first response was to threaten redoubled military pressure.

"Measures of great consequence and force" would be taken, Nixon warned Hanoi, if there were no significant progress in the peace talks by November 1, 1969—the anniversary of Johnson's bombing halt. Pentagon planners were assigned to prepare not just for resuming the bombing but for greatly intensifying it. But Hanoi ignored the threat, and there was no consensus within the American government either in favor of reescalation or that any thinkable military step would really prove decisive. The only certain result would be domestic political storms worse than any that had already occurred, and perhaps a split in the administration itself. As his self-imposed deadline neared, Nixon allowed himself—rather easily, it seems—to be talked out of following through on his ultimatum. Putting his hopes instead on the Vietnamization concept and on the possible helpful influence of China and the Soviet Union, he let November 1 pass with no dramatic gesture. The unilateral withdrawal of American troops, which had begun after the Midway summit in June, was now an irreversible policy.

Thereafter the administration's attempt was—in Kissinger's words— "to pursue a middle course between capitulation and the seemingly endless stalemate that we had inherited." That, surely, must be one of the most astonishing purposes ever advanced for continuing a large, costly war. What could lie "between" capitulation and stalemate, after all, except a sort of slow-motion defeat? If that was the implied object of the administration's policy, moreover, it could not be acknowledged. No American government could justify the deaths of 15,000 more American soldiers for such a purpose, not to mention the far larger loss of Asian lives. Perhaps for that reason, though Nixon and Kissinger had seemed to realize before taking office that the overriding U.S. interest was extrication from the war, once in power they seemed to shrink from the logic of their own perceptions.

There were, no doubt, varied personal and institutional reasons for this. Advocating a distasteful policy from outside the government was surely easier than actually beginning to carry it out. Too, once in the White House, Nixon and Kissinger were suddenly subject to a huge array of institutional pressures arising from a self-justifying system in which numerous reputations and bureaucratic interests could only be preserved by reaffirming existing policy. The information supplied by that system, while not entirely suppressing unwelcome truths, was certainly tilted toward justifying past decisions. As the settlement they had thought they could achieve kept eluding them, Nixon's and Kissinger's attitudes toward the North Vietnamese grew more baleful; it would have taken far more forgiving personalities than theirs not to begin wishing to punish those who denied them the political triumph both men thirsted for. Nixon and Kissinger were driven, also, by anger at domestic critics—particularly those who had participated in Johnson's war policies and thus seemed, to the new administration, outrageous hypocrites. And by temporizing, the new president and his adviser changed the choices before them perhaps more quickly than they had imagined would happen. Within less than a year of taking office, they no longer had the freedom to act as if undoing the mistakes of previous administrations; instead, they were compelled to vindicate the consequences of their own actions.

When their first hopeful overtures were rebuffed by Hanoi, Nixon and Kissinger spent the rest of their first year in office not disengaging from the war but imprisoning themselves in it, just as the Johnson administration had done. By the fall of 1969, Nixon's private comments no longer admitted the war was unwinnable or predicted its swift settlement. Instead, he was telling visitors, in words that could have been Lyndon Johnson's, "I will not be the first President of the United States to lose a war."

Like Johnson, too, Nixon came to see dissenters not as honorable critics but as witting or unwitting agents of treason. His administration soon began to recapitulate its predecessor's depressing descent into an intellectual and emotional state of siege. As criticism grew, his and Kissinger's differing insecurities seemed to bond, like two chemicals, into a new compound of angry, defensive rigidity. Within the fortress of their beliefs they listened, as the writer David Halberstam observed, "only to others who were believers." All doubts, whether arising from within the government or outside, were associated with weakness or disloyalty, and rejected.

Dissenting views were banished, too, as the result of Kissinger's bureaucratic style. Toward any possible competitors for power or influence, Kissinger's attitude was—no other word seems adequate—pathological. Through "incessant backbiting," as speechwriter Raymond Price called it, and by every other technique he could devise, some amazingly petty, Kissinger maneuvered to keep all rivals out of foreign policy decisions. With respect to Vietnam, he was largely successful. Among those excluded, to the extent of Kissinger's considerable ability to do so, were Defense Secretary Melvin Laird and Secretary of State William Rogers, both of whom, for various reasons, hoped to reinforce Nixon's initial impulse to extricate himself and the country from the war. Instead, Laird and Rogers were largely shut out of Vietnam decision making. More than any other U.S. endeavor of such magnitude before or since, Vietnam policy in the Nixon administration came under the utter domination of only two men, who grew steadily more impervious to any perspectives that differed from their own.

If there was a single act by which the Nixon administration closed the trap on itself, it was the decision to send U.S. forces into Cambodia at the end of April 1970.

All else they had done in Indochina, Nixon and Kissinger could claim— and the American public could agree—was a matter of cleaning up someone else's mess. But Cambodia was their own. Americans knew the half-million-man army flailing about in Vietnam was not sent there by Nixon, and they seemed willing to allow him a rather generous amount of time to extricate it in some fashion that would avoid national humiliation. They did want to see it extricated, though, and sending soldiers to fight in another Indochinese nation hardly seemed like the same thing. Neither did the strident, belligerent explanations from the White House. Cambodia could not be reconciled with Nixon's promise to end the war, and that, it seemed to me, was the real reason it generated such domestic outrage.

Anger at the Cambodian offensive was answered by an equal rage in the White House against its critics. But the more Nixon and Kissinger made the war theirs, the more damaging and painful failure appeared; and the more they had to defend their actions, the more they were compelled to assert illusory achievements and unreachable goals—like Lyndon Johnson, who was driven at last to lash out at Robert Kennedy, "We are going to win this war, and in six months all you doves will be politically dead." Nixon, too, especially after Cambodia, could only vindicate his decisions with success. That need nourished both the administration's wishful hope that Hanoi would somehow prove more flexible than it sounded and that it could be pressured into giving the U.S. an acceptable settlement, and its equally wishful overestimate of Saigon's effectiveness. Nixon's and Kissinger's expectations contradicted the realities that American influence on Vietnamese events was lessening as its military effort lessened and that there was no sustainable support for stronger measures; Hanoi, meanwhile, not the U.S., still controlled the pace and course of the war while remaining single-mindedly bent not on compromise, but victory.

Unable to resolve those contradictions, Nixon began to see the source of his frustrations in American, not Vietnamese, realities. Not Hanoi but the American antiwar movement "destroyed whatever small possibility may still have existed of ending the war in 1969," he wrote in his memoirs. His critics' motives were, in effect, treasonous. "North Vietnam cannot defeat or humiliate the United States. Only Americans can do that," he declared on November 3, 1969, in the "silent majority" speech he substituted for the military blows he had threatened. In that concept lay one significant

origin of the domestic abuses that would destroy his presidency: against
adversaries who sought the defeat of the United States, any tactic, however
extreme, could be justified.

In Indochina, meanwhile, though he carried on the war as intensely as
the domestic political environment allowed, its purposes grew steadily more
indistinct. Thoughts of victory—Johnson's "coonskin on the wall"—vanished in 1968, with Tet, the bombing halt, and the start of peace talks.
Thereafter the definition of American objectives vanished by degrees, like
Alice's Cheshire cat.

The Nixon administration first offered mutual withdrawals of U.S. and
North Vietnamese forces, but then undermined its own proposal by starting
to pull American troops out unilaterally. The concept of mutual withdrawal
remained in the peace plans but was blurred by an ambiguous ceasefire-
in-place proposal in October 1970. Subsequently, the demand for removal
of North Vietnamese troops was dropped altogether. What still prevented
agreement was only Hanoi's insistence on unacceptable political terms. The
U.S. had no prescription of its own for a political settlement, suggesting
only that the future should be decided by problematic negotiations between
the Communists and Saigon.

Thus, by 1972 the specific, concrete demands of the United States on
Hanoi had been reduced to exactly one: American prisoners must be returned. Beyond that, for American purposes, the U.S. asked Hanoi only
for restraint—that is, that it not take advantage of American disengagement
to humiliate the United States. How much restraint, and for how long,
would satisfy that condition was never clear. For South Vietnam, despite
the rhetoric of alliance that was customarily used, declared U.S. objectives
did not even specify the indefinite survival of a non-Communist government.
Washington said only that the South Vietnamese people should choose their
political future freely, and not under the threat of violence. That aim accorded with American values but unhappily not with Vietnamese conditions,
or with the historical experience of civil conflicts anywhere else in the
world, including America's own.

The disconnection of American objectives from Vietnamese realities
was not incidental or accidental or the quirk of personality or circumstance.
It was imbedded in the most fundamental strategic concepts of the nuclear
age. For the overriding consideration of American actions in Vietnam was
not to bring about any specific Vietnamese outcome, but to assist what had
become known as "credibility," the impression that the United States was
tough enough and effective enough to meet its responsibilities in the world,
defend its interests, and use its nuclear weapons for those purposes if forced
to that choice. Credibility was (and remains) the psychological component
of the deterrence concept, which holds that the only way to avoid using
nuclear arms is to possess them in enough quantity to discourage any other
possessor from using them. Similarly, if the image of credibility could be
sufficiently conveyed, its reality would never have to be demonstrated.
Appearances, in other words, as the writer Jonathan Schell pointed out in
his book *The Time of Illusion,* "were not merely important to deterrence—

they were everything. If the deterrent was used, deterrence would have failed. If the image did not do its preventive work and there was a resort to action, the whole purpose of the policy would have been defeated."

Since credibility could never be proven, the only way to establish it was to demonstrate its attributes in all other American actions in the world, while also avoiding failures or irresolution that might contradict the desired image. Thus, once U.S. forces were committed in Vietnam, the original reasons quickly lost their primacy. What became necessary for the United States was not any given set of results that could be defined as a success, but rather a display of American determination, effectiveness, and reliability as an ally. Had this not been true, the stated U.S. war aims could not have shifted so greatly during the course of the conflict. American patience was exhausted by a war whose dominant impression was of soldiers fighting again and again over the identical terrain, without advancing or retreating or winning or losing, without any apparent relationship to any other battles before or afterward, and without visible movement toward a decisive result. But that image was an accurate metaphor for the policy. The result of the war was less important to Washington than the act of fighting it.

The U.S. intervened in Vietnam initially with ideas of defeating a Communist insurgency, containing what it then saw as a menacing and expansionist China, and disproving theories of liberation war, among other reasons. By the time the Nixon administration came to power, however, what mattered fundamentally to the U.S. leadership was not what happened to the Vietnamese, much less to the Lao or the Cambodians, but what happened to the world's—and particularly the Soviet Union's—impression of American capability and resolve. Nixon's rapprochement with the Chinese leadership made much of the war's original rationale meaningless and thus made its actual outcome a matter of even less concern to him or to the American government. If some form of settlement on America's minimum terms could be reached, so much the better. But even if there were no settlement, or one that failed, that would not be critically damaging either, as long as the United States was not perceived to weaken.

Defining goals in Vietnam with regard to the American image elsewhere was not invented by the Nixon administration, by any means. As long ago as the beginning of 1962 the Joint Chiefs of Staff had argued for intervention on the grounds that, along with the defense of Southeast Asia from Communism, "of equal importance" was the "psychological impact that a firm position by the United States will have on the countries of the world—both free and Communist." The real trap lay in the negative of that proposition: "A United States political and/or military withdrawal . . . would have an adverse psychological impact," the Chiefs also warned, "of even greater proportion." This, when only a few more than 2,500 American soldiers had been sent to Vietnam and only a dozen or so had been killed or wounded.

Three years later, with the Johnson administration poised to commit major ground forces to the conflict, a Defense Department official, John McNaughton, wrote what would become one of the most widely quoted passages in the *Pentagon Papers,* expressing U.S. aims in percentage terms: "70%—to avoid a humiliating U.S. defeat (to our reputation as a guarantor). 20%—to keep SVN (and the adjacent) territory from Chinese hands. 10%—to permit the people of SVN to enjoy a better, freer way of life."

Thus, when Nixon declared in 1969 that defeat in Vietnam "would result in a collapse of confidence in American leadership not only in Asia but throughout the world" and would "promote recklessness in the councils of those great powers who have not yet abandoned their goals of world conquest," he was not being at all inconsistent with previous American reasoning. The difference, though, was that by then all *other* goals of the intervention were vanishing. Thoughts of victory had evaporated, and nearly all specific demands on Hanoi were about to do the same.

Too, the more global-minded Nixon and Kissinger spun the credibility concept much farther from any local or regional circumstances than Johnson had. Though he was aware of more distant interests, Johnson normally focused on the classic assumptions of the domino theory: a failure of American resolve in Vietnam would endanger Thailand or Malaysia or, at a slightly greater distance, Indonesia and the Philippines. Nixon's and Kissinger's was a sort of super-domino theory. If America proved ineffectual in Vietnam, they thought, it would also be weakened—a "pitiful helpless giant"—in the Middle East, in strategic arms talks, everywhere on the globe, in fact, where important U.S. interests existed. Vietnam was part of a strategy in which everything was linked to the Soviet-American nuclear confrontation, and thus everything was also linked to everything else. The war there was limited, but to the extent that it was fought for the purpose of nuclear credibility, the stakes were unlimited. Vietnam was indivisible from preventing World III and saving the entire world, including the U.S., from possible nuclear blackmail and Communist totalitarianism. As Jonathan Schell put it, "the aim of upholding American credibility superseded any conclusions drawn from a simple accounting of tangible gains and tangible losses" in Vietnam.

Such an accounting would probably have dictated to most Americans—perhaps even Nixon and Kissinger—a policy of cutting losses and withdrawing. But, as Schell wrote, "The tangible objectives of limited war had been completely eclipsed by the psychological objective. The war had become an effort directed entirely toward building up a certain image by force of arms. It had become a piece of pure theatre."

For men who prided themselves on realism, Nixon and Kissinger were remarkably myopic about a world that was, inevitably, messier in reality than in strategists' theorizing. The issues of nuclear survival and their own balance-of-power design filled their vision so completely that they seemed not to grasp that other nations had other priorities. They acted as if they expected lesser nations to subordinate their own interests to superpower needs, on the ground that the safety of the entire world must override any narrow national goal.

The loss of superpower control, Nixon and Kissinger believed, was dangerous—as was explicitly spelled out by Kissinger when, speaking not of Southeast Asia but of the Mideast, he referred to the danger created when "two groups of countries with intense local rivalries . . . [are] backed by major countries, but not fully under the control of the major countries confronting each other." This, Kissinger said, "is the sort of situation that produced World War I." If world order was menaced when local rival states were "not fully under the control" of the major powers to whom they were allied, it followed that the superpowers were not only entitled but obliged to assert that control: the United States over nations under its influence and the Soviet Union over those in the Soviet orbit, in the name of the greater good of nuclear peace.

Obviously, this reasoning is not completely groundless, any more than is the concept of nuclear credibility. Regional disputes do raise the threat of possible superpower conflict. But Nixon and Kissinger characteristically saw *only* the Soviet-American dimension of all international issues. All other aspects were blotted out. On their mental map, the rest of the countries on the globe became blank spots, without individual character or history or motive, as lacking in feature and distinctive shape as squares on a chessboard.

Thus, though for years Vietnam preoccupied U.S. policy makers more than almost any other issue, the real Vietnam with all its particularities was hardly seen at all through Washington's lenses. The Vietnamese reasons for the conflict were irrelevant because they fell outside the circular logic of the American effort: the reason Americans had to prevail was because American troops and prestige were committed to doing so. Vietnam was vital because we had declared it vital, not for any attributes of its own. We were there, in a nutshell, because we were there. The war could have been anywhere else in the world and nearly all the issues and arguments, as far as Nixon and Kissinger were concerned, would have been the same. Their perspective almost demanded disregard of Vietnamese realities, in fact, for the Vietnamese circumstances so clearly failed to justify the size or cost of the American effort there. Rather than proceeding from an assessment of the actual events and the possible advantages or disadvantages of our intervention, American policy was stagecraft. Vietnam was an abstraction. And so, in the end, was the settlement that capped four excruciating years of Henry Kissinger's diplomacy.

The Paris agreement settled nothing but the issue of American involvement. The issue over which the war was fought—who would rule South Vietnam—was not resolved at all, but left to be negotiated along with other matters that all Vietnamese on both sides knew were not really negotiable. Even Secretary of State Rogers acknowledged that the political half of the agreement was "ambiguous, but deliberately ambiguous. We never pretended that it was definite and if we had attempted to work it out we would still be fighting."

The agreement was another illusion, detached from Vietnamese reality. Nor was it ever clear what Nixon or Kissinger really thought would be its outcome, except that presumably they believed it would meet their minimum condition of avoiding a clear American humiliation. The peace, in other words, was exactly what Schell called the war: a piece of theater, in which Vietnamese actors were expected to follow a script written not to resolve the conflict that was ravaging their country, but to make an American failure look like a success and thus preserve America's reputation elsewhere in the world.

X *F U R T H E R   R E A D I N G*

Henry Brandon, *The Retreat of American Power* (1974)
Dan Caldwell, ed., *Henry Kissinger* (1983)
Raymond Garthoff, *Détente and Confrontation* (1985)
J. W. Garver, "Sino-Vietnamese Conflict and Sino-American Rapprochement," *Political Science Quarterly*, 96 (1981), 445–61
Allan E. Goodman, *The Lost Peace* (1978)
Seymour M. Hersh, *The Price of Power* (1983)
Marvin and Bernard Kalb, *Kissinger* (1974)
Henry A. Kissinger, "The Vietnam Negotiations," *Foreign Affairs*, 47 (1969) 211–34
———, *Years of Upheaval* (1983)
Robert S. Litwak, *Détente and the Nixon Doctrine* (1984)
Roger Morris, *Uncertain Greatness: Henry Kissinger and American Foreign Policy* (1977)
Richard M. Nixon, "Asia After Vietnam," *Foreign Affairs*, 46 (1967), 111–25
———, *RN: The Memoirs of Richard Nixon* (1978)
Robert E. Osgood, *Retreat from Empire?* (1973)
Jonathan Schell, *The Time of Illusion* (1975)
William Shawcross, *Sideshow: Kissinger, Nixon and the Destruction of Cambodia* (1979)
John Stoessinger, *Kissinger: The Anguish of Power* (1976)
Tad Szulc, *The Illusion of Peace* (1978)

CHAPTER

12

The Antiwar Movement and Public Opinion

The American people overwhelmingly supported government policy in Vietnam during the early years of the U.S. military buildup, much as they had other post–World War II foreign policy commitments. Even after Johnson's major escalation of 1965, dissent remained muted, with the exception of vocal protests by a handful of isolated student and intellectual groups. But as the war dragged on inconclusively and American casualties mounted throughout 1966 and 1967, protest marches and demonstrations proliferated. A symbolic march on the Pentagon in the fall of 1967 drew tens of thousands of antiwar protesters. Following the Tet offensive of early 1968, the ranks of the antiwar movement swelled.

Despite the persistence of stereotypes perpetuated in part by the media, antiwar dissidents were not confined to the young, radicals, intellectuals, and the disaffected. Indeed if one defines the antiwar movement more broadly to encompass all who came to question the efficacy of the U.S. commitment to Vietnam, by 1968 it included many powerful individuals within the business and financial communities, the media, and the government itself. Public-opinion polls conducted during the late 1960s and early 1970s revealed a steady erosion of popular support for U.S. policy. Many observers at the time noted that the war had polarized American society more than any other event since the Civil War.

The nature of the antiwar movement—its origins, purposes, and ultimate impact on policy—has long been a subject of heated controversy. Perhaps of equal importance, albeit less frequently studied, is the aggregate domestic response to Vietnam, measurable by public-opinion surveys. Who opposed the war? Why did they oppose it? What impact did antiwar activities, or changes in levels of public support, have on the actions of the Johnson and Nixon administrations?

✕ DOCUMENTS

Students for a Democratic Society (SDS), an organization that by the mid-1960s had become a leading voice for the student protest movement and New Left, announced its opposition to the war in 1965. A public statement explaining its position, issued to the press in October 1965, is the first document. The next document contains excerpts from a speech delivered by SDS president Carl Oglesby during a protest march in Washington, D.C., on November 27 of that year. His address, which was circulated widely, castigated not only the war but the system that had produced it. Martin Luther King, Jr., the preeminent civil-rights leader and Nobel Peace Prize recipient, announced his opposition to America's involvement in Vietnam on April 4, 1967. Portions of King's contro-versial speech, delivered as a sermon at New York's Riverside Church, are printed as the third document.

The military draft quickly emerged as a focus of antiwar activity. The next document, issued in the fall of 1967 by the Antidraft Resistance, led to federal prosecution of five of its signers, including famed pediatrician Benjamin Spock and Yale University chaplain William Sloane Coffin, Jr. In the following selec-tion, author and former White House speechwriter James Fallows reflects on the class inequities of the draft.

Former student activist Todd Gitlin, now a sociology professor at the Uni-versity of California, Berkeley, recalls in the sixth document the New Left's in-fatuation with the Vietcong and other Third World revolutionary movements. In the last document, John Kerry, a leader of Vietnam Veterans Against the War, bitterly attacks government policy. Now a Democratic senator from Massachu-setts, Kerry condemned the duplicity that lay behind American policy at a congressional hearing on April 22, 1971.

SDS States Opposition to the War, 1965

Students for a Democratic Society wishes to reiterate emphatically its in-tention to pursue its opposition to the war in Vietnam, undeterred by the diversionary tactics of the administration.

We feel that the war is immoral at its root, that it is fought alongside a regime with no claim to represent its people, and that *it is foreclosing the hope of making America a decent and truly democratic society.*

The commitment of SDS, and of the whole generation we represent, is clear: we are anxious to build villages; we refuse to burn them. We are anxious to help and to change our country; we refuse to destroy someone else's country. We are anxious to advance the cause of democracy; we do not believe that cause can be advanced by torture and terror.

We are fully prepared to volunteer for service to our country and to democracy. We volunteer to go into Watts to work with the people of Watts to rebuild that neighborhood to be the kind of place that the people of Watts want it to be—and when we say "rebuild," we mean socially as well as physically. We volunteer to help the Peace Corps learn, as we have been learning in the slums and in Mississippi, how to energize the hungry and desperate and defeated of the world to make the big decisions. We volunteer to serve in hospitals and schools in the slums, in the Job Corps and VISTA, in the new Teachers Corps—and to do so in such a way as to strengthen democracy at its grass-roots. And in order to make our volunteering possible, we propose to the President that all those Americans who seek so vigorously to build instead of burn be given their chance to do so. We propose that he test the young people of America: if they had a free choice, would they want to burn and torture in Vietnam or to build a democracy at home and overseas? There is only one way to make the choice real: let us see what happens if service to democracy is made grounds for exemption from the military draft. I predict that almost every member of my generation would choose to build, not to burn; to teach, not to torture; to help, not to kill. And I am sure that the overwhelming majority of our brothers and cousins in the army in Vietnam, would make the same choice if they could—to serve and build, not kill and destroy. . . .

Until the President agrees to our proposal, we have only one choice: we do in conscience object, utterly and wholeheartedly, to this war; and we will encourage every member of our generation to object, and to file his objection through the Form 150 provided by the law for conscientious objection.

Carl Oglesby Denounces the "Liberals' War," 1965

Seven months ago at the April March on Washington, Paul Potter, then President of Students for a Democratic Society, stood in approximately this spot and said that we must name the system that creates and sustains the war in Vietnam—name it, describe it, analyze it, understand it, and change it.

Today I will try to name it—to suggest an analysis which, to be quite frank, may disturb some of you—and to suggest what changing it may require of us.

We are here again to protest against a growing war. Since it is a very bad war, we acquire the habit of thinking that it must be caused by very bad men. But we only conceal reality, I think, to denounce on such grounds the menacing coalition of industrial and military power, or the brutality of the blitzkrieg we are waging against Vietnam, or the ominous signs around us that heresy may soon no longer be permitted. We must simply observe, and quite plainly say, that this coalition, this blitzkrieg, and this demand for acquiescence are creatures, all of them, of a government that since 1932 has considered itself to be fundamentally *liberal*.

The original commitment in Vietnam was made by President Truman, a mainstream liberal. It was seconded by President Eisenhower, a moderate liberal. It was intensified by the late President Kennedy, a flaming liberal. Think of the men who now engineer that war—those who study the maps, give the commands, push the buttons, and tally the dead: Bundy, McNamara, Rusk, Lodge, Goldberg, the President himself.

They are not moral monsters.
They are all honorable men.
They are all liberals.

But so, I'm sure, are many of us who are here today in protest. To understand the war, then, it seems necessary to take a closer look at this American liberalism. Maybe we are in for some surprises. Maybe we have here two quite different liberalisms: one authentically humanist, the other not so human at all.

Not long ago, I considered myself a liberal. And if someone had asked me what I meant by that, I'd perhaps have quoted Thomas Jefferson or Thomas Paine, who first made plain our nation's unprovisional commitment to human rights. But what do you think would happen if these two heroes could sit down now for a chat with President Johnson and McGeorge Bundy?

They would surely talk of the Vietnam war. Our dead revolutionaries would soon wonder why their country was fighting against what appeared to be a revolution. The living liberals would hotly deny that it is one: there are troops coming in from outside, the rebels get arms from other countries, most of the people are not on their side, and they practice terror against their own. Therefore, *not* a revolution.

What would our dead revolutionaries answer? They might say: "What fools and bandits, sirs, you make then of us. Outside help? Do you remember Lafayette? Or the 3,000 British freighters the French navy sunk for our side? Or the arms and men we got from France and Spain? And what's this about terror? Did you never hear what we did to our own loyalists? Or about the thousands of rich American Tories who fled for their lives to Canada? And as for popular support, do you not know that we had less than one third of our people with us? That, in fact, the colony of New York recruited more troops for the British than for the revolution? Should we give it all back?"

Revolutions do not take place in velvet boxes. They never have. It is only the poets who make them lovely. What the National Liberation Front is fighting in Vietnam is a complex and vicious war. This war is also a revolution, as honest a revolution as you can find anywhere in history. And this is a fact which all our intricate official denials will never change.

But it doesn't make any difference to our leaders anyway. Their aim in Vietnam is really much simpler than this implies. It is to safeguard what they take to be American interests around the world against revolution or revolutionary change, which they always call Communism—as if that were that. In the case of Vietnam, this interest is, first, the principle that revolution shall not be tolerated anywhere, and second, that South Vietnam shall never sell its rice to China—or even to North Vietnam.

There is simply no such thing now, for us, as a just revolution—never mind that for two thirds of the world's people the twentieth century might as well be the Stone Age; never mind the terrible poverty and hopelessness that are the basic facts of life for most modern men; and never mind that for these millions there is now an increasingly perceptible relationship between their sorrow and our contentment.

Can we understand why the Negroes of Watts rebelled? Then why do we need a devil theory to explain the rebellion of the South Vietnamese? Can we understand the oppression in Mississippi, or the anguish that our Northern ghettos make epidemic? Then why can't we see that our proper human struggle is not with Communism or revolutionaries, but with the social desperation that drives good men to violence, both here and abroad? . . .

Let's stare our situation coldly in the face. All of us are born to the colossus of history, our American corporate system—in many ways, an awesome organism. There is one fact that describes it: with about 5 percent of the world's people, we consume about half the world's goods. We take a richness that is in good part not our own, and we put it in our pockets, our garages, our split-levels, our bellies, and our futures.

On the *face* of it, it is a crime that so few should have so much at the expense of so many. Where is the moral imagination so abused as to call this just? Perhaps many of us feel a bit uneasy in our sleep. We are not, after all, a cruel people. And perhaps we don't really need this super-dominance that deforms others. But what can we do? The investments are made. The financial ties are established. The plants abroad are built. Our system *exists*. One is swept up into it. How intolerable—to be born moral, but addicted to a stolen and maybe surplus luxury. Our goodness threatens to become counterfeit before our eyes—unless we change. But change threatens us with uncertainty—at least.

Martin Luther King, Jr., Declares His Opposition to the War, 1967

Since I am a preacher by trade, I suppose it is not surprising that I have seven major reasons for bringing Vietnam into the field of my moral vision. There is at the outset a very obvious and almost facile connection between the war in Vietnam and the struggle I, and others, have been waging in America. A few years ago there was a shining moment in that struggle. It seemed as if there was a real promise of hope for the poor—both black and white—through the Poverty Program. Then came the build-up in Vietnam, and I watched the program broken and eviscerated as if it were some idle political plaything of a society gone mad on war, and I knew that America would never invest the necessary funds or energies in rehabilitation of its poor so long as Vietnam continued to draw men and skills and money like some demonic, destructive suction tube. So I was increasingly compelled to see the war as an enemy of the poor and to attack it as such.

Perhaps the more tragic recognition of reality took place when it became clear to me that the war was doing far more than devastating the hopes of the poor at home. It was sending their sons and their brothers and their husbands to fight and to die in extraordinarily high proportions relative to the rest of the population. We were taking the young black men who had been crippled by our society and sending them 8000 miles away to guarantee liberties in Southeast Asia which they had not found in Southwest Georgia and East Harlem. So we have been repeatedly faced with the cruel irony of watching Negro and white boys on TV screens as they kill and die together for a nation that has been unable to seat them together in the same schools. So we watch them in brutal solidarity burning the huts of a poor village, but we realize that they would never live on the same block in Detroit. I could not be silent in the face of such cruel manipulation of the poor.

My third reason grows out of my experience in the ghettos of the North over the last three years—especially the last three summers. As I have walked among the desperate, rejected and angry young men, I have told them that Molotov cocktails and rifles would not solve their problems. I have tried to offer them my deepest compassion while maintaining my conviction that social change comes most meaningfully through non-violent action. But, they asked, what about Vietnam? They asked if our own nation wasn't using massive doses of violence to solve its problems, to bring about the changes it wanted. Their questions hit home, and I knew that I could never again raise my voice against the violence of the oppressed in the ghettos without having first spoken clearly to the greatest purveyor of violence in the world today—my own government.

For those who ask the question, "Aren't you a Civil Rights leader?" and thereby mean to exclude me from the movement for peace, I have this further answer. In 1957 when a group of us formed the Southern Christian Leadership Conference, we chose as our motto: "To save the soul of America." We were convinced that we could not limit our vision to certain rights for black people, but instead affirmed the conviction that America would never be free or saved from itself unless the descendants of its slaves were loosed from the shackles they still wear.

Now, it should be incandescently clear that no one who has any concern for the integrity and life of America today can ignore the present war. If America's soul becomes totally poisoned, part of the autopsy must read "Vietnam." It can never be saved so long as it destroys the deepest hopes of men the world over.

As if the weight of such a commitment to the life and health of America were not enough, another burden of responsibility was placed upon me in 1964; and I cannot forget that the Nobel Prize for Peace was also a commission—a commission to work harder than I had ever worked before for the "brotherhood of man." This is a calling that takes me beyond national allegiances, but even if it were not present I would yet have to live with the meaning of my commitment to the ministry of Jesus Christ. To me the relationship of this ministry to the making of peace is so obvious that I sometimes marvel at those who ask me why I am speaking against the war. Could it be that they do not know that the good news was meant for all men—for communist and capitalist, for their children and ours, for black and white, for revolutionary and conservative? Have they forgotten that my ministry is in obedience to the One who loved His enemies so fully that He died for them? What then can I say to the Viet Cong or to Castro or to Mao as a faithful minister of this One? Can I threaten them with death, or must I not share with them my life?

And as I ponder the madness of Vietnam, my mind goes constantly to the people of that peninsula. I speak now not of the soldiers of each side, not of the junta in Saigon, but simply of the people who have been living under the curse of war for almost three continuous decades. I think of them, too, because it is clear to me that there will be no meaningful solution there until some attempt is made to know them and their broken cries.

They must see Americans as strange liberators. The Vietnamese proclaimed their own independence in 1945 after a combined French and Japanese occupation and before the communist revolution in China. Even though they quoted the American Declaration of Independence in their own document of freedom, we refused to recognize them. Instead, we decided to support France in its re-conquest of her former colony.

Our government felt then that the Vietnamese people were not "ready" for independence, and we again fell victim to the deadly Western arrogance that has poisoned the international atmosphere for so long. With that tragic decision, we rejected a revolutionary government seeking self-determination, and a government that had been established not by China (for whom the Vietnamese have no great love) but by clearly indigenous forces that included some communists. For the peasants, this new government meant real land reform, one of the most important needs in their lives.

For nine years following 1945 we denied the people of Vietnam the right of independence. For nine years we vigorously supported the French in their abortive effort to re-colonize Vietnam.

Before the end of the war we were meeting 80 per cent of the French war costs. Even before the French were defeated at Dien Bien Phu, they began to despair of their reckless action, but we did not. We encouraged them with our huge financial and military supplies to continue the war even after they had lost the will to do so.

After the French were defeated it looked as if independence and land reform would come again through the Geneva agreements. But instead there came the United States, determined that Ho should not unify the temporarily divided nation, and the peasants watched again as we supported one of the most vicious modern dictators—our chosen man, Premier Diem. The peasants watched and cringed as Diem ruthlessly routed out all opposition, supported their extortionist landlords and refused even to discuss reunification with the North. The peasants watched as all this was presided over by U.S. influence and then by increasing numbers of U.S. troops who came to help quell the insurgency that Diem's methods had aroused. When Diem was overthrown they may have been happy, but the long line of military dictatorships seemed to offer no real change—especially in terms of their need for land and peace.

The only change came from America as we increased our troop commitments in support of governments which were singularly corrupt, inept d without popular support. All the while, the people read our leaflets and received regular promises of peace and democracy—and land reform. Now they languish under our bombs and consider us—not their fellow Vietnamese—the real enemy. They move sadly and apathetically as we herd them off the land of their fathers into concentration camps where minimal social needs are rarely met. They know they must move or be destroyed by our bombs. So they go.

They watch as we poison their water, as we kill a million acres of their crops. They must weep as the bulldozers destroy their precious trees. They wander into the hospitals, with at least 20 casualties from American fire-power for each Viet Cong-inflicted injury. So far we may have killed a million of them—mostly children.

What do the peasants think as we ally ourselves with the landlords and as we refuse to put any action into our many words concerning land reform? What do they think as we test out our latest weapons on them, just as the Germans tested out new medicine and new tortures in the concentration camps of Europe? Where are the roots of the independent Vietnam we claim to be building?

Now there is little left to build on—save bitterness. Soon the only solid physical foundations remaining will be found at our military bases and in the concrete of the concentration camps we call "fortified hamlets." The peasants may well wonder if we plan to build our new Vietnam on such grounds as these. Could we blame them for such thoughts? We must speak for them and raise the questions they cannot raise. These too are our brothers.

Perhaps the more difficult but no less necessary task is to speak for those who have been designated as our enemies. What of the NLF—that strangely anonymous group we call VC or communists? What must they think of us in America when they realize that we permitted the repression and cruelty of Diem which helped to bring them into being as a resistance group in the South? How can they believe in our integrity when now we speak of "aggression from the North" as if there were nothing more essential to the war? How can they trust us when now we charge *them* with violence after the murderous reign of Diem, and charge *them* with violence while we pour new weapons of death into their land?

How do they judge us when our officials know that their membership is less than 25 per cent communist and yet insist on giving them the blanket name? What must they be thinking when they know that we are aware of their control of major sections of Vietnam and yet we appear ready to allow national elections in which this highly organized political parallel government will have no part? They ask how we can speak of free elections when the Saigon press is censored and controlled by the military junta. And they are surely right to wonder what kind of new government we plan to help form without them—the only party in real touch with the peasants. They question our political goals and they deny the reality of a peace settlement from which they will be excluded. Their questions are frighteningly relevant.

Here is the true meaning and value of compassion and non-violence—when it helps us to see the enemy's point of view, to hear his questions, to know of his assessment of ourselves. For from his view we may indeed see the basic weaknesses of our own condition, and if we are mature, we may learn and grow and profit from the wisdom of the brothers who are called the opposition. . . .

Somehow this madness must cease. I speak as a child of God and brother to the suffering poor of Vietnam and the poor of America who are paying the double price of smashed hopes at home and death and corruption in Vietnam. I speak as a citizen of the world, for the world as it stands aghast at the path we have taken. I speak as an American to the leaders of my own nation. The great initiative in this war is ours. The initiative to stop must be ours.

This is the message of the great Buddhist leaders of Vietnam. Recently, one of them wrote these words: "Each day the war goes on the hatred increases in the hearts of the Vietnamese and in the hearts of those of humanitarian instinct. The Americans are forcing even their friends into becoming their enemies. It is curious that the Americans, who calculate so carefully on the possibilities of military victory, do not realize that in the process they are incurring deep psychological and political defeat. The image of America will never again be the image of revolution, freedom and democracy, but the image of violence and militarism."

If we continue, there will be no doubt in my mind and in the mind of the world that we have no honorable intentions in Vietnam. It will become clear that our minimal expectation is to occupy it as an American colony, and men will not refrain from thinking that our maximum hope is to goad China into a war so that we may bomb her nuclear installations.

The world now demands a maturity of America that we may not be able to achieve. It demands that we admit that we have been wrong from the beginning of our adventure in Vietnam, that we have been detrimental to the life of her people.

In order to atone for our sins and errors in Vietnam, we should take the initiative in bringing the war to a halt. I would like to suggest five concrete things that our government should do immediately to begin the long and difficult process of extricating ourselves from this nightmare:

1. End all bombing in North and South Vietnam.
2. Declare a unilateral cease-fire in the hope that such action will create the atmosphere for negotiation.
3. Take immediate steps to prevent other battlegrounds in Southeast Asia by curtailing our military build-up in Thailand and our interference in Laos.
4. Realistically accept the fact that the National Liberation Front has substantial support in South Vietnam and must thereby play a role in any meaningful negotiations and in any future Vietnam government.
5. Set a date on which we will remove all foreign troops from Vietnam in accordance with the 1954 Geneva Agreement.

Part of our ongoing commitment might well express itself in an offer to grant asylum to any Vietnamese who fears for his life under a new regime which included the NLF. Then we must make what reparations we can for the damage we have done. We must provide the medical aid that is badly needed, in this country if necessary.

Meanwhile, we in the churches and synagogues have a continuing task while we urge our government to disengage itself from a disgraceful commitment. We must be prepared to match actions with words by seeking out every creative means of protest possible.

As we counsel young men concerning military service we must clarify for them our nation's role in Vietnam and challenge them with the alternative of conscientious objection. I am pleased to say that this is the path now being chosen by more than 70 students at my own Alma Mater, Morehouse College, and I recommend it to all who find the American course in Vietnam a dishonorable and unjust one. Moreover, I would encourage all ministers of draft age to give up their ministerial exemptions and seek status as conscientious objectors. Every man of humane convictions must decide on the protest that best suits his convictions, but we must *all* protest.

There is something seductively tempting about stopping there and sending us all off on what in some circles has become a popular crusade against the war in Vietnam. I say we must enter that struggle, but I wish to go on now to say something even more disturbing. The war in Vietnam is but a symptom of a far deeper malady within the American spirit, and if we ignore this sobering reality we will find ourselves organizing clergy- and laymen-concerned committees for the next generation. We will be marching and attending rallies without end unless there is a significant and profound change in American life and policy.

In 1957 a sensitive American official overseas said that it seemed to him that our nation was on the wrong side of a world revolution. During the past ten years we have seen emerge a pattern of suppression which now has justified the presence of U.S. military "advisors" in Venezuela. The need to maintain social stability for our investments accounts for the counterrevolutionary action of American forces in Guatemala. It tells why American helicopters are being used against guerrillas in Colombia and why American napalm and green beret forces have already been active against rebels in Peru. With such activity in mind, the words of John F. Kennedy come back to haunt us. Five years ago he said, "Those who make peaceful revolution impossible will make violent revolution inevitable."

Increasingly, by choice or by accident, this is the role our nation has taken—by refusing to give up the privileges and the pleasures that come from the immense profits of overseas investment.

I am convinced that if we are to get on the right side of the world revolution, we as a nation must undergo a radical revolution of values. When machines and computers, profit and property rights are considered more important than people, the giant triplets of racism, materialism, and militarism are incapable of being conquered.

A true revolution of values will soon cause us to question the fairness and justice of many of our past and present policies.

Proclamation of the Antidraft Resistance, 1967

To the young men of America, to the whole of the American people, and to all men of goodwill everywhere:

1. An ever growing number of young American men are finding that the American war in Vietnam so outrages their deepest moral and religious sense that they cannot contribute to it in any way. We share their moral outrage.

2. We further believe that the war is unconstitutional and illegal. Congress has not declared a war as required by the Constitution. Moreover, under the Constitution, treaties signed by the President and ratified by the Senate have the same force as the Constitution itself. The Charter of the United Nations is such a treaty. The Charter specifically obligates the United States to refrain from force or the threat of force in international relations. It requires member states to exhaust every peaceful means of settling disputes and to submit disputes which cannot be settled peacefully to the Security Council. The United States has systematically violated all of these Charter provisions for thirteen years.

3. Moreover, this war violates international agreements, treaties and principles of law which the United States Government has solemnly endorsed. The combat role of the United States troops in Vietnam violates the Geneva Accords of 1954 which our government pledged to support but has since subverted. The destruction of rice, crops and livestock; the burning and bulldozing of entire villages consisting exclusively of civilian structures; the interning of civilian non-combatants in concentration camps; the summary executions of civilians in captured villages who could not produce satisfactory evidence of their loyalties or did not wish to be removed to concentration camps; the slaughter of peasants who dared to stand up in their fields and shake their fists at American helicopters;—these are all actions of the kind which the United States and the other victorious powers of World War II declared to be crimes against humanity for which individuals were to be held personally responsible even when acting under the orders of their governments and for which Germans were sentenced at Nuremberg to long prison terms and death. The prohibition of such acts as war crimes was incorporated in treaty law by the Geneva Conventions of 1949, ratified by the United States. These are commitments to other countries and to Mankind, and they would claim our allegiance even if Congress should declare war.

4. We also believe it is an unconstitutional denial of religious liberty and equal protection of the laws to withhold draft exemption from men whose religious or profound philosophical beliefs are opposed to what in the Western religious tradition have been long known as unjust wars.

5. Therefore, we believe on all these grounds that every free man has a legal right and a moral duty to exert every effort to end this war, to avoid

collusion with it, and to encourage others to do the same. Young men in the armed forces or threatened with the draft face the most excruciating choices. For them various forms of resistance risk separation from their families and their country, destruction of their careers, loss of their freedom and loss of their lives. Each must choose the course of resistance dictated by his conscience and circumstances. Among those already in the armed forces some are refusing to obey specific illegal and immoral orders, some are attempting to educate their fellow servicemen on the murderous and barbarous nature of the war, some are absenting themselves without official leave. Among those not in the armed forces some are applying for status as conscientious objectors to American aggression in Vietnam, some are refusing to be inducted. Among both groups some are resisting openly and paying a heavy penalty, some are organizing more resistance within the United States and some have sought sanctuary in other countries.

6. We believe that each of these forms of resistance against illegitimate authority is courageous and justified. Many of us believe that open resistance to the war and the draft is the course of action most likely to strengthen the moral resolve with which all of us can oppose the war and most likely to bring an end to the war.

7. We will continue to lend our support to those who undertake resistance to this war. We will raise funds to organize draft resistance unions, to supply legal defense and bail, to support families and otherwise aid resistance to the war in whatever ways may seem appropriate.

8. We firmly believe that our statement is the sort of speech that under the First Amendment must be free, and that the actions we will undertake are as legal as is the war resistance of the young men themselves. But we recognize that the courts may find otherwise, and that if so we might all be liable to prosecution and severe punishment. In any case, we feel that we cannot shrink from fulfilling our responsibilities to the youth whom many of us teach, to the country whose freedom we cherish, and to the ancient traditions of religion and philosophy which we strive to preserve in this generation.

9. We call upon all men of good will to join us in this confrontation with immoral authority. Especially we call upon the universities to fulfill their mission of enlightenment and religious organizations to honor their heritage of brotherhood. Now is the time to resist.

James Fallows Reflects on the Draft's Inequities (1969), 1975

Many people think that the worst scars of the war years have healed. I don't. Vietnam has left us with a heritage rich in possibilities for class warfare, and I would like to start telling about it with this story:

James Fallows, "What Did You Do in the Class War Daddy?" *Washington Monthly*, October 1975, pp. 5–7. Reprinted with permission from *The Washington Monthly*. Copyright by The Washington Monthly Co., 1611 Connecticut Avenue N.W., Washington, D.C. 20009.

In the fall of 1969, I was beginning my final year in college. As the months went by, the rock on which I had unthinkingly anchored my hopes—the certainty that the war in Vietnam would be over before I could possibly fight—began to crumble. It shattered altogether on Thanksgiving weekend when, while riding back to Boston from a visit with my relatives, I heard that the draft lottery had been held and my birthdate had come up number 45. I recognized for the first time that, inflexibly, I must either be drafted or consciously find a way to prevent it.

In the atmosphere of that time, each possible choice came equipped with barbs. To answer the call was unthinkable, not only because, in my heart, I was desperately afraid of being killed, but also because, among my friends, it was axiomatic that one should not be "complicit" in the immoral war effort. Draft resistance, the course chosen by a few noble heroes of the movement, meant going to prison or leaving the country. With much the same intensity with which I wanted to stay alive, I did not want those things either. What I wanted was to go to graduate school, to get married, and to enjoy those bright prospects I had been taught that life owed me.

I learned quickly enough that there was only one way to get what I wanted. A physical deferment would restore things to the happy state I had known during four undergraduate years. The barbed alternatives would be put off. By the impartial dictates of public policy I would be free to pursue the better side of life.

Like many of my friends whose numbers had come up wrong in the lottery, I set about securing my salvation. When I was not participating in anti-war rallies, I was poring over the Army's code of physical regulations. During the winter and early spring, seminars were held in the college common rooms. There, sympathetic medical students helped us search for disqualifying conditions that we, in our many years of good health, might have overlooked. Although, on the doctors' advice, I made a half-hearted try at fainting spells, my only real possibility was beating the height and weight regulations. My normal weight was close to the cut-off point for an "underweight" disqualification, and, with a diligence born of panic, I made sure I would have a margin. I was six-feet-one-inch tall at the time. On the morning of the draft physical I weighed 120 pounds.

Before sunrise that morning I rode the subway to the Cambridge city hall, where we had been told to gather for shipment to the examination at the Boston Navy Yard. The examinations were administered on a rotating basis, one or two days each month for each of the draft boards in the area. Virtually everyone who showed up on Cambridge day at the Navy Yard was a student from Harvard or MIT.

There was no mistaking the political temperament of our group. Many of my friends wore red arm bands and stop-the-war buttons. Most chanted the familiar words, "Ho, Ho, Ho Chi Minh/NLF is Gonna Win." One of the things we had learned from the draft counselors was that disruptive behavior at the examination was a worthwhile political goal, not only because it obstructed the smooth operation of the criminal war machine, but also because it might impress the examiners with our undesirable character traits. As we climbed into the buses and as they rolled toward the Navy Yard, about half of the young men brought the chants to a crescendo. The rest of us sat rigid and silent, clutching x-rays and letters from our doctors at home.

Inside the Navy Yard, we were first confronted by a young sergeant from Long Beach, a former surfer boy no older than the rest of us and seemingly unaware that he had an unusual situation on his hands. He started reading out instructions for the intelligence tests when he was hooted down. He went out to collect his lieutenant, who clearly had been through a Cambridge day before. "We've got all the time in the world," he said, and let the chanting go on for two or three minutes. "When we're finished with you, you can go, and not a minute before."

From that point on the disruption became more purposeful and individual, largely confined to those whose deferment strategies were based on anti-authoritarian psychiatric traits. Twice I saw students walk up to young orderlies—whose hands were extended to receive the required cup of urine—and throw the vial in the orderlies' faces. The orderlies looked up, initially more astonished than angry, and went back to towel themselves off. Most of the rest of us trod quietly through the paces, waiting for the moment of confrontation when the final examiner would give his verdict. I had stepped on the scales at the very beginning of the examination. Desperate at seeing the order write down 122 pounds, I hopped back on and made sure that he lowered it to 120. I walked in a trance through the rest of the examination, until the final meeting with the fatherly physician who ruled on marginal cases such as mine. I stood there in socks and underwear, arms wrapped around me in the chilly building. I knew as I looked at the doctor's face that he understood exactly what I was doing.

"Have you ever contemplated suicide?" he asked after he finished looking over my chart. My eyes darted up to his. "Oh, suicide—yes, I've been feeling very unstable and unreliable recently." He looked at me, staring until I returned my eyes to the ground. He wrote "unqualified" on my folder, turned on his heel, and left. I was overcome by a wave of relief, which for the first time revealed to me how great my terror had been, and by the beginning of the sense of shame which remains with me to this day.

It was, initially, a generalized shame at having gotten away with my deception, but it came into sharper focus later in the day. Even as the last of the Cambridge contingent was throwing its urine and deliberately failing its color-blindness tests, buses from the next board began to arrive. These bore the boys from Chelsea, thick, dark-haired young men, the white proles of Boston. Most of them were younger than us, since they had just left high school, and it had clearly never occurred to them that there might be a way around the draft. They walked through the examination lines like so many cattle off to slaughter. I tried to avoid noticing, but the results were inescapable. While perhaps four out of five of my friends from Harvard were being deferred, just the opposite was happening to the Chelsea boys.

We returned to Cambridge that afternoon, not in government buses but as free individuals, liberated and victorious. The talk was high-spirited, but there was something close to the surface that none of us wanted to mention. We knew now who would be killed.

As other memories of the war years have faded, it is that day in the Navy Yard that will not leave my mind. . . .

We have not, however, learned the lesson of the day at the Navy Yard, or the thousands of similar scenes all across the country through all the years of the war. Five years later, two questions have yet to be faced, let alone answered. The first is why, when so many of the bright young college men opposed the war, so few were willing to resist the draft, rather than simply evade it. The second is why all the well-educated presumably humane young men, whether they opposed the war or were thinking fondly of A-bombs on Hanoi, so willingly took advantage of this most brutal form of class discrimination—what it signifies that we let the boys from Chelsea be sent off to die.

The "we" that I refer to are the mainly-white, mainly-well-educated children of mainly-comfortable parents, who are now mainly embarked on promising careers in law, medicine, business, academics. What makes them a class is that they all avoided the draft by taking one of the thinking-man's routes to escape. These included the physical deferment, by far the smartest and least painful of all; the long technical appeals through the legal jungles of the Selective Service System; the more disingenuous resorts to conscientious objector status; and, one degree further down the scale of personal inconvenience, joining the Reserves or the National Guard.

Todd Gitlin Recalls the New Left's Revolutionary Romanticism, 1987

As the war became more militant, so did the antiwar movement—in demands, in spirit, in tactics. Between 1965 and 1967, as American troops in Vietnam doubled and redoubled and redoubled twice more, most antiwar movers and shakers shook off their leftover faith in negotiations and endorsed immediate withdrawal. When doubters asked, "How can we get out of Vietnam?" the quick answer was: on boats. But the New Left wing, young and sick at heart at what it reasonably took to be empire flexing its muscles, moved beyond rebellion against American foreign policy. Much of the leadership, and some of the rank and file—it is hard to say exactly how many—slid into romance with the other side. To wear a button calling for "Victory to the National Liberation Front," to wave an NLF flag or shout, "Ho, Ho, Ho Chi Minh/The NLF is gonna win," meant more than believing that the NLF was the most popular force in South Vietnam, or that Vietnamese had flocked to it for compelling reasons, or that it represented the least bad practical alternative for Vietnam—all defensible propositions. It meant feeling the passion of the alignment and placing it at the heart of one's political identity. It meant finding heroes where the American superstate found villains and pointed its guns. It meant imagining comrades riding to *our* rescue.

This was *a* tendency, not the only one, not final or unopposed even in SDS [Students for a Democratic Society]. Its significance was certainly inflated by the prowar Right and by the attentions of a demagogic press. Although almost always greatly outnumbered by American flags turned to patriotic antiwar use, NLF flags seized a disproportionate share of the media spotlight at the giant antiwar marches. And so a too-uncomplicated endorsement of Third World revolutions—and revolutionary organizations—built a firebreak around the New Left part of the antiwar movement, sealing it off from the underbrush sympathy of the unconvinced. Surely those NLF flags were part of the explanation for one of the stunning political facts of the decade: that as the war steadily lost popularity in the late Sixties, *so did the antiwar movement*. At the growing edge of the New Left, it was as if there had to be a loyalty oath for working against the war, or American dominion in general. The napalm had to be stopped for the correct reasons. Strategy-minded antiwar liberals rudely reminded us that we were forfeiting the respect of Americans who were turning against the war but were unwilling to do so at the price of their own sense of patriotism. But the hell with them! Which side were they on, anyway?

The consequence of the New Left's Third World turn—both product and impetus of our isolation—was yet more isolation. But the reporters had not invented those NLF flags out of proverbial whole cloth. Desperate for moral companionship—America having forfeited our love—a part of ourselves looked with respect, even awe, even love, on an ideal version of ourselves who we thought existed—*had* to exist—out there in the hot climates. We needed to feel that someone, somewhere in the world, was fighting the good fight and winning. Better: that the world's good guys formed a solid front. Even better: that out of the rubble, someone, somewhere, might be constructing a good society, at least one that was decent to the impoverished and colonized. If the United States was no longer humanity's beacon—and if the movement was not building a new society itself—the light had to be found outside. The melodrama of American innocence was alive and well in the anti-American left. Henry Luce [of *Time-Life*] had been deluded when he anticipated "the American Century"; we thought this was going to be the *anti*-American Century, just as pure, just as irresistible, with a different although equivalently happy ending.

And always there was the war, which we took to be the definitive moral test of America's intentions toward the vast poor and dark-skinned world. The Third Worldist movement route began in McComb, Mississippi, and led to the Mekong Delta. With the United States pulverizing and bullying small countries, it seemed the most natural thing in the world to go prospecting among them for heroes. Their resistance was so brave, their enemies so implacable, their nationalism so noble, we could take their passions, even their slogans and styles of speech, even—in fantasy—their forms of organization for our own. And so we identified with victims who were in the process of repossessing their homelands, as we were straining to overcome our own sense of homelessness. We loved them for what we took to be their struggle for independence, as we were struggling—no mere hackneyed word—for our own. We started out feeling the suffering of peasants, defending their right to rebel, and ended up taking sides with the organizations and leaders who commanded the rebellion—all the while knowing, in anguish, that guerrilla organizations usurp the freedom which rebels are willing to die for, yet also knowing, also in anguish, that without organization (even, often, the wrong organization: dictatorship in embryo) all the bravery in the world is squandered. Some of us took seriously the dreadful histories that Communist groups had imposed, and some didn't, but the New Left tendency was to agree that American occupation was so clear and present an evil—a *homegrown* evil—that the other side would have to be forgiven its crimes. Even the movement's antiutopians thought the future of "the other side," and the morality of guerrilla war, were questions to be left until later, luxuries, or, worst of all, potential weapons in the hands of the napalmers, the question for the present being simply whether the guerrillas, or the enemy nation (the two were often confused), were entitled to have any future of their own. The issue became *how we felt* more than *what would end the war*. We would settle for nothing less than a cleaning of the historical slate.

And so, increasingly, we found our exemplars and heroes in Cuba, in China, in the Third World guerrilla movements, in Mao and Frantz Fanon and Che and Debray, most of all—decisively—in Vietnam. It no longer felt sufficient—sufficiently estranged, sufficiently furious—to say no to aggressive war; we felt driven to say yes to revolt, and unless we were careful, that yes could easily be transferred onto the Marxism-Leninism which had commandeered the revolt in the interest of practicality. Apocalypse was outfitted with a bright side. If the American flag was dripping napalm, the NLF flag was clean. If the deluded make-Vietnam-safe-for-democracy barbarism of the war could be glibly equated with the deliberate slaughter of millions in Nazi gas chambers—if the American Christ turned out to look like the Antichrist—then by this cramped either-or logic the Communist Antichrist must really have been Christ. America had betrayed us; the war, Carl Oglesby movingly said in 1965, "broke my American heart." Only true-blue believers in the promise of America could have felt so anti-American. Ours was the fury of a lover spurned. But a fury so intense, left to itself, would have consumed us. "Don't you want somebody to love?" as the Jefferson Airplane sang. So we turned where romantics have traditionally turned: to the hot-blooded peoples of the subtropics and the mysterious East. The Manichaean all-or-nothing logic of the Cold War was conserved, though inverted, as if costumes from Central Wardrobe had been rotated.

A Vietnam Veteran Opposes the War, 1971

Thank you very much, Senator Fulbright, Senator Javits, Senator Symington, Senator Pell. I would like to say for the record, and also for the men behind me who are also wearing the uniform and their medals, that my sitting here is really symbolic. I am not here as John Kerry. I am here as one member of the group of 1,000 which is a small representation of a very much larger group of veterans in this country, and were it possible for all of them to sit at this table they would be here and have the same kind of testimony. . . .

I would like to talk on behalf of all those veterans and say that several months ago in Detroit we had an investigation at which over 150 honorably discharged, and many very highly decorated, veterans testified to war crimes committed in Southeast Asia. These were not isolated incidents but crimes committed on a day to day basis with the full awareness of officers at all levels of command.

It is impossible to describe to you exactly what did happen in Detroit— the emotions in the room and the feelings of the men who were reliving their experiences in Vietnam. They relived the absolute horror of what this country, in a sense, made them do.

They told stories that at times they had personally raped, cut off ears, cut off heads, taped wires from portable telephones to human genitals and turned up the power, cut off limbs, blown up bodies, randomly shot at civilians, razed villages in fashion reminiscent of Genghis Khan, shot cattle and dogs for fun, poisoned food stocks, and generally ravaged the countryside of South Vietnam in addition to the normal ravage of war and the normal and very particular ravaging which is done by the applied bombing power of this country.

We call this investigation the Winter Soldier Investigation. The term Winter Soldier is a play on words of Thomas Paine's in 1776 when he spoke of the Sunshine Patriots and summer time soldiers who deserted at Valley Forge because the going was rough.

We who have come here to Washington have come here because we feel we have to be winter soldiers now. We could come back to this country, we could be quiet, we could hold our silence, we could not tell what went on in Vietnam, but we feel because of what threatens this country, not the reds, but the crimes which we are committing that threaten it, that we have to speak out.

I would like to talk to you a little bit about what the result is of the feelings these men carry with them after coming back from Vietnam. The country doesn't know it yet but it has created a monster, a monster in the form of millions of men who have been taught to deal and to trade in violence and who are given the chance to die for the biggest nothing in history; men who have returned with a sense of anger and a sense of betrayal which no one has yet grasped.

As a veteran and one who feels this anger I would like to talk about it. We are angry because we feel we have been used in the worst fashion by the administration of this country.

In 1970 at West Point Vice President Agnew said "some glamorize the criminal misfits of society while our best men die in Asian rice paddies to preserve the freedom which most of those misfits abuse," and this was used as a rallying point for our effort in Vietnam.

But for us, as boys in Asia whom the country was supposed to support, his statement is a terrible distortion from which we can only draw a very deep sense of revulsion, and hence the anger of some of the men who are here in Washington today. It is a distortion because we in no way consider ourselves the best men of this country; because those he calls misfits were standing up for us in a way that nobody else in this country dared to; because so many who have died would have returned to this country to join the misfits in their efforts to ask for an immediate withdrawal from South Vietnam; because so many of those best men have returned as quadriplegics and amputees—and they lie forgotten in Veterans Administration Hospitals in this country which fly the flag which so many have chosen as their own personal symbol—and we cannot consider ourselves America's best men when we are ashamed of and hated for what we were called on to do in Southeast Asia.

In our opinion, and from our experience, there is nothing in South Vietnam which could happen that realistically threatens the United States of America. And to attempt to justify the loss of one American life in Vietnam, Cambodia or Laos by linking such loss to the preservation of freedom, which those misfits supposedly abuse, is to us the height of criminal hypocrisy, and it is that kind of hypocrisy which we feel has torn this country apart.

We are probably much more angry than that, but I don't want to go into the foreign policy aspects because I am outclassed here. I know that all of you talk about every possible alternative for getting out of Vietnam. We understand that. We know you have considered the seriousness of the aspects to the utmost level and I am not going to try to dwell on that. But I want to relate to you the feeling that many of the men who have returned to this country express because we are probably angriest about all that we were told about Vietnam and about the mystical war against communism.

We found that not only was it a civil war, an effort by a people who had for years been seeking their liberation from any colonial influence whatsoever, but also we found that the Vietnamese whom we had enthusiastically molded after our own image were hard put to take up the fight against the threat we were supposedly saving them from.

We found most people didn't even know the difference between communism and democracy. They only wanted to work in rice paddies without helicopters strafing them and bombs with napalm burning their villages and tearing their country apart. They wanted everything to do with the war, particularly with this foreign presence of the United States of America, to leave them alone in peace, and they practiced the art of survival by siding with whichever military force was present at a particular time, be it Viet Cong, North Vietnamese or American.

We found also that all too often American men were dying in those rice paddies for want of support from their allies. We saw first hand how monies from American taxes were used for a corrupt dictatorial regime. We saw that many people in this country had a one-sided idea of who was kept free by our flag, and blacks provided the highest percentage of casualties. We saw Vietnam ravaged equally by American bombs and search and destroy missions, as well as by Viet Cong terrorism, and yet we listened while this country tried to blame all of the havoc on the Viet Cong.

We rationalized destroying villages in order to save them. We saw America lose her sense of morality as she accepted very coolly a My Lai and refused to give up the image of American soldiers who hand out chocolate bars and chewing gum.

We learned the meaning of free fire zones, shooting anything that moves, and we watched while America placed a cheapness on the lives of orientals.

We watched the United States falsification of body counts, in fact the glorification of body counts. We listened while month after month we were told the back of the enemy was about to break. We fought using weapons against "oriental human beings." We fought using weapons against those people which I do not believe this country would dream of using were we fighting in the European theater. We watched while men charged up hills because a general said that hill has to be taken, and after losing one platoon or two platoons they marched away to leave the hill for reoccupation by the North Vietnamese. We watched pride allow the most unimportant battles to be blown into extravaganzas, because we couldn't lose, and we couldn't retreat, and because it didn't matter how many American bodies were lost to prove that point, and so there were Hamburger Hills and Khe Sanhs and Hill 81s and Fire Base 6s, and so many others.

Now we are told that the men who fought there must watch quietly while American lives are lost so that we can exercise the incredible arrogance of Vietnamizing the Vietnamese.

Each day to facilitate the process by which the United States washes her hands of Vietnam someone has to give up his life so that the United States doesn't have to admit something that the entire world already knows, so that we can't say that we have made a mistake. Someone has to die so that President Nixon won't be, and these are his words, "the first President to lose a war."

We are asking Americans to think about that because how do you ask a man to be the last man to die in Vietnam? How do you ask a man to be the last man to die for a mistake? But we are trying to do that, and we are doing it with thousands of rationalizations, and if you read carefully the President's last speech to the people of this country, you can see that he says, and says clearly, "but the issue, gentlemen, is communism, and the question is whether or not we will leave that country to the communists or whether or not we will try to give it hope to be a free people.'' But the point is they are not a free people now under us. They are not a free people, and we cannot fight communism all over the world. I think we should have learned that lesson by now. . . .

We wish that a merciful God could wipe away our own memories of that service as easily as this administration has wiped away their memories of us. But all that they have done and all that they can do by this denial is to make more clear than ever our own determination to undertake one last mission—to search out and destroy the last vestige of this barbaric war, to pacify our own hearts, to conquer the hate and the fear that have driven this country these last ten years and more, so when 30 years from now our brothers go down the street without a leg, without an arm, or a face, and small boys ask why, we will be able to say "Vietnam" and not mean a desert, not a filthy obscene memory, but mean instead the place where America finally turned and where soldiers like us helped it in the turning.

Thank you.

✗ E S S A Y S

In the opening essay, Melvin Small of Wayne State University explores the impact of the antiwar movement on Lyndon Johnson and Richard Nixon. He contends that the protesters succeeded in capturing the attention of both presidents and affecting their policies in Vietnam to a far greater extent than most observers have suspected. The next essay, by William L. Lunch of the University of San Francisco and Peter W. Sperlich of the University of California, Berkeley, focuses on changing American public opinion toward the war. The authors identify several distinct phases of public attitudes toward it and show that, contrary to some popular stereotypes, supporters of the American effort tended to be concentrated among younger, white, male, and middle-class citizens; opponents were more likely to be older, black, female, and of lower-class background. Lunch and Sperlich speculate that, at least temporarily, the war may have changed the traditional relationship between elites and masses in the area of foreign policy.

The Impact of the Antiwar Movement
MELVIN SMALL

As I was leaving [former White House counsel] Leonard Garment's office after an interview, he asked me whether I thought antiwar dissenters had affected the decision makers. I replied that I did not know yet, as my research was incomplete. "But surely," the lawyer responded, "you must have a theory of the case."

At that time, midway through my research, I was pursuing many theories. Among the most plausible were that the movement (1) exerted pressures directly on Johnson and Nixon that contributed to their deescalation policies; (2) exerted pressures indirectly by turning the public against the war; (3) encouraged the North Vietnamese to fight on long enough to the point that Americans demanded a withdrawal from Southeast Asia; (4) influenced American political and military strategies, since Johnson and Nixon were convinced that Hanoi counted on the movement; (5) retarded the growth of general antiwar sentiment because the public perceived the protesters as unpatriotic; and (6) combinations of these theories.

Although I still cannot answer Garment's question categorically, it is clear to me now that the antiwar movement and antiwar criticism in the media and Congress had a significant impact on the Vietnam policies of both Johnson and Nixon. At two key points at least—October 1967 and October 1969—mass demonstrations affected American foreign policy. The March on the Pentagon shocked many in the Johnson administration and produced the public relations campaign that contributed to public shock after Tet. The Moratorium helped to convince Nixon that Americans would not accept the savage blows envisaged in Operation Duck Hook [a contingency plan for the massive bombing of North Vietnam's cities and blockade of its ports]. On many other occasions, involving such issues as bombing pauses, diplomatic and military initiatives, and major speeches, antiwar activities and dissent were important factors for the decision makers. Even more dramatically, the movement played a role in Lyndon Johnson's decisions not to seek a second term and to wind down the war and played a major, if latent, role in restraining Richard Nixon from reescalating. In addition, many of the Watergate crimes were related to Nixon's attempt to crush the movement. Thus, the movement played an indirect role in the first resignation of a president in American history.

The extent of the impact of the movement on decision makers cannot be gauged through an empirical approach. The most ingenious attempt, which correlated policy and opinion changes with mass demonstrations, came up with inconclusive and unconvincing findings. The historian must rely instead on traditional tools to flesh out the often impressionistic evidence that allows one to make educated guesses about policymaking.

It is never easy to determine the motivations behind any public policy. The motivations behind foreign policies are even more difficult to determine than the motivations behind domestic policies, if only because officials try to obscure the role of sordid domestic politics when they defend national security. Irrespective of the stated and attributed rationales for foreign policies, one can identify the factors that attracted the attention of the decision makers as they considered their options. Archival and published records reveal the external events that worried them enough to be taken into account as they decided what and when to bomb in Vietnam, how many soldiers to call up or send home, and what sorts of diplomatic initiatives to undertake. Further, one can assess the importance of the antiwar movement to Washington by the energies expended in monitoring and suppressing its activities. If, as the key figures often said, the movement had no impact on their foreign policies, why was it that they spent so much of their time and attention on it?

Even those who downplay the importance of the movement concede that public opinion was a crucial variable in the construction of Vietnam policies. It is in their links to public opinion that the movement and antiwar critics exercised their most profound influence on those policies. To be sure, throughout the terms of both presidents, public opinion polls revealed considerable support for whatever the military did in Vietnam. On the other hand, in both administrations, support for escalation tended to decrease as the war dragged on and as first Johnson and then Nixon proved incapable of terminating it with dispatch.

Antiwar activities helped convince more and more Americans to oppose the war, or at least begin to feel uncomfortable about the nation's involvement in Vietnam. At times, some of their activities, as framed by sensation-seeking media, may have produced a patriotic backlash. Overall, however, the movement eroded support for Johnson and Nixon, especially among college students at the best universities, their parents, and members of the attentive and informed public. Some groups of people in the United States count for more than others. The loss of Yale and the *New York Times* to Johnson and even Nixon meant more than the retention of support from state colleges in Texas and the Scripps-Howard chain of newspapers. Through their constant and often publicized attacks, experts in the movement, the media, and on the campuses helped to destroy the knee-jerk notion that "they in Washington know." This was a very important development. For the first time since 1945, major reference figures in the bipartisan establishment began to speak out against an American cold war policy and led many citizens to question the judgment and wisdom of their presidents.

From the start, it was clear that the longer the war went on, the more likely Americans would tire of their increasingly costly involvement. If the United States could not win, in the absence of a strong initial and sustained commitment to wait out the patient and dedicated enemy in Vietnam, pressures for withdrawal had to increase over time. Dean Rusk, who sees opposition rising at home because of Tet and other policy failures, irrespective of previous criticism from the antiwar movement, emphasizes this approach.

Yet that previous criticism had to be important for several reasons. First, movement activities and elite opposition in the media helped to keep the war "on the front burner" from 1965 through 1971. With the war an object of almost constant attention, presidents found it difficult to pursue military policies that the public would find objectionable. In addition, the critics presented arguments and information that provided a framework for those who did not know how to articulate their general opposition to what was becoming an endless war. The existence of any opposition helped to reinforce other opposition. Senator [Wayne] Morse's lonely stand against the war in 1964 encouraged some citizens in their opposition, as did Senator [J. William] Fulbright's hearings in early 1966, which had been encouraged by the rising opposition on elite campuses during the previous year. That opposition was legitimized to some degree when congressmen read its letters and petitions into the *Congressional Record*.

The movement's impact on the public and on the administration was enhanced by the way the antiwar argument was presented. As one critic of the movement has argued, those who opposed the war stole the moral issue from the administration early on. That issue, simplistic and naive from a Realpolitik perspective, was understood more easily than the incompetently presented limited war argument. The moral argument, with the bombing and destruction of peasant society as its cornerstone, was echoed in Western Europe as well as in neutral nations. As the war continued, the argument received "disproportionate media attention," according to Walt Rostow.

The antiwar movement plus the course of events affected the intellectual and opinion-making community, which in turn encouraged the activists and weakened the administration. Much of the nation's intellectual elite was associated with the prestigious universities where mass protests began and were nurtured. Both Johnson and Nixon blamed pied-piper professors on those campuses, more than students, for their problems there.

Whether their animosity was properly targeted, Johnson and Nixon should have expected the criticism from those opinion leaders. Irving Kristol contends that "no modern nation ever constructed a foreign policy acceptable to its intellectuals." Perhaps, but American intellectuals were not especially dovish in 1964 and 1965. By 1970, however, according to one survey, intellectuals were overwhelmingly antiwar, with more than two-thirds changing their views during the preceding years. Their favorite journals, the *New York Times*, the *New Yorker*, and the *New York Review of Books*, influenced them, and the journals, in turn, were influenced by many of the intellectuals themselves.

The alienation of the American intellectual elite did not affect the policymakers directly, in part because there was little contact between that elite and the Oval Office. That was to be expected. At the same time, the desertion of the intellectuals had an indirect impact on government officials. In a trickle-down effect, Democratic party leaders, as well as those members of the public who took their lead from favorite writers and professors, were influenced by the desertion from the cold war foreign policy consensus of many liberal intellectuals. "Trickle down" is even too vague a term to describe the relationship between intellectual discontent and the rise of the [Robert] Kennedy opposition faction within the party after 1965.

Kristol may have been correct about intellectuals generally disapproving of a nation's foreign policy, especially a policy that appears to be amoral or immoral, but it is the extent of that disapproval and the passion with which it was held that is important on the Vietnam issue. It is difficult for a democracy to operate effectively in the international sphere without the support of its intellectual leadership.

It is also clear that the disaffection of intellectuals and elite college students affected establishment types outside of government who feared for the future of their country. Respected leaders such as Dean Acheson and Clark Clifford, who worried about the establishment in the next generation, ultimately urged the administration to cut its losses before the country fell apart.

Antiwar protests, among others, in a period that witnessed unprecedented rowdy demonstrations, took a physical and emotional toll on the occupants of the White House. Neither Johnson nor Nixon could tolerate criticism, even when they expected it from the media or from liberals. Both were subjected to the most extensive and abusive criticism of any twentieth-century president. On occasion, they and their advisers went to great lengths to avoid the demonstrators, who nevertheless managed to appear almost every time the presidents stepped out of the White House. Johnson, in particular, was irritated by the incessant public manifestations of displeasure with his policies and that irritation may have been a background variable in his decision to leave Washington for the peace of his ranch.

Both Johnson and Nixon developed offensives against their critics, especially in the movement, which included the mobilization of the CIA and FBI to monitor and harass them. Both claimed that such activities were not a product of their own concern with demonstrations but their fear that Hanoi would misinterpret them. Further, both believed that some, if not most, of the antiwar movement was foreign inspired and financed; the government had to devote considerable energies to defend the country against subversion.

On the latter charge, they were mistaken. The intelligence agencies concluded in report after report that foreign influences in the antiwar movement were marginal. On the other hand, their major contention that the movement and all of its manifestations encouraged Hanoi is no doubt true. The key question, and an imponderable one at that, is whether that encouragement prolonged the war.

Without a strong antiwar movement that limited the administration's abilities to pursue a tougher military policy, goes the prolongation argument, the North Vietnamese would have accepted a half a loaf and the war would have ended much sooner. The antiwar movement here is linked to the general development of antiwar attitudes among the public.

The contest for the public's support between the government and its opponents was an important element in the making of Vietnam policy. For example, when Richard Nixon committed Washington to a Vietnamization program, domestic opinion was one "crucial variable." Vietnamization would convince the public that the war was not endless; the American commitment would decrease gradually. Domestic support would be maintained that would convince the North Vietnamese not to count on the American people to force Nixon's negotiating hand. There was a "logical flaw" in this position. If Vietnamization cooled dovish fervor in the United States, it also revealed the light at the end of the tunnel for Hanoi. Why negotiate when the last American soldier would depart Vietnam in the foreseeable future?

Moreover, the prolongation-of-the-war argument deemphasizes the commitment of Hanoi to fight on virtually forever for its goal of an independent communist Vietnam. Further, one of the major reasons Johnson and Nixon did not use tougher tactics was their fear that the Russians and Chinese might be compelled to intervene to rescue their socialist ally.

The ability to employ tougher military tactics was not just crippled by an alert antiwar movement. It is likely that the population in general, with or without the leadership of antiwar critics, would not have countenanced the bombing of the dikes in the North or the use or threatened use of tactical nuclear weapons. Americans would not have needed the movement to express their strong displeasure over the employment of such drastic means in a limited war. Here, the administrations caused their own problems. By never explaining in a convincing fashion why the war was so important, Johnson and Nixon found it impossible to escalate in a manner that would only be justified in a full-scale war vital to America's very survival. Johnson kept a low theoretical profile in the years from 1965 through 1967, in part to avoid encouraging the growth of the antiwar movement. We have come full circle. Although only strong presidential leadership and a declaration of national emergency would have given the presidents the backing to employ tougher tactics, one of the reasons they eschewed that approach was the fear of arousing the antiwar movement.

It is true that once Nixon talked and acted tougher in 1972, the communists accepted less than the whole loaf at the bargaining table. Whether that would have been the case before détente neutralized the Soviet Union, as well as before the destruction and the disbanding of the antiwar movement, is a difficult question.

Irrespective of the validity of the argument that the movement prolonged the war by encouraging Hanoi, Johnson and Nixon *believed* that the North Vietnamese counted on American opinion, influenced by the movement, as one of its main allies. Both administrations considered this alleged factor as they constructed their political and military strategies. Here, then, is irrefutable evidence of the impact of the movement on policymaking during the war, if only indirect impact.

Some critics ignore the movement and opinion and point to the media, where dissenters and dissenting commentators turned the nation around on the war. Unfair to both Johnson and Nixon, the media allegedly created the movement and undermined both administrations. George Christian thinks the press was lost by 1967. Hubert Humphrey saw the media in 1968, the crucial year of decision, as "viscerally and intellectually" anti-Johnson. In a similar vein, Edith Efron described television network news on Vietnam in the fall of 1969 as reflecting an antiadministration bias. Finally, the media were undoubtedly important in the popular understanding of Tet.

Former antiwar leader and sociologist Todd Gitlin, who does not agree with such criticism, nevertheless points out that movement ideas and activities were publicized by the media. One of his old colleagues, David Dellinger, has written that the movement had three explicit targets—the government, the public, and the activists themselves. Especially in the early days, when the public and government were not listening, media attention provided gratification for the foot soldiers who continued to turn out for the demonstrations. As the movement picked up steam, the media helped to legitimize dissent.

For the most part, however, experts do not agree with the theory of an "oppositional" media. In a study comparable to but more sophisticated than Efron's, Daniel Hallin concluded that at least as far as the *New York Times* and television news were concerned, both administrations received more than a fair break from the media. Another expert, Herbert Gans, demonstrated how, early in the war, Lyndon Johnson dominated the airwaves. Even when critical reports came in from the field through 1967, editors in New York and elsewhere either did not print them or toned them down.

Presidents' views dominate the media until major reference figures from the establishment begin to disagree with them and appear in such numbers that the media are forced to cover their criticism. Both Johnson and Nixon began with overwhelming support in the media, which declined over time. Their slowly developing criticism was legitimate and generally without malice. The presidents' failing and controversial policies, as well as their own growing antagonism to the media, led to an entirely understandable decrease in media support. Johnson, for example, blamed the media for creating the credibility gap, when in fact it was his invention.

Even the Tet argument used by the media critics can be turned around to support the notion that the press and television were more than fair to Johnson. One reason for widespread public concern over Tet was the failure of the media to prepare the nation for such an event because it accepted so uncritically the light-at-the-end-of-the-tunnel pronouncements from Washington.

The relationships between the media, the movement, public opinion, and foreign policy are complicated. They are far too complicated to blame the media for the decline of support over time for the Johnson and Nixon policies.

The antiwar movement succeeded in capturing the attention of Johnson and Nixon and affecting their policies in Vietnam. One of the important lessons one can learn from studies such as this is that government officials do not always behave the way they should according to the neat academic models of opinion formation and policymaking. Johnson and Nixon simply did not behave rationally on many occasions when they confronted media criticism and antiwar demonstrations. Surprisingly thin-skinned for professional politicians, they overreacted to criticism in unpredictable and unstructured manners. One never knew when a few demonstrators in front of the White House, or a speech on a college campus, or an editorial in the *Washington Post* might set off one or the other, even at times when they enjoyed the support of the vast majority of their constituents.

It might well be that there is less to learn here than one might suspect. Johnson and Nixon were unusual residents of the Oval Office. Both were among the most volatile, unstable, and maybe even pathological of recent presidents. Comparing their behavior and personalities to those of Roosevelt, Truman, Eisenhower, Kennedy, Ford, Carter, and Reagan, one must be leery about generalizing from Johnson and Nixon to all presidents.

Yet, as I was told time and again by such experienced presidential counselors and observers as Bryce Harlow, George Reedy, and Jack Valenti, much of the time, *all* presidents are just like everyone else. They react to criticism and challenges, even from a minority of their constituents, quite often from the gut and not from the brain. What this means is that those who exercise their rights as citizens to gather, protest, and petition in comparatively small numbers have more of an impact on their leaders than one would expect. Such a conclusion might help to sustain others who question present and future foreign policies.

American Public Opinion Toward the War

WILLIAM L. LUNCH AND PETER W. SPERLICH

Barefoot empiricism takes a few steps forward (we hope) in the following pages. We present data on the flow of American public attitudes concerning the war in Vietnam over a nine-year period (1964–73) both in the aggregate and broken down into the most notable demographic groups. This type of review strikes us as useful both because of the potential historical interest in such information and because we include summaries of the policy preferences of the American people during the war in Vietnam which we have not found elsewhere. In addition, during the war, it was difficult to find objective sources on this subject, and those who attempted to be objective were often accused of bias.

The rancor over the war and attitudes towards it are not surprising. After all, midway through the most visible phase of our involvement in Vietnam, the war there was mentioned more often than any other topic as the most important problem facing the nation. Debate among political elites over the wisdom of our role in the Vietnamese war was quite intense by the time of the 1966 national elections, and there were fist fights in the streets between mass supporters and opponents of the war a few years later. Claims and counter-claims about the preferences of "the people" flew fast and thick during this period. Part of our purpose, then, is to set the record straight.

But, like Huck Finn, while we may be barefoot, we hope to at least raise some larger questions which arise out of the American reaction to the war in Vietnam. Most notably, the war in Vietnam seems to have

William L. Lunch and Peter W. Sperlich, "American Public Opinion and the War in Vietnam," *Western Political Quarterly*, 32 (March, 1979), excerpts from pp. 21–44. Reprinted by permission.

altered, at least temporarily, the normal relationship between elites and masses in the area of foreign policy (in which elites are able to direct foreign policy largely unimpeded by masses). We comment upon this development and upon the possibility that Vietnam may have been sufficiently traumatic to produce a more permanent change in mass foreign policy attitudes. Our thoughts on these subjects are tied to the data we present, and they remain that: thoughts for further investigation.

When the first American involvement in the Vietnamese civil war occurred, in 1955, very few U.S. citizens were aware of it. As the number of advisors and the amount of military aid increased over the next nine years, public awareness of our role there grew very slowly. Even in 1964, when the United States stood poised on the verge of major military involvement, with thousands of advisors already in Vietnam and the size of our role there a campaign issue, two-thirds of the American people "said they paid little or no attention to developments in South Vietnam." This is as would be predicted from the theories of [Gabriel] Almond, [James] Rosenau, *et al.* As long as the administration seems to have foreign affairs in hand, and nothing seems unduly alarming, the vast majority of citizens are content to follow the President's leadership. As we shall see, even when these conditions no longer prevail, the old pattern of apathetic followership often prevails for surprisingly extended periods.

This pattern holds for most of the history of American involvement in Vietnam (if involvement is understood as beginning in 1955). Even if American involvement is understood to have started with the escalation of our military activity in 1965, much of the following period conforms to the predicted relationships. For example, an academic study team, surveying attitudes in the spring of 1966, fully eleven years after the first American troops had gone to Vietnam, could report that most Americans would follow presidential leadership in this area, up the escalator towards more war, or down toward some form of negotiated settlement. And, writing in that same year, Seymour Martin Lipset could say of public opinion about the war in Vietnam:

> . . . polls do not make policy so much as follow policy in most areas of international affairs. . . .
> The President makes opinion, he does not follow it. The polls tell him how good a politician he is.

This is a good shorthand statement of the conventional position on the relationship of foreign policy and public opinion. The history of the seven years which followed seem to make some revision of this view necessary.

The first indication that part of the American general (or mass) public was beginning to deviate from the expected patterns of opinion about Vietnam began to appear within about a year of the 1965 escalation, though it could hardly be recognized as such at that time. Now, in clearer hindsight we 'can see that popular uneasiness certainly began to set in by 1967, and perhaps as early as mid-1966. Increasing numbers of people began to tell pollsters that it was a "mistake" for the United States to become involved in the Vietnamese war. In this relatively mild fashion, doubt about the

Table 1   Support for the War as Measured by "No" Responses to the Mistake Question

Question asked: "In view of developments since we entered the fighting in Vietnam, do you think the U.S. made a mistake sending troops to fight in Vietnam?" (Gallup)

DATE	% NO	DATE	% NO
August 1965	61	August 1968	35
March 1966	59	October 1968	37
May 1966	49	February 1969	39
September 1966	48	October 1969	32
November 1966	51	January 1970	33
February 1967	52	April 1970	34
May 1967	50	May 1970	36
July 1967	48	January 1971	31
October 1967	44	May 1971	28
December 1967	46		
February 1968	42	At this point, Gallup stopped asking this question.	
March 1968	41		
April 1968	40		

Vietnam war begins to appear in public opinion polls on the subject. Nevertheless, very few people were bold enough to favor any real change in American *policy* in Vietnam. The initial popular reaction to escalation of the U.S. role there was to support administration policy even more than before. After a little less than a year of this stance, more Americans began to favor escalation of the war, and in 1967 this became the preferred policy of most Americans for a short time. Even in this, it might be argued that the general public was following the lead of the President, since administration policy was to slowly escalate American effort in Vietnam (more men, more money) as time went along. Still later, only after years of punishment from the war, did the American people begin to support withdrawal in a major way. By the time direct American involvement in the Vietnam war ended in 1973, complete withdrawal had become the majority preference, despite administration opposition to this course. . . .

The movement of public opinion about the war in Vietnam illustrates our contention that popular views concerning it began conventionally enough but eventually changed and produced a reordering of relationships in public opinion which may be reflective of a deeper change in the way American masses and elites now relate to one another in the area of foreign policy. As noted earlier, except for a very small group, Americans were only dimly aware of events in Vietnam, even a decade after our initial involvement there. But wars have a way of activating opinions, particularly if they go badly. If one takes the "mistake" question as a rough indicator of unfocused uneasiness and doubt about the war in Vietnam, it is clear that the efforts of both the Johnson and Nixon administrations to justify the war were failures. Though they were not prepared for a considerable period to support alternative policies, Americans did register their increasing disenchantment with the war by means of answers to the mistake question, as Table 1 . . . indicate[s].

After an initial "rally-round-the-flag" (or "round-the-President") period the American people slowly began to move away from simple acceptance of administration policy. Support for presidential policy in Vietnam declined steadily during 1966, while preferences for escalation grew. In 1967, escalation became the preferred policy of most Americans for a short time. Then, in 1968, the proportion of the public which preferred this course began to drop off. Escalation continued to lose favor until 1970, when pollsters stopped asking respondents whether they favored that course. By the end of direct American involvement in Vietnam most citizens considered the prospect of renewed military efforts there as unpalatable; at the time of the Paris peace accords in 1973, 79 percent of the public opposed the reintervention of American military troops in Vietnam even "if North Vietnam were to try to take over South Vietnam."

The figures on withdrawal sentiment tell a quite different story. They indicate that for a long period from late 1964 to late 1968, support for this option never extended beyond 20 percent. In 1967, as escalation sentiment was reaching its high point, preference for withdrawal went down to 6 percent. From this low point, it began to recoup, but it was not until after the 1968 election that preferences for withdrawal finally broke through the 20 percent level. Thereafter, despite a few reverses, preference for withdrawal increased steadily until this became the preferred policy among the American people. . . .

It is notable that by the end of American involvement in Vietnam, popular opinion had taken a clear position in opposition to administration policy on further aid to that country and that this opposition did not later change in the face of appeals from President Ford for further aid to the American-backed regime in Saigon. In light of support from the public for Presidents when crisis situations have occurred in the past, this resolute (or stubborn) position by the people would have been particularly difficult to predict using the standard model of public opinion. In the past, presidential decisions in times of international crisis have been not only accepted but lauded by the public—no matter what the nature of the decision was. Kennedy reached the highest peaks of public approval during his administration soon after the disastrous Bay of Pigs invasion while Eisenhower was helped in the 1956 election by his pacific response to the Suez crisis.

How can this new pattern be explained? What were the dynamics behind this reversal of preference, from escalation to withdrawal, from acceptance to resistance of administration policy? To answer this question, we must return to the beginning, to see how answers to the mistake question and policy preferences fit together. When this is done, four stages can be discerned in American reaction to the war in Vietnam. There is, first, the "innocence" phase, which starts with the initial polls about Vietnam in 1964 and extends to the "rally-round-the-flag" phenomenon in mid-1965. The second period might be called the "permissive majority" phase—it is visible from mid-1965 for nearly a year, until roughly the spring, 1966. The third stage could be called the "escalation" phase, and it extends from mid-1966 until late 1967 or early 1968. The late period, the "withdrawal" phase, encompasses most of 1968 and the years which followed, until direct military involvement was terminated in 1973.

1. From Innocence to Rally-Round the Flag

Before the introduction of American combat troops into Vietnam, as noted above, most people here were frankly unaware of the situation in that country. Among those who had paid attention to developments there, some uncertainty about the American role is reflected in the November 1964 sentiments for withdrawal *and* escalation, both of which were higher before the United States escalated its role in the Vietnam war in April 1965 than after that date. . . . The dramatic events surrounding the introduction of some two hundred thousand American troops into Vietnam caused two phenomena to overtake the policy-preference figures simultaneously. First, the rally-round-the-flag sentiment manifested itself among those who had held an opinion at odds with the administration before the escalation, and second, large numbers of citizens who would have otherwise remained unaware of the developments in Southeast Asia began to pay some attention. Their initial reaction was to support the President and the official policy of intervention. The percentages for both withdrawal and escalation dropped off within a month of the major American commitment.

2. A Permissive Majority

This period, which stretches for almost a year, finds both escalation and withdrawal sentiment reduced. It was during this time, from the middle of 1965 until roughly the spring of 1966 that Americans were attentive to the administration's justification of United States involvement in Vietnam. In effect, this was the period when most citizens were willing to give the new war policy a chance to work. When the results of this support were not encouraging, restlessness and uncertainty began to set in, in the form of larger numbers who began to say that U.S. involvement in Vietnam was a mistake. Between March and May 1966, the percentage of support for the war measured in this way dropped ten points. At the same time, escalation sentiment was beginning to build up. By this time (spring and early summer 1966), nearly all Americans were aware of developments in Vietnam; when the University of Michigan did its biennial survey in 1966, it had to disqualify only 7 percent of the respondents from answering questions about Vietnam due to lack of familiarity with the issue.

3. A Preference for Escalation

1967 was the year of the hawk. Escalation became the preference of most Americans while withdrawal sentiment dropped off to very small proportions. . . . It may be that the American people accepted the idea that there was a need for American participation in the Vietnamese war, but most felt that our efforts were not sufficiently vigorous to bring it to a rapid conclusion. It was during this period that the highest level of American troop concentration in Vietnam was reached. Doubt and anxiety about this role in Southeast Asia are reflected in a continuing slide in support figures as measured by the mistake question. By the middle of 1967, when escalation sentiment was at its highest point, the number of citizens who supported our involvement in Vietnam (by responding that the war was *not* a mistake) dropped permanently under 50 percent. During this period, nevertheless, the typical response of the well-known man in the street was to call for more military effort.

4. Disillusionment and Withdrawal

By November 1967, when escalation sentiment reached its highest point, there were over half a million American troops in Vietnam and the U.S. government was spending more than a billion dollars a month for the war. Still, no end to the war seemed in sight. The American public started to shift its preference from escalation to withdrawal. By November 1968, withdrawal sentiment had regained its old high-water mark at 19 percent, and after the election it continued to increase. One change which made this alteration in attitudes possible was that by 1968 opinions about the war had begun to crystalize. Philip Converse and Howard Schuman defined the process with respect to Vietnam: "Although there was a time when most Americans lacked enough information about Vietnam to form solid judgments on the nation's involvement there, experience has mounted steeply in terms of deaths, taxes, and soldiers not home for Christmas."

Another important difference after the 1968 election was recognition by mass publics that there were elites, perceived as legitimate, who opposed the war and wanted to withdraw. Antiwar demonstrations had not convinced most citizens that the United States was morally wrong in being in Vietnam and may have even slowed the development of withdrawal sentiment by acting as a negative reference point. On the other hand, during the 1968 presidential campaign, political leaders such as Robert Kennedy and Richard Nixon began to question the wisdom of our participation in the Vietnamese war. Political figures such as these, perceived as legitimate, apparently had a considerable impact on the thinking of Americans who considered themselves loyal and patriotic.

One interpretation of the public opinion figures after 1968 would emphasize that in 1969, President Nixon began a policy of slow, phased withdrawals of American troops from Vietnam, so this alternative had some support even in the White House. Another interpretation of the surge in withdrawal sentiment might be that in keeping with the opinion crystallization found by Converse and Schuman, attitudes began to turn against continued involvement in the Vietnam conflict largely independent of administration policies. By 1969 or 1970, such views certainly found more support and encouragement from more traditionally acceptable opinion leaders than in earlier years, and so identification with the disliked "protestors" did not pose such a problem for the average citizen.

No matter what the interpretation of this dovish shift (and we believe that both processes were at work simultaneously)—the effect of these events and experiences can be seen in the fact that between November 1964 and November 1968, withdrawal sentiment never rose above 19 percent, and from the low point reached in May 1967 (at 6 percent) it took eighteen months for it to regain that position. In the next comparable period withdrawal sentiment rose at a much faster pace. Put another way, from May 1967 to November 1968, sentiment for withdrawal grew at a pace of roughly seven tenths of a percentage point a month. Between November 1968 and September 1970, withdrawal sentiment increased from 19 to 55 percent, or at a monthly rate more than double the previous one. . . .

Near the end of American military involvement in Vietnam, the mistake and policy alternative questions converged again. In January 1971, Gallup found that only 31 percent of his respondents felt that the war in Vietnam was *not* a mistake, and at the same time a dichotomized question which asked if respondents favored or opposed withdrawal from Vietnam found only 28 percent opposed to withdrawal. Four months later Gallup found precisely the same percentage of his respondents who still felt that the war in Vietnam was not a mistake. So although the mistake question shows a slow, steady erosion in support for the war over a period of many years while the changes in policy preferences were far more dramatic, both questions finally settled to a very similar low level of war support.

5. A Post-Script: Wishing It Would All Go Away

Following the withdrawal of American combat troops from Vietnam, most Americans appear to have taken an attitude of studied indifference or even hostility to events in Southeast Asia. As reported above, when the Paris peace accords were signed, Gallup found widespread opposition to any continuing U.S. military role in South Vietnam. Later, as the American-backed regime in Saigon collapsed, more than three-quarters of the American people opposed sending it military aid, and a majority opposed even allowing the former U.S. clients to resettle in the United States.

Opinion about Vietnam may be a special case because of the great domestic unhappiness associated with that country; it may still be that on other foreign policy issues elites retain the freedom of action they enjoyed prior to the Vietnam war, but it may also be that domestic public opinion now constitutes a greater constraint for foreign policy makers, at least where the decision is perceived as having implications of U.S. military involvement. No matter what the actual predisposition of public opinion about foreign policy, elites may constrain themselves if they believe a negative public reaction would be registered at the next election. This familiar law of anticipated reactions is crucially important to the operation of representative polities. That American elites are more cautious in the post-Vietnam era was reflected in reports out of Washington during the 1973

Middle East war. Richard Rovere, the veteran political reporter, wrote, "American opinion, as understood here, will tolerate intervention no longer—at least when the combat zone is so remote."

The preceding discussion has used only aggregate figures, that is, it has reported the opinions and preferences of Americans as a group. In order better to evaluate the change in patterns of public opinion represented by the Vietnam war, it is important to disaggregate the total figures. The danger is that the totals may reflect dramatic shifts in one or two sub-groups, rather than a shift across the whole population spectrum.

Before going to the details, it will be helpful to have a precis of the basic result: We found that war *supporters* tended to be concentrated among the younger, white, male, and middle-class respondents. And this is one of those instances in which reversing the categories *does* provide virtually the maximum change in opinion. A typical war *opponent* was older, black, female, and of lower-class background. In the sections which follow, we hope to explain why each of these groups was located as we found them with respect to the war.

One of the recurring images of the war in Vietnam is that of youthful protestors picketing in massive numbers, singing, chanting, and venting their anger at continuing American involvement there. It is not surprising, therefore, that many people believed (and still believe) that youth and war opposition were highly correlated. The fact is that the reverse was true. As long as one sticks to measures of support for the war (in contrast to support for demonstrators), the younger the respondent, the more likely he or she was to be supportive. . . .

A number of explanations might be offered for this striking pattern, but at a minimum, it discredits the popular theory that since young men bear the burden of actually fighting wars, they will be most opposed to them. As an alternative psychologists might suggest that this pattern is an outgrowth of cognitive dissonance. That is, since young men are more exposed to involvement in wars, they would be more strongly in support of them in order to justify their participation to themselves. Since young females also suffered fairly direct privations in the case of Vietnam (loss of companionship and sex, worry and fear) they would be similarly inclined to need a means of reducing the tension between their beliefs and those problems. Historians might argue that older people have had more negative experience with war. Having gone through at least one World War and Korea, they might be more familiar than younger people with the terrors and deprivations war imposes. Sociologists could say that younger people, being closer to patriotic indoctrination in the schools would be more likely to respond aggressively in a war situation than their elders. Economists might point out that opportunities for material enrichment by young people have been better during wartime than peacetime in recent American history. Anthropologists could note that the American youth culture (especially among boys) emphasizes aggressiveness, competitiveness, courageousness, excitement and adventure—and all these elements have been present in popular presentations of war on television, in the cinema, and in journalistic accounts. Political scientists might add that young people have traditionally had the weakest attachment to political symbols, such as political party affiliation, and might therefore be more subject to government propaganda about war (particularly if it stresses patriotic themes) than older citizens who have had time to develop some independent referents and skepticism about such information. It may be that all these explanations are correct to some degree (or that none of them are). In any case, the striking fact is that the younger a person was during the Vietnam era, the more likely he or she was to support the war.

Converse and Schuman's study of public attitudes towards the war in Vietnam pointed out that "women have traditionally been unenthusiastic about war involvement, and the largest sex differences in responses emerge when policies involving strong military initiatives are at stake." Throughout the polls measuring public response to the war, females consistently exhibit more dovish attitudes than men which tends to discredit the theory of the "greater burden," as did the data for age. The annual mean support figures for the war (as measured by negative responses to the Gallup mistake question) reflect this difference. . . . It is interesting to note that as the war dragged on, the difference between men and women's opinions narrowed somewhat. . . .

Probably the most widely noted demographic aspect of public opinion about the war in Vietnam was the opposition of American blacks. By any measure, blacks were substantially more opposed to U.S. intervention in Vietnam than whites. In local referenda concerning the war held in 1966, 1967, and 1968, black precincts were likely to oppose the war more strongly than white precincts: ". . . race was associated with opposition to the war in Madison and Cambridge, where black voters comprised a small segment of the community, and in San Francisco, which contained a sizeable black population." [A] policy alternative question [posed by the Survey Research Center at the University of Michigan] also demonstrates this pattern quite clearly. . . . Blacks always favored withdrawal more than whites, and by increasing margins as the war dragged on. Moreover, blacks were consistently more unfavorable towards escalation when compared to whites. Ratios of two and three to one were the norm between the races on the question of escalation.

How can these patterns be explained? Generally, black citizens have had fewer positive experiences with their government than white citizens. A kind of generic mistrust and suspicion of white politicians and their works (which white voters were to acquire only after a number of disillusioning incidents) may provide part of the explanation for black resistance to the war in Vietnam. In addition, it is possible that many blacks believed claims that a disproportionate number of combat troops in Vietnam were black (and other minority group members), and that a disproportionate percentage of the deaths in the war were sustained by non-whites. As far as public opinion is concerned, it did not matter whether such claims were true or not; if enough non-white citizens believed them, such belief would probably appear in the form of reduced support and increased opposition to the war among such respondents. Finally, the war in Vietnam coincided with a period of quite inflamed rhetoric in the black community which sometimes branded the war in Vietnam as racist. Whether this charge was correct or not, it may have increased opposition to the war among minority groups.

Thus far, the findings have shown that war opponents were more likely to be older, rather than younger; women instead of men; and black instead of white—are these categories repetitive or additive? Do they make separate and independent contributions? That is, were black older women the most antiwar respondents, and were younger white men the most prowar? We tested all combinations of characteristics to discover the most prowar and antiwar subgroups within the population, and found that the categories are largely additive. That is, by combining men with younger respondents one gets more hawkishness than with only men or only young people, and if one further limits the test to white young men, the level of prowar opinion increases still further. . . .

One of the most widely discussed demographic characteristics of public opinion in relation to the war has been social status. Indeed, the topic has aroused considerable heat, if not light. At first, academic public opinion studies about the war in Vietnam found that there was little difference between respondents of various SES [socioeconomic] levels as measured by education, income, or occupation. The Sanford study found that:

> There is little relationship between such standard status variables as income or occupation and policy preferences on the war in Vietnam. Similarly we find little difference among sub-groups with different levels of education. . . . And neither religion nor strength of religious belief was correlated with preferences on the war. . . .
> The lack of clear relationship between social status and preferences on the war is not unexpected. The conflict, after all, does not involve domestic status politics. . . .

Those of high social status appear to have initially supported the war in Vietnam, much as they did the war in Korea. This was not true of the *best* educated members of society, but such education has never directly translated into preeminent social status in America. As the war continued (probably longer than many had initially believed it would), the well-educated and well-off members of society began to have doubts about it. This *is* a group that pays some attention to the news and is likely to respond to what they see and read. By the 1968 election they had joined the least advantaged members of American society in substantial opposition to the war. More modestly situated citizens remained more hawkish (and supportive) because, unlike the lowest status members of society, they did not have a negativism towards government born of a long history of poor treatment and privations, but their skepticism was not developed as finely as their better educated brethren, and their patriotism associated opposition to the war with disloyalty and other characteristics perceived as undesirable.

This "top-bottom" anti-war coalition is not visible in the Gallup polls because of the broad categories employed (for example, all persons with any college education are lumped together in the "college" category), but it appears in the SRC data, where greater precision is possible.

One feature of the dispute concerning the identity of war supporters and opponents centered on religious preferences. It was sometimes claimed that Catholics were more inclined to favor American intervention in Vietnam than either Protestants or Jews. The evidence on this point is mixed. If the SRC mistake question is consulted ("Do you think we did the right thing in getting into the fighting in Vietnam or should we have stayed out?"), Catholics are found to be consistently more supportive of the war than either Protestants or Jews, . . . but if the policy alternative questions are considered, Catholics and Protestants are found at virtually identical positions. This may mean that while Catholics were less troubled by the general justification for the war (perhaps due to the strongly anticommunist position of their church) than other respondents, they shared doubts about the wisdom of specific policies being pursued with the members of other denominations.

Whatever differences there may have been between Catholics and Protestants, they were quite limited, however, in comparison to the differences between Christian and Jewish respondents. Jewish Americans were clearly the most pacific religious sub-group, even if one disaggregates the Protestants into their various denominational categories. This is true no matter which measure one chooses, and no matter what year is selected for analysis. For example, in 1968, 80 percent of the Jewish respondents felt that the war in Vietnam was a mistake, compared to 64 percent of the Protestants and 56 percent of the Catholics. In specific terms, Jews were twelve to thirteen percentage points less likely to favor escalation and nineteen to twenty percentage points more likely to favor withdrawal as a solution in Vietnam. It has been suggested that non-religious persons might be as dovish as the Jewish population, and this is possible; we simply have no means of testing such a proposition since the number of respondents who are willing to admit that they have no religious affiliation to interviewers is very small. For example, when the SRC interviewed over twelve hundred people across the nation in 1968, only six identified themselves as atheists, agnostics, or otherwise as non-religious.

The Gallup mistake question demonstrates just how powerful the influence of party identification is in the United States. During the period when Lyndon Johnson was in the White House, Republican support figures by this measure are consistently lower than those for Democrats. In 1969, soon after Richard Nixon was inaugurated as President, the situation turned around; members of the GOP firmed up in their support of the war while Democrats slid down a rapid decline. By the end of the year, it was the Republicans who were more supportive and the Democrats who were less— this pattern was maintained until Gallup stopped asking this question. . . .

This pattern is entirely consistent with the perspective advanced by the authors [Angus Campbell et al.] of *The American Voter*, who suggest that party identification provides the average citizen with an easy and relatively painless and economic way to filter and order events and opinions in a complicated political world. That is, this formulation suggests that most people follow the cues provided by their most salient political reference group—their party—and that they follow, in a general fashion, the party line as a result. Since the President is the chief of his party (at least while he is serving as the national executive), Republicans will follow and generally applaud a President of their party while Democrats will tend to look askance at him. The reverse is true if a Democratic chief executive is in the White House. From this perspective, the striking reversal in partisan support for the war in general terms was to be expected.

A caveat concerning this formulation should be entered for the post-Vietnam era, however. Identification with both major parties is down, and the strength of identification among those who remain in the parties is also in decline. Both of these trends are particularly strong among young people. It is therefore possible that future mass reactions to foreign policies will be less dependent upon the party of the respondent than was the case during the Vietnam war.

With respect to specific policies, it appears that Democrats were more dovish than Republicans throughout the war, regardless of which party held the White House. . . . From 1964 to 1970, Democrats were always more supportive of withdrawal and less in favor of escalation than members of the GOP. This may be a function of the generally lower social status of Democrats, of the fact that nearly all blacks are Democrats, and/or that American Jews are predominantly Democratic. It is likely, in fact, that all three of these factors come into play and contribute to the greater dovishness of the Democrats. Sex probably makes no appreciable difference in this regard, since both parties essentially reflect the population mix with respect to it, but the age distribution in the parties probably actually worked *against* the dovishness shown above, since more young people are to be found in the Democratic party than their share of the population would suggest, and proportionally more older Americans are Republicans.

It is hardly novel to observe that American military involvement in Vietnam became extraordinarily unpopular by the time all our troops were removed from that country. The American public, considered both in the aggregate and divided into important demographic groups, clearly became very unhappy with our role there by the end.

What is less clear, but more interesting, is that in the course of changing its view of the war in Vietnam, the American general public may have changed the manner in which it reacts to foreign policies proposed by the President or other national elites. This appears to be particularly true of well-educated and high-income Americans, who are also more often found in the attentive public and among the ranks of political activists and volunteers. Since politically attentive and active persons get more attention from policy-making elites, this development could have long-term effects on the relationship between foreign policy-makers and "the public" (or those perceived to represent the public).

While it is difficult to predict what impact the Vietnam war will have on the structure of American foreign policy attitudes in the long run, a number of changes have already occurred in the aftermath of the war. Greater skepticism regarding government claims, more resistance to government plans, and considerable popular alienation from the symbols of the American political system by the American people have followed the end of American involvement in Vietnam. Attitudes and predispositions such as these make presidential leadership difficult, particularly if skeptical constituents impose constraints on the executive. Under these circumstances, Presidents are also likely to encounter policy-making limits imposed by Congress in response to popular pressures. All of this may tend to reduce the difference between the domestic and foreign policy Presidencies. The distinction found by Aaron Wildavsky between the domestic and foreign policy roles of the President was based, in large measure, on the public's lack of interest in foreign policy matters and their deference to public officials, particularly the President, in this area. The change in foreign policy attitudes, which appears to have begun with the Vietnam war, may alter the relationship between Presidents and their constituents so as to move foreign policy decisions into the more partisan arena dominated, until recently, by domestic policy questions. If this occurs, the shape of American and international politics may change quite dramatically as a consequence of attitudes which initially developed in response to our involvement in the Vietnam war.

✗ *F U R T H E R   R E A D I N G*

Edward J. Bacciocco, *The New Left in America* (1974)

Lawrence M. Baskir and William A. Strauss, *Chance and Circumstance* (1978) (on the draft)

William C. Berman, *William Fulbright and the Vietnam War* (1988)

Paul Burstein and William Fredenberg, "Changing Public Policy: The Impact of Public Opinion, Anti-War Demonstrations, and War Costs on Senate Voting on Vietnam War Motions," *American Journal of Sociology*, 84 (1978), 99–122

Charles DeBenedetti, *The Peace Reform in American History* (1980)

———, "On the Significance of Citizen Peace Activism: America, 1961–1975," *Peace and Change*, 9 (1983), 6–20

Fred Halstead, *Out Now* (1978)

Tom Hayden, *Reunion* (1988)

Godfrey Hodgson, *America in Our Time* (1976)

Milton S. Katz, "Peace Liberals and Vietnam: SANE and the Politics of 'Responsible' Protest," *Peace and Change*, 9 (1983), 21–39

Alexander Kendrick, *The Wound Within* (1974)

Allen J. Matusow, *The Unraveling of America* (1984)

Thomas Powers, *Vietnam: The War at Home* (1973)

W. J. Rorabaugh, *Berkeley at War: The University of California in the 1960s* (1989)

Milton Rosenberg, Sidney Verba, and Phillip Converse, *Vietnam and the Silent Majority* (1970)

Kirkpatrick Sale, *SDS* (1973)

Irwin Unger, *The Movement: A History of the American New Left, 1959–1972* (1974)

George R. Vickers, *The Formation of the New Left: The Early Years* (1975)
Milton Viorst, *Fire in the Streets* (1979)
James Weinstein, *Ambiguous Legacy: The Left in American Politics* (1975)
Nigel Young, *An Infantile Disorder?: The Crisis and Decline of the New Left* (1977)
Nancy Zaroulis and Gerald Sullivan, *Who Spoke Up?* (1984)

CHAPTER

13

The Media and the War

✕

Often referred to as the first media war, the Vietnam conflict was subjected to unprecedented saturation coverage by print and broadcast journalists. Most specialists agree that the stories presented and the images projected by the American media exerted a profound effect on popular attitudes toward the war. Beyond that broad generalization, however, there is little consensus among analysts with regard to the media's influence.

The following questions are among those most frequently and most intensely debated: Were American correspondents unduly critical of government policy? Did their reports deceive—or inform—the American people? Did the media have its own hidden antiwar agenda? Why, if press and television reporters initially favored U.S. involvement in Vietnam, did some turn against that policy? How did they use their influence? Was their reporting fair or biased? probing or superficial? Did the grisly images of war projected daily on American television screens help spark opposition to the conflict? And finally, how great are the power and influence of the media within American society? Toward what ends, and in whose interests, are they used?

✕ D O C U M E N T S

In the first document, an editorial published on February 14, 1962, the *New York Times* offers support for American policy while acknowledging that Vietnam might well escalate into a major conflict. In the next document, former UPI and *New York Times* correspondent Neil Sheehan recalls that nearly all members of the press in the early 1960s shared the government's desire to rout the communists. The selection is drawn from his prize-winning study of U.S. adviser John Paul Vann.

The documents that follow the Sheehan excerpt reflect growing doubts within the media about the war. Walter Lippmann, one of the most influential journalists of his generation, denounced LBJ's approach to the war in his widely read column on January 16, 1967, reprinted as the third document. The fourth document is from the July 10, 1967, issue of *Newsweek* magazine, noting that the war was beginning to make its mark on nearly every facet of American life, raising some troubling questions about the course of the conflict. Following the Tet offensive, CBS television anchorman Walter Cronkite hosted a report from Vietnam; parts of it appear as the fifth document. In the program, which aired on February 27, 1968, he characterized American policy as one "mired in stalemate." *Life* magazine, in its issue of June 27, 1969, took the extraordinary action of publishing photographs of every American killed in action between May 28 and June 3 of that year—a week, it emphasized, of no special significance. The accompanying text is reprinted here as the sixth selection; the 242 photographs are not. Finally, Don Oberdorfer, who covered the war for the Knight-Ridder newspapers and the *Washington Post*, calls charges of media bias during the war simplistic and unfair.

The *New York Times* Supports American Policy, 1962

The question of how to portray the growing American military role in South Vietnam is facing the Administration with a delicate problem.

There are now, news reports say, some 4,000 uniformed Americans in South Vietnam. They are engaged in such activities as training Vietnamese—often in combat situations flying Vietnamese troops into and out of combat and carrying out air reconnaissance and other dangerous intelligence missions. United States ships are patrolling the Vietnamese coast against military infiltration by sea from North to South Vietnam. If Americans are shot at during the course of these activities they are shooting back, and there have already been American combat casualties. Gen. Paul D. Harkins has been appointed to command the expanding American military operations in South Vietnam.

The Administration has been trying to depict the scope of this extensive American involvement in South Vietnam with as much restraint as possible. Some curbs have been put on news coverage of American activities in South Vietnam. The American role in South Vietnam is still primarily confined to assistance to the Vietnamese. American units are not independently engaged in combat. Undue publicity might well inflate the American role beyond its true proportions, and this could compromise Washington's efforts to keep the South Vietnam struggle a limited war.

There should, however, be no concealment of the possibility that what we are doing in South Vietnam may escalate into a major conflict. Whether it does will depend on just how extensively and openly Communist North Vietnam and its supporters, Communist China and Russia, choose to intervene in South Vietnam. The United States would find it difficult, if not impossible, to withdraw from the fight if they do decide to throw in major forces. There is reason to believe they will not do this, that they are also interested in keeping the conflict a limited one. But the possibility of a major war is still there, and the situation is one about which American officials ought to be candid.

"The Truth About Vietnam," editorial, February 14, 1962. Copyright © 1962 by The New York Times Company. Reprinted by permission.

Neil Sheehan Recalls Initial Press Attitudes Toward the War (1962–1963), 1988

Once a reporter had demonstrated that he would endure discomfort and expose himself to danger by marching through the paddies and spending nights in the field—that he would take this soldier's baptism—he was accepted by these amiable and sincere men, and frank discussion followed. On his next trip the exchange was freer. The advisors also noticed, from wire service dispatches printed in *Pacific Stars & Stripes*, the armed forces newspaper in the Far East, and from clippings mailed by their wives and families, that the reporters protected them by quoting anonymously or otherwise disguising the source when the remark or information was derogatory. By the time of [the battle of] Ap Bac [January 1963], I and the half dozen other American correspondents had been out on numerous operations with the 7th Division and were friendly with [U.S. Army adviser John Paul] Vann and his men. (Nick Turner of Reuters, and Peter Arnett, a New Zealander who worked for the Associated Press, counted as Americans because they held essentially the same attitude as their American colleagues.) The American reporters shared the advisors' sense of commitment to this war. Our ideological prism and cultural biases were in no way different. We regarded the conflict as our war too. We believed in what our government said it was trying to accomplish in Vietnam, and we wanted our country to win this war just as passionately as Vann and his captains did. . . .

Ho and his followers were not alone in seizing on Ap Bac. The resident newsmen in South Vietnam also seized on it. We reacted as if we had been waiting for it because, beleaguered as we felt, we *had* been waiting for it. The contradiction between the press reporting of the war and the official version being propounded by [MAAG Chief General Paul D.] Harkins and Ambassador [Frederick] Nolting had grown into an embittered confrontation.

The controversy was another issue of these years that had its origin in World War II. There had been little to argue about once the shooting had started in that war. The threat to national survival was beyond question, and the generals and admirals were sometimes brilliant and normally capable—or they were dismissed. Reporters became habituated to a role that was characterized more by support than skepticism. With some exceptions, the ability to stand aside and exercise independent and critical judgment of basic policy and of authority was lost as a result. In the postwar period the American press remained the most vigorous on earth, but where foreign affairs was concerned the reporting, while often gifted, was weighted toward the furthering of the anti-Communist crusade. When the press did cause

From *A Bright Shining Lie: John Paul Vann and America in Vietnam*, by Neil Sheehan, pp. 270–271, 314–315. Copyright © 1988 by Neil Sheehan. Reprinted by permission of Random House, Inc.

trouble the argument was over detail, not substance. The news media were also being manipulated by government to an extent they did not realize.

At the outset of the 1960s, the relationship was essentially unchanged. The military institutions, and those associated with the military in the running of American overseas interests like the State Department, were continuing to receive credit for a competence and perspicacity they no longer possessed. The reporters of the period were not accustomed to thinking of their military leaders and diplomats as deluded men, and the military leaders and diplomats were not accustomed to reporters who said that they were consistently wrong. The secrecy that shielded the meetings and written communications of the men at the top helped to perpetuate the false impression that they sought and weighed facts in their discussions. The secrecy that in the 1940s had protected the nation was by the 1960s concealing the fact that the system was no longer rational.

The resident correspondents in Vietnam were also questioning detail, not substance. We thought it our duty to help win the war by reporting the truth of what was happening in order both to inform the public and to put the facts before those in power so that they could make correct decisions. (Our ignorance and our American ideology kept us from discerning the larger truths of Vietnam beneath the surface reality we could see. Professionally, we were fortunate in our ignorance. Had any reporter been sufficiently knowledgeable and open-minded to have questioned the justice and good sense of U.S. intervention in those years, he would have been fired as a "subversive.") The confrontation had occurred because of the unprecedented consistency with which we were questioning details.

Our critical faculty did not come from any genius. One of the regular complaints Harkins and Nolting made about us was that we were "immature and inexperienced." Our youth and inexperience made it possible for us to acquire what critical faculty we were displaying. Vietnam was our first war. What we saw and what we were told by the men we most respected and most closely identified with—the advisors in the field like Vann—contradicted what we were told by higher authority. We were being forced at the beginning of our professional lives to come to grips with a constant disparity between our perception of reality and higher authority's version of it, the opposite of the experience of the World War II generation of journalists.

Walter Lippmann on a "Limited War" with "Unlimited Aims," 1967

As regards credibility about the progress of the war in Vietnam, no one in high place has been more candid and informative than Senator [John] Stennis of Mississippi. About a month ago he made a speech describing how poorly we are succeeding, saying that "under existing circumstances,

From Walter Lippmann column, *Newsweek*, 70, July 16, 1967, pp. 16–17. Reprinted by permission.

the American people must be prepared for a long-drawn-out and bloody war of attrition in Vietnam . . . which . . . may result in our being tied down in those steaming jungles for ten years or more." This estimate agrees substantially with that of General Westmoreland who, in a TV interview with CBS on Dec. 27, told Charles Collingwood, who had asked how long the war would last, that "it will be several years. I cannot be any more precise than that."

There is, however, a critical difference in their views. Senator Stennis believes the war could and should be shortened by escalating it without limit. General Westmoreland accepts the official doctrine of the Johnson Administration that he must fight a limited war. But he warns us that this will mean an indefinitely long war.

There is now under way a hard debate on whether to go beyond or to hold fast to the official doctrine of a limited war. That means a war in which the civilian population and the civilian economy of North Vietnam are in principle immune from attack, a war in which American troops are not committed to the occupation of the whole of South Vietnam and the suppression of the rebellion.

These limitations on our military action are the reason, Senator Stennis believes, why—in spite of 6,000 dead, 35,000 wounded, more than 30 billions spent—the United States is not yet in sight of winning the war. Senator Stennis cites "as an example, in the area of responsibility of one United States division there are some 131 villages. In April 1966, only ten of those villages were considered to be secure. Today . . . despite intensive efforts, only eighteen are secure."

Senator Stennis speaks for a growing number when he argues that, if this is the best that can be done with limited war, then the only choice before us is to withdraw dishonorably or to quit using "half measures," and to use any means necessary to compel the enemy to give up the fight. This is the issue which confronts the President and how he deals with it will have enormous consequences.

To hold to the present course will almost certainly mean that in order to appease Senator Stennis and the Chiefs of Staff the President will authorize some escalation, enough to wound but not enough to kill. The war will still be long, hopeless, inconclusive, cruel. And increasingly it will be an offense to the moral conscience of the American people. If, on the other hand, the President goes beyond limited war, and follows Chairman [Mendell] Rivers of the House Armed Services Committee who wants to "flatten Hanoi if necessary and let world opinion go fly a kite," there is every reason for thinking that, having adopted genocide as a national policy, the country will find itself isolated in an increasingly angry and hostile world. That would mean more than watching world opinion fly a kite. It would mean that we would be suspected and hated not only in the Communist and neutral world but in very large sections of the nations with which we are most closely allied. We would come to be regarded as the most dangerous nation in the world, and the great powers of the world would align themselves accordingly to contain us.

It would be a comfort to be able to believe that the President is still in control of the war and that he is still able and willing to review and revise his thinking. He wants so much to fight only a limited war. Why does he now find himself confronted with the agonizing fact that limited war has not worked? *Because limited war can be effective only for limited objectives.* The reason why the President is confronted with the demand for unlimited war is that he has escalated his objectives in Vietnam to an unlimited degree.

The President does not seem to understand that he has done this and that in doing it he has broken with the policy set by President Eisenhower and President Kennedy. The Johnson objectives in Vietnam are radically different from what they were under his two predecessors. Both of them insisted, as President Kennedy put it, "in the final analysis, it is their war. They are the ones who have to win it or lose it. We can help them, we can give them equipment, we can send our men out there as advisers, but they have to win it, the people of Vietnam." President Johnson has made it an American war.

In escalating his objectives he runs the danger of having to authorize unlimited escalation and the unlimited expenditure of American lives and resources to create a new Vietnamese society, one which has never existed before. The objectives which the President has pushed upon the American people are unlimited and no one should be astonished that they cannot be, that they are not being, achieved by limited means.

Newsweek Editorializes About "A Nation at Odds," 1967

The Fourth of July is a metaphor of the American dream—a sacred, self-conscious re-enactment of innocent days not quite beyond recall. All across America this week, the great pageant is being played out for the 191st time. On big-city boulevards and small-town Main Streets, the children will line the curbs waving their American flags at the marching bands, the papier-mâché floats depicting the Liberty Bell, the out-of-step Boy Scouts, the wizened Spanish-American War veterans hunched in the back-seats of gleaming convertibles lent by the local auto agency, the clangorous fire engines. Rhetoric as old as the Republic will boom from thousands of platforms bedecked with familiar bunting. Everything is as it has always been—yet a bittersweet air clings to the festivities. Cleft by doubts and tormented by frustration, the nation this Independence Day is haunted by its most corrosively ambiguous foreign adventure—a bloody, costly jungle war half a world away that has etched the tragedy of Vietnam into the American soul.

Few scars show on the surface. A stranger watching the holiday fireworks show in Detroit, the McLuhanesque march of the "transistor band" in Atlanta (50 teen-agers brandishing portable radios all tuned to the same station playing martial music), the flag-raising in the dusty, historic plaza

From "A Nation at Odds," *Newsweek*, 70, July 10, 1967, pp. 16–17, 20. Reprinted by permission.

of Sonoma (where the California Bear Republic was proclaimed 121 years ago) could easily mistake America for an omnipotent, blessedly prosperous land at peace. No war fever grips the countryside, no gasoline ration stamps dot the car windshields, no Gold Stars decorate picture windows. The casualty lists run inconspicuously on the inside pages of newspapers; wounded veterans are kept mostly out of sight, remain mostly out of mind. Save on the otherworldly mosaic of the TV screen, the war is almost invisible on the home-front. But, like a slow-spreading blight, it is inexorably making its mark on nearly every facet of American life.

The obvious costs of Vietnam are easy enough to compute: 11,373 American dead, 68,341 wounded, treasure now spent at the rate of $38,052 a minute, swelling the war's price by more than $25 billion in two years. Indeed, never have Americans been subject to such a barrage of military statistics—and never have they been so hopelessly confused by them. There are no statistics to tot up Vietnam's hidden price, but its calculus is clear: a wartime divisiveness all but unknown in America since the Blue bloodied the Gray.

In the new world's citadel of democracy, men now accuse each other of an arrogance of power and of complicity in genocide, of cowardice and disloyalty. So incendiary have feelings become that close-knit families have had to agree not to disagree about Vietnam at table. Ministers have become alienated from their flocks, parents from their children, teachers from their students and from each other, blacks from whites, hawks from doves. The crisis of conscience has spilled out into the streets—in mammoth antiwar marches like last April's big parade in New York and the "Support Our Boys" countermarch a month later. It obsesses the nation's intellectuals, spawning a bookshelf of some of the most sophisticated political analysis ever produced in America rubbing bindings with cheap charades like "MacBird!"

More than anything, Vietnam has made Americans question their fundamental assumptions about themselves and their country. In the jargony shorthand of the mid-1960s, the problem is distilled into a single, cryptic phrase: the credibility gap. For all its righteous pretensions, has America in fact stumbled into the discredited imperialist role? Are Americans henceforth doomed to fight the kind of distant, painful wars the British waged against the intractable Boers a half-century ago? Is America really in Vietnam to honor its inviolable commitments? To contain Communist China at relatively small cost? To shoulder the white man's burden of bringing democracy to the benighted? Does the military-industrial complex Dwight Eisenhower evoked in his farewell address seven years ago actually call the tune on U.S. policy? If right is on our side, Americans ask themselves, why don't *our* Vietnamese fight as well as *their* Vietnamese? Is Vietnam a colossal blunder? Or, in the hard reality of the nuclear age, are Lyndon Johnson and his advisers right after all? . . .

. . . Not since the 1930s has an American President been subjected to such scurrilous attack as has Lyndon Johnson. And rarely in American history have draft-dodging and flag-burning been so openly exalted as acts of conscience against the "immorality" of the nation's duly elected leaders. As for the thunder on the right—the eggs and red paint hurled at antiwar marchers, the Birchite muttering about Washington's "no-win" policy—it has only intensified the apocalyptic atmosphere.

The excesses of the extremists are only the frosting on the iceberg. The stubborn enigma of Vietnam has confronted reasonable men with a Hobson's choice that erodes the underpinnings of responsible politics—a cruel selection of priorities that intensifies domestic frictions, particularly in the ghettos, even as it pre-empts the resources that might soothe them. And the nation has become so committed to seeing Vietnam through to an honorable conclusion that repudiation of that commitment would unleash shock waves that would rock the country.

Thus, like a neurotic clinging desperately to set patterns of behavior, America is likely to submerge its anxieties in a brave show of business-as-usual unless the war dramatically escalates. Deep in their hearts, most Americans cherish the idea that somehow the nightmare will turn out to have a silver lining—that the U.S. will in the end achieve its limited and honorable goals in Vietnam. After all, have Americans ever failed before? Significantly though, it is the most articulate fraction of the population that has had the most profound misgivings about America's Vietnam adventure. Right or wrong, these thinkers, artists and clerics influence U.S. opinion, however slowly, and the patterns they pioneer will be felt for years.

Here, in fact, lies what may prove the most important long-range consequence of the war in Vietnam. Whatever sorrow or salvation it brings to the Vietnamese, its impact on America is almost certain to be stronger still. Almost surely, the war cannot be mastered without still greater sacrifice on the part of the American people—the latest speculation centers on an increase of 100,000 U.S. troops. And it cannot be lost or abandoned without incalculable cost to the nation's self-esteem.

The day of reckoning could come at the polls in 1968. But more likely it will come later on, after the generation of GI's and dissenters—the heroes and the hippies—take their places at the console of power. Then, the heritage of Vietnam will become visible. The danger is that it will take the form of an excruciating hunt for a scapegoat. The hope is that it will mark the birth of a cathartic realism about the true dimensions of America's world authority and its concept of itself.

Walter Cronkite Criticizes a Policy "Mired in Stalemate," 1968

Walter Cronkite: These ruins are in Saigon, capital and largest city of South Vietnam. They were left here by an act of war, Vietnamese against Vietnamese. Hundreds died here. Here in these ruins can be seen physical evi-

---

Text by Walter Cronkite found in Peter Braestrup, *Big Story: How the American Press and Television Reported and Interpreted the Crisis of Tet 1968 in Vietnam and Washington,* 1977, Vol. II.

dence of the Vietcong's Tet offensive, but far less tangible is what those ruins mean, and like everything else in this burned and blasted and weary land, they mean success or setback, victory or defeat, depending upon whom you talk to.

President Nguyen Van Thieu: I believe it gives to the VC, it shows first to the VC that the—the Vietnamese people from whom they hoped to have a general uprising, and to welcome the VC in the cities, this is a very bad test for them.

Nguyen Xuan Oanh (critic of government): I think the people have realized now that there [are] no secure areas. Your own home in the heart of the city is not secure. I am stunned myself when I see that the Vietcong can come to your door and open the door and just kill you instantly, without any warning, and without any protection from the government.

Cronkite: There are doubts about the measure of success or setback, but even more, there are doubts about the exact measure of the disaster itself. All that is known with certainty is that on the first two nights of the Tet Lunar New Year, the Vietcong and North Vietnamese Regular Forces, violating the truce agreed on for that holiday, struck across the entire length of South Vietnam, hitting the largest 35 cities, towns, and provincial capitals. How many died and how much damage was done, however, are still but approximations, despite the official figures.

The very preciseness of the figures brings them under suspicion. Anyone who has wandered through these ruins knows that an exact count is impossible. Why, just a short while ago a little old man came and told us that two VC were buried in a hastily dug grave up at the end of the block. Had they been counted? And what about these ruins? Have they gone through all of them for buried civilians and soldiers? And what about those 14 VC we found in the courtyard behind the post office at Hue? Had they been counted and tabulated? They certainly hadn't been buried.

We came to Vietnam to try to determine what all this means to the future of the war here. We talked to officials, top officials, civilian and military, Vietnamese and American. We toured damaged areas like this, and refugee centers. We paid a visit to the Battle at Hue, and to the men manning the northernmost provinces, where the next big communist offensive is expected. All of this is the subject of our report. . . .

We'd like to sum up our findings in Vietnam, an analysis that must be speculative, personal, subjective. Who won and who lost in the great Tet offensive against the cities? I'm not sure. The Vietcong did not win by a knockout, but neither did we. The referees of history may make it a draw. Another stand-off may be coming in the big battles expected south of the Demilitarized Zone. Khe Sanh could well fall, with a terrible loss in American lives, prestige, and morale, and this is a tragedy of our stubbornness there; but the bastion no longer is a key to the rest of the northern regions, and it is doubtful that the American forces can be defeated across the breadth of the DMZ with any substantial loss of ground. Another stand-off. On the political front, past performance gives no confidence that the

Vietnamese government can cope with its problems, now compounded by the attack on the cities. It may not fall, it may hold on, but it probably won't show the dynamic qualities demanded of this young nation. Another stand-off.

We have been too often disappointed by the optimism of the American leaders, both in Vietnam and Washington, to have faith any longer in the silver linings they find in the darkest clouds. They may be right, that Hanoi's winter-spring offensive has been forced by the communist realization that they could not win the longer war of attrition, and that the communists hope that any success in the offensive will improve their position for eventual negotiations. It would improve their position, and it would also require our realization, that we should have had all along, that any negotiations must be that—negotiations, not the dictation of peace terms. For it seems now more certain than ever that the bloody experience of Vietnam is to end in a stalemate. This summer's almost certain stand-off will either end in real give-and-take negotiations or terrible escalation; and for every means we have to escalate, the enemy can match us, and that applies to invasion of the North, the use of nuclear weapons, or the mere commitment of 100-, or 200-, or 300,000 more American troops to the battle. And with each escalation, the world comes closer to the brink of cosmic disaster.

To say that we are closer to victory today is to believe, in the face of the evidence, the optimists who have been wrong in the past. To suggest we are on the edge of defeat is to yield to unreasonable pessimism. To say that we are mired in stalemate seems the only realistic, yet unsatisfactory, conclusion. On the off chance that military and political analysts are right, in the next few months we must test the enemy's intentions, in case this is indeed his last gasp before negotiations. But it is increasingly clear to this reporter that the only rational way out then will be to negotiate, not as victors, but as an honorable people who lived up to their pledge to defend democracy, and did the best they could.

Life Publicizes One Week's Dead in Vietnam, 1969

The faces shown on the next pages are the faces of American men killed— in the words of the official announcement of their deaths—''in connection with the conflict in Vietnam.'' The names, 242 of them, were released by the Pentagon during the week of May 28 through June 3, a span of no special significance except that it includes Memorial Day. The numbers of the dead are average for any seven-day period during this stage of the war.

It is not the intention of this article to speak for the dead. We cannot tell with any precision what they thought of the political currents which

From *Life*, 66 (June 27, 1969). Copyright © 1969 Time, Inc. Reprinted by permission of the publisher.

drew them across the world. From the letters of some, it is possible to tell they felt strongly that they should be in Vietnam, that they had great sympathy for the Vietnamese people and were appalled at their enormous suffering. Some had voluntarily extended their tours of combat duty; some were desparate to come home. Their families provided most of these photographs, and many expressed their own feelings that their sons and husbands died in a necessary cause. Yet in a time when the numbers of Americans killed in this war—36,000—though far less than the Vietnamese losses, have exceeded the dead in the Korean War, when the nation continues week after week to be numbed by a three-digit statistic which is translated to direct anguish in hundreds of homes all over the country, we must pause to look into the faces. More than we must know *how many,* we must know *who.* The faces of one week's dead, unknown but to families and friends, are suddenly recognized by all in this gallery of young American eyes. . . .

On the back of a picture he sent home shortly before his death near Saigon, Sgt. William Anderson, 18, of Templeton, Pa., jotted a wry note: "Plain of Reeds, May 12, 1969. Here's a picture of a 2-star general awarding me my Silver Star. I didn't do anything. They just had some extra ones." His family has a few other recent photographs of the boy, including one showing him this past February helping to put a beam into place on his town's new church. His was the first military funeral held there.

Such fragments on film, in letters, in clippings and in recollection comprise the legacies of virtually every man shown in these pages. To study the smallest portion of them, even without reference to their names, is to glimpse the scope of a much broader tragedy. Writing his family just before the time he was scheduled to return to the U.S., a California man said, "I could be standing on the doorstep on the 8th [of June]. . . . As you can see from my shakey printing, the strain of getting 'short' is getting to me, so I'll close now." The ironies and sad coincidences of time hang everywhere. One Pfc. from the 101st Airborne was killed on his 21st birthday. A waiting bride had just bought her own wedding ring. A mother got flowers ordered by her son and then learned he had died the day before they arrived. A Texan had just signed up for a second two-year tour of duty when he was killed, and his ROTC instructor back home remembered with great affection that the boy, a flag-bearer, had stumbled a lot. In the state of Oregon a soldier was buried in a grave shared by the body of his brother, who had died in Vietnam two years earlier. A lieutenant was killed serving the battalion his father had commanded two years ago. A man from Colorado noted in his last letter that the Marines preferred captured North Vietnamese mortars to their own because they were lighter and much more accurate. At four that afternoon he was killed by enemy mortar fire.

Premonitions gripped many of the men. One wrote, "I have given my life as have many others for a cause in which I firmly believe." Another, writing from Hamburger Hill, said, "You may not be able to read this. I am writing it in a hurry. I see death coming up the hill." One more, who had come home on leave from Vietnam in January and had told his father he did not want to go back and was considering going AWOL, wrote last month, "Everyone's dying, they're all ripped apart. Dad, there's no one left." "I wish now I had told him to jump," the boy's father recalled. "I wish I had, but I couldn't."

Such despair was not everywhere. A lieutenant, a Notre Dame graduate, wrote home in some mild annoyance that he had not been given command of a company ("I would have jumped at the chance but there are too many Capts. floating around") and then reported with a certain pleasure that he was looking forward to his new assignment, which was leader of a reconnaissance platoon. In an entirely cheerful letter to his mother a young man from Georgia wrote, "I guess by now you are having some nice weather. Do you have tomatoes in the garden? 'A' Co. found an NVA farm two days ago with bananas, tomatoes and corn. This is real good land here. You can see why the North wants it."

There is a catalogue of fact for every face. One boy had customized his 13-year-old car and planned to buy a ranch. Another man, a combat veteran of the Korean War, leaves seven children. A third had been an organist in his church and wanted to be a singer. One had been sending his pay home to contribute to his brother's college expenses. The mother of one of the dead, whose son was the third of four to serve in the Army, insists with deep pride, "We are a patriotic family willing to pay that price." An aunt who had raised her nephew said of him, "He was really and truly a conscientious objector. He told me it was a terrible thought going into the Army and winding up in Vietnam and shooting people who hadn't done anything to him. . . . Such a waste. Such a shame."

Every photograph, every face carries its own simple and powerful message. The inscription on one boy's picture to his girl reads:

> To Miss Shirley Nash
> We shall let no Love come between Love.
> Only peace and happiness from Heaven Above.
> Love always.
> > Perpetually yours,
> > Joseph

Don Oberdorfer on Charges of Media Bias, 1987

Was the press biased in Vietnam?

Not in the simple use of the word. The coverage of Vietnam was a complicated subject, most of which is conveniently forgotten by one side or the other in the debate. For the American press, Vietnam was a learning experience—much as it was for the rest of the country and the government.

We knew very little at the beginning, but as the war progressed people in the press, along with people in the government who were our sources after all, began to get this very hazy, fuzzy situation into focus. And this picture was not the same picture that was being portrayed in the official reports. We know now, because of the Pentagon Papers, people's memoirs, and other things that the picture portrayed in the official reports was not the one that was believed by many of the policymakers.

One of the things that happened was that the consensus within the government broke down and suddenly instead of having one monolithic viewpoint presented to the press, you had conflicting viewpoints and therefore conflicting sets of sources. And if you look at the stories, it's quite clear that many of the things in Vietnam that were taken as press enterprise [came] from military or civilian officials who knew what was going on and communicated it by the back channels to the press. And they did it because they objected to the policy or objected to the deception about the policy, and also because some of them saw the press as the way to advance ideas which had been rejected from the top of the American government.

✗ E S S A Y S

In the first essay, Robert Elegant blasts his former colleagues in the media for biased reporting. A former reporter who covered Vietnam for the *Los Angeles Times*, he argues that, for the first time in modern history, the outcome of a war was determined by written and, especially, televised, coverage. The next essay, by Peter Braestrup of the Woodrow Wilson International Center for Scholars in Washington, focuses on press and television accounts of the Tet offensive and its aftermath. A former Vietnam correspondent with the *Washington Post* and the *New York Times*, Braestrup also accuses the press of distortion and superficiality, although his attack is less biting than Elegant's. In the last essay, Daniel C. Hallin, a professor of political science and communication at the University of California, San Diego, offers a different perspective. Hallin faults the media for their largely uncritical stance toward the war for most of its duration and argues that they never probed into the underlying causes of the conflict or of U.S. policy. He sees the media as a key component of the modern state, not its critic.

How to Lose a War

ROBERT ELEGANT

In the early 1960s, when the Viet Nam War became a big story, most foreign correspondents assigned to cover the story wrote primarily to win the approbation of the crowd, above all their own crowd. As a result, in my view, the self-proving system of reporting they created became ever

From Robert Elegant, "How to Lose a War," *Encounter* LVII (August 1981), excerpts from pp. 73–90. Reprinted by permission of *Encounter*.

further detached from political and military realities because it instinctively concentrated on its own self-justification. The American press, naturally dominant in an "American war," somehow felt obliged to be less objective than partisan, to take sides, for it was inspired by the *engagé* "investigative" reporting that burgeoned in the US in these impassioned years. The press was instinctively "agin the Government"—and, at least reflexively, for Saigon's enemies.

During the latter half of the 15-year American involvement in Viet Nam the media became the primary battlefield. Illusory events reported *by* the press as well as real events *within* the press corps were more decisive than the clash of arms or the contention of ideologies. For the first time in modern history, the outcome of a war was determined not on the battlefield, but on the printed page and, above all, on the television screen. Looking back coolly, I believe it can be said (surprising as it may still sound) that South Vietnamese and American forces actually won the limited military struggle. They virtually crushed the Viet Cong in the South, the "native" guerrillas who were directed, reinforced, and equipped from Hanoi; and thereafter they threw back the invasion by regular North Vietnamese divisions. None the less, the War was finally lost to the invaders *after* the US disengagement because the political pressures built up by the media had made it quite impossible for Washington to maintain even the minimal material and moral support that would have enabled the Saigon régime to continue effective resistance.

Since I am considering causes rather than effects, the demoralization of the West, particularly the United States, that preceded and followed the fall of South Viet Nam is beyond the scope of this article. It is, however, interesting to wonder whether Angola, Afghanistan, and Iran would have occurred *if* Saigon had not fallen amid nearly universal odium—that is to say, *if* the "Viet Nam Syndrome", for which the press (in my view) was largely responsible, had not afflicted the Carter Administration and paralyzed American will. On the credit side, largely despite the press, the People's Republic of China would almost certainly not have purged itself of the Maoist doctrine of "worldwide liberation through people's war" and, later, would not have come to blows with Hanoi if the defense of South Viet Nam had not been maintained for so long.

"You could be hard about it and deny that there was a brotherhood working there, but what else could you call it?" This is a question that Michael Herr asked in his *Dispatches*, a personally honest, but basically deceptive book.

> "But . . . all you ever talked about was the war, and they could come to seem like two different wars at the same time. Because who but another correspondent could talk the kind of *mythical* war you *wanted* to hear described?"

I have added the italics; for in the words "mythical" and "wanted" the essential truth is laid bare. In my own personal experience most correspondents *wanted* to talk chiefly to other correspondents to confirm their own *mythical* vision of the war. Even newcomers were pre-committed, as the American jargon has it, to the collective position most of their colleagues had already taken. What I can only call surrealistic reporting constantly fed on itself; and did not diminish thereby, but swelled into ever more grotesque shapes. I found the process equally reprehensible for being in no small part unwitting.

John le Carré (whose extravagant encomium adorns the cover of the Pan edition of *Dispatches*: "The best book I have ever read on men and war in our times") is, I feel, too clever a writer to believe he painted an even proximately accurate picture of South-east Asia in *The Honourable Schoolboy* (1972). But he brilliantly depicted the press corps and the correspondents' Asia, an encapsulated, self-defining world whirling in its own eccentric orbit. Correspondents, briefly set down in the brutally alienating milieu called Viet Nam, turned to each other for professional sustenance and emotional comfort. After all, there was nowhere else to turn, certainly not to stark reality, which was both elusive and repellent.

Most correspondents were isolated from the Vietnamese by ignorance of their language and culture, as well as by a measure of race estrangement. Most were isolated from the quixotic American Army establishment, itself often as confused as they themselves were, by their moralistic attitudes and their political prejudices. It was inevitable, in the circumstances, that they came to write, in the first instance, for each other.

To be sure, the approbation of his own crowd gave a certain fullness to the correspondent's life in exile that reached beyond the irksome routine of reporting and writing. The disapprobation of his peers could transform him into a bitterly defensive misanthrope (I think here of one industrious radio and newspaper stringer who was reputed to be the richest correspondent in Viet Nam, except, of course, for the television stars). Even the experienced correspondents, to whom Asia was "home" rather than a hostile temporary environment, formed their own little self-defensive world within the larger world of the newcomers.

It was no wonder that correspondents writing to win the approbation of other correspondents in that insidiously collegial atmosphere produced reporting that was remarkably homogeneous. After each other, correspondents wrote to win the approbation of their editors, who controlled their professional lives and who were closely linked with the intellectual community at home. The consensus of that third circle, the domestic intelligentsia, derived largely from correspondents' reports and in turn served to determine the nature of those reports. If dispatches did not accord with that consensus, approbation was withheld. Only in the last instance did correspondents address themselves to the general public, the mass of lay readers and viewers.

It was my impression that most correspondents were, in one respect, very much like the ambitious soldiers they derided. A tour in Viet Nam was almost essential to promotion for a US Regular Army officer, and a combat command was the best road to rapid advancement. Covering the biggest continuing story in the world was not absolutely essential to a correspondent's rise, but it was an invaluable cachet. Quick careers were made by spectacular reporting of the obvious fact that men, women, and children were being killed; fame or at least notoriety rewarded the correspondent who became part of the action—rather than a mere observer—by influencing events directly.

Journalists, particularly those serving in television, were therefore, like soldiers, "rotated" to Viet Nam. Few were given time to develop the knowledge, and indeed the intellectual instincts, necessary to report the War in the round. Only a few remained "in country" for years, though the experienced Far Eastern correspondents visited regularly from Hong Kong, Singapore, and Tokyo. Not surprisingly, one found that most reporting veered farther and farther from the fundamental political, economic, and military realities of the War, for these were usually *not* spectacular. Reporting Viet Nam became a closed, self-generating system sustained largely by the acclaim the participants lavished on each other in almost equal measure to the opprobrium they heaped on "the Establishment," a fashionable and very vulnerable target.

For some journalists, perhaps most, a moment of truth through self-examination was never to come. The farther they were from the real conflict, the more smugly self-approving they now remain as commentators who led the public to expect a brave new world when the North Vietnamese finally "liberated" South Viet Nam. Even those correspondents who today gingerly confess to some errors or distortions usually insist that the true fault was not theirs at all, but Washington's. The enormity of having helped in one way or another to bring tens of millions under grinding totalitarian rule—and having tilted the global balance of power—appears too great to acknowledge. It is easier to absolve one's self by blaming exclusively Johnson, Nixon, and Kissinger. . . .

Journalistic institutions are, of course, rarely afflicted by false modesty. They have not disclaimed credit for the outcome of the war, and their representatives have taken public bows for their successful intervention. The multitude of professional prizes bestowed upon the "big-story" coverage of Viet Nam certainly implied approval of the general effort.

However, the media have been rather coy; they have not declared that they played a *key* role in the conflict. They have not proudly trumpeted Hanoi's repeated expressions of gratitude to the mass media of the non-Communist world, although Hanoi has indeed affirmed that it could not have won "without the Western press." The Western press appears either unaware of the direct connection between cause (its reporting) and effect (the Western defeat in Viet Nam), or strangely reluctant to proclaim that the pen and the camera proved decisively mightier than the bayonet and ultra-modern weapons.

Nor have the media dwelt upon the glaring inconsistency between the expectation they raised of peaceful, prosperous development after Saigon's collapse and the present post-War circumstances in Indo-China. . . .

. . . Any searching analysis of fundamental premises has remained as unthinkable to "the critics" as it was during the fighting. They have remained committed to the proposition that the American role in Indo-China was totally reprehensible and inexcusable, while the North Vietnamese role—and, by extension, the roles of the Khmer Rouge in Cambodia and the Pathet Lao in Laos—was righteous, magnanimous, and just. Even the growing number who finally deplored the repressive consequences of the totalitarian victory could not bring themselves to re-examine the premises that led them to contribute so decisively to those victories. Thus William Shawcross, before his sententious book, *Sideshow*, wrote of the Communists' reshaping of Cambodian society: "The process is atrociously brutal." Although "the Khmer people are suffering horribly under their new rulers," this is how Shawcross unhesitatingly assigned the ultimate blame:

> "They have suffered every day of the last six years—ever since the beginning of one of the most destructive foreign policies the United States has ever pursued: the 'Nixon-Kissinger doctrine' in its purest form. . . ."

Most correspondents on the scene were not quite as vehement. But they were moved by the same conviction of American guilt, which was so fixed that it resisted all the evidence pointing to a much more complex reality. Employed in the service of that crusading fervor was, for the first time, the most emotionally moving medium of all.

Television, its thrusting and simplistic character shaping its message, was most shocking because it was most immediate. The Viet Nam War was a presence in homes throughout the world. Who could seriously doubt the veracity of so plausible and so moving a witness in one's own living-room?

At any given moment, a million images were available to the camera's lens in Saigon alone—and hundreds of millions throughout Indo-China. But TV crews naturally preferred the most dramatic. That, after all, was their business—show business. It was not news to film farmers peacefully tilling their rice-fields, though it might have been argued that nothing happening *was* news when the American public had been led to believe that almost every Vietnamese farmer was regularly threatened by the Viet Cong, constantly imperilled by battle, and rarely safe from indiscriminate US bombing.

A few hard, documented instances. A burning village was news, even though it was a deserted village used in a Marine training exercise—even though the television correspondent had handed his Zippo lighter to a non-commissioned officer with the suggestion that he set fire to an abandoned house. American soldiers cutting ears off a Viet Cong corpse was news—even if the cameraman had offered the soldiers his knife and "dared" them to take those grisly souvenirs. (Since the antics of the media were definitely *not* news, the network refrained from apologizing for the contrived "event" when a special investigation called the facts to its attention.) Cargo-nets full of dead South Vietnamese soldiers being lowered by helicopters were news—even if that image implicitly contradicted the prevailing conviction that the South Vietnamese never fought, but invariably threw away their weapons and ran. . . .

Equally lamentable was the failure of the Western press to cover with any thoroughness the Army of the Republic of South Viet Nam, which over the long run was doing most of the fighting. Correspondents were reluctant to commit their safety to units whose resolution they distrusted— sometimes for good reason, more often because of a kind of racist contempt—in order to get stories that interested their editors so little. Coverage of Vietnamese politics, as well as social and economic developments, was sporadic—except for military coups and political crises, and those were often misreported.

Examples of misdirected or distorted reporting could be amassed almost indefinitely. The War, after all, lasted some twenty years. A former *Washington Post* and *New York Times* correspondent, Peter Braestrup, has published a two-volume study of the coverage of the Tet Offensive of 1968. Quite significantly, it attracted little interest compared to, say, William Shawcross's *Sideshow* or Michael Herr's *Dispatches*.

Nowadays, Jean Lacouture, Anthony Lewis, and William Shawcross (among some other "Viet Nam veterans") clearly feel deceived or even betrayed by the Communists of Indo-China; yet surely, they voluntarily adopted the ideological bias that allowed Hanoi to deceive them. The Vietnamese Communists—unlike their Cambodian confrères—had, after all, openly *declared* their intention of imposing totalitarian rule upon the South. Why, then, were the "critics of the American war" so genuinely surprised by the consequences? More crucially, why did a virtual generation of Western journalists deceive itself so consistently as to the nature of the "liberation" in Indo-China? Why did the correspondents *want* to believe in the good faith of the Communists? Why did they so *want* to disbelieve the avowed motives of the United States? Why did so much of their presumably factual reporting regularly reflect their ideological bias?

The obvious explanation is not as ingenuous as it may appear: the majority of Western correspondents and commentators adopted their idiosyncratic approach to the Indo-China War precisely because other journalists had already adopted that approach. To put it more directly, it was fashionable (this was, after all, the age of Radical Chic) to be "a critic of the American war."

Decisive in the case of the Americans, who set the tone, was the normally healthy adversary relationship between the US press and the US government. American newspapermen have often felt, with some justification, that if an Administration affirmed a controversial fact, that fact— if not *prima facie* false—was at the least suspect. As the lies of successive Administrations regarding Indo-China escalated, that conviction became the credo of the press. The psychological process that began with the unfounded optimism of President John F. Kennedy's ebullient "New Frontiersmen," who were by and large believed, ended with the disastrous last stand of Richard Nixon's dour palace guard, who were believed by no one.

The reaction against official mendacity was initially healthy, but later became distorted, self-serving, and self-perpetuating. A faulty syllogism was unconsciously accepted: Washington was lying consistently; Hanoi contradicted Washington; therefore Hanoi was telling the truth.

The initial inclination to look upon Hanoi as a fount of pure truth was intelligently fostered by the Communists, who selectively rewarded "critics of the American war" with visas to North Viet Nam. A number of influential journalists and public figures (ranging from former cabinet officers to film actresses) were fêted in North Viet Nam. They were flattered not only by the attention and the presumed inside information proffered by the North Vietnamese, but by their access to a land closed to most Americans. The favored few—and the aspiring many—helped establish a climate in which it was not only fashionable but, somehow, an act of courage to follow the critical crowd in Saigon and Washington while praising Hanoi. The skeptical correspondent risked ostracism by his peers and conflicts with his editors if he did not run with "the herd of independent minds," if he did not support the consensus.

The larger reason for the tenacity of the consensus went much deeper. It welled from a new view of *this* War, which was quite different from the press's view of other wars—and from a new messianic approach to the role of the press in wartime.

The main question persists. Why was the press—whether in favor of official policy at the beginning or vehemently against the War at the end— so superficial and so biased?

Chief among many reasons was, I believe, the politicization of correspondents by the constantly intensifying clamor over Viet Nam in Europe and America. Amateur (and professional) propagandists served both sides of the question, but the champions of Hanoi were spectacularly more effective. They created an atmosphere of high pressure that made it exceedingly difficult to be objective.

In Korea, senior officers who were incensed by unfavorable reports would sometimes demand: "Who are you for—the Communists or us?" Most correspondents were detached and could answer honestly: "Personally for the UN and the US, but professionally for neither side. Just trying to tell the true story. . . ." In Viet Nam that response was virtually impossible amid growing Western horror at the "dirty, immoral war." Correspondents were almost compelled to become partisans, and most became partisans for Hanoi, or, at least, *against* Saigon and Washington.

Revulsion in Europe and America sprang as much from the nature of the correspondents' reporting as it did from the belligerents' direct manipulation of public opinion. Some of my senior colleagues had learned wisdom on a hundred battlefields, having covered World War II, the Chinese Civil War, the Viet Minh campaign against the French, and the Indonesian revolt against the Dutch. I had at least been through Korea, the Malayan "Emergency," and the fighting between Chinese Nationalists and Chinese Communists for Quemoy. But most correspondents had never seen war before their arrival in Indo-China. Many confused the beastliness of all war with the particular war in Indo-China, which they unthinkingly concluded was unique in human history because it was new to them.

This much must be said: the best of their reporting accurately conveyed the horror of war—all war. Yet it presented the suffering, barbarism, and devastation as somehow peculiar to Indo-China. It almost made it appear that other wars had been fought by mailed champions on fields remote from human habitation, while in Indo-China, for the first time, carnage brutally involved both massed military formations and the civilian populace. Since a guerrilla war is inherently not as destructive as a conventional war, human suffering and material devastation had, in reality, been markedly greater in Korea than in Viet Nam—and much, much greater on both Asian and European fronts in World War II.

Because Viet Nam did not attract many senior correspondents for extended tours, at any given time a majority of the correspondents were new to the complexities of Indo-China. Some could not even look after themselves in combat, the *sine qua non* of a successful—and surviving—war correspondent.

One afternoon in May 1968, when the Viet Cong were attacking the outskirts of Saigon, six young correspondents piled into a single mini taxi to drive to the shifting "front." They were startled when advised to take two or three taxis so that they could get out faster if they came under fire. A tall, rotund neophyte wearing a scarlet shirt paraded up and down the road the Viet Cong were attacking. He was dismayed by the pained abhorrence with which South Vietnamese paratroops regarded him, until it was explained that he was drawing rocket fire. The six clustered around a 24-year-old US 1st lieutenant, just out of the Military Academy at West Point, who was struggling to communicate with the Vietnamese major commanding and, simultaneously, to direct the gunships that swooped low, firing their machine-guns. While shells burst around them, the correspondents tried to interrogate the lieutenant on the morality of the US presence in Indo-China. . . .

The "Viet Nam Syndrome" is compounded of a variety of symptoms, none unique in itself, but unprecedented in combination and devastating in their totality. Wars have been badly reported in the past. Facts have been mis-stated, and their interpretation has been biased. Emotions have been deliberately inflamed, and reporters have ridden to fame on waves of misrepresentation. But never before Viet Nam had the collective policy of the media—no less stringent term will serve—sought by graphic and unremitting distortion the victory of the enemies of the correspondents' own side. Television coverage was, of course, new in its intensity and repetitiveness; it was crucial in shifting the emphasis from fact to emotion. And television will play the same role in future conflicts—on the Western side, of course. It will not and cannot expose the crimes of an enemy who is too shrewd to allow the cameras free play.

As long as the "Viet Nam Syndrome" afflicts the media, it seems to me that it will be virtually impossible for the West to conduct an effective foreign policy. It is apparently irrelevant that the expectations of paradise after Hanoi's victory evoked by "the critics of the American war" became the purgatory the Indo-Chinese people have suffered. Just as many denizens of the ante-bellum American South did not know that *"Damyankee"* was really two words, an entire generation in Europe and the United States behaves as if "the dirty, immoral war in Viet Nam" were an irrefutable and inseparable dogma. Merely equate El Salvador (or any other American intervention) to Viet Nam—and not only the American public, but all "liberal" Europeans will condemn it without reservation. That is all they need to know. In its final effect—what has over the last decade been called "the paralysis of political will"—it will make it especially difficult for the US to honor any political commitment anywhere in the world where small and threatened nations may expect American support for their independent existence. Before they fall to an aggressor, they will have been victimized by "the Viet Nam Syndrome."

It has long appeared to me that the medical and legal professions enjoy one enormous advantage. If they err, doctors and lawyers may be blamed. Yet, except in the most flagrant cases, the client or the patient pays them again for correcting their mistakes—if they can, and if he can. But the media on Viet Nam, it has become blatantly obvious, have enjoyed even greater advantages. Even in the most flagrant cases, they have not been blamed. They have, rather, been acclaimed for their errors. Who can, ultimately, prove it otherwise? The peoples of the non-Communist world have paid dearly for these errors—and may well continue to pay.

Missing the "Big Story"

PETER BRAESTRUP

In overall terms, the performance by the major American television and print news organizations during February and March 1968 constitutes an extreme case. Rarely has contemporary crisis-journalism turned out, in retrospect, to have veered so widely from reality. Essentially, the dominant themes of the words and film from Vietnam (rebroadcast in commentary, editorials, and much political rhetoric at home) added up to a portrait of defeat for the allies. Historians, on the contrary, have concluded that the Tet offensive resulted in a severe military-political setback for Hanoi in the South. To have portrayed such a setback for one side as a defeat for the other—in a major crisis abroad—cannot be counted as a triumph for American journalism.

Why did the media perform so unsatisfactorily? I have come to this general conclusion: The special circumstances of Tet impacted to a rare degree on modern American journalism's special susceptibilities and limitations. This peculiar conjuncture overwhelmed reporters, commentators, and their superiors alike. And it could happen again.

In most American foreign policy crises since World War II, there have been objective factors that assuaged journalistic needs and curbed journalistic excess. One thinks in particular of the 1962 Cuban missile crisis and Hanoi's 1972 offensive, the latter a far stronger military effort than

Peter Braestrup, *Big Story: How the American Press and Television Reported and Interpreted the Crisis of Tet 1968 in Vietnam and Washington*, 1977, Vol. II, pp. 705–709, 711–717, 724–727. Reprinted by permission of the author, © Peter Braestrup, 1977.

Tet. In both cases, 1962 and 1972, there were perceived forewarnings of trouble, a well-defined geographical arena, a widely shared sense of the relative strengths and capabilities of the opposing sides, a conventional confrontation remote from journalistic havens, and a coherent Presidential response. None of these reassuring elements was fully present at Tet-1968. In Vietnam, the sudden penetration of downtown Saigon by Vietcong sapper teams impacted personally on correspondents' lives. The geographical dispersion of the concurrent communist attacks elsewhere in the country led to uncertainty among newsmen about the enemy's intent, strength, and degree of success in the countryside. Journalists' unfamiliarity both with the South Vietnamese and with the relative military capabilities of each side increased this uncertainty.

Inevitably, then, the overall pattern of events in Vietnam in February 1968 was for a time obscure. But commentators and many reporters did not wait. By the time the fog of war began to lift later that month, the collective emanations of the major media were producing a kind of continuous black fog of their own, a vague conventional "disaster" image, which few newsmen attempted to reexamine and which few news managers at home sought to question. Indeed, in the case of *Newsweek*, NBC, and CBS, and of photo displays by others, the disaster theme seemed to be exploited for its own sake. The journalistic fog had thinned to a patchy haze by the time of President Johnson's March 31 speech, but it had not been penetrated by a cold, retrospective light. The record was not set straight. The hasty assumptions and judgments of February and early March were simply allowed to stand.

Was this thematic persistence due to a sudden seizure of "antiwar" feeling among newsmen, an ideological media conspiracy against Johnson Administration war policy?

One must rely for the answer on contemporary impressions and interviews obtained 18 months to two years after the fact—when time and a new set of perceptions had clouded memories. What seems fairly clear is that, in January 1968, there was little optimism among newsmen, as among congressmen, with regard to the Vietnam venture. Many, as we have indicated, were simply skeptical of any success; a few were hostile to the military and sympathetic to the academicians and senators active in the peace movement; others hoped for a negotiated settlement. Hawks were few, except on *Time*. Outspoken doves were rare, except on the *Times*. At CBS and NBC, it appears, there was both impatience with the war's length and revulsion at its horrors. In Vietnam, there was little conversation about war policy; instead, newsmen exchanged anecdotes about the war's various aspects. Overall, there seems to have been no ideological consensus *prior* to Tet that could serve as an explanation for media treatment of the crisis.

It is true that, after the attacks broke, *Newsweek* became explicit in its political stance, citing the "utter inadequacy" of Administration war policy and calling for a negotiated settlement. . . . (That magazine's Vietnam news coverage was more negative than that of the other print media.)

However, *Newsweek*'s editors may have been equally concerned about keeping up with political fashion, with the much more vocal antiwar opinion, with the pessimism of Walter Cronkite and the New York *Times*'s editorial page.

Thus, out of his own experience, and interviews with his colleagues, this writer is convinced that ideology, per se, played a relatively minor role in the media treatment of the Tet crisis. The big problems lay elsewhere, and persist to this day.

Yet, downgrading the ideological factor in Tet media coverage—a factor so heavily stressed by Nixon Administration spokesmen in 1969–72 in their attacks on the "Eastern establishment press"—should not be taken to mean that newsmen, especially those in Washington and New York, were neutral with respect to the Johnson Administration. They were suspicious and resentful, on personal-professional grounds. As was noted at the beginning of this study, the credibility among newsmen of President Johnson, Secretary McNamara, and senior officialdom by 1968 was low. Johnson, starting with his first public budget discussions in 1964, had gained a reputation in Washington for manipulation and half-truths. The public utterances of generals and civilian officials alike concerning the war had seldom been distinguished by brutal candor. And Tet, . . . came after an Administration propaganda campaign intended to shore up support for a long-term limited-war policy that embraced neither a decisive military strategy nor a plausible diplomatic ending. The policy satisfied neither hawks nor doves. Yet, this 1967 "progress" campaign had, in effect, made implicit promises that no unpleasant surprises were in store.

Although they voiced misgivings, newsmen in Vietnam (or Washington) could not *prove* in 1967 that the Administration's professed optimism was overblown. They had to report what the Administration said. But there was an underlying journalistic resentment, especially in Washington, at being thus used, and, when the crisis came, Johnson was not given the benefit of the doubt, as Presidents usually are. As several Washington reporters later noted, the primary reaction of many newsmen in the capital after Tet was to indulge in retribution for prior manipulation by the Administration. Thus, while formal ideology did not heavily flavor media treatment of Tet, to a rare degree the initial coverage reflected subjective reactions by newsmen—not only to the sights and circumstances of Tet itself, but also to the Administration's past conduct.

This coverage was also shaped by habit and convention. The press, and, most strikingly, television news since the early 1960s, have sought "themes" and "story lines" to routinize major developments and to make events intelligible. "Keep it simple," is the deskman's warning to reporters, as much for his own sake as for the reader's. Election campaigns are portrayed as horse races (with front runners and dark horses); votes on major issues in Congress are often defined as "defeats" or "victories" for the President; and, for a long time in the 1950s and 1960s, local struggles in Africa and Latin America were simplified as contests between "pro-communists" and "anticommunists." These ingrained professional habits left newsmen ill-equipped to cope with the unusual ambiguities and uncertainties surrounding Tet. In Washington, the assault on the U.S. Embassy in Saigon came as a crisis piled on top of another (apparent) crisis—the dramatic seizure of the *Pueblo* by the North Koreans—which had preoccupied news managers for a week. Moreover, . . . President Johnson did not seize the initiative in terms of information or decision-making; and although Washington newsmen do not like to admit it, their dependence on the White House for a "news agenda" and a "frame of reference," especially in crisis, is considerable. When the President is vague, or delegates the discussion of bad news to subordinates (as Johnson largely did at Tet), without demonstrably responding to the crisis himself, the government seems incoherent, the future filled with uncertainty.

We have seen that in Vietnam, too, the circumstances for newsmen were at first ambiguous and uncertain. There was the personally threatening combat in Saigon, the looming drama of Khe Sanh, the destructive urban battle in Hue. There were the fragmentary reports of action in other towns and cities. And there was Westmoreland himself predicting a second wave. To newsmen accustomed to the relatively brief, localized rural battles that characterized the war until Tet, the very persistence of communist effort in Saigon, Hue, and Khe Sanh and along the highways was unsettling. The fate of the initially inaccessible countryside, the state of the long-neglected ARVN (suddenly a key actor), the intentions and capabilities of the foe were all question marks throughout much of February. . . .

In retrospect, after all is said and done, the problem for the major bureaus in Vietnam was not lack of *opportunity* to piece together the overall picture and dispel some confusion as time went on. It lay in their initial reactions to the Tet crisis, and in the subsequent preoccupation of most reporters and their managers with more compelling matters, such as Khe Sanh and upcoming enemy moves.

Faced with ambiguities and uncertainty, the major bureaus in Saigon, for the most part, reacted in two ways. The first generalized tendency was to follow standard Vietnam operating procedure, which in turn was conditioned by standard perceptions of "news." For newspapers and AP and UPI, this meant mining and processing the most dramatic elements out of the daily communiqués and briefings in Saigon. For everyone, it meant deploying reporters to the most dramatic action elsewhere. This approach throughout an episodic war had yielded both "hard news" and vivid human-interest "features" for print, and a steady flow of filmed vignettes, oftentimes film clichés, for television. The tendency to head for "the action" (which noticeably faded among newsmen in Saigon in later years) was by no means universal in 1965–68. But it was common to the reporters most respected by their peers. Going to "the action" served the obvious professional requirements of seeing and experiencing the war one had been sent to cover; and it sustained a proud tradition in U.S. journalism. In the case of television, it also satisfied superiors' demands for GI combat stories. On another level, it legitimized (or seemed to legitimize) a newsman's claim to speak with authority on the war; it gave him a certain status. And the risks of brief exposure to danger justified his relative comfort amid so much courage and suffering.

Most newsmen in Vietnam, in their late twenties and thirties, sought the opportunity to witness a prolonged life-and-death drama of major importance to America. But their time horizons were short. Their focus was narrow. By temperament or training they were not "experts," systematic researchers, writers skilled in synthesis; they were adventurers and, to some extent, voyeurs; at their best, on some occasions, they were also shrewd observers and interrogators, and perceptive tellers of tales. To them and their superiors, the inherent drama—and importance—of Saigon, Hue, and Khe Sanh were compelling, and obviously "news." And the concentration of journalistic manpower on these dramatic but isolated stories insured that they were treated at home as the significant "news." What else was worthy of sustained firsthand attention was less obvious; and the media in Vietnam committed major sins of omission as time went on.

The second generalized reaction by the major news bureaus in Saigon was in keeping with the more ambitious, more "intellectual" journalism of the late 1950s and 1960s. It was to "explain" or "interpret" what had happened and, implicitly or explicitly, to forecast the future, especially as the fighting at Hue and Khe Sanh dragged on.

The wire services were relatively constrained in this regard; in passing, to enliven their war wrap-ups, they dwelled on the possibilities of renewed anti-cities attacks or the prospect of a second Dienbienphu at Khe Sanh. Far less constrained were *Time*, and especially *Newsweek*, where "projecting the story" was a standard technique. And on television, similar projection was used to lend added "significance" to reporters' comments (e.g., "The war is no closer to an end tonight than it was this morning").

On the *Times* and, more markedly, the [*Washington*] *Post*, some license had been given since the early 1950s to ordinary reporters (as opposed to columnists, whose independence was generally accepted) to "explain" events within the confines of conventional hard-news stories. Here, selected opinions and interpretations were often vaguely attributed to anonymous "officials," "insiders," "observers," or "senior officers," as in *Time* or *Newsweek*. Greater freedom was allowed to reporters when they wrote under the rubric of "news analysis" or "commentary." Foreign correspondents, faced with the task of explaining far-off events to American readers, were allowed the most leeway. They often went beyond observable events, attributed information, and quoted opinion to interpret developments on their own authority.

Such interpretative reporting had long been characteristic of the *Post*'s Washington coverage, occasionally to the point, in the early 1960s, where the analysis got more space and "play" than the hard news being analyzed. "News analysis" came to the *Times* in the 1950s, with James Reston among the first practitioners. The form caused early misgivings on the paper despite Reston's reputation for finding the facts, taking no sides, and eschewing the temptation to supply all the answers. But such fears eased. By Tet-1968, news analysis by *Times* reporters, especially in the Sunday "News of the Week in Review" section, was commonplace.

In the careful hands of Reston, Hanson Baldwin, Edwin Dale (the *Times* economist), and a few other specialists, the technique added considerably to reader understanding of complex matters. But no comparable competence existed among newsmen with regard to Vietnam. Indeed, as we have noted, both the war's circumstances and the media's own various organizational incentives worked against the acquisition of such competence in Vietnam (and Washington). Moreover, the problem in February 1968 for all would-be news analysts was that the Tet battlefields provided an insufficient "data base" from which to draw broad independent conclusions or to "project the story" in many areas. "Herd journalism" and the news focus on enemy threats and localized fighting in Saigon, Hue, and Khe Sanh—however important those battles might be—left many other crucial matters unexplored firsthand. Yet, the very existence of great uncertainty, added to the subjective responses noted earlier, appears to have impelled editors to publish, and reporters (and pundits) to compose, "analyses" of the crisis that would fill the vacuum. It proved a serious lapse of self-discipline. As we have seen, most analyses were the hasty reactions of the half-informed. Fewer than 15 percent of the *Times* and *Post* items about Vietnam were in explicit "commentary" categories, yet this segment of the coverage, often prominently displayed and "rebroadcast," accounted for a disproportionate share of both papers' sins of commission. And the "projection-analysis" technique, used so heavily on television and in *Newsweek*, produced more pervasive distortions.

These two immediate professional responses by major Vietnam news bureaus and their superiors back home—a focus of firsthand reporting on a few dramatic events, plus undisciplined "analysis" and "projection"—underlay the overall failure of the press and TV to cope with the formidable circumstances of February–March 1968. As often happens, these initial journalistic reactions set the tone and supplied the themes assigned to the crisis over the entire period.

The chronically short attention span of the media—four to six weeks in 1968—insured a feast-and-famine flow of information, aggravated by space and time limitations. As is usually the case in crisis, most space and "play" went to the Tet story early, when the least solid information was available. There was no institutional system within the media for keeping track of what the public had been told, no internal priority on updating initial impressions. As usual, the few catch-up or corrective stories later on were buried on back pages. This practice in turn gave Saigon correspondents little incentive to produce such stories. The *Post* was the most obvious example: On eight days in March, no story from Vietnam made page one. The networks cut their "Vietnam-related" weekday evening film reports: ABC went from 42 in the January 30–February 29 period to 24 in March; CBS, 28 to 17; NBC, 38 to 28. . . . For film reports out of Vietnam only, the networks dropped from 105 to 49. *Time* went from a weekly

February average of 99.85 column inches of text on Vietnam at home and abroad to 71.87 in March; *Newsweek*, from 126.10 to 107.50.

The result was that the media tended to leave the shock and confusion of early February, *as then perceived*, "fixed" as the final impression of Tet, and thus as a framework for news judgment and public debate at home. At Tet, the press shouted that the patient was dying, then weeks later began to whisper that he somehow seemed to be recovering—whispers apparently not heard amid the clamorous domestic reaction to the initial shouts.

There is little disagreement among historians or even journalists that the dramatic Tet surprises of late January were indeed shocking—to official Washington and the public at home, and to the U.S. Embassy and the Presidential Palace in Saigon, to say nothing of urban South Vietnamese and U.S. newsmen caught in the fighting. But drama or shock does not automatically mean a decisive turn of events, in this case "defeat" or "demoralization" on the ground. At Tet, the media managers hastily assumed it did, and led their readers to do the same. A mind-set—most obvious in the selection of page-one stories, TV film, and newspaper photographs—quickly developed: Tet was a *disaster,* not only for the highly visible 10 percent of the South Vietnamese population caught up in the urban fighting, but, actually or imminently, for the allied armies, the pacification effort, the Thieu government. Tet, belying the Johnson Administration's "progress" campaign, *thereby* showed that the war was being "lost." Tet proved that the North Vietnamese were the "winners" and their foes the "losers." Tet was a triumph for the wily Giap—in South Vietnam.

Was anything other than allied "defeat" discernible to newsmen in February–March 1968 on the ground? The answer is: Yes, starting about late February. Earlier, the newsmen in Saigon called into question MACV's hasty cumulative totals of enemy losses, and noted contradictions between the first optimistic communiqués and the realities at Hue and on Saigon's outskirts. They were skeptical of Ambassador [Ellsworth] Bunker's early (but ultimately accurate) accounting of enemy failures (no procommunist uprisings, few ARVN defections). But they neglected to echo General [Frederick C.] Weyand's sensible warning in early February that it was premature to add up the final Tet score, good or bad; and, with the "disaster" mind-set, they pressed officials for predictions of future enemy initiatives—forgetting to keep posted on what was already happening as February ended.

Yet, after the recapture of Hue on February 24, the manpower was available, at least in the larger bureaus (AP, UPI, *Time*, the networks, the *Times*), to travel about for a systematic "second look." Moreover, the reporters were enormously helped by freedom from censorship—a freedom not enjoyed by their counterparts in both World Wars and Korea, or in coverage of the Arab-Israeli wars. Thanks to official cooperation and U.S. air mobility, they had unprecedented access to the battlefield. And they had facilities for relatively rapid transmission of film and prose. By March 1, it would have been possible to observe and to report that: (1) enemy military pressure had slackened, except at Khe Sanh; (2) the fighting was shifting back to the countryside; (3) ARVN, despite its 50 percent strength level and some extraordinarily incompetent senior leadership, had held together and fought back; (4) pacification, although hit hard, was not "dead"; and (5), amid many problems and much human suffering, urban recovery was beginning here and there. In short, it was a mixed picture, but clearly neither a military nor a psychological "disaster."

Time made a good effort to catch up. The other big organizations did not. Most of the scattered *Post* and *Times* catch-up stories—dealing with localized recovery—missed page one and landed inside the paper. In mid-March, *Newsweek*, CBS, and NBC were still portraying North Vietnamese troops as holding the "initiative," if only because of a fixation with Khe Sanh. Drama was perpetuated at the expense of information.

Competition did not make for more sophisticated journalism. The fierce rivalry between UPI and AP (with the outcomes judged on the basis of clients' choices of competing agency stories) and among networks (judged on the basis of news program audience "ratings") did not lead to breadth of coverage, and hence to a comprehensive countrywide portrait of a countrywide war. It led, as often happens, to clustering of rival newsmen at the same places, so that each agency "matched" the other on the same story. The wire services put out Saigon war wrap-ups competing for "impact" back home. Competition between NBC and CBS seemed at times a contest over who could shout the same words more loudly.

But in other media, where short-range competitive success was harder to quantify—and where *Time* and the *Times* clearly outgunned their putative rivals in Vietnam—the pressures were less severe, and duplication less frequent. Indeed, in terms of *staff*-written reports from Vietnam outside Saigon, the *Times* and *Post* overlapped relatively little after the first three weeks of February.

Traditional American journalistic skills—notably in reporting what can be seen or heard—served the print media well at Da Nang, Hue, in the Delta, and in some of the Saigon street fighting. AP's John Wheeler and others reported accurately from Khe Sanh, during the early stages of the siege of that base. But the newsmen, by and large, did not *see* very much of the countrywide Tet offensive or its aftermath. There were many gaps in their information (as in that initially available to officialdom). Yet, most news managers at home were apparently willing, even eager, to supply their audiences with quick, imaginative descriptions of the strategy of the "wily Giap," the psychological impact of Tet on South Vietnamese morale, the future of the Thieu regime, the "death throes" of pacification, the enemy's "awesome" weaponry—all mostly based on guesswork and secondhand sources in Saigon or Washington.

Most important, throughout Tet, the great bulk of the wire-service output (and its refined versions in network scripts) and of the newspapers' page-one Vietnam material did not come from eyewitness reports. It was secondhand or third-hand information—reprocessed, as we have seen, several times over. To produce its war wrap-ups, the UPI, in particular, added color and spice—"words that pop out at you"—to the bare fragments.

The Saigon rewrite man sought a specific—a bombing raid, a downed aircraft, a montage of enemy mortar attacks, a "Dienbienphu angle"—to give his lead paragraphs eye appeal for jaded stateside deskmen. All this was conventional journalistic technique, but the accent on such specifics first exaggerated and then belittled the tempo of the war during February and March, since no context was provided. It was "news," but not information. It did not tell us how the war, overall, was going.

Even if one excludes the first week of Tet fighting (which heavily involved Saigon), the preponderance of Saigon stories is striking: 80 percent of all wire-service output (war wrap-ups, official statements, etc.), 80 percent of all *Times* and *Post* staff-written stories—but only 20 percent of TV film reports. (The network anchorman's nightly script, on the other hand, was largely based on wire-service Saigon war wrap-ups, and this script supplied two-thirds of all TV "reports" about Vietnam.) In the print media, news managers did indeed like eyewitness action stories, but unless it was Khe Sanh or Hue, the Saigon "headquarters" dateline got the page-one play. . . .

The Tet experience makes clear the requirement for maximum candor on the part of the President and his spokesmen *before* crisis and for Presidential coherence *during* crisis: Congress and the public cannot rely only on the specialized reactions of the press and TV to threatening events. But, ultimately, the remedies for most of the chronic flaws evident in the 1968 performance of the major news organizations lie with the media managers. Reporters and sub-editors, the myths of the craft notwithstanding, are highly responsive to firm managerial direction, either implicit or explicit. To be sure, reporters may fasten on some events and neglect others; department heads engage in bureaucratic bargaining; habits and conventions of deskmen ("gatekeepers") are strong. Budgets and owner predilection may limit managerial initiatives. Sensitivity to competitive audience ratings (in TV) and to the pattern of client response (in the wire services) may influence news selection. But, particularly in newspapers and news magazines, news policies are what the top editor and his senior editors say they are.

The February–March 1968 experience reflected in good measure a number of management policy failures persisting into the troubled 1970s. There were—and are—no universally accepted "objective standards" in the news business. However, already at Tet, there was a notable lack of management insistence on the "balance," professional discipline, and respect for the "naked facts" so often invoked as journalistic virtues. There was also a curious lack of imagination and common sense.

What did the media manager at home know when the first AP bulletins came off the ticker on January 31? He was not an "expert" on the war. But he knew, or should have known from harsh experience, that in the first days of any battle, any crisis, no one (including his staffers in Saigon in this instance) has a clear picture; that most reactions will be partisan and off-the-cuff; that political Washington, like Wall Street, tends to overreact to big news, especially big bad news. Especially in crisis, even the most authoritative sources speaking in all objectivity may be victims of the fog of war or of sheer distance from the action—a gap in perception and communication which always separates headquarters from field. The manager should have reacted with wariness to first reports—especially in terms of initial "play" and receptivity to "instant analysis"—expecting the situation to clarify, and pressing his correspondents in Vietnam for such clarification, as time went on.

Yet, we found few examples of such calls for clarification to newsmen in Saigon or Washington. By all accounts, queries on substance were rare (except in the *Time* and *Newsweek* system) and largely reflected the conventional instant wisdom at home: Wasn't the Administration covering up something? Wasn't Khe Sanh the important story, a potential Dienbienphu? Most managers did not exercise the traditional newspaper city editor's function of questioning a reporter's more sweeping assertions (a function painstakingly revived, for example, by prudent *Post* senior editors during much of the dogged 1972–73 Watergate reporting by Carl Bernstein and Bob Woodward). Instead, it would appear, some managers joined in the overreaction to Tet, and even exploited it, perhaps because they no longer felt that the Administration could supply them with a reliable context or agenda for Vietnam "news," and they had no coherent framework of their own. Amid the uncertainty and clamor at home, consciously or unconsciously, many managers simply adopted the "disaster" scenario, and thus encouraged subordinates to do the same.

We saw at Tet the first show of the more volatile journalistic style—spurred by managerial exhortation or complaisance—that has become so popular since the late 1960s. With this style came an often mindless readiness to seek out conflict, to believe the worst of the government or of authority in general, and on that basis to divide up the actors on any issue into the "good" and the "bad." It was a predilection shared by much of academia. The Army in Vietnam, then the "military-industrial complex," then the Central Intelligence Agency, among others, became the targets; their flaws were simplified, highlighted, but rarely explored in depth, and then largely forgotten. Harassment of newsmen by the Nixon Administration, followed by the monumental Watergate scandal of 1972–74, seemed abundantly to justify any "adversary" posture. But adversary journalism is, increasingly, as difficult to apply to the complexities of present-day social problems, energy crises, economic vicissitudes, and foreign policy as it was to Vietnam.

For lack of coherent managerial concepts, issues open and close swiftly in the media, like bad plays on Broadway. Only compelling dramas like Watergate and Presidential election campaigns enjoy a sustained run. It would seem that even the managers of serious newspapers and magazines have come to see television, with its emotive appeal and its fads, as a threatening rival worthy of closer emulation. At Tet, the short managerial attention span brought down the curtain while the play was still going on.

Increasingly painful limitations of time, space, and money, and the competitive quest for audiences seem to preclude easy recipes for better performance. As critics often forget, the major media do not constitute an organized, unified information conglomerate, but an array of relatively small, disparate, rival commercial organizations engaged in hurriedly assembling, variously processing, and distributing "news" which, as Walter Lippmann pointed out, is not—and cannot be—the same commodity as "truth." This "system" is easily overloaded in crisis, and tilted, and it was overloaded and tilted at Tet. Yet, some compensatory remedies emerge from examination of the Tet experience. In crisis, the major media manager can remind his producers or deskmen—those harassed gatekeepers—of the need for skepticism, of the likelihood that the "facts" will change and need explicit correction. He can underline the difference between "drama" and "significance," and allocate space or time accordingly. He can discourage instant analysis and prediction. He can order his dispersed reporters to inform one another on the state of current knowledge and to remember the need for a future overview. He can insist on intense questioning of all actors in domestic debate. On television, he can see that a minimum of context is supplied to film reports ("no microcosms" is a good rule). He can order that a running summary be kept of his organization's pertinent news output, in order to detect gaps which need filling in or initial impressions which require fresh investigation.

In slack periods, the manager often must spur his subordinates on. But in times of crisis, the audience is hungry, and journalistic adrenalin flows freely; the leader's duty then is to challenge hasty judgments, while stressing dispassionate inquiry and persistent legwork. In short, he should reinforce the proclaimed journalistic virtues.

A Critique of the Oppositional Media Thesis

DANIEL C. HALLIN

In December 1968 the *CBS Evening News* included an unusual two-part special report on the pacification program. CBS had chosen its topic well. "Pacification" involved the struggle for political support or hegemony in the villages of South Vietnam, and this was what the war was ultimately about—or at least had been when it started. So here was an opportunity, at an important point of transition between two administrations, to pause and take another look at the roots and implications of the war. The report was unusually long for television, a total of thirteen minutes, and it included a long interview with a critic of administration policy (Senator John Tunney of California), a sign that perhaps the old tendency simply to report how official policy was being carried out might be giving way at last to a real discussion of what American policy should be.

How did CBS pose the issues raised by pacification? Here are Walter

Cronkite's introduction to the report and correspondent Murray Fromson's wrap-ups to the two segments:

> *Cronkite.* American officials in Saigon came up with their most optimistic pacification report of the war today. They said that almost three-fourths of South Vietnam's seventeen million people now live in relatively secure areas controlled by the Saigon government. . . . Tonight we look at one of [the] contested areas.
>
> *Fromson (concluding Part I).* So pacification does not stand still. It moves forward, it moves back. But what is the balance? What is the trend. . . . ? An effort is being made to measure this, and we'll look at the measurements in our next report.
>
> *Fromson (concluding Part II).* Another offensive by the Communists would undermine the program. . . . But the momentum seems to be in the other direction. Since the November 1 bombing halt government and U.S. troops have taken over nearly 800 hamlets. . . . The goal is to occupy another 300 of these hamlets by the anniversary of the Tet offensive.

There was no great debate here, nor any reexamination of the roots of the war. The story was structured from beginning to end around the question of the *effectiveness* of existing policy. Reporting on the deaths of two civilians, killed when an American tank fired into the village, Fromson said, "What may be regarded as a military necessity also creates problems for the pacification team." The whole of Part II was devoted to the computerized Hamlet Evaluation System (HES), which produced the official figures on the progress of pacification. That was where Senator Tunney came in: he was not there to debate the wisdom of the justice of American policy in Vietnam, but simply to offer an opposing view on the accuracy of the figures produced by HES. At one point Fromson broached the important question of *why* the peasants of the village chose sides as they did—and not always as Americans assumed they should. "Out of fear or perhaps genuine disbelief in the government," he said, "well over half the people in Ku Chi are still influenced by the Communists." But he quickly dropped the issue, and canceled the doubts potentially raised by the phrase "genuine disbelief in the government": "The hope of winning them over depends on security," he continued, and went on to discuss the effectiveness of the local militias being organized by the government to help "break the grip" of the Vietcong.

Why this purely "technical" approach to a story that could so easily have served as a vehicle to explore more fundamental issues? Surely one reason is simply that it is easier. It is undeniably difficult for a reporter to go into a culture very different from his or her own, in a situation of political conflict vastly different from the American experience, and say anything very substantial about the causes of the conflict or its meaning to the people involved. Add to this the fact that—Vietnam being a limited war for Americans—reporters, like soldiers, served limited tours (television correspondents often served only six months, rarely much more than a year), and that almost none spoke Vietnamese (though at least one member of a three-man television crew almost always would), and it is not surprising that journalists fell back on simpler issues.

But the tendency to analyze events in terms of strategy and tactics, success and failure, "momentum" and lack of momentum is not confined to situations where the reporters are relatively ignorant outsiders. It is a general characteristic of news analysis in American journalism, most evident, in fact, in the reporting of the story reporters know best, that of the presidential election. The focus on tactics and effectiveness in coverage of the antiwar movement is another example. It is related to objectivity, and brings us around to a last look at the political consequences of the conventions of objective journalism.

Here is one final way of posing the dilemma of objectivity: on the one hand the journalist is supposed to adopt, as Lippmann put it, an attitude of "disinterested realism"; on the other hand the journalist is expected to explain the news at least to some degree, to provide background and context, and this expectation is strongest in a period like the post-Tet period of the Vietnam War, when political elites are at odds and the world seems out of joint. So the journalist has to provide interpretation and analysis without appearing to depart from objectivity. And the easiest way to accomplish this is to focus on "technical" questions that do not embroil the journalist in the conflicts of interest, perspective, and value that are the dangerous stuff of political life. It is much easier to discuss with an attitude of "disinterested realism" the accuracy of the HES than, for example, the question of whether American intervention in Vietnam was ultimately good or bad for the Vietnamese peasant.

Journalists do not, of course, only report and analyze events. They also report what people of various kinds *say* about events. But the debate over the war, as it appeared on television, was also very narrow in focus. No doubt this was due both to the quality of the debate itself and to the journalists' standards of newsworthiness. It was, as we have seen, the debate in Washington that dominated news coverage, at least as far as substantial discussion of the war is concerned. There were periods when this debate burst the normal bounds of political discussion; at the 1968 Democratic Convention there was a debate over the origins of the war and the question of whether the United States should have gotten into it to begin with. Later on there were periods when the relative power of Congress and the presidency in foreign policy were debated. But the day-to-day discussion of the war that dominated most television coverage was narrowly focused on immediate policy issues: would the invasion of Cambodia get the country into another "quagmire"? Would the Laotian operation destroy Vietnamization? Did that operation violate congressional limitations on the use of U.S. troops? Should the president announce a timetable for withdrawal?

The routines of what I have called objective journalism had particularly contradictory consequences in the later period on the war. On the one hand they continued often to be a source of power to an administration which knew how to use them to manage the news. On the other, when the morale of the troops was collapsing or Washington officials were at odds, the journalist began to look much more like the independent "watchdog" his critics and champions so often fancy him to be. The journalist clearly responded to the shifting of political boundaries, extending to a wider range of political views the right to a hearing; at the same time journalistic conventions also set bounds on the range of issues that would be seriously discussed. Many aspects of objective journalism contributed to this narrowing of the bounds of discourse. Two have been mentioned: the tendency to analyze events in technical terms and the emphasis on official Washington as the locus of political discussion. To these might be added the focus of most news on specific, day-to-day events: the issue was, "How is the war going today?" not, "What is this war about?" "How did it happen?" "What can we learn from it?"

This limiting of the focus of the news had two interrelated consequences. First, it meant that the dominant political ideology of American society was to a large extent protected from the threat Vietnam could potentially have posed; here is one more important sense in which the modern American press must be seen as an integral part, not an adversary of the state. For certain parts of the American public, mostly among the college-educated young, Vietnam led not only to dissatisfaction with certain policies or incumbent politicians, but to a questioning of basic assumptions about the character of the American political system and the American role in world politics. There was, for one thing, a questioning of the legitimacy of the foreign policy decision-making process, which resulted in large part from the revelations of the official "management" of opinion. . . . And there was a questioning of the benevolence of American power: many came to see Vietnam not merely as a "tragic miscalculation," but as an aggressive war motivated by power, comparable to the Soviet intervention in Czechoslovakia, which happened to coincide with the deepening of American divisions over Vietnam. Some of these issues are now beginning to be debated, and this is no doubt a delayed effect of Vietnam, resulting in part from the fact that the generation socialized to politics during the war is now coming into positions of power. In the reporting of Central America, for instance, there has sometimes been open discussion of the appropriateness of the Cold War perspective that has dominated U.S. foreign policy in the postwar period; there has even been discussion of whether the American role in the region has been a benevolent or an imperialistic one.

But during the Vietnam War issues of this sort were simply not on the news agenda. Never, for example, did I hear an American utter the word *imperialism* on television. On those rare occasions (rare, that is, after Tet) when the underlying reasons for American intervention were discussed explicitly, what journalists did was to defend the honorableness of American motives.

As for the legitimacy of the foreign policy decision-making process, . . . television continued to accord the administration most of the trappings and privileges of authority that previous administrations had enjoyed. There was, of course, considerable discussion of the "credibility gap" as well as debate over the power of the presidency. But the limits of discussion in this area can be seen in the fact that only seven stories in the sample contained any references—and this includes reporting of statements by domestic critics—to deliberate government deception of the public. The most substantial of these was a brief story on the Pentagon Papers, mentioning what the documents revealed about Johnson's 1964 statement that he would not send American boys to Asia. Very little of the substance of the *Pentagon Papers*, however, got into television coverage. The controversy over the leaking and publication of the Papers, on the other hand, being "hard news" rather than "mere history," was covered very extensively.

Vietnam fits a pattern that has often been observed in situations of political crisis: the media in such periods typically distance themselves from incumbent officials and their policies, moving in the direction of an "adversary" conception of their role. But they do not make the "system"— or its core beliefs—an issue, and if these are questioned, usually rise to their defense; this happened with Watergate as well.

More broadly, the narrow immediacy of television meant that none of the larger questions posed by the war was raised in any substantial way in the news. There was no discussion of the origins of revolution ("Guerrilla war, like hives, can break out any time, any place," one correspondent explained). There was no second look at the doctrine of containment or its application to a conflict like Vietnam: should such a conflict be treated as one "front" in a global struggle? There was no discussion of why this war eventually seemed to contradict so drastically the image of war and the image of themselves Americans held when they went into it: Why the violence that came to be symbolized by My Lai? Why the collapse of morale? Why the hostility of so many of those we thought we were saving, even the ones fighting with us?

The reply television people usually give to this sort of criticism is that lack of time makes it impossible for television to do more than deal with daily headlines, and that that function is performed by other elements of the news media: by documentaries, news magazines, "op-ed" articles, and the like. To this I would make several responses. First, a large part of the public learns of world affairs only from daily journalism; the typical television documentary is shown in a low-rating slot, seen by only a small fraction of the audience for the evening news. The levels of American journalism that are supposed to provide deeper reporting, moreover, including the television documentary, share many of the characteristics that limit the ability of daily news to deal with wider issues, including the focus on Washington's agenda and the technical angle in news analysis.

Finally, though it is certainly true that the time constraints imposed on television journalism by the commercial nature of the medium limit what it can do, the limits that result from ideology, culture, and journalistic routines seem much more fundamental. Television covered Vietnam nearly every day for more than seven years, producing hours of reporting on the war. Some of that reporting concerned events of great immediate significance. But the majority did not: it was taken up with routine battle coverage (several days old because most film was shipped by air); reports on technology; human-interest vignettes about the troops; occasional "light" stories about such trivia as what it is like to parachute out of an airplane; and many speeches and press conferences, relatively few of which were of real historical significance. When one looks at it all in a concentrated period of time, it is clear that a great deal of television's coverage had no significant value as information about the war. The problem with Vietnam coverage was quality, not quantity.

The media probably bear a good deal of the responsibility for the political troubles they have had in the post-Vietnam era. Americans went into Vietnam believing it was a replay on a smaller scale of World War II: a struggle to defend democracy against aggression, which we would surely win, not only because we were more powerful but because the right was clearly on our side. Television held this view strongly, perhaps more strongly than the public itself. It didn't work out that way, and eventually television brought the bad news. But it never explained *why*: it never reexamined the assumptions about the nature of the war it had helped to propagate in the early years. So to the public, the bad news must have seemed nearly as incomprehensible as an earlier "American defeat" in Asia: the "loss" of China. The Chinese revolution triumphed just when the Cold War consensus was becoming solidified, and only a few unhappy souls were so foolish as to suggest some historical development might be taking place in China that could not be reduced to the global struggle between democracy and totalitarianism. Add to this the fact that the United States had clear military superiority at the time, and it is hardly surprising that a great deal of the public should have accepted the notion that treason was the only reasonable explanation for defeat. In the same way, it is hardly surprising that Americans should gravitate toward the view that "loss of Vietnam" resulted simply from a lack of American will, which leads easily to the conclusion that the media were to blame: no more sophisticated explanations were put before them.

Did the media "lose Vietnam"? I shall argue that this is not the most important question to ask about the media's role in that war. But it is worth taking up initially, in more precise and less sensational formulation. Could American power have been used more effectively in Vietnam if officials had had more control over the media? Perhaps. But the case is by no means as strong as often supposed.

. . . Voluntary guidelines for the protection of military information worked well. There were only a handful of violations of those guidelines by the press, and there is no evidence that the military considered the press a source of significant damage to military operations. As a strictly military problem press coverage was entirely trivial compared with, say, interservice rivalries, which resulted—to name only one of many inefficiencies—in predictable American air traffic over North Vietnam.

Officials sometimes complained of diplomatic damage done by press coverage. But again there is little evidence that this was extensive. The bombing of Cambodia in 1969, for example, was kept secret, as officials have later told the story, not only to prevent opposition in the United States, but because it was believed that Sihanouk and the North Vietnamese would be more likely to protest if the bombing were officially acknowledged. They were therefore furious when the *New York Times*, using official sources, disclosed it; aside from the *Pentagon Papers* case, in which the courts concluded the government had been unable to show evidence of harm to national security, this is the episode most often cited as evidence press leaks were harming American diplomacy. But it is not obvious that it would have been of enormous significance if these protests had occurred, unless perhaps protests from Sihanouk made the bombing an issue in the United States (the bombing of Cambodia did not become a political issue until years later). And, in any case, it turned out that neither Sihanouk nor the North Vietnamese did protest. The most significant diplomatic secret of the war was Kissinger's meetings in Paris with Le Duc Tho—and this secret was kept.

So the case would seem to come down to the impact of the press on the "home front." This case can be made in a number of different ways. At times, for example, officials believed that if only the United States could send a clear enough "signal" of its resolve to the North Vietnamese, the latter could be expected to back down. And the ability to project an image of unity at home was seen as crucial to the communication of this signal. But the notion that "signaling" by itself would have induced the North Vietnamese and NLF to give up a goal they had been pursuing for decades seems very dubious—an illusion born of the assumption that the Vietnamese revolutionaries were merely proxies for the Soviet Union and China, and that Vietnam was a limited war for them just as it was for us.

The military generally believed that the war could have been won if the United States had escalated more rapidly and with fewer political limits. And it is certainly true that considerations of public opinion were in part responsible for some of the limitations placed on the use of U.S. military power. Bombing targets were limited, for instance, in part because extensive civilian casualties were seen as politically damaging. And yet it seems very likely that if Johnson had chosen to go "all out" in Southeast Asia, he could have sold that policy to the public, perhaps more easily, in fact, than the policy of limited war. Limitations on the bombing, after all, were at least as controversial a political issue as civilian casualties in the North. The *New York Times* would not have liked it if Johnson had given the military free reign, nor would the *St. Louis Post-Dispatch* or Walter Lippmann. But the *Daily News* (which was calling in 1964–65 for an invasion of China) and the *Chicago Tribune* would have been ecstatic; and my own guess is that the media in general would have been swept uneasily but powerfully into war fever. Indeed, it was in part the fear that the public would respond too vigorously to an unrestrained call to arms, pushing the country into precisely the kind of confrontation favored by the *Daily News*, that motivated the decision to keep the war limited. The Johnson administration chose to fight a limited war not so much because it felt political opposition gave it no choice, but because it was unwilling to sacrifice other political priorities to an all-out war effort, because it feared the war could grow out of control, and because many officials—an increasing number as time went on—were not convinced the expanded measures advocated by the military would bring victory at reasonable cost.

Eventually public opinion did become a powerful constraint on U.S. policy. After Tet (or, perhaps correctly, after the Johnson administration declined to take the final opportunity Tet provided to mobilize the country for all-out war) political divisions made it impossible for the United States to persist even in a limited war. So in the end one could say that public opinion was indeed decisive, as Ho Chi Minh and many others had predicted it would be.

But it is not clear that it would have been much different if the news had been censored, or television excluded, or the journalists more inclined to defer to presidential authority. It should not be forgotten that public support for the shorter and less costly limited war in Korea also dropped as its costs rose, despite the fact that television was in its infancy, censorship was tight, and the World War II ethic of the journalist serving the war effort remained strong.

A comment Dean Rusk made to reporters on the subject of censorship is revealing. "Unless we are in a formal state of war," he said, "with censorship here [in Washington], there is no point in having censorship [in Vietnam]. . . . Here is where most of the leaks come." Republicans in Washington were questioning the president's credibility on the war long before most television correspondents were. At least a year before Cronkite called the war a "bloody stalemate" and urged negotiation, the secretary of defense had reached essentially the same conclusion. The collapse of America's "will" to fight in Vietnam resulted from a political process of which the media were only one part. And that process was deeply rooted in the nature and course of the war—the fact that it was a limited war, not only in its tactics but in its relevance to vital American interests; and also the fact that it was an unsuccessful limited war, which expanded well beyond the level of commitment most policymakers would have considered rational at the outset.

The behavior of the media . . . is intimately related to the unity and clarity of the government itself, as well as to the degree of consensus in the society at large. This is not to say that the role of the press is purely reactive. Surely it made a difference, for instance, that many journalists were shocked both by the brutality of the war and by the gap between what they were told by top officials and what they saw and heard in the field, and were free to report all this. But it is also clear that the administration's problems with the "fourth branch of government" resulted in large part from political divisions at home, including those within the administration itself, which had dynamics of their own. In a sense, what is really remarkable, as [McGeorge] Bundy observed, is that the press and the public went as far with American policy in Vietnam as they did. And it is hard to see how, short of a real turn to authoritarian government, political doubt and controversy could have been contained much longer. Perhaps even a shift to authoritarian government would not have changed the outcome. It remains to be seen whether the Soviet Union will have the "will" to persist to a clear-cut victory in Afghanistan, even though Afghanistan is more comparable to Mexico than Vietnam in its relevance to Soviet security. Maybe the lesson of Vietnam is not that it is difficult for an open society to fight a limited war, but that it is difficult to fight a limited war against an enemy for whom it is not a limited war.

I have put the word *will* in quotation marks because its use implicitly begs another, more basic question: Should the United States have wanted to persist in Indochina, or to intervene there to begin with? The answer to that question of course depends on a number of others. Could the United States have won at any reasonable cost? How substantial a national interest did the United States have in the outcome of the various political struggles of Indochina? What possibilities of political compromise existed? And, finally (a question which did not in fact affect policy, but should have), what outcome was best for the people of Indochina? My own view is that the United States could not have defeated the Vietnamese revolution at any reasonable cost, to itself or to the Indochinese, and had little real national interest there, the hostility of the Vietnamese Communists to the United States being no more inevitable in the long run than that of the Chinese. I also suspect that while an early Communist government in South Vietnam might have been harsh, as revolutionary regimes usually are for some period, it would eventually, like the Chinese, have moderated and set out on a course of serious modernization within a socialist framework, probably more rapidly if it had come to power while it still had political roots and alliances in the South—before the NLF was destroyed—and through political rather than military means.

These issues . . . were never seriously discussed in news coverage of the war, not, at any rate, in *New York Times* coverage during the years when the decision was made to intervene, or in television coverage in subsequent years. They were not discussed because the constraints of ideology and of journalistic routines tying news coverage to Washington perspectives excluded them from the news agenda. From this angle the implications of government control over the media looks very different.

There is no doubt that control of images and information is central to the exercise of political power. Once a set of goals is decided upon, there are often, for example, important tactical advantages in secrecy; this is obvious to anyone who has engaged in negotiations. (There are also important advantages in publicity and credibility; this is one of the dilemmas of modern politics.) But if we learned from Machiavelli that deception is honorable in the conduct of war, we learned from Thucydides that it is prudent for a world power to consider the justice and larger political wisdom of its actions. Politics is not a football game: winning is not the only thing that counts. The wise use of power is as central to the art of politics as its effective use.

I would not be so foolish as to suggest that an open political process will always produce wise political results. Perhaps if political systems were to move in the direction of more sustained active discussion of political affairs, and a major process of political education were to take place, that would be true, at least when conflicts of interest were not sharp. But that kind of democracy is a long way off. Still, in the case of Vietnam, it seems likely that greater openness would have produced a better decision. Those who imagine that political elites would govern better without the press and the public looking over their shoulders should look back to the decision-making process of the early 1960s that led to American intervention in Vietnam; the foreign policy decision-making of that period is probably as close as the United States can come in peacetime to the ideal expressed by much of the political science of the 1950s, and, now again, by conservatives of the 1970s and 1980s, that after elections "the ordinary citizen must turn over power to elites and let them rule." It is true enough, as conservatives have argued, that every society must maintain a balance between democracy and authority. But in the case of Vietnam excessive authority looks more like the source of imbalance than excessive democracy.

✗ *F U R T H E R   R E A D I N G*

Michael Arlen, *Living-Room War* (1982)
George Bailey, "Television War: Trends in Network Coverage of Vietnam, 1965–1970, *Journal of Broadcasting*, 20 (1976), 147–158
Todd Gitlin, *The Whole World Is Watching* (1980)
David Halberstam, *The Powers that Be* (1979)
Michael Herr, *Dispatches* (1977)
Martin F. Herz, *The Prestige Press and the Christmas Bombing* (1980)
Montague Kern, Patricia W. Levering, and Ralph B. Levering, *The Kennedy Crises: The Press, the Presidency, and Foreign Policy* (1983)
Lawrence W. Lichty, "The War We Watched on Television," *American Film Institute Report*, 4 (1973), 30–37
Michael Mandelbaum, "Vietnam: The Television War," *Daedalus*, 111 (1982), 157–168
John E. Mueller, *War, Presidents and Public Opinion* (1973)
Harrison E. Salisbury, *A Time of Change* (1988)
Jonathan Schell, *The Real War* (1988)
Kathleen J. Turner, *Lyndon Johnson's Dual War* (1985) (on the press)
Sidney Verba et al., "Public Opinion and the War in Vietnam," *American Political Science Review*, 61 (June 1967), 317–333

CHAPTER
14

The Paris Peace Accords of 1973
and the Fall of South Vietnam

The Paris Peace Accords left many fundamental problems unresolved. North Vietnam had not abandoned its long-held objective of unifying the country under its direction. Nor had South Vietnam abandoned its goal of maintaining a government free of communist influence. Given those irreconcilable ambitions, it should not be surprising that the Paris agreements never brought peace to Vietnam. In fact, in the weeks immediately following the signing ceremony in January 1973, both sides were guilty of flagrant truce violations, which worsened throughout 1973 and 1974.

The United States continued to provide massive economic and military support to the Thieu regime. But with the spreading Watergate scandal, Congress reasserted its constitutional role in foreign affairs, denying or limiting many Nixon administration requests for aid to South Vietnam. Congress's hand was strengthened when the Watergate revelations forced Richard M. Nixon to resign as president in August 1974. His successor, Gerald R. Ford, faced an increasingly activist Congress that was reluctant to undertake any new commitments in Vietnam.

When North Vietnam launched a major military offensive in the spring of 1975, officials in Hanoi were evidently as stunned as those in Washington by the rapidity of South Vietnam's disintegration. Congress refused to comply with the Ford administration's last-minute request for emergency aid. On April 30, the South Vietnamese government formally capitulated. Ten years after the introduction of U.S. combat forces, and nearly thirty years after Ho Chi Minh's declaration of independence, the struggle for Vietnam was over. The triumphant northerners quickly gave Saigon a new name—Ho Chi Minh City.

This final phase of the Vietnam War has sparked much political and scholarly controversy. Why did the peace agreement break down so quickly? Which side bears primary responsibility for failing to fulfill its provisions? Why did South Vietnam collapse so swiftly in the face of North Vietnam's offensive? What role did the United States play in these events? Did Washington abandon its ally at a critical moment? Might additional American aid or military support have enabled Saigon to survive? And finally, how is the communist victory best explained?

556

✗ *D O C U M E N T S*

In a letter of January 5, 1973, Richard M. Nixon tried to reassure Nguyen Van Thieu about the future of his regime. One of a series of letters exchanged between the two leaders before the signing of the Paris Peace Accords, it is reprinted here as the first document. Key sections of the multilateral part of those accords follow. They were signed in Paris on January 27, 1973, by representatives of the United States, North Vietnam, South Vietnam, and the Provisional Revolutionary Government. On April 15, 1975, Secretary of State Henry A. Kissinger appealed to Congress to provide emergency aid to South Vietnam, then reeling from North Vietnam's military offensive; his request is reprinted as the third selection.

The final four documents are reminiscences. Secretary of Defense James R. Schlesinger, Jr., recalls the advice that he gave President Ford as South Vietnam appeared on the verge of collapse. Next, Stephen Klinkhammer, a navy hospital corpsman on the aircraft carrier *Midway*, recollects the chaos that prevailed during the evacuation of Saigon. Then, General Van Tien Dung offers a North Vietnamese perspective on the fall of Saigon. Finally, in the last document, excerpted from his memoirs, Nixon places the blame for South Vietnam's fall on Congress.

Richard M. Nixon Reassures Nguyen Van Thieu, 1973

This will acknowledge your letter of December 20, 1972.

There is nothing substantial that I can add to my many previous messages, including my December 17 letter, which clearly stated my opinions and intentions. With respect to the question of North Vietnamese troops, we will again present your views to the Communists as we have done vigorously at every other opportunity in the negotiations. The result is certain to be once more the rejection of our position. We have explained to you repeatedly why we believe the problem of North Vietnamese troops is manageable under the agreement, and I see no reason to repeat all the arguments.

We will proceed next week in Paris along the lines that General [Alexander] Haig explained to you. Accordingly, if the North Vietnamese meet our concerns on the two outstanding substantive issues in the agreement, concerning the DMZ and the method of signing, and if we can arrange acceptable supervisory machinery, we will proceed to conclude the settlement. The gravest consequences would then ensue if your government chose to reject the agreement and split off from the United States. As I said in my December 17 letter, "I am convinced that your refusal to join us would be an invitation to disaster—to the loss of all that we together have fought for over the past decade. It would be inexcusable above all because we will have lost a just and honorable alternative."

As we enter this new round of talks, I hope that our countries will now show a united front. It is imperative for our common objectives that your government take no further actions that complicate our task and would make more difficult the acceptance of the settlement by all parties. We will keep you informed of the negotiations in Paris through daily briefings of Ambassador Lam.

I can only repeat what I have so often said: The best guarantee for the survival of South Vietnam is the unity of our two countries which would be gravely jeopardized if you persist in your present course. The actions of our Congress since its return have clearly borne out the many warnings we have made.

Should you decide, as I trust you will, to go with us, you have my assurance of continued assistance in the post-settlement period and that we will respond with full force should the settlement be violated by North Vietnam. So once more I conclude with an appeal to you to close ranks with us.

The Paris Peace Accords, 1973

The Parties participating in the Paris Conference on Viet-Nam,

With a view to ending the war and restoring peace in Viet-Nam on the basis of respect for the Vietnamese people's fundamental national rights and the South Vietnamese people's right to self-determination, and to contributing to the consolidation of peace in Asia and the world,

Have agreed on the following provisions and undertake to respect and to implement them:

Chapter I   The Vietnamese People's Fundamental National Rights

Article 1.   The United States and all other countries respect the independence, sovereignty, unity, and territorial integrity of Viet-Nam as recognized by the 1954 Geneva Agreements on Viet-Nam.

Chapter II   Cessation of Hostilities—Withdrawal of Troops

Article 2.   A cease-fire shall be observed throughout South Viet-Nam as of 2400 hours G.M.T., on January 27, 1973.

At the same hour, the United States will stop all its military activities against the territory of the Democratic Republic of Viet-Nam by ground, air and naval forces, wherever they may be based, and end the mining of the territorial waters, ports, harbors, and waterways of the Democratic Republic of Viet-Nam. The United States will remove, permanently deactivate or destroy all the mines in the territorial waters, ports, harbors, and waterways of North Viet-Nam as soon as this Agreement goes into effect.

The complete cessation of hostilities mentioned in this Article shall be durable and without limit of time.

Article 3.   The parties undertake to maintain the cease-fire and to ensure a lasting and stable peace.

As soon as the cease-fire goes into effect:

a. The United States forces and those of the other foreign countries allied with the United States and the Republic of Viet-Nam shall remain in-place pending the implementation of the plan of troop withdrawal. The

Four-Party Joint Military Commission described in Article 16 shall determine the modalities.

b. The armed forces of the two South Vietnamese parties shall remain in-place. The Two-Party Joint Military Commission described in Article 17 [not included here] shall determine the areas controlled by each party and the modalities of stationing.

c. The regular forces of all services and arms and the irregular forces of the parties in South Viet-Nam shall stop all offensive activities against each other and shall strictly abide by the following stipulations:
- All acts of force on the ground, in the air, and on the sea shall be prohibited;
- All hostile acts, terrorism and reprisals by both sides will be banned.

Article 4. The United States will not continue its military involvement or intervene in the internal affairs of South Viet-Nam.

Article 5. Within sixty days of the signing of this Agreement, there will be a total withdrawal from South Viet-Nam of troops, military advisers, and military personnel, including technical military personnel and military personnel associated with the pacification program, armaments, munitions, and war material of the United States and those of the other foreign countries mentioned in Article 3 (a). Advisers from the above-mentioned countries to all paramilitary organizations and the police force will also be withdrawn within the same period of time.

Article 6. The dismantlement of all military bases in South Viet-Nam of the United States and of the other foreign countries mentioned in Article 3 (a) shall be completed within sixty days of the signing of this Agreement.

Article 7. From the enforcement of the cease-fire to the formation of the government provided for in Article 9 (b) and 14 of this Agreement, the two South Vietnamese parties shall not accept the introduction of troops, military advisers, and military personnel including technical military personnel, armaments, munitions, and war material into South Viet-Nam.

The two South Vietnamese parties shall be permitted to make periodic replacement of armaments, munitions and war material which have been destroyed, damaged, worn out or used up after the cease-fire, on the basis of piece-for-piece, of the same characteristics and properties, under the supervision of the Joint Military Commission of the two South Vietnamese parties and of the International Commission of Control and Supervision.

Chapter III   The Return of Captured Military Personnel and Foreign Civilians, and Captured and Detained Vietnamese Civilian Personnel

Article 8
a. The return of captured military personnel and foreign civilians of the parties shall be carried out simultaneously with and completed not later

than the same day as the troop withdrawal mentioned in Article 5. The parties shall exchange complete lists of the above-mentioned captured military personnel and foreign civilians on the day of the signing of this Agreement.

b. The Parties shall help each other to get information about those military personnel and foreign civilians of the parties missing in action, to determine the location and take care of the graves of the dead so as to facilitate the exhumation and repatriation of the remains, and to take any such other measures as may be required to get information about those still considered missing in action.

c. The question of the return of Vietnamese civilian personnel captured and detailed in South Viet-Nam will be resolved by the two South Vietnamese parties on the basis of the principles of Article 21 (b) of the Agreement on the Cessation of Hostilities in Viet-Nam of July 20, 1954. The two South Vietnamese parties will do so in a spirit of national reconciliation and concord, with a view to ending hatred and enmity, in order to ease suffering and to reunite families. The two South Vietnamese parties will do their utmost to resolve this question within ninety days after the cease-fire comes into effect.

Chapter IV   The Exercise of the South Vietnamese People's Right to Self-Determination

Article 9.   The Government of the United States of America and the Government of the Democratic Republic of Viet-Nam undertake to respect the following principles for the exercise of the South Vietnamese people's right to self-determination:

a. The South Vietnamese people's right to self-determination is sacred, inalienable, and shall be respected by all countries.

b. The South Vietnamese people shall decide themselves the political future of South Viet-Nam through genuinely free and democratic general elections under international supervision.

c. Foreign countries shall not impose any political tendency or personality on the South Vietnamese people.

Article 10.   The two South Vietnamese parties undertake to respect the cease-fire and maintain peace in South Viet-Nam, settle all matters of contention through negotiations, and avoid all armed conflict.

Article 11.   Immediately after the cease-fire, the two South Vietnamese parties will:

• achieve national reconciliation and concord, end hatred and enmity, prohibit all acts of reprisal and discrimination against individuals or organizations that have collaborated with one side or the other;

• ensure the democratic liberties of the people: personal freedom, freedom of speech, freedom of the press, freedom of meeting, freedom of organization, freedom of political activities, freedom of belief, freedom of movement, freedom of residence, freedom of work, right to property ownership, and right to free enterprise.

Article 12

a. Immediately after the cease-fire, the two South Vietnamese parties shall hold consultations in a spirit of national reconciliation and concord, mutual respect, and mutual non-elimination to set up a National Council of National Reconciliation and Concord of three equal segments. The Council shall operate on the principle of unanimity. After the National Council of National Reconciliation and Concord has assumed its functions, the two South Vietnamese parties will consult about the formation of councils at lower levels. The two South Vietnamese parties shall sign an agreement on the internal matters of South Viet-Nam as soon as possible and do their utmost to accomplish this within ninety days after the cease-fire comes into effect, in keeping with the South Vietnamese people's aspirations for peace, independence and democracy.

b. The National Council of National Reconciliation and Concord shall have the task of promoting the two South Vietnamese parties' implementation of this Agreement, achievement of national reconciliation and concord and ensurance of democratic liberties. The National Council of National Reconciliation and Concord will organize the free and democratic general elections provided for in Article 9 (b) and decide the procedures and modalities of these general elections. The institutions for which the general elections are to be held will be agreed upon through consultations between the two South Vietnamese parties. The National Council of National Reconciliation and Concord will also decide the procedures and modalities of such local elections as the two South Vietnamese parties agree upon.

Article 13.   The question of Vietnamese armed forces in South Viet-Nam shall be settled by the two South Vietnamese parties in a spirit of national reconciliation and concord, equality and mutual respect, without foreign interference, in accordance with the postwar situation. Among the questions to be discussed by the two South Vietnamese parties are steps to reduce their military effectives and to demobilize the troops being reduced. The two South Vietnamese parties will accomplish this as soon as possible.

Article 14.   South Viet-Nam will pursue a foreign policy of peace and independence. It will be prepared to establish relations with all countries irrespective of their political and social systems on the basis of mutual respect for independence and sovereignty and accept economic and technical aid from any country with no political conditions attached. The acceptance of military aid by South Viet-Nam in the future shall come under the authority of the government set up after the general elections in South Viet-Nam provided for in Article 9 (b).

Chapter V   The Reunification of Viet-Nam and the Relationship Between North and South Viet-Nam

Article 15.   The reunification of Viet-Nam shall be carried out step by step through peaceful means on the basis of discussions and agreements between North and South Viet-Nam, without coercion or annexation by either party, and without foreign interference. The time for reunification will be agreed upon by North and South Viet-Nam.

Pending reunification:

a. The military demarcation line between the two zones at the 17th parallel is only provisional and not a political or territorial boundary, as provided for in paragraph 6 of the Final Declaration of the 1954 Geneva Conference.

b. North and South Viet-Nam shall respect the Demilitarized Zone on either side of the Provisional Military Demarcation Line.

c. North and South Viet-Nam shall promptly start negotiations with a view to reestablishing normal relations in various fields. Among the questions to be negotiated are the modalities of civilian movement across the Provisional Military Demarcation Line.

d. North and South Viet-Nam shall not join any military alliance or military bloc and shall not allow foreign powers to maintain military bases, troops, military advisers, and military personnel on their respective territories, as stipulated in the 1954 Geneva Agreements on Viet-Nam.

Henry A. Kissinger Appeals to Congress for Emergency Aid, 1975

The long and agonizing conflict in Indochina has reached a tragic stage. The events of the past month have been discussed at great length before the Congress and require little additional elaboration. In Viet-Nam President Thieu ordered a strategic withdrawal from a number of areas he regarded as militarily untenable. However, the withdrawal took place in great haste, without adequate advance planning, and with insufficient coordination. It was further complicated by a massive flow of civilian refugees seeking to escape the advancing North Vietnamese Army. Disorganization engendered confusion; fear led to panic. The results, as we all know, were tragic losses—of territory, of population, of material, and of morale.

But to fully understand what has happened, it is necessary to have an appreciation of all that went before. The North Vietnamese offensive, and the South Vietnamese response, did not come about by chance—although chance is always an element in warfare. The origins of these events are complex, and I believe it would be useful to review them briefly.

Since January 1973, Hanoi has violated—continuously, systematically, and energetically—the most fundamental provisions of the Paris agreement. It steadily increased the numbers of its troops in the South. It improved and expanded its logistics system in the South. It increased the armaments and ammunition of its forces in the South. And as you know, it blocked all efforts to account for personnel missing in action. These are facts, and they are indisputable. All of these actions were of course in total violation of the agreement. Parallel to these efforts, Hanoi attempted—with considerable success—to immobilize the various mechanisms established by the agreement to monitor and curtail violations of the cease-fire. Thus, it assiduously prepared the way for further military actions.

South Viet-Nam's record of adherence to the agreement has not been perfect. It is, however, qualitatively and quantitatively far better than Hanoi's. South Viet-Nam did not build up its armed forces. It undertook no major offensive actions—although it traded thrusts and probes with the Communists. It cooperated fully in establishing and supporting the cease-fire control mechanisms provided for in the agreement. And it sought, as did the United States, full implementation of those provisions of the agreement calling for an accounting of soldiers missing in action.

But perhaps more relevant to an understanding of recent events are the following factors.

While North Viet-Nam had available several reserve divisions which it could commit to battle at times and places of its choosing, the South had no strategic reserves. Its forces were stretched thin, defending lines of communication and population centers throughout the country.

While North Viet-Nam, by early this year, had accumulated in South Viet-Nam enough ammunition for two years of intensive combat, South Vietnamese commanders had to ration ammunition as their stocks declined and were not replenished.

While North Viet-Nam had enough fuel in the South to operate its tanks and armored vehicles for at least 18 months, South Viet-Nam faced stringent shortages.

In sum, while Hanoi was strengthening its army in the South, the combat effectiveness of South Viet-Nam's army gradually grew weaker. While Hanoi built up its reserve divisions and accumulated ammunition, fuel, and other military supplies, U.S. aid levels to Viet-Nam were cut—first by half in 1973 and then by another third in 1974. This coincided with a worldwide inflation and a fourfold increase in fuel prices. As a result almost all of our military aid had to be devoted to ammunition and fuel. Very little was available for spare parts, and none for new equipment.

These imbalances became painfully evident when the offensive broke full force, and they contributed to the tragedy which unfolded. Moreover, the steady diminution in the resources available to the Army of South Viet-Nam unquestionably affected the morale of its officers and men. South Vietnamese units in the northern and central provinces knew full well that they faced an enemy superior both in numbers and in firepower. They knew that reinforcements and resupply would not be forthcoming. When the fighting began they also knew, as they had begun to suspect, that the United States would not respond. I would suggest that all of these factors added significantly to the sense of helplessness, despair, and, eventually, panic which we witnessed in late March and early April.

I would add that it is both inaccurate and unfair to hold South Viet-Nam responsible for blocking progress toward a political solution to the conflict. Saigon's proposals in its conversations with PRG [Provisional Revolutionary Government] representatives in Paris were in general constructive and conciliatory. There was no progress toward a compromise political settlement because Hanoi intended that there should not be. Instead, North Viet-Nam's strategy was to lay the groundwork for an eventual military offensive, one which would either bring outright victory or at least allow Hanoi to dictate the terms of a political solution.

Neither the United States nor South Viet-Nam entered into the Paris agreement with the expectation that Hanoi would abide by it in every respect. We did believe, however, that the agreement was sufficiently equitable to both sides that its major provisions could be accepted and acted upon by Hanoi and that the contest could be shifted thereby from a military to a political track. However, our two governments also recognized that, since the agreement manifestly was not self-enforcing, Hanoi's adherence depended heavily on maintaining a military parity in South Viet-Nam. So long as North Viet-Nam confronted a strong South Vietnamese army and so long as the possibility existed of U.S. intervention to offset the strategic advantages of the North, Hanoi could be expected to forgo major military action. Both of those essential conditions were dissipated over the past two years. Hanoi attained a clear military superiority, and it became increasingly convinced that U.S. intervention could be ruled out. It therefore returned to a military course, with the results we have seen.

The present situation in Viet-Nam is ominous. North Viet-Nam's combat forces far outnumber those of the South, and they are better armed. Perhaps more important, they enjoy a psychological momentum which can be as decisive as armaments in battle. South Viet-Nam must reorganize and reequip its forces, and it must restore the morale of its army and its people. These tasks will be difficult, and they can be performed only by the South Vietnamese. However, a successful defense will also require resources—arms, fuel, ammunition, and medical supplies—and these can come only from the United States.

Large quantities of equipment and supplies, totaling perhaps $800 million, were lost in South Viet-Nam's precipitous retreat from the northern and central areas. Much of this should not have been lost, and we regret that it happened. But South Viet-Nam is now faced with a different strategic and tactical situation and different military requirements. Although the amount of military assistance the President has requested is of the same general magnitude as the value of the equipment lost, we are not attempting simply to replace those losses. The President's request, based on General Weyand's [Gen. Frederick C. Weyand, Chief of Staff, United States Army] assessment, represents our best judgment as to what is needed now, in this new situation, to defend what is left of South Viet-Nam. Weapons, ammunition, and supplies to reequip four divisions, to form a number of ranger groups into divisional units, and to upgrade some territorial forces into infantry regiments will require some $326 million. The balance of our request is for ammunition, fuel, spare parts, and medical supplies to sustain up to 60 days of intensive combat and to pay for the cost of transporting those items. These are minimum requirements, and they are needed urgently.

The human tragedy of Viet-Nam has never been more acute than it now is. Hundreds of thousands of South Vietnamese have sought to flee Communist control and are homeless refugees. They have our compassion, and they must also have our help. Despite commendable efforts by the South Vietnamese Government, the burden of caring for these innocent victims is beyond its capacity. The United States has already done much to assist these people, but many remain without adequate food, shelter, or medical care. The President has asked that additional efforts and additional resources be devoted to this humanitarian effort. I ask that the Congress respond generously and quickly.

The objectives of the United States in this immensely difficult situation remain as they were when the Paris agreement was signed—to end the military conflict and establish conditions which will allow a fair political solution to be achieved. We believe that despite the tragic experience to date, the Paris agreement remains a valid framework within which to proceed toward such a solution. However, today, as in 1973, battlefield conditions will affect political perceptions and the outcome of negotiations. We therefore believe that in order for a political settlement to be reached which preserves any degree of self-determination for the people of South Viet-Nam, the present military situation must be stabilized. It is for these reasons that the President has asked Congress to appropriate urgently additional funds for military assistance for Viet-Nam.

I am acutely aware of the emotions aroused in this country by our long and difficult involvement in Viet-Nam. I understand what the cost has been for this nation and why frustration and anger continue to dominate our national debate. Many will argue that we have done more than enough for the Government and the people of South Viet-Nam. I do not agree with that proposition, however, nor do I believe that to review endlessly the wisdom of our original involvement serves a useful purpose now. For despite the agony of this nation's experience in Indochina and the substantial reappraisal which has taken place concerning our proper role there, few would deny that we are still involved or that what we do—or fail to do—will still weigh heavily in the outcome. We cannot by our actions alone insure the survival of South Viet-Nam. But we can, alone, by our inaction assure its demise.

The United States has no legal obligation to the Government and the people of South Viet-Nam of which the Congress is not aware. But we do have a deep moral obligation—rooted in the history of our involvement and sustained by the continuing efforts of our friends. We cannot easily set it aside. In addition to the obvious consequences for the people of Viet-Nam, our failure to act in accordance with that obligation would inevitably influence other nations' perceptions of our constancy and our determination.

American credibility would not collapse, and American honor would not be destroyed. But both would be weakened, to the detriment of this nation and of the peaceful world order we have sought to build.

James R. Schlesinger, Jr., Recalls the Collapse of South Vietnam (1975), 1987

My first inkling that we had lost came when the North Vietnamese began to make maneuvers toward the end of 1974 and in January of 1975 and we did not respond. They were testing us. They did not really believe that they were getting away with what they were getting away with. But given the constraints under which we had to operate, *I* knew they were going to get away with it. Then of course came the attack in the Central Highlands and the total collapse of the ARVN divisions. At that point it was all over. I had been making menacing sounds in public whenever the subject of North Vietnam had come up—they'd just better beware, and so forth. But the congressional restraints that had been established in the summer of '73 wouldn't permit our taking effective countermeasures.

Now, many of the people who were with me were people who had served there, and they had emotional ties to the country, and they just could not—and I understand it, and I'm not criticizing them—back off and say "We did our best, but it is now hopeless." They kept seeing hope where hope did not exist. [General] Fred Weyand, for example, whom Ford had sent out to Southeast Asia, was tied to Thieu and to the Vietnamese with bonds of loyalty. He came back and reported to the President, that six hundred and fifty million bucks is needed.

Before Mr. Ford asked for additional assistance in Vietnam we had a meeting of the NSC, and I said "Mr. President, it's all over." He was kind of rankled by that, quite indignant. I got sort of the Michigan fight song. And I said "Mr. President, you should go up to the Hill tomorrow and say we have suffered a severe setback, call for blood, sweat, and tears, and a national effort to deal with the consequences, but there's no way that you can persuade anybody that Vietnam is salvageable."

An American Soldier Describes the Evacuation of Saigon (1975), 1981

The evacuation of Saigon, the whole thing, was called Operation New Wind or Fresh Wind or Fresh Breeze or something like that. We got to the aircraft carrier *Midway*, and as soon as we got off the helicopter—since I was a surgical tech, my hair was always under a cap and it was rather long, about halfway down my ears—the CO [commanding officer], who

Kim Willenson et al., *The Bad War: An Oral History of the Vietnam War*, p. 316. Copyright © 1987, Newsweek, Inc. Reprinted with permission.
From *Everything We Had* by Al Santoli, pp. 256–258. Copyright © 1981 by Albert Santoli and Vietnam Veterans of America. Reprinted by permission of Random House, Inc.

was up in the tower, comes down and says, "Get those guys down for haircuts." So right away he gets on us for haircuts. The *Midway* was our base of operations. Our surgical equipment, all the green crates, never did catch up to us. That's known throughout the military, that they never catch up with you, and the *Midway* didn't have an operating room. This is about April 10 or 11.

We were real close to shore at that time, right off Saigon. We heard that we were taking on a whole bunch of civilians. We would be flying in and out with refugees, with American personnel, with reporters. The Tan Son Nhut airport was being bombed with big rockets. You could see the explosions from the sea. We were flying in and taking on refugees, and they were flying out whatever they could. With the refugees there were worms, women going into labor, TB and wounded lying on the choppers because there were a lot of shells coming in. There were a couple dead or dying on the chopper whom we couldn't save. We were landing in Tan Son Nhut. That was our staging point, where everybody was loading.

There were people coming out in boats, half-sinking boats. There were people who had their own airplanes who were flying out. There were all these choppers we had left there; they were using these to fly out, the Vietnamese. The flight deck was so full of choppers that we had to push them overboard because there was no room, we couldn't get our own choppers in. We were flying the big medevac choppers. We had an overload, packing in about twenty-five at a time, both Vietnamese and American. It was total chaos. The Purple Heart Trail, the road that came into Saigon from the paddies west of the city, was so jammed, from the air I could see columns of people that were at least twenty miles long. A lot of children crying. Some had clothes they picked off dead bodies. Most were barefoot. There were oxcarts and they were hauling what they had. There were wounded men on both sides of the road with battle dressings on. The NVA was lobbing these rockets all over the place, they were wiping out civilians . . . There were piles of wounded on the back of ambulances. They were dropping the rockets right into crowds of fleeing people. There were trucks, buses, anything they could get into. Saigon was the last stand, the capital, where the American embassy was.

A lot of American Marines were activated and had put up a perimeter guard around Tan Son Nhut. The NVA was still lobbing these rockets in. In fact, when I took off we were also flying out from the American embassy—a lot of people had been told to go there instead of Tan Son Nhut. It was really a mess. These rockets are lobbing in and a C-130 took off full of people going out to one of the aircraft carriers and it was blown out of the sky . . . that was all over the runway. There were corpses, there were burned-out tanks that people had used to come in, there were pieces of bodies lying in the fields and on the streets. It was just bananas, total chaos. It was one mess of humanity being pushed to where people were being trampled. People screaming, "I want a place on this chopper!" and not being able to communicate because of the language barrier and because they would not listen.

They were raiding the American Exchange. The image I have is this one guy holding up one of those ten-packs of Kellogg's cereal and he's waving it. They were throwing American money up in the air . . . totally berserk . . . total chaos. We were trying to get the wounded first. They were piled in these old ambulances. The refugees were coming up from the Delta as well as from the North. We were trying to get the wounded out first and a lot of them we just couldn't.

Each time we went in, a bunch of Marines would get out and cover the landing zone as we tried to get the wounded on first, but sometimes they were just overwhelmed. They had orders to shoot if they couldn't maintain order. They shot mostly over the heads. I didn't see any of the Marines shoot any civilians. The Marines set up a defensive perimeter and would return fire at the enemy, but like the rest of the war, you never saw the NVA. The ARVN were running, they were coming in, they were by-passing civilians, shooting civilians, trying to get out first all the time. The best way to describe it was every man for himself. There were pregnant women going into labor right there on the goddam landing zone. I delivered a baby right on the chopper. And I also delivered two more on the ships. It was just bananas.

We ended up with three thousand civilians aboard the *Midway*. We had taken all of our squadrons off because they had been there for offensive purposes. The civilians all stayed where the squadrons used to be. There were people sleeping on the floors, all over. Of course, they didn't know what a bathroom was. They were packed in, I'll tell you that. So we'd all take turns walking duty and if someone was puking or if someone had diarrhea or worms, we'd treat that.

On April 30 Saigon fell. South Vietnam had fallen. The Vice-President, Ky, flew out to the *Midway* in his own Cessna. Ky had with him an immense amount of gold bars. A lot of these people, some of the higher-ups in the ARVN and so on, had with them a lot of American money. We confiscated everything from civilians when they came on board. There were pounds and pounds of pure heroin, pounds and pounds of nice marijuana, which I really wanted to sample. People had little cherry-bomb grenades. We picked up guns. A lot of canned fish had to be tossed out. A lot of fever, they had a lot of malaria. So we had these three thousand people packed in there. That was the best we could do.

A North Vietnamese Commander Celebrates the "Great Spring Victory" (1975), 1977

When it was almost light, the American news services reported that [U.S. Ambassador Graham] Martin had cleared out of Saigon in a helicopter.

Van Tien Dung, *Our Great Spring Victory: An Account of the Liberation of South Vietnam*, translated by John Spragens, Jr. Copyright © 1977 by Cora Weiss. Reprinted by permission of Monthly Review Foundation.

This viceregal mandarin, the final American plenipotentiary in South Vietnam, beat a most hasty and pitiful retreat. As it happened, up until the day he left Saigon, Martin still felt certain that the quisling administration could be preserved, and that a ceasefire could be arranged, so he was halfhearted about the evacuation, waiting and watching. He went all the way out to Tan Son Nhat airfield to observe the situation. Our barrage of bombs and our fierce shelling had nearly paralyzed this vital airfield, and the fixed-wing aircraft they had intended to use for their evacuation could no longer operate. The encirclement of Saigon was growing tighter by the day. The Duong Van Minh card which they had played far too late proved useless. When Martin reported this to Washington, President Ford issued orders to begin a helicopter evacuation. Coming in waves for eighteen hours straight, they carried more than 1,000 Americans and over 5,000 of their Vietnamese retainers, along with their families, out of the South. Ford also ordered Martin to evacuate immediately "without a minute's delay."

The American evacuation was carried out from the tops of thirteen tall buildings chosen as landing pads for their helicopters. The number of these landing pads shrank gradually as tongues of fire from our advancing troops came closer. At the American embassy, the boarding point for the evacuation copters was a scene of monumental confusion, with the Americans' flunkies fighting their way in, smashing doors, climbing walls, climbing each other's backs, tussling, brawling, and trampling each other as they sought to flee. It reached the point where Martin, who wanted to return to his own house for his suitcase before he fled, had to take a back street, using the rear gate of the embassy. When "Code 2," Martin's code name, and "Lady 09," the name of the helicopter carrying him, left the embassy for the East Sea, it signaled the shameful defeat of U.S. imperialism after thirty years of intervention and military adventures in Vietnam. At the height of their invasion of Vietnam, the U.S. had used 60 percent of their total infantry, 58 percent of their marines, 32 percent of their tactical air force, 50 percent of their strategic air force, fifteen of their eighteen aircraft carriers, 800,000 American troops (counting those stationed in satellite countries who were taking part in the Vietnam war), and more than 1 million Saigon troops. They mobilized as many as 6 million American soldiers in rotation, dropped over 10 million tons of bombs, and spent over $300 billion, but in the end the U.S. ambassador had to crawl up to the helicopter pad looking for a way to flee. Today, looking back on the gigantic force the enemy had mobilized, recalling the malicious designs they admitted, and thinking about the extreme difficulties and complexities which our revolutionary sampan had had to pass through, we were all the more aware how immeasurably great this campaign to liberate Saigon and liberate the South was. . . .

The most extraordinary thing about this historic campaign was what had sprouted in the souls of our cadres and fighters. Why were our soldiers so heroic and determined during this campaign? What had given all of them this clear understanding of the great resolution of the party and of the nation, this clear understanding of our immeasurably precious opportunity, and this clear understanding of our unprecedented manner of fighting? What had made them so extraordinarily courageous and intense, so outstanding in their political acumen in this final phase of the war?

The will and competence of our soldiers were not achieved in a day, but were the result of a continuous process of carrying out the party's ideological and organizational work in the armed forces. And throughout our thirty years of struggle, there had been no campaign in which Uncle Ho had not gone into the operation with our soldiers. Going out to battle this time, our whole army had been given singular, unprecedented strength because this strategically decisive battle bore his name: Ho Chi Minh, for every one of our cadres and fighters, was faith, strength, and life. Among the myriad troops in all the advancing wings, every one of our fighters carried toward Ho Chi Minh City the hopes of the nation and a love for our land. Today each fighter could see with his own eyes the resiliency which the Fatherland had built up during these many years, and given his own resiliency there was nothing, no enemy scheme that could stop him.

Our troops advanced rapidly to the five primary objectives, and then spread out from there. Wherever they went, a forest of revolutionary flags appeared, and people poured out to cheer them, turning the streets of Saigon into a giant festival. From the Binh Phoc bridge to Quan Tre, people carrying flags, beating drums and hollow wooden fish, and calling through megaphones, chased down the enemy, disarmed enemy soldiers, neutralized traitors and spies, and guided our soldiers. In Hoc Mon on Route 1, the people all came out into the road to greet the soldiers, guide them, and point out the hiding places of enemy thugs. Everywhere people used megaphones to call on Saigon soldiers to take off their uniforms and lay down their guns. The people of the city, especially the workers, protected factories and warehouses and turned them over to our soldiers. In all the districts bordering the city—Binh Hoa, Thanh My Tay, Phu Nhuan, Go Vap, and Thu Duc—members of the revolutionary infrastructure and other people distributed leaflets, raised flags, called on enemy soldiers to drop their guns, and supplied and guided our soldiers. Before this great army entered the city, the great cause of our nation and the policies of our revolution had entered the hearts of the people.

We were very pleased to hear that the people of the city rose up when the military attacks, going one step ahead, had given them the leverage. The masses had entered this decisive battle at just the right time, not too early, but not too late. The patriotic actions of the people created a revolutionary atmosphere of vast strength on all the city's streets. This was the most precious aspect of the mass movement in Saigon-Gia Dinh, the result of many years of propaganda, education, organizing, and training by the municipal party branch. When the opportune moment arrived, those political troops had risen up with a vanguard spirit, and advanced in giant strides along with our powerful main-force divisions, resolutely, intelligently, and courageously. The people of the city not only carried flags and food and drink for the troops, but helped disperse large numbers of enemy soldiers, forced many to surrender, chased and captured many of those who were hiding out, and preserved order and security in the streets. And we will never forget the widespread and moving images of thousands, of tens of thousands of people enthusiastically giving directions to our soldiers and guiding them as they entered the city, and helping all the wings of troops strike quickly and unexpectedly at enemy positions. Those nameless heroes of Saigon-Gia Dinh brought into the general offensive the fresh and beautiful features of people's war.

As we looked at the combat operations map, the five wings of our troops seemed like five lotuses blossoming out from our five major objectives. The First Army Corps had captured Saigon's General Staff headquarters and the command compounds of all the enemy armed services. When the Third Army Corps captured Tan Son Nhat they met one wing of troops already encamped there—our military delegation at Camp Davis; it was an amazing and moving meeting. The Fourth Army Corps captured Saigon's Ministry of Defense, the Bach Dang port, and the radio station. The 232nd force took the Special Capital Zone heardquarters and the Directorate-General of Police. The Second Army Corps seized "Independence Palace," the place where the quisling leaders, those hirelings of the United States, had sold our independence, traded in human blood, and carried on their smuggling. Our soldiers immediately rushed upstairs to the place where the quisling cabinet was meeting, and arrested the whole central leadership of the Saigon administration, including their president, right on the spot. Our soldiers' vigorous actions and firm declarations revealed the spirit of a victorious army. By 11:30 A.M. on April 30 the revolutionary flag flew from "Independence Palace"; this became the meeting point for all the wings of liberating troops.

At the front headquarters, we turned on our radios to listen. The voice of the quisling president called on his troops to put down their weapons and surrender unconditionally to our troops. Saigon was completely liberated! Total victory! We were completely victorious! All of us at headquarters jumped up and shouted, embraced and carried each other around on our shoulders. The sound of applause, laughter, and happy, noisy, chattering speech was as festive as if spring had just burst upon us. It was an indescribably joyous scene. Le Duc Tho and Pham Hung embraced me and all the cadres and fighters present. We were all so happy we were choked with emotion. I lit a cigarette and smoked. Dinh Duc Thien, his eyes somewhat red, said, "Now if these eyes close, my heart will be at rest." This historic and sacred, intoxicating and completely satisfying moment was one that comes once in a generation, once in many generations. Our generation had known many victorious mornings, but there had been no morning so fresh and beautiful, so radiant, so clear and cool, so sweet-scented as this morning of total victory, a morning which made babes older than their years and made old men young again.

Nixon Blames Congress for
the Fall of South Vietnam (1975), 1978

For more than two years after the peace agreement the South Vietnamese had held their own against the Communists. This proved the will and mettle of the South Vietnamese people and their desire to live in freedom. It also proved that Vietnamization had succeeded. When Congress reneged on our obligations under the agreements, the Communists predictably rushed in to fill the gap. The congressional bombing cutoff, coupled with the limitation placed on the President by the War Powers Resolution in November 1973, set off a string of events that led to the Communist takeover in Cambodia and, on April 30, 1975, the North Vietnamese conquest of South Vietnam.

Congress denied first to me, and then to President Ford, the means to enforce the Paris agreement at a time when the North Vietnamese were openly violating it. Even more devastating and inexcusable, in 1974 Congress began cutting back on military aid for South Vietnam at a time when the Soviets were increasing their aid to North Vietnam. As a result, when the North Vietnamese launched their all-out invasion of the South in the spring of 1975, they had an advantage in arms, and the threat of American action to enforce the agreement was totally removed. A year after the collapse of South Vietnam, the field commander in charge of Hanoi's final offensive cited the cutback in American aid as a major factor in North Vietnam's victory. He remarked that Thieu "was then forced to fight a poor man's war," with his firepower reduced by 60 percent and his mobility reduced by half because of lack of aircraft, vehicles, and fuel.

The war and the peace in Indochina that America had won at such cost over twelve years of sacrifice and fighting were lost within a matter of months once Congress refused to fulfill our obligations. And it is Congress that must bear the responsibility for the tragic results. Hundreds of thousands of anti-Communist South Vietnamese and Cambodians have been murdered or starved to death by their conquerors, and the bloodbath continues.

✗ *E S S A Y S*

Allan E. Goodman, a political scientist at Georgetown University, examines the breakdown of the Paris Peace Accords in the opening essay. A former State Department official who spent several years in Vietnam, he contends that the agreement collapsed not because of any flaws in its terms or in the negotiating process but because the Saigon government proved incapable of ending the war—either through accommodation with the PRG or victory over it. In the second essay, William J. Duiker of Pennsylvania State University discusses the final communist offensive and explores the broader question of why the communists ultimately prevailed. He argues that of all the great revolutions, the Vietnamese revolution, more than any other, was above all an act of human will. Duiker emphasizes the communists' superior organizational strengths and strategic vision, which he contrasts with the chronic weaknesses of their nationalist rivals.

What Went Wrong?

ALLAN E. GOODMAN

Through the Vietnam negotiations the United States sought to legitimize the way it ended its decade of direct involvement in the war. To Henry Kissinger, what happened thereafter depended on whether the military stalemate that had made the Paris Agreement possible would last. As he observed in a press conference a year after the agreement had been signed:

> No settlement is self-enforcing. It is not possible to write an agreement whose terms, in themselves, guarantee its performance. Any agreement will last if the hostility of the parties is thereby lessened, if the parties have an incentive to observe it, and/or if the parties pay a penalty for breaking it.
>
> If those three conditions are not met, no matter what the terms of the agreement, there is a tendency toward erosion.
>
> In Viet Nam, in civil war conditions, the hostility of the parties does not significantly lessen.
>
> The incentives and penalties have been affected by many events of the past year [especially the U.S. Congress's cutoff of funds for the air war in Cambodia].
>
> So, at this moment, a great deal depends on the perception of the two sides of the existing military balance.

What had Kissinger initially expected? He initialed the Paris Agreement believing that he had achieved understandings with Le Duc Tho about the following: the future level of warfare in the south, that détente would involve a tapering off of Communist-country aid to Hanoi, that follow-up negotiations would occur if the ambiguities of the agreement created problems, and that U.S.-DRV relations would be normalized. But in mid-February 1973, when he visited Hanoi on what he called "an exploratory mission to determine how to move from hostility to normalization" of relations with the DRV, Kissinger had a disturbing meeting with North Vietnamese premier Pham Van Dong. Pham suggested that most of the DRV's Politburo saw the Paris Agreement as little more than a face-saving instrument that permitted U.S. withdrawal. He called the NCRC [National Council of Reconciliation and Concord] a transitional coalition and said that the cease-

Reprinted from *The Lost Peace: America's Search for a Negotiated Settlement of the Vietnam War* by Allan E. Goodman with permission of Hoover Institution Press, pp. 165–180. © 1978 by the Board of Trustees of the Leland Stanford Jr. University.

fire was primarily with the Americans. As Pham put it, the cease-fire-in-place definitely would not be permitted to evolve into another way of partitioning Vietnam.

Nevertheless, Kissinger hoped that the Paris Agreement would eventually lead to a peaceful political settlement. After his Hanoi trip, for example, he told the press:

> The big problem is whether Indochina can be moved from a condition of guerrilla war or even open warfare to a condition in which the energies of the peoples of that region are concentrated on constructive purposes.
>
> If that objective can be achieved, if that process can start for a period of three or four years, then any decision to resume the conflict by any of the parties will have to be taken in an environment of peace and against the experience of the population in [war-like] tasks with which they have become almost totally unfamiliar.

However, in a war in which time was a weapon and negotiation a tactic, the Paris Agreement proved neither a substitute for a military victory by Saigon nor a deterrent to the continued pursuit of military victory by Hanoi.

For Saigon, as one high GVN official remarked, the agreement permitted "continuing the war and improving our position on the battlefield with American help. The fact that there was an agreement took the edge off our American critics for a time." Saigon never believed that the causes of the war were negotiable, or that Hanoi would compromise unless it was defeated militarily in the south. Just as the war itself had seemed more important to the Americans fighting it than it did to the GVN in 1966 and 1967, so also the negotiations and the Paris Agreement were regarded by South Vietnamese officials as something far more desirable from Washington's standpoint than from Saigon's.

Throughout the negotiations, Thieu used them as a means of demonstrating his independence from the Americans and a chance to show his critics on the right, as well as the Communists, that he was no U.S. puppet. Thieu's intransigence delayed the start of substantive talks, accounted in part for the three-month delay that occurred after Henry Kissinger announced that peace was at hand, and necessitated the invention of a complicated signing ceremony in which, at Thieu's insistence, neither the GVN nor the PRG formally acknowledged the other's existence. The terms of the agreement were also not surprising to Saigon; by mid-1972 the GVN was prepared to continue the war regardless of what was agreed on in Paris. So, for Saigon, the negotiations provided time and the maximum amount of U.S. assistance possible to improve its position on the battlefield.

For Hanoi and the PRG, the negotiations provided a means to sustain the fighting, and the agreement provided a means eventually to win the war. By 1969, the kind of war Hanoi wanted to fight required a secure and uninterrupted flow of supplies from its Communist allies into the north, and thence into the south via the Ho Chi Minh trail. The bombing suspension that accompanied the negotiations provided security for the NVA's rear bases. But, as a Hanoi radio commentary pointed out on August 13, 1972: ". . . in solving the South Vietnam problem one cannot deal only with the military problem. . . . To cease-fire or to release the captured soldiers are only concrete acts; the political objective is the only problem of decisive significance. Such a cease-fire cannot eliminate the cause of the war. Instead, such a cease-fire will permanently maintain the factors for waging war again at any time." And this is precisely what the Paris Agreement did.

Indeed, as one high-level U.S. official observed in a January 1975 interview in Saigon, "Hanoi basically saw the Paris Agreement as a generous and face-saving way for the United States to end its Vietnam involvement. They then expected Thieu to be ousted, PRG territorial control to be consolidated, and the National Council of Reconciliation and Concord to be established. They still expect this. They still expect the GVN to collapse. They feel the military balance is in their favor, that Saigon's soldiers know this, and that sooner or later Thieu and his generals will blunder into a defeat."

As President Nixon wrote in his 1973 state of the world report, the Paris Agreement made it possible for the U.S. prisoners of war to be returned, and it provided Saigon with a "decent interval" of two years, in which "to demonstrate inherent strength." But the Paris Agreement did not end the war—and neither Washington, nor Saigon, nor Hanoi expected that it would. However, Kissinger did believe that the Paris Agreement would precipitate movement toward a political settlement. Speaking to newsmen shortly before the agreement was signed, he observed, ". . . it is not easy to achieve through negotiations what has not been achieved on the battlefield, and if you look at the settlements that have been made in the postwar period, the lines of demarcation have almost always followed the lines of actual control. . . . we have taken the position throughout that the agreement cannot be analyzed in terms of any one of its provisions, but it has to be seen in its totality and in terms of the evolution that it starts."

But, since neither Saigon nor Hanoi gained in Paris all that they had gained on the battlefield, both believed that further fighting was essential to achieving their basic goals. For Saigon, continuing the war would prove to the north that it could not impose a military solution once U.S. forces left Vietnam. As President Thieu declared in a speech in June 1974:

We will . . . not allow the Communists to use military means in lieu of the already agreed-to peaceful solution—the one provided for by the Paris Agreement, which calls for a cease-fire and an election. We will not let the Communists resort to war to solve the Vietnam problem. We must prove to them that they shall fail in their attempt to resort to military means, that their renewed aggression shall take them nowhere, and they had better sit down and negotiate seriously so that an election may soon be organized. All that we have done in reaction to Communist truce violations is only aimed at making the Communists realize the pointlessness of their use of force.

For Hanoi, continued fighting was essential to eliminating the "leopard spots" created by a cease-fire-in-place. As the lead editorial in the Hanoi journal *Vietnam Courier* declared in September 1973:

> The Paris Agreement recognizes the existence in South Viet Nam of two administrations, two armed forces, and two zones of control. Does this entail the threat of a new and permanent partition of Viet Nam, now split into three parts? Drawing lessons from their experiences of 1954, the Vietnamese negotiators dismissed all U.S.-Saigon proposals for regrouping belligerent forces into a number of well-defined areas: such an operation would facilitate the execution of Nguyen Van Thieu's plan to liquidate "Viet Cong pockets" at a given moment with the support of the U.S.A. or, if need be, to perpetuate the division of South Viet Nam. On insistence of the DRVN and PRG, the U.S.A. had finally to agree that the cease-fire be carried out on the spot, which makes the map of South Viet Nam look like a "leopard skin." But this very "leopard skin" must disappear within the shortest time. The existence of two zones, the recognition of which is imperative in the present phase in order to achieve a solution to South Viet Nam's internal problems, is not intended to last indefinitely.
>
> Certainly it is not a *complete* victory and this is also a question of the relation of forces reflecting itself in the Agreement concluded: the PRG . . . will have to coexist for a certain time with the puppet regime. . . . As shown by the events since January 1973, the situation "half-war, half-peace" will be the backcloth for a multisided struggle on the ground in South Viet Nam with its political, economic, and also its military aspects.

But as 1973 began, both sides were ill-prepared to expand their political support beyond areas they had controlled for decades. Much of the PRG's infrastructure was still weak: the prestige of, and latent sympathy for, the Communist movement had been much reduced by the brutality and the terrorist tactics used during and since the 1968 Tet offensive. For the non-Communists, political mobilization was still largely a product of the antagonisms among them, not a common cause designed to prepare the GVN for a political struggle with the PRG. When U.S. forces were removed from the equation, the countryside reverted to the patterns of control that each side had maintained rather consistently since the war began. It was in these areas that, the "postwar war," as my Vietnamese friends referred to it, was fought.

From the first speculations over the possibility of an agreement leading to a cease-fire-in-place through the end of the 1973 dry season (that is, from early October 1972 through spring 1973), both the PRG and the GVN concentrated on expanding the territory they controlled. Each accused the other of capturing key access points to South Vietnam, populated areas of the countryside adjacent or strategic to the defense of those areas, and certain provincial and district capitals. For the PRG, such land-grabbing made good sense; for the GVN, it was suicide.

In the first year after the Paris Agreement, Saigon alleged that it had been violated 35,673 times. The PRG charged Saigon with 301,000 violations: 34,266 land-grabbing operations, 35,532 artillery shellings, 14,749 aerial bombardments and reconnaissances, and 216,550 police and pacification operations. The initial intent of both sides was to take territory that would later have to be adjudicated by the Two Party Joint Military Commission (TPJMC) as provided for in Article 3(b) of the Paris Agreement. . . . When the TPJMC proved unable even to inspect contested areas, let alone to determine "the areas controlled by each party and modalities of [troop] stationing," both sides fought to regain the territory they had lost.

In the first eighteen months after the agreement, the PRG withdrew from more than 90 hamlets in which it had maintained a long-term presence. and from some 300 others that had been seized during land-grabbing operations in January 1973. Through deploying its forces more thinly, the GVN claimed it had increased its control over nearly 1000 hamlets. The lack of Communist aggressiveness in the land-grabbing war had long-range tactical value: in attempting to assert control over areas long ruled by the PRG, the GVN was encouraged to overextend its forces. The more the government pursued this war, the more vulnerable it became. The more it appeared to be an aggressor, the less military aid it would receive from a rebellious U.S. Congress, and the less it appeared to the population of South Vietnam to be working toward peace. "If we attack our enemies," one captured Communist directive noted, "we will suffer politically. . . . If we permit them to move into our areas, then counterattack, our political image will remain intact." Reporting from such contested areas in 1973 and 1974, U.S. journalists pointed out that GVN control was increasingly restricted to the daytime hours—a pattern reminiscent of that prevailing during most of the 1960s.

On the GVN side, what was needed was both expansion of governmental services and effective security forces that would assure the government twenty-four-hour control and, thereby, a chance for its propaganda, pacification, and economic development programs to take root. Thieu sought to accomplish this through an official administrative revolution begun in mid-spring of 1973. This involved the centralization of all program management and decision-making in the hands of officials personally chosen by Thieu. As Ngo Dinh Diem had used the government structure as a substitute for popular political mobilization, so Thieu now tried to use it as an alternative both to accommodation with the PRG and to mobilization of the popular support that would be essential if the NCRC should be established. But territory seized by the South Vietnamese government in the last moments of the 1972 war did not prove to be fertile ground for "reforms." In this respect, Thieu imitated his predecessors: Saigon governments consistently tended to apply new programs and concepts to areas in which problems were the most acute, or to launch nationwide efforts that spread resources so thinly that the population was frequently alienated from the government rather than mobilized by it.

It was a familiar pattern. Hanoi had always used lulls in the war to consolidate and strengthen the bases of its support in the south. The Saigon government used these lulls to expand its territory rather than to bring competent administration and effective security to the areas already under its control.

Along with the land-grabbing war came the struggle over a series of besieged strategic military bases. These bases alternated as tempting targets for the NVA and as strategic outposts from which the GVN could harass and occasionally interdict infiltration from the Ho Chi Minh trail into the central and northern regions of South Vietnam. They had been the scene of heavy conventional fighting in the past. One such base, Tong le Chanh, was under attack for 411 days before it fell to the North Vietnamese. Most of these bases, beginning with the fall of Le Minh base in western Pleiku on September 24, 1973, were lost to the North Vietnamese several times by the end of 1974. From the North Vietnamese viewpoint, attacks against these bases were designed as much to relieve pressure on supply routes as they were to test GVN morale and to produce in the average GVN soldier's mind the expectation of defeat.

The most intense fighting over these bases—more than 8000 soldiers on both sides were reported killed—occurred from early March through April 1974. By the first week in April, five GVN bases, many of them former U.S. Green Beret outposts, had fallen to NVA assaults. Communist spokesmen hailed the attacks as "a necessary act in order to prevent and stop Saigon land-grabbing operations." The outposts taken secured infiltration routes from Cambodia and NVA use of a newly built road extending from the demilitarized zone to the Parrot's Beak. . . .

As fighting over the strategic fire bases continued in northern and central South Vietnam, the PRG and the GVN were also fighting over the Mekong Delta's rice. There were no front lines in the rice war because the boundaries between zones of government and Communist control in the delta depended on the time of day and the season. Early in 1973, the GVN declared it would deny rice to PRG zones. That August, local GVN officials confiscated all rice in excess of a week's supply from each farming household in territory adjacent to PRG areas. Families were then given weekly withdrawal privileges from provincial storehouses. The excess rice of each household was sold to the government at prices averaging 10 to 50 percent below the market price.

The government's blockade proved ineffective: by paying two to three times the market price, the PRG retained unhindered access to all the rice it needed. Local officials meanwhile used their confiscation powers to increase their exactions from the farmers. Cash values of crops were downgraded arbitrarily, and payments were delayed for from one to several weeks. The net result of these developments was that Saigon, not the PRG, was denied access to rice. By early 1975, GVN officials estimated that fully 20 percent of the 1974 crop had been lost in this manner.

By the fall of 1974, the military balance began shifting to Hanoi's favor. . . . There were then more North Vietnamese Army (NVA) regular combat forces in South Vietnam than at any time during the past decade. Estimates of total Communist troop strength ranged from 285,000 (preferred by most

U.S. analysts) to 387,000 (suggested by GVN officials). Considerably more than half of these troops were deployed in regular infantry divisions in the area extending from the central highlands northward to the DMZ. U.S. officials feared that, if North Vietnam committed any of its estimated four to six reserve divisions to an offensive in the central highlands, or to a drive against the coastal cities of Hue or Danang, the GVN would have a less than equal chance of containing the attack. Communist artillery and armor equaled that of the GVN in number, while more than 10 percent of this inventory included weapons that could be fired completely out of the range of the ARVN's field guns. Enough ordnance had been stockpiled by the NVA to sustain an offensive at the 1972 level for a year.

Ranged against the North Vietnamese and PRG forces were 1.1 million GVN regular and paramilitary defense forces. While fully one-half to two-thirds of Saigon's forces were engaged in static defense missions, no more than 10 percent of the NVA forces were similarly deployed. Some ARVN commanders suggested that, as long as their troops had both to defend 90 percent of the population and to fight the North Vietnamese, even a delicate balance of forces no longer existed. They were right.

By 1974, both Hanoi and Saigon declared that military action was necessary to save the Paris Agreement. Their cease-fire had never been more than a less-fire. The International Commission for Control and Supervision (ICCS), and the Joint Military Commissions responsible for the maintenance of the cease-fire, were never permitted to determine which contested areas were controlled by the GVN and which by the PRG. The cease-fire and resupply inspection mechanisms were hamstrung from the start by the noncooperation of the PRG and Hanoi. The activities of the inspection forces ceased altogether after one unarmed U.S. member of the FPJMT, investigating, with the consent of the PRG, an air crash site where remains of MIAs were reported, stepped from his clearly marked helicopter and was shot dead.

Hanoi charged that it had been misled by the United States into thinking that all U.S. military installations in South Vietnam would be dismantled within sixty days of the agreement. The United States, instead, had transferred to the GVN title to all of its facilities before it signed the Paris Agreement. The North Vietnamese infiltrated additional military personnel into South Vietnam and introduced entirely new weapon systems into the south, while the United States provided Saigon with a few new F5-E fighter aircraft to replace and augment its force of F5-As. According to the terms of the agreement, both sides were permitted only to replace "armaments, munition, and war materiel which have been destroyed, damaged, worn-out or used up . . . on the basis of piece-for-piece, of the same characteristics and properties. . . ."

The agreement provided for the return of all POWs, the release of political prisoners, and a full accounting for all soldiers listed as missing in action (MIA). Only the U.S. POWs were returned to the last man. There has never been a complete accounting by Hanoi of the U.S. MIAs. The GVN charged Hanoi with imprisoning 60,000 soldiers and civilians, while political prisoners in GVN jails were released only in April 1975 when the PRG captured Saigon.

The neutrality of Cambodia and Laos was not respected, nor was an Indochina-wide cease-fire realized. Hostilities in Laos stopped for a time, but this was largely because the United States no longer needed the up-country communications complex to guide bombers to targets in North Vietnam. The Laotian forces of the right, center, and left proclaimed a cease-fire on February 21, 1973, and fourteen months later formed a coalition government. The coalition was soon dominated by the Communist Pathet Lao. Hostilities were resumed shortly thereafter, and the coalition collapsed in the wake of the fall of Phnom Penh and Saigon in the spring of 1975.

The Paris Agreement (Article 12[a]) had also provided that "the two South Vietnamese parties shall sign an agreement on the internal matters of South Vietnam as soon as possible and do their utmost to accomplish this within ninety days after the cease-fire comes into effect, in keeping with the South Vietnamese people's aspiration for peace, independence and democracy." Talks between the two parties began in late March 1973. Over a period of two years, the always acrimonious, sometimes stalled, and ultimately boycotted (after April 16, 1974) discussions revealed only that the GVN and the PRG favored establishing a National Council of Reconciliation and Concord. However, Saigon objected, as it had for the better part of a decade, to the provision in Article 12[a] that the council be composed "of three equal segments." Thieu saw this as giving the Communists undue advantage, even though the council was to function on the basis of unanimity. He argued that the third segment—called the third political tendency by its adherents in Saigon—would be dominated by the Communists, and he worked steadily to isolate, imprison, and generally weaken those associated with it. . . .

In essence, what the agreement had left up to the two South Vietnamese parties to negotiate was not negotiable. The question of who was to have power in the south, both the GVN and the PRG concluded, could only be resolved on the battlefield, not at the conference table. Hoping that international pressure might prevent any resumption of large-scale warfare, the United States arranged a conference for February 26 to March 2, 1973, . . . at which twelve countries were to guarantee the provisions of the Paris Agreement. When these signatories were later asked by the United States to urge Hanoi to halt its 1975 offensive in South Vietnam, not one agreed to do so. Kissinger's expectation that the level of military assistance reaching North Vietnam would decline also was not vindicated. By the end of 1974, Hanoi was receiving approximately twice as much aid as it had during the previous years of the war, twice what the United States was then authorized to provide Saigon.

Throughout the spring and early summer of 1973, U.S. and North Vietnamese representatives held talks on the creation of a Joint Economic Commission through which the U.S. would implement its pledge to contribute to the postwar reconstruction of the DRV. For the most part, negotiations were technical; they avoided charges and countercharges about violations of the agreement. The negotiators went relatively far in terms of talking about specific amounts and projects that would be appropriate for U.S. support. But in the fall of 1973, the U.S. Congress passed a law prohibiting any funds being given to Hanoi until Hanoi accounted for all of the U.S. MIAs. This Hanoi refused to do.

For nearly a week in June, Kissinger and Tho negotiated what they characterized as an amplification and consolidation of the original agreement. Kissinger explained to the press why such follow-up negotiation had become necessary:

> . . . during the course of March and April the United States became quite concerned about the manner in which the cease-fire agreement was being implemented. We were specifically concerned about the following points:
>
> One, the inadequate implementation of the cease-fire.
>
> Secondly, the continued infiltration into South Viet-Nam and the continued utilization of Laos and Cambodia as corridors for that infiltration.
>
> Three, we were concerned about the inadequate accounting for the missing in action.
>
> Fourth, we were concerned about the violations of the demilitarized zone.
>
> Fifth, we were concerned about the inadequate cooperation with the international control commission and the slow staffing of the two-party military commission.
>
> Sixth, we were concerned about the violations of Article 20 requiring the withdrawal of foreign troops from Laos and Cambodia.

But the resulting June communiqué . . . read like the Paris Agreement's obituary. Kissinger and Tho had met nine times that week and the communiqué was the result of more than forty hours of their work. But the hopelessness of the situation was evident: throughout the June talks both Saigon and Hanoi continued to insist on many of the very issues that had stymied the negotiations in October, November, and December 1972. At the conclusion of the June negotiations, Kissinger said that he hoped "to be able to reduce my own participation in this process [of follow-up negotiations] in order to preserve my emotional stability." In late June, the U.S. Congress voted to end all funds for U.S. air operations in Indochina on August 15, 1973. Throughout July, former White House counsel John Dean captured the nation's attention with his side of the Watergate story; by fall, the Nixon administration was under siege domestically, just as its foreign policy of détente was to face a challenge in the Middle East.

With the Cambodian bombing cut off, the president and Kissinger realized that the United States had lost its only means of enforcing the Paris Agreement. There had been debate within the administration in April 1973 over whether a resumption of the bombing of North Vietnam would be an appropriate response to, as Kissinger later put it, Hanoi's "flagrant violations of the agreements." But, Kissinger later said, "President Nixon

. . . never made a final decision . . .'' Many U.S. officials believe that, when it did become clear that U.S. air power would no longer be used in Indochina, the last obstacle to an all-out Communist offensive was removed. Kissinger and Tho met once more in December, with little result. Their talks on December 20, 1973, were designed, from Hanoi's perspective, to see if further progress could be made toward implementing U.S. postwar assistance to the DRV. Kissinger reportedly took the position that one part of the agreement could not be implemented as long as other parts of it were being violated. He stressed the need for the level of military activity in South Vietnam to be reduced, for Hanoi to account for all of the American MIAs, and for the North Vietnamese troops to withdraw from Cambodia and Laos.

With the Paris Agreement moribund, Kissinger's most difficult negotiations were those he had with Congress over future aid to Vietnam. Both he and Nixon had assured Thieu that the United States would not stand idly by in the face of continuing pressure from the NVA and that U.S. aid to Saigon would continue at appropriate levels. In November and December 1972, and again during his state visit in 1973, Thieu pressed Nixon for a specific pledge, but Nixon continually responded by saying that only Congress could make such pledges. As late as the fall of 1974, however, senior U.S. officials were still telling their South Vietnamese counterparts that Saigon would get its aid.

But the U.S. Congress ultimately proved impervious to the pleadings of many that military assistance for the 1974–1975 fiscal year be appropriated, even at the authorized level. Administration spokesmen argued that Saigon spent at the level of the actual authorization ($1 billion) and geared its defense program to that ceiling rather than to the $700 million that was appropriated in September 1974 after a surprise cut was made during House debate. And of the $700 million then available for military aid, more than $400 million were charged off for shipping costs. At the end of the pipeline was less than $300 million in military assistance. Exclusive of their shipping costs, Moscow and Peking provided Hanoi nearly $400 million in war materiel. Interviews with a variety of GVN officials acknowledged that the U.S. cut, coupled with worldwide inflation, gravely affected Saigon's capability to respond to a North Vietnamese offensive. To these pleadings and assessments congressional leaders tended to respond as did Senator Hubert Humphrey, floor manager of the Foreign Assistance Act, in a speech he gave at the time:

> After millions of words about the lessons of Vietnam, we ignore the most important lesson, that political battles cannot be resolved by force of arms.
>
> We learned this lesson at great sacrifice to our nation. Yet our policymakers now are engaged in a course of action which does not recognize this basic reality of Indochina. The United States has embarked upon a course of encouraging the funding of maximum military confrontation, hoping that somehow those we are supporting can prevail.
>
> . . . How can the policy of military confrontation be sustained when it is

clear that neither the Congress nor the American public is willing to fund the wars in Vietnam and Cambodia at high levels for the indefinite future?

Kissinger later told Barbara Walters, in an interview on the May 5, 1975, "Today Show," that he would never have negotiated the Paris Agreement if he had thought the U.S. Congress would have proved so difficult. Because of the restrictions placed on the use of American air power and the reluctance of Congress in 1974 to appropriate adequate aid for Saigon, Kissinger said he believed the resumption of the war by North Vietnam was inevitable. Ultimately, in the face of that prospect Saigon's army, and then its government, collapsed.

I originally thought it would be possible to end this study of the Vietnam negotiations with a prediction of how an eventual political settlement between the Communists and the non-Communists in South Vietnam could evolve. Such a settlement, I thought, was likely on the one hand, because of the strong anticommunism of substantial segments of Vietnamese religious and social forces, and on the other, because it was difficult for me to imagine the GVN collapsing overnight. But with a political settlement, I did expect the creation of a government not unlike the tripartite one hinted at in the Paris Agreement. Thereafter, I expected the gradual emergence of the PRG as the dominant political force in the south, just as, in 1945 and 1946, the Viet Minh—even though a minority in the north—came to dominate all other nationalist forces in the coalition government established there after World War II.

In retrospect I underestimated the PRG's prediction that the "internal contradictions" in the GVN would cause it to collapse, eliminating the need for Saigon's army to be defeated militarily. Such internal contradictions were abundant, even to the most casual observers: proclaiming an economic and social revolution, the GVN depended on the very elites who stood to lose the most from change. The peasant soldier was still led by ill-trained, urban-born scions of the elite, and army officer assignments were still largely determined by bribery. In 1975, nationalist political forces were as unprepared and unorganized for a political struggle with the PRG as they had been in 1965.

Yet, to my mind, each year that the GVN managed to survive made its collapse a little less likely. Moreover, the political opposition that Thieu faced in the fall of 1974 hardly compared with that against Diem in 1963, and the ARVN appeared to be equal to the military challenge it expected from the NVA in 1975. As one high U.S. embassy official put it that January: "We are talking about well-equipped experienced [ARVN] soldiers who know we won't do their fighting for them. The NVA is going to launch another offensive but all our indicators show that it will be nothing compared to what the ARVN withstood and pushed back at Tet 1968 or in the 1972 Easter offensive." With respect to the strength of the 1975 NVA offensive, the embassy official was right.

I traveled to Saigon in early January 1975 to conduct one last series of interviews for this book. Another dry season had begun in Vietnam and with it, the postwar war resumed against the backdrop of the breakdown of the Paris Agreement. I arrived on the eve of the fall of the provincial capital of Phuoc Long, although its loss was not confirmed by the GVN for several days. But the next day, a Vietnamese friend told me that when he saw the street banners go up proclaiming: "All compatriots support the heroic defenders of Phuoc Long," he knew the end was at hand. What I learned during the next three weeks convinced me that he was right.

After three weeks of interviewing Vietnamese officials and opposition political leaders, I concluded that the most well-organized segments of the South Vietnamese population actually expected a Communist victory. Their leaders began to use the word *accommodation* synonymously with *adaptation*. *Accommodation* had once referred to "live and let live" arrangements whereby GVN supporters coexisted with the NLF. But by January 1975, *adaptation* meant surviving while living under communism. Cabinet-level GVN officials believed that Phuoc Long was only the beginning. As one cabinet minister put it, "Much more of our territory will now be lost." I was repeatedly told that the boundary between North and South Vietnam was now, de facto, south of the seventeenth parallel and that there was to be a line drawn inside South Vietnam dividing it into eastern and western (Communist) regions.

The political opposition was equally pessimistic about both prospects for further partitioning of Vietnam and accommodation with the PRG. Consequently, the opposition was leaderless by January 1975 and no longer willing either to struggle for an alternative to Thieu or to participate in politics. The active opposition leaders who two years earlier were rarely in their offices due to their political activities in the countryside now were never in their offices due to having returned to private life. No one was coming forward to take their place.

When a strategic retreat was ordered from the central highlands in mid-March, the South Vietnamese soldiers panicked and in domino fashion abandoned outpost after outpost. They were reacting as much to the prospect of a fight with the NVA as to their future under the GVN. ARVN soldiers no longer believed (if they ever did) that they would eventually win against the NVA, and they no longer wanted war. As one U.S. embassy official put it in April 1975:

> We should have asked ourselves long ago how an army can go on functioning when it is simply a business organization in which everything is for sale, from what you eat to a transfer or a promotion. We never encouraged the Vietnamese forces to fight aggressively, to take the offensive. We fought the war for them and made them over dependent on air support. We prepared them for conventional war when the Communists were fighting unconventionally, and then, when the Communists finally adopted conventional tactics, the South Vietnamese didn't know what to do. The fact they have no leadership is largely our fault; we made them followers, so successfully that even the soldiers who were willing to fight got killed or wounded as a result of incompetence, or lost by default. . . .

From Ban Me Thuot in the central highlands, to Danang on the northern coast, and to the Mekong Delta in the south, retreating ARVN soldiers refused to believe that the future promised to them could be achieved by the government that the United States had supported in Saigon. America's lost peace in Vietnam came not only because of what was negotiated, but also because neither the process of negotiations nor the agreement itself produced a Saigon government that could end the war—through accommodation with the PRG or through victory over it.

I have not written this . . . with a view to apportioning responsibility for the whole chapter for history labeled "The Vietnam War." But such an accounting would certainly have to come to terms not only with what made a meaningful negotiated settlement unlikely, but also with the wisdom of the decision by successive American presidents to seek such a settlement, and the implications that this decision had for the strategy by which the war was fought. In retrospect, to be incremental in our military strategy and conciliatory in our negotiating strategy with an adversary who, from the outset, equated restraint with weakness, and to whom compromise was inconceivable, had the effect of obscuring what the costs of intervention in Vietnam were likely to be and, equally important, what the ultimate gains there might look like. But when U.S. policy-makers suddenly faced the end of the proverbial tunnel in Vietnam and witnessed the Saigon army fleeing the countryside—abandoning in a matter of days what it had taken a decade to secure and "pacify"—they realized there was no realistic option open that would have justified the investment. Probably there never was. Thus are the lives of men and women and the spirit of great nations wasted in adventures that ultimately bring neither the peace intended nor honor.

Why the Communists Won

WILLIAM J. DUIKER

The 1975 campaign had progressed with truly lightning speed, stunning the Saigon regime and even surpassing the expectations of the Party leadership in Hanoi. In three weeks, eight provinces had fallen to the Communists. Virtually all forces in Saigon's I and II Corps were wiped out. ARVN had lost almost half its main force units, and more than half its aircraft. The capital was in a state of evident panic, while Washington appeared impotent. On the final day of March, two days after the fall of Da Nang, the Politburo met again and concluded that the war had entered a stage of massive development. Van Tien Dung was instructed to prepare to launch a general offensive against Saigon with the objective of seizing total victory within

From William J. Duiker, *The Communist Road to Power in Vietnam*, excerpts from pp. 314–329. Reprinted by permission of the author.

four weeks: "Not only has the revolutionary war in the South entered a period of developing by leaps and bounds, but the time is ripe for carrying the general offensive and general uprising to the enemy's lair. From this moment, the final decisive battle of our army and people has begun; its aim is to complete the people's national democratic revolution in the South and bring peace and the reunification of the Fatherland."

On April 2, Van Tien Dung ordered most North Vietnamese main force units to turn south. With seaports along the northern and central coast now open and ARVN prisoners pressed into service as truck drivers, war matériel began to flow south in vast quantities, while an air shuttle was set up from the D.R.V. to Kontum and Da Nang. Two more reserve divisions were sent south and a new military headquarters was set up near Saigon to replace COSVN. Van Tien Dung was named chairman, with Pham Hung as his chief political officer. Le Duc Tho was on hand to provide a direct link with the Politburo. After several days of intensive consultation, the new military command agreed on a basic strategy for the final assault, to be labeled the "Ho Chi Minh Campaign" because of Hanoi's intention to rename Saigon for the founder of the Party. According to Dung's account, the plan was to set up a strategic encirclement of the city by cutting Route 4 from the delta and Route 1 from Tay Ninh, while main force units marching down from the north would concentrate for a major thrust on the provincial capital of Xuan Loc, east of Saigon, where the crucial Eighteenth Division was located. As those main force units prepared for the final assault on Saigon, local forces would seize suburban areas, and the Party's suicide and guerrilla units in the city would prepare to surface to incite a general uprising.

In Saigon, hopes that the situation could be stabilized were rapidly evaporating. With the earlier plan to set up a defense line anchored at Tay Ninh and Nha Trang outdated by the swift pace of events, Thieu moved to set up a line from the city of Tay Ninh, still under siege, to Phan Rang on the coast, anchored at Xuan Loc, where the Eighteenth Division formed the last major bulwark against total collapse. Even this position might soon become untenable. With half of the ARVN gone, Saigon had only about six divisions plus a few brigades and ranger groups remaining, a total of less than 100,000 troops. Prospects for U.S. support appeared dim. The Ford administration was attempting to push through Congress a $1 billion aid package, but congressional resistance to any further aid to the Saigon regime had increased and approval appeared unlikely.

With military stabilization apparently out of the question, there was increasing talk of a compromise settlement. There had been hints from various diplomatic sources that Hanoi might accept a negotiated settlement. Hanoi's presumed price for peace was the departure of President Thieu and the immediate end of any further U.S. involvement in South Vietnam. Opposition politicians in Saigon clamored for the resignation of Nguyen Van Thieu and began to explore the possibility of a peace candidate such as the popular but enigmatic general Duong Van Minh. There had been some encouragement of this line from the PRG, when on April 2 Foreign

Minister Nguyen Thi Binh had expressed a willingness to talk to Minh. Even top officials in the U.S. Embassy were cautiously optimistic that a compromise agreement could be worked out.

It is doubtful, however, that Hanoi was interested in a political settlement. With military victory now within easy reach and little likelihood of a U.S. response, there seemed no persuasive reason to compromise. As intelligence reports showed, Party leaders had decided at the end of March to settle for nothing less than total victory. A diplomatic settlement was hinted at probably to increase divisiveness in Saigon.

By the third week of April, North Vietnamese divisions had occupied Phan Rang and were beginning to encircle Xuan Loc, moving in on the highway leading to Bien Hoa, site of a major GVN airbase and weapons arsenal. From the delta, Communist units were moving north toward Saigon. All of Tay Ninh Province had been occupied except the capital, which was still under siege. As the campaign neared its climax, Saigon's resistance briefly flared. At Xuan Loc, the Eighteenth Division dug in and proved tougher than expected, slowing down the Communist blitzkrieg and stimulating a brief flurry of optimism in Saigon that total defeat could yet be averted. But the odds were too great and, after a few days of stiff resistance, ARVN units began to withdraw southward toward Vung Tau, while Communist forces bypassed Xuan Loc and began to move directly on Bien Hao and to shell its air base.

It was by now no secret that Hanoi intended to carry its offensive directly to the heart of enemy rule. The plan called for wearing down the five remaining ARVN divisions on the outskirts of the city and then launching a massive assault with main force and armored units directly into the city before government units in the suburbs could respond. The attack would be led by North Vietnamese mechanized forces, which would advance directly on the main highways into the heart of Saigon. There they would attempt to seize five major targets—the presidential palace, the headquarters of the Saigon city military command, the general police directorate, Tan Son Nhut Airport in the north-western suburbs, and the nearby headquarters of the general staff. As described by Dung, the plan was

> to use whatever forces necessary from each direction to encircle enemy forces, isolating them and preventing them from pulling back to Saigon; to wipe out and disperse the enemy main-force infantry divisions in the outer defense perimeter right on the spot; and to save the greatest number of forces to thrust in quickly and capture key positions in the outskirts. This would open the way for mechanized and tightly organized assault units to advance rapidly along the main roads and strike directly at the five chosen objectives inside the city.

The attacks in the suburbs went on schedule, as company or battalion-sized units in Go Vap, Nha Be, Binh Chanh, Hoc Mon, Thu Duc, and Cu Chi rose on April 27 and, with the aid of regular forces in the area, began to overrun military and government installations in the vicinity and to seize key bridges and guide the main force units into the city. Others were to eliminate traitors and call on ARVN soldiers to desert their units.

Meanwhile, within the city the Party's municipal apparatus activated its special action squads and sapper units and prepared to seize key government installations, while propaganda units prepared to distribute leaflets and set up loudspeakers at key points to arouse the populace to support the invading revolutionary forces. Special sapper units were organized at Nha Be and Long Tau to sabotage GVN shipping and to cut the river route to the sea. Others were active in Long Binh and Bien Hoa, while a few were infiltrated into the city to supplement the sixty special action cells and 300 armed civilians directed by the Party's municipal leadership. By the twenty-ninth, main force units were well established in key positions around the capital. In the east, routes to the south and west were cut and Bien Hoa Air Base and Vung Tau had been isolated. At command headquarters, Pham Hung and Le Duc Tho made preparations for forming a transitional revolutionary administration in the capital.

In Saigon, the situation raced to a climax. Phnom Penh had fallen to Communist forces on April 17. On the eighteenth the Ford administration, despite Ambassador Graham Martin's objections, ordered a gradual pullout of nonessential Americans. On the twenty-third President Ford announced that the war was finished as far as the United States was concerned. The South Vietnamese, he said, must confront whatever fate awaited them. Under considerable pressure, Thieu finally resigned on the twenty-first and was replaced by Tran Van Huong, a veteran Saigon politician who had achieved a moment of fame during a brief stint as prime minister in 1965. The change was futile, for the Communists refused to deal with him. Van Tien Dung described him as just a "very crafty civilian traitor" replacing a "savage military traitor." Huong resigned on the twenty-seventh and was replaced by Duong Van Minh. Minh quickly formed a new cabinet and ordered the United States to remove its personnel from the GVN in twenty-four hours. The demand had little significance, for current plans called for total evacuation by the twenty-ninth in any case. Nor had it any useful results, for the PRG contemptuously rejected negotiations with the new president.

On April 26, as the first rains began in the delta, Van Tien Dung and his subordinates had moved by car to their advance campaign headquarters near Ben Cat. That afternoon the final campaign began with an artillery barrage on the outskirts of Saigon. From all directions, North Vietnamese forces advanced toward the city and relentlessly scattered resistance from the remaining ARVN forces on the outskirts of the capital. By the evening of the twenty-ninth, Saigon was surrounded as by a vise and Hanoi's main force units, in the words of Van Tien Dung, were poised like a "divine hammer" held aloft, awaiting the word to launch the direct assault on the city of Saigon.

At 2:00 A.M. on April 30, as the last Americans were preparing to leave Vietnam from helicopter pads around the city, the PRG indicated its final refusal to the appeal for negotiations from the Saigon government. During the early morning, Hanoi's "deep strike units" began to move slowly down the major highways toward the city. Armored vehicles advanced in columns straight into the city, followed by infantry. As they entered without meeting resistance, special action squads occupied bridges while propaganda units passed out leaflets and revolutionary flags and called on the populace to welcome the revolutionary forces. There was some evidence of enthusiasm, particularly in working-class neighborhoods, but for the most part the advance was observed in silence. The attacking troops were supposed to be guided by revolutionary squads, but in at least one case, a tank commander lost his way and had to ask directions from ARVN troops standing by the side of the road.

President Duong Van Minh had met with his ministers at Independence Palace in the heart of the city and at 10:00 A.M. issued an appeal for a cease-fire. The appeal was ignored. In an indirect response, the Politburo issued a directive to its troops advancing into Saigon: "Continue the attack on Saigon according to plan, advancing in the most powerful spirit, liberate and take over the whole city, disarm enemy troops, dissolve the enemy administration at all levels, and thoroughly smash all enemy resistance." Shortly before noon, the lead tank of the Second Army Corps rumbled up Thong Nhut Boulevard and rolled onto the green lawn of the Independence Palace. Troops arrested the government ministers inside the building and raised the revolutionary flag of the PRG over the palace. Two hours later, Duong Van Minh called on all ARVN forces to lay down their arms. The war, the long bitter struggle that had lasted in one form or another for an entire generation, was finally at an end.

The predominantly military character of the final campaign has led some observers to downgrade the political significance of the Communist victory and assert that the takeover of the South was a military conquest, pure and simple. A number of high Saigon civilian and military officials echo this contention by complaining that the war was lost primarily because of the failure of the Ford administration to provide adequate military assistance to the ARVN forces in the final months. The charge is understandable. Although the 1975 campaign was described by Party spokesmen as a combined general offensive and uprising, an attack by revolutionary armed forces in rural areas coordinated with a popular uprising in the cities in the tradition of the Tet Offensive and the great August Revolution of 1945, the reality is somewhat different. The bulk of the fighting was undertaken by regular force units of the PAVN. Although the PLAF undoubtedly participated in attacks at the local level, the most damaging blows were inflicted by North Vietnamese troops. And what the Party lauded as a mass popular uprising in the cities consisted in the main of the mobilization of the Party's small municipal apparatus to welcome the North Vietnamese troops—the *bo doi*—as they entered the cities from the suburbs. While there was some organized jubilation in a few working-class areas, there was relatively little spontaneous enthusiasm among the general urban populace. It is not surprising that Hanoi would dress up the final stage of the conflict as a popular upsurge against an unpopular regime. In fact, however, the final triumph was achieved primarily by force of arms.

But the fact that the 1975 campaign was primarily a military offensive should not obscure the fundamental reality that the Party's success over a generation was attributable, above all, to nonmilitary factors. Hanoi's ability to organize and direct the insurgency and to exploit the chronic weaknesses of its adversary in Saigon were the cardinal factors in its success. Even at the end, the defeat of the GVN was probably caused less by a shortage of aircraft and ammunition than by a lack of nerve in Saigon and by the pervasive sense of malaise throughout South Vietnamese society, itself the legacy of a generation of failure by successive governments to build the foundations of a viable non-Communist society. Not least, the defeat was caused by serious deficiencies in the strategic planning of the Thieu regime. Thieu's hasty last-minute decision to abandon most of the northern provinces and the Central Highlands was ill-conceived and created a disastrous sense of confusion among top military officers as well as within the government. It contributed in no small measure to the completeness of the final collapse.

The U.S. failure to provide adequate military support in the final weeks, although not one of Washington's prouder moments, was not a decisive factor in the outcome of the war. For years the Communists had done better with less. Despite President John F. Kennedy's insistence that, in the last analysis, the war had to be waged and won by the Vietnamese, Washington's clients had come to depend heavily on U.S. largesse. It was a fatal flaw, for when the military shield represented by the power of the United States was withdrawn, the many weaknesses of the Saigon regime quickly surfaced and proved decisive.

All great revolutions are the product of multiple causes. They result from the convergence of several factors, some of them related directly to the overall political and cultural environment, others the consequence of individual human action. Marxist theory reflects this reality by locating the sources of revolution in both objective and subjective conditions. Objective conditions determine whether or not a mature revolutionary situation has arisen in a given society. Subjective conditions reflect the degree of preparedness and astute leadership provided by a revolutionary party. Revolution rarely succeeds unless both factors are present. The Marxist viewpoint is thus not simply a handy heuristic device, but a practical and often effective approach to the problem of waging revolution in human society.

But although all great revolutions share elements of both spontaneity and human will, the relative importance of these two factors has varied greatly over the years. Many of the classical revolutions in modern history—the French Revolution of 1789, the Russian Revolution of 1917, and, more recently, the revolution in Iran in the late 1970s—grew out of a relatively spontaneous eruption of popular discontent. Only after the initial stage of popular uprising did a revolutionary organization begin to manipulate these conditions to promote a final and total overthrow of existing authority.

The modern phenomenon of people's war has added a new dimension to the revolutionary process. Spontaneity has been replaced with calculation, the popular uprising with the concept of a protracted conflict. Although the presence of objective conditions favoring revolt is still considered to be ultimately essential, this factor is increasingly subordinated to the existence of a dedicated revolutionary organization whose duty it is to exacerbate the political and social tensions in societies undergoing the stress of change. The revolutionary party must serve as the catalyst to activate the latent revolutionary conditions in such societies and then take advantage of the resultant ferment to bring about a violent upheaval against the status quo and the formation of a revolutionary regime.

Although Lenin, because of his stress on the importance of individual human action in the revolutionary process, may claim partial credit for the liberation of the Marxist dialectic from the "iron laws" of history, it was Mao Tse-tung who carried Lenin's idea to its logical conclusion and, in the form of people's war, put it into practice. The Vietnamese carried on the Maoist tradition and set out deliberately to create revolutionary conditions that would topple the government and bring communism to power. Discontent against French colonial rule and later against the failures of the Saigon regime was undeniably a factor in creating the objective conditions underlying the Vietnamese revolution. But the Communist Party mobilized the inchoate frustration and anger of the mass of the Vietnamese population and fashioned it into a fierce and relentless weapon of revolutionary war.

Of all the great revolutions, then, the Vietnamese revolution was, above all, an act of human will. That does not mean that it took place in a vacuum. Even the Vietnamese Party leadership conceded that a revolutionary upsurge could not take place unless the proper opportunity—the semimystical *thoi co*—had arisen. Some of the conditions that are necessary are the classical symptoms that characterize the emergence of a prerevolutionary situation in any human society—widespread poverty, economic disorder, social inequality and unrest, an unpopular or incompetent government, and a "transfer of allegiance" on the part of the urban middle class. Such conditions, of course, do not necessarily lead to revolt. But without them, revolution is difficult, if not impossible.

At various times in its modern history, Vietnam has exhibited a number of these symptoms, and they were clearly a factor in the growth of the revolutionary movement. But it was characteristic of the situation in Vietnam that the Communists did not passively await the emergence of an economic and social crisis before launching their bid for power, but deliberately attempted to bring it about through exacerbating latent tensions in society and bringing the existing government to the point of collapse. Even in the late 1950s, when Diem's own actions had led to widespread discontent in South Vietnamese society, it was the Communists, above all, who set a match to the powder keg and thus inaugurated the revolutionary war.

In such conditions, the comparative political ability of revolutionaries and ruling elites becomes a crucial issue. And this was what was most extraordinary about the situation in Vietnam—the contrast between the chronic weakness and political ineptitude of the Saigon governing elite and the political genius of the Communist Party. The underlying reasons for the weakness of non-Communist nationalism have been the subject of scholarly analysis for decades, but satisfactory answers have been elusive. Was it merely an accident of history that could be rectified by time and effort? A generation of policymakers in Washington took this view, and based U.S. strategy on the assumption that with adequate military and economic assistance, a regime would eventually emerge that could establish an aura of political legitimacy and a popular base among the population at large. The Communists, of course, thought otherwise. They were convinced that Saigon's weaknesses were endemic and would eventually become the decisive factor in the war.

In retrospect, it appears that the Communists had a clearer view. A generation of U.S. technology and advice was unable to remedy the manifold deficiencies of the GVN. And although the mistakes of the United States may have contributed to the failure in Saigon, it seems probable that the key to the problem lay in Vietnam. The ineffectiveness of the Vietnamese nationalism during the colonial period is a matter of record. It consistently failed to produce a challenge to French rule or to provide a nucleus for a mass movement of national proportions such as those formed in a number of other colonial or semicolonial societies in the region. It is surely significant that the first non-Communist government in Vietnam did not come to power as a result of its own efforts, but was imposed from above, by the French. The governments that arose in Saigon after the Geneva settlement bore the mark of that heritage. They were concerned over the need to overcome the chronic factionalism that had characterized nationalist behavior during the colonial period, but they failed to resolve the problem or to build a constituency among the mass of the population. To the end, the only real source of Saigon's authority was the U.S. military presence.

Why were the moderate forces in Vietnam less able than their counterparts elsewhere to emerge as the central force in the struggle for independence? Over the years, a number of hypotheses have been advanced. Some observers have suggested that the root cause lay in the stifling effects of French policy, that the brutal repression of the Vietnamese nationalist movement by the colonial regime left a vacuum that was filled by the Communists. This explanation may be emotionally satisfying to critics of French colonial policy, but it is not very persuasive. On the whole, moderate nationalist forces in Vietnam received little worse treatment than they did elsewhere in colonial Southeast Asia. Only those avowedly determined to root out French rule by force, such as the VNQDD [Vietnam Nam Quoc Dan Dang, or Vietnamese Nationalist Party], were exposed to systematic persecution. Although moderate political parties in Vietnam were seldom allowed to enjoy a legal existence, they were given tacit permission to operate during the late 1930s, with no visible effects on their capabilities. A few nationalist figures were arrested and condemned to terms in prison, but most, including such fervent critics of French rule as Nguyen An Ninh and Ta Thu Thau, were soon back on the streets as the result of periodic amnesties declared in Paris. In fact, a non-Communist nationalist movement based on quasi-legal action and mass support, such as the Indian Congress Party, failed to develop in Vietnam not solely because the French prevented it, but primarily because no one attempted to form one.

It can hardly be said, then, that French brutality repressed moderate nationalists, thus leaving the field, by elimination, to the Communists. To the contrary, released documents in the French archives show that the Sûreté had become concerned about the Communists as early as 1929 and throughout much of the following decade devoted the greater part of its efforts to relentlessly pursuing the Party and preventing it from spreading its roots throughout the country. If anything, it is likely that French harassment served to toughen the Communists for the generation of struggle that lay ahead.

Party historians have a different explanation for the weakness of their rivals. Predictably, they view the issue through the prism of Marxist class analysis, and explain it as a consequence of the belated development of the Vietnamese bourgeoisie under colonial rule and its resultant failure to assume an active role in the Vietnamese revolution. By contrast, the Vietnamese working class developed early, in the mines, plantations, and factories run by French colonial interests, and was thus able to take the lead in the struggle for independence after the defeat of the VNQDD at Yen Bay in early 1930. This is an interesting hypothesis, but it lacks sufficient corroborative evidence based on a comparative analysis with other colonial societies in Southeast Asia, where similar conditions apparently existed without leading to a Communist victory. Moreover, it does not account for the fact that the Communist movement itself did not emerge directly from the Vietnamese proletariat but from among discontented members of the traditional ruling class, the sons and daughters of the patriotic scholar-gentry.

The question thus needs to be reformulated. The point is not that the Vietnamese middle class failed to assert its leadership over the nationalist movement, thereby leaving a vacuum to be filled by the proletariat. It is that such a high percentage of the most politically active elements within the educated elite chose to follow the Communists rather than their nationalist rivals, thus providing the Party with its early leadership and a significant advantage in the struggle to determine the course of the Vietnamese revolution. If such is the case, the cultural argument referred to earlier seems a more plausible hypothesis. Marxism exerted a peculiar attraction among the educated scholar-elite in Vietnam. Logical in its portrayal of the historical forces at work in the world, activist in its call for the formation of a disciplined revolutionary organization devoted to the struggle for change, ethical in its vision of a future utopia based on economic and social equality, it offered a persuasive alternative to the now discredited Confucian world view and provided patriotic Vietnamese with a basis on which to struggle for independence and build a new sense of national identity.

The fact that Marxism appealed particularly to the young generation of patriotic scholar-elites is crucial. This was the traditional ruling class in Vietnamese society. It had a heritage of educational leadership and service to society, and an equally strong awareness of the concept of Vietnamese nationhood. It was thus the logical class to lead the struggle against colonial rule. Many alienated members of this class were attracted to Marxism, giving the Party a momentum that it never relinquished. This must be recognized as one of the most significant facts in the history of modern Vietnam.

The weakness of their nationalist rivals was, of course, no guarantee that the Communists themselves would succeed. Economic and military support from Western powers provided non-Communist elites with a bulwark against social and political deterioration and a measure of protection against the spontaneous forces of popular discontent. The Communists could not wait for the proper conditions to arise. They must themselves bring them about by an act of will. Here, of course, was the challenge of people's war in South Vietnam—to hone the disparate sources of revolt into a well-oiled and highly disciplined instrument of revolutionary war. Only through the application of relentless pressure by the insurgency could the latent structural flaws in South Vietnamese society be magnified into yawning cracks that would eventually bring the entire structure to the ground. In Vietnam, there is little doubt that the Party met that challenge. If some revolutions are essentially a collapse of the old order, and others are the product of individual human action, the Vietnamese revolution is quintessentially an example of the latter.

The reasons for the Party's success have attracted considerable attention among scholars in recent years. Certainly one major factor was its comprehensive strategy of people's war. [My] primary theme . . . is the gradual evolution of that strategy from the early years of the Communist movement down to the final triumph in 1975. The strategy began as a rather unquestioning application of Bolshevik doctrine, as passed on by the Comintern in Moscow. The Russian model had little relevance to Vietnam, however, and during World War II the Party replaced it with a new strategy designed to reflect local conditions. This new strategy owed a debt to the Chinese theory and practice of people's war, but above all it was a product of the fertile mind of Ho Chi Minh. Its major components were put into practice during the revolt that took place at the end of the Pacific War. The success of the August Revolution is adequate testimony to the genius of the concept.

The strategy used during the August uprising could not be applied successfully against a highly armed adversary, and during the Franco-Vietminh conflict the Party turned more explicitly to the Chinese model of three-stage war. The strategy was generally successful, but it had certain weaknesses, among which was the excessive reliance on military factors in the later stages of the war, thus matching the Party's major area of weakness (firepower) against the primary strength of its adversary. After

Geneva, then, the Party leadership returned to the strategy used during the August Revolution. But with escalation in the early 1960s, the Party was forced once again to resort to the military option. Now, however, it appeared to recognize the limited relevance of the Maoist model and attempted to combine it with key elements from the Vietnamese approach. Specifically, it attempted to make greater use of the "political force of the masses" in an effort to achieve a better balance of political and military struggle than had obtained during the previous conflict. It also returned to the August Revolution model by seeking to use the revolutionary force of urban radicalism through the concept of a coordinated military offensive and general uprising. Finally, it now made deliberate use of diplomacy as a means of achieving a psychological advantage over the United States and eventually maneuvering it out of the war.

There is, then, a coherent pattern in the development of Vietnamese revolutionary doctrine. Clearly, however, it would be foolhardy to suggest that it had emerged full-blown from the minds of Party leaders in the mid-1940s. On the contrary, Vietnamese revolutionary strategy, in its mature form, was the product of trial and error, of a series of pragmatic decisions taken over a period of several decades and based on real contemporary situations. In the process, it periodically ran into serious difficulties. On several occasions, Party leaders miscalculated enemy intentions and capabilities. On others, they overrestimated (or underestimated) the force of the masses and their degree of support for the revolutionary cause. Not surprisingly, problems were encountered in attempting to cope with the challenges of foreign involvement. In particular, U.S. escalation in the mid-1960s presented Party strategists with a dilemma, and for a while they appeared to grope almost in desperation for a solution.

It should also be kept in mind that under the carefully cultivated impression of unity there was frequently dissension over policy within the Party leadership. Virtually every major decision was accompanied by hesitation, vacillation, and internal controversy over the strategy to be applied. There was disagreement over timing, over the relationship between political and military struggle, and over the relative priority to be assigned to revolutionary war in the South and socialist construction in the North. It would be misleading to see in such dissent indications of serious factionalism within the Party leadership. It is noteworthy that the Leninist tradition of democratic centralism was maintained throughout the struggle. But disagreement did exist. A clearer appreciation of the nature of such inner-Party tension, and the identity of the individuals involved, must await additional evidence.

Despite such problems, on the whole the strategy was effective. This must be ascribed to several factors. In the first place Party leaders possessed a clear view of the power relationships among and the security interests of the various forces involved. They correctly assessed the chronic weakness of their rivals within the nationalist camp; they correctly predicted that a significant proportion of the population could be motivated to serve the revolutionary cause in a long and difficult struggle; and they realized that France and the United States had neither the patience nor national interests sufficient to justify a protracted conflict in Indochina. In such calculations, strategists in Hanoi proved to be more clear-sighted than their counterparts in Paris and Washington.

A key factor in the Party's ability to mobilize support within Vietnam was the success of its effort to link the force of nationalism with that of social reform. The essentials of that strategy had been drawn up in 1941 with the formation of the Vietminh Front. As this study has attempted to show, this linkage was not easily achieved. Radical programs of benefit to the poor undermined the effort to win the support of moderate nationalists. But a neglect of the issue of land reform left poor peasants indifferent and difficult to mobilize for the war effort. In the late 1940s, Party strategy had placed heavier emphasis on the anti-imperialist than on the antifeudal cause. This was rectified in the early 1950s, and during the war against the United States Hanoi attempted to place relatively equal weight on both factors— the national liberation struggle and the land revolution.

How successful was the Party's effort to "walk on two legs," to construct a strategy on the dual issues of patriotism and social revolution? A definitive judgment must await further study, but available information suggests that the policy was reasonably successful. At some stages (the early years of the Party and during the first stages of the Franco-Vietminh conflict) the national issue predominated; at other times (the Nghe-Tinh revolt, the August Revolution, just prior to the 1954 settlement, and during the late 1950s) economic issues played a crucial role. During the struggle in the South, both issues contributed to support for the revolutionary cause. Interviews with prisoners and defectors show that those who joined the NLF did so for a variety of reasons. The majority were poor peasants or members of the rural proletariat, but urban volunteers were by no means rare. Most cited patriotism or personal motives as their reasons for joining, although social pressure undoubtedly played a role and there is evidence of compulsion in some instances. Members who joined before 1954 frequently mentioned patriotism as the primary reason. Those who joined after Geneva seemed to offer a wider variety of motives—a desire for adventure or for land, hopes for career advancement, a desire to avoid government conscription or to escape from personal problems. In his study of the movement in Long An Province, Jeffrey Race alluded to the importance of the NLF's ability to provide an alternate road to personal identity and upward mobility for those discontented with life under the GVN.

It is worthy to note that idealism—resentment against government corruption and injustice, or a wish to evict the U.S. imperialists—was often cited as a major factor in recruitment. Virtually all mentioned the idea of the "just cause," the "righteous war" against foreign control and the reactionary government in Saigon. It is particularly significant that patriotic motives played a part in recruitment in rural areas, a sign that nationalism had taken root among the village population. This concept of the "just war" was not just a passing enthusiasm, or one that would be easily undermined as a result of sacrifice and hardship. A surprising number of deserters gave personal reasons for leaving the movement and continued to believe that the revolutionary cause was a righteous one.

In general, then, the Party's propaganda had a fairly broad appeal within the population, and in both urban and rural areas. Still, Party leaders must have been somewhat disappointed by their failure to operate more effectively in the cities. Active support in urban areas never reached the levels apparently expected by the party. This failure was generally ascribed in internal documents to organizational weaknesses, or to the influence of the "noxious weeds" of bourgeois attitudes in the cities of South Vietnam. Whatever the reason, the failure to build a more dynamic movement in Saigon, Da Nang, and Hué was undoubtedly a factor in compelling the Party to turn to a more military approach. That in turn led to increasing reliance on troops from the North, thus diluting somewhat the issue of nationalism. Whatever the case, the concept of the popular uprising steadily lost force in Hanoi's strategy and at the end had become more the ritualistic perpetuation of a myth than a building block of victory. In the final analysis, the Communist takeover did not differ substantially from the Maoist dictum of surrounding the cities from the countryside. This was not a crucial weakness, in China or in Vietnam. In both instances Communist policy was aided by errors committed by the enemy and was thus able to prevent the urban population from committing itself wholeheartedly to the government's cause. That, in itself, was a solid achievement, and an important factor in revolutionary success.

It has been observed that the Party's achievement was a triumph of organization rather than spirit. Certainly organization, indoctrination, and the application of pressure and the threat or use of force played a major role in realizing and maintaining commitment to the revolutionary cause. The nature of the Party's organizational genius has been competently explored in previous studies, and need not detain us here. Suffice it to say that the Communists had striking success in mobilizing all available human and material resources in a total and concentrated effort to seize power. Women, children, and even the aged were put to use so that young males could be released for combat. But the effectiveness of the Party's organizational efforts should not lead us to underestimate the emotional appeal of the cause. In fact, as one American researcher reported, as late as 1964 nearly 90 percent of all members of the PLAF were volunteers.

One final factor remains to be explored. A paramount feature in almost all modern revolutions has been the existence of dynamic and charismatic leadership. It is difficult to imagine the revolts in Russia, China, or Cuba, for example, without reference to the roles played by Lenin, Mao Tsetung, and Fidel Castro. Curiously, this factor is frequently overlooked in Vietnam. Because Ho Chi Minh lacked theoretical inclinations, his role in shaping revolutionary strategy has often been ignored; because his style of leadership was quiet rather than forceful, conciliatory rather than aggressive, his influence in the decision-making process has frequently seemed ambiguous; and because his part in directing Party strategy probably diminished in the final years of his life, the importance of his influence in the latter stages of the war is difficult to substantiate. Still, over the course of the Vietnamese revolution as a whole, his influence towers. He is best known, of course, as the living symbol of the Vietnamese revolution. For more than a generation his personality, embodying the qualities of virtue, integrity, dedication, and revolutionary asceticism, transcended issues of party and ideology and came to represent, in an Eriksonian sense, the struggle for the independence and self-realization of the Vietnamese nation. Nikita Khrushchev alluded to this trait in his memoirs, when he referred to the Vietnamese leader as a "holy apostle" of the revolution, a man whose sincerity, conviction, and incorruptibility could win anyone over to belief in his cause.

But if Ho Chi Minh is best remembered as the spiritual leader of the Vietnamese revolution, his practical contributions should not be ignored. The key building blocks in the Party's revolutionary strategy bear the stamp of his genius. His fine hand can be seen in the careful attention to organization and detail, in the concern for unity (both internal and within the socialist camp as a whole), and in the delicate structure of the united front. It is perhaps most obvious in the Party's astute handling of the international situation and in its use of diplomacy as a cardinal feature of its revolutionary strategy. In an age when many of the leaders of newly independent nations in Asia lacked the administrative and organizational abilities to match their personal charisma (Sukarno and U Nu come immediately to mind), Ho Chi Minh was an unusual composite of moral leader and organizational genius, half Gandhi, half Lenin. It was a dynamic combination. It is not too much to say that, without Ho Chi Minh, there might not have been a Vietnamese revolution, at least in the form we know.

✗ F U R T H E R   R E A D I N G

Weldon A. Brown, *The Last Chopper* (1976)
Wilfred Burchett, *Grasshoppers and Elephants: Why Vietnam Fell* (1977)
David Butler, *The Fall of Saigon* (1985)
Alan Dawson, *55 Days: The Fall of South Vietnam* (1977)
Gerald R. Ford, *A Time to Heal* (1979)
P. Edward Haley, *Congress and the Fall of South Vietnam and Cambodia* (1982)
Stuart A. Herrington, *Peace with Honor?* (1983)
Stephen T. Hosmer et al., *The Fall of South Vietnam* (1980)
Nguyen Tien Hung and Jerrold L. Schecter, *The Palace File* (1986)
William E. LeGro, *Vietnam from Cease-Fire to Capitulation* (1981)
John Pilzer, *The Last Day* (1976)
Gareth Porter, *A Peace Denied* (1975)
Frank Snepp, *A Decent Interval* (1977)
Tad Szulc, "How Kissinger Did It: Behind the Vietnam Cease-Fire Agreement," *Foreign Policy*, No. 15 (1974), 21–61
Tiziano Terzani, *Giai Phong! The Fall and Liberation of South Vietnam* (1976)
Tran Van Tra, *Ending the Thirty Years' War* (1982)
Joseph J. Zasloff and MacAlister Brown, eds., *Communism in Indochina* (1975)

Consequences and Lessons

of the War

✕

Although fifteen years have elapsed since the conclusion of the Vietnam War, the debate over the war's meaning continues to rage. The proliferation of novels, memoirs, films, and television programs about Vietnam testifies to the war's continuing hold on the American people. A veritable explosion of scholarly and political accounts of the Vietnam conflict has paralleled the remarkably diverse outpourings of popular culture. Yet the picture that emerges from those diverse efforts remains hazy.

What have been the war's consequences—on America, on Asia, and on the rest of the world? How should we read the lessons of the war? Those fundamental questions have inspired a variety of conflicting answers. The documents and essays in this chapter explore those issues, continuing the debate introduced in Chapter 1 about the broader meaning of the war.

✕ D O C U M E N T S

In the first document, an excerpt from a presidential press conference of June 9, 1975, Gerald R. Ford responds to a reporter's questions about the lessons he has learned from the Vietnam experience. In the next document, President Jimmy Carter states that the war has produced a profound moral crisis for America. His comments formed part of a major foreign-policy address delivered at Notre Dame University on May 22, 1977. In a book published in 1985, part of it reprinted as the third selection, Richard M. Nixon reflected on the lessons of Vietnam, concluding that Saigon's fall represented one of the Soviet Union's greatest victories. In the next document, William Sullivan, a career foreign-service officer and former U.S. ambassador to Iran, sees some very different consequences of the war. Acknowledging its tragic nature, he argues that the war nonetheless helped bring about a strategic balance in Asia favorable to the United States. The final document is an address delivered by President Ronald Reagan at the 1988 Veterans' Day ceremony. He made his remarks, celebrating the nobility and sacrifice of Vietnam veterans, at the Vietnam Veterans' Memorial in Washington.

Gerald R. Ford on the Lessons of Vietnam, 1975

The President. I think . . . there are a number of lessons that we can learn from Vietnam. One, that we have to work with other governments that feel as we do—that freedom is vitally important. We cannot, however, fight their battles for them. Those countries who believe in freedom as we do must carry the burden. We can help them, not with U.S. military personnel but with arms and economic aid, so that they can protect their own national interest and protect the freedom of their citizens.

I think we also may have learned some lessons concerning how we would conduct a military operation. There was, of course, from the period of 1961 or 1962 through the end of our military involvement in Vietnam, a great deal of controversy whether the military operations in Vietnam were carried out in the proper way, some dispute between civilian and military leaders as to the proper prosecution of a military engagement. I think we can learn something from those differences, and if we ever become engaged in any military operation in the future—and I hope we don't—I trust we've learned something about how we should handle such an operation.

Q. Does that mean that you would not conduct a limited war again with a certain amount of restraint on the part of our bombers and so forth?

The President. I wouldn't want to pass judgment at this time on any hypothetical situation. I simply am indicating that from that unfortunate experience in Vietnam, we ought to be able to be in a better position to judge how we should conduct ourselves in the future.

Jimmy Carter Sees a "Profound Moral Crisis," 1977

For too many years, we've been willing to adopt the flawed and erroneous principles and tactics of our adversaries, sometimes abandoning our own values for theirs. We've fought fire with fire, never thinking that fire is better quenched with water. This approach failed, with Vietnam the best example of its intellectual and moral poverty. But through failure we have now found our way back to our own principles and values, and we have regained our lost confidence.

By the measure of history, our nation's 200 years are very brief, and our rise to world eminence is briefer still. It dates from 1945, when Europe and the old international order lay in ruins. Before then, America was largely on the periphery of world affairs. but since then, we have inescapably been at the center of world affairs.

Our policy during this period was guided by two principles: a belief that Soviet expansion was almost inevitable but that it must be contained, and the corresponding belief in the importance of an almost exclusive alliance among non-Communist nations on both sides of the Atlantic. That system could not last forever unchanged. Historical trends have weakened its foundation. The unifying threat of conflict with the Soviet Union has become less intensive, even though the competition has become more extensive.

The Vietnamese war produced a profound moral crisis, sapping world-wide faith in our own policy and our system of life, a crisis of confidence made even more grave by the covert pessimism of some of our leaders.

In less than a generation, we've seen the world change dramatically. The daily lives and aspirations of most human beings have been transformed. Colonialism is nearly gone. A new sense of national identity now exists in almost 100 new countries that have been formed in the last generation. Knowledge has become more widespread. Aspirations are higher. As more people have been freed from traditional constraints, more have been determined to achieve, for the first time in their lives, social justice.

The world is still divided by ideological disputes, dominated by regional conflicts, and threatened by danger that we will not resolve the differences of race and wealth without violence or without drawing into combat the major military powers. We can no longer separate the traditional issues of war and peace from the new global questions of justice, equity, and human rights.

It is a new world, but America should not fear it. It is a new world, and we should help to shape it. It is a new world that calls for a new American foreign policy—a policy based on constant decency in its values and on optimism in our historical vision.

Richard M. Nixon Reads Vietnam's Lessons, 1985

Today, after Communist governments have killed over a half million Vietnamese and over 2 million Cambodians, the conclusive moral judgment has been rendered on our effort to save Cambodia and South Vietnam: We have never fought in a more moral cause. Assertions in the antiwar news media that life in Indochina would be better after our withdrawal served to highlight in a tragic way the abysmally poor level of their reporting throughout the war. But of all their blatantly inaccurate statements over the years, none was more hideously wrong than that one.

"If wise men give up the use of power," de Gaulle once said, "what madmen will seize it, what fanatics?"

When we abandoned the use of power in Indochina, we also abandoned its people to grim fate. When the American ambassador to Cambodia, John Gunther Dean, was about to be evacuated from Phnom Penh, he offered Lon Nol's closest colleague, Sirik Matak, asylum in the United States. The former Premier responded in a letter:

Dear Excellency and Friend,

I thank you very sincerely for your letter and for your offer to transport me toward freedom. I cannot, alas, leave in such a cowardly fashion. As for you, and in particular your great country, I never believed for a moment that you would have this sentiment of abandoning a people which has chosen liberty. You have refused us your protection, and we can do nothing about it.

You leave and my wish is that you and your country will find happiness under this sky. But mark it well, that if I shall die here on the spot and in the country I love, it is too bad, because we are all born and must die one day. I have only committed this mistake of believing you.

Sisowath Sirik Matak

It was a fittingly noble, if tragically sad, epitaph for his country, his people, and himself. He was among the first whom the Khmer Rouge executed.

After we abandoned the use of power, it was seized by the North Vietnamese and Khmer Rouge Communists. Our defeat was so great a tragedy because after the peace agreement of January 1973 it was so easily avoidable. Consolidating our gains would not have taken much to accomplish—a credible threat to enforce the peace agreement through retaliatory strikes against North Vietnam and a sufficient flow of aid to Cambodia and South Vietnam. But Congress legislated an end to our involvement. It also legislated the defeat of our friends in the same stroke.

A lesson that our adversaries should learn from our intervention in Vietnam is that the United States, under resolute and strong leadership, will go to great lengths and endure great sacrifices to defend its allies and interests. We fought in Vietnam because there were important strategic interests involved. But we also fought because our idealism was at stake. If not the United States, what nation would have helped defend South Vietnam? The fact is that no other country would have fought for over a decade in a war half a world away at great cost to itself in order to save the people of a small country from Communist enslavement.

One lesson we must learn from Vietnam is that if we do not exercise power for the good, there are plenty of men like Ho Chi Minh, Le Duan, Khieu Samphan, and Pol Pot who will gladly exercise it for evil purposes. Our armed intervention in the Vietnam War was not a brutal and immoral action. That we came to the defense of innocent people under attack by totalitarian thugs is no moral indictment. That we mishandled it at times in no way taints the cause. South Vietnam and Cambodia were worthy of our help—and the 3 million people who were killed in the war's aftermath deserved to be saved. Our abandonment of them in their moment of greatest need was not worthy of our country.

Another lesson we must learn is that in the real world peace is inseparable from power. Our country has had the good fortune of being separated from our enemies by two oceans. Others, like our friends in Indochina, did not enjoy that luxury. Their enemies lived just a few miles away up the Ho Chi Minh Trail. Our mistake was not that we did too much and imposed an inhumane war on peace-loving peoples. It was that in the end we did too little to prevent totalitarians from imposing their inhumane rule on freedom-loving peoples. Our cause must be peace. But we must recognize that greater evils exist than war.

Communist troops brought peace to South Vietnam and Cambodia— but it was the peace of the grave.

The Third World war began before World War II ended. Saigon's fall ten years ago was the Soviet Union's greatest victory in one of the key battles of the Third World war. No Soviet soldiers fought in Vietnam, but it was a victory for Moscow nonetheless because its ally and client, North Vietnam, won and South Vietnam and the United States lost. After we failed to prevent Communist conquest in Vietnam, it became accepted dogma that we would fail everywhere. For six years after Vietnam, the new isolationists chanted "No more Vietnams" as the dominoes fell one by one: Laos, Cambodia, and Mozambique in 1975; Angola in 1976; Ethiopia in 1977; South Yemen in 1978; Nicaragua in 1979.

William Sullivan Identifies Some Positive Consequences, 1987

This may sound Panglossian, but a Vietnam had to happen to us sometime. This war was a very tragic event. It tore the country apart. It had consequences politically, socially, and economically from which we are still suffering. But it did draw a line under the prevailing sense of omnipotence and omniscience that the United States postwar generation had developed. When we came out of World War II we were artificially strong. We had a monopoly on nuclear weapons, the strongest conventional military forces, the most resilient economy, a vibrant political system. The rest of the world was in ruins, but it was bound to come back.

And, of course, this is the thing that is so hard to explain to the rednecks. I sometimes do lectures for the Council on Foreign Relations in places like Wichita. Why, they want to know. "Why can't it be like it was then? Goddamnit, we could snap shit and people would pay attention!" A lot of yahoos in this country never accepted that things had inevitably changed. And eventually, just by sheer force of decibels, they got us around to the point that we were prepared to behave like John Wayne and sort of knock their teeth out, knock 'em back, put 'em back in their box, blow 'em back to the Stone Age, whatever phrase you want to use. Sooner or later we were going to run into a place where we tried to do that and it didn't work.

So the Panglossian part is that just in terms of not having suffered the ruination of the country, we were damned lucky it happened in a place that didn't really matter all that much, like Indochina. Had we taken a stand in a place like Hungary, it could have blown up the world, including the United States. Fifty-eight thousand lives is too many to pay for a lesson, but it's probably smaller than we might have paid had we gone into Czechoslovakia in '68, or done something else that would have led to a direct confrontation with the Soviets or with the Chinese. So Vietnam was a tragedy but it may have been the tragic price that American hubris needed somewhere along the line to get back to reality.

Looking back on Vietnam, the supreme irony of it is that four Presidents took the United States into combat in Vietnam because they were convinced that the strategic balance in Asia was shifting against us and our friends. It wasn't just the Lao Dong [Vietnam Workers' party] moving down into South Vietnam; it was also the Chinese operations in Thailand and Malaysia and the Philippines and above all in Indonesia. What they saw was a vise tightening across the sea-lanes connecting Japan to its energy sources, isolating Australia and New Zeland, and the whole of Southeast Asia becoming Communist.

Now, that didn't happen, but I think the point that all the commentaries that were written on the tenth anniversary missed is that while we didn't win the war, *had* we won, we would have had to keep troops in South Vietnam. And had we kept troops in South Vietnam, the North Vietnamese and the Chinese would have had to patch up their differences to some extent, and the Soviets and the Chinese would have had to give them logistic support. The whole thing would have stayed glued together even though it was palpably inconsistent. Once we pulled out, everything changed. The Chinese were able then to vent their true feelings about the Vietnamese. The Soviets moved in with the Vietnamese in a way that's concerned the hell out of the Chinese. And what you got was the Chinese making this enormous change and reaching an accommodation with the United States.

And the consequence was a cosmic shift in the geostrategic position. Although the Chinese are not our allies, they act in concert with us, in intelligence and other things. We've changed our whole outlook as a result. We no longer think in terms of fighting two and a half wars; we think in terms of one and a half wars. The *Soviets* have to think about two and a half wars. It's the Chinese who keep pounding on the Soviets and the Vietnamese in Southeast Asia, and it's the Vietnamese and Soviets who keep the Chinese in check. Had we plotted it and planned it this way as Machiavellians, it couldn't have come out better.

The fact is, we stumbled into it by what turned out to be an enormously costly, traumatic national experience for the United States—not only fifty-eight thousand people killed, but also the disruption in our own society. Now I think that disruption in some milder form would have come anyway. Vietnam was not a catalyst so much as an accelerator of changes that were inevitable in our society: the civil rights movement in the South, the women's revolution, the youth revolution, the black revolution. Because it all came at once it was somehow or other in our minds associated with Vietnam. But all those things, it seems to me, have obscured the fact that in its own unintended way, the Vietnam operation turned out to be one of the master strategic strokes of the century. Lyndon Johnson would never believe it in his grave but this is so. And when the historians finally get around to it, I think a lot of the pain and the trauma that went with the sixties will be put in another perspective.

It's very easy, particularly for those who philosophically oppose these changes, to attribute them all to Vietnam and to, essentially, a failure of American will. The great right-wing myth is that the military had that war won, but the damn civilians and the press and the fuzzy intellectuals snatched defeat from the jaws of victory. You know damn well we didn't have that war won and the supreme irony is, aren't we lucky we didn't, because we've now got an equilibrium in the Pacific which is probably the best that has prevailed there since the sixteenth century.

Ronald Reagan Calls Vietnam a Noble and Just Cause, 1988

We're gathered today, just as we have gathered before, to remember those who served, those who fought, those still missing, and those who gave their last full measure of devotion for our country. We're gathered at a monument on which the names of our fallen friends and loved ones are engraved, and with crosses instead of diamonds beside them, the names of those whose fate we do not yet know. One of those who fell wrote, shortly before his death, these words: "Take what they have left and what they have taught you with their dying and keep it with your own. And take one moment to embrace those gentle heroes you left behind."

Well, today, Veterans Day, as we do every year, we take that moment to embrace the gentle heroes of Vietnam and of all our wars. We remember those who were called upon to give all a person can give, and we remember those who were prepared to make that sacrifice if it were demanded of them in the line of duty, though it never was. Most of all, we remember the devotion and gallantry with which all of them ennobled their nation as they became champions of a noble cause.

I'm not speaking provocatively here. Unlike the other wars of this century, of course, there were deep divisions about the wisdom and rightness of the Vietnam war. Both sides spoke with honesty and fervor. And what more can we ask in our democracy? And yet after more than a decade of desperate boat people, after the killing fields of Cambodia, after all that has happened in that unhappy part of the world, who can doubt that the cause for which our men fought was just? It was, after all, however imperfectly pursued, the cause of freedom; and they showed uncommon courage in its service. Perhaps at this late date we can all agree that we've learned one lesson: that young Americans must never again be sent to fight and die unless we are prepared to let them win.

But beyond that, we remember today that all our gentle heroes of Vietnam have given us a lesson in something more: a lesson in living love. Yes, for all of them, those who came back and those who did not, their love for their families lives. Their love for their buddies on the battlefields and friends back home lives. Their love of their country lives.

This memorial has become a monument to that living love. The thousands who come to see the names testify to a love that endures. The messages and mementos they leave speak with a whispering voice that passes gently through the surrounding trees and out across the breast of our peaceful nation. A childhood teddy bear, a photograph of the son or daughter born too late to know his or her father, a battle ribbon, a note— there are so many of these, and all are testimony to our living love for them. And our nation itself is testimony to the love our veterans have had for it and for us. Our liberties, our values, all for which America stands is safe today because brave men and women have been ready to face the fire at freedom's front. And we thank God for them.

Yes, gentle heroes and living love and our memories of a time when we faced great divisions here at home. And yet if this place recalls all this, both sweet and sad, it also reminds us of a great and profound truth about our nation: that from all our divisions we have always eventually emerged strengthened. Perhaps we are finding that new strength today, and if so, much of it comes from the forgiveness and healing love that our Vietnam veterans have shown.

For too long a time, they stood in a chill wind, as if on a winter night's watch. And in that night, their deeds spoke to us, but we knew them not. And their voices called to us, but we heard them not. Yet in this land that God has blessed, the dawn always at last follows the dark, and now morning has come. The night is over. We see these men and know them once again— and know how much we owe them, how much they have given us, and how much we can never fully repay. And not just as individuals but as a nation, we say we love you.

X *E S S A Y S*

In the first essay, George C. Herring of the University of Kentucky analyzes developments in Indochina since the communist victory. He explores as well the war's impact on the United States and the continuing debate about the lessons of Vietnam. In the second essay, Paul Kennedy, a Yale University historian, assesses the Vietnam War's impact on the international power system. Author of a highly acclaimed book on the rise and fall of the great powers over the past 500 years, from which this selection is drawn, Kennedy argues that the practical and symbolic consequences of the war have been profound for the United States and for the rest of the world. The last essay, by the University of Connecticut's Thomas G. Paterson, explores the parallels that have been drawn between the Vietnam experience and the more recent involvement of the United States in Central America. The debate over Central American policy has been shaped greatly by the memory of Vietnam; but, Paterson emphasizes, proponents of intervention have read the lessons of that conflict very differently from advocates of restraint.

Legacy and Lessons of the War

GEORGE C. HERRING

The fall of South Vietnam just fifty-five days after the onset of the North Vietnamese offensive was symptomatic of the malaise which had afflicted the nation since its birth. Political fragmentation, the lack of able far-sighted leaders, and a tired and corrupt elite which could not adjust to the revolution that swept Vietnam after 1945 afforded a perilously weak basis for nationhood. Given these harsh realities, the American effort to create a bastion of anti-Communism south of the seventeenth parallel was probably doomed from the start. The United States could not effect the needed changes in South Vietnamese society without jeopardizing the order it sought, and there was no long-range hope of stability without revolutionary change. The Americans could provide money and weapons, but they could not furnish the ingredients necessary for political stability and military success. Despairing of the capacity of the South Vietnamese to save themselves, the United States had assumed the burden in 1965, only to toss it back in the laps of its clients when the American people tired of the war. The dependency of the early years persisted long after the United States had shifted to Vietnamization, however. To the very end and despite overwhelming evidence to the contrary, Thieu and his cohorts clung desperately to the belief that the United States would not abandon them.

With the North Vietnamese victory, the "dominoes" in Indochina quickly toppled. Cambodia in fact fell before South Vietnam, ending a peculiarly brutal war and initiating a period of unprecedented cruelty. Between 1970 and 1972, the United States had spent over $400 million in support of Lon Nol's government and army, and heavy bombing continued until Congress legislated its end in August 1973. In six months of 1973, the bombing exceeded 250,000 tons, more than was dropped on Japan in all of World War II. Lon Nol's government and army were ineffectual even by South Vietnamese standards, however, and with extensive support from North Vietnam and China, the Khmer Rouge pressed on toward Phnom Penh, using human-wave assaults in some areas. The government collapsed in mid-April, and the Khmer Rouge took over the capital on April 17. Thousands of lives were lost in the war, and over two million people were left refugees. The country as a whole faced starvation for the first time in its history. Upon taking over, the Khmer Rouge imposed the harshest form of totalitarianism and began the forced relocation of much of the population.

The end in Laos was less convulsive. The Laotian "settlement" of 1962 had been a dead letter from the start. A flimsy coalition government nominally upheld a precarious neutrality, while outsiders waged war up and down the land. The North Vietnamese used Laotian territory for their

From *America's Longest War: The United States and Vietnam, 1950–1975*, 2nd Edition, by George C. Herring. Alfred A. Knopf, 1986, pp. 268–281. Used by permission of McGraw-Hill Publishing Company.

infiltration route into South Vietnam, and supported the insurgent Pathet Lao with supplies and as many as 20,000 "volunteers." While backing the "neutralist" government, the United States from 1962 to 1972 waged a "secret war" against North Vietnamese positions in Laos. When the bombing of North Vietnam was stopped at the end of 1968, Laos became the primary target. By 1973 the United States had dropped more than two million tons of bombs there, leaving many areas resembling a desert. At the same time, the CIA sponsored an army of Hmong or Meo tribesmen, led by General Vang Pao, which waged seasonal guerrilla warfare against the Ho Chi Minh Trail in Laos at enormous cost: more than 20,000 had been killed by the end of the war. The U.S. withdrawal from South Vietnam left the government without any chance of survival. An agreement of February 1973 created a coalition government in which the Pathet Lao held the upper hand. With the fall of Cambodia and South Vietnam, the Pathet Lao took over, making no effort to hide its subservience to North Vietnam.

The impact on world politics of America's failure in Vietnam was considerably less than U.S. policymakers had predicted. From Thailand to the Philippines, there was obvious nervousness, even demands for the removal of U.S. bases. Outside of Indochina, however, the dominoes did not fall. On the contrary, in the ten years after the end of the war, the non-Communist nations of Southeast Asia prospered and attained an unprecedented level of stability. The Soviet Union continued to build up its military arsenal. Along with Cuba, it intervened in civil wars in Angola, Zaire, and Ethiopia, and in 1979 it invaded neighboring Afghanistan. The Soviets soon bogged down in Afghanistan themselves, however, and one of the most significant and ironic effects of the end of the Vietnam War was to heighten tension among the various Communist nations, especially in Southeast Asia. The brutal Pol Pot regime launched a grisly effort to rebuild Cambodia from the "Year Zero," resulting in the death of as many as two million people. More important from the Vietnamese standpoint, Cambodia established close ties with China. To preserve a "friendly" government next door, Vietnam invaded Cambodia in 1978, drove out Pol Pot and the Khmer Rouge, and established a puppet regime. China retaliated by invading Vietnam, provoking a short and inconclusive war. Sporadic border conflicts between Vietnam and China have persisted. The United States, which had gone to war in Vietnam in 1965 to contain China, found itself in the mid-1980s indirectly supporting China's efforts to contain Vietnam.

In Vietnam itself, the principal legacy of the war has been continued human suffering. The ultimate losers, of course, were the South Vietnamese. For those who remain in Vietnam there have been poverty, oppression, forced labor, and "reeducation" camps. More than 1.4 million South Vietnamese have fled the country since 1975. As many as 50,000 of these so-called boat people perished in flight, and some still languish in squalid refugee camps scattered throughout Southeast Asia. Nearly a million Vietnamese have resettled in other countries, over 725,000 of them in the United States. Most of them had to give up all their personal possessions merely to escape, and many left family behind.

Even for the ostensible winners, victory has been a bittersweet prize. The Hanoi regime has achieved what may have been its goal from the outset—hegemony in former French Indochina—but the cost has been enormous. An estimated 180,000 soldiers remain in Cambodia, facing stubborn resistance from a number of different guerrilla groups, a drain on an economy already strained to the breaking point. The task of maintaining hegemony in Laos and Cambodia and defending against a hostile China requires one of the world's twelve poorest countries to maintain the world's fourth largest army. Vietnam's postwar aggressiveness has cost it much of the international good will it earned in the war against the United States.

Moreover, Hanoi's long-standing objective of unifying Vietnam under its control appears still to have been achieved in name only. Historic differences between north and south were sharpened during the war, and even the brutal and heavy-handed methods employed by the Hanoi regime have not forced the south into a northern-made mold. Just as it resisted American influence in the 1960s, southern Vietnam continues to resist outside influence today, making the task of consolidation quite difficult. There are also signs that in the classic tradition of the Far East, the ways of the conquered are rubbing off on the conqueror. The corruption and Western consumer culture that epitomized Saigon during the American war have carried over to postwar Ho Chi Minh City, where the black market still flourishes and bribery is necessary to accomplish anything. More significant, Saigon's mores appear to have afflicted the northern officials sent south to enforce revolutionary purity and even to have filtered north to Hanoi.

For all Vietnamese, the most pressing legacy has been economic deprivation. Thirty years of war left the country in shambles, and the regime's ill-conceived postwar efforts to promote industry and collectivize agriculture made things worse. The economic growth rate has hovered around 2 percent instead of the 14 percent optimistically projected in the five-year plan of 1975. Per capita income has averaged around $100. Inflation has run as high as 50 percent and unemployment is chronic, especially in the cities. Record rice crops in recent years have eased a severe postwar food shortage, but the food supply remains far below the needs of the population and most foods are rationed and expensive. The postwar economic crisis has forced Hanoi to abandon its central goal of socialization of southern Vietnam. New economic policies have been designed to increase production by such capitalist grimmicks as bonuses, piecework rates, and limited managerial autonomy. The collectivization of agriculture has been scrapped, at least temporarily.

A central goal of the thirty-year war was to rid Vietnam of foreign domination, and here again victory has been less than complete. Because of its poverty and its forced isolation from the United States and China, Hanoi has been forced into a dependence on the Soviet Union that causes growing uneasiness and resentment. Some 6,000 Russians administer an aid program ranging between $1 and $2 billion per year. Russian aid bears a high price tag, moreover. To many Vietnamese, the Soviet presence is increasingly obnoxious, and some appear to regard their new ally as merely another in the long line of foreigners who have exploited their country. To a considerable degree, the legacy of victory for the Vietnamese has been one of disappointed dreams and continuing sacrifice and pain. The goals of the thirty-year war have been achieved only partially, if at all.

Ten years after the fall of Saigon, Vietnam appeared eager to break out of its diplomatic isolation from the West. Hanoi probably bungled an opportunity to establish relations with the United States in 1977 by demanding $3 billion in war reparations as a precondition. Relations between the two former enemies thereafter grew steadily worse. Vietnam's seeming indifference to the fate of some 2,500 U.S. servicemen still listed as missing in action in Southeast Asia deeply antagonized Americans. Its increasing closeness to the Soviet Union and its invasion of Cambodia widened an already large chasm. On the other side, Washington's reconciliation with China in 1979 reinforced Vietnam's already strong hostility toward the United States. The need for Western aid and technology and a wish to secure recognition of its position in Cambodia encouraged Hanoi in 1985 to seek an improvement of relations. It was more cooperative than at any time since the end of the war in dealing with MIA [missing in action] issues, and it eagerly sought a settlement on Cambodia. These approaches provided the United States an opportunity to wean Vietnam from its dependence on the Soviet Union and to resolve a number of issues left from the war, but lingering hostility toward the Vietnamese and fear of China's reaction posed major obstacles to an improvement in relations.

In the United States, the effects of the war have been more in the realm of the spirit than tangible. The fall of Saigon had a profound impact. Some Americans expressed hope that the nation could finally put aside a painful episode from its past and get on with the business of the future. Among a people accustomed to celebrating peace with ticker-tape parades, however, the end of the war left a deep residue of frustration, anger, and disillusionment. Americans generally agreed that the war had been a "senseless tragedy" and a "dark moment" in their nation's history. Some comforted themselves with the notion that the United States should never have become involved in Vietnam in the first place, but for others, particularly those who had lost loved ones, this was not enough. "Now it's all gone down the drain and it hurts. What did he die for?" asked a Pennsylvanian whose son had been killed in Vietnam. Many Americans expressed anger that the civilians did not permit the military to win the war. Others regarded the failure to win as a betrayal of American ideals and a sign of national weakness which boded poorly for the future. "It was the saddest day of my life when it sank in that we had lost the war," a Virginian lamented. The fall of Vietnam came at the very time the nation was preparing to celebrate the bicentennial of its birth, and the irony was painfully obvious. "The high hopes and wishful idealism with which the American nation had been born had not been destroyed," *Newsweek* observed, "but they had been chastened by the failure of America to work its will in Indochina."

In the immediate aftermath of the war, the nation experienced a self-conscious, collective amnesia. The angry debate over who lost Vietnam, so feared by Kennedy, Johnson, and Nixon, consisted of nothing more than a few sharp exchanges between the White House and Capitol Hill over responsibility for the April 1975 debacle. Perhaps because both parties were so deeply implicated in the war, Vietnam did not become a partisan political issue; because the memories were so painful, no one cared to dredge them up. On the contrary, many public figures called for restraint. "There is no profit at this time in hashing over the might-have-beens of the past," [Senator] Mike Mansfield stated. "Nor is there any value in finger-pointing." Vietnam was all but ignored by the media. It was scarcely mentioned in the presidential campaign of 1976. "Today it is almost as though the war had never happened," the columnist Joseph C. Harsh noted in late 1975. "Americans have somehow blocked it out of their consciousness. They don't talk about it. They don't talk about its consequences."

Resentment and disillusionment nevertheless smoldered beneath the surface, provoking a sharp reaction against nearly three decades of crisis diplomacy and global intervention. Even before the war had ended, the traumatic experience of Vietnam, combined with the apparent improvement of relations with the Soviet Union and China and a growing preoccupation with domestic problems, produced a drastic reordering of national priorities. From the late 1940s to the 1960s, foreign policy had consistently headed the list of national concerns, but by the mid-1970s, it ranked well down the list. The public is "almost oblivious to foreign problems and foreign issues," opinion analyst Burns Roper remarked in late 1975. The Vietnam experience also provoked strong opposition to military intervention abroad, even in defense of America's oldest and staunchest allies. Polls taken shortly before the fall of Saigon indicated that only 36 percent of the American people felt it was important for the United States to make and keep commitments to other nations, and only 34 percent expressed willingness to send troops should the Russians attempt to take over West Berlin. A majority of Americans endorsed military intervention only in defense of Canada. "Vietnam has left a rancid aftertaste that clings to almost every mention of direct military intervention," the columnist David Broder observed. The cyclical theory of American foreign relations seemed confirmed. Having passed through a stormy period of global involvement, the United States appeared to be reverting to its more traditional role of abstention.

Those Americans who fought in the war were the primary victims of the nation's desire to forget. Younger on the average by seven years than their World War II counterparts, having endured a war far more complex and confusing, Vietnam veterans by the miracles of the jet age were whisked home virtually overnight to a nation that was hostile to the war or indifferent to their plight. Some were made to feel the guilt for the nation's moral transgressions; others, responsibility for its failure. Most simply met silence. Forced to turn inward, many veterans grew profoundly distrustful of the government that had sent them to war and deeply resentful of the nation's seeming ingratitude for their sacrifices. The great majority adjusted, although often with difficulty, but many veterans experienced problems with drugs and alcohol, joblessness, and broken homes. Many also suffered from post-traumatic stress disorder, the modern term for what had earlier been called shell shock or battle fatigue. The popular image of the Vietnam veteran in the immediate postwar years was that of a drug-crazed, gun-toting, and violence-prone individual unable to adjust to civilized society. When America in 1981 gave a lavish welcome home to a group of hostages returned from a long and much-publicized captivity in Iran, Vietnam veterans poured out the rage that had been bottled up for more than half a decade. They themselves constructed a memorial in Washington to honor the memory of the more than 58,000 comrades who did not return.

Within a short time after the end of the war, Vietnam's place in the national consciousness changed dramatically. The amnesia of the immediate postwar years proved no more than a passing phenomenon, and by the mid-1980s the war was being discussed to a degree and in ways that would have once seemed impossible. Vietnam produced a large and in some cases distinguished literature, much of it the work of veterans. Hollywood had all but ignored the war while it was going on, but in its aftermath filmmakers took up the subject in a large way, producing works ranging from the haunting *Deer Hunter*, to the surreal spectacular *Apocalypse Now*, to a series of trashy films in which American superheroes returned to Vietnam to take care of unfinished business. No television leading man was worth his salt unless he had served in Vietnam. The Vietnam veteran, sometimes branded a war criminal in the 1960s, became a popular culture hero in the 1980s, the sturdy and self-sufficient warrior who had prevailed despite being let down by his government and nation. Two million Americans a year visited the stark but moving V-shaped memorial on Washington's mall, making it the second leading tourist attraction in the nation's capital. The hoopla that accompanied the tenth anniversary of the fall of Saigon made abundantly clear how deeply embedded Vietnam was in the national psyche.

If they were more willing to talk about Vietnam, Americans remained confused and divided about its meaning, particularly its implications for U.S. foreign policy. The indifference and tendency toward withdrawal so manifest in 1975 declined sharply over the next ten years. Bitter memories of Vietnam combined with the frustration of the Iranian hostage crisis to produce a growing assertiveness, a highly nationalistic impulse to defend perceived interests, even a yearning to restore the United States to its old position in the world. The breakdown of détente, the steady growth of Soviet military power, and the use of that power in Afghanistan produced a heightened concern for American security. The defense budget soared to record proportions in the early 1980s, and support for military intervention in defense of traditional allies increased significantly.

The new nationalism was tempered by lingering memories of Vietnam, however. Many Americans remained deeply skeptical of 1960s-style globalism and dubious of such internationalist mechanisms as foreign aid or even the United Nations. Ten years after the end of the war, a whopping majority still believed that intervention in Vietnam had been a mistake. Recollection of Vietnam produced strong opposition to intervention in third-world crises in Lebanon and Central America. Thus, in the aftermath of

Vietnam, the public mood consisted of a strange amalgam of nostalgia and realism, assertiveness and caution.

The nation's foreign policy elite has been no more certain in its judgments on Vietnam than the mass public. Indeed, systematic polling of leadership groups makes clear that Vietnam was a "landmark event" that left "deep and profound" divisions. Americans agree that to construct a viable foreign policy they must learn from Vietnam. But they disagree sharply over what they should learn.

The basic issue remains the morality and wisdom of intervention in Vietnam. In the light of Hanoi's postwar actions, Americans are less likely to openly condemn their nation's intervention as immoral, an important sign of change in itself. Those who continue to feel that intervention was wrong argue that it was unnecessary or impractical or both, and most liberals still contend that at best it represented overcommitment in an area of peripheral national interest, at worst an act of questionable morality.

The conservative point of view has been more vocal in recent years and it takes two forms. Some, including President Ronald Reagan, have found in postwar events in Indochina reason to speak out anew on what they always felt was a fundamental reality—that, as Reagan has repeatedly stated, Vietnam was "in truth a noble war," a selfless attempt on the part of the United States to save a free nation from outside aggression. Others concede that the United States might have erred in getting involved in Vietnam in the first place, but they go on to insist that over time an important interest was established that had to be defended for the sake of U.S. credibility throughout the world.

The second great issue, on which Americans also sharply disagree, concerns the reasons for U.S. failure in Vietnam. Many of the leading participants in the war have concluded that America's failure was essentially instrumental, a result of the improper use of available tools. General [William] Westmoreland and others blame the "ill-considered" policy of "graduated response" imposed on the military by civilian leaders, arguing that had the United States employed its military power quickly, decisively, and without limit, the war could have been won. Other critics view the fundamental mistake as the choice of tools rather than how they were used, and they blame an unimaginative military as much as civilians. Instead of trying to fight World War II and Korea over in Vietnam, these critics argue, the military should have adapted to the unconventional war in which it found itself and shaped an appropriate counterinsurgency strategy to meet it. Still other commentators, including some military theorists, agree that military leaders were as responsible for the strategic failure as civilians. Critics such as Colonel Harry G. Summers, Jr., argue that instead of mounting costly and counterproductive search-and-destroy operations against guerrillas in South Vietnam, the United States should have used its own forces against North Vietnamese regulars along the seventeenth parallel to isolate the north from the south. Military leaders should also have insisted on a declaration of war to ensure that the war was not fought in "cold blood" and that popular support could be sustained.

The lessons drawn are as divergent as the arguments advanced. Those who feel that the United States lost because it did not act decisively conclude that if the nation becomes involved in war again, it must employ its military power with a view to winning quickly before public support erodes. Those who feel that the basic problem was the formulation rather than the execution of strategy insist that military and civilian leaders must think strategically, that they must examine more carefully the nature of the war and formulate more precisely the ways in which American power can best be used to attain clearly defined objectives.

Such lessons depend on the values and belief systems of those who pronounce them, of course, and those who opposed the war have reached quite different conclusions. To some former doves, the fundamental lesson is never to get involved in a land war in Asia; to others, it is to avoid intervention in international trouble spots unless the nation's vital interests are clearly at stake. Some commentators warn that policymakers must be wary of the sort of simplistic reasoning that produced the domino theory and the Munich analogy. Others point to the weaknesses of South Vietnam and admonish that "even a superpower can't save allies who are unable or unwilling to save themselves." For still others, the key lessons are that American power has distinct limits and that in order to be effective, American foreign policy must be true to the nation's historic ideals.

The ghost of Vietnam hovered over an increasingly divisive debate on the proper American response to revolutions in Central America. Shortly after taking office in 1981, President Reagan committed U.S. prestige to defending the government of El Salvador against a leftist-led insurgency, in part in the expectation that success there might exorcise the so-called Vietnam syndrome—the perceived reluctance of the American public in the wake of Vietnam to take on responsibilities in third-world countries. When the quick victory did not materialize, the administration expanded U.S. military aid to El Salvador, created a huge military base in Honduras, and launched a not-so-covert war to overthrow the Sandinista government of Nicaragua. The administration insisted that the United States must support non-Communist forces to avert in Central America the bloodshed and misery that followed the end of the war in Vietnam. At the same time, the military and the Defense Department have made clear that they will not go to war under the conditions that prevailed in Vietnam. On the other side, dovish critics ominously warn that U.S. intervention in Central America will lead straight into a quagmire like Vietnam.

The ongoing debate over U.S. involvement in Vietnam leaves many questions unanswered. Whether a more decisive use of military power could have brought a satisfactory conclusion to the war without causing even more disastrous consequences remains highly doubtful. Whether the adoption of a more vigorous and imaginative counterinsurgency program at an earlier stage could have wrested control of the countryside from the Vietcong can never be known, and the ability of the United States to develop such a program in an alien environment is dubious. That the United States exaggerated the importance of Vietnam, as the liberals suggest, seems clear.

But their argument begs the question of how one determines the significance of a given area and the even more difficult question of assessing the ultimate costs of intervention at an early stage.

The fundamental weakness of many of the lessons learned thus far is that they assume the continued necessity and practicability of the containment policy, at least in modified form, thereby evading or ignoring altogether the central questions raised by the war. The United States intervened in Vietnam to block the apparent march of a Soviet-directed Communism across Asia, enlarged its commitment to halt a presumably expansionist Communist China, and eventually made Vietnam a test of its determination to uphold world order. By wrongly attributing the Vietnamese conflict to external sources, the United States drastically misjudged its internal dynamics. By intervening in what was essentially a local struggle, it placed itself at the mercy of local forces, a weak client, and a determined adversary. It elevated into a major international conflict what might have remained a localized struggle. By raising the stakes into a test of its own credibility, it perilously narrowed its options. A policy so flawed in its premises cannot help but fail, and in this case the results were disastrous.

Vietnam made clear the inherent unworkability of a policy of global containment. In the 1940s the world seemed dangerous but manageable. The United States enjoyed a position of unprecedented power and influence, and achieved some notable early successes in Europe. Much of America's power derived from the weakness of other nations rather than from its own intrinsic strength, however, and Vietnam demonstrated conclusively that its power, however great, had limits. The development of significant military capabilities by the Soviet Union and China made it extremely risky for the United States to use its military power in Vietnam on a scale necessary to achieve the desired results. Conditions in Vietnam itself and the constraints imposed by domestic opinion made it impossible to reach these goals with limited means. Vietnam makes clear that the United States cannot uphold its own concept of world order in the face of a stubborn and resolute, although much weaker, foe. The war did not bring about the decline of American power, as some have suggested, but was rather symptomatic of the limits of national power in an age of international diversity and nuclear weaponry.

To assume, therefore, that the United States can simply rouse itself from the nightmare of Vietnam and resume its accustomed role in a rapidly changing world would be to invite further disaster. The world of the 1980s is even more dangerous and much less manageable than that of the 1940s and 1950s. The proliferation of nuclear weapons, the emergence of a large number of new nations, the existence of a baffling array of regional and internal conflicts, have combined to produce a more confusing and disorderly world than at any time in the recent past. The ambiguous triangular relationship between the United States, the Soviet Union, and China has had a further destabilizing effect, creating enormous uncertainty and shifting tensions and giving lesser nations increased maneuverability and opportunity for mischief. A successful American adjustment to the new conditions requires the shedding of old approaches, most notably of the traditional oscillation between crusades to reform the world and angry withdrawal from it. To carry the "Never Again" syndrome to its logical conclusion and turn away from an ungrateful and hostile world could be calamitous. To regard Vietnam as an aberration, a unique experience from which nothing can be learned, would invite further frustration. To adapt to the new era, the United States must recognize its vulnerability, accept the limits to its power, and accommodate itself to many situations it does not like. Americans must understand that they will not be able to dictate solutions to world problems or to achieve all of their goals. Like it or not, Vietnam marked the end of an era in world history and of American foreign policy, an era marked by constructive achievements but blemished by ultimate, although not irreparable, failure.

The Impact of Vietnam on America's World Role

PAUL KENNEDY

In so many ways, symbolic as well as practical, it would be difficult to exaggerate the impacts of the lengthy American campaign in Vietnam and other parts of Southeast Asia upon the international power system—or upon the national psyche of the American people themselves, most of whose perceptions of their country's role in the world still remain strongly influenced by that conflict, albeit in different ways. The fact that this was a war fought by an "open society"—and made the more open because of revelations like the Pentagon Papers, and by the daily television and press reportage of the carnage and apparent futility of it all; that this was the first war which the United States had unequivocally lost, that it confounded the victorious experiences of the Second World War and destroyed a whole array of reputations, from those of four-star generals to those of "brightest and best" intellectuals; that it coincided with, and in no small measure helped to cause, the fissuring of a consensus in American society about the nation's goals and priorities, was attended by inflation, unprecedented student protests and inner city disturbances, and was followed in turn by the Watergate crisis, which discredited the presidency itself for a time; that it seemed to many to stand in bitter and ironic contradiction to everything which the Founding Fathers had taught, and made the United States unpopular across most of the globe; and finally that the shamefaced and uncaring treatment of the GIs who came back from Vietnam would produce its own reaction a decade later and thus ensure that the memory of this conflict would continue to prey upon the public consciousness, in war memorials, books, television documentaries, and personal tragedies—all of this meant that the Vietnam War, although far smaller in terms of casualties, impacted upon the American people somewhat as had the First

From *The Rise and Fall of the Great Powers* by Paul Kennedy, pp. 404–409. Copyright © 1987 by Paul Kennedy. Reprinted by permission of Random House, Inc.

World War upon Europeans. The effects were seen, overwhelmingly, at the *personal* and *psychological* levels; more broadly, they were interpreted as a crisis in American civilization and in its constitutional arrangements. As such, they would continue to have significance quite independent of the strategical and Great Power dimensions of this conflict.

But the latter aspects are the most important ones for our survey, and require further mention here. To begin with, it provided a useful and sobering reminder that a vast superiority in military hardware and economic productivity will not always and automatically translate into military *effectiveness*. . . . Economically, the United States may have been fifty to one hundred times more productive than North Vietnam; militarily, it possessed the firepower to (as some hawks urged) bomb the enemy back into the stone age—indeed, with nuclear weapons, it had the capacity to obliterate Southeast Asia altogether. But this was *not* a war in which those superiorities could be made properly effective. Fear of domestic opinion, and of world reaction, prevented the use of atomic weapons against a foe who could never be a *vital* threat to the United States itself. Worries about the American public's opposition to heavy casualties in a conflict whose legitimacy and efficacy came increasingly under question had similarly constrained the administration's use of the conventional methods of warfare; restrictions were placed on the bombing campaign; the Ho Chi Minh Trail through neutral Laos could not be occupied; Russian vessels bearing arms to Haiphong harbor could not be seized. It was important not to provoke the two major Communist states into joining the war. This essentially reduced the fighting to a series of small-scale encounters in jungles and paddy fields, terrain which blunted the advantages of American firepower and (helicopter-borne) mobility, and instead placed an emphasis upon jungle-warfare techniques and unit cohesion—which was much less of a problem for the crack forces than for the rapidly turning over contingents of draftees. Although Johnson followed Kennedy's lead in sending more and more troops to Vietnam (it peaked at 542,000, in 1969), it was never enough to meet General Westermoreland's demands; clinging to the view that this was still a limited conflict, the government refused to mobilize the reserves, or indeed to put the economy on a war footing.

The difficulties of fighting the war on terms disadvantageous to the United States' real military strengths reflected a larger political problem—the discrepancy between means and ends (as Clausewitz might have put it). The North Vietnamese and the Vietcong were fighting for what they believed in very strongly; those who were not were undoubtedly subject to the discipline of a totalitarian, passionately nationalistic regime. The South Vietnamese governing system, by contrast, appeared corrupt, unpopular, and in a distinct minority, opposed by the Buddhist monks, unsupported by a frightened, exploited, and war-weary peasantry; those native units loyal to the regime and who often fought well were not sufficient to compensate for this inner corrosion. As the war escalated, more and more Americans questioned the efficacy of fighting for the regime in Saigon, and worried at the way in which all this was corrupting the American armed forces themselves—in the decline in morale, the rise in cynicism, indiscipline, drug-taking, prostitution, the increasing racial sneers at the "gooks," and atrocities in the field, not to mention the corrosion of the United States' own currency or of its larger strategic posture. Ho Chi Minh had declared that his forces were willing to lose men at the rate of ten to one—and when they were rash enough to emerge from the jungles to attack the cities, as in the 1968 Tet offensive, they often did; but, he continued, despite those losses they would still fight on. That sort of willpower was not evident in South Vietnam. Nor was American society itself, increasingly disturbed by the war's contradictions, willing to sacrifice everything for victory. While the latter feeling was quite understandable, given what was at stake for each side, the fact was that it proved impossible for an open democracy to wage a halfhearted war successfully. This was the fundamental contradiction, which neither [Secretary of Defense Robert] McNamara's systems analysis nor the B-52 bombers based on Guam could alter.

More than a decade after the fall of Saigon (April 1975), and with books upon all aspects of that conflict still flooding from the presses, it still remains difficult to assess clearly how it may have affected the U.S. position in the world. Viewed from a longer perspective, say, backward from the year 2000 or 2020, it might be seen as having produced a salutory shock to American global hubris (or to what Senator [J. William] Fulbright called "the arrogance of power"), and thus compelled the country to think more deeply about its political and strategical priorities and to readjust more sensibly to a world already much changed since 1945—in other words, rather like the shock which the Russians received in the Crimean War, or the British received in the Boer War, producing in their turn beneficial reforms and reassessments.

At the time, however, the short-term effects of the war could not be other than deleterious. The vast boom in spending on the war, precisely at a time when domestic expenditures upon Johnson's "Great Society" were also leaping upward, badly affected the American economy. . . . Moreover, while the United States was pouring money into Vietnam, the USSR was devoting steadily larger sums to its nuclear forces—so that it achieved a rough strategic parity—and to its navy, which in these years emerged as a major force in global gunboat diplomacy; and this increasing imbalance was worsened by the American electorate's turn against military expenditures for most of the 1970s. In 1978, "national security expenditures" were only 5 percent of GNP, lower than they had been for thirty years. Morale in the armed services plummeted, in consequence both of the war itself and of the postwar cuts. Shakeups in the CIA and other agencies, however necessary to check abuses, undoubtedly cramped their effectiveness. The American concentration upon Vietnam worried even sympathetic allies; its methods of fighting in support of a corrupt regime alienated public opinion, in western Europe as much as in the Third World, and was a major factor in what some writers have termed American "estrangement" from much of the rest of the planet. It led to a neglect of American attention toward Latin America—and a tendency to replace Kennedy's hoped-for "Alliance for Progress" with military support for undemocratic regimes and with counterrevolutionary actions (like the 1965 intervention in the Dominican Republic). The—inevitably—open post-Vietnam War debate over the regions of the globe for which the United States would or *would not* fight in the future disturbed existing allies, doubtless encouraged its foes, and caused wobbling neutrals to consider re-insuring themselves with the other side. At the United Nations debates, the American delegate appeared increasingly beleaguered and isolated. Things had come a long way since Henry Luce's assertion that the United States would be the elder brother of nations in the brotherhood of man.

The other power-political consequence of the Vietnam War was that it obscured, by perhaps as much as a decade, Washington's recognition of the extent of the Sino-Soviet split—and thus its chance to evolve a policy to handle it. It was therefore the more striking that this neglect should be put right so swiftly after the entry into the presidency of that bitter foe of Communism, Richard Nixon, in January 1969. But Nixon possessed, to use Professor [John Lewis] Gaddis's phrase, a "unique combination of ideological rigidity with political pragmatism"—and the latter was especially manifest in his dealings with foreign Great Powers. Despite Nixon's dislike of domestic radicals and animosity toward, say, Allende's Chile for its socialist policies, the president claimed to be unideological when it came to global diplomacy. To him, there was no great contradiction between ordering a massive increase in the bombing of North Vietnam in 1972—to compel Hanoi to come closer to the American bargaining position for withdrawal from the South—and journeying to China to bury the hatchet with Mao Tse-tung in the same year. Even more significant was to be his choice of Henry Kissinger as his national security adviser (and later secretary of state). Kissinger's approach to world affairs was historicist and relativistic: events had to be seen in their larger context, and related to each other; Great Powers should be judged on what they did, not on their domestic ideology; an absolutist search for security was utopian, since that would make everyone else absolutely insecure—all that one could hope to achieve was relative security, based upon a resonable balance of forces in world affairs, a mature recognition that the world scene would never be completely harmonious, and a willingness to bargain. Like the statesmen he had written about (Metternich, Castlereagh, Bismarck), Kissinger felt that "the beginning of wisdom in human as well as international affairs was knowing when to stop." His aphorisms were Palmerstonian ("We have no permanent enemies") and Bismarckian ("The hostility between China and the Soviet Union served our purposes best if we maintained closer relations with each side than they did with each other"), and were unlike anything in American diplomacy since [George] Kennan. But Kissinger had a much greater chance to direct policy than his fellow admirer of nineteenth-century European statesmen ever possessed.

Finally, Kissinger recognized the limitations upon American power, not only in the sense that the United States could not afford to fight a protracted war in the jungles of Southeast Asia *and* to maintain its other, more vital interests, but also because both he and Nixon could perceive that the world's balances were altering, and new forces were undermining the hitherto unchallenged domination of the two superpowers. The latter were still far ahead in terms of strictly military power, but in other respects the world had become more of a multipolar place: "In economic terms," he noted in 1973, "there are at least five major groupings. Politically, many more centers of influence have emerged. . . ." With echoes of (and amendments to) Kennan, he identified five important regions, the United States, the USSR, China, Japan, and western Europe; and unlike many in Washington and (perhaps) everyone in Moscow, he welcomed this change. A *concert* of large powers, balancing each other off and with no one dominating another, would be "a safer world and a better world" than a bipolar situation in which "a gain for one side appears as an absolute loss for the other." Confident in his own abilities to defend American interests in such a pluralistic world, Kissinger was urging a fundamental reshaping of American diplomacy in the largest sense of that word.

The diplomatic revolution caused by the steady Sino-American *rapprochement* after 1971 had a profound effect on the "global correlation of forces." Although taken by surprise at Washington's move, Japan felt that it at last was able to establish relations with the People's Republic of China, which thus gave a further boost to its booming Asian trade. The Cold War in Asia, it appeared, was over—or perhaps it would be better to say that it had become more complicated: Pakistan, which had been a diplomatic conduit for secret messages between Washington and Peking, received the support of both those Powers during its clash with India in 1971; Moscow, predictably, gave strong support to New Delhi. In Europe, too, the balances had been altered. Alarmed by China's hostility and taken aback by Kissinger's diplomacy, the Kremlin deemed it prudent to conclude the SALT [Strategic Arms Limitations Talks] I treaty and to encourage the various other attempts to improve relations across the Iron Curtain. It also held back when, following its tense confrontation with the United States at the time of the 1973 Arab-Israeli war, Kissinger commenced his "shuttle diplomacy" to reconcile Egypt and Israel, effectively freezing Russia out of any meaningful role.

It is difficult to know how long Kissinger could have kept up his Bismarck-style juggling act had the Watergate scandal not swept Nixon from the White House in August 1974 and made so many Americans even more suspicious of their government. As it was, the secretary of state remained in his post during Ford's tenure of the presidency, but with increasingly less freedom for maneuver. Defense budget requisitions were frequently slashed by Congress. All further aid was cut off to South Vietnam, Cambodia, and Laos in February 1975, a few months before those states were overrun. The War Powers Act sharply pared the president's capacity to commit American troops overseas. Soviet-Cuban interventions in Angola could not, Congress· had voted, be countered by sending CIA funds and weapons to the pro-western factions there. With the Republican right growing restive at this decline in American power abroad and blaming Kissinger for ceding away national interests (the Panama Canal) and old friends (Taiwan), the secretary of state's position was beginning to crumble even before Ford was swept out of power in the 1976 election.

Vietnam and Central America

THOMAS G. PATERSON

We are, the truism tells us, captives of our pasts, destined, for good or ill, whether we want to or not, to use history to find clarity in the blurred events swirling around us. Because history is our memory, it is also the most familiar and steady guide in our quest to understand and explain. Comparisons, parallels, and analogies are always springing to mind. For some, history is a cookbook that provides a host of recipes. For others, as Henry A. Kissinger put it, history "teaches by analogy and forces us to decide what, if anything, is analogous." Americans frequently remark that "history teaches," and they have been quick to draw lessons from the past, sometimes fixing them as "syndromes."

At the same time, Americans are notoriously lacking in an informed historical consciousness, and they shun close historical analysis. They may know whose statue adorns the town park, but they have only the faintest notion of the hero's place in their community's development. They may cherish the bicentennial medallions squirreled away in their treasure boxes, but they seldom ask why people rebel. Ignorance, we know too well, abounds. American's understanding of the past is selective and discriminatory. Commemoration often becomes celebration. Negatives, failures, and embarrassments become mere aberrations in the march of progress. And the lessons they draw from such a reading of history are necessarily flawed and misleading. As historians we have both the obligation and opportunity to see that Americans and their leaders get the story right, form intelligent, reasonable conclusions, and draw credible analogies based upon the fullest documentary record available.

In this essay, I have attempted to explore a case of linkage between past and present. Several questions have guided me. First, what perspectives do Americans now hold regarding the Vietnam War? What lessons have they drawn from that wrenching experience? Second, how viable is the lesson most conspicuously touted by President Ronald Reagan and his conservative allies that the Vietnam War could have been won? Was it a winnable war? Third, how sensible is the Reagan view that the U.S. role in Central America in the 1980s is not analogous to Vietnam and that triumph in the hemisphere is quite possible? And, fourth, how sound is the contrasting belief, articulated by critics of U.S. intervention in Central America, that the nation is again trudging into a Vietnam-type quagmire fraught with

Thomas G. Paterson, "Historical Memory and Illusive Victories: Vietnam and Central America," *Diplomatic History*, 12 (Winter 1988), pp. 1–18. Reprinted by permission.

peril? In short, does the analogy make sense? My fundamental assumption is that advocates on both sides of the debate over Central American policy in the 1980s hold views that have been greatly shaped by their perspectives on the Vietnam War.

Soviet leaders, masters of an "evil empire," asserted President Reagan, stood prepared "to commit any crime, to lie, to cheat" in order to achieve a Communist world. In a display of raw anticommunism reminiscent of early Cold War days, Reagan claimed that an expansionist Soviet Union "underlies all the unrest that is going on. If they weren't engaged in this game of dominoes, there wouldn't be any hot spots in the world." The president and his advisers quoted the Truman Doctrine, resuscitated the domino theory, and embraced the enduring themes of bipolarism, global containment, and Cold War confrontation, altogether happy to discard the "Vietnam syndrome" and the limits it seemed to place on the exertion of American power. Soon the Reagan Doctrine committed the United States to the active support of anti-Communist movements near and far.

The Reagan administration's attention fastened on Central America. Blaming turmoil in the region on the "Moscow-Havana axis," Reagan officials set out to defeat leftist insurgents in El Salvador, topple the Sandinista government in Nicaragua, and draw Guatemala and Honduras into closer military alignment with the United States. As the president predicted victory over "communism" in Central America, critics predicted another Vietnam. "El Salvador is Spanish for Vietnam," read one bumper sticker. The veteran diplomat George Ball, an in-house dissenter on Vietnam in the 1960s, dissented again; Reagan's policy toward El Salvador, he insisted, was a case of "plagiarization." Representative Clarence D. Long (D-MD) said that "the similarity of Vietnam is so close it is almost uncanny. There is the unwillingness of people to fight, incompetent, corrupt leadership, and calling everyone a Communist." Senator Christopher Dodd (D-CT) decried the "ignorance" of Reagan officials, who seemed "to know as little about Central America in 1983 as we knew about Indochina in 1963." Economic underdevelopment, poor medical care, illiteracy, poverty, and a rigid class structure, not Communist plotting, underlay Central American unrest, argued Dodd. Reagan not only generated debate by plunging the United States into civil wars and regional disputes, he also sparked controversy by triggering memories of Vietnam when he declared it a "noble cause." This time, in Central America, Reaganites bragged, the United States would stay the course and win. Policymakers and critics alike, then, summoned the Vietnam legacy to their debate over Central America. As a major survey has discovered, American leaders' attitudes toward the Vietnam War are the best predictors of their foreign policy views in the 1980s.

"Still in Saigon, still in Saigon, still in Saigon, in my mind," went the words of a 1981 song. But which Vietnam has stayed in American minds? That is, which lessons have Americans learned from the war that might guide them into or out of Central America? Although no consensus has formed, at least four general perspectives have become identifiable. First, the noninterventionist, "no more Vietnams" school of thought. This school holds that the United States should never again intervene in a Third World country undergoing national rebellion or civil war, because it cannot solve problems indigenous to other peoples. Americans may have the money, but they do not have the knowledge, sensitivity, patience, or muscle to rearrange other governments, especially those distant from U.S. power. Let others learn from their own mistakes; let Americans learn their own limits. Wisdom, then, lies in ending America's penchant for being the world's teacher, social worker, banker, and policeman.

A second perspective resembles the first but is more radical—the "inevitability" point of view. According to this reasoning, the United States is destined to repeat Vietnam-type experiences for several reasons. Americans must import scarce commodities and export American products; economic lifelines must be secured. Americans will likely insist on remaining "Number One," whatever that means, and this psychological factor compels an activist, interventionist foreign policy. Americans will continue, as well, to exaggerate the Communist threat and thus interpret local crises derived from internal sources as Cold War contests demanding impositions of the containment doctrine. So long as a national security bureaucracy perpetuates a warmaking machine and the imperial presidency overwhelms the checks-and-balances system and misleads the American people through deliberate "disinformation," Vietnams will darken America's future.

The third perspective we might call the "diplomatic intervention" school: the United States must be interventionist because it is a great power with global interests that must be protected against all threats, and because Americans have an obligation to help others establish democratic, prosperous states. But the means should be diplomatic rather than military. Washington should negotiate with leftist and nationalist regimes to reduce potential threats and use foreign aid to foster conditions compatible with American interests and principles. In this way, by nurturing nationalism, the United States could build a non-Communist world and, at the same time, guarantee American prosperity and security. In other words, Americans must reject the extremes of "Fortress America" (isolationism) and "Atlas America" (global policeman) in favor of "participant America." President Jimmy Carter's initial openness to the leftist government in Nicaragua and his negotiation of the Panama Canal treaties seemed to reflect this thinking. Americans, Carter once said, had to put their "inordinate fear of Communism" behind them.

The fourth perspective, often labeled the "win" or "revisionist" school, largely emerged from military officers who served in Vietnam and from conservatives and others who came to believe that the Vietnam War could have been won. Some of them promoted a "stab-in-the-back" thesis: biased journalists, antiwar critics, and meddlesome members of Congress broke America's staying power and thus assisted the enemy. America supposedly lost its will. "I don't think we were driven out of Vietnam," claimed Ambassador Jeane J. Kirkpatrick. "I think we left." According to such thinking, political leaders hampered the military through gradualist methods and should have pursued all-out war. "It takes the full strength of a tiger to kill a rabbit," lectured former General William C. Westmoreland when he made a case against incrementalism. "Remember," advised a former battalion commander, "we're watchdogs you unchain to eat up the burglar. Don't ask us to be mayors or sociologists worrying about hearts and minds. Let us eat up the burglar our own way and then put us back on the chain." Too often, but especially after the 1968 Tet Offensive, these "win" advocates have argued, the United States failed to follow up on military advantages to hurl defeat at the enemy. The military, Ronald Reagan concluded, was "denied permission to win." In short, military answers are appropriate and they can work. Others in this school of thought have declared that the war *should* have been won because it was a moral war; that is, it was quite moral for the United States to resist the tyranny of North Vietnam, whose aggression against Kampuchea and repression of Vietnamese after 1975 have revealed the Communists' brutalities.

Because Reagan's foreign policy appeared to be fueled at least in part by the notion that Vietnam was fought in the wrong way and could have been won, and hence that Central America was not a potential Vietnam, the question of victory in Vietnam became compelling. Could the war have been won with another 500,000 soldiers, billions of dollars more, unrestrained B-52 bombing raids, better counterinsurgency methods, additional equipment, and perhaps even nuclear weapons? Would all of this have delivered victory, or would the United States actually have lost more, destroying even more of what it was trying to save? Asked still another way: How could the Communist Vietnamese (the Vietcong in the South and Vietnamese of the North), outnumbered seven to one in military forces, lacking advanced weapons and bombers, using almost primitive means of communication and transportation, and receiving comparatively little foreign aid from the Soviet Union and China—how could this diminutive enemy have turned back the world's military giant?

When adherents to the "win" point of view have spoken of victory, they usually have meant either keeping a non-Communist government in power in South Vietnam or uniting under U.S. guidance the two Vietnams that had been divided by the Geneva Accords of 1954. Could either have been achieved? Many analysts have thought not, and have argued that "win" enthusiasts have failed to contend with some troubling questions and inescapable facts.

To many analysts, victory would have come only through an American invasion of North Vietnam in order to cripple Hanoi's warmaking capability. As Secretary of Defense Robert McNamara came to realize, the massive bombings of the Ho Chi Minh Trail, Laos, Kampuchea, and North Vietnamese cities had not forced the adversary to capitulate and had not halted the flow of arms and men to the South. The air terror inflicted tremendous losses on the enemy, of course, but did not break it. American planes dropped 6.7 billion tons of bombs on Indochina in 1965–73, or three times the total tonnage dumped on all enemy nations during the Second World War. Strategic bombing, we have been told, seldom works against a non-industrialized country. When Richard Nixon entered the White House in early 1969, he surmised that there were only two ways he could deliver a "knockout blow." One was to bomb the North's irrigation dikes, probably killing 100,000 civilians. The other was to use tactical nuclear weapons. He ruled out both options, in part because he recoiled from the domestic and international uproar that surely would have met such steps, and in part because either action would have wrecked the détente he hoped to cultivate with the People's Republic of China (PRC).

Even if the United States had destroyed cities, dikes, factories, and farms in North Vietnam, then what? An invasion and occupation of the territory north of the 17th parallel probably would still have been necessary. American troops would have had to slash their way across the Demilitarized Zone into the Democratic Republic of Vietnam, where a reserve army of perhaps half a million soldiers waited, and where "the whole population is dug in, with individual foxholes and an efficient civil defense." American casualties would have been staggering. Assuming the improbable, a successful invasion, the United States would have been forced to conduct an expensive and bloody occupation of indeterminate duration against a hostile people defending their homeland, probably through guerrilla warfare. And, having paid the price in lives and treasure once, would Americans have been ready to reintervene if resistance to outside authority, in the North or the South, flared significantly again? Given all of these prospects, it seems quite unlikely that an invasion would have delivered victory.

American leaders appreciated the difficulty of invading and controlling the North, but they might have opted for that drastic course had they not feared provoking a Soviet or Chinese intervention. If U.S. forces crossed the 17th parallel, Beijing had warned, the PRC would come to North Vietnam's defense. The Soviet Union, Hanoi's primary supplier, might have been dissuaded from saving its ally, but no president could gamble that both the Soviets and Chinese would stand aside. American fears were anything but casual, based as they were on prior experience in Korea, intelligence data, and strategic calculations. At the very least, an invasion would have derailed the simultaneous movement toward détente with the two Communist giants. At worst, it would have elevated a regional war to a great power conflagration. It is difficult to see, of course, how turning Vietnam into a world war would have led to an American victory.

Advocates of the "win" thesis also overlook the negative international political consequences the United States would have incurred had it prosecuted the war more vigorously. America's European allies already thought Washington had lost its senses by investing resources in a region peripheral to the West's vital interests. Members of the North Atlantic Treaty Organization became resentful and restless, further weakening the alliance. Only four of the United States' forty worldwide allies sent troops to help in Vietnam (South Korea, Thailand, Australia, and New Zealand). The Third World that the United States was trying hard to woo soured even further toward Washington, as votes against the United States in the United Nations, restrictions on American corporations, and terrorist acts against American citizens and property starkly testified when radical Islamic students stormed the American embassy in Tehran, Iran, in 1979, one of the attackers snarled to a blindfolded captive: "We're paying you back for Vietnam."

To have won the war, moreover, the United States would have had to reform significantly the Saigon government, which claimed little popular following and existed at Washington's sufferance. The clique of Southern leaders routinely jailed critics, fixed elections, refused land reform, and, as nationalists, ignored or rejected American advice. A series of conspiracies, coups, attempted coups, and American covert actions destabilized Vietnamese politics, while America's client, Ngo Dinh Diem, polarized politics by smashing the Buddhists, leaving the extreme choices of the national Liberation Front or the Saigon regime.

The American-assisted plot in 1963 to oust Diem in order to improve the chances for reform only produced more instability. By 1965, George Ball concluded, South Vietnam had only an army, not a government. "I don't think we ought to take this government seriously," Ambassador Henry Cabot Lodge told a White House meeting that same year. "There is simply no one who can do anything." South Vietnamese leaders, moreover, came to resent American criticism and bristled against their dependency upon American aid. The United States struggled with a dilemma: if it pressed Saigon to reform and manipulated the government to enhance its political standing, it risked making Southern officials appear to be puppets. Doing so would undermine the very objective of building a strong, independent government that could command popular support. In the end, American officials abandoned reform, and the weak South Vietnamese regime continued to hinder victory.

Many Vietnamese refused to fight and die for this corrupt, American-backed government and its self-serving leaders. Nor would they sacrifice for the Americans, who seemed increasingly willing to take on the responsibilities of fighting and bleeding. Marine officer Robert Muller remembered: "I served as an adviser to three separate ARVN [Army of the Republic of Vietnam] battalions, every one of which every time we were in combat, split. Not most of the time, every time!" Muller realized that "the writing was on the wall." One-third of the men in combat units deserted each year, and this high rate, not warfare or disease, accounted for the biggest loss of manpower for America's ally. ARVN forces were afflicted with the same problems that troubled their government: poor morale, corruption, self-serving politics, and nepotism.

In short, South Vietnam lacked the stable political foundation that was necessary for victory. The United States had no reliable, internal instrument for the implementation of containment and no chances of building one in the midst of a major war. As Ball has reflected, "we failed not from military ineptitude but because there was no adequate indigenous political base on which our power could be emplaced."

This incontestable evidence of the instability and ineffectiveness of the Southern government should make us doubt the postwar prescriptive analysis of Colonel Harry G. Summers, Jr., and others that a deployment of

American forces just below the Demilitarized Zone along routes into the South and a blockade of Northern ports would have stopped the movement of soldiers from the North and cut lines of supply. Under such conditions the Vietcong supposedly would have withered away. In military terms, sealing off a 900-mile frontier against a determined and versatile enemy demonstrably adept at infiltration would have been extremely difficult at best, requiring great numbers of troops. Even if such a blocking operation had worked, the fact of tortured politics and popular discontent with the Saigon coterie would have remained to ensure disarray and insurgency in the South and handicap the war effort. A different military strategy would not have altered political realities.

Another problem dogs the "win" perspective. From the postwar works of military officers and others, it seems evident that victory never could have come without a reformation of the American military establishment. The generals pursued a kill-and-destroy strategy and war of attrition that failed. Their "can-do," "no-harm-in-trying" attitude prevented them from warning the president about the serious obstacles to victory. The Joint Chiefs of Staff labored under a "group-think" or consensual approach; in order to speak with one voice to the president, they buried objections. Nor could military authorities articulate an alternative strategy for the president, because they themselves were confused about the war's objectives. They kept calling for more men and more bombs. The enemy was never beaten down to the point of surrender: hurt, to be sure, but not conquered. Their war of attrition also presumed incredible patience on the part of the American people, who eventually sensed what postwar analysts have since emphasized: American strategy was not working, and more of the same would not deliver success.

The military brass, too, sent soldiers into a war of insurgency after having trained them for combat in Europe or for an encounter similar to the Korean War. The United States largely fought a conventional war, stressing massive fire-power and technology rather than light infantry. Although the U.S. Army trained and used some special units and seemed to embrace counterinsurgency methods, its conversion to this type of warfare was "largely cosmetic." The enemy lost when it tangled with Americans in a conventional battle, but it seldom fought that way, preferring quick attacks and skirmishes in the jungles and mountains. The rotation system for officers—one year in Vietnam to "punch your ticket"—only compounded the problem; it broke continuity and squandered whatever experience had been gained. Burdened with these and other factors, the United States enjoyed tactical victory but endured strategic defeat.

The American military also engaged in deceit that made it difficult for officials in Washington to assess accurately the course of the war. Examples are legion, but a few will suffice. For twenty months, military authorities suppressed reports of the massacre of Vietnamese women, children, and elderly men at My Lai in March 1968. They played games with data, too. In jest, but illustrating the point, one former policymaker created a fictional encounter in which a military officer informed a 1967 White House meeting on the effectiveness of the air war: American planes "knocked out 78 percent of North Vietnam's petroleum reserve; since we had knocked out 86 percent three days ago and 92 percent last week, we were doing exceptionally well." In addition, military men faked body counts. Major William Lowry recalled that the "duplicity became so automatic that lower headquarters began to believe the things they were forwarding to higher headquarters. It was on paper; therefore, no matter what might have actually occurred, the paper graphs and charts became the ultimate reality." Colonel John B. Keeley, who commanded an infantry battalion in the Mekong Delta in 1967–68, provided an example: "One day my battalion spent the whole day beating the bush and flushed and killed four VC [Vietcong]. Another battalion was doing the same thing and killed two VC. We sent the number four and the number two to brigade for its body count report. There, the numbers were put side by side to make 42, not the six we actually killed."

A variety of discontents not unlike those bedeviling American society back home also troubled the American military in Vietnam. Racial tensions and drugs were rife. By spring 1971, reported American officials, 10 percent of American GIs were taking heroin, while a higher percentage was smoking marijuana. In the period 1969–72 roughly one thousand cases of fragging were registered—assaults on officers with the intent to kill, harm, or intimidate. In the years 1965–72 some 550,000 American soldiers deserted and another 570,000 American men evaded the draft. Could this military, with all its problems, from the high-level strategist in the Pentagon to the "grunt" in the field, have won the war? Reforming the behemoth military during a war that was going badly was probably impossible, yet without reform America's chances of winning remained remote.

The American people and their doubts also must figure into any discussion of why victory eluded the United States. How could their ardent support have been aroused and maintained over a long period? Summers and others have argued that a declaration of war would have mattered. It would have focused national attention on the distant war, stimulated patriotic passions, permitted the placement of restraints on television journalists, ensured adequate mobilization, and forced dissenters to rally around the flag. This argument is questionable on several scores. Americans, as the Korean War demonstrated, become impatient with limited war. As one historian has remarked, "protracted and inconclusive ground warfare will not for a long period of time command public support." Congress might not have declared war in 1965, when escalation began in earnest. At that time South Vietnam had hardly entered American consciousness as vital to the national interest. The Gulf of Tonkin incident of the year before lacked the stunning force of Pearl Harbor and could not have generated a prowar consensus. A declaration of war would not have changed the dismal status of the South Vietnamese government and military, American strategy, the continued loss of international friends, or the obstacles to invasion and occupation of the North.

Just as unlikely would have been a prolonged public tolerance for governmental controls over the flow of information. Television would probably still have brought into American homes enough pictures of death and destruction to convince many American citizens that their nation's conduct of the war was morally disgraceful. Although the credibility gap already had opened wide by 1967, Americans supported their government's decisions for a long time—not until 1970 did a majority favor withdrawal. By then many believed that their leaders had deceived them. Would a declaration of war have prevented deception? Would not Americans, with or without a declaration of war, eventually have grown weary of the returning coffins, disruptions of family life, and higher taxes? And for how long could decision makers persuade Americans that they should oppose communism in Vietnam while Washington sought détente with the two primary Communist nations, the Soviet Union and China, the latter supposedly the real enemy in Vietnam?

Data also reveal a pale popular endorsement of the war and suggest that a declaration of war and greater mobilization might have exacerbated rather than diminished protest. In addition to illegal draft evasions, lawful educational and employment deferments exempted some nine milion men from the draft. A prolonged, declared war might very well have pushed up the desertion, evasion, and avoidance statistics, created a draft crisis, and sparked more street demonstrations. In short, to have won the war, Washington would have had to undertake the daunting task of mobilizing the American people.

The obstacles to invasion and occupation of the North, the absence of allied support, the many problems besetting the American army and ARVN, the debilities of the South Vietnamese government, and the American people's shrinking endorsement of the never-ending war—all help to explain why the U.S. venture into Indochina ended in defeat. But even if the United States had overcome this litany of problems, victory would have remained elusive, because American leaders proved woefully ignorant about Indochina. They knew little and seemed not to want to know about the Vietnamese people and their ancient culture, particularly their traditional and largely successful resistance to foreign influence. American policymakers failed as well to study the long experience or heed the cautionary advice of the French, belittling their predecessors as the quitters of World War II, brutal and failed colonialists, and technologically deficient warriors. By failing to appreciate the difficulties imposed by terrain and climate on modern warfare, and by discounting the character and history of the people on whose land they were fighting, American leaders invited the disappointment they ultimately suffered.

Three points merit special consideration here. First, the environment itself was hostile. American forces had to operate in a jungle terrain of thick grasses and bamboo, leeches, and weather that alternated between hot sun and drenching rain. Boots and human skin rotted, and diseases flourished. "It is as if the sun and the land itself were in league with the Vietcong," recalled Marine officer Philip Caputo, "wearing us down, driving us mad, killing us." The Vietnam veteran Oliver Stone's provocative movie *Platoon* (1987) revealed the inhospitable country that partially negated American technological superiority. Well-hidden booby traps blasted away parts of the body, and snipers made every step of a grunt or "bonnierat" precarious. The enemy was everywhere but nowhere, often burrowed into elaborate underground tunnels or melded into the population, where every Vietnamese might be a Vietcong. No place in Vietnam seemed secure. Many veterans later suffered "post-traumatic stress disorder," an illness of nightmares and extreme nervousness.

The United States lost the war as well because its conduct alienated the Vietnamese people, some one-third of whom became refugees. Bomb craters scarred the land; the chemical defoliant Agent Orange denuded it. GIs tagged Vietnamese "gooks," and did not always distinguish between peasant farmers and the enemy. Some even sliced off Vietnamese ears as trophies. The Americans used napalm freely, blasted to bits with artillery and air strikes hamlets from which American troops had received small-arms fire, and torched villages considered friendly to the Communists. "Free-fire zones," within which any person was considered the enemy, trapped the innocent. Most American soldiers were not committing atrocities, but the record is replete with enough examples to support the conclusion of one American official that "it was as if we were trying to build a house with a bulldozer and wrecking crane." Before leaving office, Secretary McNamara complained about the bombing: "It's not just that it isn't preventing the supplies from getting down the trail. It's destroyed the countryside in the South. It's making lasting enemies." As for the village of Ben Tre, "it became necessary to destroy the town to save it," remarked an American officer.

The strategic hamlet program, begun in 1962, also uprooted people from ancestral lands and relocated them in guarded quarters surrounded by barbed wire. Although American leaders may have deliberately created a refugee population in order to separate the people from the National Liberation Front, in reality the policy meant the growth of a discontented populace and reduced agricultural production. As well, the huge influx of Americans disrupted the Vietnamese economy and helped support a debasing underworld of prostitution, drugs, and the black market. Vietnam's fragile society, already profoundly divided between Catholics and Buddhists, became further fragmented. The United States in the end was destroying the very place it was trying to defend. It is no wonder that Washington could not build a strong, popular government in the South.

The United States lost, finally, because it faced a people deeply committed to their cause, who seemed to have no "breaking point." When an American veteran returned to Vietnam as a journalist in the early 1980s, he interviewed soldiers about their endurance of great sacrifices during the war. They invariably quoted Ho Chi Minh: "Nothing is more important than independence and freedom." Although probably harboring some doubts about whether these noble aspirations had been satisfied, given the ruthlessness and warrior-state mentality of their Communist leaders in recent years, these soldiers believed in the 1960s that they were defending their divided nation against outsiders, as their ancestors had done for centuries against the Chinese, French, and Japanese. "Not only do the Viet Cong units have the recuperative power of the phoenix," General Maxwell Taylor reported in late 1964, "but they have an amazing ability to maintain morale." General Bruce Palmer remembered that "their will to persist was inextinguishable." Vietnamese nationalism and a commitment to revolution combined to thwart American victory. General Taylor summarized the general problem when he said that "we didn't know our ally. Secondly, we knew even less about the enemy. And, the last, most inexcusable of our mistakes, was not knowing our own people."

These "mistakes," Americans have been assured in the 1980s, were being avoided in El Salvador, where American military advisers and economic and military aid were at work to defeat a leftist insurgency against a conservative, American-backed government. "There is no comparison with Vietnam. There isn't going to be anything like that in this," asserted President Reagan. But critics warned against another Vietnam. "The White House did not appreciate how rapidly El Salvador would take off in the minds of the press as a Vietnam," remarked a presidential assistant.

Has the Vietnam analogy made sense, or, as some analysts have argued, was Vietnam so unique that reasonable comparisons cannot be made? Whatever our answers, Vietnam has emerged as a reference point in the debate over policy toward Central America. President Reagan seemed to think that the victory denied in Vietnam could be achieved in El Salvador. As one senator put it, El Salvador seemed a place where the United States could "win one for a change." According to Robert White, a former ambassador to El Salvador, the administration "thought it was like rolling a drunk." Why would Reagan and his advisers have thought so? Because the differences between Vietnam and El Salvador seemed favorable to a U.S. venture into Central America.

The strategic, economic, and historical contexts were quite different. Unlike Vietnam, which had China, El Salvador had no large Communist state at its border to provide supplies and sanctuary. Salvador's neighbors, Guatemala and Honduras, were actually staunch and well-armed American allies. El Salvador, moreover, was a small country about the size of Massachusetts, with only five million people. The U.S. Navy enjoyed easy access to the nation; this proximity made logistics far simpler than was the case of Vietnam, some 12,000 miles away. The Salvadoran rebels were hardly a replica of the disciplined, tenacious Vietminh or Vietcong who became battle-hardened from years of war against the French before Americans ever became combatants. The insurgents were internally divided, seemed unable to gain wide popular support, and failed to control much territory. The nationalism that drove the Vietnamese was aroused and invigorated by anticolonialism. It was not a force the Salvadoran revolutionaries could draw upon, for El Salvador already existed as a nation and no immediate colonial master lurked in the recent past, even if some Salvadorans considered the United States an imperialist intruder.

American economic and strategic interests in Central America, unlike

Vietnam, were longstanding and large. The Caribbean and Pacific sea lanes were vital to U.S. trade. North American investment in and trade with the region had always been substantial. Since the early twentieth century the United States had intervened regularly in Central America and had established strong ties with military establishments in the area. A good number of American officers spoke Spanish, whereas few had learned Vietnamese. The president of El Salvador, José Napoleón Duarte, had attended the University of Notre Dame in South Bend, Indiana. All in all, American leaders knew Central America; they had a clear view of U.S. interests; they considered it a place where Americans would no doubt fight with a staying power lacking in Vietnam. They also had a justification for intervention in the Monroe Doctrine, which had evolved by the early 1980s into a statement of U.S. hegemony in the hemisphere. Reagan officials revitalized the dormant doctrine—the conservative publicist William Buckley called it a "re-baptism"—although they sounded more like Theodore Roosevelt than James Monroe. For the Vietnam War, American leaders could not muster a declaration of such longevity, self-interest, and emotional appeal. For all of these reasons, then, presidential advisers could tell Reagan, the chances for victory in El Salvador—without the introduction of American combat troops—seemed good and certainly much better than the chances had been in Vietnam.

The Reagan administration, however, did find one difference between Vietnam and El Salvador restraining. American citizens repeatedly indicated to pollsters and members of Congress that they opposed sending American soldiers to Central America. In 1964, President Lyndon B. Johnson was able to get the Tonkin Gulf Resolution without much congressional debate, and in 1965 he was able to send American troops to Vietnam without much public discussion. In the 1980s, however, Americans were much more alert to Central American events and the prospects of an expanded American military presence. Congress cautioned the president and even, at times, prohibited U.S. aid to the contras, the anti-Sandinista forces using Honduras as a base to attack Nicaragua. Some military leaders expressed reluctance to become involved in another counterinsurgency, if only because they feared that the American people again would tire of the effort. "Remember one lesson from the Vietnam era," General William A. Knowlton lectured the 1985 Army War College class. "Those who ordered the meal were not there when the waiter brought the check." Some conservatives have agreed that the United States could not intervene militarily in Central America without a public mandate. "You first commit the nation before you commit the troops," the Texas billionaire H. Ross Perot told Colonel Oliver North of the National Security Council, who was running a clandestine aid program for the contras.

Critics of U.S. intervention in Central America believed that the similarities to Vietnam were more striking than the differences. The way American officials thought about global politics constituted the first similarity. They saw events in Central America as part of an East-West contest. As in the case of Vietnam, Washington's leaders elevated a local conflict into an international crisis. They invoked the containment doctrine to turn back "a textbook case of indirect armed aggression by Communist powers." If fear of "another China" drove decision makers in Vietnam, so fear of "another Cuba" generated policy toward Central America. Reaganites refurbished the domino theory, charging that Nicaragua, Cuba, and the Soviet Union were plotting to tip dominoes in the United States' own backyard. Remember, President Reagan said, "we are the last domino." Such threat exaggerations were typical during the Vietnam War, as were the denunciations of critics as unpatriotic apologists for Communist misdeeds. The "can-do" feeling also reemerged—the time of "self-doubt is over"—to blind leaders to the ostacles in the way of victory in another civil war. However chastened by Vietnam, American policymakers once again seemed to believe that they had answers for other people's problems.

Strategic arguments in the 1980s also resembled those of the 1960s. If Secretary of State Dean Rusk worried that China would use Vietnam as a platform for expansion into Asia, threatening such American allies as Japan and the Philippines, Secretary of State George Shultz declared that the Soviet Union was trying to use Nicaragua as a "stepping stone." Yet another similarity with Vietnam was that few U.S. allies stood with the Reagan administration. The major nations in the region, Mexico and Venezuela, have opposed Washington's emphasis on military solutions. Joining with the other members of the Contadora group, Colombia and Panama, they have urged negotiations to resolve the Salvadoran and Nicaraguan crises, which threatened to engulf all of Central America in war. But U.S. officials have rebuffed the Cantadora group's repeated overtures and plans and have flatly rejected revolutionary Salvadorans' calls for negotiations.

Still another similarity between Vietnam and Central America, claim opponents of intervention, lay in the unreliability and unsavory character of America's local allies. The contra leadership included a number of former Somoza family henchmen and National Guardsmen who had been overthrown in 1979 in large part because Nicaraguans had grown intolerant of the Somocistas' corruption and violence. Washington officials frequently have had to press the contras to reform so that they could present a better public image. In their war against the Sandinista government the contras have committed atrocities, practiced fraud with American money, and squabbled vigorously among themselves. By the late 1980s they had not demonstrated any ability to command popular support in Nicaragua. In El Salvador, although Duarte won with the help of American financing, politics remained corrupt and unpredictable, and the military and wealthy retained power. The government appeared incapable of stopping the ravaging death squads that silenced critics of all kinds. Yet another similarity flowed from these ties to local leaders: a credibility gap. If Americans came to doubt that officials were telling them the truth in the Vietnam years, they also came to question Washington's exaggerated rhetoric about Central America. Reagan's depiction of the contras as "freedom fighters" and his assurances that "democracy" was developing and "human rights" were improving in El Salvador seemed ludicrous. The official *White Paper* of 1981 on El

Salvador was so riddled with errors and unsubstantiated generalizations about Communist intrigue that the administration soon shelved it. Finally, there is the issue of international law. If the United States had violated the Geneva Accords in Vietnam, the World Court in 1986 ruled that the United States had violated international law by aiding the contras and should pay reparations to Nicaragua. Washington dismissed the court ruling and questioned its jurisdiction, even though a few years earlier American officials had appealed to that same court to punish Iran for taking Americans hostage.

. . . The outcome of U.S. intervention in Central America remains uncertain. Certainly the scenario will not follow each step of the Vietnam experience. The analogy does not work in all respects, and Reagan has vowed never to send American troops to Central America. But if the critics are right, as they seem to be, the United States will stumble in Central America for some of the same reasons it fell in Vietnam. The regions contrast sharply, but American assumptions have not changed and the drive for victory is relentless. Local conditions, once again, promise to determine the outcome. Once again the exaggerated image of a ubiquitous Communist threat takes the United States into a civil war for which there are seldom outside answers. The past directs and continues to mislead. "Here we go again," groaned Republican Senator Mark Hatfield of Oregon, "old men creating a monster for young men to destroy."

✗ *F U R T H E R   R E A D I N G*

Walter H. Capps, *The Unfinished War* (1982)
Nayan Chanda, *Brother Enemy: The War After the War* (1986)
William J. Duiker, *Vietnam Since the Fall of Saigon* (1980)
Peter Goldman, *Charlie Company: What Vietnam Did to Us* (1980)
Bob Greene, *Homecoming* (1989)
John Hellman, *American Myth and the Legacy of Vietnam* (1986)
Herbert Hendin and Ann P. Haas, *Wounds of War: The Psychological Aftermath of Combat in Vietnam* (1985)
Stanley Hoffman et al., "Vietnam Reappraised," *International Security,* 6 (1981), 3–26
Ole Holsti and James N. Rosenau, *American Leadership in World Affairs: Vietnam and the Breakdown of Consensus* (1984)
David E. Kaiser, "Vietnam: Was the System the Solution?" *International Security,* 4 (1980), 199–218
Walter LaFeber, "The Last War, the Next War, and the New Revisionists," *Democracy,* 1 (1981), 93–103
Anthony Lake, ed., *The Vietnam Legacy* (1976)
Robert Jay Lifton, *Home from the War* (1973)
Myra MacPherson, *Long Time Passing: Vietnam and the Haunted Generation* (1984)
Terry Nardin and Jerome Slater, "Vietnam Revised," *World Politics,* 33 (1981), 436–48
Norman Podhoretz, *Why We Were in Vietnam* (1982)
Earl C. Ravenal, *Never Again* (1978)
Harrison E. Salisbury, *Vietnam Reconsidered: Lessons from a War* (1984)

Robert Warren Stevens, *Vain Hopes, Grim Realities: The Economic Consequences of the Vietnam War* (1976)

W. Scott Thompson and Donaldson D. Frizzell, eds., *The Lessons of Vietnam* (1977)

John Wheeler, *Touched with Fire: The Future of the Vietnam Generation* (1984)

Marilyn B. Young, "Revisionists Revised: The Case of Vietnam," *The Society for Historians of American Foreign Relations Newsletter,* 10 (1979), 1–10